Presidents and Presidencies
in American History

Presidents and Presidencies in American History

A Social, Political, and Cultural Encyclopedia and Document Collection

VOLUME THREE: WILLIAM McKINLEY TO DWIGHT D. EISENHOWER

JOLYON P. GIRARD, EDITOR

ABC-CLIO®

An Imprint of ABC-CLIO, LLC
Santa Barbara, California • Denver, Colorado

Library of Congress Cataloging-in-Publication Data

Names: Girard, Jolyon P., 1942- editor.
Title: Presidents and presidencies in American history : a social, political, and cultural encyclopedia and document collection / edited by Jolyon P. Girard.
Description: Santa Barbara : ABC-CLIO, [2019] | Includes bibliographical references and index.
Identifiers: LCCN 2019008322 (print) | LCCN 2019012141 (ebook) | ISBN 9781440865916 (eBook) | ISBN 9781440865909 (set : alk. paper) | ISBN 9781440865923 (volume 1) | ISBN 9781440865930 (volume 2) | ISBN 9781440865947 (volume 3) | ISBN 9781440865954 (volume 4)
Subjects: LCSH: Presidents—United States—History—Encyclopedias. | Presidents—United States—Biography.
Classification: LCC E176.1 (ebook) | LCC E176.1 .P919 2019 (print) | DDC 973.09/9 [B] —dc23
LC record available at https://lccn.loc.gov/2019008322

ISBN: 978-1-4408-6590-9 (set)
       978-1-4408-6592-3 (vol. 1)
       978-1-4408-6593-0 (vol. 2)
       978-1-4408-6594-7 (vol. 3)
       978-1-4408-6595-4 (vol. 4)
       978-1-4408-6591-6 (ebook)

23 22 21 20 19   1 2 3 4 5

This book is also available as an eBook.

ABC-CLIO
An Imprint of ABC-CLIO, LLC

ABC-CLIO, LLC
147 Castilian Drive
Santa Barbara, California 93117
www.abc-clio.com

This book is printed on acid-free paper ∞
Manufactured in the United States of America

Contents

25. WILLIAM McKINLEY (1843–1901)

Presidential Term (1897–1901)

CHRONOLOGY

January 29, 1843—William McKinley is born in Niles, Ohio.

April 12, 1861—Confederate forces fire on Fort Sumter in Charleston, South Carolina, beginning the Civil War.

June 11, 1861—McKinley enlists in the army.

July 26, 1865—Brevet Major McKinley is mustered out of service.

January 25, 1871—McKinley and Ida Saxton marry in Canton, Ohio.

March 4, 1877—McKinley begins his first term in the House of Representatives.

October 1, 1890—The protectionist McKinley Tariff Act becomes law.

November 3, 1891—McKinley is elected governor of Ohio.

February 24, 1895—The Cuban revolution against Spanish rule begins.

June 18, 1896—The Republican Party nominates McKinley for president.

November 4, 1896—McKinley defeats William Jennings Bryan in the presidential election.

March 4, 1897—McKinley is inaugurated as the 25th president of the United States.

July 24, 1897—The protectionist Dingley Tariff Act becomes law, replacing the Wilson-Gorman rates.

February 2, 1898—Newspapers publish Enrique Dupuy de Lome's letter critical of President McKinley.

February 15, 1898—There is an explosion on the USS *Maine* in Havana Harbor, Cuba.

March 28, 1898—The U.S. Navy Board of Inquiry releases its report on the sinking of the *Maine*.

April 25, 1898—Congress declares war on Spain.

May 1, 1898—U.S. commodore George Dewey defeats the Spanish fleet at the Battle of Manilla Bay in the Philippines.

June 11, 1898—The first U.S. ground forces land near Guantanamo, Cuba.

June 12, 1898—U.S. forces capture Guam.

July 3, 1898—U.S. naval forces defeat the Spanish fleet in the Battle of Santiago Bay, Cuba.

July 7, 1898—The United States annexes the Hawaiian Islands.

July 25, 1898—U.S. forces land in Puerto Rico.

August 12, 1898—The United States and Spain cease hostilities and enter negotiations.

December 10, 1898—The Treaty of Paris ends the Spanish-American War.

February 3, 1899—The U.S. Senate ratifies the Treaty of Paris.

February 4, 1899—The Filipino insurrection against the United States begins.

September 6, 1899—Secretary of State John Hay sends Open Door notes to foreign powers.

March 14, 1900—The Currency Act puts the United States on the gold standard.

March 16, 1900—McKinley appoints William Howard Taft as chairman of the Second Philippines Commission.

June 20, 1900—Chinese Boxer rebels enter Peking and surround the legation district.

July 5, 1900—The Democratic Party nominates William Jennings Bryan for president.

August 14, 1900—An international armed force, including the United States, crushes the Boxer Rebellion in China.

November 6, 1900—William McKinley is reelected president of the United States.

September 6, 1901—Leon Czoglosz shoots President McKinley in Buffalo, New York.

September 14, 1901—McKinley dies from gangrene as a result of his gunshot wound. Vice President Theodore Roosevelt is sworn in as the 26th president of the United States.

December 16, 1901—The Senate ratifies the second Hay-Pauncefote Treaty.

July 2, 1902—The Filipino insurrection ends.

BIOGRAPHICAL SKETCH

A Civil War veteran, lawyer, seven-term congressman, and two-term governor of Ohio, William McKinley had a distinguished political career prior to his election as president in 1896. As president, McKinley oversaw economic prosperity, adoption of the gold standard, a successful war with Spain, overseas territorial expansion, and the establishment of the Republican Party in national political dominance for a generation. He was the third president to have died at the hand of an assassin.

William McKinley Jr. was born on January 29, 1843, in Niles, Ohio, of mixed Scots-Irish and English descent. The McKinleys were a struggling middle-class family and small-time entrepreneurs in the growing iron industry. They were devout Methodists and abolitionists. William's mother encouraged her son to become a minister. Although they lacked formal schooling themselves, his hard-working parents greatly valued learning and moved their growing family to nearby Poland, Ohio, in 1852 because it offered better education opportunities to their children. Young William was a good student and was active in the debating society. In 1860, William attended Allegheny College in Meadville, Pennsylvania, until ill health and his father's business failure forced his return home later in the year.

Like thousands of other young men, the 18-year-old William McKinley was swept up by a patriotic desire to defend the country after the rebels fired on Fort Sumter in April 1861. Yet, McKinley did not immediately respond to President Abraham Lincoln's call for volunteers three days after the attack. Instead, McKinley did what was so characteristic of him: he deliberated and coolly considered the risks and opportunities. It was after he took a trip to a nearby military camp to see off friends and thoroughly discussed the matter with others, including a cousin who accompanied him, that McKinley decided to enlist. In June 1861, he became a private in the Poland Guards.

Like every other member of his generation, the Civil War shaped William McKinley. He proved his mettle in combat. Beginning the war a private and ending it a major, he earned increasing responsibilities and promotion thanks to his work ethic, attention to details, and diligence. He emerged with a much larger vision of the world than the small-town, parochial Ohio town in which he grew up. He also made crucial connections with influential men, like future governor and president Rutherford B. Hayes, who would aid his rise in politics after the war.

After a month of training, McKinley and his regiment, the Twenty-Third Ohio Volunteers, marched into western Virginia. In August 1861, McKinley was reassigned to the quartermaster's department. He excelled in this position due to his attention to detail, organizational abilities, and conscientiousness. In April he was promoted to commissary sergeant and was responsible for provisioning the regiment.

In late August, the Twenty-Third was redeployed to Washington, D.C., to defend the national capital as Robert E. Lee's Confederate Army of Northern Virginia marched north into Maryland. The Twenty-Third fought Lee's forces at South Mountain on September 14, where it would suffer its greatest number of casualties during the entire war, and at Antietam three days later. McKinley had his most important combat experience of the war at Antietam. Realizing in the afternoon that the hungry and thirsty men of his regiment had not been fed all day, Sergeant McKinley rounded up stragglers to prepare rations and coffee. He then loaded his wagon, and against orders from an officer he happened to pass, McKinley drove his wagon through a hailstorm of bullets to feed his regiment. The men of the Twenty-Third appreciated their commissary sergeant's thoughtful act of courage. He was rewarded with a promotion to second lieutenant in November, which he received from the governor while on a recruitment assignment in Ohio with other regimental sergeants. Later in his political career, this image of him as something of a savior proved very valuable, even if opponents attempted to belittle it and overzealous supporters overinflated it by requesting he be awarded the Congressional Medal of Honor, an action the modest and embarrassed McKinley discouraged.

In early 1863, the newly promoted brigade commander, General Rutherford B. Hayes, assigned Lieutenant McKinley to the position of brigade quartermaster. In May 1864, after a quiet year, the Twenty-Third participated in General David Hunter's raid in the Shenandoah Valley. McKinley long remembered the exhaustion and gnawing hunger of the grueling retreat all the way back to Maryland as the force, with the Twenty-Third as the rearguard division, retreated while under constant pressure from the pursuing Confederates. On July 24, 1864, at the Battle of Kernstown, McKinley crossed a hail of Confederate fire to issue a retreat order to a unit that had been cut off from the main force. To observers, it seemed miraculous that he had survived, much less arrived without injury. General Hayes, who had ordered him, feared he would never see the lieutenant alive again. The next day, McKinley received promotion to captain and was chosen to by the division commander, General George Crook, to be his adjutant.

An adjutant's life was very demanding. All of the clerical functions of the division passed across his desk. Captain McKinley worked day and night to complete a mountain of paperwork that included orders, requisitions, promotions, and letters, among many others. On the other hand, during moments of combat, McKinley found himself in the middle of the action. Known throughout his life as a careful and deliberate person, he demonstrated some uncharacteristic impulsive decisions under fire during General Philip Sheridan's Shenandoah campaign. At Berryville, McKinley had a horse shot out from under him. The captain even exceeded his authority and used his position as adjutant to order troops forward. Although this might have been a wise decision to move the unit forward, he was mildly reprimanded by Crook. At Winchester, McKinley joined in a charge by his old brigade. Hayes chided his former quartermaster for this unnecessary act of bravado. McKinley responded to the effect that it was impossible for anyone to not get swept up in excitement of the moment.

William McKinley (Library of Congress)

It was during this time that he learned about freemasonry, and in May 1865 he was admitted into the order. He remained an active member throughout his life.

McKinley found camp life agreeable and applied for a position in the postwar army. However, he declined a commission when he received it, likely because, as he stated, his parents objected. In August 1865, he returned to Poland, Ohio, weeks after receiving a brevet promotion to major. Throughout the rest of his life, he would be known as and preferred to be addressed as Major McKinley.

Denying the advice of his mentor Hayes to enter the business world, where his skills stood him in a good position to earn a fair amount of money, McKinley gravitated toward law, where he could provide some service to others. In March 1867, he was admitted to the Ohio bar after a term at the Albany law school in New York state and study in a local attorney firm.

Undoubtedly, the Civil War politicized McKinley. In 1864 he cast his first presidential ballot for

Abraham Lincoln's reelection. He later supported full voting rights for the freedmen, as well as the radical Republican Reconstruction policy that deployed the army to the South to protect the civil rights of African Americans. In 1867, he campaigned for the election of Rutherford B. Hayes as governor of Ohio. The following year, McKinley organized Grant for President clubs in Canton, Ohio. In 1869 he was elected to his first political office, Stark County prosecutor. A year later, he suffered his first defeat when he lost his bid for reelection. Although McKinley did not seek elective office for another six years, he remained actively engaged in politics by speaking on behalf of the Republican Party and temperance reform.

In January 1871, William married Ida Saxton. The couple had two daughters, both of whom died in childhood. While William dealt with his grief by throwing himself into his political career, Ida McKinley never recovered from these tragic losses. She developed a seizure disorder that was quite possibly epilepsy resulting from a carriage accident. William learned to recognize the onset of these attacks. When at a rare public event such as dinner, he would drape a napkin over Ida's face until the attack subsided, acting all along as if nothing were happening. As they aged, Ida became increasingly reliant on her husband, who as a dutiful and devoted husband never questioned her needs. He left work early, stood up friends, and walked out of meetings to take Ida on a carriage ride. They were a quiet, retiring couple who preferred evenings at home reading to one another or chatting with a small circle of intimate friends over going out on the social circuit.

After vigorously campaigning for Rutherford B. Hayes's reelection as Ohio governor in 1875, McKinley decided to seek a seat in Congress. In 1876 the relatively unknown lawyer beat out several more established Republicans candidates for the nomination, and he defeated the Democrat, who had been favored, in the general election in November.

As a congressman, McKinley became known primarily for advocating one issue above all: a protective tariff. It was an issue that resonated in a district booming with industrial manufacturers. It was also an issue growing in prominence in the years following the Panic of 1873. Republicans, like their Federalist and Whig predecessors, generally supported a protective tariff that would provide the government with revenue and prevent the home market from being overrun with cheap foreign imports. With questions over Reconstruction policy dominating the federal government in the years after the end of Civil War, however, the tariff dropped down the list of party priorities. In economic policy questions, discussions over currency dominated as advocates for increased paper money circulation fought against those who wanted to retire the old greenbacks from circulation. Others wanted to increase the money supply by increasing the amount of silver coins in circulation, whereas the more conservative-minded supported President Ulysses Grant's veto of the inflation bill in 1873. McKinley was uninterested in the currency question. For him, the tariff was the central economic question. As his career progressed, he became increasingly identified with this issue, and his expertise on the subject made him an important and powerful national spokesperson on behalf of a protective tariff, an issue that came to be one of the dividing lines between Republicans and Democrats in the 1880s and the 1890s.

For McKinley, the tariff was an important patriotic or national policy that protected American industry from the harmful effects of foreign competitors dumping their cheap goods on the American market. With his family's experience in the iron industry, he understood how higher rates supported American manufacturers. More important—and this is a source of McKinley's appeal on the issue—he always stressed its value, as he believed it, to the American workers. He argued that workers benefited from a high tariff because it increased their wages and protected their jobs. McKinley always portrayed himself as a friend of the laboring man. It had led him as an attorney to take a case against powerful industrialist, and his future friend and campaign manager, Mark A. Hanna. Less admirably, it led him to vote in support of the Chinese Exclusion Act that banned immigration of Chinese laborers.

In his first act as a congressman, he delivered a petition from steel workers in his district who supported a protective tariff. The following year, he gave his first speech on the floor of the House of Representatives in denouncing a Democratic proposal to lower tariff rates. His successful opposition catapulted the freshman from Ohio into the ranks of the leading Republican spokesman on the issue of the tariff. In early 1880, McKinley's influence increased significantly when he was given a seat on the House Ways and Means Committee, which had oversight of the tariff.

In December 1881 the tariff issue again rose as President Chester Arthur called for a revision of the rates in his annual address. McKinley supported the bill to create a commission as long as it represented protectionists, which it did. But McKinley was very troubled by the commission's report that called for a significant reduction in rates, and he as even more concerned by the final bill, the so-called Mongrel Tariff, which reduced rates by less than 2 percent. Congressman McKinley was one of only six Republicans to buck the party and the president in voting with the opposition. He justified his action on the grounds that the bill threatened the interests of his district for lowering the tariff on wool and steel.

Thanks to a faltering economy, the Democrats gained control of the House of Representatives in the 1882 midterm elections. Although McKinley was declared the winner in an extremely close reelection contest, his Democrat opponent challenged the outcome because some of the ballots had been incorrectly marked. In 1884 the House Committee on Elections, now controlled by the Democrats, ruled in the favor of McKinley's opponent. Disappointed but not surprised by the outcome, McKinley returned to Canton to resume his dormant legal career.

McKinley was not out of politics long, however. He was elected to his old seat in 1884 and resumed his position as the leading advocate for protection in the House. He led the Republican opposition in the lower chamber to President Grover Cleveland's efforts to reduce the tariff rates.

In recognition of his expertise on the tariff issue, he was called upon in 1888 to write the Republican Party's plank on the subject for the upcoming presidential contest. His strong views on protection became the official policy of the party. After this success, McKinley found himself at the center of unwanted controversy at the national convention. He supported Ohio's favorite son, Senator John Sherman, for the presidential nomination. But as voting divided between Sherman and James G. Blaine of Maine, the party's 1884 nominee, the delegates looked to a unity candidate. Some put forward Congressman McKinley as that candidate. Embarrassed by the growing, unexpected ground swell of support, McKinley squashed the movement when he publicly announced that he would not accept the nomination and maintained his support of Sherman. With McKinley out of the way, Benjamin Harrison of Indiana gained the nomination. Harrison defeated the Democrat, incumbent Grover Cleveland, in the national election in November. Although McKinley resisted a movement to nominate him, he was bitten by the presidential bug and began drafting plans to win the highest elective office.

McKinley narrowly lost the Republican nomination for the Speaker of the House to Thomas B. Reed of Maine, initiating a rivalry that remained throughout the remainder of McKinley's life. As a consolation, McKinley was appointed chairman of the House Ways and Means Committee, which put him in a position to write a sweeping tariff reform measure in line with the Republican Party's campaign platform. The trick for McKinley was to retain a protectionist system while at the same time reducing revenue at a time when the federal government accumulated significant surpluses. McKinley solved this dilemma by increasing rates on items to protect American manufacturers and moving many high-volume consumer items, such as sugar, to the free list. Nonetheless, the complicated legislation was subjected to 450 amendments and alterations by the Senate. The McKinley tariff became law only a month before the midterm election that saw a significant backlash against the policies of President Benjamin Harrison and the "Billion Dollar Congress." Facing a very tough reelection in a district recently and significantly gerrymandered to include some of the most solidly Democrat areas in Ohio, McKinley lost his seat by a little over 300 votes.

As always, McKinley was unfazed and undeterred by electoral loss. In 1891 he successfully campaigned for the Republican Party nomination for the governorship and won the election by over 20,000 votes. As governor, he supported pro-labor legislation that implemented an arbitration system and punished employers who forbade their workers from joining a union. However, in 1894 he reluctantly called out the National Guard to suppress a violent strike by coal miners. He also supported state taxes on corporations and granting women the right to vote in local elections.

After Governor McKinley squashed another attempt to put his name at the top of the ticket at the 1892 Republican National Convention, the uninspired delegates nominated incumbent Benjamin Harrison. When Harrison lost his reelection in November to former president Grover Cleveland, McKinley's prospects for the future looked good. However, he unexpectedly faced his greatest challenge soon after reelection as governor in 1893. As the national economy collapsed, a close personal friend for whom McKinley had signed notes defaulted on his debts. This made McKinley responsible for tens of thousands of dollars. McKinley vowed to pay these debts, even if he had to leave politics to do so. His powerful friends, including wealthy industrialist Mark A. Hanna, created a trusteeship and raised enough money to pay off the debts. Although 21st-century voters might be alarmed with the idea of rich businessmen paying off a politician's private debts, McKinley's contemporaries appreciated that he dealt with the crisis in an honorable and responsible manner instead of defaulting.

McKinley received the Republican nomination in 1896, defeating Speaker of the House Thomas B. Reed, his closest rival. With the help of Hanna's deep pockets, McKinley ran a masterful campaign for the nomination, traveling the county, accumulating favors, and courting potential delegates. McKinley secured a plank supporting a protectionist tariff that would replace the reductions resulting from the Wilson-Gormley Tariff that had come into law without Cleveland's signature. For McKinley, this was the central economic interest. He strongly believed that the Democrats' reduction of the tariff hampered economic recovery and encouraged the outflow of gold.

McKinley was less sure of the contentious issue of currency. The Democrats completely repudiated their sitting incumbent by adopting a platform plank that called for the coinage of silver. This would, they believed, alleviate the currency shortage and its resulting deflationary spiral of commodity prices that had been plaguing the United States, especially the farmers of the West and the plains, for 20 years. This put the Republicans in a tough position. They wanted to win important electoral votes in the silver producing states in the Rocky Mountains, and they recognized the popularity of a more flexible currency. Moreover, to fully support a gold plank would ironically associate them too closely to the administration of the very unpopular Democrat incumbent, Grover Cleveland. McKinley and his party threaded this needle by calling for sound currency and proposing an international conference to discuss the silver issue. In response, a small number of western delegates, most notably Senator Henry Teller of Colorado, bolted the convention.

The campaign of 1896 was one of the most exciting in American history. The young and energetic William Jennings Bryan of Nebraska barnstormed the country in a whistle-stop campaign. McKinley had planned to run a conventional campaign, but the growing attention that Bryan gained led to a change in strategy. Understanding that he could not compete with Bryan at his own game, McKinley decided to play to his own strengths and initiated a front porch campaign. Instead of traveling the country, people would travel to his home in Canton, Ohio, where he addressed their issues of concern, met them face-to-face, and engaged in the retail politics (which was his strong suit). In a highly organized fashion and with mechanical precision, he addressed as many as 100,000 people in a single day. When the votes were counted on election day, November 3, 1896, McKinley and his vice president candidate, Garret Hobart of New Jersey, captured 60 percent of the electoral votes and 51 percent of the popular vote, winning a substantial victory by the standards of the Gilded Age. Although the Republicans lost the silver states in the West with their small electoral and popular votes, as well as the solid Democratic South, they captured all the industrial states of the Midwest, the Northeast, the border states (except for Missouri), and Iowa, Minnesota, North Dakota, California, and Oregon. Crop failures in India and Russia drove up prices for wheat, which undercut Bryan's argument that gold was depressing produce prices.

McKinley inherited a sinking economy, and his first priory upon inauguration was recovery. Naturally, he started with the revision of the tariff, and he called a special session of Congress to address this important issue. Congress quickly passed the Dingley Tariff bill, which significantly increased rates and implemented a reciprocity component that would allow the president to negotiate specific reductions with other nations in exchange for likewise considerations. As the tariff wound its way through the Congress, McKinley appointed a three-member bimetallic commission to enter discussions about an international agreement with other nations. France was the most open to some sort of international settlement for silver and worked in close conjunction with the United States. Despite this promising start, Great Britain scuttled the discussions. With the strongest financial power out of the discussions, there was little hope for any agreement on silver. Having fulfilled his promise to pursue an international agreement on silver, McKinley pivoted toward full support of the gold standard. Presidents often take undue blame when the economy fails, and they claim undue credit for times of prosperity. As the economy finally began to pull itself out of depression in 1897, McKinley associated this growth to the Dingley Tariff and its success in increasing business confidence. The discovery of mines in Alaska and South Africa that pumped new gold into the global economy deserves much great credit for the economic recovery and prosperity of the late 1890s. In 1900, McKinley signed legislation that put the United States on the gold standard.

McKinley's biggest foreign policy objective when entering the White House was to annex Hawaii. After failing to win enough votes in the Senate to secure the necessary two-thirds vote to ratify a treaty of annexation, in the summer of 1898 he convinced enough members in both chambers of the Congress to annex Hawaii through a joint resolution.

McKinley soon found himself embroiled in a foreign policy crisis with Spain over their suppression of a revolt in Cuba. Despite being personally and publicly insulted by the Spanish minister and the explosion of the USS *Maine* in Havana Harbor, which killed 268 Americans on February 15, 1898, McKinley resisted the Republican Party's imperialist faction and its call for war as long as he could. His inherent caution, bolstered with his own experience as combat veteran, led

him to consider war as the last option. Once again his opponents, even members of his own party—and in the case of Assistant Secretary of the Navy Theodore Roosevelt, within his own government—charged the old major with being weak and indecisive. By April, however, McKinley had come around to the decision that war with Spain was in the best interest of American national security.

McKinley was a very engaged war president. He created a war room in the White House and remained in direct contact with his military commanders in the field via the latest telephone and telegraph technology. Significantly, McKinley expanded the war beyond Cuba to include Guam, the Philippines, and Puerto Rico. Despite the short duration of the war, it was not without political scandal. The army was poorly equipped for the tropical conditions, and disease spread rapidly through the troops in Cuba in July and August 1898. McKinley was infuriated when army officers, led by Colonel Theodore Roosevelt, signed a round-robin letter highly critical of the slow return of troops to the United States, which they released to the press. Already concerned about the devastating effect of disease, the American public became further upset when stories spread through the newspapers about how American servicemen became sick from being served rotten canned beef.

By the time Spain sued for peace, American forces had taken possession of all four areas. Although originally unsure of what to do about the Philippines, McKinley concluded it must become a territory of the United States to prevent it from falling into the hands of either Germany or Japan. The Paris Treaty, which ended the war in November 1898, was very much along the lines of what McKinley had first proposed. Guam, Puerto Rico, and the Philippines became American possessions, whereas Cuba became an independent nation.

McKinley easily won the nomination for the Republican National Convention in 1900. The most pressing task of the convention was to select the candidate for the second spot on the ticket. Saddened by the death of Vice President Garret Hobart, whom he worked well with and had delegated a significant amount of responsibility, McKinley offered little direction on this task. The convention settled on New

York governor and war hero Theodore Roosevelt. The two had a strained relationship. As assistant secretary of the navy, colonel of the Rough Riders, and later governor, Roosevelt had been critical of McKinley's handling of the crisis with Spain from start to finish, and he famously compared the president's fortitude to that of a chocolate éclair. Yet it was in McKinley's forgiving and accommodating nature to seek harmony and agreement in politics and avoid bitter personal rivalries, especially with members of his own party. He recognized that the young Roosevelt brought many positive attributes to the ticket, even if this was not McKinley's first choice.

Unlike the previous election, McKinley did not openly campaign. He thought it was unseemly for an incumbent to do so, but he also was greatly distracted throughout the summer of 1900 by the international crisis precipitated by the Boxer Rebellion in China. McKinley authorized 2,500 American troops to be removed from the Philippines to participate in the international China Relief Force. Relying on his constitutional power as commander in chief, McKinley acted without congressional authorization. Fearing Americans in the foreign quarter in Peking were being massacred, the public largely supported the president's action, undercutting his political opponents.

In November, the McKinley-Roosevelt ticket handily defeated the Democrat ticket of William Jennings Bryan and Adlai Stevenson with 65 percent of the electoral college and 52 percent of the popular vote. With his term marked by the restoration of prosperity, a successful war, and territorial expansion, it was an almost impossible task for the opposition to defeat a popular president trusted by the public.

In the closing months of his first term and the opening days of his second term, McKinley wrestled with Congress over the thorny problems related to the government of the new colonies and a treaty with Great Britain concerning a canal through Central America. In the Philippines, he appointed William Howard Taft as governor-general of the Philippines and granted military commander's latitude to wage an aggressive campaign against pro-independence insurgents. He called elections for a constitutional convention in Cuba, and after the Platte Amendment, he secured a treaty from the new nation allowing the United States to defend the island and intervene to maintain domestic order. After the Boxer Rebellion, McKinley and Secretary of State John Hay sent a second round of Open Door notes to global powers in an effort to maintain China's sovereignty and open markets.

In the summer of 1901, McKinley traveled the country as he prepared an agenda for his second term. In September he stopped at the Buffalo Exposition. On September 6, 1901, the day after giving a widely applauded speech, the president stood in a receiving line, shaking hands, when he was shot by anarchist Leon Czolgosz. Characteristically, he called his bodyguards to not harm the gunman, and as he lay bleeding, his concerns turned to Ida. He died of gangrene a week later, on Friday, September 13, 1901. Vice President Theodore Roosevelt was sworn in as the 26th president of the United States.

For the third time in a generation, the nation mourned a murdered president. McKinley's body was returned to Washington, where it lay in state in the East Room of the White House before coming home to rest in Canton, Ohio.

HISTORICAL OVERVIEW

Politics

After three decades of a sharply, though almost evenly, divided national polity, the election of William McKinley ushered in a generation of Republican Party dominance that lasted until the Great Depression. A successful war, economic growth after years of depression, increased overseas trade, territorial expansion, and a general sense of optimism that the United States stood in a good position to meet the challenges of the 20th century marked the success of the McKinley administration and bolstered public support behind it.

With almost 30 years of political experience, McKinley was a skilled party leader. He generally made wise appointments; had a keen eye for talent, as is evident in his appointments of Charles Dawes as comptroller of the currency, John Hay as secretary of state and Elihu Root as secretary of war, among others; and toured the country in support of Republican candidates, as he did in 1898 and 1899. Some of his success was due to a conscious effort to court the press. In contrast to his predecessor, Grover Cleveland, who disdained reporters, McKinley understood the power of newspapers in shaping public opinion. He made room in the White House for the press corps, and his secretary gave nearly daily briefings to reporters.

Political patronage was the glue that bound the local and national political party organizations together in the Gilded Age. The presidents of the 19th century spent a considerable amount of time dealing with the thorny issue of filling the expanding federal bureaucracy with politically loyal appointments. However, there was also a growing awareness that this system created corruption and failed to meet the need for civil servants with specialized education or training. Since its enactment in 1883, the Pendleton Civil Service Act limited the ability of the president to make appointments to the federal bureaucracy by requiring classified positions to be staffed by qualified personnel protected from political removal. The Pendleton Act covered only 10 percent of the federal workforce, but presidents since Chester Arthur used their discretionary authority to increase the number of protected positions, mostly to prevent the opposition party from removing appointments when they came to power. In this spirit, President Cleveland, a Democrat, increased the number of protected positions before leaving office. Upon taking office, McKinley argued that many of the positions that Cleveland added to the classified list were unwise and unnecessary. Accordingly, in 1899 he repealed Cleveland's changes, making him the only president between Arthur and Theodore Roosevelt who failed to expand civil service protections among the federal workforce. The opposition used this unpopular decision to charge the president with reversing the tide of reform and spreading the worst features of the corrupt spoils system not only in the United States but now to the newly acquired overseas territories as well. McKinley's removal of a custom officer went all the way to the U.S. Supreme Court. In 1903, the Court vindicated McKinley in the case of *Shurtleff v. United States* by ruling that the president had the constitutional power to remove civil servants.

McKinley vastly expanded the political boundaries and territorial claims of the United States. The 1896 Republican Party campaign platform supported the annexation of the Hawaiian Islands. This had been an issue since American sugar growers overthrew the native monarchy in 1893. Although then president Harrison supported the United States acquiring Hawaii, he lacked support in the closing days of his term. Grover Cleveland was an anti-expansion Democrat who refused to take up the issue. In his December 1897 State of the Union address, McKinley called on the Senate to ratify an annexation treaty in the coming session. Despite heavy lobbying, the administration came up several votes short of the required two-thirds majority. McKinley revisited the matter after the declaration of war against Spain, but this time he proposed a congressional joint resolution that required a simple majority of both houses, instead of a treaty that required two-thirds of the upper chamber. This approach had been used a half century earlier to add Texas, which like Hawaii was an independent nation. After converting some anti-expansionists in his own party, McKinley secured enough votes in both houses of the Congress. In July 1898, Hawaii became a territory of the United States. Sixty-one years later, Hawaii would become the 50th state of the union.

The annexation of Hawaii alone would have been a significant accomplishment, but as a result of the Spanish-American War, McKinley added Guam, Puerto Rico, and the Philippines to the territories of the United States. With these possessions, McKinley faced the daunting new challenges of colonial government, most notably in the Philippines. After it was apparent that the Philippines would not gain its independence following the Paris Treaty between Spain and the United States, signed in November 1898, Emilio Aguinaldo, the commander of the insurrection against the Spanish, took up arms against the new imperial power. Throughout the remainder of McKinley's presidency and into that of his successor, Theodore Roosevelt, the U.S. army fought an active insurgency in the Philippines. At first, American commanders attempted to fight a standard military campaign against the rebel army, but when Aguinaldo converted to a strategy of guerrilla warfare, they were slow to adjust. Allegations of atrocities and use of tactics that the Americans had criticized the Spanish for adopting in Cuba only a couple of years prior exacerbated the challenges. McKinley responded by sending more troops and giving his military commanders increasing latitude. He appointed a commission chaired by William Howard Taft to stabilize the situation. Later, Taft would become the first American governor-general of the islands. Ironically, it was fascination of the American press with the British campaign against the Boers in South Africa that kept the bloodshed in the faraway Philippines from creating more political havoc for McKinley.

Economy

McKinley inherited an economy mired in a three-year-long depression. Business failures, unemployment, violent labor strikes, farmer unrest, shrinking prices, and an alarming flow of the gold reserves out of the United States vexed the Cleveland administration. Cleveland responded by securing repeal of the Sherman Silver Purchase Act, reforming the tariff, and making a controversial deal with banker J. P. Morgan to return gold to the United States. None of these measures seemed to be working as the 1896 election approached.

Throughout his political career, McKinley was known primarily as an advocate for a protective tariff. As an influential Congressman representing industrial districts in Ohio, he wrote protectionist planks for the 1888, 1892, and 1896 Republican Party platforms and used his powerful positions on committees to shape tariff legislation. The 1890 tariff overhaul was popularly known as the McKinley Tariff. His standing in the party had grown as the tariff increasingly became a clear dividing line between the protectionist Republicans and the more free trade–leaning Democrats. McKinley believed that a steep tariff on imported goods protected American industries from cheap, foreign competition and that higher rates correlated to job security and better wages for workers—a signature argument of his and a claim that was his contribution to the debate. Now that he occupied the White House, he considered the tariff his highest priority.

Considering the economic situation too dire to wait until December for the start of the congressional term, McKinley convened a special session on March 15, 1897. In his special message, McKinley called for hikes in the tariff rate to restore prosperity and increase revenue to shore up the federal gold reserve. Comprised of hundreds of individual lines, each affecting the economic interests of at least one district, tariff legislation could be an unwieldy and sloppy process. Under the circumstances, it is noteworthy that the House of Representatives managed to produce the Dingley Tariff on March 31.

Things got more complicated in the Senate when the tariff became entangled in the issue of an international currency agreement. McKinley had always been in favor of the amorphous term "sound currency," but he was never as rigid on the currency question as he was on the tariff. Enough of his agrarian constituents impressed on Congressman McKinley the need for a flexible currency in times of decreasing prices and deflation. Moreover, as a presidential candidate in a deeply divided political system, he understood the importance of winning every possible electoral vote. Due to the importance of the mining industry, voters in the Rocky Mountain states tended to favor the monetization of silver. In the 1896 election, the predicament became even more complex after the Democrats adopted a policy for a dramatic increase in the circulation of silver coinage. Ironically, to openly adopt the gold standard was to take the position most associated in the public mind with the very unpopular incumbent of the opposition party, a Democrat. McKinley sought to parse his way through this jumbled maze with what was an equally murky solution. Instead of adopting a unilateral policy, candidate McKinley pledged to open diplomatic negotiations to adopt a global bimetallic standard. If this could be done, he promised to support it.

France offered the most encouraging support to an international bimetallic agreement and attempted to use this as leverage to secure tariff concessions. Although this failed to gain permanent reductions in favored items such as olive oil, the strong position of France led the Senate to include a reciprocity provision that would allow the president to negotiate targeted reductions with specific nations for enumerated items.

McKinley signed the Dingley Tariff Act on July 24, 1897, the day the special session expired. His administration had stayed out of the details of specific tariff rates, leaving that contentious work to the legislature. He was satisfied with the finished product that crossed his desk. The reciprocity clause, even if that would be reassessed after only two years, pleased him.

As the tariff worked its way through the special session of Congress, McKinley appointed a commission chaired by Senator Edward Wolcott, a Colorado Republican, to negotiate an international agreement. Wolcott's commission found a sympathetic French government, but the key nation was Great Britain. In July, Wolcott presented a proposal to the British government. For the plan to work, the British would have to reopen silver mines in India that had been closed since the global depression began in 1893. Although London saw merits in an international agreement to monetize silver, the colonial government in India deemed it far too risky, especially as the global price of silver declined. On October 19, 1897, Great Britain formally rejected the Wolcott proposal, thwarting an international arrangement for the monetization of silver. Having honorably discharged a campaign promise, even if his heart was never in it, McKinley started pivoting the administration behind adoption of the gold standard. The Gold Standard Act became law in March 1900. McKinley signed the bill into law with a gold pen.

Legal

McKinley made one appointment to the U.S. Supreme Court. In January 1898, he nominated Joseph McKenna, then serving as the attorney general, to the Court. McKenna served on the bench for the next 26 years.

John Griggs replaced McKenna in the Justice Department. Like McKenna, Griggs was a conservative jurist, especially on the subject of business consolidation and the Sherman Anti-Trust Act. The trusts were increasingly becoming a hot-button political issue as the recent depression drove many small- and medium-sized companies out of business, allowing larger firms to expand their market share. Entire industries, like sugar, beef, steel, and petroleum, were falling under the dominance of trusts that colluded to control the marketplace. Books like *Wealth against Commonwealth*, an examination of Standard Oil, and public scandals like the rotten beef sold to the War Department during the war with Spain irritated a public already deeply concerned by the growing power of big business. Relying on his own reading of the antitrust statute and the

Supreme Court decision in case of *United States v. E.C. Knight* (1895) Griggs maintained that a trust had to monopolize interstate commerce, not just production. As a result, his office initiated few antitrust suits but continued those already begun by the Cleveland administration. McKenna clearly represented those who saw consolidation as a normal, perhaps even beneficial, business practice that would make the United States more competitive in the global commerce.

Comptroller of the Currency Charles Dawes was much more concerned with the trusts. As one of the young, upcoming stars of the administration and a future vice president, Dawes tried to convince McKinley that unrestrained business consolidation was leading to a dangerous and disproportionate accretion of wealth and power into the hands of a very few men. Dawes urged the president to implement a more aggressive antitrust strategy. There is some evidence that Dawes was winning over the president, such as McKinley's strong words in his 1899 State of the Union, but it is impossible to tell whether McKinley would have changed his trust policy in his second term had he not been assassinated.

In contrast to other presidents of his era, McKinley had no interest in outdoor recreation or the environment. Arthur and Cleveland were fishermen, and Benjamin Harrison and Roosevelt were hunters. McKinley made no direct contribution to the growing environmental policy in the wake of the 1891 Forest Reserve Act. He withdrew only seven million acres from the forest reserves, much less than either Harrison or Cleveland. Nevertheless, in 1897, Congress created the Division of Forestry in the Agriculture Department, and the president appointed Gifford Pinchot as its head. In the next decade, under Roosevelt's vigorous conservation policy, Pinchot would become one of the most important men in the federal government. In 1899, McKinley signed the bill creating Mount Rainier National Park in Washington State.

Social

Throughout his career in politics, William McKinley considered himself to be a friend of the laboring man. As he had done as a congressman, President McKinley argued that a protectionist tariff benefited workers by keeping wages high and jobs secure from foreign competition. Likewise, a sound currency minimized inflation and provided additional benefits to workers. The Dingley Tariff Act in 1896 and the Gold Standard Act of 1900 fulfilled McKinley's campaign pledge to American workers. McKinley did not openly support organized labor, but he made a couple of high profile appointments and consulted with American Federation of Labor president Samuel Gompers.

In addition to the tariff and the gold standard, McKinley supported the Erdman Act of 1898, which instituted a mediation process for wage disputes among interstate railroad workers, an industry that clearly fell within the federal government's constitutional prerogatives of regulating interstate commerce. President McKinley supported several other ideas that would become law in subsequent administrations, including the creation of a commerce and labor cabinet–level department and a daily hour limit for federal employees.

McKinley's record on race relations is more mixed. As a Republican Civil War veteran, he supported African American civil and electoral rights; it was one of the issues that drew the young Major McKinley into politics. On the other hand, over 30 years after Appomattox and 20 years since the end of Reconstruction, President McKinley valued sectional reconciliation. The war with Spain restored harmony between the sections as no event had done in the last three decades. This was evident in his appointment of former Confederates like General Joseph Wheeler to important commands. Black Republicans were critical of this policy because they knew that the cost of reconciliation with white Southerners was support for black voting rights in the South. McKinley did not openly abandon black voters, and he continued the practice of previous Republican administrations of appointing prominent African Americans to important patronage positions. In 1899 he went forward with a controversial decision to recruit black regiments (despite the army's opposition to this move) and deploy them to fight the insurgency in the Philippines.

Foreign Affairs

McKinley inherited a deteriorating situation 90 miles off the coast of Florida in Cuba. After most of its Central and South American colonies gained independence in the early 19th century, Cuba was the remaining jewel of the once vast Spanish Empire. Despite social, economic, class, and racial tensions on the island that frayed Cuban loyalty to Spain, including a 10-year rebellion that ended in 1878, it was untenable for any government in Spain to even speak of Cuban independence.

Cuba boiled over again in 1895 as economic depression and political turmoil in Spain triggered another colonial rebellion. With his own economic issues and anti-expansionist position, President Cleveland was reluctant to involve the United States in Cuba any deeper than an offer to mediate, which Spain declined. Fearing that the rebels would exploit any sign of weakness, the Spanish government refused to make even minor concessions. Spanish General Valeriano Weyler attempted to crush the rebellion with repression and resorted to the use of concentration camps. This aggressive policy, with its high rates of disease and mortality, won the sympathy of the American public for the rebels. Although neither the Republican candidate William McKinley nor the Democrat candidate William Jennings Bryan gave Cuba much attention in their 1896 presidential campaign, media moguls William Randolph Hearst and Joseph Pulitzer kept the issue on the front pages of the nation's newspapers throughout the campaign.

Although the economic issues of the special session absorbed President McKinley's attention in the opening months of his administration, he was concerned about the safety of thousands of Americans in Cuba, as well as the millions of business dollars invested in the island. In May 1897, at McKinley's request, Congress appropriated money to evacuate Americans from the conflict zone. McKinley addressed Cuba as sole subject of his first State of the Union address in December. He laid out the problems, perils, and dangers of a rebellion in Cuba to the United States, but he ultimately concluded it was in the interest of the United States to remain neutral by not granting the rebels any form of recognition. Imperialists in his own party demanded a more assertive policy. They considered the president weak and even naïve when he stated that Spain had acted in good faith by removing General Weyler, who was known as "the Butcher" in the American press.

In January 1898, McKinley ordered the USS *Maine*, one of the newest cruisers in the U.S. Navy, to Havana Harbor to protect American interests. On February 9, a sensational letter penned by the Spanish ambassador and highly critical of President McKinley was printed in American newspapers. He demanded an apology but did not press the issue. To his critics, the incident highlighted what they considered the president's inherent weakness and inability to act decisively or passionately. When the Spanish apology arrived, it was instantly drowned out by a more explosive event.

On February 15, 1898, the *Maine* blew up in Havana Harbor, claiming the lives of 268 Americans. Outrage swept through American public opinion, but again McKinley would not be easily stampeded into war. As a veteran who had experienced the bloody battlefield of Antietam, he understood the human cost of war. As a naval court of inquiry conducted an investigation, both sides made preparations for a possible war. The American Pacific squadron was ordered to Hong Kong, a staging point for a possible attack on the Philippines. The Spanish transferred warships to bases in Cuba. On Friday, March 18, the board of inquiry informed the president that they had determined that a mine had caused the explosion off the *Maine*, but they did not venture an opinion about who might have been responsible. The administration held the information over the weekend as it frantically attempted to obtain some diplomatic settlement from Spain before the doubtless call for war.

On April 11, after the failure of several European nations and the pope to mediate a peaceful settlement, McKinley sent a war address to Congress. He justified American military intervention in Cuba on humanitarian grounds but also cited injury to American interests, injury to American citizens, and the cost to the U.S. government as significant factors. Congress did not act immediately. For several different reasons, including racism and anti-imperialism, Congress wanted a clear definition of Cuba's status at the conclusion of a war. The adoption of the Teller Amendment, which stated that Cuba would not become part of the United States, paved the way for a successful declaration of war. On April 22, the American North Atlantic squadron left its forward base in the Florida Keys and blockaded Havana Harbor.

The two branches of the American armed forces were not on an equal footing. Although the navy had been operating according to advance plans, it possessed a modern—if modest—fleet and was ready for action. The army was poorly positioned and unprepared for war when McKinley called for 125,000 volunteers. A case in point was Commodore George Dewey's devastating assault on the Spanish fleet at Manilla on May 1, 1898. Although he would not land substantial ground forces in the Philippines until August, Dewey had neutralized the Spanish military presence with one devastating blow of naval power.

McKinley was an active war president. He created a war room in the White House with the latest maps and charts and used telegraph and telephone to directly to the important army and navy headquarters. Through these means, the commander in chief kept in daily, if not hourly, contact with his commanders in the field.

On June 14, 1898, six weeks after the initial date the president requested, the American invasion force sailed from Tampa, Florida, to Cuba under the command of General William Shafter. Less than a month after landing, the American forces won several important battles and captured control of Santiago.

As fighting in Cuba petered out and General Shafter began discussions over a cease-fire with Spanish commanders, General Nelson Miles departed Cuba with 3,300 men in late July to occupy Puerto Rico, a move that was largely unopposed by the Spanish forces on the island.

Meanwhile, yellow fever swept through American camps in Cuba, killing far more soldiers than Spanish bullets. On August 3, a group of officers signed a round-robin letter, written by Colonel Theodore Roosevelt and addressed to General Shafter, demanding the withdrawal of American forces from Cuba. The letter and its statement that anyone responsible for the delay in shipping American troops home would also be responsible for the unnecessary deaths of thousands due to disease absolutely infuriated President McKinley.

On August 12, a protocol ending hostilities was signed. This marked the culmination of a month of negotiations between Spanish authorities and General Shafter in Cuba to bring the war to an end. McKinley agreed to transport the Spanish soldiers back home across the Atlantic in U.S. ships. Meanwhile, the president appointed a peace commission to negotiate with Spanish delegates in Paris. McKinley was firm on his demands that Spain must abandon Cuba and that the United States would take possession of Puerto Rico and Guam. He was initially less certain about the Philippines. Ultimately, however, he was concerned that either the Germans or the Japanese would take possession of the islands if the United States did not. In October he wired his decision to the commissioners in Paris. Across the table, the Spanish requested to retain Puerto Rico and for the United States to assume the Spanish debt in Cuba. McKinley refused to give serious consideration to the first request. Although he did not assume the Spanish debt in Cuba, he agreed to a $20 million indemnity to Spain. After several months of work, a treaty was signed on November 28, 1898. The United States gained position of Guam, the Philippines, and Puerto Rico. Cuba became an independent nation. It took all of McKinley's legislative skills to win over two anti-imperialist Southern Democrats in order to get the two-thirds required vote for ratification by the Senate.

Under the provisions of the Teller Amendment, the United States pledged to support Cuban independence following the conclusion of the war with Spain. Although some wanted to renege on this legislation, McKinley considered himself bound by the law. He called Cuban elections in early 1901 to form a constitutional convention. However, he supported an American protectorate on the island, fearing possible German influence. Appointment of General Leonard Wood, an ardent imperialist, as governor signaled a strong position. In March 1901, Congress passed the Platt Amendment to a military appropriations bill. This called for a treaty between Cuba and the United States that would grant the United States the right to intervene to maintain domestic order as a precondition to the removal of American forces from the island. The Cuban constitutional convention requested alternations, but McKinley remained firm on the wording. With great reluctance, the new Cuban government signed the treaty in 1902. The Platt Amendment represented a form of tutelage that irritates the relations between the two countries up to this day.

The Spanish-American War and the new possession of the Philippines highlighted the need for a cross-isthmus canal through Central America. McKinley negotiated a new agreement with Great Britain that would supersede the Clayton-Bulwer Treaty of 1850, which required any such project to be a joint venture. However, the subsequent Hay-Pauncefote Treaty of 1900 proved unpopular with Republicans in the Senate because it required the canal to be neutral through guarantees from international powers and forbade the United States from building any defensive installations. Under withering criticism from his own party and with other important pending legislative matters in an election year, McKinley did not invest much presidential prestige behind the treaty. The Senate amended the agreement to remove these objectionable provisions. McKinley signed the revised treaty and forwarded it to Great Britain. After the British government rejected the amended treaty, Secretary of State John Hay entered a new round of negotiations with greater awareness of what it would take to win Senate ratification. At this juncture, however, McKinley was assassinated. The second Hay-Pauncefote Treaty removed the international guarantees and pledged the United States to neutrality but with the right to defend the canal in wartime. The new president, Theodore Roosevelt, who vehemently attacked the original version of the treaty, fully supported the second version. The Senate ratified it on December 16, 1901.

The annexation of Hawaii and the unexpected acquisition of the Philippines made the United States a Pacific power with increasing national interest in Asia. Under pressure of German and Russian expansion in 1898, it appeared that a weakened China might be dismembered. To protect American interests, Secretary John Hay proposed an international open-door policy toward China. In sum, this would protect China's sovereignty, maintain peace, and preserve equal access to markets. As Hay's notes were being considered by foreign ministers, Chinese resentment of occupation by the European powers and Japan boiled over into the Boxer Rebellion. In May 1900, the secret societies known as the Boxers entered Peking (now Beijing) and surrounded the foreign quarter, besieging embassies. Fearing their citizens would be massacred, an international force was assembled under the banner of the China Relief Expedition. McKinley pulled 2,500 troops from suppressing the insurrection in the

Philippines as the American contribution to this international force. In August, the force entered Peking and ended the Boxer Rebellion. Concerned that this incident would give a reason for the European powers and Japan to further encroachment on Chinese sovereign territory, Hay and McKinley reiterated the principles of the Open Door. Although never adopted as a treaty or binding international agreement, the Open Door notes marked an American foreign policy innovation.

Major Accomplishments and Unfinished Business

McKinley handily won reelection in 1900. This time, young war hero and governor of New York Theodore Roosevelt was his running mate. The second spot on the ballot was opened by the death of Vice President Garret Hobart, whom McKinley had worked well with and had entrusted the important task of shepherding Congress behind the administration's legislative proposals. The Democrats again nominated William Jennings Bryan, this time with Adlai Stevenson as vice presidential candidate.

On September 6, 1901, as the president greeted members of the public at the Buffalo Exposition, Leon Czolgosz shot the president in the abdomen. He died eight days later. Theodore Roosevelt became the 26th president of the United States.

Throughout his presidency, McKinley held his cards close to his vest, and it is impossible to know what he might have done in his second term had he not been assassinated. There were many important, unresolved issues that he had been working on, including antitrust policy, colonial government, a canal across Central America, tariff revision, and banking legislation, to name a few. Theodore Roosevelt tackled many of these issues in his administration, as well as several that McKinley had not even addressed (such as the conservation of natural resources).

His presidency was not without failures. Swift conclusion of the war with Spain found the administration without a clear and cohesive plan for colonial governance. The bloody insurgency in the Philippines might have been avoidable if the United States had been better prepared for the postwar challenges of colonial government. His obsession with the tariff as the most important economic issue drowned out other areas that had to be addressed later. Yet despite the fact that he could not complete his second term, McKinley left a significant list of accomplishments. He added Hawaii and expanded the interests of the United States as a global power, even if he and the nation were not quite prepared for this. His administration coincided with the restoration of prosperity and created a sense of unity and optimism that was greatly at odds with the discord and divisiveness of the previous two decades. After three decades of a weak executive office, he expanded the power of the presidency within the federal government and its influence with the public.

ANALYTICAL ESSAY

After soundly defeating the Democrat William Jennings Bryan in the exciting election of 1896, President-elect William McKinley's first task was to formulate a cabinet. The cabinet was a much more significant institution in the 19th century than it is the 21st century. Like his contemporaries, McKinley's White House staff consisted of a couple of private secretaries who provided clerical support for appointments, state papers, and the president's voluminous correspondence. Following the tradition of George Washington, presidents of the 19th century relied on the cabinet for advice, and the public expected that this body would counsel the chief executive in both normal political matters and in times of grave national crises. A proper cabinet had to balance the political factions of the party as well as state or regional interests. Managerial or administrative competence and expertise was more of a bonus than a prerequisite to appointment. McKinley's initial cabinet selections were fairly conventional, but he demonstrated a more serious appreciation of talent when later nominating successors.

The most important position of secretary of state went to fellow Ohioan John Sherman, a clear demonstration of loyalty to the Buckeye state's favorite son. However, Sherman was long past his prime, which quickly became evident during the diplomatic crisis over Cuba. McKinley eventually replaced him with the erudite John Hay. An excellent choice, Hay possessed more international experience and a superior grasp of the potential challenges and benefits resulting from the nation's rapidly growing position in the world. Lyman Gage, a gold-standard advocate who had supported both Republicans and Democrats in the past, received the appointment as secretary of the treasury. Former Michigan governor and businessman Russell Alger was given the portfolio of secretary of war. Overwhelmed by the demands of his office, Alger proved to be a very poor choice when the United States went to war with Spain; he was later replaced with the very talented Elihu Root of New York. John Long of Massachusetts, a friend of the president, became secretary of the navy. Though Long struggled with keeping his assistant, the hyperactive expansionist Theodore Roosevelt, on the same page as the administration, he efficiently performed his duties. Joseph McKenna, a Catholic from California, was chosen as attorney general. He served only a short time before McKinley elevated him to the United States Supreme Court and put John Griggs in the Justice Department. Griggs remained throughout the remainder of McKinley's first term, and Philander Knox served as McKinley's third and final Attorney General. James Wilson, a Scottish immigrant who made his political career in Iowa, received the appointment to the Agriculture Department. Wilson would continue to serve under presidents Theodore Roosevelt and William Howard Taft, becoming the longest-serving cabinet member in American history. James Gary, a Maryland businessman, became postmaster general, an important position for dispensing patronage. Finally, wealthy merchant and protective tariff advocate Cornelius Bliss assumed the post of secretary of the interior.

As president, McKinley relied on his cabinet members to run the day-to-day operations of their department. However, he freely stepped in during times of crisis when he wanted to have a firm grip on policies. As the crisis with Spain over Cuba in late 1897 and early 1898 deepened, he largely took over the diplomatic functions himself, easily bypassing the aged and feeble John Sherman. Unlike most 19th-century presidents who ignored their vice presidents, McKinley relied a great deal on Garret Hobart as a liaison to the Congress. Hobart's death in 1899 deprived McKinley of a trusted friend and adviser. For some matters, McKinley preferred the creation of commissions. By reporting directly to the president, commissions allowed McKinley a method to exercise some executive authority over policy in areas he considered important without having to get bogged down in details.

Throughout his political career, and indeed his presidency, McKinley was accused of being weak and indecisive because he rarely proclaimed a bold and definitive course of action. Instead, he was extremely cautious and conservative when considering policy, arriving at his decisions only after great deliberation. He consulted widely, including with members of his cabinet, often amiably smiling and nodding as others spoke. Like Franklin D. Roosevelt, McKinley gave the impression that he agreed with everyone to whom he spoke. Ultimately, however, McKinley largely kept his own ideas and judgments to himself. McKinley was his own man, and the policies of administrations belonged the president.

Like Franklin Roosevelt and Barack Obama, McKinley came to office at a time of economic crisis. The question of economic restoration bedeviled McKinley's predecessor, Grover Cleveland, the Democrat elected in 1892. For McKinley, the solution to the depressed economy was a protective tariff. By preventing foreign manufacturers from dumping cheap and inferior goods on the American markets, McKinley firmly believed that increased import duties would drive up wages for American workers, restore the flow of gold into the treasury department, and resuscitate economy. He had always been an advocate for a protective tariff; it was his signature political issue as a congressman who represented a district with an increasing number of factories. Increasing tariff rates was his core promise to voters in his 1896 campaign.

As soon as he took the oath of office, McKinley called a special session of Congress to address the economy; otherwise, Congress would not have met until December. Even when one equates legislation to sausage-making, tariff bills were particularly unseemly. There were thousands of lines affecting items ranging from raw materials to finished goods, from common products found in every household to luxuries like art that only a few could afford, each with its own constituency of advocates and opponents. Once the Ways and Means Committee sent its finished bill to the floor, the members of the House of Representatives offered what could be hundreds of amendments. Then it went to the Senate, where hundreds more amendments were added. Because the process often produced rival versions that were at odds with one another, a contentious conference committee had to compromise on a final bill. To further complicate the process, the tariff was more than the sum of its many lines—it was the main source of federal revenue at a time when there was serious concern about budgetary surpluses. Backed by a clear Republican majority and flush with victory, the House of Representatives overcame these challenges and produced a bill at lightning speed during the special session.

Despite the rapid pace in the House, the legislation stalled in the upper chamber as senators introduced over 400 amendments. The administration's proposed international approach to adoption of bimetallic currency further complicated matters. France hoped to leverage this in exchange for lower rates on its important products like olive oil and wine. The Senate did not oblige France directly, but it did add a reciprocity clause to the bill that would allow the president to negotiate directly with nations to lower the import duties on specific items while securing likewise treatment for U.S. exports. This had been a feature in previous tariffs, including the McKinley Tariff of 1890. The president was pleased with this compromise and signed the Dingley Tariff on July 24, 1897, when the term of the special session expired.

The Dingley Tariff introduced the highest duties on imports in American history up to that point. It remained on the books until replaced by the Payne-Aldrich Tariff of 1909, making it one of the longest-lived tariff acts in American history—a testimony to McKinley's successful strategy. By making it the focus of his presidential campaign, rallying the party around reform, calling a special session, and staying out of intricate details, McKinley enjoyed the satisfaction of delivering on his most fundamental promise to voters. The new administration projected competence that stood in sharp contrast to the previous one.

McKinley had no such success in pursuit of an international agreement on bimetallic currency, but it must also be noted that it was an issue that seemed much less important to the president, the party, and the electorate. Despite France's support, Great Britain proved the fatal obstacle to the scheme. After expressing sympathy for the proposal at first, the British government rejected it in October after colonial officials in India voiced grave concerns about reopening mines as the price of silver declined. Without the support of London, the financial capital of the world, the plan stood no chance. It is hard to tell if McKinley had much hope in an international treaty that would have standardized the exchange of both gold and silver. This was not nearly as organized as the international discussions over global finance that took place in 1933. Little ground work had been prepared in 1897, and the task was delegated to a roving commission of second- or even third-tier figures that traveled from capital to capital in hopes of persuading governments to agree to a largely U.S. program at a time when the United States was still seen as a second-rate power in Europe.

In any event, serious interest in the monetization of silver had already passed. Even during the 1896 canvass, Bryan was losing support as decreasing silver prices and increasing commodity prices seemed to undercut the foundations of his economic program. Large gold discoveries in South Africa and Alaska flushed the global economy with specie, fueling prosperity throughout the world. Instead of a cross on which to crucify mankind, gold seemed to be the bridge to a new age of wealth. In early 1900, McKinley signed legislation placing the United States on the gold standard. The currency monetization wars that had rocked American politics over the last quarter century were over. In achieving a major feat (even if it was not one he had campaigned on) and taking full credit for the gold-fueled, post-depression prosperity in an election year, McKinley bypassed the more complicated but related issue of banking reform. Thorough banking reform would have to wait until the Federal Reserve Act of 1913.

After checking off the two top items on his agenda, McKinley changed his focus from the domestic economy to foreign affairs. In doing so, the president moved into unfamiliar territory. As a congressman and governor, his political career was entirely based on domestic politics. He had almost no experience (or interest) in international affairs and diplomacy prior to becoming president; both he and Bryan had hardly mentioned the topic in their presidential campaigns. Surely it would have been a great surprise to McKinley had he known that his presidency would become dominated by questions of war and empire and that he would forever alter the role of the United States in the world.

McKinley's most immediate foreign policy objective was to add the Hawaiian Islands. President Benjamin Harrison, the last Republican president, submitted an annexation treaty to the Senate in the closing days of his administration. The treaty had been negotiated with a government consisting of a small group of wealthy American planters who had overthrown the native monarchy. The staunchly anti-imperialist Democrat Grover Cleveland withdrew it from consideration soon after taking office in 1893. McKinley lobbied senators to support an annexation treaty, but it was tough going to get commitments from the requisite two-thirds to obtain consent. A combination of fears about expanding American reach so deep into the Pacific Ocean and racist anxiety about absorbing a region where dark-skinned natives vastly outnumbered whites stalled further consideration.

Despite McKinley's desire to obtain Hawaii, he was certainly not in the camp of Republican militants like Assistant Secretary of the Navy Theodore Roosevelt or Senator Henry Cabot Lodge, who demanded that the United States shed what they considered a childish isolationism and take up the so-called "white man's burden" of imperialism. As a Civil War veteran who'd witnessed the horrors of Antietam in 1862, McKinley took his role as commander in chief seriously and did not glorify war in the way that the young imperialists did. He was not influenced, as they were, by *Influence of Sea Power on History* (1890) by Alfred Thayer Mahan or driven by existential anxiety over the closing of the frontier in 1890. If McKinley shared one trait with these younger imperialists, it was his belief that the white race was superior to the darker-skinned races. In the end, it was this belief, as much as anything, that convinced McKinley that the United States had to take on what he saw as the duties and obligations of colonial possessions in the aftermath of the Spanish-American War.

Cuba, the last bastion of the once great Spanish Empire in the Americas, suddenly grabbed the president's attention in the fall of 1897. He devoted most of his December State of the Union address to unveiling the administration's policy toward Cuba and Spain. The most recent rebellion began in 1895. Hyperbolic reporting by the so-called yellow journals convinced many Americans that Cuba suffered greatly under extreme Spanish barbarism and cruelty. The United States had long coveted the island. In the Ostend Manifesto of 1854, American ministers brashly announced the intention to annex Cuba. Over the next 20 years, several filibuster expeditions launched from ports in the United States unsuccessfully attempted to seize control of the island. In 1873, Spanish capture of one such American-registered vessel led to a crisis, but President Ulysses Grant preferred a diplomatic solution to military intervention.

It was Grant's precedent that the cautious McKinley cited to support his own decision in December 1897 against both intervention and recognition of Cuban rebels. Noting that Americans were in no imminent danger—thanks in large measure to the Congress acceding to his request for funds earlier in the year to evacuate most Americans—there was no reason to intervene. It was an anticlimactic reveal that angered Cuban rebels, Republican imperialists, pro-intervention newspaper editors, and any American citizen sympathetic to the revolutionary cause for whatever reason.

In late January 1898, McKinley, feeling the pressure of the interventionists and their allies in the press, dispatched the cruiser USS *Maine* to Cuba to demonstrate the administration's resolve. Two weeks later, over 250 people were killed when the *Maine* exploded in Havana Harbor. Although some called for war, the president refused to rush into any action or draw any hasty conclusions, and a naval board of inquiry convened to conduct an investigation. Meanwhile, as a precaution, the United States made some military preparations. Congress increased appropriations, forces were repositioned, and plans were drawn for potential conflict not just in Cuba but also in Guam, the Philippines, and Puerto Rico. On March 11, 1898, the board of inquiry reported that an external explosion had caused the tragedy. However, the report declined to speculate on who might have been responsible for the explosion. To those who had been advocating for military intervention for months, if not years, it was obvious that Spain was the culprit. However, McKinley stuck to the conclusions of the board and attempted another round of diplomacy. The fundamental fact was that due to their own domestic politics, Spain could never grant Cuba any autonomy. Having realized this and believing that the situation could only get worse, McKinley asked Congress for a declaration of war. On April 25, after the addition of the Teller Amendment, which stipulated that the United States would not take possession of Cuba after its liberation, Congress sent a bill declaring war on Spain to the White House for the president's signature.

McKinley received a great deal of criticism from the imperialists in his own party who demanded war. They claimed that American honor was at stake and that the president demonstrated an appalling case of indecision in a moment of national crisis. Those closest to McKinley noted the physical effects that the strain of events took on him as he tried to resist the drumbeat for war and ignore what could be very hurtful and personal criticism. Knowing exactly what McKinley thought at any given time is difficult because he notoriously held his cards very close to his vest and rarely disclosed his innermost thoughts. Neither did he leave much evidence of his thoughts in the form of letters. Historians have generally been sympathetic to McKinley, who they believed genuinely hoped to avoid sending young Americans to death. He had, they claimed, made good faith efforts to negotiate with Spain, and he intervened for humanitarian ends.

McKinley was an active wartime commander in chief. He had a dedicated war room created in the White House, added telephone and telegraph lines that connected him with important commanders, and centralized strategic decisions in his own hands, probably to an even greater extent than Lincoln had done. Certainly this was partly due to McKinley's sense of leadership responsibility. Like later presidents Harry Truman and John Kennedy, McKinley did not valorize war and did not fully trust his military advisers. And like Truman and Kennedy, McKinley knew this because he had served as a junior officer, had experienced combat, and had a soldier's skepticism of generals and their command decisions. Another important factor was the incompetence of Secretary of War Alger, who had, among other things, failed to prepare the army for imminent operations. It was too inexpedient to replace him at this juncture, so in effect McKinley became his own secretary of war, circumventing Alger.

During six months of active combat, the United States conducted operations in the Philippines, Puerto Rico, and Guam, in addition to Cuba. While the navy performed effectively and efficiently to capture its objectives, the army's performance was barely adequate. Its operations were poorly managed and coordinated; its commanders were lethargic and indecisive despite McKinley's nudging. Success in the ground war resulted more from the low morale and attrition already caused by Cuban rebels to the Spaniards than from superior American arms. In fact, a convincing case could be made that the Cubans would have defeated the Spanish soon enough without any American invention and secured their own independence. This position is advanced by scholars who researched Spanish language sources rarely utilized by American historians, and who argue that McKinley could be more accurately be characterized as another in the long line of Americans who had long coveted Cuba rather than as the reluctant warrior and empire builder.

Signed in December 1898, the Treaty of Paris ended the Spanish-American War. Despite his reputation for being soft, McKinley was a tough negotiator and insisted that Spain give up Cuba, Guam, Puerto Rico, and the Philippines. Spain attempted to retain Puerto Rico and sought American assumption of debts for Cuba. McKinley countered that the United States would provide $20 million in restitution to Spain for the loss of Cuba but would not relinquish on Puerto Rico. Although the terms of the Teller Amendment guaranteed Cuban independence, the United States absorbed Guam, Puerto Rico, and the Philippines as territories.

The additions of 1898 were a stunning expansion of American overseas empire. McKinley forever changed the United States and its place in the world. No longer could it claim to be aloof from global affairs. All subsequent presidents would have to adjust to the redefined United States with far-reaching national security concerns and obligations. There is some evidence that McKinley struggled with this decision, particularly the additions of the Philippines and

Puerto Rico as territories. Ultimately, McKinley concluded that to abandon them to an ill-prepared independence was to doom them to further bloodshed and struggle—and even worse, conquest by a much harsher colonial overlord such as Germany or Japan. In this manner, he convinced himself that the United States possessed a moral obligation to teach the native peoples responsible self-government. Much of McKinley's remaining time in office was spent dealing with colonial government and the fallout of new, suddenly conceived empire that the government and nation had been ill prepared to accept.

McKinley had given little thought to the postwar plans for the Philippines. The focus of the war had been Cuba, just 90 miles off the coast of Florida, and Congress had provided some direction with the Teller Amendment. No such clarity existed for the faraway archipelago in the Pacific. As McKinley moved in his usual deliberate if plodding manner while deciding how to govern the Philippines, the Filipinos took matters into their own hands by forming a constitutional convention. On January 1, 1899, they constituted a government and declared resistance leader Emilio Aguinaldo president of the new nation. Undeterred, McKinley continued at his own pace. Three weeks later, he appointed a commission to conduct an investigation of conditions on the islands and make recommendations. Aguinaldo responded by declaring war against the United States. McKinley sent reinforcements and granted his military commanders wide latitude in conducting operations against the Filipinos.

Over the next three years, bitter fighting swept through the Philippines. At its height, 75,000 American troops were deployed in the campaign to suppress the rebellion. By the time the war ended in 1902 (after McKinley's own death at the hand of an assassin), over 4,000 Americans had been killed in the fighting. However, these losses were vastly eclipsed by deaths among the Filipinos: over 20,000 insurgents and 200,000 civilians died. The death toll and the use of controversial methods that they had criticized Spain for using in Cuba embarrassed the administration. If there was one saving grace when it came to public relations, it was that much of the press was more interested in pointing out the sins of the British Empire in its war against the Boer insurgents in South Africa

than it was in examining the cost of its own nation's empire.

In tandem with the military campaign, McKinley forged ahead with the creation of civil government on the Philippines. In 1900 he appointed a second and more powerful commission under the chairmanship of future president William Howard Taft to conduct an investigation of conditions on the islands and make recommendations for future action. Concerned about the welfare of the Filipino people, Taft tried to restrain the army and clashed often with the aggressive military governor, General Arthur MacArthur. In 1902, after the war ended, many of Taft's reforms were implemented, including the establishment of a national legislature, greater economic independence, an education system, and land redistribution. McKinley ended rule by military decree and appointed Taft civil governor. Although several steps were made toward greater self-governance in the 1930s, it was not until 1946, after the World War II, that the Philippines gained its full independence from the United States.

The administration pushed several initiatives in 1899 and 1900 to meet new economic and national security interests in Asia. McKinley understood the importance of the navy for protecting the United States' new far-flung possessions. If Guam, Hawaii, and Midway were bases stretching across the Pacific to the Philippines and Asia, a canal across Central America was required to facilitate the defense over such a vast distance. In McKinley's mind, Puerto Rico was essential to protecting the eastern approaches to any future canal. The three-month voyage of the USS *Oregon* in 1898 from San Francisco, California, around South America to join the blockade in Cuba demonstrated the need for a shortcut.

The first step was to renegotiate the 1850 Clayton-Bulwer Treaty with Great Britain, which stipulated any canal across the isthmus would be a joint venture. After months of negotiations, the Hay-Pauncefote Treaty was signed in 1900. Secretary of State Hay secured American rights to build a canal but not to defend or fortify it. The Senate ratified the treaty after adding amendments to appease more militant expansionists. Great Britain refused to accept these changes, and Hay entered another round of negotiations. This second version of a treaty, which was concluded after

McKinley's death, produced a more acceptable agreement and permitted the United States to defend any canal. President Theodore Roosevelt, who had been very dissatisfied with the original version, approved the second version and forwarded it to the Senate; it was ratified in late December 1901. This might have been an important first step for construction of a canal, but it still was a long way from having a canal. It is hard to know what McKinley would have done next, or if he would have acted as decisively and swiftly as Roosevelt later did in recognizing Panama's independence from Columbia in order to build a canal.

McKinley's negotiation with Great Britain over a canal was part of a growing rapprochement between the two Anglo nations. His attitude was certainly more respectful to a treaty partner than that of his predecessor, Chester Arthur, who unilaterally declared Clayton-Bulwer null and void when he submitted the Frelinghuysen-Zavilla Treaty to the Senate in 1884. Granted Arthur's confusing reasons and failure to obtain ratification of a treaty with Nicaragua to construct a canal certainly did not offer a promising example to emulate. McKinley also worked with Great Britain for peaceful settlement of boundary issues between Alaska and Canada, and the two nations were coming to see that they had common concerns with aggressive German colonial expansion and navalism.

The United States was not the only nation expanding its overseas territorial holdings in the Pacific. European powers and Japan gobbled up ports in China and established closed spheres of influence, or zones of control. This posed a problem for American merchants who had been steadily increasing their trade in China throughout the 19th century. Just when the sudden acquisition of Guam, Hawaii, Midway, and the Philippines, combined with the possibility of a canal across Central America, offered great promise for a dramatic increase in trade with Asia, European imperialism threatened to shut the United States out of the largest market on the continent. It is with this background that Secretary of State John Hay authored the Open Door notes in September 1899. Hay proposed open and equal access to markets in China regardless of any sphere of influence. Although Hay and McKinley did not contest the creation of spheres of influence, they wanted to weaken them by eliminating any discriminatory rates or agreements in which nations would favor their own businesses over those of other powers. In addition, the open-door concept would preserve the sovereignty of China over its own territory. The Open Door notes were more an expression of an ideal that would establish a standard for international conduct toward China than it was an attempt to create an agreement that other nations pledged to support. Overall, the imperial powers opposed to varying degrees the proposal, and because they held all the cards, they saw little reason to voluntarily weaken their own position regarding China when the United States offered them little in return. The notes did not substantively alter events in China at the time, but they were an important development in American diplomatic history as the United States boldly took a much greater interest in global affairs. If the 20th century can accurately be called the American Century, characterized by emergence of the United States as a superpower that triumphed in two world wars and a 40-year cold war, it clearly began with the Spanish-American War in 1898 and proceeded through Hay's Open Door notes the following year.

American policy makers in faraway Washington, D.C., might have offered one possible solution to foreign expansion, but young Chinese patriots had a much more confrontational idea in mind. Disgusted by the weakness of their own government to resist the loss of national sovereignty, Boxers marched on the imperial capital of Peking (currently Beijing), and in June 1900 they surrounded the district that housed the foreign legations. Capitals throughout the world, including the United States, became deeply concerned about the safety of their citizens trapped by the Boxers. A hastily organized international military force dubbed the Chinese Relief Expedition (CRE) was formed, and McKinley pulled troops from the Philippines. Local commanders were upset to see their forces weakened in the middle of suppressing an insurgency, but the commander in chief felt that they were more urgently needed in China.

Renominated by the Republican Party in July for the election that fall, McKinley had a somewhat complicated balancing act. With the Democrat Party candidate, William Jennings Bryan running, an anti-imperialism campaign that was highly critical of the empire that his opponent was creating, McKinley wanted to downplay the burdens and dangers posed to Americans at the very same time that troops were fighting in China. Fortunately for McKinley, the CRE broke the siege in August and rescued the legations. Believing he possessed enough constitutional authority as commander in chief, McKinley took a bold step exerting executive power and establishing a precedent, whether he intended it or not, by committing American troops to an international military force fighting in a nation with which the United States was at peace. Americans in the 21st century are acclimated to having U.S. troops deployed throughout the globe and engaged in conflicts in several different nations, but it was a new experience for the country in 1900.

With economic recovery giving way to prosperity, growing employment in the cities and rising prices for farmers, a successful war, and a revived sense of manifest destiny, McKinley was almost assured reelection in 1900. The Republican Party nominated the young war hero as president and New York governor Theodore Roosevelt as vice president. This was not McKinley's preference because Roosevelt had been an outspoken critic of the president's foreign policy and had once referred to the commander in chief as having the fortitude of a pastry. Yet McKinley, as was characteristic of him, quickly made peace with the situation and welcomed the addition of an important electoral asset to the ticket. The McKinley-Roosevelt ticket defeated their Democrat Party rivals, William Jennings Bryan and his running mate, Adlai Stevenson.

Although McKinley increased his vote only slightly over his total from four years before, it should not obscure the importance of his victory. No president since Ulysses Grant in 1872 had been reelected. Moreover, McKinley laid the foundations of a Republican coalition associated with patriotism, prosperity, and a muscular foreign policy that would dominate the electoral politics of the nation until 1930. The election of 1900 marked a new electoral system. The era of balanced parties, close elections, and seesaw control of the White House and Congress that characterized the Gilded Age was over.

Strengthened by his reelection, McKinley spent the early months of 1901 attempting to resolve issues related to the United States' new empire before Congress went out of session in March. In the Philippines, the war against the insurrection continued, but McKinley established a civil government and appointed William Howard Taft as governor. Cuba was likewise a complicated challenge for the administration. The Teller Amendment pledged that the United States would not take possession of Cuba after the war. With American troops under the command of noted expansionist General Leonard Wood still on the island, there were some who wanted to either ignore or repeal the Teller Amendment. McKinley did not wish the United States to reverse its position in such a dramatic fashion—especially after he convened a constitutional convention—but he questioned the ability of Cuba to protect itself from becoming dominated by another power, such as Germany. Driven by these concerns, Congress adopted the Platt Amendment, which essentially made Cuba an American protectorate by granting the United States the right to oversee treaties with other nations and to intervene in instances of domestic unrest. Cuban delegates at their constitutional convention objected vehemently, but acceptance of a treaty codifying the Platt Amendment was a prerequisite to independence and withdrawal of American troops. McKinley tried to sugarcoat the bitter pill by promising a tariff reciprocity deal and economic concessions following independence. With great reluctance, the convention voted its approval.

McKinley's decisions regarding the former Spanish colonies produced consequences that continue to reverberate over a century later. Puerto Rico remains a possession of the United States. With both independence and statehood controversial topics, it seems suspended in place as a territory, just as McKinley left it in 1901. The devastating effect of Hurricane Maria in 2018 was a painful reminder of Puerto Rico's semicolonial status. Combined with the Open Door notes, the acquisition of the Philippines, Hawaii, and bases at Guam and Midway extended American commercial and national security issues deep into the Pacific Ocean and the Asian mainland. This placed the United States directly in the path of Japanese expansion, which eventually drew the United States into World War II. McKinley expressed little concern about Japan; he saw Germany as the more threatening power. The Teller and Platt Amendments rendered Cuba into a protectorate of the United States propped up by strong-armed dictators and dominated by American companies, like United Fruit, that acquired vast holdings of lands. This neocolonialism grated on the Cubans in each passing year, fueling Fidel Castro's revolution in 1958 and the creation of a Soviet-backed communist regime. Unlike the Philippines, which remained a staunch American ally in the second half of the 20th century, the antagonism in Cuba created a bitter and hostile enemy and was the scene of the most dangerous superpower nuclear showdown of the Cold War in 1962.

With the expiration of the congressional session, McKinley spent much of the summer of 1901 working on a strategy for his second term and travelling the country. As was his wont to do, he consulted widely and solicited many opinions, but he did not outwardly commit to any particular course of action. Always wanting to preserve the maximum latitude for action and keeping all options open, he kept whatever plans he had to himself. He spent much of the summer travelling the nation. The Pan-American Exposition in Buffalo, New York, was one such stop. On September 5, 1901, while greeting the public, an anarchist shot the president. William McKinley died eight days later of gangrene. Vice President Theodore Roosevelt was sworn in as the 26th president of the United States.

Long overshadowed by his dynamic successor, Theodore Roosevelt, historians began taking a renewed interest in McKinley in the late 1960s. His standing among improved throughout the 20th and 21st centuries as Americans sought a greater understanding of its place in the world, its past history of empire and fighting insurgencies, the growth of presidential power, and the development of the democratic political order. Historians have come to see that some of many of Roosevelt's significant achievements, such as construction of the Panama Canal and use of executive authority, were built on foundations laid by his predecessor. However, Roosevelt had many substantial accomplishments that could not be attributed to McKinley, such as conservation policy (an issue that McKinley had no interest) and application of the Sherman Anti-Trust Act (which McKinley never committed to doing).

McKinley's three greatest impacts on the history of the United States are the additions of territory to the United States, including the future state of Hawaii; growth of the United States as a global imperial power with a strong interest in the Pacific Ocean; expansion of executive power, including such precedents as deploying American troops overseas to suppress insurgencies; and his role in ushering a new electoral system marked by a generation of national political dominance by his Republican Party. Furthermore, he elevated several young and talented Republicans to important positions in his administration; two of them went on to become president, and one became vice president. McKinley should be seen as the first of the modern, 20th-century presidents. These are significant and enduring legacies for the 25th president of the United States.

Gregory Dehler

Further Reading

Armstrong, William H. 2000. *Major McKinley: William McKinley and the Civil War*. Kent, OH: Kent State University Press.

Calhoun, Charles W. 2010. *From Bloody Shirt to Full Dinner Pail: The Transformation of Politics and Governance in the Gilded Age*. New York: Hill and Wang.

Cherny, Robert W. 1997. *American Politics in the Gilded Age, 1868–1900*. Wheeling, IL: Harlan Davidson.

Gould, Lewis. 1980. *The Presidency of William McKinley*. Lawrence: University of Kansas Press.

Harpine, William D. 2005. *From the Front Porch to the Front Page: McKinley and Bryan in the 1896 Presidential Campaign*. College Station: Texas A&M University Press.

Morgan, H. Wayne. 1963. *William McKinley and His America*. Syracuse: Syracuse University Press.

O'Toole, G. J. A. 1984. *The Spanish War: An American Epic, 1898*. New York: W. W. Norton & Company.

Perez, Louis A. 1998. *The War of 1898: The United States & Cuba in History & Historiography*. Chapel Hill: University of North Carolina Press.

Phillips, Kevin. 2003. *William McKinley*. The American Presidents Series. Edited by Arthur M. Schlesinger Jr. New York: Times Books.

Rauchway, Eric. 2003. *Murdering McKinley: The Making of Theodore Roosevelt's America*. New York: Hill and Wang.

Rove, Karl. 2015. *The Triumph of William McKinley: Why the Election of 1896 Still Matters*. New York: Simon & Schuster.

William McKinley Papers, circa 1847–1935. n.d. Library of Congress. https://www.loc.gov/item/mm79032268/.

Williams, R. Hal. 2010. *Realigning America: McKinley, Bryan, and the Remarkable Election of 1896*. American Presidential Elections Series. Founding series editors, Donald R. McCoy, Clifford E. Griffin, and Homer E. Socolofsky. Lawrence: University Press of Kansas.

First Inaugural Address (March 4, 1897)

In McKinley's first inaugural address, which he delivered from the Capitol Building, he mainly spoke of domestic and economic issues that focused on recovering from the depression that began in 1893. He spoke little of foreign policy matters that would dominate his presidency.

Fellow-Citizens:

In obedience to the will of the people, and in their presence, by the authority vested in me by this oath, I assume the arduous and responsible duties of President of the United States, relying upon the support of my countrymen and invoking the guidance of Almighty God. Our faith teaches that there is no safer reliance than upon the God of our fathers, who has so singularly favored the American people in every national trial, and who will not forsake us so long as we obey His commandments and walk humbly in His footsteps.

The responsibilities of the high trust to which I have been called—always of grave importance—are augmented by the prevailing business conditions entailing idleness upon willing labor and loss to useful enterprises. The country is suffering from industrial disturbances from which speedy relief must be had. Our financial system needs some revision; our money is all good now, but its value must not further be threatened. It should all be put upon an enduring basis, not subject to easy attack, nor its stability to doubt or dispute. Our currency should continue under the supervision of the Government. The several forms of our paper money offer, in my judgment, a constant embarrassment to the Government and a safe balance in the Treasury. Therefore I believe it necessary to devise a system which, without diminishing the circulating medium or offering a premium for its contraction, will present a remedy for those arrangements which, temporary in their nature, might well in the years of our prosperity have been displaced by wiser provisions. With adequate revenue secured, but not until then, we can enter upon such changes in our fiscal laws as will, while insuring safety and volume to our money, no longer impose upon the Government the necessity of maintaining so large a gold reserve, with its attendant and inevitable temptations to speculation. Most of our financial laws are the outgrowth of experience and trial, and should not be amended without investigation and demonstration of the wisdom of the proposed changes. We must be both "sure we are right" and "make haste slowly." If, therefore, Congress, in its wisdom, shall deem it expedient to create a commission to take under early consideration the revision of our coinage, banking and currency laws, and give them that exhaustive, careful and dispassionate examination that their importance demands, I shall cordially concur in such action. If such power is vested in the President, it is my purpose to appoint a commission of prominent, well-informed citizens of different parties, who will command public confidence, both on account of their ability and special fitness for the work. Business experience and public training may thus be combined, and the patriotic zeal of the friends of the country be so directed that such a report will be made as to receive the support of all parties, and our finances cease to be the subject of mere partisan contention. The experiment is, at all events, worth a trial, and, in my opinion, it can but prove beneficial to the entire country.

The question of international bimetallism will have early and earnest attention. It will be my constant endeavor to secure it by co-operation with the other great commercial powers of the world. Until that condition is realized when the parity between our gold and silver money springs from and is supported by the relative value of the two metals, the value of the silver already coined and of that which may hereafter be coined, must be kept constantly at par with gold by every resource at our command. The credit of the Government, the integrity of its currency, and the inviolability of its obligations must be preserved. This was the commanding verdict of the people, and it will not be unheeded.

Economy is demanded in every branch of the Government at all times, but especially in periods, like the present, of depression in business and distress among the people. The severest economy must be observed in all public expenditures, and extravagance stopped wherever it is found, and prevented wherever in the future it may be developed. If the revenues are to remain as now, the only relief that can come must be from decreased expenditures. But the present must not become the permanent condition of the Government. It has been our uniform practice to retire, not increase our outstanding obligations, and this policy must again be resumed and vigorously enforced. Our revenues should always be large enough to meet with ease and promptness not only our current needs and the principal and interest of the public debt, but to make proper and liberal provision for that most deserving body of public creditors, the soldiers and sailors and the widows and orphans who are the pensioners of the United States.

The Government should not be permitted to run behind or increase its debt in times like the present. Suitably to provide against this is the mandate of duty—the certain and easy remedy for most of our financial difficulties. A deficiency is inevitable so long as the expenditures of the Government exceed its receipts. It can only be met by loans or an increased revenue. While a large annual surplus of revenue may invite waste and extravagance, inadequate revenue creates distrust and undermines public and private credit. Neither should be encouraged. Between more loans and more revenue there ought to be but one opinion. We should have more revenue, and that without delay, hindrance, or postponement. A surplus in the Treasury created by loans is not a permanent or safe reliance. It will suffice while it lasts, but it can not last long while the outlays of the Government are greater than its receipts, as has been the case during the past two years. Nor must it be forgotten that however much such loans may temporarily relieve the situation, the Government is still indebted for the amount of the surplus accrued, which it must ultimately pay, while its ability to pay is not strengthened, but weakened by a continued deficit. Loans are imperative in great emergencies to preserve the Government or its credit, but a failure to supply needed revenue in time of peace for the maintenance of either has no justification.

The best way for the Government to maintain its credit is to pay as it goes—not by resorting to loans, but by keeping out of debt—through an adequate income secured by a system of taxation, external or internal, or both. It is the settled policy of the Government, pursued from the beginning and practiced by all parties and Administrations, to raise the bulk of our revenue from taxes upon foreign productions entering the United States for sale and consumption, and avoiding, for the most part, every form of direct taxation, except in time of war. The country is clearly opposed to any needless additions to the subject of internal taxation, and is committed by its latest popular utterance to the system of tariff taxation. There can be no misunderstanding, either, about the principle upon which this tariff taxation shall be levied. Nothing has ever been made plainer at a general election than that the controlling principle in the raising of revenue from duties on imports is zealous care for American interests and American labor. The people have declared that such legislation should be had as will give ample protection and encouragement to the industries and the development of our country. It is, therefore, earnestly hoped and expected that Congress will, at the earliest practicable moment, enact revenue legislation that shall be fair, reasonable, conservative, and just, and which, while supplying sufficient revenue for public purposes, will still be signally beneficial and helpful to every section and every enterprise of the people. To this policy we are all, of whatever party, firmly bound by the voice of the people—a power vastly more potential than the expression of any political platform. The paramount duty of Congress is to stop deficiencies by the restoration of that protective legislation which has always been the firmest prop of the Treasury. The passage of such a law or laws would strengthen the credit of the Government both at home and abroad, and go far toward stopping the drain upon the gold reserve held for the redemption of our currency, which has been heavy and well-nigh constant for several years.

In the revision of the tariff especial attention should be given to the re-enactment and extension of the reciprocity principle of the law of 1890, under which so great a stimulus was given to our foreign trade in new and advantageous markets for our surplus agricultural and manufactured products. The brief trial given this legislation amply justifies a further experiment and additional discretionary power in the making of commercial treaties, the end in view always to be the opening up of new markets for the products of our country, by granting concessions to the products of other lands that we need and cannot produce ourselves, and which do not involve any loss of labor to our own people, but tend to increase their employment.

The depression of the past four years has fallen with especial severity upon the great body of toilers of the country, and upon none more than the holders of small farms. Agriculture has languished and labor suffered. The revival of manufacturing will be a relief to both. No portion of our population is more devoted to the institution of free government nor more loyal in their support, while none bears more cheerfully or fully its proper share in the maintenance of the Government or is better entitled to its wise and liberal care and protection. Legislation helpful to producers is beneficial to all. The depressed condition of industry on the farm and in the mine and factory has lessened the ability of the people to meet the demands upon them, and they rightfully expect that not only a system of revenue shall be established that will secure the largest income with the least burden, but that every means will be taken to decrease, rather than increase, our public expenditures. Business conditions are not the most promising. It will take time to restore the prosperity of former years. If we cannot promptly attain it, we can resolutely turn our faces in that direction and aid its return by friendly legislation. However troublesome the situation may appear, Congress will not, I am sure, be found lacking in disposition or ability to relieve it as far as legislation can do so. The restoration of confidence and the revival of business, which men of all parties so much desire, depend more largely upon the prompt, energetic, and intelligent action of Congress than upon any other single agency affecting the situation.

It is inspiring, too, to remember that no great emergency in the one hundred and eight years of our eventful national life has ever arisen that has not been met with wisdom and courage by the American people, with fidelity to their best interests and highest destiny, and to the honor of the American name. These years of glorious history have exalted mankind and advanced the cause of freedom throughout the world, and immeasurably strengthened the precious free institutions which we enjoy. The people love and will sustain these institutions. The great essential to our happiness and prosperity is that we adhere to the principles upon which the Government was established and insist upon their faithful observance. Equality of rights must prevail, and our laws be always and everywhere respected and obeyed. We may have failed in the discharge of our full duty as citizens of the great Republic, but it is consoling and encouraging to realize that free speech, a free press, free thought, free schools, the free and unmolested right of religious liberty and worship, and free and fair elections are dearer and more universally enjoyed to-day than ever before. These guaranties must be sacredly preserved and wisely strengthened. The constituted authorities must be cheerfully and vigorously upheld. Lynchings must not be tolerated in a great and civilized country like the United States; courts, not mobs, must execute the penalties of the law. The preservation of public order, the right of discussion, the integrity of courts, and the orderly administration of justice must continue forever the rock of safety upon which our Government securely rests.

One of the lessons taught by the late election, which all can rejoice in, is that the citizens of the United States are both law-respecting and law-abiding people, not easily swerved from the path of patriotism and honor. This is in entire accord with the genius of our institutions, and but emphasizes the advantages of inculcating even a greater love for law and order in the future. Immunity should be granted to none who violate the laws, whether individuals, corporations, or communities; and as the Constitution imposes upon the President the duty of both its own execution, and of the statutes enacted in pursuance of its provisions, I shall endeavor carefully to carry them into effect. The declaration of the party now restored to power has been in the past that of "opposition to all combinations of capital organized in trusts, or otherwise, to control arbitrarily the condition of trade among our citizens," and it has supported "such legislation as will prevent the execution of all schemes to oppress the people by undue charges on their supplies, or by unjust rates for the transportation of their products to the market." This purpose will be steadily pursued, both by the enforcement of the laws now in existence and the recommendation and support of such new statutes as may be necessary to carry it into effect.

Our naturalization and immigration laws should be further improved to the constant promotion of a safer, a better, and a higher citizenship. A grave peril to the Republic would be a citizenship too ignorant to understand or too vicious to appreciate the great value and beneficence of our institutions and laws, and against all who come here to make war upon them our gates must be promptly and tightly closed. Nor must we be unmindful of the need of improvement among our own citizens, but with the zeal of our forefathers encourage the spread of knowledge and free education. Illiteracy must be banished from the land if we shall attain that high destiny as the foremost of the enlightened nations of the world which, under Providence, we ought to achieve.

Reforms in the civil service must go on; but the changes should be real and genuine, not perfunctory, or prompted by a zeal in behalf of any party simply because it happens to be in power. As a member of Congress I voted and spoke in favor of the present law, and I shall attempt its enforcement in the spirit in which it was enacted. The purpose in view was to secure the most efficient service of the best men who would accept appointment under the Government, retaining faithful and devoted public servants in office, but shielding none, under the authority of any rule or custom, who are inefficient, incompetent, or unworthy. The best interests of the country demand this, and the people heartily approve the law wherever and whenever it has been thus administered.

Congress should give prompt attention to the restoration of our American merchant marine, once the pride of the seas in all the great ocean highways of commerce. To my mind, few more important subjects so imperatively demand its intelligent consideration.

The United States has progressed with marvelous rapidity in every field of enterprise and endeavor until we have become foremost in nearly all the great lines of inland trade, commerce, and industry. Yet, while this is true, our American merchant marine has been steadily declining until it is now lower, both in the percentage of tonnage and the number of vessels employed, than it was prior to the Civil War. Commendable progress has been made of late years in the upbuilding of the American Navy, but we must supplement these efforts by providing as a proper consort for it a merchant marine amply sufficient for our own carrying trade to foreign countries. The question is one that appeals both to our business necessities and the patriotic aspirations of a great people.

It has been the policy of the United States since the foundation of the Government to cultivate relations of peace and amity with all the nations of the world, and this accords with my conception of our duty now. We have cherished the policy of noninterference with affairs of foreign governments wisely inaugurated by Washington, keeping ourselves free from entanglement, either as allies or foes, content to leave undisturbed with them the settlement of their own domestic concerns. It will be our aim to pursue a firm and dignified foreign policy, which shall be just, impartial, ever watchful of our national honor, and always insisting upon the enforcement of the lawful rights of American citizens everywhere. Our diplomacy should seek nothing more and accept nothing less than is due us. We want no wars of conquest; we must avoid the temptation of territorial aggression. War should never be entered upon until every agency of peace has failed; peace is preferable to war in almost every contingency. Arbitration is the true method of settlement of international as well as local or individual differences. It was recognized as the best means of adjustment of differences between employers and employees by the Forty-ninth Congress, in 1886, and its application was extended to our diplomatic relations by the unanimous concurrence of the Senate and House of the Fifty-first Congress in 1890. The latter resolution was accepted as the basis of negotiations with us by the British House of Commons in 1893, and upon our invitation a treaty of arbitration between the United States and Great Britain was signed at

Washington and transmitted to the Senate for its ratification in January last. Since this treaty is clearly the result of our own initiative; since it has been recognized as the leading feature of our foreign policy throughout our entire national history—the adjustment of difficulties by judicial methods rather than force of arms—and since it presents to the world the glorious example of reason and peace, not passion and war, controlling the relations between two of the greatest nations in the world, an example certain to be followed by others, I respectfully urge the early action of the Senate thereon, not merely as a matter of policy, but as a duty to mankind. The importance and moral influence of the ratification of such a treaty can hardly be overestimated in the cause of advancing civilization. It may well engage the best thought of the statesmen and people of every country, and I cannot but consider it fortunate that it was reserved to the United States to have the leadership in so grand a work.

It has been the uniform practice of each President to avoid, as far as possible, the convening of Congress in extraordinary session. It is an example which, under ordinary circumstances and in the absence of a public necessity, is to be commended. But a failure to convene the representatives of the people in Congress in extra session when it involves neglect of a public duty places the responsibility of such neglect upon the Executive himself. The condition of the public Treasury, as has been indicated, demands the immediate consideration of Congress. It alone has the power to provide revenues for the Government. Not to convene it under such circumstances I can view in no other sense than the neglect of a plain duty. I do not sympathize with the sentiment that Congress in session is dangerous to our general business interests. Its members are the agents of the people, and their presence at the seat of Government in the execution of the sovereign will should not operate as an injury, but a benefit. There could be no better time to put the Government upon a sound financial and economic basis than now. The people have only recently voted that this should be done, and nothing is more binding upon the agents of their will than the obligation of immediate action. It has always seemed to me that the postponement of the meeting of Congress until more than a year after it has been chosen deprived Congress too often of the

inspiration of the popular will and the country of the corresponding benefits. It is evident, therefore, that to postpone action in the presence of so great a necessity would be unwise on the part of the Executive because unjust to the interests of the people. Our action now will be freer from mere partisan consideration than if the question of tariff revision was postponed until the regular session of Congress. We are nearly two years from a Congressional election, and politics cannot so greatly distract us as if such contest was immediately pending. We can approach the problem calmly and patriotically, without fearing its effect upon an early election.

Our fellow-citizens who may disagree with us upon the character of this legislation prefer to have the question settled now, even against their preconceived views, and perhaps settled so reasonably, as I trust and believe it will be, as to insure great permanence, than to have further uncertainty menacing the vast and varied business interests of the United States. Again, whatever action Congress may take will be given a fair opportunity for trial before the people are called to pass judgment upon it, and this I consider a great essential to the rightful and lasting settlement of the question. In view of these considerations, I shall deem it my duty as President to convene Congress in extraordinary session on Monday, the 15th day of March, 1897.

In conclusion, I congratulate the country upon the fraternal spirit of the people and the manifestations of good will everywhere so apparent. The recent election not only most fortunately demonstrated the obliteration of sectional or geographical lines, but to some extent also the prejudices which for years have distracted our councils and marred our true greatness as a nation. The triumph of the people, whose verdict is carried into effect today, is not the triumph of one section, nor wholly of one party, but of all sections and all the people. The North and the South no longer divide on the old lines, but upon principles and policies; and in this fact surely every lover of the country can find cause for true felicitation.

Let us rejoice in and cultivate this spirit; it is ennobling and will be both a gain and a blessing to our beloved country. It will be my constant aim to do nothing, and permit nothing to be done, that will arrest or disturb this growing sentiment of unity and cooperation, this revival of esteem and affiliation which now animates so many thousands in both the old antagonistic sections, but I shall cheerfully do everything possible to promote and increase it. Let me again repeat the words of the oath administered by the Chief Justice which, in their respective spheres, so far as applicable, I would have all my countrymen observe: "I will faithfully execute the office of President of the United States, and will, to the best of my ability, preserve, protect, and defend the Constitution of the United States." This is the obligation I have reverently taken before the Lord Most High. To keep it will be my single purpose, my constant prayer; and I shall confidently rely upon the forbearance and assistance of all the people in the discharge of my solemn responsibilities.

Source: Richardson, James D. *A Compilation of the Messages and Papers of the Presidents 1789–1897*. Vol. 13. New York: Bureau of National Literature, 1897, 6236–6244.

Message Regarding Special Session of Congress (March 15, 1897)

Economic recovery was McKinley's top priority upon assuming the presidency in March 1897. He considered a tariff rate increase as the best means to achieving this goal. In this message, he calls for a special session of Congress to consider this vital question. Had McKinley not called the special session, Congress would not have met until December.

To the Congress of the United States:

Regretting the necessity which has required me to call you together, I feel that your assembling in extraordinary session is indispensable because of the condition in which we find the revenues of the Government. It is conceded that its current expenditures are greater than its receipts, and that such a condition has existed for now more than three years. With unlimited means at our command, we are presenting the remarkable spectacle of increasing our public debt by borrowing money to meet the ordinary outlays incident upon even an economical and prudent administration of the Government. An examination of the subject discloses this fact in every detail and leads inevitably to the conclusion that the condition of the revenue which allows it is unjustifiable and should be corrected.

We find by the reports of the Secretary of the Treasury that the revenues for the fiscal year ending June 30, 1892, from all sources were $425,868,260.22, and the expenditures for all purposes were $415,953,806.56, leaving an excess of receipts over expenditures of $9,914,453.66. During that fiscal year $40,570,467.98 were paid upon the public debt, which had been reduced since March 1, 1889, $259,076,890, and the annual interest charge decreased $11,684,576.60. The receipts of the Government from all sources during the fiscal year ending June 30, 1893, amounted to $461,716,561.94, and its expenditures to $459,374,887.65, showing an excess of receipts over expenditures of $2,341,674.29.

Since that time the receipts of no fiscal year, and with but few exceptions of no month of any fiscal year, have exceeded the expenditures. The receipts of the Government, from all sources, during the fiscal year ending June 30, 1894, were $372,802,498.29, and its expenditures $442,605,758.87, leaving a deficit, the first since the resumption of specie payments, of $69,803,260.58. Notwithstanding there was a decrease of $16,769,128.78 in the ordinary expenses of the Government, as compared with the previous fiscal year, its income was still not sufficient to provide for its daily necessities, and the gold reserve in the Treasury for the redemption of greenbacks was drawn upon to meet them. But this did not suffice, and the Government then resorted to loans to replenish the reserve.

In February, 1894, $50,000,000 in bonds were issued, and in November following a second issue of $50,000,000 was deemed necessary. The sum of $117,171,795 was realized by the sale of these bonds, but the reserve was steadily decreased until, on February 8, 1895, a third sale of $62,315,400 in bonds, for $65,116,244, was announced to Congress.

The receipts of the Government for the fiscal year ending June 30, 1895, were $390,373,203.30, and the expenditures $433,178,426.48, showing a deficit of $42,805,223.18. A further loan of $100,000,000 was negotiated by the Government in February, 1896, the sale netting $1,166,246, and swelling the aggregate of bonds issued within three years to $262,315,400. For the fiscal year ending June 30, 1896, the revenues of the Government from all sources amounted to $409,475,408.78, while its expenditures were $434,678,654.48, or an excess of expenditures over receipts of $25,203,245.70. In other words, the total receipts for the three fiscal years ending June 30, 1896, were insufficient by $137,811,729.46 to meet the total expenditures.

Nor has this condition since improved. For the first half of the present fiscal year, the receipts of the Government, exclusive of postal revenues, were $157,507,603.76, and its expenditures, exclusive of postal service, $195,410,000.22, or an excess of expenditures over receipts of $37,902,396.46. In January of this year, the receipts, exclusive of postal revenues, were $24,316,994.05, and the expenditures, exclusive of postal service, $30,269,389.29, a deficit of $5,952,395.24 for the month. In February of this year, the receipts, exclusive of postal revenues, were $24,400,997.38, and expenditures, exclusive of postal service, $28,796,056.66, a deficit of $4,395,059.28; or a total deficiency of $186,061,580.44 for the three years and eight months ending March 1, 1897. Not only are we without a surplus in the Treasury, but with an increase in the public debt there has been a corresponding increase in the annual interest charge, from $22,893,883.20 in 1892, the lowest of any year since 1862, to $34,387,297.60 in 1896, or an increase of $11,493,414.40.

It may be urged that even if the revenues of the Government had been sufficient to meet all its ordinary expenses during the past three years, the gold reserve would still have been insufficient to meet the demands upon it, and that bonds would necessarily have been issued for its repletion. Be this as it may, it is clearly manifest, without denying or affirming the correctness of such a conclusion, that the debt would have been decreased in at least the amount of the deficiency, and business confidence immeasurably strengthened throughout the country.

Congress should promptly correct the existing condition. Ample revenues must be supplied not only for the ordinary expenses of the Government, but for the prompt payment of liberal pensions and the liquidation of the principal and interest of the public debt. In raising revenue, duties should be so levied upon foreign products as to preserve the home market, so far as possible, to our own producers; to revive and increase manufactures; to relieve and encourage agriculture; to increase our domestic and foreign commerce; to aid and develop mining and building; and to render to labor in every field of useful occupation the liberal wages and adequate rewards to which skill and industry are justly entitled. The necessity of the passage of a tariff law which shall provide ample revenue, need not be further urged. The imperative demand of the hour is the prompt enactment of such a measure, and to this object I earnestly recommend that Congress shall make every endeavor. Before other business is transacted, let us first provide sufficient revenue to faithfully administer the Government without the contracting of further debt, or the continued disturbance of our finances.

Source: Richardson, James D. *A Compilation of the Messages and Papers of the Presidents 1789–1897.* Vol. 13. New York: Bureau of National Literature, 1897, 6244–6246.

John Hay to Andrew D. White: The First Open Door Note (September 6, 1899)

As the commercial and national security interests of the United States in Asia expanded, the McKinley administration developed a far-reaching policy that served as the basis of American foreign policy throughout the 20th century. Secretary of State John Hay outlined this policy in a series of letters to American ambassadors overseas. This particular letter is addressed to Andrew D. White, the U.S. ambassador to Germany, but copies were sent to other capitals on the same date.

Department of State, Washington, September 6, 1899

At the time when the Government of the United States was informed by that of Germany that it had leased from His Majesty the Emperor of China the port of Kiao-chao and the adjacent territory in the province of Shantung, assurances were given to the ambassador of the United States at Berlin by the Imperial German minister for foreign affairs that the rights and privileges insured by treaties with China to citizens of the United States would not thereby suffer or be in anywise impaired within the area over which Germany had thus obtained control.

More recently, however, the British Government recognized by a formal agreement with Germany the exclusive right of the latter country to enjoy in said leased area and the contiguous "sphere of influence or interest" certain privileges, more especially those relating to railroads and mining enterprises; but as the exact nature and extent of the rights thus recognized have not been clearly defined, it is possible that serious conflicts of interest may at any time arise not only between British and German subjects within said area, but that the interests of our citizens may also be jeopardized thereby.

Earnestly desirous to remove any cause of irritation and to insure at the same time to the commerce of all nations in China the undoubted benefits which should accrue from a formal recognition by the various powers claiming "spheres of interest" that they shall enjoy perfect equality of treatment for their commerce and navigation within such "spheres," the Government of the United States would be pleased to see His German Majesty's Government give formal assurances, and lend its cooperation in securing like assurances from the other interested powers, that each, within its respective sphere of whatever influence—

First. Will in no way interfere with any treaty port or any vested interest within any so-called "sphere of interest" or leased territory it may have in China.

Second. That the Chinese treaty tariff of the time being shall apply to all merchandise landed or shipped to all such ports as are within said "sphere of interest" (unless they be "free ports"), no matter to what nationality it may belong, and that duties so leviable shall be collected by the Chinese Government.

Third. That it will levy no higher harbor dues on vessels of another nationality frequenting any port in such "sphere" than shall be levied on vessels of its own nationality, and no higher railroad charges over lines built, controlled, or operated within its "sphere" on merchandise belonging to citizens or subjects of other nationalities transported through such "sphere" than shall be levied on similar merchandise belonging to its own nationals transported over equal distances.

The liberal policy pursued by His Imperial German Majesty in declaring Kiao-chao a free port and in aiding the Chinese Government in the establishment there of a customhouse are so clearly in line with the proposition which this Government is anxious to see recognized that it entertains the strongest hope that Germany will give its acceptance and hearty support. The recent ukase of His Majesty the Emperor of Russia declaring the port of Ta-lien-wan open during the whole of the lease under which it is held from China to the merchant ships of all nations, coupled with the categorical assurances made to this Government by His Imperial Majesty's representative at this capital at the time and since repeated to me by the present Russian ambassador, seem to insure the support of the Emperor to the proposed measure. Our ambassador at the Court of St. Petersburg has in consequence, been instructed to submit it to the Russian Government and to request their early consideration of it. A copy of my instruction on the subject to Mr. Tower is herewith inclosed for your confidential information.

The commercial interests of Great Britain and Japan will be so clearly observed by the desired declaration of intentions, and the views of the Governments of these countries as to the desirability of the adoption of measures insuring the benefits of equality of treatment of all foreign trade throughout China are so similar to those entertained by the United States, that their acceptance of the propositions herein outlined and their cooperation in advocating their adoption by the other powers can be confidently expected. I inclose herewith copy of the instruction which I have sent to Mr. Choate on the subject.

In view of the present favorable conditions, you are instructed to submit the above considerations to His Imperial German Majesty's Minister for L Foreign Affairs, and to request his early consideration of the subject.

Source: U.S. Department of State. *Papers Relating to the Foreign Relations of the United States, 1899.* Washington, D.C.: Government Printing Office, 129–130.

Speech in Buffalo, New York (September 5, 1901)

President McKinley's speech before the Pan-American Exposition in Buffalo, New York, was much lauded at the time by the press. He spoke of trade and communication, economic growth and expansion, and the relationship between the United States and its fellow American states. Little did anyone know that this would be McKinley's last speech.

President Milburn, Director General Buchanan, Commissioners, Ladies and Gentlemen:

I am glad to be again in the city of Buffalo and exchange greetings with her people, to whose generous hospitality I am not a stranger and with whose good will I have been repeatedly and signally honored. To-day I have additional satisfaction in meeting and giving welcome to the foreign representatives assembled here, whose presence and participation in this exposition have contributed in so marked a degree to its interest and success. To the Commissioners of the Dominion of Canada and the British colonies, the French colonies, the republics of Mexico and Central and South America and the commissioners of Cuba and Puerto Rico, who share with us in this undertaking, we give the hand of fellowship and felicitate with them upon the triumphs of art, science, education and manufacture which the old has bequeathed to the new century. Expositions are the timekeepers of progress. They record the world's advancement. They stimulate the energy, enterprise and intellect of the people and quicken human genius. They go into the home. They broaden and brighten the daily life of the people. They open mighty storehouses of information to the student. Every exposition, great or small, has helped to some onward step. Comparison of ideas is always educational, and as such instruct the brain and hand of man. Friendly rivalry follows, which is the spur to industrial improvement, the inspiration to useful invention and to high endeavor in all departments of human activity. It exacts a study of the wants, comforts and even the whims of the people and recognizes the efficiency of high quality and new pieces to win their favor. The quest for trade is an incentive to men of business to devise, invent, improve and economize in the cost of production.

Business life, whether among ourselves or with other people, is ever a sharp struggle for success. It will be none the less so in the future. Without competition we would be clinging to the clumsy antiquated processes of farming and manufacture and the methods of business of long ago, and the twentieth would be no further advanced than the eighteenth century. But though commercial competitors we are, commercial enemies we must not be.

The Pan-American exposition has done its work thoroughly, presenting in its exhibits evidences of the highest skill and illustrating the progress of the human family in the western hemisphere. This portion of the earth has no cause for humiliation for the part it has performed in the march of civilization. It has not accomplished everything from it. It has simply done its best, and without vanity or boastfulness, and recognizing the manifold achievements of others, it invites the friendly rivalry of all the powers in the peaceful pursuits of trade and commerce, and will co-operate with all in advancing the highest and best interests of humanity.

The wisdom and energy of all the nations are none too great for the world's work. The success of art, science, industry and invention is an international asset and a common glory.

After all, how near one to the other is every part of the world. Modern inventions have brought into close relation widely separated peoples and made them better acquainted. Geographic and political divisions will continue to exist, but distances have been effaced. Swift ships and swift trains are becoming cosmopolitan. They invade fields Which a few years ago were impenetrable. The world's products are exchanged as never before, and with increasing transportation facilities come increasing knowledge and larger trade. Prices are fixed with mathematical precision by supply and demand. The world's selling prices are regulated by market and crop reports.

We travel greater distances in a shorter space of time and with more ease than was ever dreamed of by the fathers. Isolation is no longer possible or desirable. The same important news is read, though in different languages, the same day in all Christendom. The telegraph keeps us advised of what is occurring everywhere, and the press foreshadows, with more or less accuracy, the plans and purposes of the nations.

Market prices of products and of securities are hourly known in every commercial mart, and the investments of the people extend beyond their own national boundaries into the remotest parts of the earth. Vast transactions are conducted and international exchanges are made by the tick of the cable. Every event of interest is immediately bulletined. The quick gathering and transmission of news, like rapid transit, are of recent origin and are only made possible by the genius of the inventor and the courage of the investor. It took a special messenger of the Government, with every facility known at the time for rapid travel, nineteen days to go from the city of Washington to New Orleans with a message to General Jackson that the war with England had ceased and a treaty of peace had been signed. How different now!

We reached General Miles in Puerto Rico by cable, and he was able, through the military telegraph, to stop his army on the firing line with the message that the United States and Spain had signed a protocol suspending hostilities. We knew almost instantly of the first shots fired at Santiago, and the subsequent surrender of the Spanish forces was known at Washington within less than an hour of its consummation The first ship of Cervera's fleet had hardly emerged from that historic harbor when the fact was flashed to our capital, and the swift destruction that followed was announced immediately through the wonderful medium of telegraphy.

So accustomed are we to safe and easy communication with distant lands that its temporary interruption, even in ordinary times, results in loss and inconvenience. We shall never forget the days of anxious waiting and awful suspense when no information was permitted to be sent from Pekin, and the diplomatic representatives of the nations in China, cut off from all communication, inside and outside of the walled capital, were surrounded by an angry and misguided mob that threatened their lives; nor the joy that filled the world when a single message from the Government of the United States brought through our minister the first news of the safety of the besieged diplomats.

At the beginning of the nineteenth century there was not a mile of steam railroad on the globe. Now there are enough miles to make its circuit many times. Then there was not a line of electric telegraph; now we have a vast mileage traversing all lands and seas. God and man have linked the nations together. No nation can longer be indifferent to any other. And as we are brought more and more in touch with each other the less occasion there is for misunderstandings and the stronger the disposition, when we have differences, to adjust them in the court of arbitration, which is the noblest forum for the settlement of international disputes.

My fellow citizens, trade statistics indicate that this country is in a state of unexampled prosperity. The figures are almost appalling. They show that we are utilizing our fields and forests and mines and that we are furnishing profitable employment to the millions of workingmen throughout the United States, bringing comfort and happiness to their homes and making it possible to lay by savings for old age and disability. That all the people are participating in this great prosperity is seen in every American community, and shown by the enormous and unprecedented deposits in our savings banks. Our duty is the care and security of these deposits, and their safe investment demands the highest integrity and the best business capacity of those in charge of these depositories of the people's earnings.

We have a vast and intricate business, built up through years of toil and struggle, in which every part of the country has its stake, and will not permit of either neglect or of undue selfishness. No narrow, sordid policy will subserve it. The greatest skill and wisdom on the part of the manufacturers and producers will be required to hold and increase it. Our industrial enterprises which have grown to such great proportions affect the homes and occupations of the people and the welfare of the country. Our capacity to produce has developed so enormously and our products have so multiplied that the problem of more markets requires our urgent and immediate attention. Only a broad and enlightened policy will keep what we have. No other policy will get more. In these times of marvelous business energy and gain we ought to be looking to the future, strengthening the weak places in our industrial and commercial system, that we may be ready for any storm or strain.

By sensible trade arrangements which will not interrupt our home production we shall extend the outlets for our increasing surplus. A system which provides a mutual exchange of commodities, a mutual exchange is manifestly essential to the continued and healthful growth of our export trade. We must not repose in fancied security that we can forever sell everything and buy little or nothing. If such a thing were possible, it would not be best for us or for those with whom we deal. We should take from our customers such of their products as we can use without harm to our industries and labor. Reciprocity is the natural outgrowth of our wonderful industrial development under the domestic policy now firmly established. What we produce beyond our domestic consumption must have a vent abroad. The excess must be relieved through a foreign outlet and we should sell everywhere we can, and buy wherever the buying will enlarge our sales and productions, and thereby make a greater demand for home labor.

The period of exclusiveness is past. The expansion of our trade and commerce is the pressing problem. Commercial wars are unprofitable. A policy of good will and friendly trade relations will prevent reprisals. Reciprocity treaties are in harmony with the spirit of the times, measures of retaliation are not. If perchance some of our tariffs are no longer needed, for revenue or to encourage and protect our industries at home, why should they not be employed to extend and promote our markets abroad? Then, too, we have inadequate steamship service. New lines of steamers have already been put in commission between the Pacific coast ports of the United States and those on the western coasts of Mexico and Central and South America. These should be followed up with direct steamship lines between the eastern coast of the United States and South American ports. One of the needs of the times is to direct commercial lines from our vast fields of production to the fields of consumption that we have but barely touched. Next in advantage to having the thing. to sell is to have the convenience to carry it to the buyer. We must encourage our merchant marine. We must have more ships. They must be under the American flag, built and manned and owned by Americans. These will not only be profitable in a commercial sense; they will be messengers of peace and amity wherever they go. We must build the Isthmian canal, which will unite the two oceans and give a straight line of water communication with the western coasts of Central and South America and Mexico. The construction of a Pacific cable cannot be longer postponed.

In the furthering of these objects of national interest and concern you are performing an important part. This exposition would have touched the heart of that American statesman whose mind was ever alert and thought ever constant for a larger commerce and a truer fraternity of the republics of the new world. His broad American spirit is felt and manifested here. He needs no identification to an assemblage of Americans anywhere, for the name of Blaine is inseparably associated with the pan-American movement, which finds this practical and substantial expression, and which we all hope will be firmly advanced by the pan-American congress that assembles this autumn in the capital of Mexico. The good work will go on. It cannot be stopped. These buildings will disappear; this creation of art and beauty and industry will perish from sight, but their influence will remain to

> Make it live beyond its too short living
> With praises and thanksgiving.

Who can tell the new thoughts that have been awakened, the ambitions fired and the high achievements that will be wrought through this exposition? Gentlemen, let us ever remember that our interest is in concord, not conflict, and that our real eminence rests in the victories of peace, not those of war. We hope that all who are represented here may be moved to higher and nobler effort for their own and the world's good, and that out of this city may come, not only greater commerce and trade, but more essential than these, relations of mutual respect, confidence and friendship which will deepen and endure.

Our earnest prayer is that God will graciously vouchsafe prosperity, happiness and peace to all our neighbors, and like blessings to all the peoples and powers of earth.

Source: Richardson, James D. *A Compilation of the Messages and Papers of the Presidents 1789–1897*. Vol. 13. New York: Bureau of National Literature, 1897, 6618–6622.

26. THEODORE ROOSEVELT (1858–1919)

Presidential Term (1901–1909)

CHRONOLOGY

October 27, 1858—Theodore Roosevelt is born in New York City to Theodore Roosevelt Sr. and Martha "Mittie" Bulloch.

November 6, 1860—Abraham Lincoln is elected president of the United States.

April 12, 1861—Southern forces attack Fort Sumter in Charleston, South Carolina, beginning the Civil War.

April 9, 1865—Confederate general Robert E. Lee surrenders to Union general Ulysses S. Grant at Appomattox Court House, ending the war.

April 14, 1865—Abraham Lincoln is shot by actor and Confederate sympathizer John Wilkes Booth at Ford's Theater in Washington D.C; the president dies the following morning.

October 1876—Roosevelt enters Harvard University.

February 9, 1878—Roosevelt's father dies of stomach cancer in New York City.

June 30, 1880—Roosevelt graduates magna cum laude from Harvard University.

October 27, 1880—Roosevelt marries Alice Lee Hathaway.

November 1881—Roosevelt is elected to the New York state legislature.

February 14, 1884—Roosevelt's mother, Martha Bulloch, and wife, Alice, die at the Roosevelt home in New York City.

June 9, 1884—Roosevelt moves to the Dakota Territory.

December 2, 1886—Roosevelt marries Edith Carow.

May 1889—President Benjamin Harrison appoints Roosevelt as U.S. civil service commissioner.

February 20, 1895—African American leader Frederick Douglass dies.

May 5, 1895—Roosevelt is appointed as police commissioner of New York City.

April 19, 1897—President William McKinley appoints Roosevelt as assistant secretary of the navy.

February 15, 1898—The USS *Maine* is sunk in Havana, Cuba, leading to the deaths of 260 American sailors.

May 6, 1898—Theodore Roosevelt resigns as assistant secretary of the navy and forms the Rough Riders military unit.

November 8, 1898—Roosevelt is elected governor of New York.

February 6, 1899—The Senate ratifies the Treaty of Paris, ending the Spanish-American War.

June 21, 1900—The Republican Party nominates Roosevelt to be vice president following McKinley's nomination for president; the vice presidential nomination is considered a political dead end and a means to relegate Roosevelt to obscurity by the party.

November 6, 1900—The McKinley-Roosevelt ticket defeats William Jennings Bryan in the 1900 presidential election.

March 2, 1901—United States Steel is founded, becoming the first billion-dollar corporation.

September 6, 1901—President McKinley is assassinated in Buffalo, New York, by anarchist Leon Czolgosz; Roosevelt becomes the 26th president of the United States.

February 1902—Roosevelt's Justice Department files an antitrust suit against the Northern Securities Company under the Sherman Antitrust Act.

October 1902—Roosevelt negotiates an end to anthracite coal strike in Pennsylvania.

November 6, 1903—The United States signs the Hay-Bunau-Varilla Treaty with Panama, allowing the United States to build the Panama Canal.

November 8, 1904—Theodore Roosevelt defeats Democratic nominee Alton B. Parker in a landslide to be elected president in his own right.

December 1904—Roosevelt proclaims the Roosevelt Corollary, an addition to the Monroe Doctrine that states the United States will intervene in conflicts between European powers and Latin American countries.

September 5, 1905—Roosevelt negotiates an end to the Russo-Japanese War.

June 29, 1906—Roosevelt signs the Hepburn Act into law, increasing the power of the Interstate Commerce Commission to regulate railroads.

June 30, 1906—Following the publication of Upton Sinclair's *The Jungle*, Roosevelt signs the Meat Inspection Act and the Pure Food and Drug Act into law.

December 10, 1906—Roosevelt became the first American president to be awarded the Nobel Peace Prize for negotiating an end to the Russo-Japanese War.

December 16, 1907—The U.S. Navy's Great White Fleet departs the United States to sail around the world, a showcase of American naval strength.

June 16–19, 1908—Roosevelt honors his promise not to seek a third term, and the Republican National Convention nominates William Howard Taft for president.

November 3, 1908—William Howard Taft is elected president of the United States.

June 1910—Roosevelt returns to the United States after traveling abroad for a year in Africa and Europe.

February 1912—Roosevelt announces that he will challenge President William Howard Taft for the Republican nomination.

June 18–22, 1912—Roosevelt and his supporters claim some Republican National Convention nominating votes to be fraudulent after the convention overwhelmingly nominates Taft for president.

August 7, 1912—The Progressive Party nominates Theodore Roosevelt as its presidential nominee.

November 5, 1912—Woodrow Wilson wins the presidential election, receiving 435 electoral votes to Roosevelt's 88; Taft finishes with only 8 electoral votes.

October 4, 1913—Theodore Roosevelt departs for an expedition to South America.

August 15, 1914—The Panama Canal is completed.

January 6, 1919—Theodore Roosevelt dies at his home in Oyster Bay, New York, from a blood clot.

BIOGRAPHICAL SKETCH

Theodore Roosevelt was born on October 27, 1858, into a wealthy family in New York City. His father, Theodore Roosevelt Sr., was a wealthy businessman and philanthropist. His mother, Martha "Mittie" Bulloch, was a Southern belle from Georgia. "Teedie" (as the younger Theodore was known to his family) was a precocious child who was interested in science and military matters. Teedie was also a sickly child who suffered from asthma and nearsightedness. Throughout his life, Roosevelt sought to overcome his physical limitations with intense exercise and recreational activities. During his childhood and adolescence, Roosevelt's family made trips to Europe and the Middle East. Roosevelt was educated at home by private tutors as a child and teenager.

Roosevelt enrolled at Harvard University in 1876, where he belonged to many clubs and was inducted into Phi Beta Kappa. He was so precocious that in one class the professor reminded Roosevelt that he was not the one teaching the class. Tragedy struck Roosevelt in 1878 while attending Harvard; his father died of stomach cancer. This was a devastating blow to Roosevelt, who admired his father. At Harvard, he met the young and beautiful Alice Lee, who came from a wealthy Boston family. Roosevelt was smitten with her and eventually convinced her to marry him. They married after Roosevelt graduated from Harvard University.

After graduating from Harvard, Roosevelt shocked his family and friends by announcing that he planned to run for political office. Roosevelt ran for and won a seat in the New York state legislature. He gained a reputation as a reformer unafraid to take on the political bosses and corrupt politicians. Roosevelt worked with New York governor Grover Cleveland to enact civil service legislation. The energetic Roosevelt was dubbed the "Cyclone Assemblyman." Roosevelt eventually rose to become the leader of Republicans in the New York state legislature. To his supporters, Roosevelt was a fearless champion of reform who was unafraid to confront corrupt politicians. To his opponents, he was a self-righteous and narcissistic politician. Life was good for Roosevelt in early 1884. His political career was on the rise, and his wife, Alice, had given birth to a baby girl named Alice.

Then tragedy struck Roosevelt. On February 14, 1884, he rushed home to find that his mother and his wife were both extremely ill. He watched helplessly as they both died that same day. A distraught Roosevelt poured himself into his work. Later that year, he gave up his political seat to ranch in the Dakota Territory. Roosevelt gained the respect of the locals by working long hours in the saddles, knocking out a bully in a saloon, and chasing down boat thieves during a blizzard.

Roosevelt eventually returned to New York City in 1886, where he unsuccessfully ran for mayor. He lost the race (finishing third) but left for Europe, where he married his childhood friend Edith Carow. Edith proved to be a good match for Roosevelt, and they had six children together (Theodore Jr., Alice, Kermit, Ethel, Archie, and Quentin).

In 1889, President Benjamin Harrison rewarded Roosevelt for his support in the 1888 presidential campaign by making him civil service commissioner in Washington, D.C. As civil service commissioner, Roosevelt sought to increase the number of federal government jobs that were based on merit. As a result, he clashed with Republican political bosses, who wanted to use federal jobs to reward their supporters. This did not deter Roosevelt, and he successfully expanded the number of federal jobs under civil service. He continued to serve as civil service commissioner under both Benjamin Harrison and Grover Cleveland.

Roosevelt resigned as civil service commissioner in 1895 to accept a job as head of the New York City Police Commission. As chief New York City police commissioner, Roosevelt fired corrupt police officers

Theodore Roosevelt (Library of Congress)

and professionalized the New York City police force. He became famous for his midnight jaunts through the streets of New York City with reporters. Roosevelt experienced a backlash in New York City when he sought to enforce laws closing saloons on a Sunday. Nonetheless, Roosevelt succeeded in reforming and professionalizing the New York City police force.

Roosevelt left New York City in 1897 to accept a position as assistant secretary of the navy under President William McKinley. In this position, Roosevelt advocated a buildup of the navy. He also supported a war with Spain to help Cuba gain its independence from that country. Roosevelt disagreed with President McKinley's policy of diplomacy toward Cuba and privately remarked that McKinley had the background of a chocolate éclair. When the Spanish-American War broke out in 1898 after the sinking of the USS *Maine* in Havana Harbor, Roosevelt resigned from the Navy Department and formed a volunteer unit known as the Rough Riders. Roosevelt became the second-ranking officer in the unit (behind Leonard Wood). He experienced his moment of glory in Cuba by leading key charges up Kettle Hill and San Juan Hill. He returned from the war a military hero.

After Roosevelt returned from Cuba, he was recruited by New York Republicans to run for governor of New York in 1898. The Republican Party was mired in a corruption scandal and needed a popular candidate to win the election. Roosevelt campaigned on his war record and narrowly won the election. If Republican political bosses thought that they could control Roosevelt, they were soon disappointed. Roosevelt as governor signed a civil service reform bill into law, promoted conservation, and taxed and regulated businesses. Republican political boss Thomas C. Platt plotted to get rid or Theodore Roosevelt as governor. William McKinley's vice president, Garret Hobart, had died, and there was a vacancy on top of the Republican ticket in 1900. Platt and other New York Republicans pushed Roosevelt onto the Republican ticket with William McKinley. Roosevelt proved to be an effective campaigner who gave more speeches and traveled more miles than McKinley's Democratic rival, William Jennings Bryan. On Election Day, the ticket of William McKinley and Theodore Roosevelt easily won the election.

An active man, Roosevelt was bored by the job of vice president, which was still an insignificant office. He wrote books and thought about going to law school. However, Roosevelt was catapulted into the presidency upon the assassination of President William McKinley in Buffalo, New York, in 1901. After McKinley was shot by anarchist Leon Czolgosz, Roosevelt visited McKinley and found him in stable condition. Roosevelt returned to the Adirondack Mountains, where he went hiking with his family. He found out about McKinley's death when a messenger informed him in the mountains.

At the age of 42, Roosevelt was the youngest president to date. Conservative Republicans, such as Ohio senator Mark Hanna (and McKinley campaign manager), viewed Roosevelt as a radical who would destroy the Republican Party. Roosevelt sought to reassure conservative Republicans, who worried that he would upend the status quo, by promising to follow President McKinley's policies.

The charismatic Roosevelt became a popular president. The public was charmed by stories of his recreational activities, which included boxing, wrestling, hiking, hunting, and horseback riding. The public was also fascinated by the antics of his children. Roosevelt's son Quentin brought a pony to the White House to cheer up his brother Archie, who was ill with the measles. The public was especially fascinated by Roosevelt's rebellious daughter Alice. Alice drove fast, hung out with rich people, and smoked. Her romances were a topic of national conversation, and a new color (Alice Blue) was created to describe her striking blue eyes.

In many ways, Roosevelt was the first modern president. He was the first president to frequently meet with the press. He was the first president with a comprehensive domestic agenda (the Square Deal). He was the first president to use the presidency as a bully pulpit, in that he traveled throughout the country giving speeches to the public in support of his ideas. He was the first president to travel outside the country while in office. And he was also the first president (also the first American) to be awarded a Nobel Peace Prize for successfully negotiating an end to the Russo-Japanese War.

During his first two years in office, Roosevelt made some important domestic decisions. One decision was to use the Justice Department, in 1902, to file an antitrust suit under the Sherman Antitrust Act, breaking up the Northern Securities Company. The Northern Securities Company was a railroad monopoly whose investors included the powerful financier John Pierpont "J. P." Morgan. During his presidency, Roosevelt successfully filed suit against 44 trusts. Another key Roosevelt decision was to involve himself in a Pennsylvania coal strike that threatened to devastate the American economy. Roosevelt invited the coal operators and the United Mine Workers (which represented the striking workers) to the White House. Roosevelt found that the coal operators were unreasonable. He threatened to use the army to seize the coal mines if the coal operators did not end the strike. Both sides agreed to the creation of a commission. The commission ruled in favor of the striking workers, granting them higher wages and shorter working hours.

Roosevelt was most passionate about the issue of conservation. As an avid outdoorsman and hunter, he wanted to conserve the nation's resources for future generations. Roosevelt used his executive powers to set aside over 200 million acres for national parks, national forests, and wildlife refuges.

From the beginning of his presidency, Roosevelt took an active role in foreign policy. He believed in a strong military and increased the size of the navy during his time as president. Roosevelt's foreign policy focused on Latin America. In 1902, he watched closely as Germany, Great Britain, and Italy intervened in Venezuela to collect debts owed to them by Venezuela's leader, Cipriano Castro. Roosevelt became alarmed as foreign troops landed on Venezuelan soil. Behind the scenes, Roosevelt urged the leaders of Germany, Great Britain, and Italy to negotiate their differences with Venezuela. They listened to Roosevelt and took their grievances to the Hague tribunal, which ruled in their favor.

Another example of Roosevelt's policy in Latin America was his interest in building a canal linking the Atlantic Ocean and Pacific Ocean. In 1903, the United States signed a treaty with Colombia granting the United States the right to build a canal. However, Columbia's legislature rejected the treaty. Roosevelt looked for other ways to acquire his canal. He found his opportunity when Panama successfully revolted against Columbia, with his encouragement. Roosevelt immediately recognized Panama, which signed a treaty with the United States, giving it the right to build a canal. While Roosevelt succeeded in building the canal (the Panama Canal), critics questioned the way he had acquired it. The Panama Canal would be completed in 1914.

The Roosevelt Corollary represented Roosevelt's policy toward Latin America. A part of Roosevelt's annual message to Congress in 1904 stated that the United States would be the policeman of the Western Hemisphere and had the right to intervene in Latin American countries. To critics, the Roosevelt Corollary demonstrated that the United States was an arrogant bully pushing around Latin American countries. Defenders noted that Roosevelt's motivation for issuing the Roosevelt Corollary was to prevent European countries from gaining a foothold in the Western Hemisphere and that Roosevelt's policies were beneficial to Latin American countries. For example, Roosevelt sent in troops to Santo Domingo in 1904 when that country asked the United States to take over their customhouses because they owed money to foreign creditors. U.S. Marines occupied Santo Domingo's customhouses until that country's finances were in order. Nonetheless, Roosevelt's policies in Latin America were heavily debated both then and later.

In 1904, the popular Roosevelt ran for election in his own right. In the election, he easily defeated the colorless Alton B. Parker of New York. However, Roosevelt made a mistake after the election by announcing that he would not run for another term in 1908 because he respected the two-term tradition set by George Washington. He considered McKinley's second term his first term and the new term his second term. Though his sentiments were sincere at the time, it was a decision that he would come to regret.

In his second term, Roosevelt achieved a number of domestic victories. One domestic victory was the enactment of the Hepburn Act in 1906, which gave the Interstate Commerce Commission more power to regulate railroad rates. Two other domestic victories came about as the result of muckraking journalist Upton Sinclair's revelations in his novel *The Jungle* of the horrid conditions in the Chicago meatpacking plants. In 1906, Congress passed the Pure Food and Drug Act and the Meat Inspection Act because of Sinclair's revelations and pressure from Roosevelt. The Pure Food and Drug Act required companies to label their products, and the Meat Inspection Act stipulated that meat could not go onto the market until it had been inspected and approved by the Department of Agriculture.

In his second term, Roosevelt played the role of peacemaker in foreign policy. In 1905, he offered to mediate the end of the Russo-Japanese War between Russia and Japan. Roosevelt's motives were not wholly altruistic, as he feared that an emboldened Japan could threaten U.S. interests in the Philippines. The governments of Russia and Japan accepted Roosevelt's offer, and he negotiated the Treaty of Portsmouth, which ended the war. In the agreement, Russia gave up claims to territory in China and Korea, and in exchange, Japan did not demand reparations from Russia. For his efforts, Roosevelt was awarded the Nobel Peace Prize in 1906. In 1906, Roosevelt convinced France and Germany to negotiate their differences at the Algeciras Conference in Spain.

Roosevelt left office in 1909. He kept his promise not to run in 1908. Instead, Roosevelt convinced the Republican Party to nominate Secretary of War William Howard Taft. Taft was elected president, easily defeating William Jennings Bryan in the general election. Roosevelt went abroad so that he would not overshadow his successor. He hunted in Africa (as part of an expedition sponsored by the Smithsonian), gave commencement addresses at European universities, and formally accepted his Nobel Peace Prize in Norway.

Roosevelt turned to the United States to find dissension within the Republican Party. Unlike Roosevelt, Taft could not bridge the divide between progressives and conservatives within the party. Roosevelt listened to progressives, who argued that Taft had betrayed Roosevelt's progressive legacy. Although Taft had continued many of Roosevelt's policies—such as conservation and regulation of the trusts—Roosevelt believed that Taft had betrayed his progressive legacy.

In 1912, Roosevelt announced that he was challenging Taft for the Republican nomination. Roosevelt won most of the Republican primaries (a new innovation in 1912), including defeating Taft in his home state of Ohio. However, Taft's forces controlled the convention, and Taft won the Republican nomination. Roosevelt stormed out of the Republican convention, charging that Taft had stolen the nomination from him. He formed the Progressive Party (or Bull Moose Party, as it was popularly known). The Progressive Party favored such measures as regulation of corporations, pensions for the elderly, unemployment insurance, and women's suffrage. The Progressive Party was ahead of its time in support of these measures.

While campaigning in Milwaukee, Roosevelt was shot by bartender John Schrank, who claimed that William McKinley had told him in a dream that Roosevelt was his real assassin. Roosevelt was shot in the chest. Fortunately, the bullet was slowed down by his manuscript and eyeglass case in his breast pocket. Roosevelt proceeded to go to a scheduled speech, where he spoke for nearly two hours before agreeing to go to the hospital. Roosevelt had suffered a few fractured ribs. Both William Howard Taft and Democratic presidential nominee Woodrow Wilson suspended their campaigns while Roosevelt was in the hospital. On Election Day, Woodrow Wilson won due to the split in the Republican Party. He received 43 percent of the popular vote. Roosevelt finished a strong second with 27 percent of the popular vote and 88 electoral votes.

After the election, Theodore Roosevelt led an expedition to the Amazon River in South America, where he explored a tributary of that river. During the expedition, Roosevelt's expedition ran low on food, and he almost died from a high fever and infection. Roosevelt survived the expedition but lost a considerable amount of weight. Friends and family were shocked by his emaciated appearance when he returned to the United States. The fever that he contracted during the expedition is believed by many historians to have shortened his life.

Roosevelt focused on World War I (then known as the Great War) in the final years of his life. From the outbreak of war in 1914, Roosevelt's sympathies were clearly with the Allied powers of England and France and against Germany and the Central Powers. He denounced German atrocities in neutral Belgium and condemned the sinking of the passenger ship *Lusitania* by German submarines. From the early stages of the war, Roosevelt advocated American military preparedness. He condemned what he regarded as the weak policies of Wilson toward Germany.

To his supporters, Roosevelt was a visionary who was trying to heroically rally the American people against the German menace. To his opponents, he was a militaristic warmonger who was attempting to push the United States into a war with Germany. They also charged that his criticisms of Wilson were based on personal jealousy. In the 1916 presidential election, voters appeared to reject Roosevelt's views when they reelected Wilson over Republican presidential nominee Charles Evans Hughes. Wilson promised to keep the United States out of war. However, Wilson was unable to keep his promise because of unrestricted submarine warfare on the part of the Germans as well as the discovery that the German government sought to encourage Mexico to attack the United States. In April 1917, the United States declared war on Germany.

When the United States entered the war in 1917, Roosevelt eagerly volunteered his services. He offered to lead a volunteer military unit modeled on the Rough Riders from the Spanish-American War. However, his offer was rejected by President Wilson, which only increased distrust between the two men. Although he supported the war, Roosevelt consistently criticized what he considered to be Wilson's weak and inefficient war policies. Roosevelt raised money for the war effort and sent his four sons (Theodore Jr., Kermit, Archie, and Quentin) to fight in the war. All four sons distinguished themselves in battle. Sadly for Roosevelt, his son Quentin was killed in combat in 1918 when his plane was shot down over France. A devastated Roosevelt never recovered from Quentin's death.

Roosevelt's political fortunes appeared to turn when Republicans won control of Congress during the 1918 midterm election. This was a repudiation of Wilson, who had urged voters to vote for Democrats if they supported the war effort. The election results were seen as a vindication of Roosevelt, and Republicans discussed him as their presidential nominee in 1920. Unfortunately, it was not to be. Roosevelt died from a blood clot on January 6, 1919, at his home in Oyster Bay, New York.

Theodore Roosevelt was a larger-than-life figure who transformed the presidency at the turn of the 20th century. Whether traveling across the country to promote his domestic agenda or negotiating an end to the Russo-Japanese War, Roosevelt created the modern presidency. The charismatic and controversial Roosevelt left an indelible stamp on the American presidency.

HISTORICAL OVERVIEW

Dramatic changes occurred during Theodore Roosevelt's lifetime, from 1858 to 1919. In this period, the United States became the preeminent industrial power and a major world power. The country experienced significant changes during the Civil War, Reconstruction, the Gilded Age, and World War I. Theodore Roosevelt was shaped by and responded to these changes and events.

Demographics

The U.S. census two years after Theodore Roosevelt's birth in 1860 showed that the population was approximately 30 million people. A year after Roosevelt's death in 1920, the census indicated that the population was approximately 106 million people. At the time of Roosevelt's birth, the United States was still primarily a rural country. By 1920, the urban population surpassed the rural population for the first time. When Theodore Roosevelt was born, the majority of immigrants came to the United States from Northern and Western Europe. After 1880, the majority of immigrants arriving in the United States were from Southern and Eastern Europe.

Civil War

The primary cause of the Civil War was the issue of slavery in the territories. It was an issue that appeared to be resolved when Speaker of the House Henry Clay negotiated the Missouri Compromise of 1820, which allowed Missouri to come in as a slave state and Maine to be admitted as a free state; it also set Missouri's southern boundary line as the dividing line between future free and slave states. However, the issue was reopened during the Mexican-American War (1846–1848) when Pennsylvania congressman David Wilmot unsuccessfully proposed an amendment to a defense appropriations bill that would have banned slavery in any territory acquired through war. In the aftermath of the Mexican-American War, there was a passionate debate over the extension of slavery into the territories newly acquired from Mexico (the future states of California, Arizona, New Mexico, and Utah). Southerners threatened to leave the union if California was admitted as a free state. Senator Henry Clay sought to resolve the situation with a series of compromises, known as the Compromise of 1850. His proposals included admitting California as a free state; abolishing the slave trade (but not slavery itself) in Washington, D.C.; allowing the people of New Mexico, Arizona, and Utah to decide whether they wanted slavery; and more rigorously enforcing the fugitive slave laws. These proposals were passed by Congress and signed into law in 1850, and they temporarily stabilized the situation. However, the Compromise of 1850 was not a true compromise because each measure had to be passed piecemeal, and neither Northern nor Southern politicians had truly compromised.

The Kansas-Nebraska Act of 1854 further heightened the divide between North and South on the issue of slavery in the territories. Proposed by Senator Stephen A. Douglas of Illinois, it allowed the newly organized Kansas and Nebraska Territories to decide whether they wanted to be admitted into the union as free or slave states. The problem with the Kansas-Nebraska Act for many Northerners was that it violated the Missouri Compromise. Kansas and Nebraska were north of Missouri's southern boundary line, where slavery was supposed to be banned under the Missouri Compromise. In response to the Kansas-Nebraska Act, the Republican Party was created in opposition to the expansion of slavery into the territories.

In the aftermath of the Kansas-Nebraska Act, Kansas became a bloody battleground between pro-slavery and antislavery forces. In essence, there was a civil war before the Civil War in Kansas. The *Dred Scott* decision of 1857 further exacerbated sectional tensions. The case involved the slave Dred Scott, whose owner (an army surgeon) took him to live in Illinois (a free state) and Wisconsin (then a free territory). After his owner's death, Dred Scott sued for his freedom, arguing that he could not have been a slave if he had lived in a free territory and a free state.

The case came before the Supreme Court in 1857. Chief Justice Roger Taney ruled for a majority of the Supreme Court against Dred Scott, controversially claiming that African Americans had no rights under the Constitution that any white man was bound to respect. Taney added as an aside that the federal government did not have authority to regulate slavery in the territories. Critics pointed out that this was not true, as the federal government had banned slavery in the Northwest Territory under the Northwest Ordinance of 1787 and slavery had been banned north of Missouri's southern boundary line under the Missouri Compromise of 1820.

Divisions between North and South were wider than ever after abolitionist John Brown's unsuccessful raid on the arsenal at Harper's Ferry, Virginia. In the aftermath of the raid, John Brown was captured (by future Confederate general Robert E. Lee) and executed by the state of Virginia. To Southerners, Brown was a terrorist whose actions reinforced their fears that abolitionists wanted to violently overthrow slavery. To many Northerners, Brown was a heroic figure who sacrificed his life for the worthy cause of abolishing slavery.

The election of Republican presidential candidate Abraham Lincoln to the presidency in 1860 precipitated the secession of Southern states. Southerners feared that Lincoln would abolish slavery, even though Lincoln said repeatedly that he only wanted to prevent the extension of slavery into the territories and would not touch slavery in the South. By the time of Lincoln's inauguration on March 4, 1861, most Southern states had seceded from the Union. Lincoln repeated his assurances that he did not intend to abolish slavery, but he also insisted that secession was illegal and that he would defend all federal possessions in the South (including forts and post offices).

On April 12, 1861, the Confederate States of America started the Civil War by attacking Fort Sumter, in Charleston, South Carolina. This attack started a bloody war that would last four years and cost at least 620,000 lives on both sides. The North had many advantages at the beginning of the Civil War, including a larger population, an extensive system of railroads, and most of the industry in the United States. Yet, the South benefited from the home field advantage (most of the battles were fought in the South), shorter supply lines, and superior military leadership (at the beginning of the war). The South also believed that it could count on England and France to support them because those countries wanted Southern cotton.

The South experienced success in the Eastern theater of the war, winning victories at First Bull Run, the Battle of the Seven Days, Second Bull Run, Fredericksburg, and Chancellorsville. Most of these victories were won under the brilliant military leadership of Robert E. Lee and Thomas Jonathan "Stonewall" Jackson. However, Robert E. Lee failed to win the crucial battles of Antietam and Gettysburg. A victory in September 1862 at the Battle of Antietam, in Maryland, by Robert E. Lee would have demoralized the Northern public and could have led England and France to recognize the Confederate States of America. Instead, a draw at Antietam was considered enough of a victory for Abraham Lincoln to issue the Emancipation Proclamation, which made the abolition of slavery a Union war aim.

Robert E. Lee's army was never the same after its crushing loss at the Battle of Gettysburg, in

Pennsylvania, in 1863. In the Western theater, Union forces experienced greater success, winning crucial victories under the skillful military leadership of Ulysses S. Grant at Fort Henry, Fort Donelson, Shiloh, and Vicksburg. Grant's capture of the garrison at Vicksburg, Mississippi, in July 1863 split the Confederacy in half and ensured Union domination of the Mississippi River.

The year 1864 was the most crucial year of the Civil War. Bloody battles between Union general Ulysses S. Grant and Confederate general Robert E. Lee in the Eastern theater contributed to Northern war weariness, The Northern public was also alarmed that Union general William T. Sherman had not taken Atlanta by the summer of 1864. Peace Democrats (referred to as "Copperheads" by their critics) blamed Lincoln for the stalemate and argued that he should negotiate an end to the war, even if it meant bringing Southern states back into the union with slavery.

In the summer of 1864, it appeared that Abraham Lincoln would be a one-term President. Fortunately for Lincoln, a series of Union victories in the fall of 1864 ensured his reelection. These included William T. Sherman's capture of Atlanta and Phil Sheridan's victories in the Shenandoah Valley of Virginia. In November, Lincoln was easily reelected president. With Lincoln's reelection, it was clear that the South had no chance of winning the Civil War. Realizing that victory was futile, Robert E. Lee, on April 9, 1865, surrendered to Ulysses S. Grant at Appomattox Court House. For all intents and purposes, this was the end of the war. Tragically, Lincoln did not have the opportunity to savor the Union victory. On April 14, 1865, he was assassinated by actor and Confederate sympathizer John Wilkes Booth at Ford's Theater.

The Civil War preserved the union and finally demonstrated that the federal government did have supremacy over the states. More significantly, it led to the abolition of the long-standing institution of slavery. Slavery was formally abolished with the ratification of the Thirteenth Amendment in December 1865.

The formative event of Theodore Roosevelt's childhood was the Civil War. The Roosevelt family was divided over the war along sectional lines. Roosevelt's father, Theodore Roosevelt Sr., was a New Yorker who supported the North, but his mother,

Martha "Mittie" Bulloch, was a Georgian who supported the South. Two of her brothers served in the Confederate Navy during the Civil War. For the sake of family harmony, Roosevelt's father hired a substitute to fight in his place. It was a decision that haunted Theodore Roosevelt. He viewed his father's decision not to fight as a blemish on an otherwise honorable record.

Roosevelt's father had worked closely with President Abraham Lincoln during the Civil War, and he had also created a system that allowed Union soldiers to send money home to their family members. One of Roosevelt's earliest memories was watching Abraham Lincoln's funeral from the window of his family's home in 1865. For the rest of his life, Roosevelt retained his admiration for Lincoln. He never doubted that the North was on the right side of the Civil War. It was one reason for Roosevelt's lifelong affiliation with the Republican Party.

Reconstruction

Even before the end of the Civil War, the North had begun plans to reconstruct the South. In 1863, President Abraham Lincoln proposed the Ten Percent Plan, which would allow a Southern state to reenter the union if 10 percent of the state's residents signed an oath of loyalty to the union and agreed to abolish slavery. Radical Republicans, such as Thaddeus Stevens of Pennsylvania and Charles Sumner of Massachusetts, disagreed with the Ten Percent Plan, considering it too lenient toward the South. Instead, they supported the Wade-Davis Bill (proposed by Benjamin Wade of Ohio and Henry Davis of Maryland), which required 50 percent of residents in a state to sign a loyalty oath to the union and agree to abolish slavery and support civil and political rights for African Americans. Lincoln considered the Wade-Davis Bill too harsh and pocket vetoed it at the end of the legislative session in 1864. In his last speech before he was assassinated, Lincoln supported voting rights for African Americans who were literate and had fought in the Civil War.

Andrew Johnson (Abraham Lincoln's vice president) became president upon Lincoln's death. Although critical of large slaveholders throughout his political career in Tennessee, as president, the North

Carolina–born Johnson proved to be sympathetic toward the South. His identity as a white Southerner and support for white supremacy overcame any hatred that he once possessed for large slaveholders. He pardoned hundreds of former Confederate military officers and politicians. In addition, he vetoed the Civil Rights Act of 1866 and the extension of the Freedmen's Bureau. Both vetoes were overridden by a Republican-controlled Congress.

In the aftermath of the 1866 midterm elections, Republicans gained a supermajority in Congress. They increasingly took control of Reconstruction in the South. Republicans passed the Fourteenth Amendment in 1866 (it was later ratified by the states in 1868), which gave African Americans citizenship rights. The Reconstruction Acts of 1866 divided the South into five military districts until Southern states wrote state constitutions acceptable to Congress. Andrew Johnson sought to obstruct Republicans' Reconstruction plans, which was one of the reasons that he was impeached in 1868.

The official reason for Andrew Johnson's impeachment was the firing of Secretary of War Edwin Stanton, who was sympathetic to the policies of the Radical Republicans. Republicans in the House of Representatives impeached Johnson as a result of Stanton's firing because they said it violated the Tenure of Office Act, which required the president to consult the Senate before firing a cabinet officer. Johnson's lawyers argued that Johnson did not violate the Tenure of Office Act because Stanton was originally appointed by Abraham Lincoln. Although Johnson survived his impeachment trial in the Senate by one vote, he was a lame duck president for the rest of his presidency. In addition, Congress passed the Fifteenth Amendment, giving African American males the right to vote in 1869 (it was ratified by the states in 1870). Congress also passed the Enforcement Acts in 1870 and 1871 to go after terrorist organizations in the South, such as the Ku Klux Klan.

However, by the early 1870s, the Northern people were beginning to lose interest in Reconstruction. Reconstruction was the focal point of the 1876 presidential election between Republican nominee Rutherford B. Hayes and Democratic nominee Samuel Tilden. Tilden won the popular vote, but the electoral vote was in dispute. Both sides claimed that they won

Louisiana, South Carolina, and Florida. The House of Representatives created a commission to determine which candidate would receive those states' electoral votes. The commission voted along partisan lines to award those disputed electoral votes to Rutherford B. Hayes, giving him a majority in the Electoral College.

Reconstruction formally ended with the Compromise of 1877, when President Rutherford B. Hayes withdrew all remaining federal troops from the South after Southern Democrats agreed to support Hayes's election. In the decades after Reconstruction, Southern politicians failed to keep their promise to Hayes that they would uphold the Reconstruction laws in the South. Instead, white Southerners enacted a series of laws to ensure that African Americans would be third-class citizens in the South. Southern leaders used methods such as the poll tax, the literacy test, and the grandfather clause to dramatically restrict the voting rights of African Americans. By the early 20th century, only a small number of African Americans voted in the South. In addition, Southern politicians implemented segregation laws that mandated separate facilities for white and black Southerners. The Supreme Court gave segregation legal sanction when it ruled in its 1896 *Plessy v. Ferguson* decision that separate facilities were legal as long as they were of equal quality. However, most black facilities were far from equal. To the frustration of African Americans in the South, the federal government failed to enforce the Reconstruction laws for many decades.

Throughout his life, Roosevelt had mixed views on issues of race. On the one hand, Roosevelt took pride in the fact that his Republican Party had been instrumental in abolishing slavery at the end of the Civil War. As governor of New York and later as president of the United States, Roosevelt dined with African Americans (most notably the African American educator Booker T. Washington). He condemned lynching during his presidency and appointed African Americans to federal offices. Roosevelt frequently said that he believed government policies should treat everyone fairly, regardless of class, religion, gender, or race. On the other hand, Roosevelt did not always live up to his professed ideals on race. At times, he confessed to friends that it may have been a mistake to give African Americans the right to vote during Reconstruction.

Roosevelt also made no effort to enforce the Reconstruction laws. In one of the lowest moments of his presidency, he dishonorably discharged highly decorated black soldiers accused of shooting up the town of Brownsville, Texas. As head of the Progressive Party ticket in 1912, Roosevelt controversially refused to seat African American delegates from Southern states (though he allowed the seating of African American delegates from Northern states) in a bid to win over white Southern voters.

The courtship of the South failed, and prominent African American intellectuals such as W. E. B. DuBois and William Monroe Trotter were so outraged by Roosevelt's actions that they endorsed Democratic nominee Woodrow Wilson. On the other hand, Roosevelt condemned attacks on African Americans during the East St. Louis Riots in 1918, and in his final speech, he stood beside W. E. B. DuBois and praised the contributions of African American troops during World War I.

American Frontier

During Theodore Roosevelt's lifetime, Americans expanded westward. Many western territories were admitted into the union, including Colorado, Montana, South Dakota, North Dakota, Idaho, Utah, and Oklahoma. Many factors facilitated the settlement of the American frontier. One factor was the passage of the Homestead Act in 1862, which encouraged settlers to move west by offering them land if they paid a small fee and lived on the land for five years. A second factor was the construction of the Transcontinental Railroad in 1869, which linked the Union Pacific and Central Pacific together. This was the first truly national railroad in American history, and it made travel westward quicker and cheaper for settlers. A third factor was the defeat of Indian tribes on the frontier. Indian tribes resisted throughout the 19th century as American settlers encroached upon their land.

During the late 19th century, Americans possessed a romanticized view of the American West. The former army scout William F. Cody popularized the West with his famous Buffalo Bill's Wild West Show. Theodore Roosevelt was one of those Americans fascinated by the American West. He traveled out West with his brother Elliot on a hunting trip. After the deaths of his wife and mother, Roosevelt moved to the Dakota Territory to recover from his grief (now North Dakota) and purchased two ranches. Many Roosevelt biographers have noted the pivotal influence of the West on Theodore Roosevelt's life. His Western experience transformed Roosevelt physically, and it enabled him to identify himself as a Westerner (instead of as a wealthy New Yorker). Roosevelt later said that he never would have become president if he had never lived in the West.

Roosevelt frequently wrote about the American West. He wrote about his personal experiences out West in *Hunting Trips of a Ranchman* and *Ranch Life and the Hunting Trail*. His most influential book about the West was his multivolume *The Winning of the West*. The four-volume work was a history of westward expansion. The heroes of the work were American settlers and frontiersman such as Daniel Boone. While Roosevelt praised Native Americans as brave warriors, he justified the taking of their land by American settlers. Roosevelt argued that it was not their land because all they did was roam and graze the land. Like many Americans, Roosevelt celebrated the settlement of the American frontier. To Roosevelt, Native Americans were in the way of progress and civilization. As president, Roosevelt worked to improve conditions on Indian reservations and befriended Native American leaders such as Quanah Parker.

The Western influence on Roosevelt could be seen in his creation of the volunteer military unit known as the Rough Riders during the Spanish-American War. The unit included cowboys and Native Americans in addition to graduates of Ivy League schools. The heroics of Theodore Roosevelt and the Rough Riders helped propel Roosevelt into the governorship of New York and the presidency.

The historian Frederick Jackson Turner influenced perceptions of the American West with his argument that the frontier had been settled by 1890 (though later historians would dispute this argument). Both Turner and Roosevelt believed that the (white) Western inhabitants represented the best of America.

Gilded Age

Theodore Roosevelt's formative political experience was during the Gilded Age. This was a period characterized by massive voter participation, widespread political corruption, rapid industrialization, the rise of big business, and clashes between business and labor.

The Gilded Age was a period of high voter turnout and close elections. During this period, voter turnout averaged between 70 percent and 80 percent. Presidential elections between Democrats and Republicans tended to be very competitive and were determined by a few swing states (usually New York and Ohio). The popular vote margin was often less than 1 percent between the winning and losing candidates. In two presidential elections (1876 and 1888), the winning candidate won the electoral vote, even though he lost the popular vote. The power base of the Democratic Party was in the South, and the Democratic Party was the party of states' rights and limited government. The power base of the Republican Party was in the North, and it was the party of a strong central government.

Voter turnout was high because voters strongly identified with the Democratic and Republican Parties. They considered politics a form of entertainment, whether in the holding of parades or political speeches. Voter turnout was also high because of the appeal of the spoils system. Loyal Democrats and Republicans knew that they would be rewarded with a cushy government job if their candidate won. Under the spoils system, political loyalty was more important than one's qualifications. It was not until the passage of the Pendleton Act (in response to the assassination of President James A. Garfield by disgruntled office seeker Charles Guiteau) that some federal government jobs were based on the applicant's abilities rather than their political connections.

The Gilded Age was a period of widespread political corruption. A prime example of political corruption was the Tammany Hall (New York City's Democratic political machine) political boss William Marcy Tweed. "Boss Tweed," as he was known, took bribes from businessmen, stuffed ballot boxes, and defrauded New York City out of $100 million. His most notorious scheme was the building of a courthouse that was supposed to cost around $250,00 but ultimately cost over $12 million. The reason that the courthouse cost so much was that Tweed and his political associates were pocketing the money. Tweed stayed in power so long because he was able to appeal to poor Irish Catholic immigrants by providing them with food, jobs, and housing in exchange for their support. Tweed's power began to fade when he was lampooned by political cartoonist Thomas Nast. Tweed went to jail for corruption but escaped from jail. He fled to Spain, where he was ultimately captured by authorities, having identified him from Thomas Nast's cartoons. Tweed was extradited back to the United States, where he died in prison.

Political corruption was also common in the Republican Party during the Gilded Age. Ulysses S. Grant's administration was embroiled in a number of political scandals, including the Whiskey Ring and the Credit Mobilier scandals.

The Gilded Age was a period of rapid industrialization. Railroads were the first big business in the United States. In 1869, the Transcontinental Railroad was built, linking the Union Pacific and Central Pacific in Utah. This was the first truly national railroad in American history and made it cheaper and quicker for passengers to travel across the country. It also made it easier to move goods across the country. Other big industries emerged, including the steel industry (controlled by industrialist Andrew Carnegie) and the oil industry (controlled by John D. Rockefeller's Standard Oil Company). By the end of the 19th century, the United States produced more oil, coal, and steel than its European counterparts.

Supporters of the large industrialists considered them visionary industrial statesman who were primarily responsible for the nation's economic prosperity. They cited the theory of Social Darwinism, which contends that the rich are rich because they deserve to be rich, and the poor are poor because they deserve to be poor. Critics considered the industrialists to be robber barons who exploited the nations resources, crushed competition, and bribed politicians. They were alarmed by the power of financier J. P. Morgan. Morgan served on the boards of hundreds of companies and engineered mergers that led to a few companies controlling a single industry. He was so powerful that, in 1894, he bailed out the federal government when it ran low on gold. Although Congress passed the Sherman Antitrust Act in 1890 to regulate the big business combinations known as trusts, the law was not enforced until the presidency of Theodore Roosevelt.

In the Gilded Age, there were frequent clashes between labor and business. In many respects, the Gilded Age was a period of economic prosperity, but this was not the case for many workers. Workers typically worked at least 12 hours a day over a six-day work week. They did not receive workmen's compensation if they were injured on the job, nor did they receive unemployment benefits if they lost their jobs. This drastic situation led to the creation of labor unions. Two major unions were founded during the Gilded Age. One was the Knights of Labor founded by Terrence Powderly in 1869. The Knights of Labor included women, immigrants, and African Americans. It was regarded as a more radical labor union. The other major labor union was the American Federation of Labor (AFL), which was founded by Samuel Gompers in 1886. The AFL was a more exclusive labor union that catered to skilled laborers and emphasized bread-and-butter issues such as higher wages, shorter hours, and better working conditions.

Business owners actively sought to crush labor unions and were quick to fire workers who joined them. Judges usually sided with business owners in labor disputes. They argued that the factory was the owner's private property and that the owner was free to determine wages and working hours. The federal government sometimes sent federal troops to crush labor strikes. A notable example was the 1894 Pullman Strike, when President Grover Cleveland sent in federal troops to crush the strike, citing the need to deliver the mail. It would not be until Theodore Roosevelt's presidency that a national leader treated labor unions fairly.

Theodore Roosevelt came of age politically during the Gilded Age. The personal and political were intertwined for Roosevelt. In 1877, Roosevelt's father (considered a reformer in New York City politics) was nominated by Rutherford B. Hayes to be the commissioner for the Port Authority of New York. Unfortunately, Theodore Roosevelt Sr.'s nomination was blocked by Senator (and Republican political boss) Roscoe P. Conkling of New York. Theodore Roosevelt Sr. never recovered from the rejection and died a year later, in 1878. Young Theodore Roosevelt would never

forget this personal slight to his father, and it would influence his hatred of the patronage system and his support for civil service reform (government jobs based on merit).

After graduating from Harvard, Roosevelt successfully ran for a seat in the New York state legislature. In the legislature, Roosevelt exposed a corrupt judge bribed by industrialist Jay Gould, and he convinced New York governor Grover Cleveland to sign civil service reform into law. In the state legislature, Roosevelt's views evolved toward business and labor. He came into the state legislature believing in the sanctity of private property and resistant to the regulation of business. However, Roosevelt's views began to change when labor leader Samuel Gompers took him to tenements where residents made cigars in miserable conditions. The encounters convinced Roosevelt to support legislation regulating the production of cigars.

This was the beginning of Roosevelt's belief that the government should regulate business. Roosevelt's attitudes during the Gilded Age could be seen in his strong support for civil service reform during his time as civil service commissioner and in his relentless crusade against corruption while New York City police commissioner.

Progressive Era

The Progressive era was a period of major reform during the early part of the 20th century. Many of the progressive reforms were motivated by concerns about urbanization and industrialization. While many progressives grew up in cities and viewed them as a sign of progress, progressive reformers were concerned about poor conditions in tenement housing and political corruption. While progressive reformers considered the rise of big business a positive development, they worried about the seemingly unlimited power of industrialists such as J. P. Morgan, John D. Rockefeller, and Andrew Carnegie. They also worried about the long hours, low pay, and dangerous conditions experienced by many workers. Progressives were horrified that young children worked in dangerous conditions. Progressives supported regulation of the trusts, workmen's compensation for workers injured on the job, and restrictions on child labor. Progressive reforms often started at the local level with reformers like Jane Addams, who sought to improve the lives of immigrants at her settlement house in Chicago and crusaded against political corruption and supported women's suffrage. Progressive reforms continued at the state level with the energetic support of progressive governors such as Robert LaFollette of Wisconsin, Charles Evans Hughes of New York, and Hiram Johnson of California. These governors fought against political corruption and successfully regulated businesses and railroads. Progressive policies culminated at the national level with the support of Presidents Theodore Roosevelt and Woodrow Wilson.

Progressive reforms benefited from the support of a truly national media. Publications like *Cosmopolitan* and *McClure's* had national circulations and promoted progressive reforms. Journalist Jacob Riis highlighted the poor conditions in tenement housing in his book *How the Other Half Live*. Lincoln Steffen exposed widespread corruption throughout the country in his book *The Shame of the Cities*. Ida Tarbell publicized the ruthless business techniques of John D. Rockefeller in her book *The History of the Standard Oil Company*. Most famously, the socialist Upton Sinclair shocked and outraged the nation by revealing the horrible conditions in meatpacking plants in his novel *The Jungle*.

Theodore Roosevelt supported many of the progressive reforms as governor of New York, as president, and during his unsuccessful run for president as the Progressive Party candidate in 1912. As governor of New York, Roosevelt regulated conditions in factories, taxed and regulated corporations, established an eight-hour day for state workers, and created state parks and forests. As president, he implemented progressive ideas by regulating the trusts, supporting the demands of coal miners during a strike for higher wages and shorter hours, convincing Congress to pass legislation further regulating the railroads, successfully convincing Congress to pass the Meat Inspection Act and Pure Food and Drug Act, and setting aside over 200 million acres of land for national parks, national forests, national monuments, and wildlife preserves. Roosevelt considered himself a pragmatic progressive who was willing to compromise to achieve his goals. In this regard, he differed from more ideological progressives, such as Robert LaFollette, who believed that it violated one's principles to compromise. While Roosevelt supported and benefited from many of the exposés of progressive journalists, he thought that too often they dwelled on the darker side of American life and labeled them as "muckrakers."

Roosevelt continued his support for progressive ideas as the Progressive Party candidate for president in 1912 (after losing the Republican nomination to President William Howard Taft). During the campaign, he supported women's suffrage, a federal income tax, workmen's compensation, pensions for the elderly, and the abolition of child labor. Although Democratic candidate Woodrow Wilson won the election, Roosevelt finished a strong second with 27 percent of the popular vote and 88 electoral votes. Even though Roosevelt disbanded the Progressive Party in 1916, he continued to support progressive policies for the rest of his life.

Foreign Relations

U.S. foreign policy changed dramatically during Theodore Roosevelt's lifetime. For much of American history, American policy makers followed George Washington's admonition to avoid entangling alliances. After the Monroe Doctrine of 1823, there was an emphasis in preventing European powers from colonizing the Western Hemisphere. In the decades after the Civil War, the United States played a more active role in foreign affairs. The key event that signaled the rise of the United States as a world power was the Spanish-American War of 1898, in which the United States decisively defeated Spain and acquired Guam, Puerto Rico, and the Philippines. In China, the United States asserted the right of Western powers to have equal access to China's markets and was instrumental in crushing the Boxer Rebellion.

Theodore Roosevelt had a unique perspective on U.S. foreign relations. As a child and an adolescent, he had traveled throughout Europe and the Middle East. At one point, he and his siblings lived with a German family. His two honeymoons were spent in Europe. The best man at his second wedding was the British diplomat Cecil Spring Rice. As the civil service commissioner in Washington, D.C., he often socialized with foreign diplomats. Roosevelt liked to read the history and literature of other countries. Many of his hobbies had a foreign tinge, whether it was engaging in sumo wrestling or jiujitsu. In essence, few American leaders possessed Roosevelt's firsthand knowledge and experience with foreign affairs.

Roosevelt was instrumental in the change in U.S. foreign policy by the 1890s. As assistant secretary of the navy, Roosevelt advocated a naval buildup and pushed for a war with Spain. Once the Spanish-American War occurred, Roosevelt resigned as assistant secretary of the navy and formed a volunteer military unit known as the Rough Riders. Roosevelt's heroics in Cuba propelled him into the governorship of New York, the vice presidency, and, ultimately, the presidency. As president, Roosevelt continued an active foreign policy. He built up the U.S. Navy and sent the Great White Fleet around the world in a show of American power. Roosevelt demonstrated his diplomatic skills by negotiating an end to the Russo-Japanese War. He expanded U.S. power in Latin America with the formulation of the Roosevelt Corollary, which asserted that the United States was the policeman of the Western Hemisphere. Roosevelt helped to end a blockade of Venezuela by European powers, temporarily occupied Santo Domingo until its finances were stabilized, and began the construction of the Panama Canal. Roosevelt's activist policies in Latin America continued under his successors, William Howard Taft and Woodrow Wilson. Taft and Wilson intervened more frequently and violently in Latin America than Theodore Roosevelt. Most notably, Woodrow Wilson intervened in Nicaragua, Honduras, Haiti, the Dominican Republic, and Mexico. Wilson's intervention in Mexico (in response to Mexican outlaw Pancho Villa's attack on Columbus, New Mexico) almost led to war.

World War I

The assassination of Archduke Franz Ferdinand of Austria-Hungry in Sarajevo, Bosnia, by Gavrilo Princip on June 28, 1914, was the event that sparked World War I. However, there were underlying causes to the war, including the race for colonies in Asia and Africa among European powers, the naval arms race, and the system of alliances. Of the three underlying causes, the system of alliances was the most likely explanation for war.

On the eve of war, Europe was split into two alliances. One alliance was the Triple Alliance, which consisted of Germany, Austria-Hungary, and Italy. This alliance was created by Germany, and the purpose was to isolate France. The other major alliance was the Triple Entente, which consisted of England, France, and Russia. The system of alliances divided Europe into two armed camps and restricted the diplomatic flexibility of the countries in these alliances.

After Archduke Franz Ferdinand's assassination, Austria-Hungary declared war on Serbia. Russia responded by declaring war on Austria-Hungary. Germany declared war on France and invaded neutral Belgium. In response to Germany's invasion of Belgium, England declared war on Germany. By the end of the summer, Europe was at war. On one side, there were the Allied powers, consisting of England, France, and Russia. On the other side, there were the Central Powers, consisting of Germany, Austria-Hungary, and the Ottoman Empire. The war turned into a bloody stalemate that cost the lives of over 6 million people on both sides. The war was made especially deadly by new weapons, such as poison gas, machine guns, tanks, airplanes, and submarines.

The war quickly divided Americans. Many German Americans supported Germany, and many Americans in the Northeast sympathized with the Allied powers (especially England). Theodore Roosevelt was an early supporter of the Allied powers and condemned Germany early in the war for atrocities committed in Belgium. Many Americans in the Midwest and West believed that the United States should stay out of the war. For example, Senator George Norris argued that the United States should not be dragged into what he considered an imperialist war. Reflecting his lifelong commitment to military preparedness, Roosevelt advocated an American military buildup. President Woodrow Wilson said that the United States must be neutral in both thought and in action. During the war, he constantly offered to mediate between the Allied powers and Central Powers but was rebuffed. The United States was not completely neutral, though, as the United States loaned the Allied powers over $2 billion, compared to just $27 million to Germany.

German submarine warfare put Wilson in a difficult position. Many of the ships that they sunk carried American passengers. The most famous ship sunk by the Germans was the British ocean liner the *Lusitania*. It was sunk by a German U-boat off the coast of Ireland in 1915. Over 1,000 people died, including over 100 Americans. Wilson's initial response was to say that sometimes a man is too proud to fight. Theodore Roosevelt condemned Woodrow Wilson's reaction and charged that Germany's action was piracy on the high seas. Eventually, Wilson demanded an apology from Germany. However, his response was more vigorous when a German U-boat sunk the *Sussex*, which was also carrying American passengers. In response, Wilson threatened to cut off diplomatic relations with Germany. As a result of Wilson's strong response, Germany promised to only attack military vessels.

In the 1916 campaign, the war was front and center as Wilson campaigned on a slogan of "He Kept Us Out of War." During the campaign, Theodore Roosevelt supported the Republican nominee, Charles Evans Hughes, and condemned what he regarded as Wilson's weak policies toward Germany. Wilson's promise to keep the United States out of the war was a major factor in his narrow reelection win.

Yet, it proved to be a promise that Wilson could not keep. Events pushed the United States into the war. At the end of January 1917, Germany announced that it was renewing its unrestricted submarine warfare. In February, the Zimmerman Telegram was released, which revealed that Germany had asked Mexico to attack the United States and in exchange would help Mexico regain territory that it lost to the United States during the Mexican-American War. In April 1917, Woodrow Wilson went before Congress to ask for a declaration of war. He framed the war in an idealistic light, contending that the United States had no ulterior motives and was fighting to make the world safe for democracy. In response, Congress overwhelmingly voted for war.

Roosevelt was enthusiastic about Wilson's speech and the declaration of war. He met with Wilson and offered to raise a division to fight in Europe. Although the meeting was cordial, Wilson rejected his offer. Roosevelt saw the rejection as a vindictive and petty move on the part of Wilson. However, many military leaders (including John J. Pershing) questioned Roosevelt's military experience and his health, and they pointed out that this was a different war than the Spanish-American War in which Theodore Roosevelt had fought. Although Roosevelt did not fight this time, his sons (Theodore Jr., Kermit, Archie, and Quentin) served in the war. Ted, Kermit, and Archie distinguished themselves in combat. Tragically, Roosevelt's son Quentin died in combat when his plane was shot down by the Germans.

Throughout the war, Wilson failed to reach out to Roosevelt for help. As a result, Roosevelt became Wilson's most vocal critic during the war. Roosevelt argued that Wilson had left the United States poorly prepared to fight in the war. To his critics, Roosevelt was a jealous and vindictive man who was attacking Wilson for personal reasons. To his supporters, Roosevelt was a patriotic man whose charges of unpreparedness were supported by congressional investigations. As the war neared its end, Roosevelt became more popular. In the 1918 midterm elections, Wilson made the mistake of urging voters to vote for Democratic candidates if they supported the war. The move backfired, and Republicans won control of Congress in the midterm elections. By the end of the war, Roosevelt was seen as the leader of the Republican Party and the favorite to win the presidency in 1920. Unfortunately for Roosevelt, he died from a blood clot on January 6, 1919.

Conclusion

Theodore Roosevelt witnessed many significant changes in his lifetime. He was shaped by the Civil War and Reconstruction, his travels abroad as a young man, and by the Gilded Age. Roosevelt responded to and influenced events in American foreign policy, the Progressive era, and World War I. He would not live to see even more dramatic changes in foreign and domestic affairs in the succeeding decades.

ANALYTICAL ESSAY

Theodore Roosevelt served as president of the United States from 1901 to 1909. Roosevelt became president in 1901 upon the assassination of President William McKinley (Roosevelt was McKinley's vice president).

Domestically, Roosevelt sought to limit the power of big business monopolies known as trusts. He did this by using the Sherman Antitrust Act to break up trusts—most famously financier J. P. Morgan's Northern Securities Company. Unlike previous presidents, he sought to treat labor unions fairly, most notably in his handling of the 1902 anthracite coal strike. Roosevelt convinced Congress to pass legislation to regulate the inspection of meat and to require the labeling of products. In foreign policy, Roosevelt enhanced the role of the United States. In Latin America, Roosevelt asserted the right of the United States to intervene in Latin America through the Roosevelt Corollary. He began the construction of the Panama Canal (completed after his presidency in 1914). Roosevelt became the first president to be awarded the Nobel Peace Prize after successfully negotiating an end to the Russo-Japanese War in 1905. A firm supporter of a strong navy, Roosevelt increased the size of the U.S. Navy and sent a modernized fleet (known as the Great White Fleet) around the world in 1907.

Few people were as well prepared to assume the presidency as Theodore Roosevelt. Born in 1858 to a wealthy New York family, he had held a variety of offices before assuming the presidency upon William McKinley's assassination in 1901. Roosevelt had served as a New York state legislator, civil service commissioner, New York City police commissioner, assistant secretary of the navy, and governor of New York. Although only 42 years old when he became president, Roosevelt had extensive political experience. In many of these jobs, Roosevelt had proven himself to be a superb administrator. Through most of his career, Roosevelt was a reformer who worked within the political system and through the Republican Party. The sole exception occurred when he broke away from the Republican Party in 1912 to run as the presidential nominee of the Progressive Party. However, by 1916, Roosevelt had scrapped the Progressive Party and returned to the Republican fold.

One of Roosevelt's most pressing challenges as president was how to respond to the growing power of the big business combinations known as the trusts. Trusts dominated whole industries. For example, John D. Rockefeller's Standard Oil Company dominated 90 percent of the oil-refining industry. One of the largest

trusts was the U.S. Steel Corporation, which was formed in 1900 when steel magnate Andrew Carnegie sold his business to the financier John Pierpont "J. P." Morgan. U.S. Steel was the first billion-dollar company in American history. Even though Congress passed the Sherman Antitrust Act in 1890 to regulate the power of the trusts, it had not been seriously enforced. Instead, the law had been used against labor unions.

Roosevelt was the first president to enforce the Sherman Antitrust Act and regulate the trusts. The Justice Department filed an antitrust suit in 1902 against a railroad monopoly known as the Northern Securities Company. This suit was significant because one of the investors in the Northern Securities Company was the financier J. P. Morgan, widely regarded as the most powerful man in the country. In filing the suit against the Northern Securities Company, Roosevelt was sending the message that not even someone as powerful as J. P. Morgan was above the law.

The Supreme Court later upheld the Justice Department's antitrust suit. This was the beginning of 44 successful antitrust suits during Roosevelt's presidency, which included the breakup of the Duke tobacco trust and John D. Rockefeller's Standard Oil Company. Although known as a trust buster, Roosevelt did not seek to break up all trusts. Instead, he differentiated between "good" and "bad" trusts. "Good" trusts were those that allowed some competition and treated their workers fairly, and "bad" trusts were those that undermined competition and treated their workers poorly. It was more important for Roosevelt to establish the precedent that the federal government possessed the ability to limit the power of the trusts.

During Roosevelt's presidency, he sought to demonstrate that he could be evenhanded in disputes between business and labor. A good example of this was his handling of the 1902 anthracite coal strike. The nation's economy threatened to shut down over the coal strike, which began in Pennsylvania. Coal was a necessity, whether it was heating homes or fueling ships and trains. Roosevelt sought to resolve the strike by holding a conference at the White House. This was a departure from the policies of his predecessors, who tended to use troops to crush strikes. Roosevelt found the workers' demands (represented by John Mitchell of the United Mine Workers) for higher wages and shorter hours to be reasonable. On the other hand, he found the coal operators to be arrogant and inflexible. They denounced the workers as radicals and asserted that God was on their side.

Roosevelt warned the coal operators that if they did not resolve the strike that the U.S. Army would operate the mines. As a result, the workers' union and the coal operators agreed to the creation of commission composed of representatives from both groups. The commission ruled in favor of the striking workers, giving them higher wages and shorter hours. The strike came to an end, and Roosevelt received the credit for mediating between the two groups. Roosevelt's handling of the anthracite coal strike represented his Square Deal policies of asserting a "square deal" for everyone, regardless of class, religion, race, or gender. Square Deal became the nickname for Roosevelt's domestic agenda as president.

Another issue that confronted Theodore Roosevelt during his presidency was the awful conditions in the meatpacking industry in Chicago. These conditions were exposed by the journalist Upton Sinclair in his 1906 novel *The Jungle*. *The Jungle* revealed that people were eating tainted and diseased meat. Sinclair was a socialist who hoped that people would read his work and convert to socialism. However, Sinclair was disappointed that people did not want radical revolution but rather reform of the meatpacking industry.

One of the people horrified by the revelations from *The Jungle* was Theodore Roosevelt. Although distrustful of the radical Sinclair, Roosevelt requested that the Department of Agriculture investigate Sinclair's allegations. The conclusion of the investigation was that Sinclair's allegations were true. Roosevelt used the report to pressure Congress to pass the Meat Inspection Act, which required that meat not go to the market unless it had been inspected and approved by the Department of Agriculture. Along with the Meat Inspection Act, Congress also passed the Pure Food and Drug Act, which required companies to post their ingredients on products that were consumed by the public (such as patent medicines, drugs, and beverages) and created the Food and Drug Administration (FDA) to monitor the safety of food and drug products.

During his presidency, Roosevelt sought to regulate the railroads. In 1903, he convinced Congress to pass the Elkins Act, which outlawed preferential shipping to large companies. Industrialists such as oil baron John D. Rockefeller of the Standard Oil Company had benefited from preferential treatment from railroad companies. In Roosevelt's second term, he lobbied Congress for further railroad regulation. He used his popularity to appeal to the public to support legislation. Roosevelt also used the threat of tariff revision (the Republican Party supported high tariffs at this point) to convince conservative leaders in Congress to support the legislation. As a result, Congress passed the Hepburn Act in 1906, which strengthened the power of the Interstate Commerce Commission to regulate railroad rates. In this battle, Roosevelt demonstrated his ability to successfully rally the public to his side and to negotiate with Congress to achieve his goals.

A major challenge during Theodore Roosevelt's presidency was how to handle the issue of civil rights. The Republican Party was perceived by many African Americans as the "Party of Lincoln" that had freed the slaves. On the other hand, the Republicans had not done much for African Americans since the Reconstruction era. This was partly due the racism prevalent in the American public as well as the desire of the Republican Party to make gains in the South. During his presidency, Roosevelt appointed African Americans to federal government positions. He also condemned lynching in his public pronouncements.

Roosevelt found how difficult the issue of civil rights was when he invited African American educator Booker T. Washington to the White House in October 1901. As the founder of the vocational Tuskegee Institution in Alabama, Washington was the most famous African American in the country. Roosevelt was dining in the White House with Booker T. Washington because they had a friendship that went back to the days before Roosevelt was president. Washington's message of self-help and individualism appealed to Roosevelt. Washington was also invited to the White House because he was a Republican who could give Roosevelt advice on how the Republican Party could improve its performance in the South. The invitation to Washington demonstrated that Roosevelt (unlike many white Americans) was comfortable dining with a black man. During his tenure as governor of New

York, Roosevelt had dined with African Americans and allowed them to stay overnight with him in the governor's mansion.

There was a negative reaction in the country (particularly the South) when word leaked out of Roosevelt's dinner with Washington. Southerners charged that Roosevelt favored the intermixing of the races and probably wanted to marry off his children to Booker T. Washington's children. Roosevelt defended Washington as a great man who was the equal of any white man. However, Roosevelt never invited Washington back to the White House after the backlash, although he did continue to consult Washington.

Roosevelt also confronted the difficulty of race issues in the aftermath of the Brownsville Riots in 1906. A military unit of highly decorated African American soldiers had been accused of shooting up the town of Brownsville, Texas. Roosevelt dishonorably discharged the whole military unit of black troopers, even though there was no evidence of wrongdoing on their part. Roosevelt's actions angered and disillusioned the African American community, which felt that Roosevelt had acted rashly on the basis of no evidence. Roosevelt's actions damaged his relationship with the African American community for the rest of his presidency.

Roosevelt's record on civil rights was mixed. He appointed African Americans to federal jobs, condemned lynching, and invited Booker T. Washington to the White House. On the other hand, he dishonorably discharged the black troopers in Brownsville, Texas, with no evidence, and Roosevelt made no effort to overturn the system of Jim Crow discrimination against African Americans in the South. In his private letters, Roosevelt confided to friends that the Fifteenth Amendment (giving African American males the right to vote) may have been a mistake because he believed that there were many African Americans that were not qualified to vote.

In his later years, Roosevelt continued to struggle with the issue of civil rights. During the 1912 campaign, he was criticized by African American leaders for insisting on all-white delegations to the Progressive Party from the South. Yet, Roosevelt also condemned race riots in East St. Louis in 1917, in which African Americans were attacked, and in his final speech, he appeared on stage with African American leader W. E. B. DuBois to praise the contributions of African American soldiers.

The issue that generated the most passion from Roosevelt was conservation. An ardent naturalist since early childhood, he wanted to preserve the nation's resources for future generations. Roosevelt was an avid hunter and birdwatcher who had an encyclopedic knowledge of birds and animals. He befriended prominent naturalists such as John Burroughs and John Muir and worked with them to conserve the nation's resources. As governor of New York, Roosevelt set aside land for state parks and state forests. Roosevelt used executive orders as president to set aside over 200 million acres of land for national parks, national monuments, and national forests. He created the U.S. Forest Service in 1905 to oversee and protect the country's natural resources.

Roosevelt's policies were carried out with the energetic assistance of Gifford Pinchot, the head of the U.S. Forest Service. Among the areas created by President Roosevelt were the Grand Canyon in Arizona, Crater Lake National Park in Oregon, Mesa Verde National Park in Colorado, Devil's Tower in Wyoming, and the Petrified Forest in Arizona. While business leaders felt Roosevelt's actions intruded on their bottom line and many state politicians required Roosevelt's executive orders as a power grab, Roosevelt's conservation record is his most enduring legacy and is appreciated by the many tourists who visit the nation's national monuments and national parks every year.

The economy during Roosevelt's presidency was generally prosperous. However, the public experienced a scare during the Panic of 1907 when the stock market collapsed and the banking system was on the verge of failure. Business leaders blamed the regulatory policies of Roosevelt, and Roosevelt blamed overspeculation by investors. Financial ruin was averted when the powerful financier J. P. Morgan intervened by using his influence and money to save the banks. During the Panic of 1907, Roosevelt allowed J. P. Morgan to acquire the Tennessee Coal & Iron company. He accepted Morgan's explanation that the merger was necessary to end the economic downturn. However, critics then and later argued that

Roosevelt was tricked into agreeing to a merger that benefited Morgan.

During his presidency, Roosevelt had the opportunity to make three appointments to the Supreme Court: Oliver Wendell Holmes Jr. in 1902, William Rufus Day in 1903, and William Henry Moody in 1906. Of the three appointments, Holmes turned out to be the biggest disappointment for Roosevelt. Roosevelt had great hopes for Holmes, a Civil War veteran and judge on the Massachusetts Supreme Court with a reputation for supporting progressive causes. Roosevelt picked Holmes, believing that he would support Roosevelt's progressive policies on the Supreme Court. However, Holmes disappointed Roosevelt with his dissent in the *U.S. v. Northern Securities Case* in 1904.

Two years earlier, the Justice Department had filed an antitrust suit under the Sherman Antitrust Act to break up the Northern Securities Company. The Northern Securities Company was a railroad monopoly whose investors included J. P. Morgan. Although a majority of the Supreme Court justices voted to support the Justice Department's decision, Holmes dissented in the case. He argued that the Northern Securities Company did not violate the Sherman Antitrust Act because it was not in restraint of trade. Key decisions issued by the Supreme Court during Roosevelt's presidency included *Lochner v. New York* (1905) and *Muller v. Oregon* (1908). In *Lochner*, the Supreme Court ruled that it was unconstitutional for the state of New York to regulate working hours. In *Muller*, the Supreme Court ruled that the state of Oregon could limit the working hours of women. Throughout his career, Roosevelt criticized the courts as an obstacle to progressive reforms. After he left the presidency, he controversially called for the recall of judges at the state level who struck down progressive measures.

Roosevelt's progressive record has been passionately debated by historians. Historians such as Richard Hofstadter, John Morton Blum, and Gabriel Kolko have questioned Roosevelt's progressive record. To Hofstadter, Roosevelt was an opportunistic politician whose reforms were purely ornamental in nature. Blum considered Roosevelt a conservative and argued that his progressive reforms were driven by his fear of radicalism. To Kolko, the Progressive era was not progressive but instead the "triumph of conservatism." He argued that Roosevelt, in pursuing reforms (such as the Meat Inspection Act), followed the lead of corporate leaders who wanted the reforms because they promoted predictability and stability and disadvantaged smaller competitors. On the other hand, more recent historians, such as Kathleen Dalton, have argued that Roosevelt was committed to progressive causes throughout his political career. The historian Edward Kohn has noted Roosevelt's support for progressive issues during his years as a politician in New York City.

In foreign policy, Roosevelt believed in the importance of a strong military. This was a recurring theme throughout his life and career. Roosevelt's fascination with the navy can traced back to his childhood, where he learned about the exploits of his uncles James and Irving Bulloch, who were Confederate naval officers in the Civil War. After graduating from Harvard, Roosevelt wrote the highly regarded *The Naval War of 1812*, which was a thoroughly researched account of naval battles between the United States and England during the War of 1812. As assistant secretary of the navy, he was instrumental in preparing the United States for the Spanish-American War. During his presidency, Roosevelt increased the size of the U.S. Navy. By the time he left office, the United States possessed the second-largest navy in the world (second only to England). He believed that a strong military (especially a powerful navy) was crucial to support any warnings that he might deliver to foreign nations.

Earlier historians believed that Roosevelt's emphasis on a strong military represented his militaristic and belligerent nature. However, in recent decades, historians such as Frederick Marks and William Tilchin have highlighted Roosevelt's diplomatic skills. They point out that Roosevelt saw no contradiction between military preparedness and maintaining peaceful relations with other countries. Like George Washington, Roosevelt believed that the best way to keep the peace was to be prepared for war. These historians note that, in his seven years as president, Roosevelt did not initiate a war and was awarded the Nobel Peace Prize for successfully negotiating an end to the Russo-Japanese War.

In the Western Hemisphere, Roosevelt enhanced the power of the United States. In late 1902 and early

1903, Roosevelt became alarmed when Germany, England, and Italy sent a fleet to the Western Hemisphere to collect debts owed to them by the Venezuelan government of Cipriano Castro. He was especially concerned when those countries landed troops on Venezuelan soil. Behind the scenes, Roosevelt urged the European countries to pull out of Venezuela and confronted them with a series of ultimatums. By early 1903, the governments of England, Germany, and Italy had withdrawn their troops from the Western Hemisphere and agreed to negotiate the dispute before The Hague Tribunal in the Netherlands. The Hague Tribunal eventually ruled in favor of the European countries, and Roosevelt publicly congratulated them on their victory.

For the rest of his presidency, Roosevelt worried about the European countries establishing a foothold in the Western Hemisphere. As a result of his experiences with the European powers in Venezuela, in 1904, Roosevelt formulated the Roosevelt Corollary, which stated that the United States would act as the policeman of the Western Hemisphere. That same year, Roosevelt, at the invitation of the government of Santo Domingo (which feared that European creditors would occupy them), sent troops to occupy that country's customhouses until it was able to pay its European creditors. Once Santo Domingo was able to pay its bills, U.S. forces left the country.

More controversially, in 1903, Roosevelt intervened in Panama's revolution against Colombia in order to acquire a canal that would connect the Atlantic and Pacific Oceans. This appealed to Roosevelt because it would make it easier to connect the United States' Atlantic and Pacific fleets in the event of a war or emergency. Roosevelt encouraged the Panamanian revolution after Colombia rejected a treaty with the United States to build a canal. Once Panama successfully revolted against Colombia, Roosevelt quickly recognized the new country and signed a treaty with Panama to build a canal. By 1914, the Panama Canal was completed.

While Roosevelt regarded the Panama Canal as his greatest achievement, critics condemned Roosevelt for the bullying and high-handed way that he had acquired the Panama Canal. To many in Latin America, the way in which Roosevelt acquired the canal reinforced perceptions of the United States as an imperialist bully. On the other hand, Roosevelt's interventions in Latin America (especially compared to his successors, William Howard Taft and Woodrow Wilson) tended to be infrequent and nonviolent.

In Asia, Roosevelt closely followed the Russo-Japanese War between Russia and Japan, which started in 1904 when Japan attacked Russia over disputed claims between the two countries in Manchuria and Korea. Roosevelt regarded the Russians as autocratic barbarians who could not be trusted. He publicly criticized the Russian government for its persecution of Jewish citizens. On the other hand, Roosevelt admired the fighting qualities of the Japanese and regarded Japan as a Western country. However, Roosevelt became concerned when it became clear that Japan was winning the Russo-Japanese War. He feared that if Japan won a decisive victory, it could threaten U.S. interests in the Philippines. As a result, Roosevelt offered to mediate an end to the war between Russia and Japan. Both Russia and Japan accepted Roosevelt's offer. As a result of Roosevelt's efforts, the Treaty of Portsmouth was negotiated in 1905. Russia agreed to give up all claims to Manchuria and Korea, and in exchange, Japan did not ask Russia for reparations. Roosevelt was awarded the Nobel Peace Prize in 1906 for his successful efforts to end the Russo-Japanese War.

However, the Japanese government did not tell their people that they willingly gave up reparations, and there were riots in Japan. Roosevelt took a number of steps to protect U.S. interests in the Philippines. He realized that the United States was in a vulnerable position there. He sent Secretary of War William Howard Taft to Asia to negotiate the secret Taft-Katsura Agreement with Japan in 1905. In this secret agreement, Japan promised to recognize U.S. control of the Philippines if the United States recognized Japan's control of Korea. Roosevelt also negotiated the Root-Takahira Agreement in 1908 with Japan. Both sides agreed to abide by the Open Door policy in China (which allowed European powers equal access to China's markets), to support the status quo in Asia, and to support each other in the event of an emergency in Asia. Roosevelt also attempted to impress Japan by sending the Great White Fleet (a modernized naval fleet) around the world. One of the places that the fleet stopped was in Japan.

In California, Roosevelt attempted to avert problems with Japan over the state of California's discriminatory treatment of Japanese immigrants, fearing that it could lead to war with Japan. In 1907, Roosevelt negotiated the Gentlemen's Agreement between the state of California and the government of Japan. Under the Gentlemen's Agreement, the state of California would treat Japanese immigrants like any other American citizen. In addition, the Japanese government agreed to limit the number of Japanese coming to California.

In Europe, Roosevelt worked to avoid a war between France and Germany. In 1905, the impulsive and erratic Kaiser Wilhelm II of Germany demanded that France give Germany an open door in Morocco or else fight a war with Germany. Roosevelt averted a war between France and Germany by getting both sides to hold a conference in Algeciras, Spain. He convinced France, through his close friend, French ambassador Jules Jusserand, that it could not win a war with Germany (which had the most powerful army in Europe) and would be better off negotiating a settlement. He assured the French government that the United States would support them if a conference were held. Roosevelt convinced Kaiser Wilhelm II to hold a conference by using flattery. He wrote Kaiser Wilhelm II that a conference would cement his legacy. At the conference, the United States and other European countries outmaneuvered Germany. France's control of Morocco was preserved, and a potential war between France and Germany was prevented.

Roosevelt's presidency from 1901 to 1909 was a consequential one. Domestically, he was the first president to enforce the Sherman Antitrust Act and the first president to treat labor fairly in business-labor disputes. Roosevelt succeeded in convincing Congress to pass key domestic reforms, including the Meat Inspection Act, the Pure Food and Drug Act, and the Hepburn Act. He energetically used his executive powers to set aside land to be used for national parks, national forests, and national monuments. In foreign policy, Roosevelt strengthened the navy, enhanced the role of the United States in the Western Hemisphere, began the process of building the Panama Canal, successfully negotiated an end to the Russo-Japanese War (for which he was awarded the Nobel Peace Prize), and averted a war between France and Germany at the Algeciras Conference. The United States played a more active role in foreign policy during Roosevelt's presidency. Roosevelt established the model for a strong president in the 20th century that was followed by succeeding presidents such as Woodrow Wilson and Franklin D. Roosevelt.

There were issues left unresolved at the end of Theodore Roosevelt's presidency. One issue was the state of race relations. On the one hand, Roosevelt had condemned the lynchings of African Americans, appointed African Americans to government positions, and invited Booker T. Washington to the White House. On the other hand, he dishonorably discharged black troops in the Brownsville Riots with little evidence, and he failed to enforce the Fourteenth Amendment (which provided equal protection for all citizens, including African Americans) and Fifteenth Amendment (which provided African American males the right to vote) in the South.

Roosevelt also left the issue of the tariffs unresolved. Although he had doubts about a high tariff and had threatened tariff revisions in negotiations with congressional leaders over the Hepburn Act, Roosevelt made no effort to revise the tariff. Roosevelt knew that high tariffs were Republican doctrine and that to propose tariff reductions would divide the Republican Party.

A third unresolved issue was the state of the banking system. The banking system had been rattled by the Panic of 1907, and many banks were on the verge of collapse. They would have collapsed but for the energetic actions of the powerful financier J. P. Morgan. When Roosevelt left office in 1909, the United States lacked a centralized banking system.

A fourth unresolved issue was the uneasy relationship between progressives and conservatives in the Republican Party. As a shrewd politician, Roosevelt was able to hold both groups together during his seven years as president. However, the divisions between conservatives and progressives would widen under Roosevelt's successor, William Howard Taft.

Jason Roberts

Further Reading

Beale, Howard K. 1956. *Theodore Roosevelt and the Rise of America to World Power*. Baltimore: Johns Hopkins Press.

Brands, H. W. 1997. *TR: The Last Romantic*. New York: Basic Books.

Brinkley, Douglas. 2009. *Wilderness Warrior: Theodore Roosevelt and the Crusade for America*. New York: Harper Perennial.

Cooper, John Milton. 1985. *The Warrior and the Priest: Woodrow Wilson and Theodore Roosevelt*. Cambridge, MA: Belknap Press

Dalton, Kathleen. 2001. *Theodore Roosevelt: A Strenuous Life*. New York: Vintage Books.

Marks, Frederick W. 1982. *Velvet on Iron: The Diplomacy of Theodore Roosevelt*. Lincoln: University of Nebraska Press.

Miller, Nathan. 1992. *Theodore Roosevelt: A Life*. New York: William Morrow and Company.

Morris, Edmund. 1979. *The Rise of Theodore Roosevelt*. New York: Coward, McCann, & Geoghegan.

Morris, Edmund. 2001. *Theodore Rex*. New York: Random House.

Morris, Edmund. 2010. *Colonel Roosevelt*. New York: Random House.

Mowry, George. 1946. *Theodore Roosevelt and the Progressive Movement*. New York: Hill and Wang.

Mowry, George. 1958. *The Era of Theodore Roosevelt: 1900–1912*. New York: Harper & Row.

Square Deal Speech (September 7, 1903)

Theodore Roosevelt delivered this speech at the New York State Fair. In this speech, Roosevelt famously argued for a "square deal" for the American people. He asserted that every American should be treated fairly regardless of whether he or she were rich or poor.

In speaking on Labor Day at the annual fair of the New York State Agricultural Association, it is natural to keep especially in mind the two bodies who compose the majority of our people and upon whose welfare depends the welfare of the entire State. If circumstances are such that thrift, energy, industry, and forethought enable the farmer, the tiller of the soil, on the one hand, and the wage-worker on the other, to keep themselves, their wives, and their children in reasonable comfort, then the State is well off, and we can be assured that the other classes in the community will likewise prosper. On the other hand, if there is in the long run a lack of prosperity among the two classes named, then all other prosperity is sure to be more seeming than real.

It has been our profound good fortune as a nation that hitherto, disregarding exceptional periods of depression and the normal and inevitable fluctuations, there has been on the whole from the beginning of our government to the present day a progressive betterment alike in the condition of the tiller of the soil and in the condition of the man who, by his manual skill and labor, supports himself and his family, and endeavors to bring up his children so that they may be at least as well off as, and, if possible, better off than, he himself has been. There are, of course, exceptions, but as a whole the standard of living among the farmers of our country has risen from generation to generation, and the wealth represented on the farms has steadily increased, while the wages of labor have likewise risen, both as regards the actual money paid and as regards the purchasing power which that money represents.

Side by side with this increase in the prosperity of the wage-worker and the tiller of the soil has gone on a great increase in prosperity among the business men and among certain classes of professional men; and the prosperity of these men has been partly the cause and partly the consequence of the prosperity of farmer and wage-worker. It cannot be too often repeated that in this country, in the long run, we all of us tend to go up or go down together. If the average of well-being is high, it means that the average wage-worker, the average farmer, and the average business man are all alike well-off. If the average shrinks, there is not one of these classes which will not feel the shrinkage. Of course, there are always some men who are not affected by good times, just as there are some men who are not affected by bad times. But speaking broadly, it is true that if prosperity comes, all of us tend to share more or less therein, and that if adversity comes each of us, to a greater or less extent, feels the tension.

Unfortunately, in this world the innocent frequently find themselves obliged to pay some of the penalty for the misdeeds of the guilty; and so if hard times come, whether they be due to our own fault or to our misfortune, whether they be due to some burst of speculative frenzy that has caused a portion of the business world to lose its head—a loss which no legislation can possibly supply—or whether they be due to any lack of wisdom in a portion of the world of labor—in each case, the trouble once started is felt more or less in every walk of life.

It is all-essential to the continuance of our healthy national life that we should recognize this community of interest among our people. The welfare of each of us is dependent fundamentally upon the welfare of all of us, and therefore in public life that man is the best representative of each of us who seeks to do good to each by doing good to all; in other words, whose endeavor it is not to represent any special class and promote merely that class's selfish interests, but to represent all true and honest men of all sections and all classes and to work for their interests by working for our common country.

We can keep our government on a sane and healthy basis, we can make and keep our social system what it should be, only on condition of judging each man, not as a member of a class, but on his worth as a man. It is an infamous thing in our American life, and fundamentally treacherous to our institutions, to apply to any man any test save that of his personal worth, or to draw between two sets of men any distinction save the distinction of conduct, the distinction that marks off those who do well and wisely from those who do ill and foolishly. There are good citizens and bad citizens in every class as in every locality, and the attitude of decent people toward great public and social questions should be determined, not by the accidental questions of employment or locality, but by those deep-set principles which represent the innermost souls of men.

The failure in public and in private life thus to treat each man on his own merits, the recognition of this government as being either for the poor as such or for the rich as such, would prove fatal to our Republic, as such failure and such recognition have always proved fatal in the past to other republics. A healthy republican government must rest upon individuals, not upon classes or sections. As soon as it becomes government by a class or by a section, it departs from the old American ideal.

Many qualities are needed by a people which would preserve the power of self-government in fact as well as in name. Among these qualities are forethought, shrewdness, self-restraint, the courage which refuses to abandon one's own rights, and the disinterested and kindly good sense which enables one to do justice to the rights of others. Lack of strength and lack of courage and unfit men for self-government on the one hand; and on the other, brutal arrogance, envy—in short, any manifestation of the spirit of selfish disregard, whether of one's own duties or of the rights of others, are equally fatal.

In the history of mankind many republics have risen, have flourished for a less or greater time, and then have fallen because their citizens lost the power of governing themselves and thereby of governing their state; and in no way has this loss of power been so often and so clearly shown as in the tendency to turn the government into a government primarily for the benefit of one class instead of a government for the benefit of the people as a whole. Again and again in the republics of ancient Greece, in those of medieval Italy and medieval Flanders, this tendency was shown, and wherever the tendency became a habit it invariably and inevitably proved fatal to the state. In the final result, it mattered not one whit whether the movement was in favor of one class or of another.

The outcome was equally fatal, whether the country fell into the hands of a wealthy oligarchy which exploited the poor or whether it fell under the domination of a turbulent mob which plundered the rich. In both cases there resulted violent alternations between tyranny and disorder, and a final complete loss of liberty to all citizens—destruction in the end overtaking the class which had for the moment been victorious as well as that which had momentarily been defeated. The death-knell of the Republic had rung as soon as the active power became lodged in the hands of those who sought, not to do justice to all citizens, rich and poor alike, but to stand for one special class and for its interests as opposed to the interests of others.

The reason why our future is assured lies in the fact that our people are genuinely skilled in and fitted for self-government and therefore will spurn the leadership of those who seek to excite this ferocious and foolish class antagonism. The average American knows not only that he himself intends to do what is right, but that his average fellow countryman has the same intention and the same power to make his intention effective. He knows, whether he be business man, professional man, farmer, mechanic, employer, or wage-worker, that the welfare of each of these men is bound up with the welfare of all the others; that each is neighbor to the other, is actuated by the same hopes and fears, has fundamentally the same ideals, and that all alike have much the same virtues and the same faults. Our average fellow citizen is a sane and healthy man who believes in decency and has a wholesome mind. He therefore feels an equal scorn alike for the man of wealth guilty of the mean and base spirit of arrogance toward those who are less well off, and for the man of small means who in his turn either feels, or seeks to excite in others the feeling of mean and base envy for those who are better off. The two feelings, envy and arrogance, are but opposite sides of the same shield, but different developments of the same spirit. . . .

The line of cleavage between good citizenship and bad citizenship separates the rich man who does well from the rich man who does ill, the poor man of good conduct from the poor man of bad conduct. This line of cleavage lies at right angles to any such arbitrary line of division as that separating one class from another, one locality from another, or men with a certain degree of property from those of a less degree of property.

The good citizen is the man who, whatever his wealth or his poverty, strives manfully to do his duty to himself, to his family, to his neighbor, to the States; who is incapable of the baseness which manifests itself either in arrogance or in envy, but who while demanding justice for himself is no less scrupulous to do justice to others. It is because the average American citizen, rich or poor, is of just this type that we have cause for our profound faith in the future of the Republic.

There is no worse enemy of the wage-worker than the man who condones mob violence in any shape or who preaches class hatred; and surely the slightest acquaintance with our industrial history should teach even the most short-sighted that the times of most suffering for our people as a whole, the times when business is stagnant, and capital suffers from shrinkage and gets no return from its investments, are exactly the times of hardship, and want, and grim disaster among

the poor. If all the existing instrumentalities of wealth could be abolished, the first and severest suffering would come among those of us who are least well-off at present. The wage-worker is well off only when the rest of the country is well-off; and he can best contribute to this general well-being by showing sanity and a firm purpose to do justice to others.

In his turn, the capitalist who is really a conservative, the man who has forethought as well as patriotism, should heartily welcome every effort, legislative or otherwise, which has for its object to secure fair dealing by capital, corporate or individual, toward the public and toward the employee. Such laws as the franchise-tax law in this State, which the Court of Appeals recently unanimously decided constitutional- such a law as that passed in Congress last year for the purpose of establishing a Department of Commerce and Labor, under which there should be a bureau to oversee and secure publicity from the great corporations which do an interstate business—such a law as that passed at the same time for the regulation of the great highways of commerce so as to keep these roads clear on fair terms to all producers in getting their goods to market—these laws are in the interest not merely of the people as a whole, but of the propertied classes. For in no way is the stability of property better assured than by making it patent to our people that property bears its proper share of the burdens of the State; that property is handled not only in the interest of the owner, but in the interest of the whole community.

Among ourselves we differ in many qualities of body, head, and heart; we are unequally developed, mentally as well as physically. But each of us has the right to ask that he shall be protected from wrongdoing as he does his work and carries his burden through life. No man needs sympathy because he has to work, because he has a burden to carry. Far and away the best prize that life offers is the chance to work hard at work worth doing; and this is a prize open to every man, for there can be no better worth doing than that done to keep in health and comfort and with reasonable advantages those immediately dependent upon the husband, the father, or the son. There is no room in our healthy American life for the mere idler, for the man or the woman whose object it is throughout life to shirk the duties which life ought to bring. Life can mean nothing worth meaning, unless its prime aim is the doing of duty, the achievement of results worth achieving. A recent writer has finely said: "After all, the saddest thing that can happen to a man is to carry no burdens. To be bent under too great a load is bad; to be crushed by it is lamentable; but even in that there are possibilities that are glorious. But to carry no load at all—there is nothing in that. No one seems to arrive at any goal really worth reaching in this world who does not come to it heavy laden."

Surely from our own experience each one of us knows that this is true. From the greatest to the smallest, happiness and usefulness are largely found in the same soul, and the joy of life is won in its deepest and truest sense only by those who have not shirked life's burdens. The men whom we most delight to honor in all this land are those who, in the iron years from '61 to '65, bore on their shoulders the burden of saving the Union. They did not choose the easy task. They did not shirk the difficult duty. Deliberately and of their own free will they strove for an ideal, upward and onward across the stony slopes of greatness. They did the hardest work that was then to be done; they bore the heaviest burden that any generation of Americans ever had to bear; and because they did this they have won such proud joy as it has fallen to the lot of no other men to win, and have written their names forevermore on the golden honor-roll of the nation. As it is with the soldier, so it is with the civilian. To win success in the business world, to become a first-class mechanic, a successful farmer, an able lawyer or doctor, means that the man has devoted his best energy and power through long years to the achievement of his ends. So it is in the life of the family, upon which in the last analysis the whole welfare of the nation rests. The man or woman who, as bread-winner and home-maker, or as wife and mother, has done all that he or she can do, patiently and uncomplainingly, is to be honored; and is to be envied by all those who have never had the good fortune to feel the need and duty of doing such work. The woman who has borne, and who has reared as they should be reared, a family of children, has in the most emphatic manner deserved well of the Republic. Her burden has been heavy, and she has been able to bear it worthily only by the possession of resolution, of good sense, of conscience, and of unselfishness. But if she has borne it well, then to her shall come the supreme blessing, for in the words of the oldest and greatest of books, "Her children shall rise up and call her blessed;" and among the benefactors of the land, her place must be with those who have done the best and the hardest work, whether as lawgivers or as soldiers, whether in public or private life.

This is not a soft and easy creed to preach. It is a creed willingly learned only by men and women who, together with the softer virtues, possess also the stronger; who can do, and dare, and die at need, but who while life lasts will never flinch from their allotted task. You farmers, and wage-workers, and business men of this great State, of this mighty and wonderful nation, are gathered together today, proud of your State and still prouder of your nation, because your forefathers and predecessors have lived up to just this creed. You have received from their hands a great inheritance, and you will leave an even greater inheritance to your children, and your children's children, provided only that you practice alike in your private and your public lives the strong virtues that have given us as a people greatness in the past. It is not enough to be well-meaning and kindly, but weak; neither is it enough to be strong, unless morality and decency go hand in hand with strength. We must possess the qualities which make us do our duty in our homes and among our neighbors, and in addition we must possess the qualities which are indispensable to the make-up of every great and masterful nation—the qualities of courage and hardihood, of individual initiative and yet of power to combine for a common end, and above all, the resolute determination to permit no man and no set of men to sunder us one from the other by lines of caste or creed or section.

We must act upon the motto of all for each and each for all. There must be ever present in our minds the fundamental truth that in a republic such as ours the only safety is to stand neither for nor against any man because he is rich or because he is poor, because he is engaged in one occupation or another, because he works with his brains or because he works with his hands. We must treat each man on his worth and merits as a man. We must see that each is given a square deal, because he is entitled to no more and should receive no less.

Finally, we must keep ever in mind that a republic such as ours can exist only by virtue of the orderly liberty which comes through the equal domination of the law over all men alike, and through its administration in such resolute and fearless fashion as shall teach all that no man is above it and no man below it.

Source: *The Works of Theodore Roosevelt. Presidential Addresses and State Papers, Part Two.* New York: P. F. Collier & Son, 1901, 466–481.

The Roosevelt Corollary (December 6, 1904)

As part of his annual message to Congress, Roosevelt formulated what became known as the Roosevelt Corollary. He argued that the United States had the right to act as the policeman of the Western Hemisphere if Latin American countries engaged in wrongdoing or were unable to pay their debts to foreign creditors.

It is not true that the United States feels any land hunger or entertains any projects as regards the other nations of the Western Hemisphere save such as are for their welfare. All that this country desires is to see the neighboring countries stable, orderly, and prosperous. Any country whose people conduct themselves well can count upon our hearty friendship. If a nation shows that it knows how to act with reasonable efficiency and decency in social and political matters, if it keeps order and pays its obligations, it need fear no interference from the United States. Chronic wrongdoing, or an impotence which results in a general loosening of the ties of civilized society, may in America, as elsewhere, ultimately require intervention by some civilized nation, and in the Western Hemisphere the adherence of the United States to the Monroe Doctrine may force the United States, however reluctantly, in flagrant cases of such wrongdoing or impotence, to the exercise of an international police power. If every country washed by the Caribbean Sea would show the progress in stable and just civilization which with the aid of the Platt amendment Cuba has shown since our troops left the island, and which so many of the republics in both Americas are constantly and brilliantly showing, all question of interference by this Nation with their affairs would be at an end. Our interests and those of our southern neighbors are in reality identical. They have great natural riches, and if within their borders the reign of law and justice obtains, prosperity is sure to come to them. While they thus obey the primary laws of civilized society they may rest assured that they will be treated by us in a spirit of cordial and helpful sympathy. We would interfere with them only in the last resort, and then only if it became evident that their inability or unwillingness to do justice at home and abroad had violated the rights of the United States or had invited foreign aggression to the detriment of the entire body of American nations. It is a mere truism to say that every nation, whether in America or anywhere else, which desires to maintain its freedom, its independence, must ultimately realize that the right of such independence can not be separated from the responsibility of making good use of it.

In asserting the Monroe Doctrine, in taking such steps as we have taken in regard to Cuba, Venezuela, and Panama, and in endeavoring to circumscribe the theater of war in the Far East, and to secure the open door in China, we have acted in our own interest as well as in the interest of humanity at large. There are, however, cases in which, while our own interests are not greatly involved, strong appeal is made to our sympathies. Ordinarily it is very much wiser and more useful for us to concern ourselves with striving for our own moral and material betterment here at home than to concern ourselves with trying to better the condition of things in other nations. We have plenty of sins of our own to war against, and under ordinary circumstances we can do more for the general uplifting of humanity by striving with heart and soul to put a stop to civic corruption, to brutal lawlessness and violent race prejudices here at home than by passing resolutions about wrongdoing elsewhere. Nevertheless there are occasional crimes committed on so vast a scale and of such peculiar horror as to make us doubt whether it is not our manifest duty to endeavor at least to show our disapproval of the deed and our sympathy with those who have suffered by it. The cases must be extreme in which such a course is justifiable. There must be no effort made to remove the mote from our brother's eye if we refuse to remove the beam from our own. But in extreme cases action may be justifiable and proper. What form the action shall take must depend upon the circumstances of the case; that is, upon the degree of the atrocity and upon our power to remedy it. The cases in which we could interfere by force of arms as we interfered to put a stop to intolerable conditions in Cuba are necessarily very few. Yet it is not to be expected that a people like ours, which in spite of certain very obvious shortcomings, nevertheless as a whole shows by its consistent practice its belief in the principles of civil and religious liberty and of orderly freedom, a people among whom even the worst crime, like the crime of lynching, is never more than sporadic, so that individuals and not classes are molested in their fundamental rights—it is inevitable that such a nation should desire eagerly to give expression to its horror on an occasion like that of the massacre of the Jews in Kishenef, or when it witnesses such systematic and long-extended cruelty and oppression as the cruelty and oppression of which the Armenians have been the victims, and which have won for them the indignant pity of the civilized world.

Source: Theodore Roosevelt's Annual Message to Congress for 1904; House Records HR 58A-K2; Records of the U.S. House of Representatives; Record Group 233; Center for Legislative Archives; National Archives.

The Man with the Muckrake (April 14, 1906)

This speech was delivered in Washington, D.C. In this speech, Roosevelt condemned what he regarded as the sensationalistic methods of many investigative journalists. Roosevelt coined the term muckraker *to describe these journalists.*

Over a century ago Washington laid the corner stone of the Capitol in what was then little more than a tract of wooded wilderness here beside the Potomac. We now find it necessary to provide by great additional buildings for the business of the Government. This growth in the need for the housing of the Government is but a proof and example of the way in which the nation has grown and the sphere of action of the National Government has grown. We now administer the affairs of a nation in which the extraordinary growth of population has been outstripped by the growth of wealth and the growth in complex interests. The material problems that face us to-day are not such as they were in Washington's time, but the underlying facts of human nature are the same now as they were then. Under altered external form we war with the same tendencies toward evil that were evident in Washington's time, and are helped by the same tendencies for good. It is about some of these that I wish to say a word to-day.

In Bunyan's Pilgrim's Progress you may recall the description of the Man with the Muck-rake, the man who could look no way but downward, with the muck-rake in his hand; who was offered a celestial crown for his muck-rake, but who would neither look up nor regard the crown he was offered, but continued to rake to himself the filth of the floor.

In Pilgrim's Progress the Man with the Muck-rake is set forth as the example of him whose vision is fixed on carnal instead of on spiritual things. Yet he also typifies the man who in this life consistently refuses to see aught that is lofty, and fixes his eyes with solemn intentness only on that which is vile and debasing. Now, it is very necessary that we should not flinch from seeing what is vile and debasing. There is filth on the floor, and it must be scraped up with the muck-rake; and there are times and places where this service is the most needed of all the services that can be performed. But the man who never does anything else, who never thinks or speaks or writes, save of his feats with the muck-rake, speedily becomes, not a help to society, not an incitement to good, but one of the most potent forces for evil.

There are, in the body politic, economic and social, many and grave evils, and there is urgent necessity for the sternest war upon them. There should be relentless exposure of and attack upon every evil man whether politician or business man, every evil practice, whether in politics, in business, or in social life. I hail as a benefactor every writer or speaker, every man who, on the platform, or in book, magazine, or newspaper, with merciless severity makes such attack, provided always that he in his turn remembers that the attack is of use only if it is absolutely truthful. The liar is no whit better than the thief, and if his mendacity takes the form of slander, he may be worse than most thieves. It puts a premium upon knavery untruthfully to attack an honest man, or even with hysterical exaggeration to assail a bad man with untruth. An epidemic of indiscriminate assault upon character does not good, but very great harm. The soul of every scoundrel is gladdened whenever an honest man is assailed, or even when a scoundrel is untruthfully assailed.

Now, it is easy to twist out of shape what I have just said, easy to affect to misunderstand it, and, if it is slurred over in repetition, not difficult really to misunderstand it. Some persons are sincerely incapable of understanding that to denounce mud slinging does not mean the endorsement of whitewashing; and both the interested individuals who need whitewashing, and those others who practice mud slinging, like to encourage such confusion of ideas. One of the chief counts against those who make indiscriminate assault upon men in business or men in public life, is that they invite a reaction which is sure to tell powerfully in favor of the unscrupulous scoundrel who really ought to be attacked, who ought to be exposed, who ought, if possible, to be put in the penitentiary. If Aristides is praised overmuch as just, people get tired of hearing it; and overcensure of the unjust finally and from similar reasons results in their favor.

Any excess is almost sure to invite a reaction; and, unfortunately, the reaction, instead of taking the form of punishment of those guilty of the excess, is very apt to take the form either of punishment of the unoffending or of giving immunity, and even strength, to offenders. The effort to make financial or political profit out of the destruction of character can only result in public calamity. Gross and reckless assaults on character, whether on the stump or in newspaper, magazine, or book, create a morbid and vicious public sentiment, and at the same time act as a profound deterrent to able men of normal sensitiveness and tend to prevent them from entering the public service at any price. As an instance in point, I may mention that one serious difficulty encountered in getting the right type of men to dig the Panama Canal is the certainty that they will be exposed, both without, and, I am sorry to say, sometimes within, Congress, to utterly reckless assaults on their character and capacity.

At the risk of repetition let me say again that my plea is, not for immunity to but for the most unsparing exposure of the politician who betrays his trust, of the big business man who makes or spends his fortune in illegitimate or corrupt ways. There should be a resolute effort to hunt every such man out of the position he has disgraced. Expose the crime, and hunt down the criminal; but remember that even in the case of crime, if it is attacked in sensational, lurid, and untruthful fashion, the attack may do more damage to the public mind than the crime itself. It is because I feel that there should be no rest in the endless war against the forces of evil that I ask that the war be conducted with sanity as well as with resolution. The men with the muck-rakes are often indispensable to the well-being of society; but only if they know when to stop raking the muck, and to look upward to the celestial crown above them, to the crown of worthy endeavor. There are beautiful things above and round about them; and if they gradually grow to feel that the whole world is nothing but muck, their power of usefulness is gone. If the whole picture is painted black there remains no hue whereby to single out the rascals for distinction from their fellows. Such painting finally induces a kind of moral color-blindness; and people affected by it come to the conclusion that no man is really black, and no man really white, but they are all gray. In other words, they neither believe in the truth of the attack, nor in the honesty of the man who is attacked; they grow as suspicious of the accusation as of the offense; it becomes well-nigh hopeless to stir them either to wrath against wrongdoing or to enthusiasm for what is right; and such a mental attitude in the public gives hope to every knave, and is the despair of honest men.

To assail the great and admitted evils of our political and industrial life with such crude and sweeping generalizations as to include decent men in the general condemnation means the searing of the public conscience. There results a general attitude either of cynical belief in and indifference to public corruption or else of a distrustful inability to discriminate between the good and the bad. Either attitude is fraught with untold damage to the country as a whole. The fool who has not sense to discriminate between what is good and what is bad is well-nigh as dangerous as the man who does discriminate and yet chooses the bad. There is nothing more distressing to every good patriot, to every good American, than the hard, scoffing spirit which treats the allegation of dishonesty in a public man as a cause for laughter. Such laughter is worse than the crackling of thorns under a pot, for it denotes not merely the vacant mind, but the heart in which high emotions have been choked before they could grow to fruition.

There is any amount of good in the world, and there never was a time when loftier and more disinterested work for the betterment of mankind was being done than now. The forces that tend for evil are great and terrible, but the forces of truth and love and courage and honesty and generosity and sympathy are also stronger than ever before. It is a foolish and timid, no less than a wicked thing, to blink the fact that the forces of evil are strong, but it is even worse to fail to take into account the strength of the forces that tell for good. Hysterical sensationalism is the very poorest weapon wherewith to fight for lasting righteousness. The men who with stern sobriety and truth assail the many evils of our time, whether in the public press or in magazines, or in books, are the leaders and allies of all engaged in the work for social and political betterment. But if they give good reason for distrust of what they say, if they chill the ardor of those who demand truth as a primary virtue, they thereby betray the good cause, and play into the hands of the very men against whom they are nominally at war.

In his "Ecclesiastical Polity" that fine old Elizabethan divine, Bishop Hooker, wrote:

> He that goeth about to persuade a multitude that they are not so well governed as they ought to be, shall never want attentive and favorable hearers; because they know the manifold defects whereunto every kind of regimen is subject, but the secret lets and difficulties, which in public proceedings are innumerable and inevitable, they have not ordinarily the judgment to consider.

This truth should be kept constantly in mind by every free people desiring to preserve the sanity and poise indispensable to the permanent success of self-government. Yet, on the other hand, it is vital not to permit this spirit to sanity and self-command to degenerate into mere mental stagnation. Bad though a state of hysterical excitement is, and evil though the results

are which come from the violent oscillations such excitement invariably produces, yet a sodden acquiescence in evil is even worse. At this moment we are passing through a period of great unrest—social, political, and industrial unrest. It is of the utmost importance for our future that this should prove to be not the unrest of mere rebelliousness against life, of mere dissatisfaction with the inevitable inequality of conditions, but the unrest of a resolute and eager ambition to secure the betterment of the individual and the nation. So far as this movement of agitation throughout the country takes the form of a fierce discontent with evil, of a determination to punish the authors of evil, whether in industry or politics, the feeling is to be heartily welcomed as a sign of healthy life.

If, on the other hand, it turns into a mere crusade of appetite against appetite, of a contest between the brutal greed of the "have-nots" and the brutal greed of the "haves," then it has no significance for good, but only for evil. If it seeks to establish a line of cleavage, not along the line which divides good men from bad, but along that other line, running at right angles thereto, which divides those who are well off from those who are less well off, then it will be fraught with immeasurable harm to the body politic.

We can no more and no less afford to condone evil in the man of capital than evil in the man of no capital. The wealthy man who exults because there is a failure of justice in the effort to bring some trust magnate to an account for his misdeeds is as bad as, and no worse than, the so-called labor leader who clamorously strives to excite a foul class feeling on behalf of some other labor leader who is implicated in murder. One attitude is as bad as the other, and no worse; in each case the accused is entitled to exact justice; and in neither case is there need of action by others which can be construed into an expression of sympathy for crime.

It is a prime necessity that if the present unrest is to result in permanent good the emotion shall be translated into action, and that the action shall be marked by honesty, sanity, and self-restraint. There is mighty little good in a mere spasm of reform. The reform that counts is that which comes through steady, continuous growth; violent emotionalism leads to exhaustion.

It is important to this people to grapple with the problems connected with the amassing of enormous fortunes, and the use of those fortunes, both corporate and individual, in business. We should discriminate in the sharpest way between fortunes well-won and fortunes ill-won; between those gained as an incident to performing great services to the community as a whole, and those gained in evil fashion by keeping just within the limits of mere law-honesty. Of course no amount of charity in spending such fortunes in any way compensates for misconduct in making them. As a matter of personal conviction, and without pretending to discuss the details or formulate the system, I feel that we shall ultimately have to consider the adoption of some such scheme as that of a progressive tax on all fortunes, beyond a certain amount either given in life or devised or bequeathed upon death to any individual—a tax so framed as to put it out of the power of the owner of one of these enormous fortunes to hand on more than a certain amount to any one individual; the tax, of course, to be imposed by the National and not the State government. Such taxation should, of course, be aimed merely at the inheritance or transmission in their entirety of those fortunes swollen beyond all healthy limits.

Again, the National Government must in some form exercise supervision over corporations engaged in interstate business—and all large corporations are engaged in interstate business—whether by license or otherwise, so as to permit us to deal with the far-reaching evils of overcapitalization. This year we are making a beginning in the direction of serious effort to settle some of these economic problems by the railway-rate legislation. Such legislation, if so framed, as I am sure it will be, as to secure definite and tangible results, will amount to something of itself; and it will amount to a great deal more in so far as it is taken as a first step in the direction of a policy of superintendence and control over corporate wealth engaged in interstate commerce, this superintendence and control not to be exercised in a spirit of malevolence toward the men who have created the wealth, but with the firm purpose both to do justice to them and to see that they in their turn do justice to the public at large.

The first requisite in the public servants who are to deal in this shape with corporations, whether as legislators or as executives, is honesty. This honesty can be no respecter of persons. There can be no such thing as unilateral honesty. The danger is not really from corrupt corporations; it springs from the corruption itself, whether exercised for or against corporations.

The eighth commandment reads, "Thou shalt not steal." It does not read, "Thou shalt not steal from the rich man." It does not read, "Thou shalt not steal from the poor man." It reads simply and plainly, "Thou shalt not steal." No good whatever will come from that warped and mock morality which denounces the misdeeds of men of wealth and forgets the misdeeds practiced at their expense; which denounces bribery, but blinds itself to blackmail; which foams with rage if a corporation secures favors by improper methods, and merely leers with hideous mirth if the corporation is itself wronged. The only public servant who can be trusted honestly to protect the rights of the public against the misdeed of a corporation is that public man who will just as surely protect the corporation itself from wrongful aggression. If a public man is willing to yield to popular clamor and do wrong to the men of wealth or to rich corporations, it may be set down as certain that if the opportunity comes he will secretly and furtively do wrong to the public in the interest of a corporation.

But, in addition to honesty, we need sanity. No honesty will make public man useful if that man is timid or foolish, if he is a hot-headed zealot or an impracticable visionary. As we strive for reform we find that it is not at all merely the case of a long uphill pull. On the contrary, there is almost as much of breeching work as of collar work; to depend only on traces means that there will soon be a runaway and an upset. The men of wealth who to-day are trying to prevent the regulation and control of their business in the interest of the public by the proper Government authorities will not succeed, in my judgment, in checking the progress of the movement. But if they did succeed they would find that they had sown the wind and would surely reap the whirlwind, for they would ultimately provoke the violent excesses which accompany a reform coming by convulsion instead of by steady and natural growth.

On the other hand, the wild preachers of unrest and discontent, the wild agitators against the entire existing order, the men who act crookedly, whether because of sinister design or from mere puzzle-headedness, the men who preach destruction without proposing any substitute for what they intend to destroy, or who propose a substitute which would be far worse than the existing evils—all these men are the most dangerous opponents of real reform. If they get their way they will lead the people into a deeper pit than any into which they could fall under the present system. If they fail to get their way they will still do incalculable harm by provoking the kind of reaction which, in its revolt against the senseless evil of their teaching, would enthrone more securely than ever the very evils which their misguided followers believe they are attacking.

More important than aught else is the development of the broadest sympathy of man for man. The welfare of the wage-worker, the welfare of the tiller of the soil, upon these depend the welfare of the entire country; their good is not to be sought in pulling down others; but their good must be the prime object of all our statesmanship.

Materially we must strive to secure a broader economic opportunity for all men, so that each shall have a better chance to show the stuff of which he is made. Spiritually and ethically we must strive to bring about clean living and right thinking. We appreciate that the things of the body are important; but we appreciate also that the things of the soul are immeasurably more important. The foundation stone of national life is, and ever must be, the high individual character of the average citizen.

Source: Roosevelt, Theodore. "Address of President Roosevelt at the Laying of the Corner Stone of the Office Building of the House of Representatives Saturday, April 14, 1906." Washington, D.C.: Government Printing Office, 1906.

27. WILLIAM HOWARD TAFT (1857–1930)

Presidential Term (1909–1913)

CHRONOLOGY

September 15, 1857—William Howard Taft is born in Cincinnati, Ohio.

Spring 1878—Taft graduates from Yale University.

Spring 1880—Taft graduates from Cincinnati Law School.

June 19, 1886—Taft marries Helen "Nellie" O'Herron.

1890–1892—Taft serves as U.S. solicitor general.

July 2, 1890—President Benjamin Harrison signs the Sherman Antitrust Act into law.

November 3, 1896—William McKinley is elected the 25th president of the United States.

April–August 1898—The Spanish-American War takes place.

November 6, 1900—McKinley is reelected to a second term as president.

July 4, 1901—Taft becomes governor-general of the Philippines, territory gained from Spain in the Spanish-American War.

September 14, 1901—President McKinley dies from complications resulting from an assassination attempt on September 6. Theodore Roosevelt becomes the 26th president of the United States.

February 1, 1904—President Roosevelt appoints Taft secretary of war.

November 8, 1904—Roosevelt wins election to a term of his own as president.

June 19, 1908—After Roosevelt endorses Taft as his successor, the Republican National Convention nominates Taft for president.

November 3, 1908—Taft defeats William Jennings Bryan to become the 27th president of the United States.

August 6, 1909—President Taft signs the Payne-Aldrich Tariff into law.

November 1910—A divided Republican Party suffers major losses in the midterm elections, allowing Democrats to regain control of the House of Representatives.

May 15, 1911—In *Standard Oil Co. of New Jersey v. United States*, the Supreme Court orders the breakup of Standard Oil.

February 1912—Angered by Taft's shift to the right, Roosevelt announces that he will challenge Taft for the Republican nomination.

June 18–22, 1912—Roosevelt and his supporters claim some Republican National Convention nominating votes to be fraudulent after the convention overwhelmingly nominates Taft for president.

August 7, 1912—The Progressive Party nominates Theodore Roosevelt as its presidential nominee.

November 5, 1912—Taft finishes third in the presidential election behind winner Woodrow Wilson, who received 435 electoral votes, and Roosevelt, who finished with 88; Taft earned only 8 electoral votes.

November 2, 1920—Warren G. Harding is elected the 29th president of the United States.

May 19, 1921—U.S. Supreme Court Justice Edward Douglass White, appointed by Taft, dies while in office.

June 30, 1921—The Senate confirms Harding's appointment of Taft to be chief justice, 61–4.

July 11, 1921—Taft is sworn in as chief justice of the United States, the first and only person to date to serve as president and chief justice.

February 3, 1930—Due to declining health, Taft resigns as chief justice; he is succeeded by Charles Evans Hughes.

March 8, 1930—Taft dies in Washington, D.C.

BIOGRAPHICAL SKETCH

William Howard Taft was the 27th president of the United States. Following in the footsteps of the charismatic and tremendously popular Theodore Roosevelt, Taft, whose true and ultimately achieved ambition was to be chief justice, struggled to be his own man while still seeking to further Roosevelt's progressive program. In the end, his more conservative approach led to a major clash with his mentor, Roosevelt, and a major split in the Republican Party, one that resulted in the election of Democrat Woodrow Wilson as president in 1912.

William Howard Taft was born on September 15, 1857, in Cincinnati, Ohio, to Alphonso Taft and his wife, the former Louisa Maria Torrey. Taft's father, an attorney, had a distinguished career in public service as a judge on the Cincinnati Superior Court and as both secretary of war and attorney general under president Ulysses S. Grant. He was also the minister to Austria-Hungary in 1882, before finally serving as minister to Russia under President Chester A. Arthur. Taft worshipped his father, but the amiable procrastinator sometimes struggled to meet his father's exacting standards. At the same time, their shared reverence for the judiciary was a touchstone of Taft's life and career.

Taft got his early education in the local public schools in Cincinnati. He graduated from the city's Woodward High School in 1874 before attending Yale University from 1874 to 1878. Active in the Yale community, he was an accomplished wrestler, a talented rower, and a skilled debater, and he also joined Skull and Bones, the school's prestigious secret society of which his father had been a founder. An outstanding student, Taft graduated as the salutatorian of his class in 1878. From Yale, Taft returned to home, attending the University of Cincinnati law school. Taft, who worked part-time as a courthouse reporter for the *Cincinnati Commercial* during his student days, completed his studies in 1880 and was admitted to the Ohio bar in May of that year.

Following law school, the young attorney turned down an opportunity to serve as a full-time reporter for the *Commercial* and instead took a job as assistant prosecutor for Hamilton County, a post he held from 1881 to 1882. He also got his first taste of electoral politics, as the office's political ties meant that working on behalf of the local Republican candidates was an unstated expectation. He then served for a year as the collector of internal revenue for Cincinnati's First District, becoming the country's youngest tax collector, before going into private practice, forming a partnership with Harlan Page Lloyd. Returning to the public arena in 1885, Taft served as assistant solicitor for Hamilton County from 1885 to 1887.

Recognizing that he was best suited for the judiciary, and with an eye to ultimately serving on the U.S. Supreme Court, Taft accepted an appointment to a seat on the Cincinnati Superior Court in 1887, a post he held until 1890. He followed that with a stint as U.S. solicitor general from 1890 to 1892. In that post, he burnished his reputation through his work in the dispute with Great Britain over the Bering Sea fisheries as well as the McKinley Tariff cases. At the same time, while the opportunity to argue before the Supreme Court was invaluable, it also reinforced Taft's belief that he was better as a judge than as an advocate. Consequently, in 1892, he was very receptive to President Benjamin Harrison's offer of a seat on the U.S. Sixth Circuit Court as well as an ex officio member of the Sixth Circuit Court of Appeals, which had jurisdiction over Ohio, Michigan, Kentucky, and Tennessee. As a circuit court judge, he was involved in a number of important labor cases, including one related to the famous 1894 Pullman Strike, in which he declared secondary boycotts illegal. In addition to his judicial duties, during the period from 1896 to 1900, Taft also served as a professor of law and dean of the University of Cincinnati law school.

In 1901, a reluctant Taft stepped down from the bench to accept an appointment as commissioner of the Philippines, a territory acquired in the Spanish-American War. Preferring to remain on the bench, Taft initially advised President McKinley that he did not think the United States should even keep the islands, and while McKinley did not wholly disagree, he countered by expressing his belief that someone who did not want them would likely be a better steward of the interests of the Filipino people than someone who did. In the end, with prodding from his ever-ambitious wife and bowing to his well-developed sense of service, he accepted the appointment, determined to make real the president's directive of establishing a civil government in the newly acquired territory.

Although he clashed with Arthur MacArthur, the U.S. military governor, whom he criticized for his disdainful attitude toward the Philippine natives, Taft played a critical role in the development of the islands' government, being a primary contributor in the drafting of the territory's governing documents. These called for eventual independence and included a bill of rights almost identical to the one added to the U.S. Constitution. Promoted to the post of Governor General in 1901, Taft skillfully oversaw the transition of America's role from that of an overseer of military rule to that of civil government. Under his leadership, the United States was able to put down a rebellion led by dissident Emilio Aguinaldo, reform the judicial system, and establish a civil service system. In addition, under Taft's direction, the Filipinos were able to open English-language schools, improve health standards, and begin to make improvements in the islands' harbors and roads. He helped negotiate a major land purchase from the Vatican and then oversaw a program where, through low-cost mortgages, the newly acquired land was distributed to thousands of Filipino peasants. Deeply committed to the interests of the Filipino people, and determined to see this program through to completion, Taft twice refused offers by President Theodore Roosevelt to serve on the Supreme Court, being unwilling to abandon his post while things were still in flux.

Ultimately, his efforts in the Philippines earned Taft much acclaim, and in 1904, President Theodore Roosevelt brought him back to the United States, seeking to use his impressive administrative skills on the home front. As the newly appointed secretary of war, Taft oversaw preparations for the construction of the Panama Canal and personally inspected the site near the end of 1904. He also had meetings with the Japanese, securing an agreement that protected the Philippines, whose welfare remained of deep personal concern, from Japanese aggression. Adding to Taft's portfolio, in 1905, he served as acting secretary of state while John Hay was ill, and in the face of an impending rebellion, he traveled to Cuba, where he negotiated a settlement that made U.S. military

William Howard Taft (Library of Congress)

intervention unnecessary. Finally, to further stabilize things, for a brief time in the fall of 1906, he served as provisional governor of the island.

Taft's judicious and efficient performances in these varied roles only enhanced his stature in Washington's political circles. Yet, while he continued to profess that his greatest ambition was a seat on the Supreme Court, especially the chief justiceship, he nevertheless showed an impressive commitment to his duties, such that, in 1906, Taft again turned down yet another offer from Roosevelt of a seat on the Supreme Court. Meanwhile, Taft's increased public profile and the acclaim with which his efforts were received were leading to talk of the presidency, which was encouraged by both his wife, Nellie, and Roosevelt, who, despite his youth and obvious love of the job, had announced back when he was elected in 1904 that he would not seek another term.

Given all of this, in many ways, the contest for the Republican presidential nomination in 1908 was more a coronation than a political contest. As the widely recognized designated heir of the popular Roosevelt in a party that Roosevelt so dominated, there was no real opportunity for other potential leaders to emerge, Taft easily won the nomination at the party's Chicago convention. In addition, the delegates chose New York congressman James Sherman to be his running mate. The party platform on which they would run pointed to the accomplishments of the Roosevelt administration, highlighting antitrust efforts, improved worker safety, and tariff reform. With the Democrats again running William Jennings Bryan, the low-key campaign centered on the question of which candidate could best further the Roosevelt agenda. While Taft was clearly the designated heir, Bryan contended that Roosevelt had in fact co-opted the Democratic platform on which he had previously run and that, as a result, he was best suited to continue the effort. The verdict of the voters was that it was Taft, Roosevelt's right-hand man for the last four years, who would be the best steward of his legacy, as the genial secretary of war won 29 states to Bryan's 17, resulting in 321 electoral votes to Bryan's 162. Meanwhile, his 51.6 percent of the vote gave him an almost 10 percent popular vote margin over the 43 percent won by the Democrats' veteran standard-bearer.

Central to Taft's rise was the support of his wife, Helen "Nellie" Herron, whom he married on June 19, 1886, in Cincinnati. The couple would ultimately have three children, Robert, Helen, and Charles. Nellie was four years younger than Taft and also from Cincinnati. Her father, an attorney, was a college classmate and one-time partner of Rutherford B. Hayes, to whom she is reported to have expressed her intention to marry a man who would be president. By all accounts, the ambitious and energetic Nellie would play an important role in Taft's political success, providing no small amount of the ambition that ultimately resulted in his rise to the presidency. Indeed, reflective of her drive is a famous story, possibly apocryphal, but revealing nevertheless, that circulated in Washington as the 1908 presidential campaign loomed. The story had the Tafts visiting the Roosevelts in the White House. After dinner, the president undertook to conduct a séance. With a typically dramatic flair, the president said that while he saw a new and higher office looming in Taft's future, one that would bring great honor and prestige,

he could not make out exactly what it was. At this point, Taft was reported to have said, "Make it the chief justiceship." But Nellie was said to have cried out, "Make it the presidency." And when her husband achieved her ambition, she initially reveled in his accomplishment and in the social opportunity it afforded her.

In fact, by the time Taft won election to the presidency, Nellie Taft had already established herself as her husband's public partner. While in the Philippines, she had worked hard to improve the quality of life for the country's poor, but she made a special effort to help the women, working hard to convince the local residents to take advantage of the food and medical supplies that were arriving from the United States. She also founded the Drop of Milk program, which offered instructions to local residents in how to sterilize milk. In addition, like her husband, she worked to improve American attitudes toward the Filipinos. She and her husband both urged their fellow Americans to treat the country's people with respect, and their own efforts set a powerful and important example. In addition, foreshadowing some of her efforts as first lady, the adventuresome Nellie was the first white female to tour the dangerous Luzon Mountain region. That same spirit was on full display in the immediate aftermath of Taft's swearing in when Nellie joined her husband, becoming the first first lady to accompany the president on the parade route back to the White House. Historically, it was a role assumed by the outgoing chief executive, but Roosevelt had already departed. The first lady filled the void, joyously dismissing critics and calling the experience the proudest moment of her life.

Unhappily, but befitting his fortunes as president, in the middle of May 1909, Nellie Taft suffered a stroke that left her speech impaired. It would be almost a year until she recovered. In the meantime, the new chief executive was himself handicapped on two levels: not only was he beside himself with worry about the well-being of his wife, whom he revered, but he was also denied her advice and counsel, something he had always relied on. It was a political and personal blow from which he would never fully recover. Happily, Nellie did recover, and she made the most of the last three years of Taft's presidency. She undertook a major White House redecorating effort while also resuming her role as an influential counselor to the president. And she was an outspoken advocate for women's suffrage, although she expressed the belief that women should not seek elective office.

Nellie Taft sought to improve life in the nation's capital. She actively participated in the effort to create the West Potomac Park, and she was instrumental in starting the weekly U.S. Marine Band performances that began during the Taft presidency. Perhaps her greatest legacy was the planting of the Japanese cherry blossom trees, whose blooming each April signals the arrival of spring. She had discovered them on a visit to Japan while her husband was secretary of war. After the mayor of Tokyo presented her with 3,000 trees, she presented them to the government, and the gorgeous display was created.

The final chapter in Taft's long and distinguished pubic career began in 1921, when he was appointed by President Warren Harding to the position of chief justice of the United States, a long-held dream. It was a job he would fill with distinction for the rest of the decade. But before that and following his defeat in the 1912 election, Taft returned to his alma mater, Yale, having been appointed to the Kent professorship of law. (Always self-deprecating about his weight, he was reported to have said that he was not sure that a "chair" at the school would be adequate. But if the university could offer a "sofa of law," he was sure it could be worked out.) At Yale, he taught both government and international law. He also lectured widely and wrote articles that appeared in numerous national magazines. Collecting some of his writings and lectures, he published *Popular Government: Its Essence, Its Permanence, and Its Perils* in 1913. The following year, he produced *The Anti-Trust Act and the Supreme Court*. Finally, in 1916, Taft published *Our Chief Magistrate and His Powers*. All these works offered interesting insights into Taft's views on the changing nature of the democratic process in the American system of government, the antitrust laws that had been so much a part of his early judicial and subsequent presidential years, and the powers, responsibilities, and limits on the office of president. With the law still his passion, he was active in the legal community and served a term as president of the American Bar Association.

Taft also remained active in Republican and national politics. Seeking to restore a united Republican Party to power, he campaigned vigorously for its presidential nominee, Charles Evans Hughes, in 1916, and while that effort was unsuccessful, following the election, he crossed party lines in supporting President Wilson's efforts to keep the United States out of war. However, earlier in 1916, he had been a leader in the unsuccessful effort to prevent the confirmation of Wilson's nominee, Louis D. Brandeis, to the Supreme Court.

Once the United States entered the war, Wilson appointed Taft a cochair of the National War Labor Board. His work in that role, where he helped keep the labor peace necessary to furthering the war effort while also securing better conditions for the working men and women, not only helped rehabilitate his reputation but also made him more aware of working conditions at the lower levels, a sensitivity that would inform some of his later work on the Supreme Court. He also favored a draft once the United States had entered the war. During the conflict, Taft also devoted considerable time to the American Red Cross. In that same period, Taft and Roosevelt reconciled when a chance encounter in a hotel restaurant led to conversation and a rekindling of the human spark and connection that had made them such close friends and productive partners in the first decade of the 20th century.

At this same time, Taft was a vocal opponent of Prohibition. He was concerned about both the expansion of congressional power that he believed it represented as well as the challenges of enforcing it, correctly predicting that the manufacture and sale of liquor would continue but would be taken over by the nation's criminal class. On a personal level, after the adoption of the Eighteenth Amendment and the Volstead Act, out of respect for the law, the former chief executive kept a dry home, a decision that provoked probably the only major marital disagreement of Taft and Nellie's over four-decade-long marriage; it was an issue they simply did not discuss. Meanwhile, ever the loyal Republican, Taft stumped actively for the Republican nominee, Ohio senator Warren G. Harding, for president, and he was both gratified and optimistic when Harding defeated Ohio governor James Cox in a landslide.

Indeed, Harding's election rekindled all of Taft's ambitions for the chief justiceship, and when a postelection visit between Harding and Taft included a virtual promise of just that, Taft could only bide his time, waiting on the chief justice's health the way a vice president might on that of the president. Ultimately, on May 19, 1921, lightning struck with the sudden death of Chief Justice Edward Douglass White. While Harding hesitated briefly, Taft's core support in the Republican Party and his bipartisan efforts during the war years combined to create a wealth of support and good feeling. On June 30, Harding finally made the appointment. Indeed, his nomination, confirmed by the Senate on the same day it was submitted, represented not just the realization of a dream, and the successful culmination of a campaign aimed at President Harding to secure the appointment, but it also served as a salve on the wounds he had suffered as a result of his overwhelming rejection by the voters in 1912. Those efforts, coupled with what some saw as divine intervention in terms of the creation of the vacancy, marked the start of a decade of historic service, one that transcended his role on the Court, for his influence with the president did not subside once Taft took his seat. Indeed, some have gone so far to say that Taft was Harding's last appointment, with the implication being clear that it was in fact Taft who made the call on the other three seats that Harding filled. While that is not a wholly fair characterization, there can be no denying that the independence of the judiciary was at least a little bit strained when the sitting chief justice became the president's frequent sounding board for judicial appointments.

On the Court, Taft proved himself to be a superb administrator. Intent on dispatching the Court's backlog, he traveled to England in 1922 to study their system, and upon returning to the United States, he implemented procedures to do just that while also successfully lobbying in a way he had never thought proper as president for the passage of the Judiciary Act of 1925. The legislation, also known as the Judges Bill, represented a procedural breakthrough. It gave the Court considerably greater control over its own docket, as it eliminated many of the previously mandated automatic appeals, a change that in the final analysis allowed the nation's top court to focus on the important constitutional questions that only it could authoritatively address.

Leading by example, Taft wrote almost 250 opinions over his tenure, almost one-sixth of the Court's total during that time. Also, having worked hard to limit dissents and have the Court present a united front, something he knew enhanced the Court's authority and influence, he dissented only about 20 times and only wrote 4 dissents. Among his more memorable and important rulings was *Carroll v. United States* (1925), in which, writing for a 7–2 majority, he created the "automobile exception" to the Fourth Amendment, upholding the distinction established by Congress in enacting the Volstead Act between searches of residences where warrants were required and cars where they were not. In the 1928 case *Olmstead v. United States*, Taft also wrote for a 5–4 majority in upholding the warrantless wiretapping of one of the nation's most renowned bootleggers. While the case is best known for Brandeis's dissent, a prescient defense of electronic privacy, Taft's opinion was well grounded in the existent view of the framers' ideas of "reasonable searches and seizures." Another of his important opinions was *Truax v. Corrigan* (1921). Writing for the Court in an opinion that reaffirmed his reputation as the "father of injunctions," he struck down a section of the Clayton Anti-Trust Act, which had barred injunctions against peaceful picketing, determining that such picketing, if it led to a financial loss for the business, represented the deprivation of property without due process. Taft did author a powerful dissent in *Adkins v. Children's Hospital* (1923), a controversial case in which the Court struck down a minimum wage law for women, reminding his colleagues, in words that would resonate deeply over the next decade and a half, that "it is not the function of this court to hold Congressional acts invalid simply because they are passed to carry out economic views which the court believes to be unwise or unsound."

In what some saw as an interesting turnaround for a man who regularly spoke of the constitutional limits on the president's powers, Taft wrote the opinion of the Court in *Myers v. United States* (1926). The decision invalidated the Tenure of Office Act of 1867, the controversial law whose violation by President Andrew Johnson had been at the center of the impeachment proceedings against the embattled chief executive. It also invalidated a more recent enactment at the heart of the dispute, upholding the president's power to remove a federal official that he had appointed, even those requiring Senate confirmation, a ruling that certainly reaffirmed, if not enhanced, presidential power. Taft believed it was his most important opinion.

Taft's time on the Court not only represented the realization of a lifelong dream but also the chance to redefine and reshape his historical reputation and legacy. But while these years were undoubtedly the happiest of his life, they took a toll on his health, and after suffering two heart attacks, the rigors of an active and public life finally began to take their toll. After almost a decade on the Supreme Court, on February 3, 1930, his failing health having made it impossible for him to carry out his responsibilities, Taft reluctantly submitted his resignation to President Herbert Hoover. How bad his health had become was revealed less than a month later, when, on March 8, 1930, the only man to serve as both president and chief justice died at his home in Washington. He had been suffering from arteriosclerotic heart disease as well as high blood pressure and an inflamed bladder. Following his death, he lay in state at the U.S. Capitol with Cass Gilbert's model of the soon-to-be-built Supreme Court building exhibited alongside him. A simple funeral service was held at All Soul's Unitarian Church, and William Howard Taft was buried in Arlington National Cemetery, the first president to be so honored. In a fitting final gesture, a picture of Taft was placed in the cornerstone of the new Court building during the October 1932 groundbreaking ceremony.

HISTORICAL OVERVIEW

Taft's ascension to the presidency and the transition of power from one administration to the next was as smooth as any in American history. And yet, for all its apparent ease, in reality, following in Roosevelt's footsteps presented no small challenge—even for, or perhaps especially for, someone who had so loyally served the dynamic president. Indeed, Roosevelt's larger-than-life personality along with the fact that Taft was rightly seen as his handpicked successor

made it hard for Taft to establish himself as an independent entity. In fact, they were so closely linked that there was an ever-present question of whether the American people wanted an independent President Taft or TR round two. Further complicating things was the fact that although Taft was for the most part seen as Roosevelt redux, in reality, he mirrored Roosevelt in neither style nor temperament. And Roosevelt's still-evolving political views only exacerbated the situation when he returned from his postpresidential travels to find that Taft had sought to be his own man.

Indeed, throughout his presidency, Taft was dogged by the shadow of Roosevelt, one that was made even longer by the former president's image. Nowhere was this clearer than in the perceptions related to their efforts in the area of antitrust work. Utilizing both his unparalleled public relations talent as well as an eye for headline-catching cases, TR garnered the image of a crusading trustbuster, and there is no denying that he utilized and energized the Sherman Act in unprecedented ways. But the efforts of the Taft administration in fact dwarfed Roosevelt's while also holding up to public scrutiny a couple of agreements that the more pragmatic and politically savvy Roosevelt had allowed. With his strict legalistic view of the issue, Taft made none of the distinctions that Roosevelt had between good and bad trusts. Consequently, Attorney General Wickersham, wholly backed by the president, initiated more than twice as many antitrust suits as Roosevelt and in barely half the time. And even more noteworthy was the fact that the administration's strict enforcement of the Sherman Anti-Trust Act led to the breakup of industrial giants American Tobacco Company and the Standard Oil Company. An announced plan to pursue a suit against U.S. Steel was ultimately unsuccessful, but not before court filings made public that Roosevelt had either turned a blind eye to the ramifications of the steel giant's acquisition of Tennessee Coal and Iron Company or been hoodwinked by banking titan J. P. Morgan. Either way, the Taft administration's effort infuriated Roosevelt and served as a final push in the direction of his 1912 challenge to Taft for the 1912 Republican nomination as well as the end of their friendship.

None of that would have been expected in March 1909, when Taft succeeded his mentor and friend as president. Give the smooth succession, as well as Taft's predilection to be a loyal party member, his cabinet included a number of respected party stalwarts, all of whom served in loyal and solid fashion. In the beginning, there was comparatively little turnover, but while Taft had spoken of retaining TR's team early on, he ultimately decided not to. Instead, his choices, befitting the solid, consistent nature of Taft's approach, resulted in six of the cabinet members being corporate attorneys. While they were a group with impressive reputations, it was still not enough to prevent criticism from those who both feared an excessive corporate influence and that such changes ran counter to Taft's pledge to continue Roosevelt's policies.

Heading the cabinet was former corporate lawyer Philander C. Knox, who served as secretary of state for the whole of Taft's term. Franklin MacVeagh, a Chicago banker, also served as the secretary of the treasury for the entire Taft administration. His advice led Taft to overrule Attorney General Wickersham in allowing subsidiaries of bank holding companies to make investments in the stock market. His tenure as secretary was marked by efforts to increase efficiency, a process that was helped by the abolition of 450 positions. In addition, he oversaw the rehabilitation of the U.S. Customs Service as well as the introduction of electric automatic weighing devices and the acceptance of certified checks for customs and internal revenue payments.

Jacob M. Dickinson of Tennessee was Taft's original choice for secretary of war. As a Democrat, he provided both the Southern and bipartisan representation that Taft sought in his cabinet. An attorney and one-time law professor who had served in the Justice Department, Dickinson resigned in May 1911 and was succeeded by former U.S. attorney and 1910 New York gubernatorial candidate Henry L. Stimson, who served for the duration of the term.

George W. Wickersham, one of the pillars of the nation's legal establishment, served as attorney general. True to Taft's philosophy, Wickersham actively pursued Sherman Anti-Trust Act violations, achieving the breakup of both Standard Oil and the American Tobacco Company. In addition, he played a key role in securing passage of the Mann-Elkins Act.

George von L. Meyer served as secretary of the navy throughout the Taft administration to little real

effect, while the U.S. Postal Service was headed by Frank H. Hitchcock. As postmaster general, Hitchcock was a big booster of the development of airmail service, and he also helped establish both the postal savings bank as well as parcel post.

The tenure of Secretary of the Interior Richard Ballinger, of Washington State, would be marked by major controversies that contributed significantly to the Taft-Roosevelt split. As the commissioner of public lands under Roosevelt, Ballinger seemed a logical choice for the post, but he soon clashed with Roosevelt protégé and chief of the Forest Service Gifford Pinchot concerning federal land reserves in Alaska. When Taft stood by Ballinger and fired Pinchot, it became a cause célèbre that divided the party. Additional charges by Interior employee Louis Glavin led to a House investigation that cleared Ballinger of any wrongdoing, although that verdict did nothing to assuage the concerns of Progressives, who feared that the administration was backtracking on previous commitments to protect the environment. The treatment of Pinchot also contributed to the developing party divide. Seeking a restoration of his health and finances, Ballinger resigned in March 1911, when he was replaced by Walter L. Fisher of Illinois, who served out the term. During his time as secretary, Fisher encouraged the development of Alaska while also pushing for the creation of additional national parks. He also advocated for the conservation of the nation's natural resources.

Taft's choice as secretary of agriculture was James Wilson, who had begun as secretary in 1897 under McKinley. Kept on by Roosevelt, he was a popular figure in the farming community, and while Taft also reappointed him, by the end of his term, the president was unhappy with his administrative efforts.

Taft chose Charles Nagel to serve as secretary of the Department of Commerce and Labor. A corporate attorney from St. Louis, Missouri, who served for the whole of the Taft administration, Nagel was the last person to hold the position before the department was divided into separate Commerce and Labor Departments with individual heads. As secretary, Nagel, who would later found the U.S. Chamber of Commerce, worked to make the Department of Commerce and Labor more accessible to the needs of the business community. In addition, while expanding the Bureau of Immigration and Naturalization, he also successfully urged Taft to veto a bill that would have required a literacy test as part of the nation's immigrant admission policy.

With his time in the Philippines and his tenure as secretary of war, Taft was not a novice in the workings of foreign affairs, and over the course of his term, his administration adopted a distinctive approach that came to be known as "dollar diplomacy." Reflective of Taft's conservative view of the presidency, and despite the fact that his prepresidential career made him as well prepared as any of his predecessors to take an active role in the development and implementation of his administration's foreign policy, he was in fact content to set out broad parameters and leave the rest to Secretary of State Philander Knox. And Knox was ready and willing to do that. Indeed, as a first step in that effort, upon assuming office, Knox reorganized the department in a geopolitical manner, with Europe, the Far East, and Latin America each getting its own division. Then, under his direction, the administration sought to use its military power and diplomatic influence to further American economic interests overseas. While the administration encouraged American investments in an effort to construct railroads in China, the Chinese, who were also in discussions with Great Britain, France, and Germany, were reluctant to commit. But as things were nearing a possible agreement, a leadership change in China made any such resolution impossible. A lesser comprehensive agreement, one involving a considerably smaller investment, was achieved in mid-1910, but in the end, that whole episode had fanned the flames of anti-foreign feeling in China, a growing sentiment that would culminate with the Revolution of 1911 and the establishment in 1912 of the Chinese Republic. Another part of the American effort to pull China within the American economic circle involved Manchuria, but with its desire to build a railroad that spanned the area being shared by Britain and France, and with Manchuria itself being an area long dominated by Japan and Russia, the ability to find common ground upon which all interested parties could agree proved impossible. In fact, in the end, the multifaceted discussions seemed to leave the United States on the outside, while Russia and Japan seemed to have emerged with an enhanced relationship, although all parties essentially agreed on the continuation of the status quo in Manchuria.

Closer to home, U.S. business involvement in the Caribbean was more successful, with American investors helping to rescue a troubled Honduran regime while also securing a major stake in Haiti. After first urging the new Nicaraguan government to accept some large loans from a group of Wall Street banks in hopes of stabilizing its economy, continuing instability forced Taft to send marines into the country to help put down a rebellion aimed at overthrowing a regime that was very friendly toward American business interests. While the approach was controversial, Taft had no qualms defending it, maintaining that the administration's approach represented little more than an extension of the Monroe Doctrine and that its ultimate goal was the protection of the Central American nations, a goal that was furthered when U.S. businesses helped finance the development and rehabilitation of local economies.

Another foreign policy challenge lay right along the nation's southern border in Mexico. Seeking to put a personal face on the diplomatic process, in October 1909, Taft made a quick visit to Mexico to exchange pleasantries with Mexican dictator Porfirio Diaz, with whom he also issued a joint statement affirming the strong friendship shared by both the men and their nations. Unfortunately for Diaz, the friendship did not remain a strong one. Indeed, over the next three years, Mexico was the site of much internal unrest. Diaz's regime was challenged and eventually overthrown by opposition forces headed by Francisco Madero, who was purchasing his guns in the United States. Despite pleas from Diaz, the United States refused to shut down Madero's operations, maintaining, a bit disingenuously, that he was simply engaging in commercial activity and was not staging his efforts in the United States. As the situation worsened, the U.S. ambassador intervened on Diaz's behalf. In March 1911, Taft mobilized 200,000 troops along the border after the U.S. ambassador to Mexico, Henry Lane Wilson, warned that the safety of the Americans then living in Mexico could be at risk. However, Diaz was not placated nor were tensions eased when two Americans were killed in a cross fire at the Arizona border in April 1911. Things continued to deteriorate, and by the summer of 1911, Madero had overthrown Diaz. But the change in regime did not bring calm. In fact, while the Taft administration stayed scrupulously neutral, in February 1913, Madero was overthrown by General Victoriano Huerta, marking the second Mexican revolution of Taft's presidency, with the result being something that would greet Woodrow Wilson as he came into office.

At the same time, the administration did see some other foreign policy achievements that reinforced the president's faith in the power of arbitration. Among these was the successful conclusion of a long-running dispute with Great Britain over fishing rights off Newfoundland as well as two cases where U.S.-sponsored arbitration successfully settled border disputes between Peru and Ecuador in 1910 and Haiti and the Dominican Republic in 1911.

Meanwhile, beyond the signature dollar diplomacy for which the administration became known, there were other lesser-known initiatives. Taft negotiated a treaty with Great Britain that protected Pacific seals, and the administration also signed arbitration treaties with France and England; although with Roosevelt and his close friend and political ally Senator Henry Cabot Lodge leading the opposition, they were never ratified.

In general, when it came to foreign policy, Taft sought to expand U.S. economic influence in Asia, while in keeping with the Monroe Doctrine, he was intent on keeping Europe out of the Western Hemisphere. Meanwhile, the lawyer/jurist in him was a firm believer in the use of arbitration as a means of preserving world peace, and he left office able to point to more than a few arbitration-based accomplishments.

On the domestic front, despite his best intentions and his determination to address an issue central to the party's platform, Taft got off to a rocky start with the Payne-Aldrich Tariff, which was perceived by Progressives as a wholesale surrender by Taft to the party's business wing, a group that TR had, or so legend had it, gotten under control. Ironically, the Payne-Aldrich Tariff was a response to a Taft initiative—tariff reform—that he and the party had promised to pursue at both the convention and on the campaign trail. No less ironic was the fact that it also represented an effort to address an issue that Roosevelt had skillfully but

knowingly ignored throughout his presidency. However, while Taft, intent on fulfilling the party's platform promise to achieve tariff reform, called Congress into special session within days of his inauguration to address the issue, it would ultimately lead to a series of events that would result in nothing but political trouble. No less interesting was the fact that the legislative process culminating in the passage of the tariff offered a preview of the president's approach to the lawmaking process, an approach that bore no resemblance to his predecessor. Indeed, while Taft was happy to fulfill his constitutional duty to call a special session and then to offer a proposal to address the situation at hand, it was at that point that the constitutionally hidebound chief executive handed off the responsibility to the legislative branch, whose responsibility it was, at least in his view, to respond to his 343-word message and address the matter at hand. And they did.

In seeking to address the many issues stemming from the last major tariff reform effort, the Dingley Tariff, enacted in 1897 under McKinley, the divisions that marked the Republican Party at that time were revealed. Indeed, after the legislation sponsored by Representative Sereno Payne that called for reduced tariffs pretty much across the board was overwhelmingly passed by the House, Rhode Island senator Nelson W. Aldrich, a longtime spokesman for the nation's big business interests, substituted an alternative version that not only reduced some of the House cuts but actually raised some of the rates. When the Senate's passed version went back to the House, it was passed, but while the final legislation, signed by Taft in August 1913, did lower the overall rate, the reduction from 46 percent to 41 percent did not begin to meet reformers' expectations. Given the fact that some rates were being raised, the overall impact was deemed disappointing. Indeed, Democrats and progressive Republicans both saw it as little more than political window dressing and hocus pocus aimed at obscuring what was in fact a reaffirmation of the party's long-standing protectionist policies. It became a central issue in the 1910 midterm election—one that saw the Democrats winning control of the House—after Taft, in defending the bill, committed a political faux pas when he termed it "the best tariff bill that the Republicans ever passed." He added that if people wanted a revenue tariff, free trade, and lower prices along with business failures, which he said would accompany all of that, then they should put the Democrats in power. It was not one of Taft's finest hours, and it further divided the party.

Knowing that he did not have the personal touch of his predecessor, Taft sought to make himself better known to the American people and earn support for his programs by undertaking a series of speaking tours. Leaving Washington in mid-September 1909, the nation's chief executive undertook an extensive national tour, delighting people from all over who excitedly sought a glimpse of the president. He was gone for almost two months, and the White House reported that he gave 259 speeches. That effort would be followed by others, and by the end of his term, Taft had traveled approximately 150,000 miles, the most of any president up to that time.

Not long after his return, in November 1909, Taft found himself forced to defend Secretary of the Interior Richard Ballinger against charges from Louis Glavis, the chief of the Interior Department's Field Division, that had been published in *Collier's Weekly* magazine that accused Ballinger of conspiring to defraud the public domain in the Alaskan coal fields. The article also said that the administration was involved in Ballinger's efforts. The situation was exacerbated in January 1910 when Taft fired Gifford Pinchot, the head of the U.S. Forest Service and one of Theodore Roosevelt's closest political allies, after Pinchot had written letters to Senator Dolliver of Iowa in support of two Interior employees who had been implicated in the Ballinger case. The congressional investigation into the matter ultimately cleared both Ballinger and Taft of any substantive wrongdoing, although evidence of some minor improprieties was made public, hurting the reputations of both men. However, the incident's biggest impact was the effect it had on the Taft-Roosevelt relationship. Indeed, in clashing with Pinchot, Taft had made a major political mistake, one that served only to exacerbate Roosevelt's developing doubts and disappointment regarding his successor. Since Roosevelt had left the country, Pinchot had been feeding him a steady diet of information and opinion, little of which did Taft any good. Indeed, over the course of the fall, their once close friendship had deteriorated beyond recognition.

Any chance of salvaging the relationship was lost when Taft failed to greet the conquering hero upon his return to the United States, which was itself followed by Roosevelt declining Taft's invitation to come to the White House. The final straw appeared to be Taft's unwillingness to accept an award jointly honoring Taft and Roosevelt. The dinner at which the presentation was to be made was to take place only days after Roosevelt had given his "New Nationalism" speech, an address that outlined a new progressive agenda, one which, he made clear, was necessary given the disappointing and ineffectual efforts of the incumbent administration. A partnership that had once done great good for the nation had unraveled under the pressures of the nation's highest office and the egos of two proud men.

The decline in Taft's political fortunes was confirmed in the 1910 midterm elections. With the Republican Party beginning to splinter and a progressive wing that, in some cases, not only abandoned the party regulars but mounted direct electoral challenges, the Democrats won control of the House of Representatives for the first time since 1894. Although the Republicans retained control of the Senate, they lost eight seats. It was a tremendous rebuke to the administration's efforts and left party leaders deeply concerned about their prospects for 1912.

Yet, for all his early political challenges and setbacks, Taft continued to try to address the issues central to the United States at that time. Recognizing the need to address the income lost from the reduction in tariff rates, Taft proposed a tax on the net income of all corporations except banks. Also, given the Supreme Court's striking down of an earlier effort by Congress to impose a personal income tax, Taft also called for Congress to adopt a constitutional amendment that would allow the imposition of such a revenue measure. This recommendation got a positive reception from Congress, resulting in the Sixteenth Amendment, which achieved ratification shortly before Taft left office. Indeed, his administration saw the passage by Congress of both the Sixteenth and Seventeenth Amendments to the Constitution. The Sixteenth, which allowed for the income tax, was ratified a month before Taft left office and was the basis for the subsequent imposition of an income tax under President Woodrow Wilson. Meanwhile, the

Seventeenth Amendment, which called for the direct election of senators, was in the middle of the ratification process when Taft left office. The ratification was secured in April 1913, and the 1914 midterm elections witnessed the first round of senators elected by popular vote, a change that would markedly alter the American political process.

Notwithstanding his belief in the limited powers of the federal government, and especially the executive, the Taft administration chalked up a number of major legislative accomplishments. Indeed, showing no reluctance to exercise the government's growing regulatory power, Taft successfully pushed for the passage of the Mann-Elkins Act. The legislation, passed in 1910, gave additional power to the Interstate Commerce Commission (ICC), expanding its authority to include the ability to set maximum rates charged to shippers by the railroads while also eliminating the practice of charging more for short-haul transports than long-haul services. In addition, the act added the developing telephone, telegraph, and radio services to the ICC's regulatory agenda. Always a stickler for efficiency and skilled administration, Taft was also able to secure the establishment of a Commission on Economy and Efficiency, an effort that has been seen as an early model for the modern Office of Management and Budget.

Despite portrayals as a loyal party man, Taft reduced the overall appointment rolls, putting 35,000 postmasters, 20,000 skilled navy shipyard workers, and diplomats in the civil service system. After first calling for a national budget, he unified the federal budget and supported the successful division into two separate departments, Commerce and Labor, with both being accorded cabinet-level status.

Under Taft, the postal service established a savings bank system designed to aid small depositors, and rural areas of the United States were provided with parcel post delivery at a rate less expensive than the express company service that had previously been their only real option.

Taft's efforts to strengthen the economy and promote American industry included more than just the Payne-Aldrich Tariff. In July 1911, he signed the Canadian Tariff Reciprocity Agreement, although the effort came to naught when the Canadian Parliament voted it down. In August 1911, Taft vetoed tariff reductions on wool and woolen goods that had been passed by Congress. However, it was a decision that said much about his judicial- and procedure-based approach to his responsibilities. He explained his somewhat surprising action by asserting that the legislation was premature, given that Tariff Board had not completed its investigation of the issue.

Because Taft was more deferential to Congress than Roosevelt had been, his efforts related to conservation were frequently misunderstood and underappreciated. Indeed, many saw him retreating on the conservation front, especially after Congress passed the Withdrawal Act, a piece of legislation under which Congress authorized the president to withdraw public lands from entry and reserve them for "water-power sites, irrigation, classification of lands, or other public purposes." In addition, the new law reaffirmed its ban on the creation or enlargement of national forests in six western states. At the same time, however, Congress passed a bill establishing Glacier National Park, Montana, and Taft issued a proclamation establishing Rainbow Bridge National Monument in Utah. In an impressive show of foresight, as well as a recognition of the growing problem of large-scale urban water pollution, Congress passed legislation to prevent the dumping of garbage in Lake Michigan or near Chicago.

In the end, the Taft administration set aside almost as much land as Roosevelt had—and in a shorter period of time—but reflective of the leader, it was accomplished through a more judicial and administratively based approach. However, that approach did not appear to have the same impact and was certainly not perceived in the same way. Impressions about his efforts in this area were further influenced by the political reality that he was not only following in Roosevelt's footsteps but that he had alienated progressives by his falling out with Roosevelt favorite and progressive leader Gifford Pinchot.

While even his wife said his speeches often read like judicial opinions, in general, notwithstanding his self-imposed restraint, Taft was an effective, if understated, legislative leader. At the same time, he was periodically rebuffed by Congress, with one such override, perhaps offering a preview of things to come, being the Webb-Kenyon Interstate Liquor Shipments Act of 1913, where the lame duck Taft's veto of the law, which barred the interstate transportation of liquor into dry states, was overridden.

Another area in which President William Howard Taft, both appropriately and ironically, had a large hand was in the shaping of the Supreme Court. Notwithstanding his status as Theodore Roosevelt's designated heir when he was elected president in 1908, Taft's lifelong dream was to be chief justice of the United States, a goal he refused to abandon even upon assuming the presidency. Given this ambition, it was highly ironic that not only did Taft have the opportunity to shape the nation's judicial policy through the appointment of six justices in his four-year term—a number exceeded only by Washington, who, of course, was starting from scratch, and FDR, who served longer than anyone—but he also had the opportunity to appoint a chief justice. One can only imagine the anguish he must have felt in giving the job of his dreams to someone else. Indeed, while the story may be apocryphal, it has been reported that when it came time to make that fateful selection, Taft, having narrowed the choice to a pair of associate justices, 65-year-old Edward Douglass White and 48-year-old Charles Evans Hughes, chose White at least in part because his more advanced age left open the greater possibility that he might die or retire in time for Taft to succeed him, a possibility highly unlikely with the younger Hughes. While there is no definitive evidence that this was what Taft was thinking, when White died in 1921, President Warren Harding offered Taft the center seat, making the former president's dream come true.

As to his other appointments, Taft's criteria was straightforward if a bit broad: he wanted men of integrity, men he knew, and, ideally, they all had to have judicial experience. In addition, in making his choices, he gave great consideration to what one author terms "their real politics." Taft was not a boat rocker; he revered the stability he believed the Constitution represented, and he wanted no "liberals," people who would be "destroyers of the Constitution." In the end, all of his choices fit that limited if innocuous criteria, but they also did little to embolden the Court or make a truly distinctive mark. In fact, with the exception of

Hughes, none of Taft's other selections—Justices Horace Lurton, Edward Douglass White, Willis Van Devanter, Joseph Lamar, and Mahlon Pitney—were more than average, nor did any serve with more distinction than Taft upon his subsequent appointment. Indeed, in a reality tinged with further irony, while later serving alongside his own appointees, Taft came to see how limited they were.

The 1912 presidential election was a personal disaster for Taft. Roosevelt's disappointment with Taft's performance as president coupled with his own regrets about having stepped down prematurely from a job he loved, all fueled by the progressive wing of the party that revered the former president and saw him as the man who could redirect its effort, led Roosevelt to challenge his former protégé. After dropping numerous hints, in February 1912, fulfilling a prediction that Nellie Taft had made shortly after her husband had entered the Oval Office, Roosevelt finally determined to make the move. Espousing his belief in the power of pure democracy, the former president outlined a populist program that would eventually evolve into what became known as New Nationalism, and Roosevelt took his case to the people. In the first truly newsworthy and impactful state presidential primaries in American history, Taft and Roosevelt went head to head, to no real effect, in a limited number of state contests. While Roosevelt's won more states, more votes, and more primary-determined delegates, as president, Taft retained full control of the party machinery, and it was the party, and not the small sampling represented in the primaries, that ultimately determined the nominee. Consequently, despite much bluster and a political performance worthy of the charismatic and outsized figure that Roosevelt was, Taft and the party regulars put down the Roosevelt challenge only to have Roosevelt and his followers reconvene in a convention of their own making where they nominated the former chief executive as the candidate of the Progressive Party. Meanwhile, after a tumultuous battle, the Democrats, sensing a chance for victory over a divided Republican Party, nominated New Jersey's progressive governor Woodrow Wilson on a then record 46th ballot. The three major candidates were joined by socialist Eugene Debs, who would poll an unprecedented 6 percent of the vote.

In some respects, the general election was almost anticlimactic, and Taft had no illusions about his chances for victory. At the same time, bridling at what he saw as the overly populist and democratic approaches of both Roosevelt's New Nationalism and Wilson's New Freedom, Taft proudly offered a defense of his record and his vision of a presidency rooted in the defined limits of the Constitution. But, in the end, with Roosevelt earning 27 percent and Taft getting 23 percent, the divided Republican vote was deeply split, allowing Wilson, with 42 percent of the popular vote—the lowest winning total since Lincoln—to win. Indeed, the Republican divide allowed Wilson to win an overwhelming victory in the Electoral College, as he accumulated 435 electoral votes to Roosevelt's 88 and Taft's 8 to become the first Democrat since Grover Cleveland in 1892 to be elected to the White House. Taft's performance was the poorest by any incumbent in American in history.

Before it was all over, Taft could also boast of enlarging the country, as his presidency saw the admission of two new states, New Mexico and Arizona, in 1912, bringing the nation's total to 48. The process did not occur until after Taft, true to form, had taken a stand on an issue of critical personal importance—the idea of an independent judiciary. Both of the prospective state constitutions included provisions allowing for judicial recall, a definitive deal breaker for Taft, who vetoed their admission. However, upon resubmission of revised constitutions with the recall provision removed, statehood was approved. These additions would be the last for almost a half century before the 1959 additions of Alaska and Hawaii.

It was with a sense of relief that William Howard Taft saw his presidency come to an end. He did not waver in his commitment to the office or the American people. Indeed, In February 1913, with less than a month to go in his term, Taft took a stand for human dignity when he vetoed a bill that mandated literacy tests for immigrants. That stance actually went hand in hand with his earlier expressed opposition to an ultimately successful effort by California to discriminate against Japanese aliens. Reflecting the more common Progressive viewpoint, Roosevelt would later express his belief that the United States should be able to exclude any group of aliens it wanted.

In the end, Taft appreciated his time as president, but even as he left office, the 55-year-old former jurist expressed the hope that he might yet again return to the bench.

ANALYTICAL ESSAY

As a historical figure, William Howard Taft often seems more caricature than real, more a collection of titles than a human being. He is known far and wide as the fattest president as well as the only person to serve as both president and chief justice, and yet, if one can get beyond the one-dimensional descriptions, one discovers a man whose impact—both in and out of the White House—on American history was both real and far-reaching. Indeed, for all the talk of his being Roosevelt's handpicked successor, that status was not bestowed on him out of generosity but as a hard-earned designation, the product of an impressive record in the delicate positions of governor of the Philippines, secretary of war, and all around presidential trouble-shooter at an important time in history.

Taft was not an innately political man; his preference for a life in law was made clear countless times, and his work as a federal judge, as solicitor general, as a law professor, and as an administrator were all far more fulfilling than any political office–seeking task he ever undertook. Indeed, both his successful 1908 campaign and his unsuccessful 1912 campaign were examples of his undertaking responsibilities that he felt he could not shirk than they were either the achievement of a long-held ambition or the culmination of a deep-seated desire to do a particular job. This was a paradox to be sure, especially given the lengths to which modern men go to be president. But in many ways, for Taft, the office sought the man, and he would gladly have traded it for the center seat on the Court. It is not a surprise that Taft reached the heaviest weight he would ever be while president, but he was almost 100 pounds lighter while enjoying his tenure on the bench. In the end, the contrast was insightfully encapsulated by a former nemesis turned appreciative colleague Louis Brandeis, who late in Taft's life asked, "How could such a good Chief Justice have been such a bad President?" Indeed, Taft was a fine chief justice.

Taft's previous experience made him a highly effective spokesman for the branch that well into the 20th century still did not have a permanent home. Indeed, it was Taft, as much as any other man, who was responsible for the construction of the U.S. Supreme Court building. He lobbied Congress for the money to buy the land and to construct the building, and he selected the architect, Cass Gilbert. While it has been criticized as a veritable palace, its physical stature compares favorably with both the White House and the U.S. Capitol, and in that way, it is a physical symbol as well as a reminder to the American people that it is one of three coequal branches, a proposition to which Taft was wholeheartedly committed. Beyond that, Taft was a superb administrator, running the Court in an efficient and effective manner, consistently and humanely recognizing the inherent value of each member, each of whom was treated with respect whatever their ideological predilections. There is no better testament to Taft's impact than to note that the Court had significantly improved, in countless ways, after his ascension to the bench a decade before. Being chief justice had been a lifelong ambition, and he had made the most of it.

And yet, while the Court represented the pinnacle of his dreams and saw Taft at his happiest, his presidency was not the disaster that it is sometimes portrayed as being and was in fact an administration that reflected the ideas and vision of its occupant, even if they did not measure up to the imaginings of both outsiders and the omnipresence of Theodore Roosevelt, which was central to the perceptions, then and now, of Taft's presidency. Indeed, few things illustrate the size of the shadow under which Taft came into office than the joke that made the rounds in the capital prior to Taft's assumption of the presidency, which declared slyly, if unkindly, that Taft stood for "Take Advice from Theodore."

In fact, William Howard Taft's ascension to the Oval Office represented one of the most unusual political climbs in American political history. Few individuals have arrived in the White House as the all but anointed successor, all obstacles—including, perhaps, his own doubts—to his ascension wiped away, and yet few, if any, have wanted it less. At the same time, possessing as deep a sense of public service and devotion

to his country as anyone who has ever held the job, when Taft assumed the presidency, he intended to do right by the office as he pursued his own vision, even if that meant, however unexpectedly, the loss of his political sponsor and closest friend. Despite Taft's lack of ambition, he was a proud man, and once the bear was poked and his honor challenged, his deep pride was triggered. In securing renomination, he undertook a game of political combat that would have been the envy of any big city party boss. He may not have wanted it, but once there, he did his best. He was ready and willing to defend both his own honor and the office he sought to honor through his principled approach to his responsibilities.

Taft had nothing but respect for the office of the president, and he had strived to serve previous occupants to the best of his ability. But he also knew that the office really belonged to the American people and was not one man's toy to be played with before being handed over to another to enjoy before being taken back at the "owner's" whim. Yes, Taft brought a conservative view of a limited chief executive and a limited view of federal power at a time when the powers and the reach of both the president and the federal government were being stretched and expanded in ways never before imagined. And yet, that did not mean that his approach was illegitimate nor that it could not work, and it did not mean that it had no value or support. Rather, in a distinct contrast to both his predecessor Theodore Roosevelt and his successor Woodrow Wilson, both of whom in their own ways had larger-than-life personalities, the human Taft, the largest man to hold the office, took an approach to the presidency that was devoid of personality.

In looking at President William Howard Taft, one sees an approach not dominated by the president's personality but rather by the president's distinctive and well-defined conception of the office and its role within the American constitutional system. While those who have served as president represent a wide range of legal experiences, Taft is the only president who brought the full-scale mind-set and mentality of a judge to the presidency and to his responsibilities in that office. That reality impacted every action he took and every decision he made as president. That approach and mind-set were central to this presidency.

For Taft, the presidency was a constitutional office, not a political one. He believed that the Founders had established a republic, not a democracy, and that the ideas of the people were to be filtered through their representatives, who would give them serious consideration. He was deeply opposed to the democratic ideas of the Progressive era, things like referendum, recall, and party primaries. At the same time, however, his opposition to those ideas was mild compared to his fierce disdain for those who called for the recall of judges. But neither of them rivaled his belief that those like Roosevelt, who proposed that the people be allowed to override judicial decisions by a popular vote, were attacking a fundamental tenet of the American system of government and especially of an independent judiciary.

Taft's legalistic and constitutionally oriented approach to the presidency was evident in his pledge to put a legal foundation under many of the executive orders that Roosevelt had issued. Indeed, loath to rely on the executive orders that had characterized many of Roosevelt's advances, Taft worked hard to construct a legislative scaffolding under the progressive agenda. It was a necessary and important advancement, one that provided an important foundation for future efforts, but was not something that got much attention. Nor did the fact that in his nomination acceptance speech he pledged justice for all men, without regard to race or color, and to unhesitatingly pursue enforcement of the Thirteenth, Fourteenth, and Fifteenth Amendments. Similarly, Taft supported the right of unions to strike, but in a preview of later legislation, especially the Taft-Hartley Act that bore the name of his oldest son, he was unequivocal in his opposition to secondary boycotts.

Taft's judicial mind-set also impacted his view of publicity and public relations. He was not a much of a newspaper reader, and as a result, he did not appreciate how they impacted public opinion. Consequently, giving little thought to how they might influence the pursuit of his legislative agenda, Taft never worried about the timing of public statements and did not recognize the impact such efforts might have on achieving his goals. This approach only reinforced another issue that contributed to Taft's problems; in addition to a restricted view of executive power, Taft was hampered by a lack of practical political experience.

Government experience he had in abundance, and it was part of what made his stints in the Philippines and in the War Department so successful. But the lack of interaction with party workers and patronage appointees left him lacking an understanding of the mind-set of elective office seekers. For him, the office had always sought the man, and as a result, he did not understand the pressures nor the motivations of those for whom elective office was a prize. Indeed, he had little to no patience for those who sought a place on the federal payroll as a reward for their efforts. Unhappily for Taft, his noble and service-oriented mind-set made him unduly trusting of others, and he was sometimes burned by the trust he placed in other officeholders, whose motives were not as pure as his. To his credit, friends and observers often spoke of his fitness, indeed his unwillingness, to engage in the pettiness that so often characterized politics, and even in his break with Roosevelt, he was the last to acknowledge the irretrievable nature of the split, a fact that led more people than he ever wanted to admit, including his wife, to tell him, "I told you so."

All of this, ideology and personality, was very much mirrored in his idea of executive leadership. A typical example was his approach to his signature tariff reform effort, where he sent Congress a 340-word legalistic message and then sat back to watch Congress do its constitutional duty. The tariff battle offered an early preview of Taft's approach while laying the seeds for the Progressives' subsequent discontent; there was a fundamental misunderstanding of Taft's role and approach, one that was clear in his mind but not to those who looked through a political lens rather than Taft's constitutional one. Indeed, in his view, the Constitution authorized the president to recommend laws but not to lobby for them. Anything more was beyond the scope of the office's designated authority. For anyone who had truly watched Taft's early career, such an approach should not have been a surprise, but at the time and since, the Taft presidency has been seen as representing a short interim period—a brief and perhaps final period of congressional preeminence, marking time between the unprecedented exercise of executive power under Roosevelt and the president as prime minster model that would characterize the Wilson years.

For the most part, Taft took little initiative in the legislative arena, in one instance sitting by while Congress added over 800 amendments to the tariff reform bill that was to be a centerpiece of his early legislative program. And yet, he never truly saw it as his legislative program, and such actions were very much in line with Taft's philosophical approach to the presidency, one that was not out of line with the then accepted model. The emergence of the executive branch as the driving force of the federal government was starting, but while Roosevelt and Wilson would offer a model for a more active executive, the presidencies of Harding, Coolidge, and Hoover were all more akin to Taft's than to those of Roosevelt or Wilson. Indeed, it would take the convergence of events (the Great Depression and World War II) and personality (Franklin Roosevelt) to quash the long accepted and constitutionally designed model of congressional dominance—a system in which Taft was very comfortable.

The reality is that beyond his philosophy, what is critical to judging Taft and his presidency is context. Compared to Roosevelt, who had broken the presidential mold, Taft was very different. Indeed, for those who liked TR and expected a second Roosevelt, there was only disappointment, if not disillusionment. To view Taft on his own terms, he was a conservative constitutionalist who believed that TR had expanded the powers of the executive beyond their proper borders and who sought to restrain the potentially disruptive democratic forces that TR and other progressives had sought to unleash; he wanted to protect the republican form of government that he believed the Founders had intended.

In many ways, Taft's presidency represented a period of consolidation following the well-promoted activism and, in some cases, the unprecedented initiatives that had characterized the Roosevelt presidency. And yet, whether it was a product of their differing styles or the fact that Roosevelt had burst through the door, whereas Taft was simply following the old established path, his efforts, which often exceeded Roosevelt's, frequently seemed to be undervalued. His trust-busting efforts, which were by almost any measure at least the equal of Roosevelt's but lacking his predecessor's flair, did not begin to garner the same attention. In addition, Taft achieved numerous small

victories that moved the progressive agenda forward. Typical of these smaller but no less significant accomplishments was the establishment of the Children's Bureau in the Department of Commerce in 1912. Given the important task of monitoring child welfare, the agency was at the heart of the progressive agenda. And Taft's appointment of reformer Julia Lathrop to head the bureau, an appointment that made her the highest-ranking woman in the federal government, reflected his willingness to do things differently as the task warranted. Another similar achievement was the passage of a law authorizing an eight-hour day for all workers operating under federal contracts.

Similarly, on the foreign policy front, while dollar diplomacy has become the hallmark of assessments of Taft foreign policy and served as an inspiration for the further development of American economic interests in Asia, the administration was no less committed to forestalling any European colonial ambitions in the Western Hemisphere that would run afoul of the Monroe Doctrine, which the Roosevelt Corollary had recently reenergized. In addition, with Taft's foreign policy reflecting the president's legalistic tendencies, it added the use of arbitration as a viable option in the effort to preserve world peace, and the administration's numerous successful uses of the process helped add to its credibility worldwide. These success were balanced by the unsettled situation that still reigned in Mexico when Taft left office, but to his credit, he had managed to limit direct U.S. involvement while helping the country navigate among competing factions.

On the domestic front, despite his best intentions and his determination to address an issue central to the party's platform, Taft took a political beating, but one that might well have been expected. Meanwhile, on the more specific economic front, in addition to his trust-busting efforts, which as noted were more extensive if less publicized than those of his predecessor, Taft showed both a deep-seated commitment to a balanced budget as well as an economy that served, rather than exploited, American workers and small businesses. All of this was evident in some of the regulatory acts he supported as well as his effort to make possible an income tax. No less important was his effort to have the president, rather than the wide range of federal agencies, submit a single budget, an action that Congress prohibited but which nevertheless started the efforts that would eventually result in the creation in 1921 of the executive budget under the Budget and Accounting Act. In fact, in the domestic and economic realms, for all the criticism he received, his was a presidency that lacked far more in recognition than it did in accomplishment.

Ironically, while Taft hoped that his refusal to weigh in on legislative matters would preclude party divisions, his insistence that the Constitution prohibited him from adopting such a role actually served to fracture the party. Yet, he had sought to fulfill the party's pledge to achieve tariff reform, and while it led to a political firestorm, it also represented not only the first effort at tariff reform in two decades but was also an initiative in an area that Roosevelt had purposely avoided. Taft also pursued other revenue options, proposing constitutional amendments for an income tax and a corporate income tax. In an effort to scale back the government that TR had exploded, Taft wanted the tariff reform to not only reduce trade barriers but also to help achieve a balanced budget. Combined with major spending cuts, the Taft administration reduced the deficit from $89 million in TR's last year to $11 million in Taft's first year, followed by surpluses of $11 and $3 million. In addition, but seemingly unbeknownst to the American people, in the conservation area, Taft withdrew more land for federal protection in his single term than Roosevelt had in two, and he also created 10 national parks. But certainly at the time, if not since, the Ballinger-Pinchot affair overshadowed all of that.

In the end, with incidents like the Ballinger-Pinchot affair, among others, serving to overshadow his substantive accomplishments while dominating the perceptions of his presidency, as the 1912 presidential election approach, Taft found himself challenged from within his own party and by his onetime mentor. While to some, including his wife, it was a case of "I told you so" for the proud, principled, and sensitive Taft, the challenge represented a personal affront, and so believing he had been unfairly wronged, not to mention misunderstood, William Howard Taft turned the presidential campaign into a defense of a constitutional vision. It was a battle between competing, indeed conflicting, philosophies, with Taft and Roosevelt offering competing views of presidential power: TR believed that the

president could do anything that was not forbidden by the Constitution, while Taft believed he could only do what the Constitution specifically allowed. To the chief executive with the judicial temperament, both Roosevelt and Wilson were demagogic populists advocating the use of unauthorized power. For Taft, the 1912 election was a clash of visions—his of the presidency as an office of limited power as defined and limited by the Constitution versus the popularly elected office directly accountable to the people that Roosevelt and Wilson envisioned.

Ultimately, Taft's presidency was in many ways a reflection of the man himself. With an optimistic, cheerful, upbeat personality, he was a popular man who had lots of friends but few intimates. As a result, he had few to whom he could go for unvarnished, candid advice, and when Nellie, his biggest supporter and closest counsel, suffered a stroke early in his administration, Taft was left adrift. He had been the counselor and source of support for much of Roosevelt's term, but he had no one to play that role for him. He needed someone to help Taft be Taft—something that every chief executive needs—but given the circumstances of his rise to power, it was absolutely critical to any attempt by Taft to effectively establish himself as an independent officeholder.

For too long and in the eyes of too many, Taft's accomplishments have been overshadowed by his girth. He was viewed by some as disinterested, which was exacerbated by the fact that he suffered from a form of sleep apnea that prevented him from getting a full and restful night's sleep, causing a series of embarrassing incidents in which he fell asleep in meetings or public events. Indeed, in the public memory and imagination, he is more likely to be associated with oversized bathtubs than legislative accomplishments or even groundbreaking judicial pronouncements. And yet, for all the ridicule to which he was subjected, the ever-congenial and warm-hearted Taft, although sensitive to political criticism, in large part because his actions were, in his view, so rooted in doing what was right, could readily laugh at himself. Indeed, while he struggled with his weight, something that was under control when he was happy or content with his station in life, he nevertheless often entertained audiences with humorous stories about himself, a favorite being the time he reported to Secretary of War Elihu Roots that he was feeling well after a long horseback ride, to which Root replied, "How is the horse?" It is a pleasant quip, one that Taft did not disavow, but it also encapsulated much of the public image of a man whose deep devotion and selfless service it overshadowed.

Taft's was not a flashy presidency—especially as compared with the two-term efforts of Roosevelt and Wilson that surrounded it. And yet, it was a period of overlooked accomplishment and necessary consolidation, critical for the acceptance of the Roosevelt effort while serving to firm up the foundation for the Wilsonian initiatives that would follow. But much of that has gone unrecognized. Perhaps historians and commentators have been overwhelmed, or at least influenced, by the stylistic dazzle of Roosevelt and Wilson, or maybe they have taken refuge in the fact that Taft has still been able to get his historical due because of his postpresidential career on the Supreme Court. But in looking back at his seemingly star-crossed presidency, at his four years in the national saddle, it is fair to echo Root and ask, "How was the country?" The answer, upon reflection, was, "Pretty good."

Bill H. Pruden

Further Reading

Anderson, Donald F. 1973. *William Howard Taft: A Conservative Conception of the Presidency.* Ithaca, NY: Cornell University Press.

Anderson, Judith Icke. 1981. *William Howard Taft: An Intimate History.* New York: W. W. Norton & Company.

Goodwin, Doris Kearns. 2013. *The Bully Pulpit: Theodore Roosevelt, William Howard Taft, and the Golden Age of Journalism.* New York: Simon & Schuster.

Gould, Lewis L. 2009. *The William Howard Taft Presidency.* Lawrence: University Press of Kansas.

Lurie, Jonathan. 2011. *William Howard Taft: The Travails of a Progressive Conservative.* New York: Cambridge University Press.

Rosen, Jeffrey. 2018. *William Howard Taft.* The American Presidents Series. Edited by Arthur M. Schlesinger Jr. and Sean Wilentz. New York: Times Books/Henry Holt and Company.

William H. Taft Papers, 1784–1973. n.d. Library of Congress. https://www.loc.gov/item/mm78042234/.

Inaugural Address (March 4, 1909)

The inaugural address of President Taft offers both a vivid example of his judiciously based style of communication and his limited view of presidential power. At the same time, it also offers insight into his programmatic priorities as well as his approach to addressing the challenges that he had inherited.

My Fellow-Citizens:

Anyone who has taken the oath I have just taken must feel a heavy weight of responsibility. If not, he has no conception of the powers and duties of the office upon which he is about to enter, or he is lacking in a proper sense of the obligation which the oath imposes.

The office of an inaugural address is to give a summary outline of the main policies of the new administration, so far as they can be anticipated. I have had the honor to be one of the advisers of my distinguished predecessor, and, as such, to hold up his hands in the reforms he has initiated. I should be untrue to myself, to my promises, and to the declarations of the party platform upon which I was elected to office, if I did not make the maintenance and enforcement of those reforms a most important feature of my administration. They were directed to the suppression of the lawlessness and abuses of power of the great combinations of capital invested in railroads and in industrial enterprises carrying on interstate commerce. The steps which my predecessor took and the legislation passed on his recommendation have accomplished much, have caused a general halt in the vicious policies which created popular alarm, and have brought about in the business affected a much higher regard for existing law.

To render the reforms lasting, however, and to secure at the same time freedom from alarm on the part of those pursuing proper and progressive business methods, further legislative and executive action are needed. Relief of the railroads from certain restrictions of the antitrust law have been urged by my predecessor and will be urged by me. On the other hand, the administration is pledged to legislation looking to a proper federal supervision and restriction to prevent excessive issues of bonds and stock by companies owning and operating interstate commerce railroads.

Then, too, a reorganization of the Department of Justice, of the Bureau of Corporations in the Department of Commerce and Labor, and of the Interstate Commerce Commission, looking to effective cooperation of these agencies, is needed to secure a more rapid and certain enforcement of the laws affecting interstate railroads and industrial combinations.

I hope to be able to submit at the first regular session of the incoming Congress, in December next, definite suggestions in respect to the needed amendments to the antitrust and the interstate commerce law and the changes required in the executive departments concerned in their enforcement. . . .

The work of formulating into practical shape such changes is creative word of the highest order, and requires all the deliberation possible in the interval. I believe that the amendments to be proposed are just as necessary in the protection of legitimate business as in the clinching of the reforms which properly bear the name of my predecessor.

A matter of most pressing importance is the revision of the tariff. In accordance with the promises of the platform upon which I was elected, I shall call Congress into extra session to meet on the 15th day of March, in order that consideration may be at once given to a bill revising the Dingley Act. This should secure an adequate revenue and adjust the duties in such a manner as to afford to labor and to all industries in this country, whether of the farm, mine or factory, protection by tariff equal to the difference between the cost of production abroad and the cost of production here, and have a provision which shall put into force, upon executive determination of certain facts, a higher or maximum tariff against those countries whose trade policy toward us equitably requires such discrimination. It is thought that there has been such a change in conditions since the enactment of the Dingley Act, drafted on a similarly protective principle, that the measure of the tariff above stated will permit the reduction of rates in certain schedules and will require the advancement of few, if any.

. . . It is not that the tariff is more important in the long run than the perfecting of the reforms in respect to antitrust legislation and interstate commerce regulation, but the need for action when the revision of the tariff has been determined upon is more immediate to avoid embarrassment of business. To secure the needed speed in the passage of the tariff bill, it would seem wise to attempt no other legislation at the extra session. I venture this as a suggestion only, for the course to be taken by Congress, upon the call of the Executive, is wholly within its discretion. . . .

The obligation on the part of those responsible for the expenditures made to carry on the Government, to be as economical as possible, and to make the burden of taxation as light as possible, is plain, and should be affirmed in every declaration of government policy. This is especially true when we are face to face with a heavy deficit. But when the desire to win the popular approval leads to the cutting off of expenditures really needed to make the Government effective and to enable it to accomplish its proper objects, the result is as much to be condemned as the waste of government funds in unnecessary expenditure. The scope of a modern government in what it can and ought to accomplish for its people has been widened far beyond the principles laid down by the old "laissez faire" school of political writers, and this widening has met popular approval. . . .

The putting into force of laws which shall secure the conservation of our resources, so far as they may be within the jurisdiction of the Federal Government, including the most important work of saving and restoring our forests and the great improvement of waterways, are all proper government functions which must involve large expenditure if properly performed. While some of them, like the reclamation of and lands, are made to pay for themselves, others are of such an indirect benefit that this cannot be expected of them. A permanent improvement, like the Panama Canal, should be treated as a distinct enterprise, and should be paid for by the proceeds of bonds, the issue of which will distribute its cost between the present and future generations in accordance with the benefits derived. It may well be submitted to the serious consideration of Congress whether the deepening and control of the channel of a great river system, like that of the Ohio or of the Mississippi, when definite and practical plans for the enterprise have been approved and determined upon, should not be provided for in the same way.

Then, too, there are expenditures of Government absolutely necessary if our country is to maintain its proper place among the nations of the world, and is to exercise its proper influence in defense of its own trade interests in the maintenance of traditional American policy against the colonization of European monarchies in this hemisphere, and in the promotion of peace and international morality. I refer to the cost of maintaining a proper army, a proper navy, and suitable fortifications upon the mainland of the United States and in its dependencies.

We should have an army so organized and so officered as to be capable in time of emergency, in cooperation with the national militia and under the provisions of a proper national volunteer law, rapidly to expand into a force sufficient to resist all probable invasion from abroad and to furnish a respectable expeditionary force if necessary in the maintenance of our traditional American policy which bears the name of President Monroe. . . .

What has been said of the army may be affirmed in even a more emphatic way of the navy. A modern navy cannot be improvised. It must be built and in existence when the emergency arises which calls for its use and operation. My distinguished predecessor has in many speeches and messages set out with great force and striking language the necessity for maintaining a strong navy commensurate with the coast line, the governmental resources, and the foreign trade of our Nation; and I wish to reiterate all the reasons which he has presented in favor of the policy of maintaining a strong navy as the best conservator of our peace with other nations, and the best means of securing respect for the assertion of our rights, the defense of our interests, and the exercise of our influence in international matters.

Our international policy is always to promote peace. We shall enter into any war with a full consciousness of the awful consequences that it always entails, whether successful or not, and we, of course, shall make every effort consistent with national honor and the highest national interest to avoid a resort to arms. We favor every instrumentality, like that of the Hague Tribunal and arbitration treaties made with a view to its use in all international controversies, in order to maintain peace and to avoid war. But we should be blind to existing conditions and should allow ourselves to become foolish idealists if we did

not realize that, with all the nations of the world armed and prepared for war, we must be ourselves in a similar condition, in order to prevent other nations from taking advantage of us and of our inability to defend our interests and assert our rights with a strong hand.

In the international controversies that are likely to arise in the Orient growing out of the question of the open door and other issues the United States can maintain her interests intact and can secure respect for her just demands. She will not be able to do so, however, if it is understood that she never intends to back up her assertion of right and her defense of her interest by anything but mere verbal protest and diplomatic note. . . Our Government is able to afford a suitable army and a suitable navy. It may maintain them without the slightest danger to the Republic or the cause of free institutions, and fear of additional taxation ought not to change a proper policy in this regard.

The policy of the United States in the Spanish war and since has given it a position of influence among the nations that it never had before, and should be constantly exerted to securing to its bona fide citizens, whether native or naturalized, respect for them as such in foreign countries. We should make every effort to prevent humiliating and degrading prohibition against any of our citizens wishing temporarily to sojourn in foreign countries because of race or religion.

The admission of Asiatic immigrants who cannot be amalgamated with our population has been made the subject either of prohibitory clauses in our treaties and statutes or of strict administrative regulation secured by diplomatic negotiation. I sincerely hope that we may continue to minimize the evils likely to arise from such immigration without unnecessary friction and by mutual concessions between self-respecting governments. . . .

This leads me to point out a serious defect in the present federal jurisdiction, which ought to be remedied at once. Having assured to other countries by treaty the protection of our laws for such of their subjects or citizens as we permit to come within our jurisdiction, we now leave to a state or a city, not under the control of the Federal Government, the duty of performing our international obligations in this respect. . . . We cannot permit the possible failure of justice, due to local prejudice in any State or municipal government, to expose us to the risk of a war which might be avoided if federal jurisdiction was asserted by suitable legislation by Congress and carried out by proper proceedings instituted by the Executive in the courts of the National Government.

One of the reforms to be carried out during the incoming administration is a change of our monetary and banking laws, so as to secure greater elasticity in the forms of currency available for trade and to prevent the limitations of law from operating to increase the embarrassment of a financial panic. The monetary commission, lately appointed, is giving full consideration to existing conditions and to all proposed remedies, and will doubtless suggest one that will meet the requirements of business and of public interest. . . .

The incoming Congress should promptly fulfill the promise of the Republican platform and pass a proper postal savings bank bill. . . .

I sincerely hope that the incoming Congress will be alive, as it should be, to the importance of our foreign trade and of encouraging it in every way feasible. The possibility of increasing this trade in the Orient, in the Philippines, and in South America are known to everyone who has given the matter attention. The direct effect of free trade between this country and the Philippines will be marked upon our sales of cottons. . . . The necessity of the establishment of direct lines of steamers between North and South America has been brought to the attention of Congress by my predecessor…and I sincerely hope that Congress may be induced to see the wisdom of a tentative effort to establish such lines by the use of mail subsidies. . . .

The Panama Canal will have a most important bearing upon the trade between the eastern and far western sections of our country . . . and may possibly revolutionize the transcontinental rates with respect to bulky merchandise. It will also have a most beneficial effect to increase the trade between the eastern seaboard of the United States and the western coast of South America, and, indeed, with some of the important ports on the east coast of South America reached by rail from the west coast. . . .

The governments of our dependencies in Porto Rico and the Philippines are progressing as favorably as could be desired. The prosperity of Porto Rico continues unabated. The business conditions in the Philippines are not all that we could wish them to be, but with the passage of the new tariff bill permitting free trade between the United States and the archipelago, with such limitations on sugar and tobacco as shall prevent injury to domestic interests in those products, we can count on an improvement in business conditions in the Philippines and the development of a mutually profitable trade between this country and the islands. Meantime our Government in each dependency is upholding the traditions of civil liberty and increasing popular control which might be expected under American auspices. The work which we are doing there redounds to our credit as a nation.

I look forward with hope to increasing the already good feeling between the South and the other sections of the country. My chief purpose is not to effect a change in the electoral vote of the Southern States. That is a secondary consideration. What I look forward to is an increase in the tolerance of political views of all kinds and their advocacy throughout the South, and the existence of a respectable political opposition in every State; even more than this, to an increased feeling on the part of all the people in the South that this Government is their Government, and that its officers in their states are their officers.

The consideration of this question cannot, however, be complete and full without reference to the negro race, its progress and its present condition. . . . The thirteenth and fourteenth amendments have been generally enforced and have secured the objects for which they are intended. While the fifteenth amendment has not been generally observed in the past, it ought to be observed, and the tendency of Southern legislation today is toward the enactment of electoral qualifications which shall square with that amendment. Of course, the mere adoption of a constitutional law is only one step in the right direction. It must be fairly and justly enforced as well. In time both will come. . . . The colored men must base their hope on the results of their own industry, self-restraint, thrift, and business success, as well as upon the aid and comfort and sympathy which they may receive from their white neighbors of the South.

. . . What remains is the fifteenth amendment to the Constitution and the right to have statutes of States specifying qualifications for electors subjected to the test of compliance with that amendment. This is a great protection to the negro. It never will be repealed, and it never ought to be repealed. If it had not passed, it might be difficult now to adopt it; but with it in our fundamental law, the policy of Southern legislation must and will tend to obey it, and so long as the statutes of the States meet the test of this amendment and are not otherwise in conflict with the Constitution and laws of the United States, it is not the disposition or within the province of the Federal Government to interfere with the regulation by Southern States of their domestic affairs. There is in the South a stronger feeling than ever among the intelligent well-to-do, and influential element in favor of the industrial education of the negro and the encouragement of the race to make themselves useful members of the community. The progress which the negro has made in the last fifty years, from slavery, when its statistics are reviewed, is marvelous, and it furnishes every reason to hope that in the next twenty-five years a still greater improvement in his condition as a productive member of society, on the farm, and in the shop, and in other occupations may come.

The negroes are now Americans. Their ancestors came here years ago against their will, and this is their only country and their only flag. They have shown themselves anxious to live for it and to die for it. Encountering the race feeling against them, subjected at times to cruel injustice growing out of it, they may well have our profound sympathy and aid in the struggle they are making. We are charged with the sacred duty of making their path as smooth and easy as we can. Any recognition of their distinguished men, any appointment to office from among their number, is properly taken as an encouragement and an appreciation of their progress, and this just policy should be pursued when suitable occasion offers. . . .

Personally, I have not the slightest race prejudice or feeling. . . . Meantime, if nothing is done to prevent it, a better feeling between the negroes and the whites in the South will continue to grow, and more and more of the white people will come to realize that the future of the South is to be much benefited by the industrial and intellectual progress of the negro. The exercise of political franchises by those of this race who are intelligent and well to do will be acquiesced in, and the right to vote will be withheld only from the ignorant and irresponsible of both races.

There is one other matter to which I shall refer. It was made the subject of great controversy during the election and calls for at least a passing reference now. My distinguished predecessor has given much attention to the cause of labor, with whose struggle for better things he has shown the sincerest sympathy. At his instance Congress . . . passed the bill. Additional legislation of this kind was passed by the outgoing Congress.

I wish to say that insofar as I can I hope to promote the enactment of further legislation of this character. I am strongly convinced that the Government should make itself as responsible to employees injured in its employ as an interstate-railway corporation is made responsible by federal law to its employees; and I shall be glad, whenever any additional reasonable safety device can be invented to reduce the loss of life and limb among railway employees, to urge Congress to require its adoption by interstate railways.

Another labor question has arisen which has awakened the most excited discussion. That is in respect to the power of the federal courts to issue injunctions in industrial disputes. As to that, my convictions are fixed. Take away from the courts, if it could be taken away, the power to issue injunctions in labor disputes, and it would create a privileged class among the laborers and save the lawless among their number from a most needful remedy available to all men for the protection of their business against lawless invasion. . . . The secondary boycott is an instrument of tyranny, and ought not to be made legitimate.

The issue of a temporary restraining order without notice has in several instances been abused by its inconsiderate exercise, and to remedy this the platform upon which I was elected recommends the formulation in a statute of the conditions under which such a temporary restraining order ought to issue. A statute can and ought to be framed to embody the best modern practice, and can bring the subject so closely to the attention of the court as to make abuses of the process unlikely in the future. . . .

Having thus reviewed the questions likely to recur during my administration, and having expressed in a summary way the position which I expect to take in recommendations to Congress and in my conduct as an Executive, I invoke the considerate sympathy and support of my fellow-citizens and the aid of the Almighty God in the discharge of my responsible duties.

Source: Richardson, James D. *A Compilation of the Messages and Papers of the Presidents 1789–1897*. Vol. 15. New York: Bureau of National Literature, 1897, 7368–7379.

Message to the Special Session of Congress Called to Address the Issue of Tariff Reform (March 16, 1909)

President Taft's statement to Congress about tariff reform is a document that offers a window into Taft's approach to presidential leadership and the role of the president in the legislative process. Succinct and direct, it fulfills his limited role as he sees it, but no more.

To The Senate and House of Representatives:

I have convened Congress in this extra session in order to enable it to give immediate consideration to the revision of the Dingley tariff act. Conditions affecting production, manufacture, and business generally have so changed in the last twelve years as to require a readjustment and revision of the import duties imposed by that act. More than this, the present tariff act, with the other sources of government revenue, does not furnish income enough to pay the authorized expenditures. By July 1 next the excess of expenses over receipts for the current fiscal year will equal $100,000,000.

The successful party in the late lection is pledged to a revision of the tariff. The country, and the business community especially, expect it. The prospect of a change in the rates of import duties always causes a suspension or halt in business because of the uncertainty as to the changes to be made and their effect. It is therefore of the highest importance that the new bill should be agreed upon and passed with as much speed as possible consistent with its due and thorough consideration. For these reasons, I have deemed the present to be an extraordinary occasion within the meaning of the Constitution, justifying and requiring the calling of an extra session. In my inaugural address I stated in a summary way the principles upon which,

in my judgment, the revision of the tariff should proceed, and indicated at least one new source of revenue that might be properly resorted to in order to avoid a future deficit It is not necessary for me to repeat what I then said.

I venture to suggest that the vital business interests of the country require that the attention of the Congress in this session be chiefly devoted to the consideration of the new tariff bill, and that the less time given to other subjects of legislation in this session, the better for the country.

Source: Richardson, James D. *A Compilation of the Messages and Papers of the Presidents 1789–1897*. Vol. 15. New York: Bureau of National Literature, 1897, 7379.

Address on the Tariff Law of 1909 (November 17, 1909)

The statement by President Taft analyzing and defending the Payne-Aldrich Tariff offers a window into one of the administration's most controversial efforts, one that left Taft in serious political trouble. It offers a good sense of Taft's approach to governing as well as his steadfast party loyalty. It also makes clear why the tariff, as well as comparable subsequent efforts, left the president vulnerable to political attacks by the party's progressive wing.

MY FELLOW CITIZENS: As long ago as August, 1906, in the congressional campaign in Maine, I ventured to announce that I was a tariff revisionist and thought that the time had come for a readjustment of the schedules. I pointed out that it had been ten years prior to that time that the Dingley bill had been passed; that great changes had taken place in the conditions surrounding the productions of the farm, the factory, and the mine, and that under the theory of protection in that time the rates imposed in the Dingley bill in many instances might have become excessive; that is, might have been greater than the difference between the cost of production abroad and the cost of production at home with a sufficient allowance for a reasonable rate of profit to the American producer. I said that the party was divided on the issue, but that in my judgment the opinion of the party was crystallizing and would probably result in the near future in an effort to make such revision. I pointed out the difficulty that there always was in a revision of the tariff, due to the threatened disturbance of industries to be affected and the suspension of business, in a way which made it unwise to have too many revisions. In the summer of 1907 my position on the tariff was challenged, and I then entered into a somewhat fuller discussion of the matter. It was contended by the so-called "standpatters" that rates beyond the necessary measure of protection were not objectionable, because behind the tariff wall competition always reduced the prices, and thus saved the consumer. But I pointed out in that speech what seems to me as true to-day as it then was, that the danger of excessive rates was in the temptation they created to form monopolies in the protected articles, and thus to take advantage of the excessive rates by increasing the prices, and therefore, and in order to avoid such a danger, it was wise at regular intervals to examine the question of what the effect of the rates had been upon the industries in this country, and whether the conditions with respect to the cost of production here had so changed as to warrant a reduction in the tariff, and to make a lower rate truly protective of the industry.

It will be observed that the object of the revision under such a statement was not to destroy protected industries in this country, but it was to continue to protect them where lower rates offered a sufficient protection to prevent injury by foreign competition. That was the object of the revision as advocated by me, and it was certainly the object of the revision as promised in the Republican platform.

I want to make as clear as I can this proposition, because, in order to determine whether a bill is a compliance with the terms of that platform, it must be understood what the platform means. A free trader is opposed to any protected rate because he thinks that our manufacturers, our farmers, and our miners ought to withstand the competition of foreign manufacturers and miners and farmers, or else go out of business and find something else more profitable to do. Now, certainly the promises of the platform did not contemplate the downward revision of the tariff rates to such a point that any industry theretofore protected should

be injured. Hence, those who contend that the promise of the platform was to reduce prices by letting in foreign competition are contending for a free trade, and not for anything that they had the right to infer from the Republican platform. . . .

Mr. Payne reported a bill—the Payne Tariff bill—which went to the Senate and was amended in the Senate by increasing the duty on some things and decreasing it on others. The difference between the House bill and the Senate bill was very much less than the newspapers represented. It turns out upon examination that the reductions in the Senate were about equal to those in the House, though they differed in character. Now, there is nothing quite so difficult as the discussion of a tariff bill, for the reason that it covers so many different items, and the meaning of the terms and the percentages are very hard to understand. The passage of a new bill, especially where a change in the method of assessing the duties has been followed, presents an opportunity for various modes and calculations of the percentages of increases and decreases that are most misleading and really throw no light at all upon the changes made. . . .

Now, the promise of the Republican platform was not to revise everything downward, and in the speeches which have been taken as interpreting that platform, which I made in the campaign, I did not promise that everything should go downward. What I promised was, that there should be many decreases, and that in some few things increases would be found to be necessary; but that on the whole I conceived that the change of conditions would make the revision necessarily downward—and that, I contend, under the showing which I have made, has been the result of the Payne bill. I did not agree, nor did the Republican party agree, that we would reduce rates to such a point as to reduce prices by the introduction of foreign competition. That is what the free traders desire. That is what the revenue tariff reformers desire; but that is not what the Republican platform promised, and it is not what the Republican party wished to bring about. . . .

I have never known a subject that will evoke so much contradictory evidence as the question of tariff rates and the question of cost of production at home and abroad. . . .

On the whole, however, I am bound to say that I think the Payne tariff bill is the best tariff bill that the Republican party ever passed; that in it the party has conceded the necessity for following the changed conditions and reducing tariff rates accordingly. This is a substantial achievement in the direction of lower tariffs and downward revision, and it ought to be accepted as such. . . .

. . . Living has increased everywhere in cost—in countries where there is free trade and in countries where there is protection—and that increase has been chiefly seen in the cost of food products. In other words we have had to pay more for the products of the farmer, for meat, for grain, for everything that enters into food. Now, certainly no one will contend that protection has increased the cost of food in this country, when the fact is that we have been the greatest exporters of food products in the world . . . but what I wish to emphasize is that the recent increases in the cost of living in this country have not been due to the tariff. We have a much higher standard of living in this country than they have abroad, and this has been made possible by higher income for the workingman, the farmer, and all classes. Higher wages have been made possible by the encouragement of diversified industries, built up and fostered by the tariff.

Now, the revision downward of the tariff that I have favored will not, I hope, destroy the industries of the country. Certainly it is not intended to. All that it is intended to do, and that is what I wish to repeat, is to put the tariff where it will protect industries here from foreign competition, but will not enable those who will wish to monopolize to raise prices by taking advantage of excessive rates beyond the normal difference in the cost of production.

If the country desires free trade, and the country desires a revenue tariff and wishes the manufacturers all over the country to go out of business, and to have cheaper prices at the expense of the sacrifice of many of our manufacturing interests, then it ought to say so and ought to put the Democratic party in power if it thinks that party can be trusted to carry out any affirmative policy in favor of a revenue tariff. Certainly in the discussions in the Senate there was no great manifestation on the part of our Democratic friends in favor of reducing rates on necessities. They voted to maintain the tariff rates on everything that came from their particular sections. If we are to have free trade, certainly it cannot be had through the maintenance of Republican majorities in the Senate and House and a Republican administration. . . .

This is a government by a majority of the people. It is a representative government. People select some 400 members to constitute the lower House and some 92 members to constitute the upper House through their legislatures, and the varying views of a majority of the voters in eighty or ninety millions of people are reduced to one resultant force to take affirmative steps in carrying on a government by a system of parties. Without parties popular government would be absolutely impossible. In a party, those who join it, if they would make it effective, must surrender their personal predilections on matters comparatively of less importance in order to accomplish the good which united action on the most important principles at issue secures.

. . . When I could say without hesitation that this is the best tariff bill that the Republican party has ever passed, and therefore the best tariff bill that has been passed at all, I do not feel that I could have reconciled any other course to my conscience than that of signing the bill. . . . Of course, if I had vetoed the bill I would have received the applause of many Republicans who may be called low-tariff Republicans, and who think deeply on that subject, and of all the Democracy. Our friends the Democrats would have applauded, and then laughed in their sleeve at the condition in which the party would have been left; but, more than this, and waiving considerations of party, where would the country have been had the bill been vetoed, or been lost by a vote? It would have left the question of the revision of the tariff open for further discussion during the next session. It would have suspended the settlement of all our business down to a known basis upon which prosperity could proceed and investments be made, and it would have held up the coming of prosperity to this country certainly for a year and probably longer. These are the reasons why I signed it.

Source: Richardson, James D. *A Compilation of the Messages and Papers of the Presidents 1789–1897*. Vols. 15–16. New York: Bureau of National Literature, 1897, vol. 15, 7393 to vol. 16, 7409.

Special Message on Canadian Reciprocity (January 26, 1911)

President Taft's statement on Canadian reciprocity offers a good look at his views on both an aspect of foreign policy and international commerce. In the statement, Taft offers a sense for how his foreign policy and economic policy work together serving both U.S. economic and international interests. It is methodical and thoughtful, which is typical of an approach that once led his wife to comment that all of Taft's public statements read like legal opinions, but in that way, it also is a fine example of his style.

To the Senate and House of Representatives:

In my annual message of December 6, 1910, I stated that the policy of broader and closer trade relations with the Dominion of Canada, which was initiated in the adjustment of the maximum and minimum provisions of the tariff act of August 5, 1909, had proved mutually beneficial and that it justified further efforts for the readjustment of the commercial relations of the two countries. I also informed you that, by my direction, the Secretary of State had dispatched two representatives of the Department of State as special commissioners to Ottawa to confer with representatives of the Dominion Government, that they were authorized to take steps to formulate a reciprocal trade agreement, and that the Ottawa conferences thus begun, had been adjourned to be resumed in Washington.

On the 7th of the present month two cabinet ministers came to Washington as representatives of the Dominion Government, and the conferences were continued between them and the Secretary of State. The result of the negotiations was that on the 21st instant a reciprocal trade agreement was reached, the text of which is herewith transmitted with accompanying correspondence and other data.

One by one the controversies resulting from the uncertainties which attended the partition of British territory on the American Continent at the close of the Revolution, and which were inevitable under the then conditions, have been eliminated—some by arbitration and some by direct negotiation. The merits of these disputes, many of them extending through a century, need not now be reviewed. They related to the settlement of boundaries, the definition of rights of navigation, the interpretation of treaties, and many other subjects.

Through the friendly sentiments, the energetic efforts, and the broadly patriotic views of successive administrations, and especially of that of my immediate predecessor, all these questions have been settled. The most acute related to the Atlantic fisheries, and this longstanding controversy, after amicable negotiation, was referred to The Hague Tribunal. The judgment of that august international court has been accepted by the people of both countries and a satisfactory agreement in pursuance of the judgment has ended completely the controversy. An equitable arrangement has recently been reached between our Interstate Commerce Commission and the similar body in Canada in regard to through rates on the transportation lines between the two countries.

The path having been thus opened for the improvement of commercial relations, a reciprocal trade agreement is the logical sequence of all that has been accomplished in disposing of matters of a diplomatic and controversial character. The identity of interest of two peoples linked together by race, language, political institutions, and geographical proximity offers the foundation. The contribution to the industrial advancement of our own country by the migration across the boundary of the thrifty and industrious Canadians of English, Scotch, and French origin is now repaid by the movement of large numbers of our own sturdy farmers to the northwest of Canada, thus giving their labor, their means, and their experience to the development of that section; with its agricultural possibilities.

The guiding motive in seeking adjustment of trade relations between two countries so situated geographically should be to give play to productive forces as far as practicable, regardless of political boundaries. While equivalency should be sought in an arrangement of this character, an exact balance of financial gain is neither imperative nor attainable. No yardstick can measure the benefits to the two peoples of this freer commercial intercourse and no trade agreement should be judged wholly by custom house statistics.

We have reached a stage in our own development that calls for a statesmanlike and broad view of our future economic status and its requirements. We have drawn upon our natural resources in such a way as to invite attention to their necessary limit. This has properly aroused effort to conserve them, to avoid their waste, and to restrict their use to our necessities. We have so increased in population and in our consumption of food products and the other necessities of life, hitherto supplied largely from our own country, that unless we materially increase our production we can see before us a change in our economic position, from that of a country selling to the world food and natural products of the farm and forest, to one consuming and importing them. . . . A farsighted policy requires that if we can enlarge our supply of natural resources, and especially of food products and the necessities of life, without substantial injury to any of our producing and manufacturing classes, we should take steps to do so now. We have on the north of us a country contiguous to ours for three thousand miles, with natural resources of the same character as ours which have not been drawn upon as ours have been, and in the development of which the conditions as to wages and character of the wage earner and transportation to market differ but little from those prevailing with us. The difference is not greater than it is between different States of our own country or between different Provinces of the Dominion of Canada. Ought we not, then, to arrange a commercial agreement with Canada, if we can, by which we shall have direct access to her great supply of natural products without an obstructing or prohibitory tariff? This is not a violation of the protective principle, as that has been authoritatively announced by those who uphold it, because that principle does not call for a tariff between this country and one whose conditions as to production, population, and wages are so like ours, and when our common boundary line of three thousand miles in itself must make a radical distinction between our commercial treatment of Canada and of any other country.

The Dominion has greatly prospered. It has an active, aggressive, and intelligent people. They are coming to the parting of the ways. They must soon decide, whether they are to regard themselves as isolated permanently from our markets by a perpetual wall or whether we are to be commercial friends. . . . Should we not now, therefore, before their policy has become too crystallized and fixed for change, meet them in a spirit of real concession, facilitate commerce between the two countries, and thus greatly increase the natural resources available to our people?

I do not wish to hold out the prospect that the unrestricted interchange of food products will greatly and at once reduce their cost to the people of this country. . . . But a source of supply as near as Canada would certainly help to prevent speculative fluctuations, would steady local price movements, and would postpone the effect of a further world increase in the price of leading commodities entering into the cost of living, if that be inevitable.

In the reciprocal trade agreement numerous additions are made to the free list. . . . By giving our people access to Canadian forests we shall reduce the consumption of our own, which, in the hands of comparatively few owners, now have a value that requires the enlargement of our available timber resources.

Natural, and especially food, products being placed on the free list, the logical development of a policy of reciprocity in rates on secondary food products, or foodstuffs partly manufactured, is, where they cannot also be entirely exempted from duty, to lower the duties in accord with the exemption of the raw material from duty. This has been followed in the trade agreement which has been negotiated. . . .

Both countries in their industrial development have to meet the competition of lower priced labor in other parts of the world. Both follow the policy of encouraging the development of home industries by protective duties within reasonable limits. This has made it difficult to extend the principle of reciprocal rates to many manufactured commodities, but after much negotiation and effort we have succeeded in doing so in various and important instances.

The benefit to our widespread agricultural implement industry from the reduction of Canadian duties in the agreement is clear. . . .

My purpose in making a reciprocal trade agreement with Canada has been not only to obtain one which would be mutually advantageous to both countries, but one which also would be truly national in its scope as applied to our own country and would be of benefit to all sections. . . . That the broadening of the sources of food supplies, that the opening of the timber resources of the Dominion to our needs, that the addition to the supply of raw materials, will be limited to no particular section does not require demonstration. The same observation applies to the markets which the Dominion offers us in exchange. As an illustration, it has been found possible to obtain free entry into Canada for fresh fruits and vegetables—a matter of special value to the South and to the Pacific coast in disposing of their products in their season. It also has been practicable to obtain free entry for the cottonseed oil of the South—a most important product with a rapidly expanding consumption in the Dominion. . . .

Reciprocity with Canada must necessarily be chiefly confined in its effect on the cost of living to food and forest products. The question of the cost of clothing as affected by duty on textiles and their raw materials, so much mooted, is not within the scope of an agreement with Canada, because she raises comparatively few wool sheep, and her textile manufactures are unimportant.

This trade agreement, if entered into, will cement the friendly relations with the Dominion which have resulted from the satisfactory settlement of the controversies that have lasted for a century, and further promote good feeling between kindred peoples. It will extend the market for numerous products of the United States among the inhabitants of a prosperous neighboring country with an increasing population and an increasing purchasing power. It will deepen and widen the sources of food supply in contiguous territory, and will facilitate the movement and distribution of these foodstuffs.

The geographical proximity, the closer relation of blood, common sympathies, and identical moral and social ideas furnish very real and striking reasons why this agreement ought to be viewed from a high plane.

Since becoming a nation, Canada has been our good neighbor, immediately contiguous across a wide continent without artificial or natural barrier except navigable waters used in common.

She has cost us nothing in the way of preparations for defense against her possible assault, and she never will. She has sought to agree with us quickly when differences have disturbed our relations. She shares with us common traditions and aspirations. I feel I have correctly interpreted the wish of the American people by expressing in the arrangement now submitted to Congress for its approval, their desire for a more intimate and cordial relationship with Canada. I therefore earnestly hope that the measure will be promptly enacted into law.

Source: Richardson, James D. *A Compilation of the Messages and Papers of the Presidents 1789–1897*. Vol. 16. New York: Bureau of National Literature, 1897, 7581–7586.

28. WOODROW WILSON (1856–1924)

Presidential Term (1913–1921)

CHRONOLOGY

December 28, 1856—Woodrow Wilson is born in Staunton, Virginia.

September 29, 1879—Wilson attends Princeton College (University).

June 24, 1885—Wilson marries Ellen Louise Axon.

April 16, 1886—The couple's first daughter, Margaret, is born.

May 1886—Wilson earns a PhD from Johns Hopkins University.

August 28, 1887—Daughter Jessie is born while Wilson is teaching at Bryn Mawr College.

August 16, 1889—Daughter Eleanor is born while Wilson is teaching at Wesleyan University.

June 9, 1902—Wilson is named president of Princeton.

November 8, 1910—Wilson, a Democrat, is elected governor of New Jersey.

November 6, 1912—With a split Republican Party, Wilson wins the presidential election, beating Progressive Party candidate Theodore Roosevelt and Republican incumbent William Howard Taft.

April 3, 1913—Henry Ford produces the first assembly line Motel T automobile.

April 8, 1913—States ratify the Seventeenth Amendment, making way for the popular election of U.S. senators.

October 3, 1913—Wilson signs the Underwood Tariff, which reestablishes a federal income tax.

October 10, 1913—The Panama Canal is completed and later opens on August 15, 1914.

December 23, 1913—President Wilson signs the Federal Reserve Act, establishing the Federal Reserve System as a central bank in the United States.

July 28, 1914—World War I begins; Wilson declares U.S. neutrality.

May 7, 1915—A German submarine sinks the British passenger liner *Lusitania*, killing 1,198 passengers and crew, including 128 Americans.

December 18, 1915—Wilson marries Edith Bolling Gait.

October 16, 1916—Margaret Sanger opens the first birth control clinic in Brooklyn, New York.

November 7, 1916—Wilson wins a second term as president, defeating Democrat Charles Evans Hughes.

March 3, 1917—The secret Zimmerman Note, a telegram from the German Foreign Office sent in January to the German ambassador to Mexico suggesting a German-Mexican military alliance, is released to the public.

April 2, 1917—Jeanette Rankin becomes the first woman elected to House of Representatives.

April 2, 1917—The United States declares war against Germany.

January 8, 1918—Wilson delivers his Fourteen Points address to Congress, stating the U.S. principles for peace.

November 11, 1918—An armistice ends World War I.

January 18, 1919—The Paris Peace Conference begins.

January 29, 1919—Congress ratifies the Eighteenth Amendment, prohibiting the sale and manufacture of alcohol in the United States.

June 29, 1919—The Versailles Treaty is signed, which includes the creation of the League of Nations.

September 25, 1919—Wilson begins an extensive train trip to promote the League of Nations.

November 16, 1919—President Wilson suffers a stroke and returns to Washington.

March 19, 1920—The Senate rejects the Versailles Treaty and the League of Nations.

August 18, 1920—Tennessee ratifies the Nineteenth Amendment, giving women the right to vote; it is the last state ratification needed to amend the Constitution.

November 2, 1920—Republican Warren G. Harding defeats James Cox in the presidential election.

December 19, 1920—Wilson receives the Nobel Peace Prize.

February 3, 1924—President Wilson dies.

BIOGRAPHICAL SKETCH

Woodrow Wilson served as the 28th president of the United States. Through a succession of vocational changes, he became first a lawyer, a college professor, and then the president of Princeton University. Thereafter, the opportunity to run for the governorship of New Jersey presented itself, and he ran for that office and won, serving in that capacity from 1911 to 1913. Subsequently, Wilson ran for president of the United States, won the election, and served from 1913 to 1921.

On December 28, 1856, Thomas Woodrow Wilson was born in Staunton, Virginia, to Joseph Ruggles Wilson, an ambitious clergyman who aspired to advance his reputation in the Presbyterian Church, and Janet Woodrow, who came from a family of long-distinguished ministers in the same church. Wilson's middle name, Woodrow, was chosen to emphasize the prominence of his mother's family. Wilson grew up in the South, and most of his education rook place there. However, his interests over the years became increasingly focused on the politics of the United States and on its government and its policies.

Woodrow Wilson's early life was closely connected to the Presbyterian Church. During the Civil War (1861–1865), the Southern branch of the Presbyterian Church separated from the Northern church, and the Reverend Dr. Wilson was involved in the organization of the Southern Presbyterians. When he was nine years old, Wilson had a close relationship with his mother and father, but it was his father who became his mentor and counseled him, even when he later attended college at Princeton. During his childhood, Wilson had difficulty reading. His parents never considered this a serious problem and praised his other high mental abilities.

In 1870, the Wilson family moved to Columbia, South Carolina, where Wilson's father became professor at the Columbia Theological Seminary. During this period, Wilson enjoyed music and played baseball. In 1873, he entered Davidson College in North Carolina for a year, where he took great interest in the debating and literary societies. Meanwhile, he prepared to enter the College of New Jersey, popularly called Princeton. He entered Princeton in 1875 and made intellectual headway. By his senior year, he wrote for *The Princetonian*, the college newspaper, and was its managing editor.

In 1879, now 22 years old, he started going by the name Woodrow Wilson and entered law school at the University of Virginia. For years, Wilson's father prepared for him to become a lawyer, and Woodrow was a dutiful son, but he found the rigor of studying law tedious. Even though he was an excellent debater, the competition at Virginia was daunting. Nonetheless, he made numerous friends and polished his debating and writing skills.

In January 1882, Wilson moved to Atlanta, Georgia, and began practicing law with Edward L. Renick, a classmate of his at University of Virginia. The law partnership languished for a year. By this time, Wilson considered the practice of law drudgery. In September 1883, he decided to study for a new profession as a professor and applied to graduate school at Johns Hopkins University in Baltimore. Earlier, while in Atlanta, he fell in love with Ellen Axson and planned on proposing to her. As he was traveling north to Johns Hopkins in January 1883, he accidentally crossed paths with Ellen in Asheville, North Carolina. He proposed to her, and she accepted.

When Wilson arrived at Johns Hopkins, he was one of numerous political science graduate students. From January to September 1884, Wilson wrote a book, *Congressional Government*, published in January 1885, which received considerable attention and advanced his career. He received his PhD at Johns Hopkins in 1886.

On May 18, 1884, Ellen's father, Samuel, died. Wilson helped her settle her father's estate, and she used part of the money to enroll in the Art Students

League in New York. Still unmarried, Wilson began looking for employment. An associate professor of history position turned up at Bryn Mawr, a new women's college in Pennsylvania. In May 1885, Ellen Axson and Woodrow Wilson married in an inauspicious ceremony conducted by his father, Joseph, and Ellen's grandfather, Isaac Axson.

When the Wilsons headed north to Bryn Mawr, Ellen was pregnant with her first child, Margaret. Later, she had two more daughters, Jessie and Eleanor. Wilson continued his prolific writing at Bryn Mawr, publishing as well as teaching. His growing, impressive list of publications continued to earn him a solid reputation, and he convinced Bryn Mawr to raise his salary and hire an assistant for him.

In 1888, when Bryn Mawr failed to hire an assistant, Wilson's lawyer used this omission as a pretext for Woodrow to move on to Wesleyan University in Middleton, Connecticut, at a higher salary with fewer duties. His goal was a professorship at Princeton. Meanwhile, he used his network of friends at Princeton to aid him in getting on at the school. In 1890, he finally became the chair of Jurisprudence and Political Economy at Princeton, where many of his old classmates filled key positions. Wilson discovered the college had grown in size since he'd attended there, but not in vision. He saw opportunities to advance his educational ideas by emphasizing a broader perspective in academics at Princeton. The president at the time, Francis Patton, posed a roadblock to his plans. Wilson, meanwhile, became the most popular teacher at the school. In 1896, however, he suffered numbness in his right hand, indicating he might have had a mild, early stroke.

In 1898, the University of Virginia, with the backing of Virginia's governor and school faculty, attempted to recruit Wilson. Princeton reacted by raising his salary. In 1902, Princeton's faculty, along with Andrew Fleming West, the dean of the graduate school and a close coterie of Wilson's faculty friends and school trustees, agitated for Wilson to replace the unimaginative Patton as president. Patton got wind of the scheme and offered to accept generous terms from the school in return for resigning. Woodrow Wilson then took the helm.

Wilson was inaugurated as the president of Princeton on October 15, 1902. Wilson was entering a new

Woodrow Wilson (Library of Congress)

phase in life, made clear by the luminaries who attended his ceremony: former president Grover Cleveland, financier J. P. Morgan, William Dean Howells, Booker T. Washington, and several prominent publishers. Wilson wasted no time informing the university trustees that Princeton was underfunded, its faculty was poorly paid, and a campaign to raise money was his top priority. He envisioned transforming Princeton into a top-ranked university. Wilson immediately targeted the richest men in the nation for donations—men like Andrew Carnegie and J. P. Morgan. Wilson intended to recruit some of the best teachers in the nation, and he skillfully conducted their interviews. Wilson also picked talented faculty for his staff as well as fresh talent from other universities. He chose trusted friend John Hibben as his second in command and continued Andrew Fleming West as dean of the graduate school.

Meanwhile, Wilson organized the college into 11 departments and established a tutorial system managed by 46 "preceptors," most of them PhDs. Each advised and instructed small groups of students and suggested their reading programs. Wilson then agitated for what he called his "Quadrangle plan." His objective was to create a more socially integrated, intellectual campus life. The plan would organize the undergraduates into residential units where they would be monitored by faculty. Greek-letter fraternities at Princeton were eliminated earlier and replaced with "eating clubs," which served the role of establishing a social hierarchy. Wilson's misperception of the power and entrenchment of the eating club advocates and his controlling manner ultimately aroused widespread resistance at Princeton when he sought to abolish the clubs. As president of Princeton, after five years of infighting with his opponents over his attempts to democratize the school, Wilson was being edged out of his position at the university.

Wilson recognized his support at the college had diminished and began looking for a new career. Having presented hundreds of speeches over the previous several years, Wilson had encountered many important people, one of whom encouraged him to run for political office, George Harvey, of *Harper's Weekly*, who mentored him on his political chances, had contacts with big city bosses and the "boss machine" in New Jersey. He contacted James "Sugar Jim" Smith, a former U.S. senator, and persuaded him to support Wilson for governor. Harvey and Smith perceived Wilson as a conservative and believed he could be controlled politically.

Wilson was invited to the Democratic Convention in Trenton on September 15, 1910, where Smith and Harvey rounded up enough votes for Wilson to win the nomination. When he accepted the nomination the next day, he said he would single-mindedly serve the people and honor no pledges violating that promise. The bosses figured this was just usual loose political talk. When Wilson ran against his Republican opponent, Vivian M. Lewis, he accused the Republicans of running an unholy alliance with the moneyed class. On November 8, Wilson was elected by a wide margin and began carrying out his "progressive" policies. His conservative backers were astonished and enraged. Nonetheless, Wilson began initiating a number of laws to remedy corrupt elections, control corporations, economize government, equalize taxes, and enforce employers' liability for workplace injuries. Instead of dropping these prospective laws in the lawmakers' laps, Wilson went to the legislatures and promoted and explained each law in detail, and they were passed.

Wilson's many innovations in New Jersey government and the impact of his early victories faded by 1912, however, when his Democratic opponents and progressive Republicans combined to create a Republican-dominated legislature. Afterward, control of the legislature alternated and Wilson's attention became engaged in the presidential election campaign.

As 1912 edged closer, George Harvey, Wilson's mentor when he gained the governorship of New Jersey, groomed him to run for president. Republican President William H. Taft, in the meantime, decided to run for reelection, and his former mentor and predecessor, Theodore Roosevelt, disappointed by Taft's lackluster administration, decided to run against him. Roosevelt split from the Republicans and created the Progressive Party, known as the Bull Moose Party. Wilson and Harvey saw this division in the Republicans as a huge opportunity for the Democrats.

When the Democrats conducted their convention in Baltimore, only two candidates seemed capable of winning: Representative James Beauchamp "Champ" Clark of Missouri and Governor Woodrow Wilson. Handlers for both candidates attempted to collect a majority of the needed votes, but Wilson captured the nomination when William Jennings Bryan released his Democratic delegates to Wilson, but not until the 46th ballot.

When the campaign opened, Taft continued in the race but stayed home at the White House. Roosevelt and Wilson immediately set out on nationwide tours. Wilson described his political program as "New Freedom," attacked trusts and monopolies, advocated greater power for unions, and supported an income tax, stronger regulations on drugs and food, and reforms of public utilities. Ultimately, Wilson won the election by a plurality of 42 percent of the popular vote and 435 electoral votes. Roosevelt trailed with 27 percent of the popular vote and 88 electoral votes. The new president warned the political bosses that no one would receive special favors from him.

President Wilson took office in March 1913 and began enacting his progressive reforms. He chose not to send a State of the Union message to Congress but went directly to a joint session of Congress and outlined his case for lower tariffs and saw the Underwood Tariff bill enacted, lowering rates from 41 to 27 percent.

Next, Wilson placed restrictions on the banking system, convincing both houses to pass a law limiting the power of monopolies and creating a Federal Trade Commission, which ensured fairer business practices. He also introduced the Clayton Antitrust Act, passed to strengthen the Sherman Antitrust Act (1890). Meanwhile, labor and agricultural organizations were exempted from being considered trusts.

Meanwhile, news from Europe dampened American spirits. World War I in Europe commenced on July 28, 1914, creating fear among Americans that the United States would get drawn into the struggle. Wilson hoped to avoid entanglements but was wary. He hoped to continue his domestic program. Meanwhile, another tragedy occurred in Wilson's family when his wife, Ellen, died unexpectedly of nephritis in August. This desolated Wilson so much that he had difficulty carrying out his duties. Fortunately for his mental state, he was soon introduced to a Virginia widow, the wealthy Edith Galt (1872–1961), who became his friend and lifted his spirits. She became his fiancée, and they married on December 18, 1915.

Another crisis soon unfolded. The United States became involved in a threat of war with Mexico. Relations between the two countries had become strained in 1913 after President Francisco Madera was deposed by revolting units of the Mexican Army, and General Victoriano Huerta, who replaced him as president, had Madera killed. Important American business interests pressured Wilson to recognize the new leader, but he refused, and relations between the two countries became tense. When Mexican authorities arrested American sailors in Tampico, the conflict heated up further. The U.S. sailors were eventually released, but many Americans were angry.

The commander of the U.S. fleet at Tampico, Rear Admiral Henry Mayo, demanded that Huerta raise the American flag over Tampico and give the United States a 21-gun salute. Huerta refused. On April 21, 1914, Wilson sent troops to Veracruz and occupied the town. Further engagements became unnecessary,

though, when Argentina, Brazil, and Chile offered to act as mediators and Huerta resigned. Venustiano Carranza was installed as the new president, but many Mexicans were displeased.

In May 7, 1915, the United States learned that a German U-boat had attacked a British passenger liner, the *Lusitania*, and 1,200 lives were lost, including 128 Americans. Wilson's advisors failed to agree on a response to this crisis. Some believed it called for war, but Secretary of State William Jennings Bryan vigorously opposed that alternative. Bryan also opposed Wilson when he sent an acrimonious letter to the German government scolding them for their actions, which had caused the deaths of innocent people. The Germans' hostile response angered Wilson, and he warned the Germans against further attacks, saying that they would be considered attacks on the United States. Bryan disagreed with this policy and resigned.

On March 9, 1916, Pancho Villa, a revolutionary leader, led a raid on Camp Furlong, New Mexico, which was repulsed. In fleeing, the Mexicans rode through Columbus and killed eight American civilians. Consequently, Wilson sent General John Pershing and the U.S. Expeditionary Force into Mexico to capture Villa, but they were unsuccessful, and Wilson eventually recalled them.

In 1916, Wilson's campaign for reelection required all the ingenuity and organizational genius he and his staff could generate to gain success. The demographics suggested failure for Wilson. Roosevelt would not be in the campaign this time, so Wilson would not have the power that divisions in the Republican Party gave him the first time. Nonetheless, Wilson had had a successful first four years in the White House and sought to parlay that into another win. This time, he developed a platform that would generate progressive votes: laws promoting workers' health and safety, an unemployment compensation law, child labor proscriptions, a minimum wage law, a six-day workweek, eight-hour workdays, and pro-women's suffrage support.

But Wilson's opponent, Supreme Court Justice Charles Evans Hughes, was no pushover. He was handsome, had great speaking abilities, and was a hard campaigner. Like Wilson, he had little charisma and demonstrated a cold personality. Wilson's main advantage was his campaign slogan, "He kept us out of war." No one realized how tenuous that promise would be. When the vote came in, it was one of the tightest elections on record, with Wilson winning the electoral vote by only 24 votes. Wilson won California by only 3,806 votes; had he lost the state, Wilson would have lost the election.

After his reelection, Wilson focused on how he would address the war in Europe, which he knew the United States was likely to enter. He had made few preparations for the United States to enter the war. Wilson soon learned that the Atlantic Ocean no longer offered the protection it once had. The United States' position of isolationism disappeared when British intelligence decoded a telegram between German foreign minister Arthur Zimmerman and the German ambassador in Mexico. The message advocated an alliance between Germany and Mexico should the United States engage in the war supporting the Allies (Britain, France, and Russia). Moreover, the Germans were offering to financially support Mexico so it could reconquer New Mexico, Arizona, California, and Texas. Weeks earlier, Wilson also learned that Germany intended to resume unrestricted submarine warfare in the Atlantic and had ordered the German ambassador to leave the country.

On April 2, 1917, President Wilson addressed a joint session of Congress and asked for a declaration of war against Germany, which was approved on April 6, 1917. Allied leaders were relieved and planned to use U.S. troops as replacements for their own. Wilson refused that plan, however, and placed U.S. soldiers under General John J. Pershing, commander of the American Expeditionary Force (AEF). A draft was introduced, and a War Industries Board was formed.

When American forces began arriving in Europe in large numbers in late 1917, the balance of military power swung steadily to the Allies. The Germans were desperate, and on May 21, 1918, they launched the Ludendorff Offensive, which sought to defeat the Allies before more American power could arrive. Ludendorff's attack was repulsed, however, and Germany's situation worsened, riots erupted, and Germany's allies began suing for peace. On November 11, 1918, an Armistice was signed.

Wilson foresaw the defeat of Germany as early as January 1918, when he announced his Fourteen Points, which he insisted would provide a foundation for world peace when the war ended. The points were eventually agreed to by England, France, and Italy, but punitive changes were incorporated later, when conversation turned to land grabbing and talk of war reparations by Germany. The Allied leaders agreed on Wilson's concept of a League of Nations, which was included in the Treaty of Versailles, signed in June 1919. But Wilson was never able to convince the Senate to ratify that part of the treaty. While attempting to persuade Senators to do so, he suffered a debilitating stroke, which disabled him and severely limited his ability to perform his presidential duties. His wife, Edith, and his cabinet concealed the full extent of their knowledge concerning his condition until the close of his presidency, and Edith acted as gatekeeper for any contacts with Wilson.

With the inauguration of Republican president Warren G. Harding in 1920, Wilson left the White House and returned to private life. His health improved somewhat, and he remained involved in Democratic Party politics for the next four years until February 3, 1924, when his physical condition steadily deteriorated and he died. Thomas Woodrow Wilson's dying words were, "I am ready. When the machine is broken . . . I am ready" (*New York Times*, February 3–4, 1924).

HISTORICAL OVERVIEW

President Woodrow Wilson's experience in public life as he transitioned from professor to college president of Princeton University, governor of New Jersey, and president of the United States was dramatic. Indeed, he advanced to the last two positions within two years, demonstrating a meteoric rise to a high estate. The conditions in the United States immediately before and during Wilson's rise to power reveal the political trends apparent during his two terms as president from 1913 to 1921, when Wilson managed his momentous accomplishments and established himself as one of the United States' most productive presidents.

He proactively addressed some of these important trends apparent in the United States before and during his political career by introducing legislation to positively affect them. He was generally aloof to, ignored, or was disinterested in some other trends. For instance, most of Wilson's education took place in the South not long after the Civil War. Yet that war and the attitudes and resentments it engendered in most Southerners did not seem to affect him.

Although Wilson experienced the dislocating effects of the South's reconstruction period during his youth and witnessed the domination of the Southern people by Northern troops and carpetbaggers, he never acquired the bitterness that many Southerners felt about the war and the harsh Northern control of his area after it. Later in life, he defended the centralized government that brought on the South's defeat. In later years, some say, he did not even exhibit a trace of a Southern accent. But he did understand and share the general Southern ethos, especially in reference to black people, although not in as pronounced a degree as some other Southerners.

Other social and historical influences, however, made an enduring impression on Wilson before he finally took up politics at the age of 54. Populism was one of these powerful influences. Populism became recognizable in the 1870s and prominent around 1880, and its effects continued through World War I (1914–1918). Populism originated among Midwesterners and Southerners and began in the creation of farmer's alliances in the 1880s, in which the farmers organized politically to lessen the distress experienced by rural economies caused by falling prices, extensive crop failures, insufficient credit facilities, and poor marketing advantages. During the 1892 national election, farmers formed the Populist (or People's) Party and advocated the unlimited minting of silver, which they believed would create inflation and lessen the impact and severity of their personal debts. Their candidate, James B. Weaver, received more than a million votes—a far from insignificant outcome, but worth only 22 electoral votes.

By 1896, the populists united with the Democrats and chose William Jennings Bryan as their presidential candidate, and he became the national leader of the Free Silver Movement. Through their affiliation with the Democratic Party, populists advocated the increased coining of silver by the government at a ratio to gold of 16 to 1. Bryan made an impassioned, famous speech for silver at the Democratic National Convention at Chicago that year, referred to as his "Cross of Gold Speech." Nonetheless, Bryan was defeated by Republican William McKinley, 271 electoral votes to 176. Bryan ran against McKinley once more in 1900, and he lost to him again. Bryan ran for the presidency again in 1908 and lost to William Howard Taft. After that election, the populists lost much of their power, but some of their spirit remained in the Democratic Party. In 1913, Bryan became President Woodrow Wilson's secretary of state after securing the nomination for Wilson by turning his delegates over to him during the national convention. Later, Bryan resigned his position over a disagreement with President Wilson concerning what he considered Wilson's intemperate second message to Germany protesting the sinking of the *Lusitania* on June 8, 1915.

During the early 20th century, "muckrakers" proved effective in creating an impact on Wilson as well as many other Americans. These investigative journalists made their living by exposing governmental and business abuses, as they saw them, and backing up their contentions with evidence. They attacked the existence of slums, child labor, overpricing of needed goods, racial prejudice and discrimination, price extortion, and the quality of foods on the market. Their emphasis was on scandals, and their easy targets were often the wealthy and privileged of society.

John D. Rockefeller and his company Standard Oil were favorite targets, despite the fact that through forming monopolies, titans like Rockefeller were producing the lowest prices ever for gasoline. Their means and ways of obtaining success, however, seemed to be their main vices to the muckrakers, and other considerations were irrelevant. Muckraker figures like Ida Tarbell and Henry Demarest Lloyd became famous. Tarbell authored *The History of the Standard Oil Company* (1904), and Lloyd wrote "The Story of the Great Monopoly" (March 1881) in the *Atlantic Monthly*. Magazines like *Collier's*, *McClure's*, and *Everybody's* carried word of scandals. *McClure's* also published an article by Lincoln Steffens, "The Shame of the Cities," which resonated with Americans. Author Upton Sinclair's fictional book, *The Jungle* (1906), captured the reality of the American meat-packing industry and its tainted foods and excoriated the horrible working conditions suffered by people in that industry. His book inspired a new Food and Drug Act (1906). Another exposé led to the Hepburn Act (1906) enforcing regulations on the American railroads. Weeklies like the *Nation* and *New Republic* appealed to the upper middle class, elites, and upper crust with their scathing revelations. All such articles and books were meant to cast aspersions on corporate power and vices, anti–social exploitation, and unscrupulous business practices. These critical efforts inspired Americans to demand reforms, and Wilson, first as governor of New Jersey and then as president of the United States, was acutely aware of these sentiments, interests, and social trends, exploiting them thoroughly to advance his political fortune.

Another social influence was progressivism. The term applied to a variety of responses to the economic and social problems resulting from rapid industrialization introduced into the United States during the late 19th and early 20th centuries. Progressivism began as a social movement and evolved into a political movement. The early progressives rejected the late 19th and early 20th century concept of social Darwinism, which was used to justify imperialism, political conservatism, and racism designed to discourage interventionism and reform. In other words, progressives believed that the problems society faced—poverty, violence, greed, racism, and class warfare—were not natural and could best be addressed by providing good education, safe environments, and clean workplaces. Progressive leaders lived mainly in urban areas, were college educated, and believed that government could be used as a tool for change. Social reformers and writers like Jane Addams, Jacob Riis, Henry Lloyd, Lincoln Steffens, Upton Sinclair, and Ida Tarbell agitated for social change as progressives. The evils of corporate greed were censured, and tolerance and protections were sought for immigrants and the downtrodden in the spirit of democracy.

Progressive leaders urged all American voters to seek candidates who would fight political corruption and encouraged citizens to vote for leaders who would improve their lives. By voting for the first progressive president, Theodore Roosevelt—a Republican who attacked monopolies and the domination of the government by elite corporate heads and millionaires

through their control of members of Congress—the poor and less powerful believed they could ameliorate their economic and social situations. When Theodore Roosevelt became president in 1901, he urged federal regulations to curb monopolies, but his efforts were largely ineffectual. After the 1912 election, President Wilson continued the campaign of regulating the business community and personally took one bill after another to Congress, explained them in detail, and saw them passed into law, among them the Underwood Tariff Act (1913), which significantly lowered tariffs and resulted in cheaper prices for food and other necessary items used by most people. Under the Wilson administration, the Federal Trade Commission (FTC), established in 1914, was used to harness the power of businesses and corporations, supplement the Clayton Antitrust Act (1914), and bolster the earlier Sherman Antitrust Act (1890). The Clayton Antitrust Act called for the prosecution of directors and officers of companies who violated antitrust laws, and it defined unfair trade practices (such as predatory pricing, acquiring stock, and interfering with competition) and rules opposing interlocking directorates by companies that traded with one another. The Clayton Antitrust Act proved effective, but FTC actions proved ineffective and were frequently challenged in the courts.

In many respects, progressivism was curtailed during World War I, perhaps to facilitate the war effort. There was also a growing antagonism and cynicism toward Wilson when his 1916 reelection campaign slogan, "He kept us out of war," was remembered bitterly by many Americans and came back to haunt him. Scarcely five months after his reelection, Wilson asked Congress for a declaration of war against Germany so that the world could "be made safe for democracy."

After the breakout of World War I in Europe in 1914, Wilson carefully observed the war as he sought to avoid American entrance into it. Indeed, most Americans favored staying out of the war. By May 1916, Wilson was considering the formation of a League of Nations, a peacemaking organization and conference, which might arrange terms upon which the World War I combatants could agree and, in so doing, settle the war and end the fighting. On May 27, Wilson was invited to speak to an organization called the League to Enforce Peace (LEP), which was led by former president William Howard Taft. The LEP advocated a rough, general prototype for the later League of Nations, which was eventually proposed by Wilson and accepted by the Allies (Britain, France, and Russia). In mid-1916, Wilson and the LEP were already thinking ahead to the end of World War I and to an organization to prevent another such international conflict. Some of the ideas later incorporated into the League of Nations were discussed by the LEP in their meeting with Wilson. The president shared the speaker's platform with his longtime, bitter opponent, Massachusetts Republican Senator Henry Cabot Lodge, who a year earlier had called for great nations to unite in some form of organization to enforce peace. The "league of nations" concept was being entertained by a large number of politicians and intellectuals in the Unites States and elsewhere before the end of the war and as a reaction to its virulence, during which tens of millions of people died. In his speech, Wilson expressed his support of an international organization to enforce peace and to include peace negotiations to ensure the right of sovereignty to all nations, small or large. Wilson also proposed that all nations in the future should be made secure from aggression by other nations and interference in their sovereign rights.

In November 1916, while the war in Europe raged on but the United States remained neutral, Wilson met with Colonel Edward House, his full-time, unpaid adviser, about the need for a group to devise a plan for eventual peace talks and negotiations when Germany surrendered, which by this time Wilson considered a foregone conclusion. House led the search for such a group of Americans, enlisted their help, and guided them toward the formulation of a viable plan for peace. Of course, Wilson was continuously kept informed of the group's progress, helped clarify its objectives, and suggested possible points of departure. The group, called the Inquiry, operated "quietly," which in Wilson's lexicon meant "secret." It was an early think tank composed of knowledgeable and bright, first-rate thinkers operating outside the purview of the U.S. State Department. Specifically, it would gather and analyze information in relation to a projected future peace conference, and it would define a possible settlement. One of the better known members of the Inquiry was Walter Lippmann, the famous columnist

and intellectual. Others were academics and experts enlisted from Harvard, Princeton, Columbia, Yale, and the University of Chicago.

In October 1917, the Bolsheviks (Russian communists) seized control of the Russian government and opened up a civil war. Mutinies had occurred within the French Army. The situation for the Allies and the Central Powers (Germany, the Austro-Hungarian Empire, and the Ottoman Empire) was shaky, and countries in both belligerent alliances were nearing physical and economic collapse. Meanwhile, Wilson continued to announce to the world, the Allies, and especially the Central Powers that as president of the United States, he had no desire to see a change in national borders in Germany or in the Austro-Hungarian Empire. The United States, Wilson insisted, was not fighting for "aggression or indemnity," but for a "peace without victory." Ironically, most of these promises were not the aims of the Allies, which may have misinformed the Germans and the world of the Allies' real intentions when Wilson's statements were made. Moreover, the members of the Central Powers appeared to listen too much to the voluble Wilson and not enough to the leaders of Great Britain and France, which were the countries who later assessed the real costs of surrender of the Central Powers to the Allies. These heavy burdens were planned so as to inflict painful and damaging consequences for Germany, the Austro-Hungarian Empire, and the Ottoman Empire in land, treasure, and power. Britain and France effectively decided the fate of Germany. Wilson's Fourteen Points, which Wilson essentially added to the document along with his suggestion of a League of Nations, and Article XIV, which he termed its "Covenant," were characterized by some as fuzzy idealism and window dressing. The Fourteen Points left much unstated while the Allies (primarily Britain and France) passionately restructured Europe in their own self-interested way, which proved to include a punishing dismantling of much of Germany, Austria-Hungary, and the Ottoman Empire despite Wilson's objections. Huge monetary reparations were also exacted from Germany, which many believe inspired Germany to rearm and initiate World War II in 1939. Ironically, Wilson predicted all of this but could not prevent it.

Finally, on January 8, 1918, Wilson revealed his latest plans for an eventual peace conference and peace treaty to Congress, inspired by data compiled by Wilson's Inquiry group. These plans included Wilson's own guidance and inclusions, which was later called the Fourteen Points. These included the following:

I. The advocacy of open treaties instead of secret ones;
II. Freedom of the seas
III. Removal of tariff barriers to commerce
IV. Disarmament, except for that necessary for domestic, national security
V. Restructuring of colonies consistent with the interests of the colonial peoples
VI. Russia should be "unhampered and unembarrassed" by any limitations to her sovereignty
VII. German forces in Russia, France, Poland, and the Balkans were to be evacuated
VIII. Alsace-Lorraine was to be returned to France
IX. Italy should have borders "along clearly recognized lines of nationality"
X. Self-determination should be ensured for the various peoples of the former Austria-Hungary
XI. Independence of the "several Balkan States" should be enforced
XII. Sovereignty was to be offered to the ethnic Turks and "autonomous development" to other nationalities in the extinct Ottoman Empire
XIII. Poland was to be independent and identified by nationality and provided with "a free and secure access to the sea"
XIV. "A general association of nations must be formed under specific covenants for the purpose of affording mutual guarantees of political independence and territorial integrity to great and small states alike"

The 14th point included Wilson's suggestion for an international organization, which became the League of Nations (Link 1966–1993, 536–538). Whereas before Wilson talked fervently about wishing to stay out of World War I or to personally mediate its end, his thoughts and actions soon drifted steadily toward war and showed an urgency to enter the war.

Wilson's original objective in his Fourteen Points was to end the conflict and create an enduring peace settlement. He perceived of himself as the catalyst for such a peace, the leader of a demonstrated powerful country who would introduce this treaty to the Allies and eventually secure its acceptance. Wilson clearly overestimated his power and persuasiveness and quickly discovered that the Allied leaders had their own firm ideas of the final treaty outcome, which were not only far different from his own but also precluded his.

In October 1918, Germany, close to a military collapse, contacted Wilson to secure an armistice based on his Fourteen Points and other propositions that the president had voiced earlier. Wilson passed on the offer to the Allies, which was acceptable to them, except that Britain wanted to adjust the "free seas" stipulation in the Fourteen Points and both Britain and France insisted on unspecified German war reparations for civilian properties destroyed or damaged during the fighting. Also, the details of how the Central Powers were to be dismantled were left largely unspecified. In January 1919, a conference was convened in Paris. In his typical style, Wilson aggressively entered into a discussion with his Allied equals and tried vigorously to sell his Fourteen Points as the basis for a peace settlement. Instead, British Prime Minister David Lloyd George, Italian Prime Minister Vittorio Orlando, and French Prime Minister George Clemenceau revealed their own, quite different ideas regarding a proper settlement. They steadily and firmly outlined the settlement they wanted, and they listed in great detail what the immense war reparations Germany would suffer, with the payments continuing for years.

The European Allies considered World War I as Germany's fault, knew they were on the point of total military collapse now that the American Expeditionary Force (AEF) was fully committed, and intended to make the Germans pay a huge price for their weakness and defeat. Wilson had to have been shocked by his reception at the Paris conference and was sobered by his obvious lack of negotiating strength among his peers. He was forced to negotiate away many of the promises he'd made to the Germans and seriously compromised some of the tenets of his Fourteen Points, which he had proposed to Congress as a fair basis for peace. Meanwhile, in violating some of the principles of the Fourteen Points, the Allies, in the fashion of realpolitik, were intervening in the Russian Revolution. Indeed, so would Wilson in short order by sending small contingents of American soldiers to northern Russia and to Siberia, violating Wilson's own Covenant and its stated belief in self-determination for all nations. Wilson did get the Allies to use his Covenant and the League of Nations in the Versailles Treaty, and he helped preserve some of the integrity of most of Germany, except for the area adjoining Poland and Alsace-Loraine.

While the American public looked with approval on the signing of such a treaty, Wilson's blind trust that Congress would necessarily approve of the public's and president's wishes was thoroughly misguided. Wilson brought the treaty to Congress on July 10, 1919, and gave a 40-minute, flowery speech on its contents. The Senate balked at the treaty, and Wilson sought an up-and-down vote, but the Senate would not agree to do so. One congressman called Wilson's speech "soap bubbles and a soufflé." Another said it was "a fine lot of glittering generalities." An Arizona senator said, "His audience wanted raw meat, he fed them cold turnips" (Cooper 2011, 509). Lodge minced no words about his resistance to the treaty, which violated the United States' long-standing belief from the time of the Founding Fathers that the nation should avoid international entanglements in the form of binding treaties involving war. Senator Lodge authored a paper, ironically specifying 14 *objections* he and his Republican colleagues had with the treaty, especially Article XIV of the Covenant, which called for the United States to come to the aid of any of the signers of the treaty should they become involved in fighting a war. The Republicans insisted that Congress must have the sole right to decide when U.S. forces mobilize for war.

The crestfallen Wilson decided, as he usually did in serious conflicts, to resist domination, and he took the matter of the treaty to the people for them to decide. Wilson maintained that to give in to Lodge and his Republican colleagues' objections to Article XIV was a nullification of the treaty. Wilson made a long speaking tour in September 1919, which ended in his physical breakdown followed by a serious stroke on

October 2. When acceptance of the treaty was voted on again on November 19, 1919, and once more on March 19, 1920, the treaty failed ratification by a two-thirds majority.

A number of national political issues had developed during the war that blemished Wilson's presidency. War fervor in the United States ran high during World War I, but it was higher yet in the offices of the president and his cabinet. German and Italian immigrants were numerous in the country, some recent arrivals and others (in much larger numbers) long-term residents. Friction and suspicion existed throughout the nation from the start, some warranted but much of it not. Wilson addressed this nagging, dangerous problem of dissent with a rigid program of suppression. Wilson and the United States' leadership were compelled to consider possible subversive behavior by some Americans during World War I and to counter it when it was detected. World War I fighting was the most fierce, widespread, and brutal in European and American history, with 10s of millions of soldiers and civilians killed and wounded. The war had elicited feverish attempts by both sides to win, and animosities that had developed between the Allied countries and those of the Central Powers were extreme. The propaganda programs waged by both sides were exaggerated, often filled with falsehoods and scurrilous attacks. To offset possible disloyalty to the war effort in the United States, Wilson, through Congress, had two repressive laws passed in hopes of stifling American dissent, the Espionage Act of June 15, 1917, and the more severe Sedition Act of 1918. The Espionage Act called for imprisonment of anyone stating or spreading disloyal, profane, scurrilous, or abusive language against the U.S. government, military, flag, or president. The Sedition Act threatened imprisonment for those protesting the draft or criticizing the American government. In 1918 alone, 1,500 Americans were arrested for violating these laws.

Before the passage of the two bills, normal freedom of speech in the United States had allowed normal propagandists in some newspapers to promote evasions of the draft, but now that threatened the increasing need by the United States to induct soldiers to fight in Europe, and it interfered with Wilson's attempt to get American soldiers on the battlefields of

Western Europe as fast as possible to relieve the sagging defenses of the Allies and catch the increasingly vulnerable Germans unprepared for the huge influx of American fighting men entering the war on the side of the Allies. Nevertheless, draft boards across the country had called out draft numbers, already enlisting over 687,000 draftees in the struggle. Blacks were called into service as well as whites, and conscientious objectors were tried and usually imprisoned if they did not answer the call. Wilson also sought to censor the press, but his effort failed when the Congress deleted that portion of a new bill effecting newspaper censorship.

During this period, long-standing German American citizens experienced some of the most egregious suppressions of their rights when many of their schools where German was taught and spoken were closed. In addition, some orchestras fired German musicians or banned the use of German composers such as Beethoven, Brahms, and Mozart. Meanwhile, Wilson ignored or failed to criticize such actions. Moreover, some 1,000 workmen of the Industrial Workers of the World (IWW), a union, were arrested by a posse in Bisbee, Arizona; wrestled into boxcars; and taken to the middle of the desert and deposited there without food, water, or shelter. Furthermore, President Wilson ordered his attorney general, Thomas W. Gregory, to deploy a special committee of his agents, named by the president, to investigate the IWW in 33 cities. In early September 1917, Gregory's agents in his department's Bureau of Investigation, aided by the local police, seized the files and records of the IWW in these cities across the country. In September 1917, some 166 IWW leaders were indicted in Chicago, including the union's president, William D. "Big Bill" Haywood. Woodrow Wilson was intimately aware of all these actions performed by his subordinates and made no comments or exceptions to their actions.

Another government program and board, created in 1917 at the instigation of President Wilson, was the Committee of Public Information (CPI). Leadership of the organization was assigned to one-time muckraker George Creel. The idea driving the organization was to mobilize public opinion through various media, such as artistic posters, pamphlets, speeches, and films. Some of its artistic guidance and vision came from Austro-American Edward Bernays, nephew of

Dr. Sigmund Freud. Like his uncle, Bernays was inspired by symbols that suggested greater meaning than the discrete images themselves imparted. This knowledge could be tailored for the use of propaganda purveyors. Bernays was made head of the CPI's export service, which made him useful in the distribution of propaganda. To destroy the popular estimation of American and foreign Germans was one of the CPI's aims. One of the CPI's promoted films was *The Heart of Humanity*, which showed the bald-headed producer, actor, and director Erich von Stroheim donning a monocle (characteristic of some Germans) and acting in the role of a brutish "Hun," who is shown attempting to rape a woman and then throw a baby out of a window. One poster produced by the CPI showed Germans portrayed as drooling apes chasing after Lady Liberty. In addition, the CPI sent some 75,000 speakers throughout the United States to give 750,000 speeches to 11 million spectators in an attempt to interest them more intensely in the war and influence them to accept the same viewpoint as the Wilson administration. Wilson's goal was to disseminate what he termed as true information to the public, but in reality what was passed on was meant to influence Americans into thinking and feeling in ways consistent with U.S. policies, right or wrong. The CPI did not limit its propaganda reach to the United States but reached out to all the Allied nations with a steady flow of information to galvanize Allied (as well as American) support of the war.

For decades, Elizabeth Cady Stanton and Susan B. Anthony, through the National American Woman Suffrage Association (NAWSA), had agitated for the right for women to vote. By 1915, the organization was led by Dr. Anna Howard Shaw, a medical doctor, and Carrie Chapman Catt, a former teacher. The association sought to pressure the federal government into providing women suffrage, but their agitation failed. President Wilson convinced the women that they would be more successful by pursuing a state-by-state acquisition of voting rights, which would lead ultimately to national voting rights through an amendment to the Constitution. Meanwhile, NAWSA was contested by another women's suffrage group, the National Woman's Party (NWP), formed in 1916. Led by the youthful Alice Paul, the NWP advocated more aggressive tactics and a fight, including hunger strikes and picketing. This caused turmoil and wrangling with the government and police, but it obtained visibility for their organization. The NWP picketed Wilson's White House and chained themselves to the front fence. Consequently, they were arrested and fined $250 each, a huge fine, but they refused to pay it and were sentenced to seven months in a workhouse. When Wilson learned of the arrests, he was enraged and pardoned the ladies, but they refused the pardons and remained imprisoned. Alice Paul went on a hunger strike, and the authorities placed a tube down her throat and force-fed her. Finally, the ladies agreed to accept their freedom.

Meanwhile, NAWSA's campaign continued to focus on obtaining individual voting rights for women in as many states as possible. Already women had gained the vote in Wyoming Territory (1869), Utah Territory (1870), Washington Territory (1883), Colorado (1893), and Idaho (1896). NAWSA accelerated its campaign to obtain voting rights for women and gained voting rights in 15 states and partial rights in 26 other states. The Nineteenth Amendment to the Constitution was soon passed by the requisite number of states, and full voting rights were secured by a vote of Congress in 1920. Women in the United States were two years behind British women in obtaining their voting rights.

The American people had expected much of Woodrow Wilson's presidency, and they got it. When he became president, he immediately introduced, promoted, and saw through passage a number of far-reaching progressive bills: the Underwood Tariff Act, leading to cheaper prices of goods; the Clayton Anti-Trust Act, giving teeth to earlier bills introduced by President Theodore Roosevelt that had proved ineffective; and the installment of the Federal Trade Commission, used to further control and regulate powerful business cartels owned by prominent millionaires and to curb price fixing. Congress weakened these last two bills before passing them. The curbs on freedom of speech and assembly promulgated by Wilson during World War I, though, have received little current support, and neither have his cautious support of Women's suffrage or his weak attention to the plight of black people after the Civil War. Many believe these

last issues left a stain on his presidency. Nonetheless, Woodrow Wilson is still regarded as one of the nation's most admired presidents.

ANALYTICAL ESSAY

Great presidents have far from unblemished records. This includes the highly productive presidency of Woodrow Wilson. Leadership is a difficult task and draws on a wide variety of skills, knowledge, and insights in its effective accomplishment. In the case of Wilson's impressive political life, there were striking successes, as well as sometimes deficiencies that marred the final results of his successes as a leader. His strengths lay in his strong network of friends, his excellent communication skills, and his broad and insightful visions concerning politics and advancing his own ideas. However, the latter also served as a weakness at times when he pushed too hard for his own agenda instead of remaining flexible, as well as his idealistic approach to international affairs, an area in which he lacked a strong network of allies, and his power of persuasion proved unequal to the task.

Some of Wilson's traits as a leader were imbued in him as a youngster. Much of his early, effective training was the result of schooling and training by his father, a prominent Presbyterian minister, Joseph Ruggles Wilson. It was Joseph who introduced Tommy (as he was called within his family) in the adroit use of words and their manner of being spoken. Joseph taught his son how to talk and write effectively, to think sharply, and to express himself orally with great clarity, emulating in many respects language as it is spoken not so much as commonly written. Father and son, from the time Wilson was eight years old until he entered Princeton in 1875, talked about his father's Sunday sermons on the day afterward, discussing their content and the manner of their presentation and analyzing them in detail. Joseph taught Tommy to write and speak succinctly, expressing himself in direct and clear points. These skills were invaluable to him in his early, formal schooling at Princeton and other universities, and some of their effects were still dramatically apparent when Wilson became president of Princeton, served as governor of New Jersey, and ascended to the presidency of the United States. This training by his father in the use of language and its power in persuasion empowered Wilson in his campaigns, especially when he was challenged by reporters. His language skills later made him potent in promoting his various legislative proposals and bills in Congress and fending off congressmen who challenged him.

The religion Wilson absorbed through reading and talking with his father also infused in him a religious framework for his life, a belief that he was an instrument of God's will. This had both a positive and negative effect on his conduct. Such certainty in his beliefs led Wilson to assert himself strongly, aggressively, and successfully on his own behalf, believing that he had a deeper insight than others might have about what was true and good in politics, morality, and personal conduct. In Wilson's case, however, his certitude on behalf of his political aims was sometimes considered by others as intransigent, stubborn, and authoritarian, and that created resistance to his aims.

Although Wilson did not take up politics formally until he was 54 years old, he practiced many of the components of political leadership most of his life. Many leadership skills are general skills practiced during one's lifetime; for instance, networking is the creation of a mutual aid system by individuals, assisting them in forwarding their successful careers. Other components of leadership are organizing plans and initiatives, supporting a cause or causes, speaking in public, showing aggressiveness and initiative when necessary to stabilize interpersonal situations, learning to cooperate with others for common goals, acquiring skills to persuade others to your opinions, and developing necessary stratagems (sometimes to accomplish compromises). Wilson brought all these sorts of skills to the table when he took up politics and when he became president. By the time he became a professional politician, he was well grounded in many adaptable political skills. Someone once asked Wilson if he had difficulty operating as a politician in the hard-hitting world of professional politics. Wilson answered that if one compared politics as it is practiced in state legislatures and Congress with similar practices in universities, the applications of politics in a university were even more trying and demanding than those in Congress. Thus, so many qualities and skills that Wilson brought to the presidency were finely polished in his earlier experiences as a teacher and a colleague among peers in a university setting. This gave him the rigorous experience in interpersonal relationships necessary in a president of the United States and honed his confidence and poise.

In 1873, Wilson entered Davidson College in North Carolina and attended that school for a year, with plans to transfer to Princeton University. At Davidson, he fit in nicely and joined the local literary and debating societies. These activities indicated his interest in public speaking and a more intimate knowledge of writing, both adaptable to politics and the presidency. When Wilson enrolled at Princeton in 1875, his personality developed more maturity. At that time, Princeton had a long and famous history. One of its presidents was Jonathon Edwards, an esteemed Puritan divine who was a renowned master of the English language, and President James Madison, an alumnus of Princeton. The school was a staid Presbyterian one, and Wilson used this opportunity to expand his mind and read voraciously. Although he did not seek academic honors, he nonetheless remained in the top quarter of his class. He was pleased that his debating society emphasized politics, and this period opened up that subject for him; his interest in writing flourished as well. Both these clubs became the foundation for skills of use to a politician as well as for a skilled writer and speaker. These skills became instrumental when he ran for the presidency and took office. Wilson also became the general manager and a writer for the *Princetonian*, Princeton's college newspaper, and he exercised this opportunity to write on political subjects. Meanwhile, he developed his understanding of the need for the public to be better educated in political processes, and this became a tenet of his concept of leadership in politics. Already, Wilson insinuated himself steadily into leadership roles and demonstrated initiative, an essential political trait.

During his senior year, Wilson, now 21 years old, took time to write a fine essay, "Cabinet Government in the United States," which he submitted to the *International Review*, a prominent journal edited by a young Harvard University instructor, Henry Cabot Lodge, who later became a famous senator. By this time, Wilson was becoming interested in the possibility of eventually becoming a politician. His new writing success offered him a springboard into that profession through developing a reputation for himself as a political thinker and author. Wilson was able to bypass the ordinary low-level political maneuvering and office-holding contests by demonstrating his profound understanding of politics through his speaking and writing achievements.

In 1879, Wilson entered the law school of the University of Virginia with the goal of becoming a lawyer. His father had always encouraged him to become a lawyer. He found Virginia University compatible, made many friends there, joined a fraternity, continued to develop his writing skills, and became an expert debater. He spent the next 18 months living with his family in Wilmington while he studied for the bar. In the meantime, he published an essay in the *New York Evening Post* in February 1881, adding to his publishing résumé, this time on the national level. A good friend of his at Princeton, Robert Bridges, was now on the staff of the *Evening Post* and was a cog in his political network.

In January 1882, Wilson began a law practice in Augusta, Georgia, with Edwin I. Renick, a former classmate at the University of Virginia. In October 1882, Woodrow passed the Georgia bar examination with the highest score given and received permission to practice in the federal district court. Renick's and Wilson's law partnership was unsuccessful, but Wilson did have the opportunity to address the Tariff Commission, a congressional investigative body that met in Atlanta in August 1882, which earned a fine newspaper review by a friend of Renick's, Walter Hines Page of the *New York World*. Woodrow learned the advantage of connections and continued his relationship with Page for a number of years, with advantages for both. Wilson's Atlanta speech was one of his first in a long succession of speeches that he performed in the years to come, which eventually marked him as a leading political speaker, thinker, leader, and political performer—traits essential to a politician aspiring to high office.

In spring 1883, Wilson abandoned his law practice to become a college teacher and further develop his intellectual life. Wilson found the law stultifying and boring. By this time, and before leaving for graduate school at Johns Hopkins University, Wilson met a well-connected, beautiful, young Presbyterian girl, Ellen Axson, and fell in love. On the way to Johns Hopkins, he asked her to marry him, and she accepted. In 1884, Woodrow submitted a book manuscript to Houghton Mifflin, and it was accepted for publication in September 1884 and published in January 1885. Titled *Congressional Government*, it was immediately acclaimed widely and established Wilson as a first-rate writer and intellectual.

Upon leaving Johns Hopkins, Wilson began weighing his employment possibilities. A job soon materialized in January 1885 at Bryn Mawr, an associate in history position at a newly formed women's college in Pennsylvania. Wilson accepted it. By June 1885, he was married to Ellen Axson, and two months later, as they moved north to Bryn Mawr to establish their new home, they were expecting their first child, Margaret. In May 1886, he received his PhD from Johns Hopkins. This led to a three-year contract at Bryn Mawr at $2,000 a year. Wilson's reputation in academic circles continued to spread with his continued publication of articles and a textbook, and in June 1888 he received a job offer from Wesleyan University, Middletown, Connecticut, which offered him a higher salary than Bryn Mawr ($2,500) and a full professorship. Earlier, when he had accepted his new contract from Bryn Mawr, he had asked for and was promised an assistant to aid him with his classes. Because the administration failed to comply with that promise, Wilson used that lapse as a pretext, along with a lawyer's leverage, to break his contract and move on to Wesleyan, a men's college and his preference. Wilson was continually advancing to positions that would be essential to qualifying him for a high position, which would eventually culminate with the presidency of the United States.

During his tenure at Bryn Mawr, Wilson also taught classes at Johns Hopkins, and by 1889 he was receiving employment feelers from Princeton University, his favored academic destination. So far they were not aggressively interested in him, but his network friend, Bob Bridges, and other wealthy former classmates of his at Princeton—Cleveland Dodge, Cyrus McCormick, and Moses Taylor Pyne, the latter two now trustees at Princeton—were agitating on his behalf. The current president of Princeton, Francis

Landey Patton, finally relented to this pressure, and Moses Pyne sent Wilson a telegram on February 13, 1890, offering him a professorship at $3,000 a year. Wilson's addition to the faculty of Princeton saw the emergence of a new leader on campus and illustrates how leaders often emerge as the product of their networks as well as due to their own mental strengths and initiative. Most often, leadership is a composite of diverse qualities. Princeton served as an incubator, so to speak, for the further development of Wilson's leadership abilities.

When Wilson began his teaching at Princeton, still called the College of New Jersey in the fall of 1890, he found that the college had not improved or advanced in the 11 years since he graduated—in fact, it had regressed in his estimation. Wilson was quite aware of this situation and began to mull over it for several years, determining what the school needed to correct this situation and achieve respect as one of the United States' most distinguished educational institutions. Meanwhile, through dint of much hard planning and brilliant execution, he became the school's most popular lecturer for six consecutive years. During this period, he augmented his teaching salary with a rigorous schedule of contracted speeches and through writing articles in major journals. This was profitable for Wilson and advanced his reputation.

In the meantime, through his many personal contacts, Wilson developed a wide range of friendships at his college, including trustees and faculty, and also other important contacts when he gave speeches at various cities in the East and mid-South, many of which proved beneficial to him when he became a politician and ascended in stages to the presidency. As an example of his expanding reputation, the University of Illinois offered him its presidency, a high leadership position, at a salary of $6,000 in 1892, and the University of Virginia offered Wilson their presidency in 1898. He turned down both.

In 1895–1896, Wilson accepted contracts to write a serialized biography, *George Washington*, and twelve installments of *A History of the American People*, for which he would be paid a total of $42,000. That sum dwarfed his yearly salary and would amount to close to a half million dollars in today's money. President Theodore Roosevelt was aware of Wilson, had become one of his friends, and solicited him for educational advice. By this time, Wilson's thoughts on the deficiencies in the educational system at Princeton and elsewhere were becoming crystallized. In 1894, he had written an article, "University Training and Citizenship," in which he proposed that universities should expand the necessary reading in their curricula; he believed wide reading was the basis for high mental development. He suggested that colleges and universities should hire young tutors to guide manageable groups of students in their reading. At other times, he also suggested that Princeton should recruit better qualified instructors and professors and generate the needed funds to promote this important change. Through his wide friendships at Princeton and his publications, his thoughts became known throughout the university and beyond, and it developed an active advocacy for Wilson by many within the faculty and trustees. By 1900, a revolt was brewing against the current, unimaginative president of Princeton, Francis Patton, and the reform leadership included wealthy trustees, Moses Pyne and Cyrus McCormick, Wilson's friends, and Cornelius Cuyler. Patton's days as president were numbered. The faculty and trustees were looking for a dramatic, innovative change in leadership, and Dr. Woodrow Wilson was that change.

Wilson had taught at Princeton for over 10 years and was a highly respected teacher and intellectual leader; in fact, he was the faculty's star. His high reputation near and far also made him the natural man to replace Patton. Wilson was an obvious leader. What was more, he had the politics and the power within the trustees of the university to ensure that he obtained that position. Thus, Wilson was inaugurated on October 25, 1902, in a celebratory ceremony graced by some of the most prominent figures in America: former president Grover Cleveland; financier J. P. Morgan; Speaker of the House of Representatives Thomas B. Reed; Robert Todd Lincoln, Abraham Lincoln's only surviving son; prominent author William Dean Howells; Booker T. Washington; and numerous prominent national publishers (Wilson's associates). Although Andrew Carnegie was not present, he would be solicited to aid Wilson in obtaining the necessary monies to make his new educational programs work. Wilson was now a national figure.

Wilson did not wait for his inauguration to state his plans and objectives for Princeton, but during the summer of 1902 in a special status report to the trustees, he boldly outlined his intentions and plans:

1. Calling the university's situation critical, Wilson said the curriculum needed a radical new method. He maintained that "Reading subjects," such as economics, history, literature, politics, and philosophy, should be modified and augmented by what he called the "English Tutorial System."
2. To implement the system would require the hiring of 50 young teachers provided with contracts lasting a minimum of five years.
3. A number of distinguished professors should be hired to augment the current staff, and the science department needed improved facilities.
4. The above program would require an increase of $2.2 million in the existing monies on hand.
5. Money must be found to provide for these improvements, and Wilson would lead the search and interact personally to get the monies (with face-to-face leadership).
6. A graduate college was also needed to include a residential building, and two new schools were imperative: a law school and an advanced engineering school.

This plan was bold, farseeing, and a hands-on demonstration of intellectual and managerial leadership and brainpower. It captured the imagination of students, faculty, and trustees. Key to this plan was the acquisition of funds to make it happen. Wilson took that responsibility and initiative fully on his own shoulders, and he immediately began raising capital funds to pay for the plan by creating a list of patrons and visiting these wealthy men. He personally contacted and met with many other possible donors who had intermediate financial means and convinced them to help. Andrew Carnegie and J. P. Morgan were at the top of Wilson's list. Wilson's plan was a brilliant one characterized by considerable analysis, planning, initiative, and projected means of execution—a model of outstanding leadership, all the way from marshaling support for his proposals, explaining their scope, and outlining their costs and from where the money would

come. In all this effort on his part, Wilson demonstrated outstanding leadership.

By 1905, Wilson began recruiting 50 new teachers, preponderantly PhDs, to staff what he called a "preceptorial system" at Princeton to revitalize its instruction. These teachers were bright young men personally interviewed and chosen by Wilson, who would each lead and mentor a group of students at the college, which was at the heart of the system. This plan proved highly successful and popular with the trustees and faculty, and it reflected well on Wilson and enhanced his already impressive reputation. In mid-1906, however, Wilson had another physical problem when he arose one morning to find himself blind in one eye. He learned later it was caused by hardening of the arteries, and he took a two-month vacation, expecting to recover.

While Wilson basked in the admiration he received for his new ideas, he was driven to seek even more innovations. One of his new programs was to create new common buildings, residential units, where students would be supervised by their preceptors, and also a new graduate school building, which Wilson sought to build in the middle of the campus. He called it his Quad Plan.

But much fussing by the faculty began over how it should be done and where, and Wilson started squabbling with his peers over the details. His natural authoritarian nature, his stubbornness, and his general disposition to refuse to compromise or adjudicate differences with his scholarly brothers came into play—negative leadership characteristics. Furthermore, Wilson sought to do away with what they called "eating clubs" at Princeton, which served as substitutes for Greek letter societies at the college and were social discriminators. Wilson vehemently opposed the eating clubs and wanted them abolished. Before the dispute was resolved, the extinguishing of the eating clubs became a bridge too far, and a bitter feud developed in which Wilson's unyielding stand and his acrimony toward his opponents and refusal to compromise led to a failure in his leadership; and the trustees were discussing his removal. The end of his presidency appeared imminent, and he knew it. This was a learning moment for Wilson. One of the most important components of leadership is judgment. Wilson's reorganization of the building and instructional program at Princeton exhibited profound good judgment. His actions related to the eating clubs demonstrated failed judgment.

By 1910, Wilson's life at Princeton was finished. He had several options, of course. As it turned out, he did not want a quiet life as a professor, and neither was he perfectly set on another position as a college president. Thus, it was fortuitous that one of his network of friends, the prominent George Harvey of *Harper's Weekly*, suggested a new possible career for him in politics. To bolster his suggestion, Harvey had firm connections with Democratic politicians in New Jersey and prominent city bosses. He suggested to Wilson that these men could become interested in him as their candidate for governor of New Jersey through Harvey's intercession. These men were conservatives, and Wilson was not a known progressive (liberal), so Harvey thought that because of Wilson's reputation in New Jersey, he had an excellent chance to become the Democrats' winning candidate for governor.

One of Harvey's contacts was the wealthy James "Sugar Jim" Smith Jr., a former New Jersey senator and political boss. Smith's son-in-law, James Nugent, ran the Democratic political machine in Newark. In January 1910, Harvey assured Wilson that he had fixed it with Democratic leaders for Wilson to be their candidate for governor. On September 14, 1910, the day before the Democratic convention occurred in Trenton, New Jersey, various delegates met at the Trenton House Hotel, where Smith, Harvey, and Nugent went to the various hotel rooms gathering delegates committed to Wilson, resulting in his selection.

The next day, Wilson spoke to the Democratic convention and explained his political program. The party bosses likely believed he would fudge on these proposals once in office, and they believed he would be loyal to them instead of his plans. Wilson was a highly practiced speaker and created a powerful vision of his beliefs that day, captivating the progressive members of the party, some of whom cried during his talk. But the delegates who helped ensure Wilson's nomination were the political enemies of the bosses. Jim Smith even provided $50,000 for Wilson's upcoming campaign. Later, one of the progressives at the speech, Joseph Patrick Tumulty, became Wilson's

loyal right-hand man for most of his subsequent political career. Wilson traveled around the state in a hard-hitting contest that bowled over his Republican opponent, Vivian M. Lewis, a prominent lawyer. Toward the end of the campaign, on October 20 Wilson was forced by the trustees at Princeton to resign as president—a rancorous ending to his tenure there. But two weeks later, Wilson won the governorship race over Lewis by a wide margin. Wilson's victory received widespread coverage in New Jersey and the nation. He was riding a progressive wave of support, which extended across the country.

Meanwhile, Wilson ingratiated himself with many of the legislators at social gatherings and in a meeting with them at his office in Princeton, hoping to gain more leadership traction. Though somewhat stiff, Wilson could be charming in small doses. Next, he decided to take his comprehensive program of progressive legislation to the assembly, boldly going face-to-face with them, where he explained his proposals in great clarity and detail, exhibiting his capacity to lead. He covertly developed a coalition as well with some of the Republican legislators. His initiatives were extensive and far-reaching calling for (1) election reform, (2) public utility regulations, (3) an employers' liability law, (4) corrupt election changes, (5) stronger corporate regulations, (6) direct primary elections, (7) referendum and recall legislation, (8) tax reform, (9) addressing corrupt practices, and (10) campaign finance reform. Wilson became a dynamic, organizational genius and caucus leader, and he astonishingly won almost everything he sought. Meanwhile, he had learned how to bargain and compromise, and he created a national reputation for his leadership abilities. His last two years in office were more subdued, however, affected by the increasing resistance to his administration by the city political bosses and by Wilson's efforts to organize a national political campaign for the U.S. presidency.

In the early part of 1911, a campaign to gain Wilson the Democratic presidential nomination coalesced under the direction of three men who knew Wilson well and were part of his network of advocates. They sought to run their friend for president of the United States, a complex venture. The men first met on February 24, 1911, to organize their drive to obtain the nomination for Wilson, which included fundraising, a publicity strategy, and a western speaking tour. In addition, the governor needed to broaden his network of supporters to include William Jennings Bryan, who would be critical to his campaign. That March, Ellen Wilson, always alert to any advantage for her husband, learned that Bryan was soon to give a speech at Princeton Theological Seminary. She immediately telegraphed Wilson to come home now (he was out of town), and she invited Bryan to dine with them. The two men had never had cordial relations hitherto, and this was meant to bring the two men together. Mrs. Wilson believed this meeting got her husband in the White House. It wasn't that easy, but it was a good start, and Bryan's support was essential. Meanwhile, Wilson continued to give speeches widely. In the summer of 1911, Wilson replaced his campaign manager with William Gibbs McAdoo, a railroad manager and a Southern expatriate, like all of Wilson's handlers.

James Beauchamp "Champ" Clark, speaker of the House of Representatives, soon emerged as the leading candidate in the race and was difficult for Wilson to dislodge. Bryan was the X factor in the contest, however: he was the man who wielded a sizeable bloc of supporters and could decide the issue. After a number of ups and downs, Wilson's chances appeared dismal, Bryan's votes were still lined up for Clark, and Wilson's supporters were despondent. However, corrupt Tammany Hall (the Democrat political party machine who controlled much of the politics in New York City and the state of New York) added its New York votes to Clark's. This infuriated Bryan, and he ordered his followers to switch their votes from Clark to Wilson. Soon, votes began tumbling Wilson's way, and astonishingly he was victorious.

Wilson's opponents in the 1912 election were incumbent president William Howard Taft, former president Theodore Roosevelt, and Socialist Party candidate Eugene V. Debs. Roosevelt, denied the Republican nomination in favor of Taft, was forced to organize a new Progressive Party and vie with Wilson for progressive votes. Neither Wilson nor Roosevelt considered Taft competition and saved their barbs for each other. Wilson made himself open for advice, and many party leaders offered it. The most valuable suggestions came from Louis D. Brandeis, a brilliant,

well-respected lawyer, who provided Wilson with tactics to fend off his opponents on the critical subject of the trusts. Both Roosevelt and Wilson opposed the trusts, but the key was in how to fight them. Roosevelt wanted to regulate the trusts outright, whereas Wilson originally sought to destroy them. Brandeis suggested to Wilson a more workable alternative that would avoid direct government interference in the trusts. Brandeis's suggestion was to regulate competition *before* trusts formed. Wilson, an astute leader, exploited the genius of one of his followers.

An intense campaign now unfolded between Roosevelt and Wilson and spanned the nation. On October 14, 1912, as Roosevelt left a hotel in Milwaukee, a fanatic shot him in the chest, the bullet traveling through his steel eyeglass case and through a thick speech he carried with him, which may have saved his life. In typical heroic fashion, Roosevelt went on to give his speech until he faltered physically and was led off the stage. When Roosevelt temporarily suspended his tour, Wilson gallantly did the same. When the election finally commenced, Wilson went home to Princeton, and his phone jangled incessantly. Steady, positive reports continued to roll in. Finally, a loud bell rang outside, the Wilsons opened their front door, and Wilson's secretary, Tumulty, dashed in screaming, "He's elected, Mrs. Wilson!" Through intense effort, Wilson had mobilized his staff, campaigned skillfully, and led the Democratic Party to victory.

Almost immediately, Wilson launched into his new duties, one of which was to choose his new cabinet. This was a difficult problem seeing that Wilson was not part of the Washington scene and lacked the inside knowledge of who was best to fill the positions. Friends who had done service for Wilson were high on the list but would not fill all the necessary slots. In his typical leadership style, Wilson reached out to his wide range of advisors and friends, which included William Jennings Bryan, his most vocal and knowledgeable helpmate; Carter Glass of Virginia, chairman of the House Banking and Currency Committee; Colonel Edward M. House, who was quickly becoming his principal adviser; Professor H. Parker Willis; and Louis D. Brandeis. Some of the key people in his late campaign would receive favors: Bryan, as secretary of state; William Gibbs McAdoo, as secretary of the treasury; and Joseph Tumulty, as Wilson's secretary. Wilson listened to a lot of counseling about the other posts, but in the end he made his own decisions, tempered by the advice he had received—typical of his own leadership style.

Similar to his bold actions with the New Jersey legislature, Wilson met face-to-face with Congress and presented his progressive agenda in 1913. He had great strength in the House of Representatives but a small majority in the Senate, six seats. Nonetheless, Wilson was instrumental in getting the Underwood-Simmons Tariff Bill passed in 1913, which lowered tariff rates 14 percent but on condition of the ratification of the Sixteenth Amendment, which authorized the levying of the first constitutional tax on income, which was part of the tariff legislation. Wilson was brilliant in his stewardship of the bill through Congress after many failures by previous presidents. Two chairmen useful in the passage were given gold pens. Emboldened by his success with Congress on the tariff bill, Wilson began his campaign to pass a banking bill, ultimately titled the Federal Reserve Act. Wilson expected easy passage, but the conflict lasted eight months and involved continual wrangling over the bill until each group of partisans got something but none was happy. Wilson learned to control his temper and exasperation. The act was signed into law on December 22, 1913. In 1914, a Clayton bill proved equally difficult to pass; it was intended to strengthen the Sherman Anti-Trust Act, which had lacked strong enforcement provisions. Wilson tried to force its passage through Congress with some teeth left in it, but the bill ran into hornets' nests along the way in the form of senatorial and labor obstructions, so that when the bill passed on October 15, 1914, Wilson hardly acknowledged its passage. It became a failure. No gold pens were given on its passage, nor deserved to be.

By this time, World War I broke out in Europe, and Wilson's wife, Ellen, tragically died. At the same time, a Federal Trade Commission Act (1914) passed, which was meant to strengthen the earlier, anemic Clayton Act. Although it was lauded at the time, it had little effect on monopolies—its intention—and gave few advantages to labor. Wilson led and was a catalyst in the passage of all the above laws, and he repeatedly interacted with representatives in and out of the halls of Congress in a dynamic leadership manner.

In 1913, the United States was involved in an altercation with Mexican General Victoriano Huerta and, later in early 1916 to early 1917, with Francisco "Pancho" Villa after his forces entered New Mexico in a raid, but these situations were resolved. The United States was more concerned now with the extremely explosive war in Europe, where millions of soldiers were being killed and wounded. On May 7, 1915, 128 Americans lost their lives when a British liner, the *Lusitania*, was sunk by a German U-boat. Wilson sent a tough message to the Imperial German government. However, Secretary Bryan took exception with its abrasiveness and resigned; he was replaced by Robert Lansing. Other ships with Americans aboard were later sunk, with each incident followed by German "regrets." Wilson's attention at this time was also on his reelection campaign in 1916, in which he ran against Supreme Court Justice Charles Evans Hughes, a tough campaigner. The election ended in very close victory for Wilson, secured perhaps by his favorite campaign slogan, "He kept us out of war."

Meanwhile, the situation in Europe became grave. Word was received by Wilson on January 31, 1917, that Germany had resumed unrestricted submarine warfare. This act ratcheted up the cry for war in the United States, even among Wilson's cabinet, but the president still sought a peaceful resolution. Nonetheless, he broke diplomatic relations with Germany. On February 28, 1917, the impasse ended when news of a German telegram intercepted and decoded by British intelligence in mid-January reached the United States and was passed on to Wilson. It was the Zimmerman Telegram, a message sent from German Undersecretary for Foreign Affairs Arthur Zimmermann to the German ambassador in Mexico, ordering him to encourage Mexican President Venustiano Carranza to ally with Germany against the United States. The eventual reward for this alliance included a promise of money to Mexico as well as the opportunity for Mexico to regain its lost territory in Texas, California, Arizona, and New Mexico. Meanwhile, on March 5, Wilson was inaugurated for his second term as president. On Friday, March 30, 1916, at 8:32 p.m., Wilson went before a joint session of Congress and called for a declaration of war against Germany. Congress responded affirmatively on April 6.

Wilson's job now was to mobilize the United States for the war in Europe. The Allied powers wanted U.S. troops as replacements for their own decimated ranks. General John J. Pershing, consulted by Wilson, refused to agree to this plan and said that American soldiers should only fight in presently constituted U.S. units, and only when adequately trained for fighting. Wilson agreed. The U.S. Army, meanwhile, was designated the American Expeditionary Force (AEF). A War Industries Board was formed to ensure that military and industrial leaders efficiently coordinated the purchasing and pricing of war supplies, and it ensured mass production. Meanwhile, Wilson sought to facilitate the broad development of a war machine by cutting as much red tape as possible and injecting highly experienced leaders into key positions who could make quick and wise judgments as to what must be done and how to do it.

By this time, American forces began arriving in Europe in sizeable numbers, stabilizing the shaky Allied position. Germany's armies were nearing exhaustion, but they nonetheless moved large forces from the Russian front to make one last, desperate attack on the Allied forces in Western Europe, hoping to break through its defenses and defeat it before more American forces arrived. The German plan, called the Ludendorff Offensive, commenced on March 21, 1917. The British Fifth Army was driven back 30 miles by the German advance, causing the loss of 100,000 soldiers. French general and Allied supreme commander Marshal Ferdinand Foch managed to finally stabilize the Allied lines, however, and Ludendorff's gamble failed. Some 1.5 million combined casualties were the result. Om 1918, the AEF, adequately trained, finally entered the contest in force and won battles at Cantigny (May), Belleau Wood (June), Château Thierry (July), St. Mihiel (September), and Argonne Forest (September to the Armistice in November), but at a cost of 116,506 U.S. soldiers killed and another 204,002 wounded. Nonetheless, the Allied victories convinced the Central Powers that they were beaten, and amid German riots, they sued for peace and signed an Armistice on November 11, 1918.

Wilson and his entourage traveled to France to participate in the Paris Peace Conference, held in the Hall of Mirrors in the Palace of Versailles outside of Paris on December 3, 1918. The president was confident he could make a positive impact on the conference and obtain most of his objectives, including his concept of a League of Nations and his Fourteen Points Covenant, which outlined a settlement of the war. Wilson and some others under his direction had worked on this concept for a treaty as early as 1916, and the quest had culminated in a working group called the Inquiry in November 1917, which created what Wilson liked to call his Covenant. For the next several months, Wilson and his staff worked in Paris, returning periodically to the United States to regroup, and then they went to Paris again to continue hammering out an agreement. It was not easy. The principal representative for France, Foreign Minister George Clemenceau, and Britain's Foreign Minister David Lloyd George wanted to punish Germany, make it admit its fault for starting the war, and to force it to pay a horrendous amount of money as well as relinquish German territory as reparations.

Finally, after settling on an agreement with the Allies—in which Wilson lost most of his battles—he took the finished Treaty of Versailles home for Congress to ratify, which proved impossible because the Republicans and some Democrats had serious reservations about Article XIV of the Covenant, which called for the United States to give military support to any of the signers of the treaty involved in a future war. Republicans believed this concession violated the Monroe Doctrine, which warned Americans against entangling foreign alliances. Wilson sailed back to Europe in an attempt to gain further concessions from the Allies necessary to overcome congressional obstacles, but he did not succeed. When Wilson brought his treaty to Congress for approval, it twice failed to receive enough votes. Wilson, in failing health, began campaigning around the country to elicit public support to pressure Congress to sign the treaty. During these tours, he suffered two strokes, the last one of which permanently disabled him. President Woodrow Wilson was a great leader with considerable talents, but ultimately he met obstacles he could not overcome. His power in Congress was insufficient, and his connections and influence in Europe were feeble.

Presidential leadership is a complex phenomenon, the result of multifaceted and evolving experiences by a president. The capacity for leadership is molded over time. In the case of President Wilson, this knowledge and training included his exceptional early education during more than a decade of his life under the tutelage of his highly intellectual father, Dr. Joseph Ruggles Wilson, who took him under his wing and gave him (besides his public education) a thorough grounding in sophisticated rhetoric, molding his use of language into a sophisticated, persuasive tool for his later educational and lifetime pursuits. When Wilson attended Davidson College, he joined the debate team and developed his skills in presenting arguments and refuting those of others, which was ideal training for the law (which he later entered) and politics.

Along the way, Wilson collected a network of progressively important and influential people to aid him in his vocational advancement, a major tool of leaders. These personal ties opened up opportunities for him to gain prominent positions in academia (president of Princeton), the governor ship of New Jersey, and soon thereafter a triumph in a national election against a tough field of candidates for president. As a result of these various devices of leadership, his intellectual arguments, powers of persuasion, and connections in Congress, Wilson introduced and saw through passage a long list of legislative bills. He became the champion of a progressive program that transformed U.S. government and the nation. These victories were the climax of his intellectual growth and the tactics of successful leadership. Later, his efforts to persuade Congress to ratify the Treaty of Versailles and join the League of Nations failed. Nonetheless, Woodrow Wilson had won many more victories that placed him in the pantheon of successful American presidents.

Donald L. Gilmore

Further Reading

Annin, Robert Edwards. 1924. *Woodrow Wilson: A Character Study*. New York: Dodd, Mead.

Beaty, Mary D. 1988. *A History of Davidson College*. Davidson, NC: Briarpatch.

Berg, A. Scott. 2013. *Wilson*. New York: Berkley Books.

Blum, John Morton. 1951. *Joe Tumulty and the Wilson Era*. Boston: Houghton Mifflin.

Bragdon, Henry Wilkinson. 1967. *Woodrow Wilson: The Academic Years*. Cambridge, MA: Belknap Press of Harvard University Press.

Bryan, William Jennings. 1925. *The Memoirs of William Jennings Bryan*. Edited by Mary Bryan. Philadelphia: John C. Winston.

Calero, Manuel. 1916. *The Mexican Policy of President Woodrow Wilson: As It Appears to a Mexican*. New York: Smith & Thomson.

Churchill, Winston. 1923. *The World Crisis, 1911–1918*. London and New York: Thornton Butterworth and Charles Scribner's Sons.

Coffman, Edward M. 1968. *The War to End All Wars: The American Military Experience in World War I*. New York: Oxford University Press.

Cooper, John Milton, Jr. 1911. *Woodrow Wilson: A Biography*. New York: Vintage Books.

Hodgson, Godfrey. 2006. *Woodrow Wilson's Right Hand: The Life of Colonel Edward M. House*. New Haven, CT: Yale University Press.

Hoover, Herbert. 1958. *The Ordeal of Woodrow Wilson*. New York: McGraw-Hill.

House, Edward M. 1926. *The Intimate Papers of Colonel House, Arranged as a Narrative by Charles Seymour*. 4 vols. Boston: Houghton Mifflin.

Houston, David F. 1926. *Eight Years with Wilson's Cabinet, 1913–1921*. 2 vols. Garden City, NY: Doubleday, Page.

Lansing, Robert. 1935. *War Memoirs*. Indianapolis, IN: Bobbs-Merrill.

Link, Arthur S., et al., eds. 1966–1993. *The Papers of Woodrow Wilson*. Princeton, NJ: Princeton University Press.

Lodge, Henry Cabot. 1925. *The Senate and the League of Nations*. New York: Charles Scribner's Sons.

McMath, Robert C. 1989. *American Populism: A Social History 1877–1893*. New York: Hill & Wang.

Smith, Gene. 1964. *When the Cheering Stopped: The Last Years of Woodrow Wilson*. New York: William Morrow.

Tarbell, Ida. 1904. *The History of the Standard Oil Company*. New York: McClure Phillips & Co.

White, William Allen. 1924. *Woodrow Wilson, the Man, His Times, and His Task*. Boston: Houghton Mifflin.

First Inaugural Address (March 4, 1913)

Only one Democrat, Grover Cleveland, had been president since James Buchanan left the White House in 1861. Woodrow Wilson took advantage of a party split among the Republicans in the 1912 election and became the second. On a cool, overcast day, Chief Justice Edward White administered the oath of office to Wilson on the east portico of the U.S. Capitol.

There has been a change of government. It began two years ago, when the House of Representatives became Democratic by a decisive majority. It has now been completed. The Senate about to assemble will also be Democratic. The offices of President and Vice-President have been put into the hands of Democrats. What does the change mean? That is the question that is uppermost in our minds to-day. That is the question I am going to try to answer, in order, if I may, to interpret the occasion.

It means much more than the mere success of a party. The success of a party means little except when the Nation is using that party for a large and definite purpose. No one can mistake the purpose for which the Nation now seeks to use the Democratic Party. It seeks to use it to interpret a change in its own plans and point of view. Some old things with which we had grown familiar, and which had begun to creep into the very habit of our thought and of our lives, have altered their aspect as we have latterly looked critically upon them, with fresh, awakened eyes; have dropped their disguises and shown themselves alien and sinister. Some new things, as we look frankly upon them, willing to comprehend their real character, have come to assume the aspect of things long believed in and familiar, stuff of our own convictions. We have been refreshed by a new insight into our own life.

We see that in many things that life is very great. It is incomparably great in its material aspects, in its body of wealth, in the diversity and sweep of its energy, in the industries which have been conceived and built up by the genius of individual men and the limitless enterprise of groups of men. It is great, also, very great, in its moral force. Nowhere else in the world have noble men and women exhibited in more striking forms the beauty and the energy of sympathy and helpfulness and counsel in their efforts to rectify wrong, alleviate suffering, and set the weak in the way of strength and hope. We have built up, moreover, a great system of government, which has stood through a long age as in many respects a model for those who seek to set liberty upon foundations that will endure against fortuitous change, against storm and accident. Our life contains every great thing, and contains it in rich abundance.

But the evil has come with the good, and much fine gold has been corroded. With riches has come inexcusable waste. We have squandered a great part of what we might have used, and have not stopped to conserve the exceeding bounty of nature, without which our genius for enterprise would have been worthless and impotent, scorning to be careful, shamefully prodigal as well as admirably efficient. We have been proud of our industrial achievements, but we have not hitherto stopped thoughtfully enough to count the human cost, the cost of lives snuffed out, of energies overtaxed and broken, the fearful physical and spiritual cost to the men and women and children upon whom the dead weight and burden of it all has fallen pitilessly the years through. The groans and agony of it all had not yet reached our ears, the solemn, moving undertone of our life, coming up out of the mines and factories, and out of every home where the struggle had its intimate and familiar seat. With the great Government went many deep secret things which we too long delayed to look into and scrutinize with candid, fearless eyes. The great Government we loved has too often been made use of for private and selfish purposes, and those who used it had forgotten the people.

At last a vision has been vouchsafed us of our life as a whole. We see the bad with the good, the debased and decadent with the sound and vital. With this vision we approach new affairs. Our duty is to cleanse, to reconsider, to restore, to correct the evil without impairing the good, to purify and humanize every process of our common life without weakening or sentimentalizing it. There has been something crude and heartless and unfeeling in our haste to succeed and be great. Our thought has been "Let every man look out for himself, let every generation look out for itself," while we reared giant machinery which made it impossible that any but those who stood at the levers of control should have a chance to look out for themselves. We had not forgotten our morals. We remembered well enough that we had set up a policy which was meant to serve the humblest as well as the most powerful, with an eye single to the standards of justice and fair play, and remembered it with pride. But we were very heedless and in a hurry to be great.

We have come now to the sober second thought. The scales of heedlessness have fallen from our eyes. We have made up our minds to square every process of our national life again with the standards we so proudly set up at the beginning and have always carried at our hearts. Our work is a work of restoration.

We have itemized with some degree of particularity the things that ought to be altered and here are some of the chief items: A tariff which cuts us off from our proper part in the commerce of the world, violates the just principles of taxation, and makes the Government a facile instrument in the hand of private interests; a banking and currency system based upon the necessity of the Government to sell its bonds fifty years ago and perfectly adapted to concentrating cash and restricting credits; an industrial system which, take it on all its sides, financial as well as administrative, holds capital in leading strings, restricts the liberties and limits the opportunities of labor, and exploits without renewing or conserving the natural resources of the country; a body of agricultural activities never yet given the efficiency of great business undertakings or served as it should be through the instrumentality of science taken directly to the farm, or afforded the facilities of credit best suited to its practical needs; watercourses undeveloped, waste places unreclaimed, forests untended, fast disappearing without plan or prospect of renewal, unregarded waste heaps at every mine. We have studied as perhaps no other nation has the most effective means of production, but we have not studied cost or economy as we should either as organizers of industry, as statesmen, or as individuals.

Nor have we studied and perfected the means by which government may be put at the service of humanity, in safeguarding the health of the Nation, the health of its men and its women and its children, as well as their rights in the struggle for existence. This is no sentimental duty. The firm basis of government is justice, not pity. These are matters of justice. There can be no equality or opportunity, the first essential of justice in the body politic, if men and women and children be not shielded in their lives, their very vitality, from the consequences of great industrial and social processes which they can not alter, control, or singly cope with. Society must see to it that it does not itself crush or weaken or damage its own constituent parts. The first duty of law is to keep sound the society it serves. Sanitary laws, pure food laws, and laws determining conditions of labor which individuals are powerless to determine for themselves are intimate parts of the very business of justice and legal efficiency.

These are some of the things we ought to do, and not leave the others undone, the old-fashioned, never-to-be-neglected, fundamental safeguarding of property and of individual right. This is the high enterprise of the new day: To lift everything that concerns our life as a Nation to the light that shines from the hearthfire of every man's conscience and vision of the right. It is inconceivable that we should do this as partisans; it is inconceivable we should do it in ignorance of the facts as they are or in blind haste. We shall restore, not destroy. We shall deal with our economic system as it is and as it may be modified, not as it might be if we had a clean sheet of paper to write upon; and step by step we shall make it what it should be, in the spirit of those who question their own wisdom and seek counsel and knowledge, not shallow self-satisfaction or the excitement of excursions whither they can not tell. Justice, and only justice, shall always be our motto.

And yet it will be no cool process of mere science. The Nation has been deeply stirred, stirred by a solemn passion, stirred by the knowledge of wrong, of ideals lost, of government too often debauched and made an instrument of evil. The feelings with which we face this new age of right and opportunity sweep across our heartstrings like some air out of God's own presence, where justice and mercy are reconciled and the judge and the brother are one. We know our task to be no mere task of politics but a task which shall search us through and through, whether we be able to understand our time and the need of our people, whether we be indeed their spokesmen and interpreters, whether we have the pure heart to comprehend and the rectified will to choose our high course of action.

This is not a day of triumph; it is a day of dedication. Here muster, not the forces of party, but the forces of humanity. Men's hearts wait upon us; men's lives hang in the balance; men's hopes call upon us to say what we will do. Who shall live up to the great trust? Who dares fail to try? I summon all honest men, all patriotic, all forward-looking men, to my side. God helping me, I will not fail them, if they will but counsel and sustain me!

Source: Richardson, James D. *A Compilation of the Messages and Papers of the Presidents 1789–1897*. Vol. 16. New York: Bureau of National Literature, 1897, 7868–7871.

Annual Message to Congress (December 2, 1913)

Presidents George Washington and John Adams had delivered annual State of the Union messages in personal addresses. Thomas Jefferson, the nation's third president, opted not to do so and instead sent a written message to Congress. He was not a good public speaker, and he considered the practice too "royal" in its style. Since that time, every other American president had sent a written annual message to Congress—until Wilson. On December 2, he went to the U.S. Capitol and delivered his remarks in a prepared speech he had written himself on his personal typewriter.

In pursuance of my constitutional duty to "give to the Congress information of the state of the Union," I take the liberty of addressing you on several matters which ought, as it seems to me, particularly to engage the attention of your honorable bodies, as of all who study the welfare and progress of the Nation.

I shall ask your indulgence if I venture to depart in some degree from the usual custom of setting before you in formal review the many matters which have engaged the attention and called for the action of the several departments of the Government or which look to them for early treatment in the future, because the list is long, very long, and would suffer in the abbreviation to which I should have to subject it. I shall submit to you the reports of the heads of the several departments, in which these subjects are set forth in careful detail, and beg that they may receive the thoughtful attention of your committees and of all Members of the Congress who may have the leisure to study them. Their obvious importance, as constituting the very substance of the business of the Government, makes comment and emphasis on my part unnecessary.

The country, I am thankful to say, is at peace with all the world, and many happy manifestations multiply about us of a growing cordiality and sense of community of interest among the nations, foreshadowing an age of settled peace and good will. More and more readily each decade do the nations manifest their willingness to bind themselves by solemn treaty to the processes of peace, the processes of frankness and fair concession. So far the United States has stood at the front of such negotiations. She will, I earnestly hope and confidently believe, give fresh proof of her sincere adherence to the cause of international friendship by ratifying the several treaties of arbitration awaiting renewal by the Senate. In addition to these, it has been the privilege of the Department of State to gain the assent, in principle, of no less than 31 nations, representing four-fifths of the population of the world, to the negotiation of treaties by which it shall be agreed that whenever differences of interest or of policy arise which can not be resolved by the ordinary processes of diplomacy they shall be publicly analyzed, discussed, and reported upon by a tribunal chosen by the parties before either nation determines its course of action.

There is only one possible standard by which to determine controversies between the United States and other nations, and that is compounded of these two elements: Our own honor and our obligations to the peace of the world. A test so compounded ought easily to be made to govern both the establishment of new treaty obligations and the interpretation of those already assumed.

There is but one cloud upon our horizon. That has shown itself to the south of us, and hangs over Mexico. There can be no certain prospect of peace in America until Gen. Huerta has surrendered his usurped authority in Mexico; until it is understood on all hands, indeed, that such pretended governments will not be countenanced or dealt with by the Government of the United States. We are the friends of constitutional government in America; we are more than its friends, we are its champions; because in no other way can our neighbors, to whom we would wish in every way to make proof of our friendship, work out their own development in peace and liberty. Mexico has no Government. . . .

I turn to matters of domestic concern. You already have under consideration a bill for the reform of our system of banking and currency, for which the country waits with impatience, as for something fundamental to its whole business life and necessary to set credit free from arbitrary and artificial restraints. I need not say how earnestly I hope for its early enactment into law. I take leave to beg that the whole energy and attention of the Senate be concentrated upon it till the matter is successfully disposed of. And yet I feel that the request is not needed-that the Members of that great House need no urging in this service to the country. . . .

It has, singularly enough, come to pass that we have allowed the industry of our farms to lag behind the other activities of the country in its development. I need not stop to tell you how fundamental to the life of the Nation is the production of its food. Our thoughts may ordinarily be concentrated upon the cities and the hives of industry, upon the cries of the crowded market place and the clangor of the factory, but it is from the quiet interspaces of the open valleys and the free hillsides that we draw the sources of life and of prosperity, from the farm and the ranch, from the forest and the mine. Without these every street would be silent, every office deserted, every factory fallen into disrepair. And yet the farmer does not stand upon the same footing with the forester and the miner in the market of credit. He is the servant of the seasons. Nature determines how long he must wait for his crops, and will not be hurried in her processes. He may give his note, but the season of its maturity depends upon the season

when his crop matures, lies at the gates of the market where his products are sold. And the security he gives is of a character not known in the broker's office or as familiarly as it might be on the counter of the banker. . . .

Turn from the farm to the world of business which centers in the city and in the factory, and I think that all thoughtful observers will agree that the immediate service we owe the business communities of the country is to prevent private monopoly more effectually than it has yet been prevented. I think it will be easily agreed that we should let the Sherman anti-trust law stand, unaltered, as it is, with its debatable ground about it, but that we should as much as possible reduce the area of that debatable ground by further and more explicit legislation; and should also supplement that great act by legislation which will not only clarify it but also facilitate its administration and make it fairer to all concerned. . . .

I turn to a subject which I hope can be handled promptly and without serious controversy of any kind. I mean the method of selecting nominees for the Presidency of the United States. I feel confident that I do not misinterpret the wishes or the expectations of the country when I urge the prompt enactment of legislation which will provide for primary elections throughout the country at which the voters of the several parties may choose their nominees for the Presidency without the intervention of nominating conventions. I venture the suggestion that this legislation should provide for the retention of party conventions, but only for the purpose of declaring and accepting the verdict of the primaries and formulating the platforms of the parties; and I suggest that these conventions should consist not of delegates chosen for this single purpose, but of the nominees for Congress, the nominees for vacant seats in the Senate of the United States, the Senators whose terms have not yet closed, the national committees, and the candidates for the Presidency themselves, in order that platforms may be framed by those responsible to the people for carrying them into effect.

These are all matters of vital domestic concern, and besides them, outside the charmed circle of our own national life in which our affections command us, as well as our consciences, there stand out our obligations toward our territories over sea. Here we are trustees. Porto Rico, Hawaii, the Philippines, are ours, indeed, but not ours to do what we please with. Such territories, once regarded as mere possessions, are no longer to be selfishly exploited; they are part of the domain of public conscience and of serviceable and enlightened statesmanship. We must administer them for the people who live in them and with the same sense of responsibility to them as toward our own people in our domestic affairs. No doubt we shall successfully enough bind Porto Rico and the Hawaiian Islands to ourselves by ties of justice and interest and affection, but the performance of our duty toward the Philippines is a more difficult and debatable matter. We can satisfy the obligations of generous justice toward the people of Porto Rico by giving them the ample and familiar rights and privileges accorded our own citizens in our own territories and our obligations toward the people of Hawaii by perfecting the provisions for self-government already granted them, but in the Philippines we must go further. We must hold steadily in view their ultimate independence, and we must move toward the time of that independence as steadily as the way can be cleared and the foundations thoughtfully and permanently laid. . . .

A duty faces us with regard to Alaska which seems to me very pressing and very imperative; perhaps I should say a double duty, for it concerns both the political and the material development of the Territory. The people of Alaska should be given the full Territorial form of government, and Alaska, as a storehouse, should be unlocked. One key to it is a system of railways. These the Government should itself build and administer, and the ports and terminals it should itself control in the interest of all who wish to use them for the service and development of the country and its people. . . .

Three or four matters of special importance and significance I beg, that you will permit me to mention in closing.

Our Bureau of Mines ought to be equipped and empowered to render even more effectual service than it renders now in improving the conditions of mine labor and making the mines more economically productive as well as more safe. This is an all-important part of the work of conservation; and the conservation of human life and energy lies even nearer to our interests than the preservation from waste of our material resources.

We owe it, in mere justice to the railway employees of the country, to provide for them a fair and effective employers' liability act; and a law that we can stand by in this matter will be no less to the advantage of those who administer the railroads of the country than to the advantage of those whom they employ. The experience of a large number of the States abundantly proves that.

We ought to devote ourselves to meeting pressing demands of plain justice like this as earnestly as to the accomplishment of political and economic reforms. Social justice comes first. Law is the machinery for its realization and is vital only as it expresses and embodies it.

An international congress for the discussion of all questions that affect safety at sea is now sitting in London at the suggestion of our own Government. So soon as the conclusions of that congress can be learned and considered we ought to address ourselves, among other things, to the prompt alleviation of the very unsafe, unjust, and burdensome conditions which now surround the employment of sailors and render it extremely difficult to obtain the services of spirited and competent men such as every ship needs if it is to be safely handled and brought to port.

May I not express the very real pleasure I have experienced in co-operating with this Congress and sharing with it the labors of common service to which it has devoted itself so unreservedly during the past seven months of uncomplaining concentration upon the business of legislation? Surely it is a proper and pertinent part of my report on "the state of the Union" to express my admiration for the diligence, the good temper, and the full comprehension of public duty which has already been manifested by both the Houses; and I hope that it may not be deemed an impertinent intrusion of myself into the picture if I say with how much and how constant satisfaction I have availed myself of the privilege of putting my time and energy at their disposal alike in counsel and in action.

Source: Richardson, James D. *A Compilation of the Messages and Papers of the Presidents 1789–1897*. Vol. 17. New York: Bureau of National Literature, 1897, 7906–7913.

Neutrality Speech (August 24, 1914)

World War I had erupted in Europe in July 1914, and the major European powers had become involved in a conflict that shortly spread across the globe. Since George Washington's presidency, the United States' time-honored policy had been to declare neutrality in European wars. President Wilson not only planned to honor that tradition, but he believed fervently in the need to remain clear of the spreading crisis. His hopes, however, failed. In April 1917, the United States went to war.

My Fellow-Countrymen:

I suppose that every thoughtful man in America has asked himself, during these last troubled weeks, what influence the European war may exert upon the United States, and I take the liberty of addressing a few words to you in order to point out that it is entirely within our own choice what its effects upon us will be and to urge very earnestly upon you the sort of speech and conduct which will best safeguard the Nation against distress and disaster.

The effect of the war upon the United States will depend upon what American citizens say and do. Every man who really loves America will act and speak in the true spirit of neutrality, which is the spirit of impartiality and fairness and friendliness to all concerned. The spirit of the Nation in this critical matter will be determined largely by what individuals and society and those gathered in public meetings do and say, upon what newspapers and magazines contain, upon what ministers utter in their pulpits, and men proclaim as their opinions on the street.

The people of the United States are drawn from many nations, and chiefly from the nations now at war. It is natural and inevitable that there should be the utmost variety of sympathy and desire among them with regard to the issues and circumstances of the conflict. Some will wish one nation, others another, to succeed in the momentous struggle. It will be easy to excite passion and difficult to allay it. Those responsible for exciting it will assume a heavy responsibility, responsibility for no less a thing than that the people of the United States, whose love of their country and whose loyalty to its Government should unite them as Americans all, bound in honor and affection to think first of her and her interests, may be divided in camps of hostile opinion, hot against each other, involved in the war itself in impulse and opinion if not in action.

Such divisions among us would be fatal to our peace of mind and might seriously stand in the way of the proper performance of our duty as the one great nation at peace, the one people holding itself ready to play a part of impartial mediation and speak the counsels of peace and accommodation, not as a partisan, but as a friend.

I venture, therefore, my fellow countrymen, to speak a solemn word of warning to you against that deepest, most subtle, most essential breach of neutrality which may spring out of partisanship, out of passionately taking sides. The United States must be neutral in fact as well as in name during these days that are to try men's souls. We must be impartial in thought as well as in action, must put a curb upon our sentiments as well as upon every transaction that might be construed as a preference of one party to the struggle before another.

My thought is of America. I am speaking, I feel sure, the earnest wish and purpose of every thoughtful American that this great country of ours, which is, of course, the first in our thoughts and in our hearts, should show herself in this time of peculiar trial a Nation fit beyond others to exhibit the fine poise of undisturbed judgment, the dignity of self-control, the efficiency of dispassionate action; a Nation that neither sits in judgment upon others nor is disturbed in her own counsels and which keeps herself fit and free to do what is honest and disinterested and truly serviceable for the peace of the world.

Shall we not resolve to put upon ourselves the restraints which will bring to our people the happiness and the great and lasting influence for peace we covet for them?

Source: Richardson, James D. *A Compilation of the Messages and Papers of the Presidents 1789–1897.* Vol. 17. New York: Bureau of National Literature, 1897, 7978–7979.

Declaration of War (April 2, 1917)

Between the president's declaration of neutrality in August 1914 and his call for a declaration of war on

April 2, Wilson had sought to keep the United States neutral during World War I. However, a variety of factors ultimately made his initial sincere efforts impossible. German submarine warfare challenged U.S. maritime policy, a secret German cablegram (the Zimmerman Note) suggested an alliance with Mexico, heavy private U.S. loans were granted to Germany's allies, and other factors prodded Wilson and the nation toward entering the conflict. On April 6, the House voted 373–50 and the Senate voted 82–6 in favor of the president's request.

I have called the Congress into extraordinary session because there are serious, very serious, choices of policy to be made, and made immediately, which it was neither right nor constitutionally permissible that I should assume the responsibility of making. On the 3rd of February last, I officially laid before you the extraordinary announcement of the Imperial German government that on and after the 1st day of February it was its purpose to put aside all restraints of law or of humanity and use its submarines to sink every vessel that sought to approach either the ports of Great Britain and Ireland or the western coasts of Europe or any of the ports controlled by the enemies of Germany within the Mediterranean.

That had seemed to be the object of the German submarine warfare earlier in the war, but since April of last year the Imperial government had somewhat restrained the commanders of its undersea craft in conformity with its promise then given to us that passenger boats should not be sunk and that due warning would be given to all other vessels which its submarines might seek to destroy, when no resistance was offered or escape attempted, and care taken that their crews were given at least a fair chance to save their lives in their open boats. The precautions taken were meager and haphazard enough, as was proved in distressing instance after instance in the progress of the cruel and unmanly business, but a certain degree of restraint was observed.

The new policy has swept every restriction aside. Vessels of every kind, whatever their flag, their character, their cargo, their destination, their errand, have been ruthlessly sent to the bottom without warning and without thought of help or mercy for those on board, the vessels of friendly neutrals along with those of belligerents. Even hospital ships and ships carrying relief to the sorely bereaved and stricken people of Belgium, though the latter were provided with safe conduct through the proscribed areas by the German government itself and were distinguished by unmistakable marks of identity, have been sunk with the same reckless lack of compassion or of principle.

I was for a little while unable to believe that such things would in fact be done by any government that had hitherto subscribed to the humane practices of civilized nations. International law had its origin in the attempt to set up some law which would be respected and observed upon the seas, where no nation had right of dominion and where lay the free highways of the world. By painful stage after stage has that law been built up, with meager enough results, indeed, after all was accomplished that could be accomplished, but always with a clear view, at least, of what the heart and conscience of mankind demanded.

This minimum of right the German government has swept aside under the plea of retaliation and necessity and because it had no weapons which it could use at sea except these which it is impossible to employ as it is employing them without throwing to the winds all scruples of humanity or of respect for the understandings that were supposed to underlie the intercourse of the world. I am not now thinking of the loss of property involved, immense and serious as that is, but only of the wanton and wholesale destruction of the lives of noncombatants, men, women, and children, engaged in pursuits which have always, even in the darkest periods of modern history, been deemed innocent and legitimate. Property can be paid for; the lives of peaceful and innocent people cannot be.

The present German submarine warfare against commerce is a warfare against mankind. It is a war against all nations. American ships have been sunk, American lives taken in ways which it has stirred us very deeply to learn of; but the ships and people of other neutral and friendly nations have been sunk and overwhelmed in the waters in the same way. There has been no discrimination. The challenge is to all mankind.

Each nation must decide for itself how it will meet it. The choice we make for ourselves must be made with a moderation of counsel and a temperateness of judgment befitting our character and our motives as a nation. We must put excited feeling away. Our motive will not be revenge or the victorious assertion of the physical might of the nation, but only the vindication of right, of human right, of which we are only a single champion.

When I addressed the Congress on the 26th of February last, I thought that it would suffice to assert our neutral rights with arms, our right to use the seas against unlawful interference, our right to keep our people safe against unlawful violence. But armed neutrality, it now appears, is impracticable. Because submarines are in effect outlaws when used as the German submarines have been used against merchant shipping, it is impossible to defend ships against their attacks as the law of nations has assumed that merchantmen would defend themselves against privateers or cruisers, visible craft giving chase upon the open sea.

It is common prudence in such circumstances, grim necessity indeed, to endeavor to destroy them before they have shown their own intention. They must be dealt with upon sight, if dealt with at all. The German government denies the right of neutrals to use arms at all within the areas of the sea which it has proscribed, even in the defense of rights which no modern publicist has ever before questioned their right to defend. The intimation is conveyed that the armed guards which we have placed on our merchant ships will be treated as beyond the pale of law and subject to be dealt with as pirates would be.

Armed neutrality is ineffectual enough at best; in such circumstances and in the face of such pretensions it is worse than ineffectual: it is likely only to produce what it was meant to prevent; it is practically certain to draw us into the war without either the rights or the effectiveness of belligerents. There is one choice we cannot make, we are incapable of making: we will not choose the path of submission and suffer the most sacred rights of our nation and our people to be ignored or violated. The wrongs against which we now array ourselves are no common wrongs; they cut to the very roots of human life.

With a profound sense of the solemn and even tragical character of the step I am taking and of the grave responsibilities which it involves, but in unhesitating obedience to what I deem my constitutional duty, I advise that the Congress declare the recent course of the Imperial German government to be in fact nothing less than war against the government and people of the United States; that it formally accept the status of belligerent which has thus been thrust upon it; and that it take immediate steps, not only to put the country in a more thorough state of defense but also to exert all its power and employ all its resources to bring the government of the German Empire to terms and end the war.

What this will involve is clear. It will involve the utmost practicable cooperation in counsel and action with the governments now at war with Germany and, as incident to that, the extension to those governments of the most liberal financial credits, in order that our resources may so far as possible be added to theirs. It will involve the organization and mobilization of all the material resources of the country to supply the materials of war and serve the incidental needs of the nation in the most abundant and yet the most economical and efficient way possible. It will involve the immediate full equipment of the Navy in all respects but particularly in supplying it with the best means of dealing with the enemy's submarines. It will involve the immediate addition to the armed forces of the United States already provided for by law in case of war at least 500,000 men, who should, in my opinion, be chosen upon the principle of universal liability to service, and also the authorization of subsequent additional increments of equal force so soon as they may be needed and can be handled in training. . . .

While we do these things, these deeply momentous things, let us be very clear, and make very clear to all the world, what our motives and our objects are. My own thought has not been driven from its habitual and normal course by the unhappy events of the last two months, and I do not believe that the thought of the nation has been altered or clouded by them. I have exactly the same things in mind now that I had in mind when I addressed the Senate on the 22nd of January last; the same that I had in mind when I addressed the Congress on the 3rd of February and on the 26th of February.

Our object now, as then, is to vindicate the principles of peace and justice in the life of the world as against selfish and autocratic power and to set up among the really free and self-governed peoples of the world such a concert of purpose and of action as will henceforth ensure the observance of those principles. Neutrality is no longer feasible or desirable where the peace of the world is involved and the freedom of its peoples, and the menace to that peace and freedom lies in the existence of autocratic governments backed by organized force which is controlled wholly by their will, not by the will of their people. We have seen the last of neutrality in such circumstances. We are at the beginning of an age in which it will be insisted that the same standards of conduct and of responsibility for wrong done shall be observed among nations and their governments that are observed among the individual citizens of civilized states.

We have no quarrel with the German people. We have no feeling toward them but one of sympathy and friendship. It was not upon their impulse that their government acted in entering this war. It was not with their previous knowledge or approval. It was a war determined upon as wars used to be determined upon in the old, unhappy days when peoples were nowhere consulted by their rulers and wars were provoked and waged in the interest of dynasties or of little groups of ambitious men who were accustomed to use their fellowmen as pawns and tools. . . .

We are accepting this challenge of hostile purpose because we know that in such a government, following such methods, we can never have a friend; and that in the presence of its organized power, always lying in wait to accomplish we know not what purpose, there can be no assured security for the democratic governments of the world. We are now about to accept gauge of battle with this natural foe to liberty and shall, if necessary, spend the whole force of the nation to check and nullify its pretensions and its power. We are glad, now that we see the facts with no veil of false pretense about them, to fight thus for the ultimate peace of the world and for the liberation of its peoples, the German peoples included: for the rights of nations great and small and the privilege of men everywhere to choose their way of life and of obedience.

The world must be made safe for democracy. Its peace must be planted upon the tested foundations of political liberty. We have no selfish ends to serve. We desire no conquest, no dominion. We seek no indemnities for ourselves, no material compensation for the sacrifices we shall freely make. We are but one of the champions of the rights of mankind. We shall be satisfied when those rights have been made as secure as the faith and the freedom of nations can make them.

Just because we fight without rancor and without selfish object, seeking nothing for ourselves but what we shall wish to share with all free peoples, we shall, I feel confident, conduct our operations as belligerents without passion and ourselves observe with proud punctilio the principles of right and of fair play we profess to be fighting for. . . .

It is a distressing and oppressive duty, gentlemen of the Congress, which I have performed in thus addressing you. There are, it may be, many months of fiery trial and sacrifice ahead of us. It is a fearful thing to lead this great peaceful people into war, into the most terrible and disastrous of all wars, civilization itself seeming to be in the balance. But the right is more precious than peace, and we shall fight for the things which we have always carried nearest our hearts-for democracy, for the right of those who submit to authority to have a voice in their own governments, for the rights and liberties of small nations, for a universal dominion of right by such a concert of free peoples as shall bring peace and safety to all nations and make the world itself at last free.

To such a task we can dedicate our lives and our fortunes, everything that we are and everything that we have, with the pride of those who know that the day has come when America is privileged to spend her blood and her might for the principles that gave her birth and happiness and the peace which she has treasured. God helping her, she can do no other.

Source: Horne, Charles F., ed. *Source Records of the Great War.* Vol. 5. New York: National Alumni, 1923, 107–117.

Fourteen Points (January 8, 1918)

As the U.S. armed forces joined the enemies of Germany as an "associate power" in France, President Wilson believed it necessary to explain to the nation and the world that the country had gone to war for moral reasons and hoped to end war forever. The

January 8 speech laid out his famous Fourteen Points as a plan to make World War I a "war to end all wars." George Creel, Wilson's head of the Committee on Public Information, printed millions of copies of the Fourteen Points and distributed them around the world to propagandize Wilson's message. The fourteenth point called for the creation of a postwar League of Nations.

Gentlemen of the Congress: . . .

We entered this war because violations of right had occurred which touched us to the quick and made the life of our own people impossible unless they were corrected and the world secured once for all against their recurrence. What we demand in this war, therefore, is nothing peculiar to ourselves. It is that the world be made fit and safe to live in; and particularly that it be made safe for every peace-loving nation which, like our own, wishes to live its own life, determine its own institutions, be assured of justice and fair dealing by the other peoples of the world as against force and selfish aggression. All the peoples of the world are in effect partners in this interest, and for our own part we see very clearly that unless justice be done to others it will not be done to us. The program of the world's peace, therefore, is our program; and that program, the only possible program, as we see it, is this:

I. Open covenants of peace, openly arrived at, after which there shall be no private international understandings of any kind, but diplomacy shall proceed always frankly and in the public view.

II. Absolute freedom of navigation upon the seas, outside territorial waters, alike in peace and in war, except as the seas may be closed in whole or in part by international action for the enforcement of international covenants.

III. The removal, so far as possible, of all economic barriers and the establishment of an equality of trade conditions among all the nations consenting to the peace and associating themselves for its maintenance.

IV. Adequate guarantees given and taken that national armaments will be reduced to the lowest point consistent with domestic safety.

V. A free, open-minded, and absolutely impartial adjustment of all colonial claims, based upon a strict observance of the principle that in determining all such questions of sovereignty the interests of the populations concerned must have equal weight with the equitable claims of the government whose title is to be determined.

VI. The evacuation of all Russian territory and such a settlement of all questions affecting Russia as will secure the best and freest cooperation of the other nations of the world in obtaining for her an unhampered and unembarrassed opportunity for the independent determination of her own political development and national policy and assure her of a sincere welcome into the society of free nations under institutions of her own choosing; and, more than a welcome, assistance also of every kind that she may need and may herself desire. The treatment accorded Russia by her sister nations in the months to come will be the acid test of their good will, of their comprehension of her needs as distinguished from their own interests, and of their intelligent and unselfish sympathy.

VII. Belgium, the whole world will agree, must be evacuated and restored, without any attempt to limit the sovereignty which she enjoys in common with all other free nations. No other single act will serve as this will serve to restore confidence among the nations in the laws which they have themselves set and determined for the government of their relations with one another. Without this healing act the whole structure and validity of international law is forever impaired.

VIII. All French territory should be freed and the invaded portions restored, and the wrong done to France by Prussia in 1871 in the matter of Alsace-Lorraine, which has unsettled the peace of the world for nearly fifty years, should be righted, in order that peace may once more be made secure in the interest of all.

IX. A readjustment of the frontiers of Italy should be effected along clearly recognizable lines of nationality.

X. The peoples of Austria-Hungary, whose place among the nations we wish to see safeguarded and assured, should be accorded the freest opportunity of autonomous development.

XI. Rumania, Serbia, and Montenegro should be evacuated; occupied territories restored; Serbia accorded free and secure access to the sea; and the relations of the several Balkan states to one another determined by friendly counsel along historically established lines of allegiance and nationality; and international guarantees of the political and economic independence and territorial integrity of the several Balkan states should be entered into.

XII. The Turkish portions of the present Ottoman Empire should be assured a secure sovereignty, but the other nationalities which are now under Turkish rule should be assured an undoubted security of life and an absolutely unmolested opportunity of autonomous development and the Dardanelles should be permanently opened as a free passage to the ships and commerce of all nations under international guarantees.

XIII. An independent Polish state should be erected which should include the territories inhabited by indisputably Polish populations, which should be assured a free and secure access to the sea, and whose political and economic independence and territorial integrity should be guaranteed by international covenant.

XIV. A general association of nations must be formed under specific covenants for the purpose of affording mutual guarantees of political independence and territorial integrity to great and small states alike.

In regard to these essential rectifications of wrong and assertions of right we feel ourselves to be intimate partners of all the governments and peoples associated together against the Imperialists. We cannot be separated in interest or divided in purpose. We stand together until the end.

For such arrangements and covenants we are willing to fight and to continue to fight until they are achieved; but only because we wish the right to prevail and desire a just and stable peace such as can be secured only by removing the chief provocations to war, which this program does remove. We have no jealousy of German greatness, and there is nothing in this program that impairs it. We grudge her no achievement or distinction of learning or of pacific enterprise such as have made her record very bright and very enviable. We do not wish to injure her or to block in any way her legitimate influence or power. We do not wish to fight her either with arms or with hostile arrangements of trade if she is willing to associate herself with us and the other peace-loving nations of the world in covenants of justice and law and fair dealing. We wish her only to accept a place of equality among the peoples of the world,—the new world in which we now live,—instead of a place of mastery.

Neither do we presume to suggest to her any alteration or modification of her institutions. But it is necessary, we must frankly say, and necessary as a preliminary to any intelligent dealings with her on our part, that we should know whom her spokesmen speak for when they speak to us, whether for the Reichstag majority or for the military party and the men whose creed is imperial domination.

We have spoken now, surely, in terms too concrete to admit of any further doubt or question. An evident principle runs through the whole program I have outlined. It is the principle of justice to all peoples and nationalities, and their right to live on equal terms of liberty and safety with one another, whether they be strong or weak. Unless this principle be made its foundation no part of the structure of international justice can stand. The people of the United States could act upon no other principle; and to the vindication of this principle they are ready to devote their lives, their honor, and everything that they possess. The moral climax of this the culminating and final war for human liberty has come, and they are ready to put their own strength, their own highest purpose, their own integrity and devotion to the test.

Source: President Wilson's Message to Congress, January 8, 1918; Records of the United States Senate: Record Group 4; Records of the United States Senate; National Archives.

29. WARREN G. HARDING (1865–1923)

Presidential Term (1921–1923)

CHRONOLOGY

November 2, 1865—Warren G. Harding is born in Blooming Grove, Ohio.

February 24, 1868—The House of Representatives votes to impeach President Andrew Johnson.

May 10, 1869—The Transcontinental Railroad is completed with a symbolic golden spike in Promontory, Utah.

February 3, 1870—The Senate ratifies the Fifteenth Amendment guaranteeing voting rights for all male citizens.

March 1, 1875—Congress passes the Civil Rights Act prohibiting discrimination in any public facility. The Supreme Court rules the act unconstitutional in 1883.

March 1879—Fourteen-year-old Warren Harding enters Ohio Central College.

May 6, 1882—President Chester A. Arthur signs the Chinese Exclusion Act, the first law specifically limiting immigration into the United States.

September 18, 1889—Jane Addams and Ellen Gates Starr cofound Hull House, a settlement home for newly immigrated European women in Chicago, Illinois.

May 1892—Harding moves to Marion, Ohio. He buys a local newspaper, the *Marion Star*, and begins his career as a journalist.

April 25, 1898—The United States declares war on Spain.

September 6, 1901—Leon Czolgosz shoots President William McKinley. The president dies eight days later. Theodore Roosevelt assumes the office.

November 1903—Ohio voters elect Harding lieutenant governor as a Republican.

February 12, 1909—Civil rights advocates found the National Association for the Advancement of Colored People in Buffalo, New York.

July 1914—World War I begins in Europe and quickly becomes a global conflict. On August 19, President Wilson declares U.S. neutrality.

November 1914—Harding is elected to the U.S. Senate.

May 1915—D. W. Griffith's film *Birth of a Nation* opens.

April 2, 1917—Senator Harding votes in support of President Wilson's request for a declaration of war against Germany.

November 11, 1918—The Allies and Germany sign an armistice, ending hostilities in World War I.

June 4, 1919—Harding votes to ratify the Nineteenth Amendment guaranteeing women the vote.

October 28, 1919—Harding votes with a majority of the Senate to override President Wilson's veto of the Volstead Act (prohibition).

January 1, 1920—African American musicians in New Orleans, Louisiana, begin playing a new form of popular music—jazz.

January 2, 1920—Under the direction of Attorney General A. Mitchell Palmer, federal agents begin nationwide raids on suspected anarchists, communists, and political "radicals."

November 2, 1920—Republican Warren Harding defeats his Democratic opponent, James Cox, to win the presidency.

November 2, 1920—KDKA Radio in Pittsburgh, Pennsylvania, the first commercial station, broadcasts the results of the Harding-Cox election.

May 31, 1921—The trial of Nicola Sacco and Bartolomeo Vanzetti, two accused radicals, begins in Braintree, Massachusetts.

December 23, 1921—Harding pardons socialist activist Eugene V. Debs and 23 others found guilty under the wartime Espionage Act.

April 1922—The Teapot Dome Scandal breaks during congressional hearings. Albert Fall's involvement, Harding's Interior Secretary, taints the president's administration.

June 20, 1923—Harding and his wife embark on a transcontinental speaking tour, the "voyage of understanding," to reassure the public about his administration in light of scandals.

August 2, 1923—President Harding develops pneumonia while on his speaking tour and dies in San Francisco, California, at the age of 57.

BIOGRAPHICAL SKETCH

Warren Harding, the 29th president of the United States, came to the White House in 1921 during an auspicious time for himself and the Republican Party he represented. World War I had ended in 1918 with U.S. victory. However, a bitter struggle developed between President Woodrow Wilson, a Democrat, and a Republican majority Senate over American entry into the postwar League of Nations. It left the country in a cynical mood regarding foreign affairs.

At the same time, two decades of domestic progressive reform that prompted changes in government, commerce, and society appeared to have lost its zeal and commitment. Many voters indicated they wanted political leaders who would not be so energetic in pursuing broad international and domestic changes to American life. In Warren G. Harding, they found that president in 1921. In Harding, the nation selected a leader and administration that saw little benefit in continuing the aggressive domestic reform laws and legislation of the previous two decades. Neither did the president see any point in developing foreign policy goals tied to an international organization like the League of Nations.

President Harding was 55 years old when he swore the oath of office in Washington, D.C., in March 1921. His life in Ohio during that half century had shaped his background, ideas, and values.

He was born on November 2, 1865, in Blooming Grove, Ohio, a small farming town in the northcentral part of the state. The eldest child of George Tyron Harding and Phoebe Elizabeth Dickerson Harding, he grew up in a hard-working, religious family that attended Methodist services each Sunday. His mother served as the "religious glue" that molded the Harding family, and her eldest son would remember her fondly throughout his life. Between Warren's birth in 1865 and Elizabeth's daughter Phoebe's in 1879, she had eight children. While raising a growing family, she volunteered regularly at the Methodist Church and was a local practicing midwife.

His father owned and worked a small farm, but he also taught in the local school, studied medicine, and became a licensed physician. None of those ventures ever provided the financial security and respectability that Tyron Harding hoped to obtain. The desire to achieve those goals eluded him as the family moved periodically. The local Blooming Grove community respected the family, but political issues and a lack of livable income caused them to leave the town.

In 1873, the Hardings moved to Caledonia, Ohio. As outspoken abolitionists, they found the new home more receptive to their views opposing slavery. Tyron Harding purchased a printing press and began publishing a local newspaper, the *Argus*. In his new role as editor and publisher, he used the paper to print local news items and antislavery editorials. His oldest son worked at his side and learned the basics of the newspaper business from an early age. The experience would become a major part of his adult life.

Living in Caledonia, Harding enjoyed an almost carefree youth. He had worked on his father's farm in Blooming Grove but hated the hard work that farming required. His time at the *Argus* proved far easier. Even though he was new in the town, he got on well with a local group of boys, and out of school they engaged in the things that youngsters did in the summer. They swam regularly in the local creek, fished, played pickup baseball games, and raced their horses. Described as "robust and large" even as a preteen, Harding's friends also saw him as lazy and lacking focus. Friendly and easygoing would remain descriptive of Harding all of his life.

When Harding was 10, his uncle gave him a cornet. Learning to play the instrument became one, if not the only, passion in his youth. He learned to play so well that a local band made him a member. The group was invited to Chicago to perform at an event celebrating the opening of the Erie Railroad. It would not be the last time Harding visited the city that would play a key location in Republican Party politics. He would continue to enjoy his music well into adulthood.

In 1878, the 13-year-old boy experienced the first real tragedy in his life. His younger brother and sister, Charles and Pricilla, died after a short illness, possibly the flu. A year later, he enrolled for the fall term at his father's college. At 14, Harding had reached the height of six feet and weighed almost 170 pounds. He was a big, strong young teenager moving on in his life.

In 1879, Iberia College (later Ohio Central College) had three faculty members and an enrollment of fewer than 50 students. Studying a general liberal arts curriculum, he proved a good student and an active member of the campus community. With his experience in the newspaper business, he and a friend began publishing a school paper, the *Iberia Spectator*. It served both the college and the local community. Harding expressed no specific career goals and indicated no clear postgraduate plans or interests. Still a teenager, he seemed happy with his studies, his college friends, and the school newspaper. He had already developed the personality that made him popular.

In his senior year, his father moved the family again, this time to Marion, Ohio. For the remainder of his life, Warren Harding would consider Marion his home. He spoke fondly of his memories in the small farming town. For him, it defined a positive, conservative, midwestern American culture that valued family, religion, and the benefits of small town life. If Blooming Grove and Caldonia had shaped his views, Marion confirmed them. Yet Marion in the 1880s had changed. It was no longer a small county seat with only farming families, and several rail lines connected the city with the outside world in Ohio and beyond. Manufacturing businesses, banks, and increasing shops and stores came to town. A reasonably diverse economy and growing population had turned Marion into a city.

In 1883, Harding graduated with two other seniors and gave the commencement address. Harding tried a variety of jobs. He taught school, sold insurance for a time, and considered the study of law. None of those possibilities drew his full attention or commitment. He

Warren G. Harding (Library of Congress)

played his coronet in a band, became the manager and substitute first baseman on the local baseball team, and spent his evenings playing poker at a bar near the city train station. He had developed a reputation as a womanizer and become one of the more popular men about town. Many of the local woman liked his strong, self-confident attitude and friendly demeanor. His male friends saw the same traits. As he grew older, Harding simply refined those attributes.

At 19, he finally decided to return to his earlier involvement with the newspaper business. With $300, he purchased the *Marion Star* in late 1883. The *Star*, one of three local papers, had the fewest advertisements and smallest circulation. Harding struggled to keep it afloat. His editorials adopted a Republican Party perspective, and in July 1884, he attended the Republican National Convention in Chicago, Illinois. Harding had been to Chicago as a boy, but he had not mingled with other journalists, politicians, and businesspeople who crowded into the city to attend the nomination of James G. Blaine. The cosmopolitan quality of the event impressed him, and Harding returned to Marion with a commitment to make his paper, and himself, a major figure in the community. Unfortunately, a sheriff's sale had closed the *Star* for unpaid debts. Forced to take a job with a rival paper, the *Democratic Mirror,* Harding chafed at having to write news supporting the 1884 Democratic candidate, Grover Cleveland.

Within a year, with his father's financial support, Harding paid his debts and began reprinting the *Marion Star*. His efforts became a local success story. The *Star* put out a daily edition, the only one in Marion; most local papers printed fortnightly editions. The citizens in the town had tended to vote Republican, but the county remained Democrat. To appeal to as many customers as possible, the *Star* adopted a moderate, pro-Republican position that avoided offending virtually any reader. Once, again, Harding's fundamental attitude aimed at limiting confrontation. It worked. He also spent time visiting Marion businesses (even investing in some), talking to the locals, and using his affable, easygoing manner to build a positive, personal reputation in Marion. The town was growing. He seemed to sense its energy and sought to play a key role in its future. In 1880, it numbered 4,000 citizens. In 1890, it was 8,000. And in 1900, Marion had climbed in numbers to 12,000. The *Star* grew right along with the city. In short order, the paper's success led to the closing of the other Republican paper in Merion, and the *Star* and *Democratic Mirror* competed. Harding's journal quickly surpassed its remaining competitor.

While his business prospered, Harding's personal life did as well. In 1886, he met and began to court Florence Kling, five years his senior and the daughter of a successful Marion banker and land developer Amos Kling. Florence had earlier married Peter deWolfe against her father's wishes and left town; she returned a year later with a year-old son and no husband. The elder Kling agreed to care for his grandson but not his daughter, who made a living as a piano teacher. One of her students, Harding's sister Chat, introduced her to Harding, and they began seeing each other.

Mrs. deWolfe divorced her husband in 1886 and agreed to marry the local newspaper editor, again against her father's wishes. Amos Kling despised Harding because the *Star* had written a number of editorials and news stories critical of King's business practices. The banker even launched a rumor that Harding had "African blood" in his heritage and appealed to the citizenry to boycott the *Star*. The racial claim would follow Harding to his presidency. In any event, perhaps to spite her father, Florence married Warren in July, 1891. Mrs. Harding was aware of her husband's former relationships with other women, but her own tenacity worked to control any wandering eye in his behavior. Never considered attractive by the standards of the time, her willpower served as Florence's greatest asset, and Harding respected her single-minded intelligence throughout their marriage.

She had a major role in his life, both personal and political. They had no children, so Florence focused on almost every aspect of her husband's day-to-day affairs. She took over the business management of the newspaper, guided his future political ambitions, and even controlled his appearance, clothes, and manners. Harding referred to Florence as "the Duchess," and both contemporaries and historians have wondered whether he meant it as a compliment or a complaint. Yet he followed her advice and listened to her instructions.

Harding's political ambitions grew when he attended the Republican Convention in 1884. He became an avid supporter of Joseph Foraker, who became Ohio's Republican governor and then the state's U.S. senator. He also met Mark Hanna, Ohio's other Republican senator and the powerful chairman of the Republican National Committee. Foraker helped him to gain a place as a delegate to the state convention in 1888. Harding lost a local, county election for auditor in 1895, his first venture into elective politics. During the 1896 election, however, Republican leaders in Ohio asked him to campaign around the state for the party's presidential nominee, William McKinley.

Harding made a good impression with Foraker, Hanna, and other key Republicans during the campaign. Handsome, friendly, and tempered in his speeches, he appealed to average voters and seemed to identify with their concerns. Insiders saw a potential future for the journalist, and they opened elective opportunities for him. In 1899, with strong party backing, Harding won a two-year term as state senator. He then won a second term in 1901. He got on well at the state capitol in Columbus. Colleagues liked his demeanor, tact, and easygoing personality. At the same time, he voted a Republican party line even while the leaders had begun an internal political struggle between Conservative and Progressive wings.

Harding met Harry M. Daugherty in 1899. A former state senator, Daugherty became a lobbyist and influential insider in Ohio Republican politics. At a chance meeting while stumping for the presidential candidate, the two men stayed in the same hotel in Richwood, Ohio. Legend suggests that Harding offered Daugherty a chew of tobacco one morning. He accepted, and they struck up a conversation that would turn into an acquaintance. As the Marion journalist walked away from the meeting, Daugherty later remembered his parting remark: "What a great-looking president he'd make." Harding still courted the advice and patronage of Joe Foraker and Mark Hanna, but Daugherty became his key political advisor and would remain so until he won the presidency

In 1903, as his second term in the state senate came to a close, Harding sought the nomination for governor. The party opted for Myron Herrick but added Harding on the ticket as lieutenant governor. The two won handily, but the Republican Party in Ohio remained divided as the United States' Progressive movement split old-line conservatives from a new breed of progressive leaders.

The dissention within Republican Party ranks failed to harm Harding's growing influence. His moderation and apparent tact on issues enabled him to make few enemies as the political battle continued. In the 1908 presidential campaign, Harding initially endorsed his old mentor, Joe Foraker, against William Howard Taft. When it became clear that Foraker's conservativism no longer appealed to voters, however, the *Star* and its owner shifted support to Taft. Harding had concluded that the progressive wing of the Ohio Republican Party appeared the political path for the future, and he went with the new direction.

The Marion newspaper owner continued his own political goals as Taft became president in 1909. Harding sought and won the nomination for Ohio governor

in 1910, but he lost to incumbent Democrat Judson Harmon. By, 1912, the Republican Party split had gone nationwide. Theodore Roosevelt lost the party's nomination running against Taft and formed an independent Progressive Party. That split enabled Woodrow Wilson to win the 1912 election.

The states had ratified the Seventeenth Amendment in 1913, which made the popular election of U.S. senators the new procedure for holding the office. Four Ohio Democrats sought the nomination: Theodore Burton, a sitting senator; Joe Foraker, the "old" conservative; Congressman Ralph Cole; and Warren Harding. Burton dropped out of the race, and Harding's continued appeal to moderation, toleration, and goodwill worked in his favor as it always had. He won the nomination and used the same style of campaigning to defeat his Democratic opponent, state attorney general Timothy Hogan, by 100,000 votes.

As a junior senator, Harding received some minor committee assignments, but he performed the way he had through his entire career. Moderate, friendly, and quick to hear both sides of an argument, he became a popular member of the Senate in a short time. He consistently voted with the Republican minority but remained careful to court conservatives and progressives in the party. He even got along with some Democrats. The two issues that drew Senate attention focused on suffrage and prohibition. Harding kept his personal views on suffrage to himself, and he told constituents that he would wait to see how Ohio would respond to an amendment; he would then vote accordingly. Harding drank liquor regularly, but he supported the Eighteenth Amendment and the Volstead Act. In effect, he came down on the right side politically as the Eighteenth Amendment (1919) and Nineteenth Amendment (1920) won ratification.

In 1916, the Republican Party assigned Harding to serve as chairman of the Republican National Convention, again held in Chicago. He also gave the keynote address. His star had risen. The party's nominee, Charles Evans Hughes, lost in a narrow race with Woodrow Wilson, who was seeking a second term. Unlike the previous election, where Roosevelt's split with the party had divided Republican voters, those issues appeared resolved, and the election was close.

In Washington and around the nation, attention had turned to the 1914 outbreak of World War I. Senator Harding supported President Wilson's August declaration of neutrality. Like many Americans, he believed in the traditional policy position that George Washington had established. The United States should avoid involvement in Europe's wars. When a series of events between 1914 and 1917 drew the nation away from neutrality, however, he backed the president when Wilson asked Congress for a declaration of war against Germany. Harding supported most of the president's wartime policies, as did many Republicans, but in 1918 that position changed.

The bipartisan politics of wartime diplomacy collapsed when President Wilson publicly asked voters to return Democratic majorities to the Congress in 1918 midterm elections. Many Republican leaders concluded that Wilson had betrayed an agreed-upon party cooperation, and they mounted a strong campaign to take control of the House and Senate. Republicans won a narrow victory in the Senate and were poised to challenge whatever postwar plans Wilson might pursue, specifically his call for the creation of an international League of Nations. Appointed to the Senate Foreign Relations Committee, Harding attached his loyalty to the committee chairman, Henry Cabot Lodge, and other senior senators determined to limit or block Wilson's efforts to use the Paris Peace Conference as a vehicle to establish a league and join the United States to the organization.

The battle between the president and the Senate occupied the nation's interest from the end of World War I, in November 1918, until March 1920. Harding played a role in the debate, and Senate Republicans were able to block Wilson's plans and keep the United States from joining the League of Nations. That decision and the Senate vote would remain one of the party's foreign policy platforms and position throughout the decade, both in Congress and the White House.

The 1920 presidential election seemed ripe for the Republicans to regain control of the White House. The American public appeared weary with the political battle over the League of Nations and the energetic idealism that had fueled the Progressive movement. Something was in the wind, and a change of direction in political thinking seemed likely. Theodore Roosevelt became an early front runner for the Republican nomination, but he died in 1919, and a host of candidates emerged to fill the vacancy. Warren Harding was one of the many. His political mentor, Harry Daugherty, and his wife, Florence, prodded him to seek the nomination even though more well-known and respected figures came to the Chicago Republican Convention on June 8.

By 1920, 16 states conducted primaries, and in those, Harding had not done well. Daugherty and Mrs. Harding badgered him into staying in the race, so he arrived in Chicago as a dark horse candidate. A surprising deadlock between the two front-runners, Leonard Wood and Frank Lowden awarded neither the necessary votes, and the convention was thrown open to a compromise candidate. A myth emerged that in a "smoke-filled room" in the Blackstone Hotel, the party bosses picked Harding because he had few enemies and "looked presidential" (the old Daugherty quip). Although no direct evidence supports the claim, it may be true. Harding did become the compromise candidate on June 12, and the party selected Calvin Coolidge from Massachusetts to run as the vice presidential candidate.

One thing had concerned the party bosses about Harding's nomination. It involved his personal life and the possibility of an election scandal. In 1905, while Ohio's lieutenant governor, he had begun an affair with Carrie Fulton Phillips, a married woman and a friend of his wife. That relationship lasted off and on until 1920. In a meeting with a small group of Republican leaders, the senator admitted the affair and also told them that Phillips had blackmailed him. In a rare instance in factual backroom politics, the party power brokers agreed to pay Phillips for her silence, which she kept. That solved the problem—or at least the problem of Carrie Phillips.

Unbeknown to them, however, in 1905 Harding had begun another affair with an 18-year-old woman from Marion named Nan Britton. Harding had met her when she was a teenager in Marion. She had taken a job as a secretary in New York and regularly traveled to Washington to be with him. The affair continued until his death in 1923. Mrs. Harding may have been aware of both infidelities, but her interest in his political career probably outweighed her concerns. The affair with Britton remained secret throughout the campaign and Harding's presidency—except perhaps to the Secret Service agents who protected him.

The 1920 presidential campaign pitted Harding and Coolidge against James Cox, governor of Ohio, and Franklin D. Roosevelt of New York, Cox's running mate. Both Harding and Cox had been dark horse candidates at their respective conventions. Rather than attack Cox politically, Harding's campaign focused on criticizing Woodrow Wilson—both his international policies and his domestic progressive reform programs. The Republican position seemed moving back to an old Jacksonian idea that "the government that governs best, governs least." It worked. In November, Harding won more than 60 percent of the popular vote and 404 electoral votes. The Republican Party also increased its majority in both Houses of Congress. It would begin a decade of Republican power in the White House and the legislature.

Harding gave a short, tempered inaugural address, and the social functions following the inaugural proved limited and inexpensive. The new president seemed to set a tone suggesting his administration might practice governing in the same style. "Our most dangerous tendency," Harding had warned, "is to expect too much from the government."

Harding never acted comfortably as president. He enjoyed the more provincial atmosphere of small town Marion and continued to savor his bourbon and cigars while playing poker with old friends like Daugherty, whom he appointed attorney general. The cerebral secretary of state, Charles Evans Hughes, and the well-known, energetic secretary of commerce, Herbert Hoover may have intimidated the president. Later scandals in the Veterans Bureau and the Teapot Dome affairs would frustrate Harding because they took place under the leadership of friends he had appointed to positions of authority. (Harding's policies, both constructive and scandalous, will be examined in the analytical essay.) What remains clear is that Warren Harding's last two years in office proved unhappy ones for him.

In June 1923, President Harding planned an extensive tour and speaking trip that he called his "Voyage of Discovery." He would travel by train cross-country, giving speeches in Kansas City and Denver. Upon reaching the West Coast, Harding would sail to Alaska,

the first American chief executive to visit the U.S. territory. Moving back down the coast, he planned to stop in Vancouver, British Columbia; speak a day later in Seattle; and arrive in San Francisco in late July. From there, Harding's itinerary had scheduled a further trip down the Pacific Ocean through the Panama Canal, on to Puerto Rico, and back to Washington, D.C., by late August. It was an ambitious and trying venture for anyone. It had become clear, however, that President Harding was not well.

As early as 1919, doctors had diagnosed that Harding had a serious heart condition; his drinking, smoking, and dietary habits had caused it. At the same time, the demands of his political career, emerging scandals in the administration, and concerns about Mrs. Harding's medical problems increased his fatigue and a growing depression. Yet in the early part of his tour, he did well. Harding spoke to enthusiastic and large audiences in Kansas City and Denver and made a great public impression by visiting the sites in Alaska, where he spent two weeks. The first sitting president to visit Canada, the United States' northern neighbors appeared equally delighted with his visit to Vancouver and named a public park in Harding's honor.

On July 27, he gave a speech at the University of Washington in Seattle, again to a large, cheering audience. A few hours afterward, he became ill, and doctors forced him to rest and limit his appearances. Off and on, Harding seemed to recover, and he performed so well at speeches he delivered in San Francisco on July 29 that he asked Florence Harding to read editorials lauding his remarks while he rested in his bed in the Palace Hotel.

At 7:30 p.m. on August 2, Florence, reading one of the favorable editorials, asked if she should continue. Harding replied, "That's good, read some more." A minute later, he was dead at 57 years of age. Doctors initially listed the cause of death as cerebral hemorrhage, but later analysis determined he had died of a heart attack.

The president's body was taken by train to Washington for funeral services in the nation's capital. Then he returned to his home in Marion. Harding's vice president, Calvin Coolidge; Chief Justice William Howard Taft; Harding's wife; and Harding's father followed a horse-drawn hearse through the town and past his newspaper office to the Marion Cemetery for final burial.

The American public and media generally liked and admired President Harding. The crowds that gathered in Washington and Marion were large and somber. Editorials were equally remorseful. As Senate investigations and newspaper coverage began to reveal the number of administration scandals that had occurred during his presidency, however, that popularity suffered. President Harding may not have been directly involved in the scandals, and neither did he know much about them; the revelations occurred after his death. Still, he was the president and was ultimately deemed responsible not as complicit but as ignorant of the events.

Florence Harding survived her husband by a year. She had planned to live in Washington, D.C., after her husband's death and hoped to tour Europe. However, her doctor convinced her to return to Marion and settle in his medical sanitarium. Diagnosed with renal failure, she died on November 21, 1924. The Hardings had no children, but Florence's two grandchildren by her first marriage received the balance of the Harding family estate.

Historians have concluded that Warren Harding was ill prepared for the office, and they have cited the various problems in his administration as evidence. He died while beginning to see that his legacy might well be an unfavorable one, and it has been.

HISTORICAL OVERVIEW

Warren Harding lived during a period of significant change in the United States. Born in 1865, just seven months after the American Civil War ended, he died in 1923, fewer than five years after the end of World War I. Between those two conflicts, significant in their own right, fundamental changes occurred in the United States. They would affect the ideas, beliefs, and attitudes of the newspaper owner turned politician as his career evolved from Marion, Ohio, to Washington, D.C. The nature of history is a study in change. The time between Harding's birth in 1865 and death in 1923 saw alterations in American life often difficult to assess or even accept by the people who lived through those years. Both society as a whole and a political leader like Harding would experience a profound learning curve during the last decades of the 19th century and the first two decades of the 20th century.

Demographics

Five years after the Civil War, the U.S. population numbered 38.5 million residents living in 36 states and a huge frontier wilderness. Decade by decade, that number soared. In 1890, 62.9 million people lived in America—a better than 40 percent increase. When Warren Harding campaigned for the presidency in 1920, 106 million populated 48 states. Only the territories of Alaska and Hawaii waited admission to the union as states.

Where Americans lived had also changed. In 1870, only 26 percent of Americans lived in cities. By 1900 it was 40 percent, and in 1920, 51 percent inhabited urban locations. Cities were growing, and farm populations had declined.

While the population grew and movement to cities increased, the racial makeup of the American scene remained fairly steady during the 50 years from 1870 to 1920. African Americans made up 12–13 percent of the population but declined to less than 10 percent by 1920. Hispanic, Asian, and Native American numbers remained at single-digit percentages, often 1–2 percent.

More than 25 million immigrants came to the United States between 1870 and 1920: 12 million from Northern Europe, 12 million from Eastern and Southern Europe, 2 million from Latin America, and half a million from Asia. Those families, leaving their homes for economic or political reasons, not only enhanced the nation's population but also brought new cultural values and ideas to American society that were often novel but sometimes unwelcome. The "Americanization of immigrants" that served as a major aspect of Frederick Jackson Turner's Frontier Thesis demanded new attention in society.

Finally, advances in health and medical knowledge, aided the United States rise in population. Throughout most of the 1800s, life expectancy for men and women in the United States hovered around 40 to 45 years of age. By the beginning of the 20th century, the age average began to rise into the mid-fifties.

Essentially, during Warren Harding's lifetime, the United States had become much larger in numbers, more urban, more ethnically diverse, and healthier. By the first decades of the 1900s, those demographic changes required politicians like Harding to confront and respond differently to American life than they would have only a generation or two before.

The Frontier

In 1870, the official map of the U.S. Census Bureau designated most U.S. land west of the Mississippi river as an unsettled frontier. Between St. Louis, Missouri, and San Francisco, California, a Trans-Mississippi wilderness invited the possibility of settlement. Although numerous Native American tribes occupied the territory as their own, the American government continued to pursue a policy to move them, whether by treaty or force.

The Republican Congress had passed the Homestead Act in May 1862 allowing Americans, including freed slaves, to claim 160 acres of free land in the frontier region. A generation of settlers in the postwar decades would begin a migration into that "wilderness" and change the national demographic. Settlers would eventually file 1.6 million claims through the 420,000 square miles available. The completion of the transcontinental railroad in May 1869 not only made it easier for them to move west from Missouri but also made the transport of natural resources, livestock, and farm products more efficient. Towns, and then cities, grew up along the rail lines to support the railroad economy. Chicago, Illinois, the city that hosted Republican Conventions on a regular basis and the large urban center that first impressed Warren Harding, grew along with the railroads. So too did its population.

In 1890, the Census Bureau issued a new map indicating that the American frontier no longer existed. The transcontinental country was "settled." Two years later, Frederick Jackson Turner, a history professor at the University of Wisconsin, wrote a seminal article, "The Influence of the Frontier in American History," in the *Mississippi Valley Historical Review*. It argued that the national confrontation with the wilderness since colonial times had shaped the United States' democratic form of government, its free market

economics, and its "Americanization" of immigrants Turner believed the nation's constant struggle to tame the wilderness shaped the character of the United States. He wondered how the country and its people would continue to evolve without that influence.

In the same year that Turner published his work, Warren Harding had just celebrated his 27th birthday. Through most of his early life, the settlement of the trans-Mississippi frontier had been part of the mainstream of the nation's ethos. His Ohio upbringing in the former Northwest Territory, a rural, agricultural, small town region, had many of the attributes that shaped his thinking. Professor Turner wrote about those ideas, and Harding accepted the conclusion that sturdy, western, rural family values provided the main spring of American life. By the time he entered national political life, however, that image (whether myth or reality) had changed. Factories, not farms, had become the nation's new economic identity.

The Industrial Revolution

The industrial revolution began in Great Britain and Western Europe at the beginning of the 1800s, and it grew slowly by midcentury. After the Civil War, it exploded in the United States as well as Europe. The development of the mass production of goods and services, the increased capital that fueled it, the millions of workers necessary to make the goods, and the innovations in science and technology to speed the process (just conceived when Harding was born) would witness both success and problems by the beginning of the 20th century. Yet more than the frontier, industrialism shaped the nation that Harding would lead as president.

After the Civil War, the United States possessed the money, the natural resources, a generation of peace, and political backing to generate an industrial boom. It needed only cheap labor, locations for plants and factories, consumers, and entrepreneurs to generate the calculus of industrialism.

A wave of new immigration swept into the United States and supplied both labor and consumers. Between 1880 and 1920, 20 million immigrants arrived in the United States. In the past, most had come from Northern and Western Europe. Many still did, but new arrivals also came from Central, Eastern, and Southern Europe, as well as Asia. The broad majority of people looked to improve their economic future as they always had. The country's streets were not paved with gold, but jobs became available in the mines, plants, and factories.

The influx of people from new environments concerned many "homegrown" Americans. Forms of nativism surfaced, critical of the newcomers. Their religions, social and cultural ideas, and affection for their former homelands led to nativist expressions of outright bigotry and oppression. However, the immigrants were needed to drive the economy, and their labor did so.

Harding himself had to adapt. He grew to maturity in a predominantly white, Western European, Protestant environment. It was a place that the prolific novelist Sinclair Lewis described in *Main Street* (1920) and *Babbitt* (1922) as suspicious, parochial, and bigoted. Although the new Americans may have been necessary to provide cheap labor, they often remained unwelcome in his society.

The labor-immigration demand worked, however. The 1890 census saw the U.S. population rise to 62,979,766, a 25 percent increase since the 1880 census. Like it or not, older generations and their politicians, like Harding, had to adapt. Not only did American business owners need the workers, but politicians needed their votes.

Urbanization was a direct result of industrialism. In 1870, the U.S. urban population made up 25.7 percent of the nation. By 1920, when Harding ran for president, 51.2 percent lived in cities, many first- and second-generation immigrants. That demographic shift had an impact on the political environment as Republicans and Democrats began to rethink their appeal to the new voters. Harding, always a moderate in expressing his views, avoided any expression of nativism throughout his political life.

The accumulation of wealth in the hands of a few "robber barons," and the government's wide support of the process of laissez-faire capitalism and big business would, by 1900, make the United States the most productive industrial state in the world. Although that success benefited many Americans, it also created social, political, and economic concerns about an "other America" of poverty, slums, and injustice. Those concerns prompted a major reform movement, the Progressive era. Changes in the United States since 1870 forced the nation to examine the role of government, economics, and social justice as the new century dawned.

The Progressive Era

As the 20th century began, a major reform movement emerged in the United States. It had earlier roots in agrarian populist concerns about the rise of industrialism, corporate capitalism, and the power of Eastern business "robber barons." Between 1900 and 1918, however, the Progressive movement became a national, grass roots, middle-class cause, both rural and urban, that demanded major changes in the United States. Reformers looked at three broad issues.

The growth of industrial capitalism, they believed, placed too much power in the hands of wealthy bankers and business tycoons. As a result, both workers and consumers had few protections from the greed and exploitation of big business. The only source powerful enough to check the behavior of capitalism, progressives argued, required government oversight at every level, local, state, and federal.

Progressives also concluded, however, that most elected or appointed politicians had come to serve the interests of corporate, industrial leaders. Men like J. P. Morgan, Andrew Carnegie, and John D. Rockefeller controlled monopolies in banking, railroads, oil, and steel production that destroyed healthy competition and exploited the public. Those "robber barons" appeared to possess more power than the government. Since the end of the Civil War, Republicans and Democrats had adopted a laissez-faire, supportive attitude toward the exploding growth and profits of the industrial boom and the men who led it. The United States needed a new breed of political leaders who were honest, efficient, and committed to curbing the excesses of big business and its greedy leadership.

Additionally, Progressives turned their attention to social justice. They believed that immigrants, laborers, women, African Americans, and others had been shut out of the opportunity to achieve true success in a nation that prided itself on exceptionalism. Nativism, anti-unionism, sexism, and racism, which were endemic in the early 1900s, continued to stain the belief that the United States was a place of liberty and opportunity.

Applauding the growth of big cities made little sense when many of them contained tenement slums, hunger, dangerous factors, and poverty. Freedom from slavery for African Americans made little sense when Jim Crow segregation in Southern states was little better. And women still lacked the vote except in Wyoming (1890). By the 1920 presidential election, only 14 states granted the franchise to women.

The growing movement had no central leadership or even a clear direction beyond those three basic concerns. How to achieve their goals differed widely with the men and women who supported progressivism. From anarchists, socialists, labor union organizers, and moderates, reformers of all stripes sought their own methods to achieve the basic goals of progressive thinking. The two major parties, however, had to determine the most expedient way to control and direct its impulse.

As a rising Republican politician, Warren Harding—always moderate, calculating, and determined to offend the fewest leaders and voters—considered how best to respond to the growing popularity of progressive reform. His party divided on the issue. "Old Guard" Republicans opposed major efforts to change, yet Theodore Roosevelt led the party as president from 1901 to 1909 and advocated aspects of economic, political, and social reform with the support of another faction within the party.

When Harding ran for Ohio's Senate seat in 1914, he took his typical, moderate position. His supporters attacked his opponent, Tom Hogan, with vicious nativist attacks because he was a Roman Catholic. Harding never endorsed those attacks, but neither did he condemn them. When asked his position on the Nineteenth Amendment, granting the vote to women, Harding adroitly responded that he would support what the voters in Ohio decided. He drank liquor regularly, never favored Prohibition, but voted with party regulars to override President Wilson's veto to ratify the Eighteenth Amendment. Throughout the Progressive era, Senator Harding maintained a low-key involvement in the broad variety of new laws and programs that implemented major changes in the nation's economic and political response to the new era of growing industrial success and government's involvement in its evolution.

Harding had grown to maturity in a country that Professor Richard Hofstater claimed had been settled and dominated by "white, protestant farmers" (Hofsater 1955). As the 20th century began, the United States was an altogether different place. The freeing of millions of African American slaves had removed them from the misery of slavery and exposed the reality that they too had been in the United States as long as those "protestant farmers." How would they be treated in the post–Civil War decades? History would offer a shabby, racist response that would confront Harding and other political leaders well into the new century and beyond.

Civil rights influenced American life while the newspaper owner from Marion, Ohio, grew to maturity. The Reconstruction Era (1865–1877) sought briefly to respond justly to former African American slaves. The Thirteenth, Fourteenth, and Fifteenth Amendments aimed to first free slaves and then provide them with political citizenship and civil rights. Racial prejudice, and a Southern reclaiming of state's rights, betrayed that hope, as did a dwindling Northern concern for blacks as well. By the beginning of the 1880s, an age of Jim Crow segregation would condemn the nation's African American population to generations of prejudice and oppression.

When Harding became president in 1921, black civil rights leaders like W. E. B. DuBois, Ida Wells, Booker T. Washington, and many others had sparked a turn-of-the-century movement that led to the founding of the National Association for the Advancement of Colored People (NAACP) and a broad commitment to overturn Jim Crow racism and oppression. Both as a senator and president, Harding tended to support their goals, but with his usual moderation. As senator, he voted in favor of the 1918 Dyer Anti-Lynching Law. Southern Democrats blocked passage of Dyer's bill using filibusters in 1922, 1923, and 1924. In 1922, as president, Harding gave a controversial speech in Birmingham, Alabama, calling for support of renewed antilynching legislation and better racial relations in the South.

At the same time, American women began their own struggle for equality and social justice. The suffrage movement sought the vote, the first stage of a long social and political drive to enhance the rights of females. It would persist until 1920, when Congress ratified the Nineteenth Amendment, the year the nation elected Warren Harding president. His political career from state office to the Congress, Senate, and White House dealt regularly with the social and political issues that focused on suffrage, but he was careful. He noted that he would vote to support the amendment only if his constituents in Ohio supported the idea. When they did so, the amendment received his support. Whether Harding acted as a full-fledged political progressive committed to the basic reforms demanded by African Americans and women is open to question. As a good Republican, he tended to support his party's direction.

The United States' conflict with Native Americans had existed since the earliest days of colonial settlement in the 1600s. It seemed both a shameful and expected history fueled by a vague sense of Manifest Destiny. Although the nation technically treated Indians tribes as sovereign states, the inevitable goal of U.S. policy acted to remove Native Americans from their land in order to provide space for its own immigrants. From Harding's birth in 1865 to the last decade of the 19th century, the United States pursued a relentless policy of achieving that result, either by treaty or war. As Harding grew up, he read accounts of General George Custer's defeat at the Battle of Little Big Horn in the Dakotas in 1876 and the last years of the Apache wars in the late 1880s. The reservation system grew during Harding's rise to political power. Not until 1924, a year after his death, did the United States grant citizenship rights to American Indians.

Foreign Relations

Just as in domestic life, the United States experienced major shifts in international affairs. Throughout the 19th century, it pursued two basic goals; contiguous territorial expansion across the continent and nonintervention in European political issues.

Both guided U.S. foreign policy from George Washington's farewell address to the United States' entry into World War I in 1917. The new nation wanted to avoid "entangling" alliances with European states, convinced that their crises and conflicts might threaten its peaceful and prosperous development. U.S. leaders also came to believe that "Old" Europe should leave the "New World" alone. They concluded, hopefully, that the wide Atlantic Ocean would provide a strategic moat to protect the country.

The 1823 Monroe Doctrine warned Europeans to cease further colonization in the hemisphere and supported the success of Latin American revolutions to end Spanish rule. It implied, however, that the United States had a special role to play in the region. The United States was the first nation to recognize independence for the new governments to the South, but it prompted skepticism among Latin American states that their Yankee neighbors had their own plans to dominate the area. Their suspicions were well founded. In effect, the diplomatic thinking and practice in the United States reflected a nation on the defensive, suspicious and fearful of powerful European nations but not constrained in its own ambitions.

By the decade of the 1890s, however, American foreign policy began to change as its power grew. In 1898, the United States annexed the islands of Hawaii. The country went to war with Spain that same year and "freed" Cuba from Spain's colonial control. It then annexed Puerto Rico, the Philippines, and Guam, former Spanish colonies, to begin a period of overseas imperial expansion. Those forms of expansion, limited compared to European imperialism, coupled with economic influence in Latin American as well. In many ways, the nation's economic influence served as another form of traditional imperialism.

When the United States undertook the construction of the Panama Canal between 1903 and 1914, three American presidents had established a privileged, U.S. protectorate in the heart of Central America. Under the influence of Alfred T. Mahan, a noted U.S. naval theorist, the country had built a fleet, rivaled only by Great Britain, to protect its growing interests in the Caribbean and Central America. In 1903, President Theodore Roosevelt added a corollary to the Monroe Doctrine claiming the United States' right to intervene in the affairs of other hemisphere nations to protect the nation's interests. American military forces would enter a number of independent states in the Caribbean and Central America during the next two decades in what historians have described as aggressive "Big Stick Diplomacy" or "Dollar Diplomacy."

By the time Harding came to the Senate in 1915, the U.S. policy of the past, one of defensive thinking, had shifted to that of a world power prone to more aggressive behavior in the international arena. As former secretary of state John Hay had remarked at the beginning of the Spanish-American War, we had become a world power "willy-nilly."

World War I and the League of Nations

The European conflict that erupted in July–August 1914 quickly became a world war that involved dozens of nations. Great Britain, France, Russia and Italy (the Entente) fought against Germany, Austria-Hungary, and the Ottoman Empire (the Triple Alliance). Modern weapons, huge military forces, and total national commitment to the conflict combined to create a devastating result. By the end of the war in 1918, 9–11 million military deaths and 5–6 million civilian lives died worldwide. Those wounded or missing numbered over 40 million people. A flu pandemic that may have begun in the military camps in Europe at the end of the war spread across the globe and caused the death of 20–50 million people—the worst medical tragedy in history. The emotional, psychological, and practical impact of the war scarred a generation.

On August 19, 1914, as the war in Europe began, President Woodrow Wilson acted in a diplomatic tradition established during George Washington's administration: he declared U.S. neutrality. While campaigning for the Senate, Harding approved, as did most Americans. During the next three years, however, as the war intensified, different factors drew the United States into the conflict. Economic concerns involving loans and sales to the combatants, German submarine warfare that caused U.S. civilian deaths, and other issues pushed Wilson's administration toward war. Before he won a second term in 1916, Wilson warned Germany to cease U-boat attacks on ships carrying American civilians, and he drew a

proverbial red line. The German government agreed to do so, issuing the Sussex Pledge in March 1916, six months before the presidential election. In January 1917, however, it changed policy by announcing the beginning of unrestricted submarine warfare in the Atlantic Ocean. Germany had violated the Sussex Pledge and crossed Wilson's red line.

On April 2, 1917, the president asked Congress for a declaration of war against Germany. The Senate, including Harding, supported the request 82–6. The House followed with a vote of 373–50. Two million Americans served in Europe between June 1917 and November 1918. When World War I ended in an armistice on November 11, over 100,000 members of the American Expeditionary Force (AEF) had died, and more than 200,000 were listed as casualties.

The nation's involvement in the war and treaty decisions following the armistice provoked a serious public debate and involved Harding as a member of the Senate Foreign Relations Committee. Upon attending the Paris Peace Conference in 1919, President Wilson sought to create a League of Nations as an integral part of the treaty ending the war. His belief in an international organization to prevent future threats of war clashed with a Republican Senate that won majority control of that body in the 1918 off-year elections. When President Wilson returned from Europe in the summer of 1919, Republicans in the Senate had already warned him they would not support his efforts in Paris either at all or with serious, restrictive reservations and amendments.

A lengthy battle over U.S. entry into the league pitted Wilsonian internationalists against a small group of Republican isolationists and a larger number of Republican reservationists, who wanted to limit or control the United States' postwar membership in the organization. The Senate ultimately won the battle. By March 1920, as the presidential election campaign began, Republican nominee Harding had already cast his vote in the Senate to prevent U.S. entry into the League of Nations.

The Republican Party and its nominee had reverted to a form of neo-isolationism. As powerful as the United States had become by 1920, Harding and his party saw little need to enhance or protect that power through membership in an international body. While running for president, Harding made his criticism of Wilson's goals a major campaign issue. During a decade of Republican control of Congress and the White House, the broad policy of avoiding collective-internationalism guided American foreign policy.

Postwar Economy

As Warren Harding began his presidential campaign, a postwar recession caused a brief period of financial slowdown. By July, however, the recession ended, and the United States began a booming economic revival that would last until 1928. Between those years, the nation's Gross National Product (GNP) grew 42 percent. Unemployment fell below 4 percent; average annual income rose from $6,400 to $8,016. While income inequality rose sharply and saw the top 1 percent earn 14 percent of income, most American's credited the Republican Party, and President Harding, with the general economic growth.

Even before the war, technical innovations created cheaper mass production methods and new goods and services. Better advertising, new markets in Latin America, and the growth of banking and the stock market fueled the expanding success of American business and financial investment opportunities. Equally important, full employment gave the broad public spending money to purchase the goods and services necessary to grow the economy. The devastation in Europe in the aftermath of war also limited, for a time, strong competition from abroad. By mid-decade, the United States produced half the world's economic output. Although President Harding had little direct input in the prosperity, he did reduce the top tax rate to 58 percent, a significant drop from Progressive Era rates that amounted to 77 percent by 1918. His administration and the Republican Congress became supporters of American business. The Progressive Era efforts to provide oversight and restrictions lapsed.

While the decade of prosperity grew, some Americans did suffer. Farming as a percentage of the national economy dropped, and small farmers suffered the most. Labor unions failed to win the support of Republican administrations. An "Other America" of African American sharecroppers, and blacks in general, still failed to receive the same employment opportunities and wages as most Americans. In that regard, little had changed, though a majority of Americans had begun to define the postwar era as the Roaring Twenties.

Taking advantage of the mood, the Republicans ran their political campaigns on the slogan "Peace, Prosperity, and Security." Americans kept voting for them.

Society and Culture from the Gilded Age to the Roaring Twenties

George Santayana, a Spanish-born Harvard professor, wrote in *The Genteel Tradition: Nine Essays* (1935), "America is a young country with an old mentality." He suggested that the United States had grown from "infancy" to "senility" without a period of "maturity." During Warren Harding's lifetime, however, American society and culture accomplished remarkable contributions in every aspect of social and cultural life. In literature, art, music, and recreation—both elite and popular forms of culture—the nation's contributions rivaled any society in the world. American exceptionalism made its mark in all of those endeavors.

The nation's size alone predicted the accomplishment. By 1900, the United States had more symphony orchestras, ballet companies, art galleries, museums, and public libraries than any country in Europe or elsewhere. American writers, artists, and musicians rivaled global competitors. The nation verged on creating a mass consumer culture that took advantage of industrialism, urbanization, immigration, and a growing middle class able to pursue its own choices in recreation and amusement.

When Mark Twain and Charles Dudley Warren wrote *The Gilded Age: A Tale of Today* (1873), they attacked the excess and waste that the industrial revolution's success had produced among the wealthy. The term "Gilded Age" came to define the last generation of the 1800s not just because of excess wealth among the few but because the whole society seemed changing. Though belief in family, religion, propriety, and local customs and values still persisted, they faced the challenges that not always conformed with mid-19th-century American culture.

A practical response to those changes produced the Progressive Era. However, it dealt with economic, political, and justice concerns. Subtle changes in culture evolved beneath the surface of laws, legislation, and constitutional amendments. Urbanization alone brought together large numbers of people seeking forms of entertainment and amusement with change left over from their employment. Mass popular culture rose to provide it.

Newspapers and magazines (print media) dominated American journalism as thousands of local and national editors sold their efforts to the public in every city across the nation. Papers now included sports sections, comic strips, and even astrology readings. The "penny press" searched for a mass audience. Warren Harding's *Marion Star* competed locally in a widely expanding business, but his traditional layout failed to compete with the new press. Famous owners like William Randolph Hearst and Joseph Pulitzer, whose *New York Journal* and *New York World,* respectively, became synonymous with "Yellow Press" sensational reporting and editorial competition in the 1890s. Ultimately, commercial radio would also compete, but when Harding became president in 1921, newspapers ruled the information cycle, and they had evolved into a mass audience medium.

New forms of entertainment like records and moving pictures also loomed on the horizon. Thomas Edison, W. K. Dickson, George Eastman, and others invented early versions of film (kinetoscope) displayed at the 1893 Chicago World's Fair. By 1909, 9,000 movie theaters played single reel films to growing audiences in American cities. Edison had also invented the phonograph in 1877, and by 1885, music publishers and writers in New York City's "Tin Pan Alley" not only published sheet music but also produced records to play on the new machines.

Historians have always seen the evolution of automobile transportation as a cultural as well as technical and economic success story. By 1899, 30 manufactures produced 2,500 automobiles for sale. In 1908, Henry T. Ford and William Durant created two new companies, Ford Motor Company and General Motors, respectively. Five years later, they sold 485,000 cars between them. They sought a broad market, so prices were reasonably low. Socially and culturally, the automobile offered a way for owners, particularly young people, to escape the local, narrow society of their

town and find recreation and privacy beyond the prying eyes of parents and neighbors.

College and professional athletics witnessed similar popularity. Baseball had been an American pastime since the Civil War, and 100s of different teams of amateurs and professionals barnstormed through rural towns. By 1901, however, the National and American Leagues organized, and their professional teams centered in big cities. The leagues became segregated, and African Americans developed their own teams and performed for their own spectators. Football remained a popular college level sport that drew huge crowds, but professionals formed their own league in 1892. In 1922, it became the National Football League (NFL).

Gerald Early, a contemporary essayist and professor at Washington University in St. Louis, wrote, "There are only three things that America will be remembered for 2,000 years from now when they study civilization; the Constitution, jazz music, and baseball." Warren Harding may not have been around for the first, but during his lifetime, he was there for the last two—and much more—as the culture grew broader, more available, and certainly more diverse.

As the 1920s and Harding's presidency began, the nation had become a different place than it was when he was a boy in Ohio: bigger, powerful, industrial, urban, and diverse. Yet the surface benefits of those accomplishments appeared to produce a more cynical view of American life even while many enjoyed the options of the Roaring Twenties or Jazz Age in nightclubs, speakeasies, ballparks, and movie theaters.

ANALYTICAL ESSAY

It remains difficult to write an analysis of Warren Harding's presidency. History and historians have been unkind to the Ohio chief executive. When he won the office in 1920, however, he had broad popular support. When he died in 1923, even though several scandals in his administration had surfaced, Harding still remained a popular, admired leader.

In 1948, the historian Arthur Schlesinger Sr. conducted a survey among 55 leading scholars to rate the best and worst presidents. Harding ended in the bottom tier. Similar surveys have taken place since, from 1948 to 2014. In every instance, the 29th president has finished among the bottom 10 chief executives, often as low as one of the five worst.

As he campaigned in 1920, Warren Harding had assets and practical experiences that qualified him for the nation's highest office. He possessed a college education—not Harvard or Yale, though most presidents didn't enjoy that privilege. As a relatively successful newspaper editor and journalist, he kept current with the evolving political and economic issues not only in Ohio but throughout the nation. Harding had experience in Ohio politics, elected as a state senator and lieutenant governor. He also served for six years in the U.S. Senate. Any number of presidents, including Abraham Lincoln, who often ranked first in surveys failed to match his formal educational background or active political experience.

Most scholars who have studied Harding seem unimpressed with his intellect, his lack of extensive reading in history or politics, or the fact that he had failed to develop a thoughtful world view about the job he held. A contemporary in the White House remembered Harding admitting, "I am a man of limited talents from a small town." It may have prompted one of his major biographers, Francis Russell, to title his work *The Shadow of Blooming Grove* (1968). Both the title and the book itself suggested that Harding's life in a small-town Ohio environment may have hindered his performance as president. Apparently, Harding may have thought so as well.

However, any number of American presidents were born and raised in small towns across the country, attended little known colleges, and did not read extensively or ponder deeply the issues of the day. Something has colored history's negative interpretation of Warren Harding.

A general critique of his presidency offers several basic conclusions. First, Warren Harding did lack the intellectual capacity to do the job; he knew it, and so did others. Second, he took no real interest in his role as president and turned decision-making over to Congress, his cabinet, and other subordinates. In effect, Harding failed to lead; he preferred to follow. Finally, President Harding never grasped the monumental changes that confronted the United States in the second decade of the century and remained stuck in a 19th-century vision of a rural, small-town, agricultural

society. Critics of Harding see that flaw as a reason for his rejection of Wilsonian internationalism and progressive reform. Yet the Republican Party also rejected both ideas in general. So too did the voters.

As a U.S. senator, from 1915 to 1920, Harding voted the Republican Party line on every key issue. He introduced no major legislation, gave no important speeches on the floor, and did not do much to advance his career there as had future presidents like Lyndon Johnson. He was a minor figure on the Senate Foreign Relations Committee who simply backed the chairman, Henry Cabot Lodge. The powerful Massachusetts senator, a personal and political enemy of President Woodrow Wilson, used his position to defeat Wilson's efforts to have the United States join the League of Nations following World War I.

Harding may not have understood the nuance of Lodge's use of amendments and reservations to attack the league, but he quickly assessed the fundamental argument. Article X of the League of Nations' Covenant opened the possibility of American military forces used to enforce the league's policies. That challenged the Constitution. War-making powers required Senate approval, and a loose interpretation of Article X might preclude that authority. When the United States went to war in 1917, Harding had favored Wilson's decision and supported his policies during the conflict. In 1918, however, he aligned his interests with the Republican disavowal of U.S. entry into the league and voted with Lodge and the so-called Reservationists. His position bore political fruit.

The 1920 Republican National Convention that finally selected Harding as its nominee to run for the presidency did so because the front-runners split delegate votes and could not win the number necessary. A dark horse compromise candidate appeared necessary to end the contentious voting and send the delegates home.

Throughout the nomination process, Harry Daugherty, Harding's political advisor, served as his campaign manager and played a key role in his victory. He and Mrs. Harding kept the senator in the race, even when he thought of dropping out. They remained important advisors throughout the presidential campaign and when Harding went to the White House. Daugherty would prove a scandalous figure as attorney general during Harding's administration, but he proved invaluable persuading party leaders and delegates to support his man. No evidence suggests that Harding's choice troubled the Republican Party, and most of its leaders believed he could win the 1920 election.

The 1920 presidential campaign pitted Harding and Coolidge against Democrats James Cox of Ohio and Franklin D. Roosevelt of New York. Woodrow Wilson wanted to run for a third term, but the Democrats decided that his popularity had dwindled following the League of Nations defeat. Oddly, Cox and Roosevelt adopted many of Wilson's views on international relations and progressive reform. The Democrats believed it was Wilson himself the public disliked, but it turned out to be his ideas. They should have taken heed of a new American view of the postwar environment.

With hindsight, two factors emerged in 1920. Voters had become disenchanted with Wilsonian internationalism following World War I. They had also become skeptical regarding Progressive Era domestic policies. Yet the Democratic platform and its candidates continued to support entry into the league and the continuation of progressive reform legislation. Cox and Roosevelt were not Wilson, but they advocated his policies, as did their party. Harding sensed the change in the public's thinking, tailored his campaign accordingly, and explained the difference in clear, understandable terms.

Throughout 1919 and 1920, a series of problems confronted the nation: a postwar recession, labor unrest and strikes, race riots in a number of American cities, and anarchist attacks on Wall Street. Unrest and revolutions in Europe added to the disquiet. Rather than attack Cox, Harding focused on Wilson's legacy and suggested that his administration had created the problems. He maintained that Cox was just a carbon copy of the former president. In a May 14 speech in Boston, he coined the phrase "Return to Normalcy," and a careful reading of his comments laid bare the Republican position. It was a blunt condemnation of everything progressivism had produced, both domestically and internationally. It resonated with the American public. The candidate may not have been an intellectual heavyweight, but he knew his audience and their mood.

In November, Harding won a smashing victory. He polled 16,114,093 popular votes to Cox's 9,139,661. In the Electoral College, he won 404 votes and 37 states. Cox won 127 votes and 11 states (all in the South). In Congress, the Republicans had a 59–37 majority in the Senate and a 303–131 majority in the House. The president and the Republican Party had dismantled progressive reform and internationalism for a decade.

Remarkably, the former newspaper owner from Marion. Ohio had accomplished the improbable. A one-term senator with little national notoriety had gone to Chicago an unlikely potential presidential candidate. Taking advantage of a split among party regulars, he won the nomination. Whether Harding had personally used his own skills to achieve that conclusion was irrelevant. He took advantage of the situation and capitalized on it. His modesty and temperament played a role in the decision. Harding was likeable, and that had always served him well in the political arena. His victory in 1920 was pure Warren G. Harding.

Although it may have been a foregone conclusion that the Republican Party would win the presidency and gain solid majorities in Congress, things might have gone wrong. Harding could have made mistakes on the campaign trail that threatened that inevitability. He did not. He adroitly sensed the mood of the voters, refused to attack Cox, and concentrated on the disenchantment Americans felt regarding Wilson. Perhaps as a result of his own views about the United States in the postwar era, he wanted to return to a simpler time, and so did they. That symbiosis between candidate and voter resonated in the huge victory that Harding achieved. If, as critics would claim, Harding failed to see a changed country, the voters seemed to agree with him. They wanted relief from the high energy days of reform politics, both at home and abroad.

On Friday, March 21, 1921, President Warren G. Harding swore the oath of office as the nation's 29th chief executive. He gave a balanced, conciliatory inaugural address that emphasized what he had argued on the campaign trail. The United States, he said, recognized the problems caused by the Great War, but he believed the nation had the power, legacy, and commitment to deal with them. Both at home and overseas, he maintained confidently, the United States could enter a new decade of prosperity and peace spurred on by commercial growth and honest relations with its neighbors. He appeared sure and ready for the task of leading the nation.

Critics then and now would maintain that Harding's first flaw as president centered on his cabinet appointments. They argued that he filled positions with patronage appointments, the so-called Ohio Gang that caused so much later trouble in his administration. In fact, however, only one of his cabinet officers was from the state, and many of them had the necessary qualifications and background to hold their positions. Secretary of State Charles Evans Hughes had served as New York's governor and ran for president in 1916. Herbert Hoover, secretary of commerce, was a Quaker from Iowa and had earned international acclaim for his food relief efforts in Europe at the end of the war. Andrew Mellon, a Pittsburgh millionaire, acted as treasury secretary. The only cabinet position from Ohio went to Harding's campaign manager and political advisor Harry Daugherty.

Harding's relationship with the cabinet may have stemmed from his belief in his own limitations. He usually allowed them a free hand in the day-to-day conduct of official business. He also deferred to Congress on many issues. Hughes and the Republican Senate virtually directed American foreign policy. Mellon, an astute, conservative business entrepreneur, guided fiscal policy and served both Calvin Coolidge and Herbert Hoover during their administrations. Hoover, as commerce secretary, worked well with Hughes and Mellon to construct a broad foreign and domestic policy for the administration. If Harding himself failed to initiate or conceive those major goals, he possessed the good sense to allow his subordinates to do so with his knowledge and support.

Domestic policy during Harding's administration focused on promoting business and commercial growth and careful management of the federal budget. The 1920 Fordney-McCumber Tariff had hiked rates to protect American businesses. Under the president's urging, Congress passed the Budget and Accounting Act in June 1921. It allowed a budget director, Charles Dawes, to manage expenditures throughout the government. The 1921 Revenue Act cut surtax rates from 65 to 50 percent. The administration blocked an effort to pass a Soldier's Bonus Act as too costly. Similarly, efforts to fund a revitalized merchant marine fleet failed for the same reason. Dawes and Mellon developed a fiscal model designed to cut spending, utilize protective tariffs to support U.S. business, and reduce taxes. By the time of Harding's death in 1923, various forms of legislation and policies that fit that plan had gone into effect. Critics have questioned those actions, but they neatly fit the mainstream Republican thinking at the time.

Harding also maintained a sound working relationship with Henry Wallace, the administration's competent secretary of agriculture. The president had championed the farming community, particularly the declining number of small farm owners. During his campaign, he pledged to look out for their interests, and he did so. By 1922, at his urging, Congress had passed six farm bills to protect farmers from price discrimination and manipulations by expanding mega-agriculture businesses, railroads, and marketing firms.

While proactive in some areas, Harding (and the Republicans in every branch) refused to support the interests or goals of organized labor. That was not unusual in either party at the time, and the concept of collective bargaining as a method to improve the wages and life of workers simply did not fit Andrew Mellon's or Warren Harding's mind-set. At the same time, the administration and Congress put the brakes on immigration. For the first time in American history, the government passed legislation to slow and reduce the arrival of immigrants from any foreign nation. Where previous immigration restrictions aimed specifically at China, the 1921 Immigration Act limited to 3 percent annually the number of immigrants entering the United States from anywhere.

Harding was not an aggressive champion of African American civil rights, but he nonetheless appeared more outspoken about segregation and Jim Crow oppression of blacks than Woodrow Wilson or previous occupants of the White House. As a senator, he voted in favor of antilynching legislation even though Southern Democrats filibustered and blocked their passage. He brought that attitude to the White House. On October 26, 1921, President Harding traveled to Birmingham, Alabama, in the heart of Jim Crow racism and the oppressive actions of the Ku Klux Klan.

His speech before a large audience stunned both black and white listeners. It was not a cry for complete equality, but Harding supported the right of African Americans to vote and seek equality in employment. He called on white society to recognize the significance of African Americans in the United States and suggested that although legal segregation might be culturally understandable, it should not be unequal in its opportunities. His remarks met with silence from the white audience and broad applause from black listeners.

The Birmingham speech produced no positive results, and neither did it spark an increased move of black voters to the Republican Party; they already voted Republican. At the time, however, the United States witnessed an increased awareness in black civil rights. The NAACP, founded in 1909, had become a national organization aimed at protecting African American rights. In New York City, a cultural awakening (often called the Harlem Renaissance) evolved in the second decade of the century. Writers, artists, and musicians produced a full expression of the black experience. Harding had nothing to do with either political or cultural movement, but perhaps he sensed the direction that both signified in the modern United States. More likely, his moderate, friendly personality saw a basic injustice, still tainted by his era's fundamental racism.

Secretary of State Charles Evans Hughes proved a valuable asset as he worked with President Harding to form the administration's postwar foreign policy. As a former New York governor and 1916 presidential candidate, Hughes had experience and intelligence. He served Harding well, and the president trusted him. Hughes also worked well with Commerce Secretary Hoover and Treasury Secretary Mellon as the three devised commercial policies to expand U.S. international business interests.

Both the president and Congress had rejected U.S. commitment to the League of Nations and sought a process of unilateral diplomacy that involved actions that such organizations might restrain or misdirect. That did not suggest, however, that U.S. foreign policy would fail to engage in the key international issues of the decade. Harding, Hughes, and the Republican Senate recognized the need to interact with other nations so long as they could do so from a traditional unilateral posture.

At the urging of Senator William E. Borah (R-Idaho), with Hughes' support, President Harding invited nine nations to send representatives to Washington. Between November 12, 1921, and February 6, 1922, they discussed naval arms limitations and crucial diplomatic issues in the Pacific. A postwar naval arms race developed after World War I, and the United States, Great Britain, and Japan competed to enhance their battleship fleets. At the same time, regions in the Pacific and Far East had emerged as flash points, increasing diplomatic tensions between a number of nations that had interests there. The Washington Naval Conference sought to address both concerns. In addition to the United States, Britain, and Japan, France, Italy, Belgium, China, Portugal, and the Netherlands sent delegations.

The conference produced three treaties that set ratios on the size of battleship tonnage and resolved concerns about the territorial integrity of China. For a time, those agreements limited or stalled the arms race and protected China from efforts on the part of Japan and European nations to seize territory there (a reinterpretation of the 1898 Open Door Notes). The agreements took place without the involvement of the League of Nations. Borah, Hughes, and Harding could point out that the United States had the ability to conduct effective international relations without depending on membership in the league.

At the same time, the United States had become involved in a touchy situation in Europe, one that Hughes and Harding had to ultimately resolve. At the Paris Peace Conference, President Wilson had agreed to create a Rhineland Commission to control German territory west of that river until the League of Nations approved Germany's right to reclaim control of the region. To enforce the commission, French, British, Belgian, and U.S. military forces occupied the Rhineland. As a result, 15,000 U.S. troops stationed at Coblenz did so while Wilson and the Senate battled over the League of Nations.

When Harding became president, he ordered a reduction in the military presence but opted to keep a small American contingent in Coblenz. He and Hughes believed that they served as an "unbiased, if reluctant, umpire" to balance and protect both France and Germany from a potential confrontation. The continued U.S. presence would assure the French that the United States remained their postwar ally. It would also convince Germany that the United States hoped to protect their vulnerability from possible French aggression.

In a clash with the Republican Senate, Harding blocked its efforts to remove the American troops until January 1923, when French military units crossed the Rhine and occupied German territory east of the river in the Ruhr Valley. At that point, fearing U.S. forces might get caught in a potential conflict, Harding ordered the withdrawal of the U.S. forces and complied with a Senate resolution to do so.

In the spring of 1823, the Senate also rejected Harding's efforts to have the United States join the International Court of Justice. It had no direct connection with the League of Nations, established headquarters in the Hague, and lobbied Harding and Hughes to have the United States become a member. Both men wanted to do so, but Senate isolationists remained unwilling.

The diplomatic actions of the Harding administration do not suggest that the president had become a Wilsonian internationalist. They do indicate, however, that he listened to Hughes and others and that he appeared willing to moderate strong isolationist thinking and respond to individual foreign policy decisions carefully.

In United States' relations with its Latin American neighbors, the Harding administration began to change the nation's approach. Since the Spanish-American War in 1898, U.S. diplomacy in the hemisphere had become more aggressive and intrusive. Annexing Puerto Rico, creating a protectorate in Cuba, and expanding business interests in the region and building the Panama Canal drew the nation more forcefully into Latin American affairs. In 1904, President Theodore Roosevelt's State of the Union address included a policy statement defined broadly as the Roosevelt Corollary to the Monroe Doctrine. He stated that to protect the security of the United States and the hemisphere, the United States reserved the right to intervene directly in Latin American nations to prevent foreign threats to the area. It provoked a wide negative response throughout the hemisphere, and the belief of a "Yankee Colossus" became a catchphrase in numerous capitals in the hemisphere.

That concern proved legitimate. During the next two decades, the United States practiced a policy of "Big Stick Diplomacy" and "Dollar Diplomacy" that saw the continuous use of American military forces to enforce policy in Central America and the Caribbean. At the same time, Roosevelt's administration virtually stole Panama from Colombia, fomented a revolution there, and proceeded to build the Panama Canal. Roosevelt, Taft, and Wilson followed that basic intervention policy. It culminated with Wilson sending forces into Mexico because he disapproved of their election results.

The three presidents all had the best interests of the United States in mind. Both for security and commercial reasons, they believed in their policy actions. However, those actions had created deep animosity toward the United States throughout the hemisphere. Harding, Hughes, Hoover, and Mellon hoped to change that perception. Beginning in 1921, the new administration began to remove American forces still stationed in Central America, paid an indemnity to Colombia over the Panama issue, cavalierly refused to use future armed forces, and opted for a more diplomatic method to resolve interhemisphere concerns. The Harding administration set the stage for the "Good Neighbor Policy" that Franklin Roosevelt's presidency would pursue in the 1930s.

A reasoned analysis of Harding's foreign policy performance warrants a conclusion of balanced diplomacy. He did not pursue a rigid, isolationist approach to international affairs, and neither did his cabinet officials. They did, however, conduct foreign relations from a unilateral posture. It appeared a better approach in Latin America than previous administrations, and for a time, it stemmed potential crises in Europe and Asia.

Harding's court appointments influenced judicial decisions in the nation well into the 1930s. He appointed four new members to the Supreme Court: Chief Justice William Howard Taft (former president) and Associate Justices Pierce Butler, Edward Sanford, and George Sutherland. In addition, six justices joined courts of appeal, and 42 judges were named to U.S. district courts.

Taft's Supreme Court rendered business0related decisions that supported the private sector versus the government. Interpreting the "commerce clause" in the Constitution, majority decisions came down firmly on the side of business. In other cases, however, decisions both in the Supreme Court and in other federal jurisdictions tended to be balanced and moderate, protecting individual liberties, Fourteenth Amendment cases, and cases that did not involve commerce. Again, even if President Harding showed little personal interest in the courts, he nominated jurists who did their job. Wilson's Supreme Court appointments, like Louis Brandeis, chaffed at the conservative majority's decisions. However, even Brandeis recognized the oft-used political axiom "elections have consequences." If conservatives had disliked and disapproved of progressive laws and legislation, in 1921, the tide had turned.

Unfortunately, Warren Harding failed to prevent the series of scandals and crises that developed as a result of his less honest or qualified subordinates. His political advisor, friend, and attorney general Harry Daugherty played a part in two of those. In July 1922 a railroad union strike saw 400,000 workers join picket lines demanding better wages and working conditions. Daugherty used favorable judges to issue injunctions and ordered federal marshals to back owners. Ten strikers were killed in clashes during the summer. Hoover and Labor Secretary James Davis wanted to arbitrate a resolution, but on September 1, the district court in Illinois, with Daugherty's influence, declared the strike illegal and ordered the union members back to work. Critics began to question whether the attorney general had received kickbacks from owners.

In a more egregious action, Daugherty and members of his staff received payoffs from bootleggers engaged in the illegal transport and sale of alcohol. For financial favors, the attorney general's Justice Department guaranteed immunity from prosecution for their violation of the Volstead Act. The facts would not become public until 1924. Senator Burton K. Wheeler (D-Montana) chaired a Senate investigation that exposed the scandal. One Justice Department official, Jess Smith, committed suicide, and others went to jail. Though Daugherty never faced criminal charges in the affair, he certainly knew it had occurred.

The Veterans Bureau also scandalized the Harding administration. Not only had Harding refused to support a Veterans' Bonus Bill, but the Bureau granted leases to construction companies to build a series of veteran's hospitals without proper and legal bidding procedures. Initially under the authority of the Treasury Department, members of the American Legion (a new and powerful veteran's lobby group) had the bureau operate as an independent entity. Colonel Charles Forbes served as its head. Leasing contracts to two construction firms, Forbes received millions of dollars in paybacks for the deal. An attorney for the bureau, Charles Cranmer, committed suicide. Forbes resigned and fled to Europe in 1923; he returned in 1924, stood trial for bribery and corruption, and received a two-year prison sentence.

The most infamous scandal during Harding's presidency centered on oil leasing: the Teapot Dome affair. The U.S. Navy had begun to shift from coal to petroleum to fuel its ships. To secure and store surplus oil for national emergencies, the government established a series of petroleum reserve sites throughout the United States. One was located in Teapot Dome, Wyoming. Two additional reserves held fuel in California, in Elk Hill and Buena Vista. Private companies could use the reserve facilities under strict guidelines and open, public bidding procedures. Beginning in 1922, however, Interior Secretary Albert Fall allowed Henry Sinclair's Mammoth Oil and Edward Doheny's Pan American Petroleum to tap oil from the reserves at low cost with no bidding—both violations of federal law.

From 1921 to 1923, Fall received thousands of dollars in gifts and no interest loans from the two owners. The issue surfaced after Harding's death when Senator Thomas Walsh (D-Montana) began an investigation that shocked the nation. Fall became the first cabinet officer sentenced to prison for his involvement in the affair.

Harding was not complicit in any of the emerging scandals, but neither did he control or oversee the behavior of the men who were. Perhaps Harding could trust that his best cabinet members would do their jobs honestly and effectively. They did. His tragic flaw hinged on placing the same faith in less honest or competent subordinates.

A public image emerged of the people involved meeting at a "little green house" at 1625 K Street in Washington. There, they drank bourbon smoked cigars, played poker, and entertained women. And there, the Ohio Gang, whoever they were, concocted the deals that finally scandalized Harding's presidency. Hoover, Mellon, and Hughes refused to go to K Street, but Daugherty remained a prominent host, and the president visited as well. Some historians, and his critics in the press at the time, believed he felt more comfortable there than in the White House. Editorials referred to him as "President Hardly" because he rarely made decisions on his own. Quotes attributed to Harding advance the conclusion that he felt incompetent: "I knew the job was too much for me" and "I am not fit for this office and should never have been here." Many presidents, however, had experienced moments of doubt about their ability to hold the office.

Even his extramarital infidelities appear less scandalous given the knowledge that other chief executives since have done the same, including presidents with more generous historical evaluations.

As obvious as his flaws may have been, Harding's administration nonetheless helped create three years of peace, prosperity, and security, the political mantra of the Republican Party. Historians have tended to see the accomplishments of the Harding administration as the result of the actions of its best cabinet leaders. They attribute its flaws and scandals to the president's weaknesses.

When he died in San Francisco in August 1923, Calvin Coolidge (and then Herbert Hoover) retained party control of the White House, and the Republicans maintained a majority in the Congress until the Great Depression. Both Coolidge and Hoover may have been better prepared to serve as president, but history has not been kind to either, and neither proved more popular with the American public than the man they followed.

Jolyon P. Girard

Further Reading

Allen, Frederick Lewis. 1931. *Only Yesterday: An Informal History of the 1920s*. New York: Harper and Row.

Bates, Leonard J. 1963. *The Origins of Teapot Dome*. Urbana: University of Illinois Press.

Dean, John W. 2004. *Warren G. Harding*. The American Presidents Series. Edited by Arthur M. Schlesinger Jr. New York: Henry Holt & Co.

Girard, Jolyon P. 1979. *Bridge on the Rhine: American Diplomacy and the Rhineland, 1919–1923*. College Park: University of Maryland Press.

Goldberg, David, and Stanley Cutler. 1999. *Discontented America: The United States in the 1920s*. Baltimore, MD: Johns Hopkins University Press.

Hofstater, Richard. 1955. *The Age of Reform: From Bryan to F. D. R.* Baltimore, MD: Johns Hopkins University Press.

Miller, Nathan. 2003. *New World Coming: The 1920s and the Making of Modern America*. New York: Simon and Schuster.

Murray, Robert. 1969. *The Harding Era: Warren G. Harding and His Administration*. Newtown, CT: American Political Biography Press.

Pietrusza, David. 2007. *1920: The Year of Six Presidents*. New York: Carroll Graf Publishers.

Russell, Francis. 1968. *The Shadow of Blooming Grove: Warren G. Harding in His Times*. New York: McGraw Hill.

Sinclair, Andrew. 1965. *The Available Man: The Life behind the Masks of Warren Gamaliel Harding*. New York: Macmillan.

Warren G. Harding Papers. n.d. Library of Congress. https://www.loc.gov/item/mm80050773.

Speech Opposing the League of Nations (January 20, 1920)

Senator Harding gave the speech to members of the Ohio Society of New York at the Waldorf Hotel. He explained his reason for voting to reject U.S. entry into the postwar League of Nations. The speech essentially argued that joining the league would mean the surrender of the United States' independent nationalism.

My countrymen, the first flaming torch of Americanism was lighted in framing the Federal Constitution in 1787. The pilgrims signed their simple and majestic covenant a full century and a half before, and set aflame their beacon of liberty on the coast of Massachusetts. Other pioneers of New World's freedom were rearing their new standards of liberty from Jamestown to Plymouth for five generations before Lexington and Concord heralded the new era. It is all American in the destined result, yet all of it lacked the soul of nationality.

In simple truth, there was no thought of nationality in the revolution for American independence. The colonists were resisting a wrong, and freedom was their solace. Once it was achieved, nationality was the only agency suited to its preservation. Americanism really began when robed in nationality. The American Republic began the blazed trail of representative popular government. Representative democracy was proclaimed the safe agency of highest human freedom. America headed the forward procession of civil, human, and religious liberty, which ultimately will affect the liberation of all mankind. The Federal Constitution is the very base of all Americanism, the "Ark of the Covenant" of American liberty, the very temple of equal rights. The Constitution does abide and ever will, so long as the Republic survives.

Let us hesitate before we surrender the nationality which is the very soul of highest Americanism. This republic has never failed humanity, or endangered civilization. We have been tardy sometimes—like when we were proclaiming democracy and neutrality, and yet ignored our national rights—but the ultimate and helpful part we played in the Great War will be the pride of Americans so long as the world recites the story. We do not mean to hold aloof, we choose no isolation, we shun no duty. I like to rejoice in an American conscience; and in a big conception of our obligation to liberty, justice, and civilization—aye, and more. I like to think of Columbia's helping hand to new republics which are seeking the blessings portrayed in our example. But I have a confidence in our America that requires no council of foreign powers to point the way of American duty. We wish to counsel, cooperate, and contribute, but we arrogate to ourselves the keeping of the American conscience, and every concept of our moral obligation.

It is time to idealize, but it's very practical to make sure our own house is in perfect order before we attempt the miracle of Old World stabilization. Call it selfishness of nationality if you will, I think it an inspiration to patriotic devotion—to safeguard America

first, to stabilize America first, to prosper America first, to think of America first, to exalt America first, to live for and revere America first.

Let the internationalist dream and the Bolshevist destroy. God pity him for whom no minstrel raptures swell. In the spirit of the Republic we proclaim Americanism and acclaim America.

Source: Schortemeier, Frederick E. *Rededicating America: Life and Recent Speeches of Warren G. Harding.* Indianapolis: Bobbs-Merrill Company, 1920, 103–114.

Loyalty Speech (March 31, 1921)

After less than a month in office, Harding delivered short remarks from the White House that addressed immigrants' loyalty to their former countries in Europe. He basically challenged all Americans to direct their loyalty to the United States. He tied his remarks to the continued Republican position on avoiding "entanglements" with European affairs through membership in some misguided "super government" like the League of Nations.

My countrymen, the pioneers to whom I have alluded, these stalwart makers of America, could have no conception of our present-day attainment. Hamilton, who conceived, and Washington, who sponsored, little dreamed of either a development or a solution like ours of today. But they were right in fundamentals. They knew what safe and preached security was. One may doubt if either of them, if any of the founders, would wish America to hold aloof from the world. But there has come to us lately a new realization of the menace to our America in European entanglements which emphasizes the prudence of Washington, though he could little have dreamed the thought which is in my mind.

When I sat on the Senate Committee on Foreign Relations and listened to American delegations appealing in behalf of kinsman or old home folks across the seas, I caught the aspirations of nationality, and the perfectly natural sympathy among kindred in this republic. But I little realized then how we might rend the concord of American citizenship in our seeking to solve Old World problems. There have come to me, not at all unbecomingly, the expressed anxieties of Americans foreign born who are asking our country's future attitude on territorial awards in the adjustment of peace. They are Americans all, but they have a proper and a natural interest in the fortunes of kinsfolk and native lands. One cannot blame them. If our land is to settle the envies, rivalries, jealousies, and hatreds of all civilization, these adopted sons of the Republic want the settlement favorable to the land from which they came.

The misfortune is not alone that it rends the concord of nations. The greater pity is that it rends the concord of our citizenship at home. It's folly to think of blending Greek and Bulgar, Italian and Slovak, or making any of them rejoicingly American, when the land of adoption sits in judgement on the land from which he came. We need to be rescued from divisionary and fruitless pursuit of peace through super government. I do not want Americans of foreign birth making their party alignments on what we mean to do for some nation in the old world. We want them to be Republican because of what we mean to do for the United States of America. Our call is for unison, not rivaling sympathies. Our need is concord, not the antipathies of long inheritance.

Surely no one stopped to think where the great world experiment was leading. Frankly, no one could know. We're only learning now. It would be a sorry day for this republic if we allowed our activities in seeking for peace in the Old World to blind us to the essentials of peace at home. We want a free America again. We want America free at home, and free in the world. We want to silence the outcry of nation against nation, in the fullness of understanding. And we wish to silence the cry of class against class, and stifle the party appeal to class, so that we may ensure tranquility in our own freedom. If I could choose but one, I had rather have industrial and social peace at home, than command the international peace of all the world.

Source: "Nationalism and Americanism." New York: Nation's Forum, 1920. Available at the Library of Congress.

First Annual Address to Congress (December 6, 1921)

Article II, Section 3, Clause 1, of the U.S. Constitution requires the president to provide a "State of the Union" message to Congress. Until Woodrow Wilson went to the U.S. Capitol to deliver his address, most presidents had sent a written message. Harding's was a typical review of his first year in office, heralding the administration's accomplishments. His 1922 annual address was the first broadcast on radio.

It is a very gratifying privilege to come to the Congress with the Republic at peace with all the nations of the world. More, it is equally gratifying to report that our country is not only free from every impending, menace of war, but there are growing assurances of the permanency of the peace which we so deeply cherish.

For approximately ten years we have dwelt amid menaces of war or as participants in war's actualities, and the inevitable aftermath, with its disordered conditions, bits added to the difficulties of government which adequately can not be appraised except by, those who are in immediate contact and know the responsibilities. Our tasks would be less difficult if we had only ourselves to consider, but so much of the world was involved, the disordered conditions are so well-nigh universal, even among nations not engaged in actual warfare, that no permanent readjustments can be affected without consideration of our inescapable relationship to world affairs in finance and trade. Indeed, we should be unworthy of our best traditions if we were unmindful of social, moral, and political conditions which are not of direct concern to us, but which do appeal to the human sympathies and the very becoming interest of a people blest with our national good fortune.

It is not my purpose to bring to you a program of world restoration. In the main such a program must be worked out by the nations more directly concerned. They must themselves turn to the heroic remedies for the menacing conditions under which they are struggling, then we can help, and we mean to help. We shall do so unselfishly because there is compensation in the consciousness of assisting, selfishly because the commerce and international exchanges in trade, which marked our high tide of fortunate advancement, are possible only when the nations of all continents are restored to stable order and normal relationship.

In the main the contribution of this Republic to restored normalcy in the world must come through the initiative of the executive branch of the Government, but the best of intentions and most carefully considered purposes would fail utterly if the sanction and the cooperation of Congress were not cheerfully accorded.

I am very sure we shall have no conflict of opinion about constitutional duties or authority. During the anxieties of war, when necessity seemed compelling there were excessive grants of authority and all extraordinary concentration of powers in the Chief Executive. The repeal of war-time legislation and the automatic expirations which attended the peace proclamations have put an end to these emergency excesses but I have the wish to go further than that. I want to join you in restoring, in the most cordial way, the spirit of coordination and cooperation, and that mutuality of confidence and respect which is necessary ill representative popular government.

Encroachment upon the functions of Congress or attempted dictation of its policy are not to be thought of, much less attempted, but there is all insistent call for harmony of purpose and concord of action to speed the solution of the difficult problems confronting both the legislative and executive branches of the Government.

It is worth while to make allusion here to the character of our Government, mindful as one must be that an address to you is no less a message to all our people, for whom you speak most intimately. Ours is it popular Government through political parties. We divide along political lines, and I would ever have it so. I do not mean that partisan preferences should hinder any public servant in the performance of a conscientious and patriotic official duty. We saw partisan lines utterly obliterated when war imperiled, and our faith in the Republic was riveted anew. We ought not to find these partisan lines obstructing the expeditious solution of the urgent problems of peace.

Granting that we are fundamentally a representative popular Government, with political parties the governing agencies, I believe the political party in power should assume responsibility, determine upon policies ill the conference which supplements conventions and election campaigns, and then strive for achievement through adherence to the accepted policy.

There is vastly greater security, immensely more of the national viewpoint, much larger and prompter accomplishment where our divisions are along party lines, in the broader and loftier sense, than to divide geographically, or according to pursuits, or personal following. For a century and a third, parties have been charged with responsibility and held to strict accounting. When they fail, they are relieved of authority; and the system has brought us to a national eminence no less than a world example.

Necessarily legislation is a matter of compromise. The full ideal is seldom attained. In that meeting of minds necessary to insure results, there must and will be accommodations and compromises, but in the estimate of convictions and sincere purposes the supreme responsibility to national interest must not be ignored. The shield to the high-minded public servant who adheres to party policy is manifest, but the higher purpose is the good of the Republic as a whole.

It would be ungracious to withhold acknowledgment of the really large volume and excellent quality of work accomplished by the extraordinary session of Congress which so recently adjourned. I am not unmindful of the very difficult tasks with which you were called to deal, and no one can ignore the insistent conditions which, during recent years, have called for the continued and almost exclusive attention of your membership to public work. It would suggest insincerity if I expressed complete accord with every expression recorded in your roll calls, but we are all agreed about the difficulties and the inevitable divergence of opinion in seeking the reduction, amelioration and readjustment of the burdens of taxation. Later on, when other problems are solved, I shall make some recommendations about renewed consideration of our tax program, but for the immediate time before us we must be content with the billion dollar reduction in the tax draft upon the people, and diminished irritations, banished uncertainty and improved methods of collection. By your sustainment of the rigid economies already inaugurated, with hoped-for extension of these economies and added efficiencies in administration, I believe further reductions may be enacted and hindering burdens abolished.

In these urgent economies we shall be immensely assisted by the budget system for which you made provision in the extraordinary session. The first budget is before you. Its preparation is a signal achievement, and the perfection of the system, a thing impossible in the few months available for its initial trial, will mark its enactment as the beginning of the greatest reformation in governmental practices since the beginning of the Republic.

There is pending a grant of authority to the administrative branch of the Government for the funding and settlement of our vast foreign loans growing out of our grant of war credits. With the hands of the executive branch held impotent to deal with these debts we are hindering urgent readjustments among our debtors and accomplishing nothing for ourselves. I think it is fair for the Congress to assume that the executive branch of the Government would adopt no major policy in dealing with these matters which would conflict with the purpose of Congress in authorizing the loans, certainly not without asking congressional approval, but there are minor problems incident to prudent loan transactions and the safeguarding of our interests which can not even be attempted without this authorization. It will be helpful to ourselves and it will improve conditions among our debtors if funding and the settlement of defaulted interest may be negotiated.

The previous Congress, deeply concerned in behalf of our merchant marine, in 1920 enacted the existing shipping law, designed for the upbuilding of the American merchant marine. Among other things provided to encourage our shipping on the world's seas, the Executive was directed to give notice of the termination of all existing commercial treaties in order to admit of reduced duties on imports carried in American bottoms. During the life of the act no Executive has complied with this order of the Congress. When the present administration came into responsibility it began an early inquiry into the failure to execute the expressed purpose of the Jones Act. Only one conclusion has been possible. Frankly, Members of House and Senate, eager as I am to join you in the making of an American merchant marine commensurate with our commerce, the denouncement of out-commercial treaties would involve us in a chaos of trade relationships and add indescribably to the confusion of the already disordered commercial world. Our power to do so is not disputed, but power and ships, without comity of relationship, will not give us the expanded trade which is inseparably linked with a great merchant marine. Moreover, the applied reduction of duty, for which the treaty denouncements were necessary, encouraged

only the carrying of dutiable imports to our shores, while the tonnage which unfurls the flag on the seas is both free and dutiable, and the cargoes which make it nation eminent in trade are outgoing, rather than incoming.

It is not my thought to lay the problem before you in detail today. It is desired only to say to you that the executive branch of the Government, uninfluenced by the protest of any nation, for none has been made, is well convinced that your proposal, highly intended and heartily supported here, is so fraught with difficulties and so marked by tendencies to discourage trade expansion, that I invite your tolerance of noncompliance for only a few weeks until a plan may be presented which contemplates no greater draft upon the Public Treasury, and which, though yet too crude to offer it to-day, gives such promise of expanding our merchant marine, that it will argue its own approval. It is enough to say to-day that we are so possessed of ships, and the American intention to establish it merchant marine is so unalterable, that a plain of reimbursement, at no other cost than is contemplated in the existing act, will appeal to the pride and encourage the hope of all the American people.

There is before you the completion of the enactment of what has been termed a "permanent" tariff law, the word "permanent" being used to distinguish it from the emergency act which the Congress expedited early in the extraordinary session, and which is the law today. I can not too strongly urge in early completion of this necessary legislation. It is needed to stabilize our industry at home; it is essential to make more definite our trade relations abroad. More, it is vital to the preservation of many of our own industries which contribute so notably to the very lifeblood of our Nation.

There is now, and there always will be, a storm of conflicting opinion about any tariff revision. We can not go far wrong when we base our tariffs on the policy of preserving the productive activities which enhance employment and add to our national prosperity.

Again comes the reminder that we must not be unmindful of world conditions, that peoples are struggling for industrial rehabilitation and that we can not dwell in industrial and commercial exclusion and at the same time do the just thing in aiding world reconstruction and readjustment. We do not seek a selfish aloofness, and we could not profit by it, were it possible. We recognize the necessity of buying wherever we sell, and the permanency of trade lies in its acceptable exchanges. In our pursuit of markets we must give as well as receive. We can not sell to others who do not produce, nor can we buy unless we produce at home. Sensible of every obligation of humanity, commerce and finance, linked as they are in the present world condition, it is not to be argued that we need destroy ourselves to be helpful to others. With all my heart I wish restoration to the peoples blighted by the awful World War, but the process of restoration does not lie in our acceptance of like conditions. It were better to remain on firm ground, strive for ample employment and high standards of wage at home, and point the way to balanced budgets, rigid economies, and resolute, efficient work as the necessary remedies to cure disaster.

Everything relating to trade, among ourselves and among nations, has been expanded, excessive, inflated, abnormal, and there is a madness in finance which no American policy alone will cure. We are a creditor Nation, not by normal processes, but made so by war. It is not an unworthy selfishness to seek to save ourselves, when the processes of that salvation are not only not denied to others, but commended to them. We seek to undermine for others no industry by which they subsist; we are obligated to permit the undermining of none of our own which make for employment and maintained activities.

Every contemplation, it little matters in which direction one turns, magnifies the difficulty of tariff legislation, but the necessity of the revision is magnified with it. Doubtless we are justified in seeking .1 More flexible policy than we have provided heretofore. I hope a way will be found to make for flexibility and elasticity, so that rates may be adjusted to meet unusual and changing conditions which can not be accurately anticipated. There are problems incident to unfair practices, and to exchanges which madness in money have made almost unsolvable. I know of no manner in which to effect this flexibility other than the extension of the powers of the Tariff Commission so that it can adapt itself to it scientific and wholly just administration of the law.

I am not unmindful of the constitutional difficulties. These can be met by giving authority to the Chief Executive, who could proclaim additional duties to meet conditions which the Congress may designate.

At this point I must disavow any desire to enlarge the Executive's powers or add to the responsibilities of the office. They are already too large. If there were any other plan I would prefer it.

The grant of authority to proclaim would necessarily bring the Tariff Commission into new and enlarged activities, because no Executive could discharge such a duty except upon the information acquired and recommendations made by this commission. But the plan is feasible, and the proper functioning of the board would give its it better administration of a defined policy than ever can be made possible by tariff duties prescribed without flexibility.

There is a manifest difference of opinion about the merits of American valuation. Many nations have adopted delivery valuation as the basis for collecting duties; that is, they take the cost of the imports delivered at the port of entry as the basis for levying duty. It is no radical departure, in view of varying conditions and the disordered state of money values, to provide for American valuation, but there can not be ignored the danger of such a valuation, brought to the level of our own production costs, making our tariffs prohibitive. It might do so in many instances where imports ought to be encouraged. I believe Congress ought well consider the desirability of the only promising alternative, namely, a provision authorizing proclaimed American valuation, under prescribed conditions, on any given list of articles imported.

In this proposed flexibility, authorizing increases to meet conditions so likely to change, there should also be provision for decreases. A rate may be just to-day, and entirely out of proportion six months from to-day. If our tariffs are to be made equitable, and not necessarily burden our imports and hinder our trade abroad, frequent adjustment will be necessary for years to come. Knowing the impossibility of modification by act of Congress for any one or a score of lines without involving a long array of schedules, I think we shall go a long ways toward stabilization, if there is recognition of the Tariff Commission's fitness to recommend urgent changes by proclamation.

I am sure about public opinion favoring the early determination of our tariff policy. There have been reassuring signs of a business revival from the deep slump which all the world has been experiencing. Our unemployment, which gave its deep concern only a few weeks ago, has grown encouragingly less, and new assurances and renewed confidence will attend the congressional declaration that American industry will be held secure.

Much has been said about the protective policy for ourselves making it impossible for our debtors to discharge their obligations to us. This is a contention not now pressing for decision. If we must choose between a people in idleness pressing for the payment of indebtedness, or a people resuming the normal ways of employment and carrying the credit, let us choose the latter. Sometimes we appraise largest the human ill most vivid in our minds. We have been giving, and are giving now, of our influence and appeals to minimize the likelihood of war and throw off the crushing burdens of armament. It is all very earnest, with a national soul impelling. But a people unemployed, and gaunt with hunger, face a situation quite as disheartening as war, and our greater obligation to-day is to do the Government's part toward resuming productivity and promoting fortunate and remunerative employment.

Something more than tariff protection is required by American agriculture. To the farmer has come the earlier and the heavier burdens of readjustment. There is actual depression in our agricultural industry, while agricultural prosperity is absolutely essential to the general prosperity of the country.

Congress has sought very earnestly to provide relief. It has promptly given such temporary relief as has been possible, but the call is insistent for the permanent solution. It is inevitable that large crops lower the prices and short crops advance them. No legislation can cure that fundamental law. But there must be some economic solution for the excessive variation in returns for agricultural production.

It is rather shocking to be told, and to have the statement strongly supported, that 9,000,000 bales of cotton, raised on American plantations in a given year, will actually be worth more to the producers than 13,000,000 bales would have been. Equally shocking is the statement that 700,000,000 bushels of wheat, raised by American farmers, would bring them more money than a billion bushels. Yet these are not exaggerated statements. In a world where there are tens of millions who need food and clothing which they can not get, such a condition is sure to indict the social system which makes it possible.

In the main the remedy lies in distribution and marketing. Every proper encouragement should be given to the cooperative marketing programs. These have proven very helpful to the cooperating communities in Europe. In Russia the cooperative community has become the recognized bulwark of law and order, and saved individualism from engulfment in social paralysis. Ultimately, they will be accredited with the salvation of the Russian State.

There is the appeal for this experiment. Why not try it? No one challenges the right of the farmer to a larger share of the consumer's pay for his product, no one disputes that we can not live without the farmer. He is justified in rebelling against the transportation cost. Given a fair return for his labor, he will have less occasion to appeal for financial aid; and given assurance that his labors shall not be in vain, we reassure all the people of a production sufficient to meet our National requirement and guard against disaster.

The base of the pyramid of civilization which rests upon the soil is shrinking through the drift of population from farm to city. For a generation we have been expressing more or less concern about this tendency. Economists have warned and statesmen have deplored. We thought for at time that modern conveniences and the more intimate contact would halt the movement, but it has gone steadily on. Perhaps only grim necessity will correct it, but we ought to find a less drastic remedy.

The existing scheme of adjusting freight rates has been favoring the basing points, until industries are attracted to some centers and repelled from others. A great volume of uneconomic and wasteful transportation has attended, and the cost increased accordingly. The grain-milling and meat-packing industries afford ample illustration, and the attending concentration is readily apparent. The menaces in concentration are not limited to the retarding influences on agriculture. Manifestly the conditions and terms of railway transportation ought not be permitted to increase this undesirable tendency. We have a just pride in our great cities, but we shall find a greater pride in the Nation, which has it larger distribution of its population into the country, where comparatively self-sufficient smaller communities may blend agricultural and manufacturing interests in harmonious helpfulness and enhanced good fortune. Such a movement contemplates no destruction of things wrought, of investments made, or wealth involved. It only looks to a general policy of transportation of distributed industry, and of highway construction, to encourage the spread of our population and restore the proper balance between city and country. The problem may well have your earnest attention.

It has been perhaps the proudest claim of our American civilization that in dealing with human relationships it has constantly moved toward such justice in distributing the product of human energy that it has improved continuously the economic status of the mass of people. Ours has been a highly productive social organization. On the way up from the elemental stages of society we have eliminated slavery and serfdom and are now far on the way to the elimination of poverty.

Through the eradication of illiteracy and the diffusion of education mankind has reached a stage where we may fairly say that in the United States equality of opportunity has been attained, though all are not prepared to embrace it. There is, indeed, a too great divergence between the economic conditions of the most and the least favored classes in the community. But even that divergence has now come to the point where we bracket the very poor and the very rich together as the least fortunate classes. Our efforts may well be directed to improving the status of both.

While this set of problems is commonly comprehended under the general phrase "Capital and Labor," it is really vastly broader. It is a question of social and economic organization. Labor has become a large contributor, through its savings, to the stock of capital; while the people who own the largest individual aggregates of capital are themselves often hard and earnest laborers. Very often it is extremely difficult to draw the line of demarcation between the two groups; to determine whether a particular individual is entitled to be set down as laborer or as capitalist. In a very large proportion of cases he is both, and when he is both he is the most useful citizen.

The right of labor to organize is just as fundamental and necessary as is the right of capital to organize. The right of labor to negotiate, to deal with and solve its particular problems in an organized way, through its chosen agents, is just as essential as is the right of capital to organize, to maintain corporations, to limit the liabilities of stockholders. Indeed, we have come to recognize that the limited liability of the citizen as a member of a labor organization closely parallels the limitation of liability of the citizen as a stockholder in a corporation for profit. Along this line of reasoning we shall make the greatest progress toward solution of our problem of capital and labor.

In the case of the corporation which enjoys the privilege of limited liability of stockholders, particularly when engaged in in the public service, it is recognized that the outside public has a large concern which must be protected; and so we provide regulations, restrictions, and in some cases detailed supervision. Likewise in the case of labor organizations, we might well apply similar and equally well-defined principles of regulation and supervision in order to conserve the public's interests as affected by their operations.

Just as it is not desirable that a corporation shall be allowed to impose undue exactions upon the public, so it is not desirable that a labor organization shall be permitted to exact unfair terms of employment or subject the public to actual distresses in order to enforce its terms. Finally, just as we are earnestly seeking for procedures whereby to adjust and settle political differences between nations without resort to war, so we may well look about for means to settle the differences between organized capital and organized labor without resort to those forms of warfare which we recognize under the name of strikes, lockouts, boycotts, and the like.

As we have great bodies of law carefully regulating the organization and operations of industrial and financial corporations, as we have treaties and compacts among nations which look to the settlement of differences without the necessity of conflict in arms, so we might well have plans of conference, of common counsel, of mediation, arbitration, and judicial determination in controversies between labor and capital. To accomplish this would involve the necessity to develop a thoroughgoing code of practice in dealing with such affairs It might be well to frankly set forth the superior interest of the community as a whole to either the labor group or the capital group. With rights, privileges, immunities, and modes of organization thus carefully defined, it should be possible to set up judicial or quasi judicial tribunals for the consideration and determination of all disputes which menace the public welfare.

In an industrial society such as ours the strike, the lockout, and the boycott are as much out of place and as disastrous in their results as is war or armed revolution in the domain of politics. The same disposition to reasonableness, to conciliation, to recognition of the other side's point of view, the same provision of fair and recognized tribunals and processes, ought to make it possible to solve the one set of questions as easily as the other. I believe the solution is possible.

The consideration of such a policy would necessitate the exercise of care and deliberation in the construction of a code and a charter of elemental rights, dealing with the relations of employer and employee. This foundation in the law, dealing with the modern conditions of social and economic life, would hasten the building of the temple of peace in industry which a rejoicing nation would acclaim.

After each war, until the last, the Government has been enabled to give homes to its returned soldiers, and a large part of our settlement and development has attended this generous provision of land for the Nation's defenders.

There is yet unreserved approximately 200,000,000 acres in the public domain, 20,000,000 acres of which are known to be susceptible of reclamation and made fit for homes by provision for irrigation.

The Government has been assisting in the development of its remaining lands, until the estimated increase in land values in the irrigated sections is full $500,000,000 and the crops of 1920 alone on these lands are estimated to exceed $100,000,000. Under the law authorization these expenditures for development the advances are to be returned and it would be good business for the Government to provide for the reclamation of the remaining 20,000,000 acres, in addition to expediting the completion of projects long under way.

Under what is known as the coal and gas lease law, applicable also to deposits of phosphates and other minerals on the public domain, leases are now being made on the royalty basis, and are producing large revenues to the Government. Under this legislation, 10 per centum of all royalties is to be paid directly to the Federal Treasury, and of the remainder 50 per centum is to be used for reclamation of arid lands by irrigation, and 40 per centum is to be paid to the States, in which the operations are located, to be used by them for school and road purposes.

These resources are so vast, and the development is affording so reliable a basis of estimate, that the Interior Department expresses the belief that ultimately the present law will add in royalties and payments to the treasuries of the Federal Government and the States containing these public lands a total of $12,000,000,000. This means, of course, an added wealth of many times that sum. These prospects seem to afford every justification of Government advances in reclamation and irrigation.

Contemplating the inevitable and desirable increase of population, there is another phase of reclamation full worthy of consideration. There are 79,000,000 acres of swamp and cut-over lands which may be reclaimed and made as valuable as any farm lands we possess. These acres are largely located in Southern States, and the greater proportion is owned by the States or by private citizens. Congress has a report of the survey of this field for reclamation, and the feasibility is established. I gladly commend Federal aid, by way of advances, where State and private participation is assured.

Home making is one of the greater benefits which government can bestow. Measures are pending embodying this sound policy to which we may well adhere. It is easily possible to make available permanent homes which will provide, in turn, for prosperous American families, without injurious competition with established activities, or imposition on wealth already acquired.

While we are thinking of promoting the fortunes of our own people, I am sure there is room in the sympathetic thought of America for fellow human beings who are suffering and dying of starvation in Russia. A severe drought in the Valley of the Volga has plunged 15,000,000 people into grievous famine. Our voluntary agencies are exerting themselves to the utmost to save the lives of children in this area, but it is now evident that unless relief is afforded the loss of life will extend into many millions. America can not be deaf to such a call as that.

We do not recognize the government of Russia, nor tolerate the propaganda which emanates therefrom, but we do not forget the traditions of Russian friendship. We may put aside our consideration of all international politics and fundamental differences in government. The big thing is the call of the suffering and the dying. Unreservedly I recommend the appropriation necessary to supply the American Relief Administration with 10,000,000 bushels of corn and 1,000,000 bushels of seed grains, not alone to halt the wave of death through starvation, but to enable spring planting in areas where the seed grains have been exhausted temporarily to stem starvation.

The American Relief Administration is directed in Russia by former officers of our own armies, and has fully demonstrated its ability to transport and distribute relief through American hands without hindrance or loss. The time has come to add the Government's support to the wonderful relief already wrought out of the generosity of the American private purse.

I am not unaware that we have suffering and privation at home. When it exceeds the capacity for the relief within the States concerned, it will have Federal consideration. It seems to me we should be indifferent to our own heart promptings, and out of accord with the spirit which acclaims the Christmastide, if we do not give out of our national abundance to lighten this burden of woe upon a people blameless and helpless in famine's peril.

There are a full score of topics concerning which it would be becoming to address you, and on which I hope to make report at a later time. I have alluded to the things requiring your earlier attention. However, I can not end this limited address without a suggested amendment to the organic law.

Many of us belong to that school of thought which is hesitant about altering the fundamental law. I think our tax problems, the tendency of wealth to seek nontaxable investment, and the menacing increase of public debt, Federal, State and municipal—all justify a proposal to change the Constitution so as to end the issue of nontaxable bonds. No action can change the status of the many billions outstanding, but we can guard against future encouragement of capital's paralysis, while a halt in the growth of public indebtedness would be beneficial throughout our whole land.

Such a change in the Constitution must be very thoroughly considered before submission. There ought to be known what influence it will have on the inevitable refunding of our vast national debt, how it will operate on the necessary refunding of State and municipal debt, how the advantages of Nation over State and municipality, or the contrary, may be avoided. Clearly the States would not ratify to their own apparent disadvantage. I suggest the consideration because the drift of wealth into nontaxable securities is hindering the flow of large capital to our industries, manufacturing, agricultural, and carrying, until we are discouraging the very activities which make our wealth.

Agreeable to your expressed desire and in complete accord with the purposes of the executive branch of the Government, there is in Washington, as you happily know, an International Conference now most earnestly at work on plans for the limitation of armament, a naval holiday, and the just settlement of problems which might develop into causes of international disagreement.

It is easy to believe a world-hope is centered on this Capital City. A most gratifying world-accomplishment is not improbable.

Source: *Papers Relating to the Foreign Relations of the United States*. 1921, Vol. 1. Washington, D.C.: Government Printing Office, 1936, xx–xxxii.

30. CALVIN COOLIDGE (1872–1933)

Presidential Term (1923–1929)

CHRONOLOGY

July 4, 1872—Calvin Coolidge is born in Plymouth Notch, Vermont.

Spring 1895—Coolidge graduates from Amherst College.

1897—Coolidge is admitted to the Massachusetts bar.

October 4, 1905—Coolidge marries Grace Goodhue.

November 5, 1918—Coolidge is elected governor of Massachusetts.

January 16, 1919—The states ratify the Eighteenth Amendment, prohibiting the sale or manufacture of alcohol.

June 28, 1919—The signing of the Treaty of Versailles ends World War I.

September 19, 1919—Responding to the Boston Police Strike, Governor Coolidge declares, "There is no right to strike against the public safety by anybody, anywhere, anytime."

August 18, 1920—States ratify the Nineteenth Amendment, providing for women's suffrage.

November 2, 1920—Harding is elected as the 29th president of the United States; Coolidge is elected vice president.

November 2, 1920—The first commercial radio broadcast is made.

August 2, 1923—President Harding dies in San Francisco while on a speaking tour of the country.

August 3, 1923—Coolidge is sworn in as the 30th president of the United States.

May 1924—Congress enacts the National Origins Act, restricting immigration.

September 1924—The Dawes Plan addressing Germany's World War I debt is put into effect.

November 4, 1924—Coolidge wins a term of his own as president.

February 26, 1926—Coolidge signs the Revenue Act, lowering income taxes, a move that further damages the floundering economy.

April 29, 1926—The United States and France sign a pact that eliminates 60 percent of French debt from World War I.

August 2, 1927—Coolidge declares, "I choose not to run," regarding another term as president.

July 25, 1928—The United States recognizes the National Government of Chiang Kai-shek in China.

August 27, 1928—The United States joins 15 other nations in signing the mostly symbolic Kellogg-Briand Pact, which outlaws war as a means to settle disputes between nations.

November 6, 1928—Herbert Hoover wins election as the 31st president of the United States.

October 24–29, 1929—From "Black Thursday" on October 24 to "Black Tuesday" on October 29, share prices on the New York Stock Exchange collapse, ushering in the Great Depression.

November 8, 1932—Franklin D. Roosevelt is elected the 32nd president of the United States.

January 5, 1933—Calvin Coolidge dies in Northampton, Massachusetts.

BIOGRAPHICAL SKETCH

Calvin Coolidge was the 30th president of the United States. After ascending to the presidency following the sudden death of President Warren Harding, the quiet and reserved Coolidge almost immediately found

Calvin Coolidge (Library of Congress)

inspired Coolidge's sense of duty and service, introducing the youngster, who often accompanied his father to meetings and political gatherings, to the realities of the political world. Unhappily, Coolidge's mother, whom he adored, died at the age of 39, only months before Calvin's 13th birthday. Five years later, his sister Abigail, four years younger than Calvin but his favorite companion, died suddenly from appendicitis. Beyond these emotional setbacks, Coolidge was a sickly boy growing up. He suffered from a variety of ailments and had respiratory and digestive problems that dogged him for much of the rest of his life. Even as president, he had attacks of asthma and hay fever and took numerous different medications to address ailments that ranged from swollen sinuses to bronchitis. He was easily fatigued, and even as an adult, he took regular afternoon naps.

Coolidge got his earliest education in the local elementary school in Plymouth before enrolling at Black River Academy in 1886. Following his graduation, he failed the entrance exam for Amherst College. Consequently, he spent the 1890–1891 school year at St. Johnsbury Academy in Ludlow, Vermont, preparing for the exams. He successfully completed the St. Johnsbury program, and because he had earned a college entrance certificate, he was automatically qualified for acceptance at Amherst, which he entered in 1891. While at Amherst, Coolidge was something of a loner and was not much involved in either extracurricular activities or athletics. While he got off to a slow start in the classroom, his academic performance markedly improved over his final two years when he focused on both history and philosophy, allowing him to ultimately graduate cum laude. As a member of the College's Young Republicans, his essay "The Principles Fought for in the American Revolution" won First Prize, a $150 gold medal, in a contest sponsored by the Sons of the American Revolution. In addition, and ironically given his future reputation, while at Amherst, Coolidge developed a reputation as something of a campus wit, and as a result, he was chosen to deliver the Grove Oration, an address that traditionally was notable for its irreverence and satirical bent.

Following Coolidge's graduation from Amherst in 1895, he studied law in the office of Northampton, Massachusetts, attorneys John C. Hammond and

himself facing a breaking political scandal involving some of Harding's major appointees. Acting decisively, Coolidge quickly addressed the situation, and in doing so, he not only restored the people's faith in the nation's governmental system but established himself as a man of integrity. This all but guaranteed his election to a term of his own, during which he presided over a growing economy while furthering the Republican Party's conservative social agenda.

John Calvin Coolidge was born on July 4, 1872, in Plymouth, Vermont. He was named after his father, and from his earliest years, the future president was known as Calvin or Cal to avoid confusion. He completely dropped the use of his first name after his graduation from college, and throughout his public career, he was known simply as Calvin Coolidge.

Coolidge led a rather solitary life as a child. He mentioned no childhood friends in his autobiography, and most biographers only make note of friends beginning in college. He worshipped his father, whose service in countless town and local governmental positions

Henry P. Field, pillars of the local legal and civic community. The experience not only prepared him for his legal career but got him his first taste of politics when he helped in Field's successful run for mayor of Northampton. He also gained some local acclaim with a piece in the local paper defending the gold standard in response to Democratic presidential candidate William Jennings Bryan's call for free silver.

Coolidge was admitted to the bar in 1897. He opened a law practice in Northampton that same year and quickly plunged ever deeper into the activities of the local Republican Party. His local involvement represented the first step in a public career in which Coolidge's ultimate ascension to the presidency was the culmination of a methodical but determined climb up the political ladder. Soon after he opened his practice, the party invited him to serve on its city committee, a body that helped select nominees for local offices.

In 1898, the young attorney made his own first foray into the electoral arena, winning election to the Northampton City Council, where he served from 1899 to 1900. That unpaid post was followed by his selection by the city council as city solicitor, a post he filled from 1900 to 1902. He then filled the unexpired term of the Hampshire County clerk of court in 1903 before being named chairman of the local Republican Party in 1904. The following year, Coolidge suffered the only electoral loss of his career, making an unsuccessful bid for a seat on the Northampton School Board.

Clearly dedicated to the pursuit of public office, an undaunted Coolidge returned to the public arena the next year, winning a seat in the state legislature, in what was then known as the Massachusetts General Court. Serving from 1907 to 1908, he made a reputation as a progressive, supporting both a six-day work week as well as protective legislation in the area of women and child labor. As an advocate of ever broader democracy, Coolidge was a supporter of both the direct election of senators and women's suffrage, two ideas that would come to fruition as constitutional amendments in the coming decade and a half. In addition, true to his deep commitment to free enterprise, Coolidge also fought for legislation aimed at limiting the kind of price cutting that was used to undermine economic competition. He also played a role in the effort to codify the state's banking laws.

Returning to politics at the local level, Coolidge served as mayor of Northampton from 1910 to 1911, and in that role, he cut taxes while also reducing the city's debt. In addition, he expanded the town's police and fire departments and improved the local streets and sidewalks. Again shifting gears, Coolidge next moved on to the Massachusetts State Senate, where he served four terms from 1912 to 1915, with the last two years occupying the chair as senate president. During his senate career, he helped mediate the Lawrence textile strike that shook the city in 1912, and he organized the votes needed to override a gubernatorial veto of a bill that brought the extension of rail service to his district.

Coolidge burnished his already recognized progressive *bona fides* by supporting an income tax, the legalization of labor pickets, and a minimum wage for women. He also opposed the insurance industry's effort to prevent banks from underwriting life insurance policies, a program pioneered in Massachusetts to much acclaim, especially among labor. At the same time, for all his progressive efforts, Coolidge was a loyal establishment Republican who supported the reelection of President Taft in 1912.

From the top spot in the state senate, Coolidge rose to the office of lieutenant governor, winning election to that office in 1916. While he was relegated to a typical supporting role as lieutenant governor, he nevertheless managed to make a mark heading a commission that worked to rescue the financially imperiled Boston Elevated Street Railway. He also had a voice in the governor's appointments and pardons. He campaigned actively on behalf of Republican presidential nominee Charles Evans Hughes in 1916, and when the United States went to war the following year, Coolidge traveled the state encouraging activities in support of the war effort. His long and steady climb in Massachusetts politics was capped in 1918 when, aided by campaign appearances by former presidents Theodore Roosevelt and William Howard Taft, Coolidge won a narrow 16,000 vote victory over Democrat Richard Long, a wealthy aspirant who had financed his own campaign, in the governor's race.

As governor, Coolidge made a major effort to address the postwar housing shortage while also supporting cost-of-living increases for public employees and limiting working hours for women and children. Coolidge, who never served in the military, strongly supported legislation providing benefits to returning World War I veterans. Appreciative of the region's natural beauty, the Vermont native also supported the regulation of outdoor advertising and also helped set up a state budget system. True to his conservative fiscal beliefs, he vetoed a bill that raised the salaries of the state legislators by 50 percent. Dubbed the "Salary Grab Bill" by critics, Coolidge's veto was overridden by the unapologetic legislature, but he earned considerable public support for his effort in trying to stop the bill. But for all of this, it was his response to a strike by the Boston police in 1919 that brought him to national attention. Amid the postwar fear of radical influence and the labor upheaval that gripped the country, Coolidge's declaration, "There is no right to strike against the public safety by anybody, anywhere anytime," resonated with a nation in turmoil and helped Coolidge secure an overwhelming victory in the 1919 rematch with Richard Long.

The declaration itself was a classic example of Coolidge's managerial approach, as it had followed a period of temporizing while he held off getting involved, giving the local officials and the police commissioner an opportunity to settle the strike themselves. Coolidge only weighed in when all of that had failed. In the end, it was a political masterstroke, and one his advisers tried to take advantage of it in a party that had no obvious choice as its presidential nominee. Indeed, Coolidge's longtime friend, businessman Frank Stearns, arranged for the publication of a collection of a number of Coolidge's speeches. The subsequent book, *Have Faith in Massachusetts*, became one of the most successful campaign volumes in history. At the same time, his adviser, public relations guru Bruce Barton, was looking to strategically raise Coolidge's public profile beyond the borders of Massachusetts.

However, for all their work, with Senator Henry Cabot Lodge refusing to support the governor, he could not even boast a united Massachusetts delegation at the convention, and as a result, the effort gained no real traction. But after the party leaders imposed Ohio senator Warren G. Harding on the delegates as the presidential nominee, the delegates started to rebel, resisting the leadership's effort to impose Wisconsin

senator Irvine Lenroot on the other half of the ticket. Instead, as events unfolded, Coolidge emerged as the favorite of a convention that had never followed the script, winning the nomination for vice president on the first ballot. In the end, the quiet East Coast governor provided a nice balance to the Ohio orator, and together they crushed the Democratic ticket of Ohio governor James Cox and Assistant Secretary of the Navy Franklin D. Roosevelt. Promising a "return to normalcy," while also repudiating President Woodrow Wilson's Treaty of Versailles and the League of Nations, Harding and Coolidge won an overwhelming victory. Garnering a then record 60.3 percent of the popular vote, the ticket carried 37 states with 404 electoral votes and returned the White House to Republican hands.

Having served as Massachusetts' lieutenant governor, Coolidge knew what it was like to be in a position with limited responsibility. As vice president, Coolidge attended cabinet meetings, but in a White House dominated by presidential friends and cronies, a group that would become known as the "Ohio gang," the taciturn Coolidge was very much an outsider. His formal duties were basically limited to presiding over the Senate in a way that only reinforced every stereotype of a vanished vice president that had ever been offered.

However, on the night of August 2, 1923, while vacationing at the family home in Plymouth Notch, Vermont, Coolidge's life changed forever. While Coolidge was quietly enjoying time with his family in a house that had no phone, President Harding, in the middle of a major cross-country trip, suddenly died in San Francisco, California. Getting word of the president's death, Coolidge's stenographer, a chauffeur, and a newspaper reporter drove in the middle of the night from Bridgewater, Vermont, to deliver the news. After awakening the family, at 2:47 a.m., on August 3, 1923, they shared the news with Coolidge, who was then sworn in to his new office by his father, a local justice of the peace and a notary, in the sitting room of the family home. Befitting his image, President Calvin Coolidge then went back to sleep.

On the personal front, Coolidge had married Grace Anna Goodhue, an only child, at her parents' home in Burlington, Vermont, in 1905. Grace had graduated from the University of Vermont and then taken a job as a lipreading instructor at the Clark Institute for the Deaf in Northampton, Massachusetts. A chance meeting in 1903 led to a more formal introduction, and a relationship developed. Never warming to her son-in-law, Grace's mother tried to postpone the wedding, and not only was her relationship with Coolidge little more than formal, she later credited her daughter with being responsible for most of Coolidge's political success. Despite these tensions, Grace's vivacity and spirit served as an ideal complement to Coolidge's reserve, and they were devoted to each other for almost three decades of marriage. Grace was not a political confidant; in fact, Coolidge's announcement that he would not seek another term in 1928 caught her by surprise.

However, as first lady, Grace Coolidge was a popular hostess whose own warmth and personality helped humanize the public's impression of the reserved and often taciturn president. She enthusiastically performed the duties of first lady, happily undertaking such events as the opening of rest homes for veterans and laying cornerstones for new buildings. She also encouraged women to take advantage of their newfound right to vote, participating in a photo session that showed her filling out her absentee ballot at the White House in advance of an upcoming election.

After leaving the White House in March 1929, Coolidge and his wife returned to Northampton, Massachusetts. His attendance at a July 1929 celebration of the signing of the Kellogg-Briand Treaty represented his only return to Washington, as otherwise he pretty much left public life behind. He did write an autobiography as well as articles for a number of national magazines, including the *Saturday Evening Post* and *Colliers*. In addition, he wrote a daily column titled "Thinking Things Over with Calvin Coolidge" for the McClure Newspaper Syndicate from 1930 to 1931.

Coolidge rebuffed numerous offers to promote a range of products, although he did serve on the board of directors of the New York Life Insurance Company. However, that experience went awry when an October 1931 radio speech warning listeners about insurance agents who would attempt to alter policies resulted in a lawsuit by an agent who claimed that the speech had

cost him $100,000 of lost business. Anxious to avoid a trial, the publicity-shy Coolidge settled out of court for $2,500.

While his retirement saw him withdrawing from active political involvement, he was reported to have resented the fact that Hoover had never consulted the former president on anything. However, Coolidge did deliver one major address in Madison Square Garden as well as a radio address on behalf of the beleaguered incumbent in his 1932 race against Democrat Franklin Roosevelt.

Coolidge's efforts on behalf of Hoover proved the last of his public career. He had complained that fall of difficulty breathing as well as indigestion, and he evidenced an overall listlessness and lack of energy, which, for all his low-key persona, was not the norm. On January 5, 1933, Coolidge spent the first part of the morning in his office in Northampton, but he returned home before lunch. He then worked for a brief time on a jigsaw puzzle of George Washington before heading upstairs to his bedroom around noon. When Mrs. Coolidge went to check on him about an hour later, she found him deceased, at the age of 60. Doctors determined that he had suffered a coronary thrombosis.

News of his death was met by a major public outpouring of grief, and the simple funeral service held in Northampton at the Edwards Congregational Church was attended by the president and first lady, former secretary of state and then chief justice Charles Evans Hughes, Justice Harlan Fiske Stone, and Eleanor Roosevelt, among others. Following the short service, Coolidge's body was transported to the family plot in Plymouth Notch, Vermont.

HISTORICAL OVERVIEW

For all the calm he showed upon becoming president, the challenges that Coolidge faced were not insignificant. In fact, Coolidge assumed the office at a time when the Harding administration was beginning to come apart, for unbeknownst to the new president, the administration was racked by scandal. Indeed, prior to his death, Harding had learned that Charles Forbes, the director of the Veteran's Bureau, had either stolen or misused almost a quarter of a million dollars. Forbes was ultimately indicted for fraud and bribery related to government hospital supply contracts, but reflective of Harding's somewhat lax ethical code, he initially allowed Forbes to resign his post and then escape overseas. Forbes would ultimately serve over a year and a half in prison in 1926 and 1927. Meanwhile, in the aftermath of Harding's death, it was revealed that Attorney General Harry Daugherty had taken bribes from businessmen, bootleggers, and others. However, despite the best efforts of the Coolidge administration, Daugherty escaped jail when his trial resulted in a hung jury. But the biggest scandal that President Coolidge had to address was what became known as the Teapot Dome scandal. With Harding's acquiescence, Secretary of the Interior Albert Fall (a former Senate colleague of the president's) had arranged to have two oil deposits, one an oil reserve called Teapot Dome in Wyoming, put under the jurisdiction of the Department of the Interior. Fall then leased the oil reserves—important components of the nation's defense supplies—to private companies, receiving a hefty fee for the effort. In the aftermath of Harding's death, all of this began to emerge, and Fall was ultimately convicted. When he began serving his prison term in 1929, he became the first person to go to jail for illegal acts committed while serving in the cabinet.

All of this was coming to a head as Coolidge assumed office, and from the outset, he had to navigate a fine line between a former administration's agenda that he was now committed to carry out and whose members now worked for him and increasing calls, sometimes motivated by the politics of the day, for action. Indeed, after vowing early on to enforce the law while also promising to appoint a special prosecutor, he stumbled with his early choices before finally landing on former senator Atlee Pomerene and future Supreme Court justice Owen Roberts. Their efforts, coupled with the congressional investigations headed by Senators Robert LaFollette and Thomas Walsh, all supported by a Justice Department that had seen the disgraced Daugherty replaced by Harlan Fiske Stone, the former dean of Columbia Law School and an Amherst classmate of Coolidge's, brought the perpetrators to justice. In the end, the clean-up effort did much to restore people's faith in the integrity of the government while also allowing the nation to move on. It also allowed Coolidge to pursue his own agenda, as his efforts to unravel the mess of his predecessor not only enhanced his reputation for integrity but, to the dismay of the Democrats who had hoped to use the scandal in the upcoming campaign, served to put some distance between Coolidge and members of the tainted Harding team.

In addition to cleaning up the mess resulting from the Tea Pot Dome scandal, Coolidge also brought to completion a number of important items on the Harding and Republican Party agendas. He helped secure passage of the Immigration Act of 1924, a measure that reduced the overall number of American immigrants who could enter the country and changed the formula for the allocation of those who could enter the country. The result of the change was a substantive reduction in people coming from Southern and Eastern Europe, such as Italians and Jews, while the chances of those who sought to emigrate from Northern Europe were enhanced. In addition, effective in 1927, a new ceiling of 150,000 was placed on the total number of immigrants who could enter the country on an annual basis. Finally, immigrants from Japan were completely excluded, but the total exemption from any quotas that Canada and Mexico had long enjoyed remained in effect.

Despite these early successes, Coolidge did not have smooth sailing. Throughout his presidency, he would regularly find the Republican-controlled Congress unwilling to follow the presidential lead. He suffered an early setback when his 1924 veto of the World War Adjusted Compensation Act, more commonly known as the Bonus Act, was overridden. An earlier versions of the act, strongly supported by the American Legion, had been passed, but it was vetoed by President Harding. Coolidge made clear his own opposition, saying that "patriotism bought and paid for is not patriotism." At the same time, backers of the bill argued that it was not a "bonus" but simply the completion of compensation earned by the veterans for their wartime service. In the end, Coolidge's veto could not be upheld because Republican leaders feared, as they had from the start, that the presidential commitment to fiscal integrity would have an adverse effect on the party's electoral prospects. Congress ultimately overrode Coolidge's veto. A desire by veterans suffering in the Great Depression to receive the payments early would subsequently lead to the controversial Bonus March of 1932.

While these efforts reflected that Coolidge had effected a comparatively successful, if challenging, transition to the presidency, in fact, Coolidge had barely assumed office when he and the Republican Party had to turn their attention to the upcoming presidential election. Although his status as president gave him a leg up, to many he was little more than a placeholder, yet another in the line of men—starting with John Tyler and continuing through Millard Fillmore, Andrew Johnson, Chester Arthur, and Theodore Roosevelt—who had ascended to the presidency but then, except for Roosevelt, had been shunted aside, not even being nominated to run for a full term.

Yet, Coolidge proved more politically adroit than his historical predecessors, and he quickly dispatched his two most likely challengers, Pennsylvania governor and former Roosevelt protégé Gifford Pinchot and auto magnate Henry Ford. Once they had been maneuvered to the sidelines, the contest was never really in doubt, although at one point the candidate himself gave serious consideration to withdrawing from the race.

Indeed, amid what should have been a time of professional and personal celebration, Calvin and Grace Coolidge had to deal with every parent's nightmare, the death of a child. On June 30, less than three weeks after the Republican convention in Cleveland, Ohio, that had overwhelmingly nominated the president to run for a full term of his own, Calvin Jr. and his brother John were playing tennis on the White House courts when Calvin Jr., who had been playing tennis without socks, developed a blood blister on the middle toe of his right foot. Within a couple of days, the sixteen-year-old began to feel weak and developed a fever, swollen glands, and other symptoms, which led doctors to believe he had a bacterial infection. Tests confirmed that a staph infection had poisoned his bloodstream. Every type of medication then in existence was administered to the boy, but his condition only worsened. Surgery also offered no relief, and at 10:20 p.m., on the night of July 7, 1924, Calvin Coolidge Jr. died.

The Coolidges were the recipients of a national outpouring of sympathy, with letters and telegrams flooding the White House. The Democrats adjourned their convention upon hearing the news. The president was devastated and inconsolable, saying, "When he went, the power and glory of the Presidency went with him." He often remarked later that he was never the same after young Calvin's death. Indeed, for months afterward, even in the midst of his greatest political triumph, he was an emotional wreck, no longer, in the view of one visitor, the president, but simply a father who had tragically lost his son.

And yet, while Coolidge was suffering, his party was in fine fettle. The economy was humming, and the cloud that the Tea Pot Dome scandal might have cast over their efforts had been erased through the president's and Congress's quick and decisive response, actions that sent a clear message to the nation. Adding to the Republicans' good fortune was a deeply divided Democratic Party, one that needed 103 ballots before settling on former congressman and solicitor general John W. Davis, a compromise candidate, who it was hoped could bridge the divide that had been personified by New York's governor Al Smith—a "wet" urban Catholic on the one side and the Southern native, now California-based, William Gibbs McAdoo, Woodrow Wilson's son-in-law and former treasury secretary, whose "dry" rural-based candidacy had been given at least tacit seal of approval from the Ku Klux Klan, on the other. Adding to the intrigue was the independent Progressive Party candidate from Wisconsin, Senator Robert LaFollette, who believed that both major parties had become hostages of the nation's business community.

Despite the strong prospects, neither Coolidge nor the party took anything for granted. Not surprisingly, given his ongoing mourning over Calvin Jr.'s death, Coolidge was happy to leave the bulk of the active campaigning to others. He did emerge in the campaign's final days to deliver a pro-business address to the U.S. Chamber of Commerce, but in general, it was surrogates who spread throughout the country, praised the president's calm but decisive leadership, and urged people to "Keep Cool with Coolidge," a memorable if insubstantial slogan.

Coolidge's campaign pioneered some new public relations approaches that would ultimately transform the electoral process. Working with professional public relations figures Bruce Barton and Edward

Bernays, the campaign put an unprecedented emphasis on the candidate and his personality, in contrast to the time-honored focus on the party and its programs. Putting a new focus on radio, where Coolidge was able to reach more people in fewer speeches, thus lending each a greater air of importance, Coolidge was able to get his message out while connecting, at least over the airwaves, with larger and larger audiences. Radio addresses also allowed Coolidge to make targeted addresses to smaller audiences. It was a forum in which he shined. From his initial use of the airwaves to accept the Republican nomination to individual addresses sprinkled throughout the campaign, all complemented by celebrity testimonials and newsreel footage that helped to further humanize the nation's accidental chief executive, the public relations campaign continued to urge people to "Keep Cool with Coolidge." In the end, that is exactly what the American people decided to do, giving the incumbent 54 percent of the vote in the three-party race, with Davis getting 28.8 percent and LaFollette garnering a mere 16.6 percent.

With a strong electoral victory behind him and now ensconced in the Oval Office on his own merits, Coolidge continued to pursue the small government, laissez-faire policies at the heart of the party's agenda. He also began to remake his administration. Given the circumstances of his ascension to the presidency, most of Harding's cabinet stayed on at least through the election. Secretary of States Charles Evans Hughes, the Republican presidential nominee in 1916 and a former Supreme Court justice, remained in office until after the election and was succeeded by Frank B. Kellogg, who had previously served as ambassador to Great Britain and who remained at the head of the State Department until Coolidge left office.

Meanwhile, Secretary of the Treasury Andrew W. Mellon, who was equally committed to the free market policies that Coolidge espoused, oversaw a booming economy. Originally appointed by President Harding, Mellon served throughout the Coolidge years and into the Hoover administration as well. Indeed, working closely with Mellon, Secretary of Commerce Herbert Hoover was also a key member of the Harding-Coolidge economic team, and his efforts in that role, coupled with his earlier work overseeing humanitarian relief in Europe following World War I, made him a major figure in the Republican Party and led to his ultimate selection as the party's nominee for president in 1928. Upon that designation, he resigned from the cabinet and was replaced by William F. Whiting, a Massachusetts Republican whose family had long been active in party affairs.

In the post of Secretary of War, Coolidge inherited John W. Weeks, a Massachusetts native who was well known to the former Bay State governor, having represented the state in both the House and the Senate before joining the cabinet. Poor health forced Weeks to retire in October 1925, and he died the following July. In the aftermath of Week's resignation, Coolidge elevated the assistant secretary, Dwight Davis, who served the remainder of the term. But Davis's greater historical stature perhaps comes from the prize, the Davis Cup, that he donated for the international tennis competition.

One of the quicker exits from the Coolidge cabinet was that of Attorney General Harry Daugherty, arguably Harding's closest adviser, but one whose corrupt performance in office was a stain on the administration's record. As his activities became known—it was ultimately revealed that he had taken bribes from businessmen, bootleggers, and others—Coolidge quickly moved to replace him and clean up the Justice Department. By appointing an old Amherst classmate, Harlan Fiske Stone, who was then serving as dean of the Columbia Law School and had a sterling reputation in the nation's legal community, Coolidge went a long way toward restoring confidence in the department, although, despite their best efforts, Daugherty escaped jail when his trial resulted in a hung jury. In the end, Stone's tenure as attorney general, while highly impactful, was comparatively short-lived, for when a vacancy arose on the Supreme Court in 1925, Coolidge appointed the scholarly Stone to the seat, where he would carve out a distinguished career.

Coolidge originally sought to replace Stone with Charles Warren of Michigan. Although he was a long-time Republican stalwart, having served as ambassador to both Japan and Mexico, his arrogance had left him an unpopular figure in party circles. That personal aspect, coupled with his work for a company under investigation by the Justice Department, coupled with poor headcounts by the Senate floor mangers, resulted in a 40–40 vote, which Vice President Dawes, having returned to his hotel room for a nap, was unable to get back to the Senate in time to break. Coolidge was livid on many levels, but a second attempt to nominate Warren resulted in an outright rebuke of the president, who ended up settling on John G. Sargent of Vermont to serve the remainder of the term. In that capacity, Sargent struggled with the effort to enforce Prohibition, trying his best to address a problem that had been a challenge since the passage of the Eighteenth Amendment and the enactment of the Volstead Act.

Coolidge's original secretary of the navy, Edwin Denby, was another Harding holdover who got involved, apparently unwittingly, in the Teapot Dome scandal, when he acceded to the request from Interior Secretary Fall to have the navy relinquish control over the nation's oil reserves, transferring them instead to the Interior Department. As the dimensions of the scandal became known, Congress called on Denby to resign, which he did, but in accepting his resignation, the president expressed his faith in Denby's honesty.

Despite his own belief in Denby's character, Coolidge recognized the need to shore up public confidence in the navy. Seeking to do that, he named Curtis D. Wilbur of California, a Naval Academy graduate active in Republican political circles, whose work first as an associate justice and then as chief justice of the California Supreme Court had earned him a sterling reputation for probity and integrity that had served the administration well. Policy wise, Wilbur led an effort to enlarge and modernize the fleet, and he sought to make greater use of the developing aircraft through the establishment of the naval air force.

The nation's ever-advancing air capabilities also played a major part in the efforts of Coolidge's postmaster general, Harry S. New of Indiana. Originally appointed to his post by Harding, New served throughout Coolidge's presidency and played a central role in the efforts to improve and expand the nation's airmail service.

Following the resignation of Albert Fall, as a result of his involvement with the Tea Pot Dome scandal, Coolidge sought to restore public confidence by appointing Hubert Work as secretary of the interior. Working with the Justice Department, he helped

reestablish the department's reputation before resigning in July 1928 to manage Herbert Hoover's presidential campaign. Roy O. West of Illinois served out the remainder of the term.

Coolidge's first secretary of agriculture was Henry C. Wallace, a holdover from the Harding administration. Wallace died on October 24, only 10 days before the election. He was replaced before the end of the year by Howard R. Gore, who was promoted from assistant secretary, but his tenure was short-lived, as he resigned in March to become governor of West Virginia. He was succeeded by William M. Jardine, who at the time of his appointment was serving as president of the Agricultural College in Manhattan College. He served the remainder of Coolidge's term.

Secretary of Labor James Davis, from Pennsylvania, was a holdover from the Harding administration who not only stayed on through the end of Coolidge's presidency but served under Hoover for two years before winning election to the U.S. Senate.

With a team of his own in place, Coolidge sought to continue the economic growth and prosperity that had thus far characterized the Republican decade, and as he had indicated in his inaugural address, he remained committed to pursuing programs that would continue to yield that same kind of economic prosperity. Rebuffing, if not outright dismissing, calls for approaches that might more directly impact the poor or impose higher taxes on the wealthy, Coolidge had shared with the inauguration day audience his view that "the wise and correct course to follow in taxation and all other economic legislation is not to destroy those who have already secured success but to create conditions under which everyone will have a better chance to be successful."

In that vein, he secured passage of the Tax Reduction Act of 1926, which, coupled with the version enacted in 1924, reduced both income and inheritance taxes while also abolishing not only the existing gift tax but also most of the excise taxes that had been imposed during World War I. The intent of the legislation was to free up more money for investment, which, it was believed, would further fuel economic growth. In reality, it would lead to a flurry of speculation that would play no small role in the stock market crash and the attendant depression that wreaked such havoc after Coolidge left office.

At the same time, Coolidge held firm in regard to congressional efforts to address a developing problem in the economy's agricultural sector. The McNary-Haugen Bill sought to support farm prices through the creation of a government corporation that would buy certain surplus crops for ultimate resale abroad. Under the plan, the government would store the crops until prices rose or simply dump them at a loss, but in either case, the farmer would be protected from the vagaries of Mother Nature and uncertain markets that so often dogged the world of agriculture. Twice, in both 1927 and 1928, Congress passed versions of the act, and twice Coolidge vetoed it. In his veto message, Coolidge lashed out at what he saw as an attempt at price fixing, a concept that was anathema to a free market advocate like himself, and something he deemed a danger from which the country should be protected.

On a less contentious note, the administration secured passage of the Air Commerce Act, which placed civil aviation under the direction of the Commerce Department and approved the establishment of the nation's first two commercial air routes: a Transcontinental Airway route which would connect New York and Los Angeles/San Francisco via a variety of connections, which included Salt Lake City, Chicago, and Cleveland, and one through Southwestern Airways, which linked Chicago and Dallas with connections at a number of cities, including Tulsa, Kansas City, and Fort Wayne. Additional routes between Boston and Miami; Southern California and Portland, Oregon; and St. Louis and New Orleans were being planned.

In general, foreign policy under Coolidge reflected the president's overarching view of government. Akin to his approach on the domestic side, in the foreign arena, he preferred a noninterventionist pose unless U.S. financial interests were at stake. An example of this was his support of legislation that funded an expanded merchant marine, which he in turn believed would afford the United States greater international trade opportunities. In this same vein, he actively encouraged a joint U.S.-Canadian construction of the St. Lawrence Seaway which he believed could serve as a gateway for the trade between the Great Lakes and Europe.

Despite the general reluctance of the administration to initiate much in the area of international affairs, if only because of the actions of other parties, under Coolidge, the United States was in fact active, if reactive, from the beginning.

In May 1924, Coolidge and his foreign policy team completed the ongoing negotiations and finalized the Pact of Anapala. In one of many efforts by the United States to keep Honduran president Rafael Gutiérrez in power, Nicaragua, Guatemala, and El Salvador, in conjunction with the United States, agreed to cut off aid to the rebel forces that sought to mount an insurgent campaign against Gutiérrez. The pact was successful in the short run, but Gutiérrez would ultimately be overthrown in 1933.

Meanwhile, shortly after the 1924 Republican convention, the Coolidge administration celebrated the signing of the Dawes Plan on August 30. The plan, drawn up by Charles G. Dawes, a member of the Allied Reparations Commission as well as a banker, a sometime governmental official and diplomat, and ultimately Coolidge's running mate in 1924, sought to aid the struggling German economy by offering an alternative reparation schedule to the one that had been imposed on the defeated nation following the war and which was strangling the country's economy. The Dawes Plan, which was signed by representatives from the United States, France, Great Britain, Italy, and Belgium, based Germany's reparation payments on what they could pay rather than on the punitive amount that had previously been dictated. For his effort, Dawes would receive the Nobel Peace Prize the following year.

Only a few weeks later, the United States withdrew its troops from Santo Domingo, the final step in a process of disengagement initiated by Secretary of State Charles Evans Hughes after taking office in 1921. These troops, which had been originally dispatched by President Wilson in 1916, had helped stabilize the country and prepare it for free elections and, eventually, independence. It represented an end to a decades-long involvement in the developing nation, a role justified by Coolidge as necessary under the Monroe Doctrine.

The following year, the administration tied up a long dangling loose end on a treaty that had been pending before the Senate since 1904, securing Senate ratification of the Isle of Pines Treaty, which recognized

Cuba's possession of the Isle of Pines. In January 1926, the Senate adopted a resolution that allowed the United States to join the World Court. However, it attached five conditions, and when one went unsatisfied, the Senate rejected full U.S. participation. Coolidge was a strong advocate of American membership in the court, and he would push for it during the remainder of his term. But despite his efforts, as well as those by Hoover that followed, it was something that never came to fruition.

Believing that the Soviet Union was easing some of its more restrictive policies, Coolidge floated the possibility of U.S. recognition of the Soviet Union. However, when the Soviets refused to comply with the conditions the president laid out, including an end to communist propaganda aimed at the United States and payment for confiscated property and recognition of formerly repudiated debts, the administration withheld the recognition, a policy the United States continued until 1933.

Southern neighbor Mexico was also the object of an effort to repair relations that had been strained by a U.S. military invasion under Wilson as well as Germany's efforts to use the country in the war. At the same time, Coolidge also sought to secure a stable investment climate in the area, a particularly important consideration at a time when, because of the war having disrupted much of the European economy, many of the Latin and South American countries were now turning to the United States to borrow money while also being the recipients of increased amounts of American exports. Although Mexican president Elias Calles's actions, in 1925, that were aimed at nationalizing American industries created a new crisis, a solution crafted by the president's Amherst classmate Dwight Morrow prevented the nationalization, and once that was settled, the countries were able to move forward and develop a more mutually advantageous partnership.

Meanwhile, the big foreign policy triumph of Coolidge's full term was the Kellogg-Brian Pact completed in 1928. Under the terms of the agreement, 15 of the world's major nations, led by the United States, Great Britain, Germany, France, and Japan, agreed to outlaw war as a means for settling international disputes. While the agreement, ultimately joined by

another 47 countries, was hailed at the time, in the end, it proved to be little more than a parchment barrier, unable to halt or even slow the rising militarism of the 1930s, which would eventually lead to World War II.

Not surprisingly, Coolidge made only one foray onto foreign soil. Traveling to Havana, Cuba, to attend the Sixth International Conference of American States, he gave the opening address at the conference, where he expressed his desire to achieve greater harmony between the United Sates and the nations in the Southern Hemisphere.

Finally, the Coolidge administration gave diplomatic recognition to the National Government in China.

Although seemingly known as much for what he did not say as what he did, Silent Cal was in fact a more consistent communicator and more available to the media than almost any of his fellow chief executives. Over the course of 67 months in office, he held 520 press conferences, averaging almost eight a month. He also spoke at least once a month to a national radio audience. He was willing to put himself in front of the American public for a range of photographs. Indeed, photographers were thrilled when he donned a full Indian headdress during an address to a crowd of 10,000 Sioux. They were no less pleased when he willingly posed in old-fashioned overalls while working on his father's farm and in cowboy chaps and hat while on vacation in South Dakota. In addition, he was the first to appear in a talking film when a speech was recorded, and his State of the Union address in 1923, his acceptance speech at the 1924 Republican National Convention, and his inaugural address in 1925 were all aired over the radio. Comfortable in his own skin, he easily played to his audience.

Despite his often dour expressions, he was known as someone who liked to make people laugh, and in addition to being renowned among his friends for his dry, lean wit, he was also known to emerge from his famous silences to utter pithy remarks. All of this represented a marked contrast to his formal addresses, where he projected a high-minded, serious, and dignified demeanor. Communication was also a policy issue, and prodded by Commerce Secretary Hoover, Coolidge supported the passage of the Radio Act, which brought the developing radio industry under the nation's regulatory umbrella. It was declared public property and thus subject to regulation by the new Federal Radio Commission, which would evolve into the Federal Communications Commission (FCC).

While few doubted the sincerity of his deep-seated philosophical abhorrence of governmental activism or overreach, it could sometimes make him appear unfeeling and callous. Nowhere was that more evident than in his response to the Great Mississippi Flood of April 1927. The flood was a disaster that ultimately left hundreds dead and almost half a million people homeless. It also left hundreds of millions of dollars of damage in its wake. It was an incident that cried out for government assistance, and yet Coolidge was reluctant to have the federal government get too heavily involved.

While he did call on his secretary of commerce, Herbert Hoover, the man who had led the U.S. effort to provide food to a starving Europe after World War I, to head up a relief effort, Hoover's efforts were hamstrung by a lack of funds. Despite the fact that private sources of aid proved inadequate, Coolidge refused to allow his name to be used to help the Red Cross raise funds for the victims, and he was also unwilling to broadcast a national radio appeal. He rebuffed calls from countless officeholders that he visit the area. All of this reluctance was apparently based in his concern that, if he took center stage, it would heighten the demand for federal intervention. He deeply feared the precedent he would set if the federal government got involved in what he saw as a regional issues that should be solved by the state and local governing bodies. He also feared the impact of such aid on the budget surpluses that he had so carefully achieved. At the same time, despite his resistance, the cries for help from the federal government only grew. What the president saw as a principled stance was viewed by outsiders and especially flood victims as evidence of an uncaring and insensitive ideologue.

Despite increased pressure from many quarters, Coolidge refused to call a special session of Congress, and it was only in late 1927, after the Republican-led House Flood Control Committee held hearings, that the president was forced to act. In his December State of the Union address, he expressed his support for federal flood control measures, although he insisted most of the costs be borne by local governments and property owners. In addition, his proposal called for much less funding than the House and Senate bills. Negotiations continued with Coolidge, who not only called the congressional plans "radical and dangerous" but who also expressed his concerns about corruption. Fearing that the funds would not be directed to the victims, he remained intent on limiting the role of the federal government.

Finally, in early May 1928, an agreement was reached. To the president's delight, the federal government was only financially responsible for the areas flooded in 1927. Meanwhile, local contributions were limited. In addition, the bill established a federal board to improve the physical engineering around the river. Perhaps most importantly, it declared the flooding in the region to be a matter national interest. Satisfied, but not pleased, on May 15, Coolidge signed the bill in private rather than holding a formal signing ceremony.

Despite over five years as president, Calvin Coolidge made only one appointment to the Supreme Court. And yet, for a chief executive whose legacy continues to be debated and reassessed, his appointment of Harlan Fiske Stone to the Court has never been seen as anything but an undeniable triumph, one that had an important and lasting impact on the nation's legal, political, and social landscape. The appointment's political roots lay in the challenges Coolidge faced from the start of his presidency, when the multifaceted corruption within the late president's administration, a web that became known as the Teapot Dome scandal, began to reveal itself. Coolidge's response included firing Attorney General Harry Daugherty, a major player in the scandal, and replacing him with an old college classmate, the highly respected dean of the Columbia Law School, Harlan Fiske Stone. With a clear directive from Coolidge, Stone worked with Congress to clean up the mess.

Stone's efforts, complemented by his impressive academic reputation, earned Stone an appointment to the Court in 1925, upon the retirement of Justice Joseph McKenna. In that role, he proved to be a leader in moving the Court in a more activist direction, one that saw it energizing and elevating the freedoms encapsulated in the Bill of Rights. His initial dissent and subsequent opinion in the flag salute cases were a testament to the freedoms that American soldiers were fighting for, and his famous footnote in the *Carolene Products* cases offered a foundation upon which many of the Court's subsequent historic civil rights decisions were based. Later elevated to the post of chief justice by Franklin Roosevelt, Stone's legal credentials, recognized with the initial appointment by Coolidge and manifested in his singular performance as an associate justice, and not his position as chief justice, as solid as that effort was, cemented his historic stature as well as that part of Coolidge's legacy.

Surprisingly perhaps, given the timing of his tenure, Coolidge also had a record on civil rights that deserves attention. While no one would confuse him with future trailblazers, he was arguably ahead of his times and certainly represented an improvement over Wilson's resegregation of the capital, an effort that reminded Americans that the former governor of New Jersey was in fact born and bred in the Confederacy.

Coolidge's first noteworthy effort in this area came while he was still in the Massachusetts legislature. There, in April 1915, while serving as the president of the Massachusetts Senate in the aftermath of race riots that had greeted the premier of D. W. Griffith's controversial film *The Birth of a Nation*, which exulted the Ku Klux Klan's efforts in the postwar South, in an action that free speech advocates might have had qualms about, Coolidge cast the deciding vote on a bill that banned the showing of the film.

Ironically, given his reputation for silence, most of Coolidge's efforts in this area centered on public addresses, opportunities in which he used the bully pulpit of the presidency to try and impact the nation's mind-set. Indeed, soon after becoming president, the usually taciturn and reserved president took a firm stand, one that reminded people that he was the head of the "Party of Lincoln." In his first State of the Union address, in 1923, Coolidge called for major funding for the capital's historically black Howard University. Asking $500,000, he announced his intention to help with the education of 500 black doctors annually. The following year, on June 2, 1924, expressing his admiration for the high rate of Native American enlistment in the army during World War I, Coolidge signed the Indian Citizenship Act. Just days later, on June 6,

1924, Coolidge shined a spotlight on black achievement when he delivered the commencement address, "The Progress of a People," at Howard University.

Later that summer, Coolidge penned a letter titled, "Equality of Rights," in which he strongly responded to a statement that had questioned the appropriateness of a black man running for the Republican nomination for a congressional seat. While some believed the president could have taken an even stronger stand against the notorious Ku Klux Klan, the prominent African American newspaper the *Chicago Defender* praised the president's statement, headlining its front page with "Cal Coolidge Tells Kluxers When to Stop." Similarly, reflecting his belief in the multiculturalism that was becoming an increasing hallmark of the United States, he gave addresses at a wide and varied array of places, including a September 1924 address before the Catholic Holy Name Society, where he spoke on "Authority and Religious Liberty"; a May 3, 1925, address, "The Spiritual Unification of America," at a dedication of the Jewish Community Center in Washington, D.C.; and the October 6, 1925, address "Tolerance and Liberalism," a ringing statement on tolerance, that he delivered before the American Legion Convention at Omaha, Nebraska. Meanwhile, in 1929, with the end of his term approaching, Coolidge signed a bill that called for a memorial to celebrate the achievements of the nation's black population.

In general, while there was little in the way of federal legislative action, which was no real surprise given Coolidge's philosophical bent, this series of efforts did reflect his clear recognition of the power of the president to set a tone and help foster a culture on these issues of national importance. In addition, following the lead of Harding, Coolidge also made clear his opposition to the lynchings that were an all too common part of Southern life. However, after numerous Republican-backed federal anti-lynching laws had been passed by the House only to be blocked by Southern Democrats, by the end of his term, he had given up pursuing further efforts.

Having never recovered emotionally or psychologically from the sudden death of his son in 1924, and despite his popularity and the overwhelming likelihood of winning reelection, on August 2, 1927, President Calvin Coolidge made an announcement that shocked the nation. Vacationing in his "Summer White House" in the Black Hills of South Dakota, he walked outside to the waiting reporters, and in his typically calm and dispassionate way, he handed each of them a slip of paper that read simply: "I do not choose to run for President in nineteen-twenty-eight." Taking no questions, Coolidge silently walked back inside his house—the remaining year and half of his term, notwithstanding—and out of the presidency.

Over the years, speculation about why Coolidge opted to forgo another run for the White House has been abundant, although there is much evidence to indicate that he had made clear to at least some confidants as early as 1924 that he would not seek another term. His own preference for privacy was certainly a factor, and the issue of the two-term tradition was also likely a factor, given that Theodore Roosevelt's decision not to run in 1908 had set the precedent that partial terms like his and Coolidge's counted. Indeed, he was reported to have said that, had he won a second term, his time in office would have ultimately been almost 10 years, a tenure he believed was too long for anyone. At the same time, despite those subsequent remarks, some have speculated that Coolidge hoped to be drafted, although his subsequent active opposition to the effort that did arise undermines that idea. Meanwhile, others think the man, who was reported to have admitted that he had spent much of his presidency avoiding the big problems, simply did not have the drive, desire, or energy to address the challenges that he for one recognized lay ahead.

Some have also seen it as reflective of two fundamental aspects of the man and his philosophy. On the hand, while he had committed almost three decades to public service and public office, he had never evinced a lust for power, so when he felt it was done—and there was no ongoing project or undertaking that needed to be brought to a close—he simply said enough. At the same time, for a man who believed to his core in limited government, that same principle applied to the people who ran it. For all his time in office, his tenure as president was the longest single office he ever held, and as he would later say, that was enough; another four would have been too much. In the end, whatever the reason, one of the most atypical politicians ever to hold the office seems to have simply followed his own atypical path and, in doing so, walked away from power.

In the aftermath of Coolidge's surprising decision not to seek another term, the Republicans looked for a successor. With Coolidge refusing to support any individual candidate, many expressed interest, but Herbert Hoover quickly emerged as the clear front-runner. Coolidge had long had mixed feelings about his commerce secretary. He saw him as overly ambitious and too much of a self-promoter. At the same time, he welcomed the way the man he had dismissed as "Wonder Boy" would willingly take on almost any project, which the ever ready to delegate president appreciated. For all of his misgivings, Coolidge did nothing to encourage the "Stop Hoover" movement that developed at the convention and was led by supporters of Kansas senator Charles Curtis nor the group that sought to draft Coolidge, and in the end, Hoover won an overwhelming victory on the first ballot. In addition, Curtis was nominated for vice president after an effort to renominate Dawes was rebuffed when word was circulated that the president, who had come to loathe his vice president, would consider it a personal insult if Dawes were selected. Indeed such an action was unlikely at a convention that was, however unconsciously, a tribute to the Coolidge years, featuring a platform that praised the administration's many accomplishments and pledged to continue the same responsible economic and social programs.

ANALYTICAL ESSAY

President Calvin Coolidge was a man of and for his time. For almost three-quarters of a century, beginning with the turmoil leading up to the Civil War, the United States had been a nation on the move. The nation emerged from that divisive armed conflict and awkwardly moved into an unprecedented period of Reconstruction, one in which millions of previously enslaved people had to suddenly figure out where they fit in—and yet it was no less a puzzle for those with whom they had to fit. It represented a new beginning for everyone, and the answers did not come easily. Then, on the heels of this human dilemma, there were technological advances that only complicated the equation. The industrial revolution, coupled with an ever-greater western expansion and immigrant-fueled growth and development, further turned the country into a place that the Founding Fathers would likely have found unrecognizable. Too, arising from these changes were some first tentative steps into a formerly scorned international arena. At the same time, the Progressive movement emerged to address some of the unanticipated residue and impacts of the fast-moving advancement on the economic and industrial fronts. Then came World War I, and the nation that emerged from that conflict bore little resemblance to the one that had gone to war with itself 60 years before.

Such was the setting when Calvin Coolidge assumed the presidency. Warren G. Harding, his running mate and predecessor, had campaigned with a promise of a return to normalcy, but while the phrase certainly had a nice ring to it, in the campaign of the time, few could really say what it meant. In fact, the nation needed less of a return to normalcy than a chance to catch its breath and see exactly where it was, what kind of nation it had become, and where it stood in relation to the broader global community, one from which it had long shrunk but in which it now had real and inescapable role, if not responsibility. To all of these problems and challenges, Coolidge brought an ideological bent toward laissez-faire economics and a hands-off approach to government, which, coupled with a low-key personality, served to slow things down, allowing the country to begin at least to try to figure things out.

But at the same time, while Coolidge may have slowed the wheels of government, American society continued to move, leading to inevitable questions about whether Coolidge should have more actively moved with it. Perhaps he should have intervened more, but the battles over immigration as seen through the lens of the Sacco and Vanzetti case and the issues raised by the Scopes trial and the revival of the Ku Klux Klan reflected a country trying to figure out where it was 150 years after it had been founded with a proclamation that all men were created equal even while millions were enslaved. As a result, even if one believes that Coolidge should have acted more aggressively, it is hard to know exactly where and how, given the nation's divide, it should have been done.

Indeed, the American political and social landscape of the 1920s represented a work in progress, a canvas on which an unprecedented experiment in democracy could play out. Reflective of this turmoil, the election of 1912 showed a deep desire for progressive change, with Wilson, Roosevelt, and Debs combining for 75.2 percent of the vote, while the "establishment" candidate, the upholder of the status quo, Taft, limped in with only 23.2 percent of the vote. And yet, by 1924, the tables had turned, with Coolidge winning a strong 54 percent, while Democrat John W. Davis, a conservative compromise standard-bearer, got 28.8 percent. Meanwhile, Robert LaFollette, seeking to uphold the progressive banner, limped in with 16.6 percent. It was a dramatic reversal that demonstrated the shift in the national psyche, as the forces of calm and continuity had triumphed—at least at the ballot box. Change was afoot, but neither the people nor their institutional leaders were fomenting it. Rather, it was coming from individuals, entrepreneurs, performers, and adventurers, from Babe Ruth to Charles Lindbergh. It was a different time, and Calvin Coolidge, in his own way, not only represented it but oversaw it in a manner that was right at the time.

Indeed, for all the seeming calm, the return to normalcy that Harding's election was purported to have ushered in, not to mention the prosperity of the Roaring Twenties, Coolidge presided over a nation that was becoming increasingly divided. While it may not have been immediately evident, given the many signs of good times and prosperity, there were cracks in the armor, and normalcy no longer had the same meaning. From the return of the Ku Klux Klan (KKK), albeit with its new focus on immigrants and Catholics, to the passage of the newly restrictive immigration law, all coupled with the questions and approaches to life raised by the Scopes Trial and the Sacco and Vanzetti case, Americans were not as happy or carefree as one might have thought. Indeed, the expansion of the electorate to include women had altered some of the political discussions, and Prohibition served as something of a test as to how people viewed law, order, and authority in the modern United States. Meanwhile, legendary cultural figures, such as Charles Lindbergh and his transatlantic plane flight, Babe Ruth and his remaking of the national pastime, and Red Grange's gridiron heroics, along with Flappers, "talkies," and commercial radio, bespoke an energy and a life in the

United States that was not reflected in the occupant of the White House. And yet, in the midst of a country that was changing, the United States found solace and comfort in the quiet consistency that Coolidge brought to the Oval Office. While historians continue to debate how much he or his fellow Republicans might have done to address the conditions that contributed to the Great Depression, at the time, he was seen as a conscientious steward of his responsibilities and a man who believed in the limits of the office he held and governed accordingly.

In assessing Coolidge's efforts, one must recognize that Coolidge faced two major challenges upon becoming president: he had to ensure the continuation of the prosperity that the American people had come to enjoy, and he had to both clean up the direct damage wreaked by the corruption, broadly labeled the Tea Pot Dome scandal, of the Harding years and restore the confidence in the government that the scandal had done so much to undermine. While the way he did it may have represented a stark contrast from the often larger-than-life figures who had held the office in the previous two decades, in his own low-key way, Coolidge achieved those goals, and no assessment of his record can ignore that reality.

Despite first running for office while still in his midtwenties, Calvin Coolidge was the most unnatural of politicians. He was deeply shy, undemonstrative, and restrained in public and with those he did not know. He spoke of the absolute terror he felt as a young boy growing up when he heard unfamiliar voices in the family kitchen, dreading the inevitable meeting he would have when he finally, as he knew he must, ventured into the room. He described how he recognized, at around 10 years old, that that he could not continue responding this way, and he willed himself not to do it. However, years later, he noted that, although he was comfortable with friends, there remained times when meeting new people still ignited memories of his family kitchen and his fear of meeting new people. It was certainly not the response one would expect from a man who was basically a career politician. But it certainly worked for him.

In fact, throughout his political climb, Coolidge developed a reputation as a man of quiet action. Frequently characterized as "Silent Cal," he often seems

better known for what he supposedly did not say than what he did, and he has become the butt of innumerable jokes as a result. However, in truth, he not only served the country faithfully while grieving over the tragic and sudden death of his son in the middle of the 1924 campaign, but he also jumped unhesitatingly into the political thicket that was the Harding scandals, exerting strong and important presidential leadership to address the issue and, in doing so, restored trust and confidence in the presidency.

Central to both his public image and historical reputation was a taciturn nature that became the stuff of legends. Stories and comments about the president included a string of acerbic observations from critics, who observed that he could be silent in five languages and that, at a press conference, he had answered nothing more than "no" to any single question, but still admonished the attendant reporters not to quote him. And of course, there is the widely repeated story of the young woman, who, sidling up to the president at a dinner, told him that she had just bet a friend that she could get him to say at least three words. To which he was reported to have replied, "You lose."

At the same time, many saw a flintiness that bordered on outright cruelty, and he was reportedly not well liked by the White House staff of his presidency. While he was accessible to the press, the circumstances under which they interacted yielded something less than easy, flowing communication. Most press conferences included questions submitted in advance, and even then, they seldom left the press with anything truly newsworthy. Coolidge was also usually reluctant to allow himself to be quoted.

And yet, by the end of his presidency, figures as diverse as New York governor and 1928 Democratic presidential nominee Al Smith, chief justice and former president William Howard Taft, and associate justice Oliver Wendell Holmes Jr. were applauding and encouraging his lack of action. Indeed, the justices had made clear their view that the public sought no surprises. Only a couple years after Coolidge left office, Smith observed, "Mr. Coolidge belongs rather in the class of Presidents who were distinguished for character more than for heroic achievement. His great task was to restore the dignity and prestige of the Presidency when it had reached the lowest ebb in our history, and to afford, in a time of extravagance and waste, a public shining example of the simple and homely virtues which came down to him from his New England ancestors."

Regardless of one's views of the end product, even his critics had to acknowledge that what Coolidge did—and in some cases, more importantly, did not do—was based in a solid and consistently applied philosophy. Stylistically, his governmental and management philosophies merged, making him someone who was a hands-off leader. He believed in setting the tone and offering the broad vision and direction but then leaving it to his subordinates and, as president, his cabinet as well as the states to implement and resolve the problems of the time. It was the rarest of situations in which he would deem bold federal action either the wisest or the most appropriate course.

Not surprisingly, this philosophy meant that, as chief executive, Coolidge was a hands-off administrator who set a clear agenda for his administration and then left it up to his executive team to implement it. At the same time, his actions and approach were grounded in a definitive philosophy of government, in which he believed that problems were best solved by the local and state governments that were on the scene. His commitment to small government was sincere and intense, reflected clearly in his assertion that, were the federal government to cease operations, the average citizens would not notice the difference. At the same time, Coolidge's unwillingness to unleash the potential power of the federal government only reinforced its lack of impact on people's lives, leaving open to debate the impacts that involvement and regulation might have had in such areas as agriculture or the stock market.

Indeed, his stewardship of the economy represents one of the great conundrums in assessing the Coolidge presidency. While no one can deny the impressive economic growth of the Coolidge years, one can also not deny that the policies that fueled that growth also furthered the growing American economic divide, which left a society whose unparalleled production was paired with a consumer class whose buying power was incapable of keeping up, an economic imbalance that certainly contributed to the ultimate onset of the Great Depression. At the same time, with fiscal responsibility intended to help achieve economic growth at the

heart of Coolidge's agenda, he could proudly point to series of not just balanced budgets but surpluses, which allowed him to reduce the national debt. In keeping with his minimalist philosophy, he did not take action against the risky practice of buying on margin that was driving the stock market by the end of his term. And yet, while his reluctance to act may have been rooted in sincerely held beliefs—a belief that has interestingly been buttressed by reports that Coolidge's decision not to run in 1928 was based, at least in part, on the fact that he did recognize some of the problems looming on the economic horizon but also recognized that he was neither temperamentally nor philosophically capable of addressing them in the manner they required—it nevertheless begs the question about whether he and his fellow political leaders should have foreseen the ultimate results and intervened. Even those who place more of the responsibility on the global aspects of the Great Depression have recognized the impact of the decade-long weak agricultural economy as well as the dangers of excessive margin buying—which could have been addressed by the federal government—that fueled the stock market rise of the era. Of course, the extent and exact nature of any intervention remains a source of debate among even those say there was no option. All of these, of course, are questions that have occupied generations of historians to no definitive resolution.

Coolidge's belief in limited governmental activism was not limited to the domestic side of the ledger. Indeed, while it was not surprising for a politician who spent the first two decades of his public life in local and state offices, Coolidge's efforts in the international arena were similarly less assertive and reactive. Part of this was simply a product of the fact that he was less interested in foreign policy, but to his credit, he had the good sense to rely on his capable secretaries of state, Charles Evans Hughes and Frank B. Kellogg. Former secretary of state Elihu Root once quipped that Coolidge "did not have an international hair on his head," but the president made no pretense to know more than he did. At the same time, while observers would likely have been surprised that Coolidge, who had little foreign policy experience, was an advocate of a strong and aggressive diplomacy, the argument, however, can also be made that the lack of such initiatives stemmed more from Coolidge's predisposition to respond to public opinion rather than try to shape it. This was an approach that certainly left him at the mercy of a populace rooted in a historic tradition of isolationism and burned by its recent World War I outreach. But given this, it was an approach which, in the midst of peace and prosperity, seemingly served him well.

Given the extent of his popularity while in office, one must ask whether a part of Coolidge's historical reputation was a product of the increased public focus on personality as opposed to a traditional institutional view of the office. Indeed, his quiet demeanor did little to dominate the news of the day, but as modern observers look back on his tenure, has he been a victim of the increased focus on the personality of a public official and especially the president? While accessible to an unprecedented degree, Coolidge fit under no one's definition of colorful. At the same time, while he was arguably as image laden as any president, in Coolidge's case, the image is often clouded with negative connotations. And yet, Coolidge had an advanced sense of public relations and the importance of image in politics. Coached from the earliest days of his presidency by his friend Bruce Barton, an advertising pioneer, Coolidge was a willing pupil whose own sense of himself and how best to connect with voters was strong. While many of the photos that have come down through history seem silly, at the time, they were often breakthrough moments that not only showed his willingness to reach out to different groups and constituencies but also the power of those mediums.

Interestingly, for a popular chief executive, Coolidge often struggled with Congress. Indeed, perhaps because his political climb had been just that, a climb through a succession of offices, a process which meant, in the end, more elections than legislative sessions, he seemed a better campaign politician than a legislative one. At the same time, his limited view of the government generally and the executive in particular, like Taft before him, may have also been a factor. Whereas Taft was limited by his concept of the presidency, one under which he was free to propose things to Congress, but it was left to Congress to act, Coolidge's tendency to lay out the basic idea or plan and then delegate the implementation or even development

of the specifics to his staff may also have impacted the process and the overall results.

Central to the debate is Coolidge's role as an exemplar of old-fashioned virtues and values. For some, he is a man that time had passed by. For others, he is the symbol of what we have lost and someone about whom it can be said, if we were like Coolidge, if we had not strayed from his values, things would be better. Ironically, while he sought to stay above the developing culture wars in his own time, he has become a central part of the modern ones.

Coolidge was not so much a reactionary as some have charged; he was simply an advocate of limited government. There were no efforts on the part of his administration to roll back the progressive advances of the prewar period. To the degree that the twenties saw some of that, it was more a result of the Supreme Court's decisions, which given his appointment of the judicially liberal Harlan Fiske Stone, was not something to which Coolidge contributed. Indeed, Coolidge should be seen as a transitional figure from the Progressive era that preceded him and the New Deal that followed, a chief executive who presided over a period that linked, however awkwardly, those two periods of governmental activism.

In the end, while his personal habits were not representative of the developing consumer-oriented new era that emerged on his watch, Coolidge made no effort to thwart its development. He may have frowned on the culture—speakeasies, celebrity, and the like—that developed over time, but he seemed to happily accept it as an almost inevitable offshoot of the rising standard of living that made it all possible. The business of the United States being business had cultural ramifications of which Coolidge was not unaware, but he was also not going to sacrifice the one to halt the other. Indeed, however unconsciously, at least on a personal level (for his advisers, it would appear to be a matter of total intent), it was candidate and then president Calvin Coolidge who took full advantage of, and even furthered, the developing celebratory culture of the 1920s. Indeed, as the newsreels- and radio-fueled media propelled people like Babe Ruth, Al Jolson, and Charles Lindbergh, to name just a few, to previously unimagined heights of recognition and attention, Coolidge and his advisers used it to his great advantage, taking personality-based political image making to new heights, a fact tinged with no small irony given the many critics who argued that Coolidge had no discernible personality.

With all of this being said, in looking at Coolidge and his presidency, one sees a man whose efforts embody the ebb and flow and the shifting nature of presidential reputations. Few have ever denied him credit for restoring the nation's confidence and faith in its politics in the aftermath of the Harding scandals, and he has never been seen as anything other than an exemplar of virtue and high character—although to some commentators, he seemed to take that to an extreme, demonstrating a prudishness or priggishness that seemed very out of step with the Roaring Twenties that were taking place around him. And yet, few doubted the sincerity of his convictions.

At the same time, his policies and his approach to the presidency and executive power have been viewed with far less unanimity. As noted, he was extremely popular upon his exit from office and even upon his death, and the causes, not to mention the full impact of the Great Depression, were still being debated. Yet, in a country soon caught up in the energy and precedent-shattering activism of the Roosevelt presidency, an administration headed by a larger-than-life political personality, Coolidge soon became lumped with his fellow Republican presidents as one of the trio of mediocrities under whose watch during the 1920s the seeds for the Great Depression were sown. And of course, the contrast in personalities between the taciturn Coolidge and the ebullient FDR was no less damning.

Much of that began to change, or at least became open to change, in the aftermath of the Great Society, as questions of about the role of "big government" became a part of the national political discourse. Similarly, the rise of the imperial presidency left many casting an admiring eye backward, to a time when the chief executives were more about executing the will of the people rather than orchestrating the efforts of an overreaching federal government. All of this was further fueled by the expressed admiration for the 30th president by the 40th, Ronald Reagan, who not only made clear his belief that Coolidge had long been one of the nation's most underrated chief executives but proceeded to shine a spotlight on the Vermont native's

efforts by hanging Coolidge's portrait in the Cabinet Room.

Critics were not surprised by the admiration expressed by the former California governor, arguing that his tax cuts and the trickle-down theory of economics were little more than a 1980s version of the program that Coolidge had espoused and which, they argued, had paved the way for the Great Depression. Conservatives, commentators, and historians alike pushed back, focusing on both the peace and prosperity over which Coolidge presided as well as the perils of big government that Reagan was working to reduce, an effort that to many would see its ultimate triumph when Democrat Bill Clinton announced that "the era of big government is over." Coolidge had won. Reagan also enhanced Coolidge's reputation, or at least brought him out his historical shadows, with his hard line in the 1981 air traffic controllers strike. While Reagan himself did not make a direct reference to Coolidge's handling of the Boston Police Strike, his equally emphatic declaration against public employees who struck against the public interest echoed Coolidge's efforts, reminding the public of the then Massachusetts governor's efforts to send an equally clear message, one that resonated with the public in the same way it had in 1919, when it helped turn an obscure governor into a national figure.

While the Reagan years ushered in a new era of Coolidge study, introducing him to a whole new generation of Americans, it did not necessarily revise public perceptions. Indeed, critics argued that aspects of the Reagan programs seemed like throwbacks to Coolidge's time, but the contrasts in their personalities led to a different public perception, for despite the fact that Coolidge had been in the forefront of the 1920s communication revolution, no one confused "Silent Cal" with the "Great Communicator" who remade the Republican Party in the 1980s. Rather, his public reemergence seemed to establish Coolidge as something of a political Rorschach test, a hero to advocates of small government and a heartless ideologue to those who believe government has a responsibility to provide a safety net for its most vulnerable citizens. At the same time, regardless of their views on his performance and his approach to the presidency, few would deny that Coolidge was a dedicated public servant who was deeply committed to doing the best he could, as he saw it, for the country he loved.

Bill H. Pruden

Further Reading

Calvin Coolidge Papers, 1915–1932. n.d. Library of Congress. https://www.loc.gov/item/mm79016741.

Coolidge, Calvin. 2004. *The Autobiography of Calvin Coolidge*. Honolulu, HI: University Press of the Pacific.

Greenberg, David. 2006. *Calvin Coolidge*. The American Presidents Series. Edited by Arthur M. Schlesinger Jr. New York: Times Books/Henry Holt and Company.

Johnson, Charles C. 2013. *Why Coolidge Matters: Leadership Lessons from America's Most Underrated President*. New York: Encounter Books.

McCoy, Donald R. 2000. *Calvin Coolidge: The Quiet President*. Newtown, CT: American Political Biography Press.

Shlaes, Amity. 2013. *Coolidge*. New York: Harper.

Sobel, Robert. 1998. *Coolidge: An American Enigma*. Washington, D.C.: Regnery Publishing.

Second Annual Message (December 3, 1924)

President Coolidge's annual message of 1924 offers a valuable look at his views on the state of the nation. While it reinforces the idea of a limited federal government, it nevertheless illustrates Coolidge's recognition of the many challenges that lay ahead. Indeed, he mentions an exhaustive list of topics, and his treatment of them makes for interesting reading. In that way, it is a very telling document.

To the Congress of the United States:

The present state of the Union, upon which it is customary for the President to report to the Congress under the provisions of the Constitution, is such that it may be regarded with encouragement and satisfaction by every American. Our country is almost unique in its ability to discharge fully and promptly all its obligations at home and abroad, and provide for all its inhabitants an increase in material resources, in intellectual vigor and in moral power. The Nation holds a position unsurpassed in all former human experience. This does not mean that we do not have any problems. It is elementary that the increasing breadth of our experience necessarily increases the problems of our national life. But it does mean that if all will but apply ourselves industriously and honestly, we have ample powers with which to meet our problems and provide for I heir speedy solution. I do not profess that we can secure an era of perfection in human existence, but we can provide an era of peace and prosperity, attended with freedom and justice and made more and more satisfying by the ministrations of the charities and humanities of life.

Our domestic problems are for the most part economic. We have our enormous debt to pay, and we are paying it. We have the high cost of government to diminish, and we are diminishing it. We have a heavy burden of taxation to reduce, and we are reducing it. . . . There yet exists this enormous field for the application of economy. . . .

The fallacy of the claim that the costs of government are borne by the rich and those who make a direct contribution to the National Treasury cannot be too often exposed. No system has been devised, I do not think any system could be devised, under which any person living in this country could escape being affected by the cost of our government. It has a direct effect both upon the rate and the purchasing power of wages. It is felt in the price of those prime necessities of existence, food, clothing, fuel and shelter. It would appear to be elementary that the more the Government expends the more it must require every producer to contribute out of his production to the Public Treasury, and the less he will have for his own benefit. The continuing costs of public administration can be met in only one way—by the work of the people. The higher they become, the more the people must work for the Government. The less they are, the more the people can work for themselves.

The present estimated margin between public receipts and expenditures for this fiscal year is very small. Perhaps the most important work that this session of the Congress can do is to continue a policy of economy and further reduce the cost of government, in order that we may have a reduction of taxes for the next fiscal year. Nothing is more likely to produce that public confidence which is the forerunner and the mainstay of prosperity, encourage and enlarge business opportunity with ample opportunity for employment at good wages, provide a larger market for agricultural products, and put our country in a stronger position to be able to meet the world competition in trade, than a continuing policy of economy. Of course necessary costs must be met, proper functions of the Government performed, and constant investments for capital account and reproductive effort must be carried on by our various departments. But the people must know that their Government is placing upon them no unnecessary burden.

TAXES

Everyone desires a reduction of taxes, and there is a great preponderance of sentiment in favor of taxation reform. When I approved the present tax law, I stated publicly that I did so in spite of certain provisions which I believed unwise and harmful. One of the most glaring of these was the making public of the amounts assessed against different income-tax payers. Although that damage has now been done, I believe its continuation to be detrimental to the public welfare and bound to decrease public revenues, so that it ought to be repealed.

Anybody can reduce taxes, but it is not so easy to stand in the gap and resist the passage of increasing appropriation bills which would make tax reduction impossible. It will be very easy to measure the strength of the attachment to reduced taxation by the power with which increased appropriations are resisted. If at the close of the present session the Congress has kept within the budget which I propose to present, it will then be possible to have a moderate amount of tax reduction and all the tax reform that the Congress may wish for during the next fiscal year. . . . I am convinced that the larger incomes of the country would actually yield more revenue to the Government if the basis of taxation were scientifically revised downward. Moreover the effect of the present method of this taxation is to increase the cost of interest on productive enterprise and to increase the burden of rent. It is altogether

likely that such reduction would so encourage and stimulate investment that it would firmly establish our country in the economic leadership of the world.

WATERWAYS

Meantime our internal development should go on. Provision should be made for flood control of such rivers as the Mississippi and the Colorado, and for the opening up of our inland waterways to commerce. Consideration is due to the project of better navigation from the Great Lakes to the Gulf. Every effort is being made to promote an agreement with Canada to build the, St. Lawrence waterway. There are pending before the Congress bills for further development of the Mississippi Basin, for the taking over of the Cape Cod Canal in accordance with a moral obligation which seems to have been incurred during the war, and for the improvement of harbors on both the Pacific and the Atlantic coasts. While this last should be divested of some of its projects and we must proceed slowly, these bills in general have my approval. Such works are productive of wealth and in the long run tend to a reduction of the tax burden.

RECLAMATION

Our country has a well-defined policy of reclamation established under statutory authority. This policy should be continued and made a self-sustaining activity administered in a manner that will meet local requirements and bring our and lands into a profitable state of cultivation as fast as there is a market for their products. Legislation is pending based on the report of the Fact Finding Commission for the proper relief of those needing extension of time in which to meet their payments on irrigated land, and for additional amendments and reforms of our reclamation laws, which are all exceedingly important and should be enacted at once.

No more important development has taken place in the last year than the beginning of a restoration of agriculture to a prosperous condition. We must permit no division of classes in this country, with one occupation striving to secure advantage over another. Each must proceed under open opportunities and with a fair prospect of economic equality. The Government cannot

938 | **Presidents and Presidencies in American History**

successfully insure prosperity or fix prices by legislative fiat. Every business has its risk and its times of depression. It is well known that in the long run there will be a more even prosperity and a more satisfactory range of prices under the natural working out of economic laws than when the Government undertakes the artificial support of markets and industries. Still we can so order our affairs, so protect our own people from foreign competition, so arrange our national finances, so administer our monetary system, so provide for the extension of credits, so improve methods of distribution, as to provide a better working machinery for the transaction of the business of the Nation with the least possible friction and loss. The Government has been constantly increasing its efforts in these directions for the relief and permanent establishment of agriculture on a sound and equal basis with other business. . . .

MUSCLE SHOALS

The production of nitrogen for plant food in peace and explosives in war is more and more important. It is one of the chief sustaining elements of life. It is estimated that soil exhaustion each year is represented by about 9,000,000 tons and replenishment by 5,450,000 tons. The deficit of 3,550,000 tons is reported to represent the impairment of 118,000,000 acres of farm lands each year.

To meet these necessities the Government has been developing a water power project at Muscle Shoals to be equipped to produce nitrogen for explosives and fertilizer. It is my opinion that the support of agriculture is the chief problem to consider in connection with this property. It could by no means supply the present needs for nitrogen, but it would help and its development would encourage bringing other water powers into like use. . . .

RAILWAYS

The railways during the past year have made still further progress in recuperation from the war, with large rains in efficiency and ability expeditiously to handle the traffic of the country. We have now passed through several periods of peak traffic without the car shortages which so frequently in the past have brought havoc to our agriculture and industries. The condition of many of our great freight terminals is still one of

difficulty and results in imposing, large costs on the public for inward-bound freight, and on the railways for outward-bound freight. Owing to the growth of our large cities and the great increase in the volume of traffic, particularly in perishables, the problem is not only difficult of solution, but in some cases not wholly solvable by railway action alone. . . .

The consolidations need to be carried out with due regard to public interest and to the rights and established life of various communities in our country. It does not seem to me necessary that we endeavor to anticipate any final plan or adhere to an artificial and unchangeable project which shall stipulate a fixed number of systems, but rather we ought to approach the problem with such a latitude of action that it can be worked out step by step in accordance with a comprehensive consideration of public interest. Whether the number of ultimate systems shall be more or less seems to me can only be determined by time and actual experience in the development of such consolidations.

Those portions of the present law contemplating consolidations are not sufficiently effective in producing expeditious action and need amplification of the authority of the Interstate Commerce Commission, particularly in affording a period for voluntary proposals to the commission and in supplying Government pressure to secure action after the expiration of such a period. . . .

Another matter before the Congress is legislation affecting the labor sections of the transportation act. Much criticism has been directed at the workings of this section and experience has shown that some useful amendment could be made to these provisions.

It would be helpful if a plan could be adopted which, while retaining the practice of systematic collective bargaining with conciliation voluntary arbitration of labor differences, could also provide simplicity in relations and more direct local responsibility of employees and managers. But such legislation will not meet the requirements of the situation unless it recognizes the principle that t e public has a right to the uninterrupted service of transportation, and therefore a right to be heard when there is danger that the Nation may suffer great injury through the interruption of operations because of labor disputes. If these elements are not comprehended in proposed legislation, it would be better to gain further experience with the present organization for dealing with these questions before undertaking a change.

SHIPPING BOARD

The form of the organization of the Shipping Board was based originally on its functions as a semi judicial body in regulation of rates. During the war it was loaded with enormous administrative duties. It has been demonstrated time and again that this form of organization results in indecision, division of opinion and administrative functions, which make a wholly inadequate foundation for the conduct of a great business enterprise. The first principle in securing the objective set out by Congress in building up the American merchant marine upon the great trade routes and subsequently disposing of it into private operation cannot proceed with effectiveness until the entire functions of the board are reorganized. The immediate requirement is to transfer into the Emergency Fleet, Corporation the whole responsibility of operation of the fleet and other property, leaving to the Shipping Board solely the duty of determining certain major policies which require deliberative action. . . .

NATIONAL ELECTIONS

Nothing is so fundamental to the integrity of a republican form of government as honesty in all that relates to the conduct of elections. I am of the opinion that the national laws governing the choice of members of the Congress should be extended to include appropriate representation of the respective parties at the ballot box ant equality of representation on the various registration boards, wherever they exist.

THE JUDICIARY

The docket of the Supreme Court is becoming congested. At the opening term last year it had 592 cases, while this year it had 687 cases. Justice long delayed is justice refused. Unless the court be given power by preliminary and summary consideration to determine the importance of cases, and by disposing of those which are not of public moment reserve its time for the more extended consideration of the remainder, the congestion of the docket is likely to increase. It is also desirable that Supreme Court should have power to improve and reform procedure in suits at law in the Federal courts through the adoption of appropriate rules. The Judiciary Committee of the Senate has reported favorably upon two bills providing for these reforms which should have the immediate favorable consideration of the Congress.

I further recommend that provision be made for the appointment of a commission, to consist of two or three members of the Federal judiciary and as many members of the bar, to examine the present criminal code of procedure and recommend to the Congress measures which may reform and expedite court procedure in the administration and enforcement of our criminal laws.

PRISON REFORM

Pending before the Congress is a bill which has already passed one House providing for a reformatory to which could be committed first offenders and young men for the purpose of segregating them from contact with banned criminals and providing them with special training in order to reestablish in them the power to pursue a law-abiding existence in the social and economic life of the Nation. This is a matter of so much importance as to warrant the early attention of the present session. Further provision should also be made, for a like reason, for a separate reformatory for women.

NATIONAL POLICE BUREAU

Representatives of the International Police Conference will bring to the attention of the Congress a proposal for the establishment of a national police bureau. Such action would provide a central point for gathering, compiling, and later distributing to local police authorities much information which would be helpful in the prevention and detection of crime. I believe this bureau is needed, and I recommend favorable consideration of this proposal.

DISTRICT OF COLUMBIA WELFARE

The welfare work of the District of Columbia is administered by several different boards dealing with charities and various correctional efforts. It would be an improvement if this work were consolidated and placed under the direction of a single commission.

FRENCH SPOLIATION CLAIMS

During the last session of the Congress legislation was introduced looking to the payment of the remaining claims generally referred to as the French spoliation claims. The Congress has provided for the payment of many similar claims. Those that remain unpaid have been long pending. The beneficiaries thereunder have every reason to expect payment. These claims have been examined by the Court of Claims and their validity and amount determined. The United States ought to pay its debts. I recommend action by the Congress which will permit of the payment of these remaining claims.

THE WAGE EARNER

Two very important policies have been adopted by this country which, while extending their benefits also in other directions, have been of the utmost importance to the wage earners. One of these is the protective tariff, which enables our people to live according to a better standard and receive a better rate of compensation than any people, any time, anywhere on earth, ever enjoyed. This saves the American market for the products of the American workmen. The other is a policy of more recent origin and seeks to shield our wage earners from the disastrous competition of a great influx of foreign peoples. This has been done by the restrictive immigration law. This saves the American job for the American workmen. I should like to see the administrative features of this law rendered a little more humane for the purpose of permitting those already here a greater latitude in securing admission of members of their own families. But I believe this law in principle is necessary and sound, and destined to increase greatly the public welfare. We must maintain our own economic position, we must defend our own national integrity. . . .

THE NEGRO

These developments have brought about a very remarkable improvement in the condition of the negro race. Gradually, but surely, with the almost universal sympathy of those among whom they live, the colored people are working out their own destiny. I firmly believe that it is better for all concerned that they should be cheerfully accorded their full constitutional rights, that they should be protected from all of those impositions to which, from their position, they naturally fall a prey, especially from the crime of lynching and that they should receive every encouragement to become full partakers in all the blessings of our common American citizenship.

CIVIL SERVICE

The merit system has long been recognized as the correct basis for employment in our, civil service. I believe that first second, and third class postmasters, and without covering in the present membership tile field force of prohibition enforcement, should be brought within the classified service by statute law. Otherwise the Executive order of one administration is changed by the Executive order of another administration, and little real progress is made. Whatever its defects, the merit system is certainly to be preferred to the spoils system.

DEPARTMENTAL REORGANIZATION

One way to save public money would be to pass the pending bill for the reorganization of the various departments. This project has been pending for some time, and has had the most careful consideration of experts and the thorough study of a special congressional committee. This legislation is vital as a companion piece to the Budget law. Legal authority for a thorough reorganization of the Federal structure with some latitude of action to the Executive in the rearrangement of secondary functions would make for continuing economy in the shift of government activities which must follow every change in a developing country. Beyond this many of the independent agencies of the Government must be placed under responsible Cabinet officials, if we are to have safeguards of efficiency, economy, and probity.

ARMY AND NAVY

Little has developed in relation to our national defense which needs special attention. Progress is constantly being made in air navigation and requires encouragement and development. Army aviators have made a successful trip around the world, for which I recommend suitable recognition through provisions for promotion, compensation, and retirement. Under the direction of the Navy a new Zeppelin has been successfully brought from Europe across the Atlantic to our own country.

Due to the efficient supervision of the Secretary of War the Army of the United States has been organized with a small body of Regulars and a moderate National Guard and Reserve. The defense test of September 12 demonstrated the efficiency of the operating plans.

These methods and operations are well worthy of congressional support.

Under the limitation of armaments treaty a large saving in outlay and a considerable decrease in maintenance of the Navy has been accomplished. We should maintain the policy of constantly working toward the full treaty strength of the Navy. Careful investigation is being made in this department of the relative importance of aircraft, surface and submarine vessels, in order that we may not fail to take advantage of all modern improvements for our national defense. A special commission also is investigating the problem of petroleum oil for the Navy, considering the best policy to insure the future supply of fuel oil and prevent the threatened drainage of naval oil reserves. Legislative action is required to carry on experiments in oil shale reduction, as large deposits of this type have been set aside for the use of the Navy. . . .

Our country has definitely relinquished the old standard of dealing with other countries by terror and force, and is definitely committed to the new standard of dealing with them through friendship and understanding. This new policy should be constantly kept in mind by the guiding forces of the Army and Navy, by the. Congress and by the country at large. I believe it holds a promise of great benefit to humanity. I shall resist any attempt to resort to the old methods and the old standards. I am especially solicitous that foreign nations should comprehend the candor and sincerity with which we have adopted this position. While we propose to maintain defensive and supplementary police forces by land and sea, and to train them through inspections and maneuvers upon appropriate occasions in order to maintain their efficiency, I wish every other nation to understand that this does not express any unfriendliness or convey any hostile intent. I want the armed forces of America to be considered by all peoples not as enemies but as friends as the contribution which is made by this country for the maintenance of the peace and security of the world.

VETERANS

With the authorization for general hospitalization of the veterans of all wars provided during the present year, the care and treatment of those who have served their country in time of peril and the attitude of the Government toward them is not now so much one of needed legislation as one of careful, generous and humane administration. It will ever be recognized that their welfare is of the first concern and always entitled to the most solicitous consideration oil the part of their fellow citizens. They are organized in various associations, of which the chief and most representative is the American Legion. Through its officers the Legion will present to the Congress numerous suggestions for legislation. They cover such a wide variety of subjects that it is impossible to discuss them within the scope of this message. With many of the proposals I join in hearty approval and commend them all to the sympathetic investigation and consideration of the Congress.

FOREIGN RELATIONS

At no period in the past 12 years have our foreign relations been in such a satisfactory condition as they are at the present time. Our actions in the recent months have greatly strengthened the American policy of permanent peace with independence. The attitude which our Government took and maintained toward an adjustment of European reparations, by pointing out that it wits not a political but a business problem, has demonstrated its wisdom by its actual results. We desire to see Europe restored that it may resume its productivity in the increase of industry and its support in the advance of civilization. We look with great gratification at the hopeful prospect of recuperation in Europe through the Dawes plan. Such assistance as can be given through the action of the public authorities and of our private citizens, through friendly counsel and cooperation, and through economic and financial support, not for any warlike effort but for reproductive enterprise, not to provide means for unsound government financing but to establish sound business administration ' should be unhesitatingly provided. . . .

It is not necessary to stress the general desire of all the people of this country for the promotion of peace. It is the leading principle of all our foreign relations. We have on every occasion tried to cooperate to this end in all ways that were consistent with our proper independence and our traditional policies. It will be my constant effort to maintain these principles, and to reinforce them by all appropriate agreements and treaties. While we desire always to cooperate and to help, we are equally determined to be independent and free. Right and truth and justice and humanitarian efforts will have the moral support of this country all over the world. But we do not wish to become involved in the political controversies of others. Nor is the country disposed to become a member of the League of Nations or to assume the obligations imposed by its covenant.

INTERNATIONAL COURT
America has been one of the foremost nations in advocating tribunals for the settlement of international disputes of a justiciable character. Our representatives took a leading in those conferences which resulted in the establishment of League Tribunal, and later in providing for a Permanent Court of International Justice. I believe it would be for the advantage of this country and helpful to the stability of other nations for us to adhere to the protocol establishing, that court upon the conditions stated in the recommendation which is now before the Senate, and further that our country shall not be bound by advisory opinions which may be, rendered by the court upon questions which we have not voluntarily submitted for its judgment. This court would provide a practical and convenient tribunal before which we could go voluntarily, but to which we could not be summoned, for a determination of justiciable questions when they fail to be resolved by diplomatic negotiations.

DISARMAMENT CONFERENCE
Many times I have expressed my desire to see the work of the Washington Conference on Limitation of Armaments appropriately supplemented by further agreements for a further reduction M for the purpose of diminishing the menace and waste of the competition in preparing instruments of international war. It has been and is my expectation that we might hopefully approach other great powers for further conference on this subject as soon as the carrying out of the present reparation plan as the established and settled policy of Europe has created a favorable opportunity. But on account of proposals which have already been made by other governments for a European conference, it will be necessary to wait to see what the outcome of their actions may be. I should not wish to propose or have representatives attend a conference which would contemplate commitments opposed to the freedom of action we desire to maintain unimpaired with respect to our purely domestic policies.

INTERNATIONAL LAW
Our country should also support efforts which are being made toward the codification of international law. We can look more hopefully, in the first instance, for research and studies that are likely to be productive of results, to a cooperation among representatives of the bar and members of international law institutes and societies, than to a conference of those who are technically representative of their respective governments, although, when projects have been developed, they must go to the governments for their approval. These expert professional studies are going on in certain quarters and should have our constant encouragement and approval.

OUTLAW OF WAR
Much interest has of late been manifested in this country in the discussion of various proposals to outlaw aggressive war. I look with great sympathy upon the examination of this subject. It is in harmony with the traditional policy of our country, which is against aggressive war and for the maintenance of permanent and honorable peace. While, as I have said, we must safeguard our liberty to deal according to our own judgment with our domestic policies, we cannot fail to view with sympathetic interest all progress to this desired end or carefully to study the measures that may be proposed to attain it.

LATIN AMERICA
While we are desirous of promoting peace in every quarter of the globe, we have a special interest in the peace of this hemisphere. It is our constant desire that all causes of dispute in this area may be tranquilly and satisfactorily adjusted. Along with our desire for peace is the earnest hope for the increased prosperity of our sister republics of Latin America, and our constant purpose to promote cooperation with them which may be mutually beneficial and always inspired by the most cordial friendships.

FOREIGN DEBTS

About $12,000,000,000 is due to our Government from abroad, mostly from European Governments. Great Britain, Finland, Hungary, Lithuania and Poland have negotiated settlements amounting close to $5,000,000,000. This represents the funding of over 42 per cent of the debt since the creation of the special Foreign Debt Commission. As the life of this commission is about to expire, its term should be extended. I am opposed to the cancellation of these debts and believe it for the best welfare of the world that they should be liquidated and paid as fast as possible. I do not favor oppressive measures, but unless money that is borrowed is repaid credit cannot be secured in time of necessity, and there exists besides a moral obligation which our country cannot ignore and no other country can evade. Terms and conditions may have to conform to differences in the financial abilities of the countries concerned, but the principle that each country should meet its obligation admits of no differences and is of universal application.

It is axiomatic that our country cannot stand still. It would seem to be perfectly plain from recent events that it is determined to go forward. But it wants no pretenses, it wants no vagaries. It is determined to advance in an orderly, sound and common-sense way. It does not propose to abandon the theory of the Declaration that the people have inalienable rights which no majority and no power of government can destroy. It does not propose to abandon the practice of the Constitution that provides for the protection of these rights. It believes that within these limitations, which are imposed not by the fiat of man but by the law of the Creator, self-government is just and wise. It is convinced that it will be impossible for the people to provide their own government unless they continue to own their own property.

These are the very foundations of America. On them has been erected a Government of freedom and equality, of justice and mercy, of education and charity. Living under it and supporting it the people have come into great possessions on the material and spiritual sides of life. I want to continue in this direction. I know that the Congress shares with me that desire. I want our institutions to be more and more expressive of these principles. I want the people of all the earth to see in the American flag the symbol of a Government which intends no oppression at home and no aggression abroad, which in the spirit of a common brotherhood provides assistance in time of distress.

Source: *Congressional Record*, Senate, December 3, 1924. Washington, D.C.: Government Printing Office, 1924, 52–56.

Message Regarding the Relationship of Church and State (October 20, 1925)

President Coolidge's remarks on the separation of church and state offer an interesting look into his views on the relationship between religion and government. In addition, they offer a window into his views about the spiritual and moral dimensions of both public life and the nation's culture. It is a look into ideas that are not often at the forefront of people's views of political figures but that can be interesting when explored.

Mr. Moderator, Members Of The Council:

It is my understanding that the purpose of this Council is to enlarge and improve the moral and spiritual life of the Nation. While I appreciate that its purpose is religious rather than political, I have felt a propriety in coming here because of my belief in the necessity for a growing reliance of the political success of our Government upon the religious convictions of our people.

Everyone recognizes that our modern life has become more and more complex. It has become more and more interdependent. This is true in our economic life; it is true in our political life. With the extension of knowledge and science, with the new powers that these have conferred, there are a multitude of ways and opportunities for committing crime, for doing wrongs which result in personal and property injury to others, and for perverting that which ought to minister to our well-being to the service of evil ends which in former days did not exist. New occasions have been opened for the turning of the instrumentalities of government, which ought to be used for the public welfare, into the service of selfish and misguided interests. Temptations have been both multiplied and intensified. The perils both to the individual and to society have in numerous ways been increased many fold.

It is notorious that crime and violence always follow in the wake of war. It appears to be the rule that there is a dissolution of the old restraints, brought about by the reaction which follows from the severe discipline and nervous tension of an era of conflict. These may be, and probably are, a temporary state which will tend to disappear with the mere passage of time. But too many of our people have found oftentimes to their sorrow that the privileges of liberty instead of being easy to enjoy are in reality highly difficult responsibilities, requiring the utmost of effort for success. Nor can it be denied that on the part of some there is a tendency to disregard too many of the former standards of society and too much of the former influence of authority.

Another characteristic of our present state of civilization, which has already been noted and commented upon, is the disposition of those who are less well equipped to receive the benefits of the modern state of society through bearing its burdens to attempt to resist all efforts to subject them to the necessary restraints and discipline, and to try to tear down and destroy the results which others have secured by generations of constant effort. What others have accumulated through industry and self-denial they propose to seize and to dissipate and destroy through indolence and self-indulgence, without compensation to its rightful owners. Lawlessness is altogether too prevalent, and a lack of respect for government and the conventions of enlightened society is altogether too apparent.

It is because I do not know of any political method of adequately dealing with these difficulties that I have ventured to bring them to the attention of this Council.

It is natural to attempt to shift the blame from ourselves to others when evil conditions arise. It is always easy to criticize the Government for failure[s] . . . I have great faith in the local and national governments of the United States, but much of this field is beyond their reach. The chief function of organized government is to maintain order, provide security for persons and property, and set up the instrumentalities for the administration of justice. This means the making, interpretation, and the execution of the law through the legislature, the judiciary, the executive, and all the various machinery of administration which these imply. But it ought always to be remembered that our institutions have undertaken to recognize that the human mind is and must be free. This is one of the reasons why it is neither practical nor justifiable to impose upon the Government the responsibility for the ultimate provision of the instrumentalities which minister to the spiritual life.

It is true that the Government can aid, and is aiding, in the solution of some of the problems to which I have already referred. Without doubt the law acts as a deterrent to wrong-doing and will usually go a long way in the repression of crime. But this reaches its highest application only when there is a very healthy and determined public sentiment in favor of the observance of the law. Such a determination cannot be produced by the Government. My own opinion is that it is furnished by religion.

Another contribution of great benefit, which is carried on so successfully by the local public authorities, is that of education. It is well known that ignorance and vice and crime all flourish together. Our local schools which are sanctioned by the States and cherished by the National Government are institutions of enormous value not only in providing earning for our youth but in removing the prejudices which naturally would exist among various racial groups and bringing the rising generation of our people to a common understanding. A more thorough comprehension of our political and social institutions has rarely failed to produce a more loyal citizen. With few exceptions those who come to us as enemies of society are so because they have always found society enemies to them. Education in the elements and fundamentals of the American principles of human relationship has seldom failed to secure their allegiance. But the mere sharpening of the wits, the bare training of the intellect, the naked acquisition of science, while they would greatly increase the power for good, likewise increase the power for evil. An intellectual growth will only add to our confusion unless it is accompanied by a moral growth. I do not know of any source of more power other than that which comes from religion.

But there is another and more basic reason why the Government cannot supply the source and motive for the complete reformation of society. In the progress of the human race religious beliefs were developed before the formation of governments. It is my understanding that government rests on religion. While in our own country we have wisely separated the church and the state in order to emancipate faith from all political interference, nevertheless the forms and theories of our Government were laid in accordance with the prevailing religious convictions of the people. The great revival of the middle of the eighteenth century had a marked influence upon our Revolutionary period. The claim to the right to freedom, the claim to the right to equality, with the resultant right to self-government—the rule of the people—have no foundation other than the common brotherhood of man derived from the common fatherhood of God. The righteous authority of the law depends for its sanction upon its harmony with the righteous authority of the Almighty. If this faith is set aside, the foundations of our institutions fail, the citizen is deposed from the high estate which he holds as amenable to a universal conscience, society reverts to a system of class and caste, and the Government instead of being imposed by reason from within is imposed by force from without. Freedom and democracy would give way to despotism and slavery. I do not know of any adequate support for our form of government except that which comes from religion.

Our history has been marked by the contributions which have been made by clergymen to the cause of education and government. . . . These contributions were not made in any narrow or lay sense, but resulted from the broad general teachings of the necessity for an enlightened and consecrated people, and from the conclusions drawn from their theology as to the relations of men to each other and to their God. The teaching of religion necessarily taught education and government.

It is on this theory that our institutions of government rest. We do not look upon the authority of the state as something imposed by a selected few upon the masses of the people through the special dispensation of divine right or by the force of military power, but we rather recognize the universal divine right including all the people to govern themselves in accordance with the dictates of a common conscience. If the people are the government it cannot rise above them; it cannot furnish them with something they do not have; it will be what they are. This is true representation.

The government will be able to get out of the people only such virtue as religion has placed there. If society resists wrongdoing by punishment, as it must do unless it is willing to approve it through failure to resist it, for there is no middle ground, it may protect itself as it is justified in doing by restraining a criminal, but that in and of itself does not reform him. It is only a treatment of a symptom. It does not eradicate the disease. It does not make the community virtuous. No amount of restraint, no amount of law can do that. If our political and social standards are the result of an enlightened conscience, then their perfection depends upon securing a more enlightened conscience . . . It is necessary to do something more than to have government treat symptoms. If we are to preserve what we already have and provide for further reformation, we must become a nation of partakers of the spirit of Shepherd and Hooker and Wise, or, as the clergy tell us, we must become partakers of the spirit of the Great Master. This way is outside of the government. It is the realm of religion.

It is this absolute necessity for support of the Government outside itself, through religion, that I wish to impress upon this assembly. Without that support political effort would be practically fruitless. It is not in any denominational or any narrow and technical sense that I refer to religion. I mean to include all that can be brought within that broad general definition. . . . While certain formalities of the past may have lost the hold they once had, I do not see any diminution in the steadfastness of the religious convictions of the people. If these were broken down, society might go on for a time under its own momentum, but it would be had for destruction. We do not possess any other enlightening force. We do not have any other hope for the reform and perfection of society. There is no other method by which we can "have life and have it more abundantly."

While I have pointed out some of the difficulties and perils with which we are threatened at the present time, and while I believe we may well heed them and be warned by them, it is by no means my desire to sound any note of discouragement. The very fact that amid all the complexities and distractions of our present life we are still maintaining unimpaired the foundations of our institutions, constantly increasing the rectitude with which the great business affairs of our country are conducted, all the while improving our educational facilities, answering more and more generously to the calls of public and private charity, continually enlarging the field of art, giving more and more attention to the humanities, and becoming more and more responsive to spiritual things, appears to more to be incontrovertible evidence that though it may be practiced in a somewhat different manner than formerly the deep and abiding faith of our people in religion has not diminished but has increased.

I have tried to indicate what I think the country needs in the way of help under present conditions. It needs more religion. If there are any general failures in the enforcement of the law, it is because there have first been general failures in the disposition to observe the law. I can conceive of no adequate remedy for the evils which beset society except through the influences of religion. There is no form of education which will not fail, there is no form of government which will not fail, there is no form of reward which will not fail. Redemption must come through sacrifice, and sacrifice is the essence of religion. It will be of untold benefit if there is a broader comprehension of this principle by the public and a continued preaching of this crusade by the clergy. It is only through these avenues, by a constant renewal and extension of our faith, that we can expect to enlarge and improve the moral and spiritual life of the Nation. Without that faith all that we have of an enlightened civilization cannot endure.

Source: *Reports of Commissions and Mission Boards, Moderator's Address, Council Sermon, Minutes, Roll of Delegates, Constitution and By-laws, etc.* New York: National Council of the Congregational Churches of the United States, 1925, 71.

Address at the Opening of Work on Mount Rushmore (August 10, 1927)

President Coolidge's comments at the opening of the work on the Mount Rushmore Memorial offer an interesting look at Coolidge's views as seen through his vignettes of the work of the four presidential predecessors to whom the monument paid tribute. The highlights of their presidencies that he chooses to cite offer insight into his own values and display a patriotism and love of country that was central to the longtime public officeholder's career.

We have come here to dedicate a cornerstone that was laid by the hand of the Almighty. On this towering wall of Rushmore, in the heart of the Black Hills, is to be inscribed a memorial which will represent some of the outstanding features of four of our Presidents, laid on by the hand of a great artist in sculpture. This memorial will crown the height of land between the Rocky Mountains and the Atlantic Seaboard, where coming generations may view it for all time.

It is but natural that such a design should begin with George Washington, for with him begins that which is truly characteristic of America. He represents our independence, our Constitution, our liberty. He formed the highest aspirations that were entertained by any people into the permanent institutions of our Government. He stands as the foremost disciple of ordered liberty, a statesman with an inspired vision who is not outranked by any mortal greatness.

Next to him will come Thomas Jefferson, whose wisdom insured that the Government which Washington had formed should be entrusted to the administration of the people. He emphasized the element of self-government which had been enshrined in American institutions in such a way as to demonstrate that it was practical and would be permanent. In him was likewise embodied the spirit of expansion. Recognizing the destiny of this Country, he added to its territory. By removing the possibility of any powerful opposition from a neighboring state, he gave new guaranties to the rule of the people.

After our country had been established, enlarged from sea to sea, and was dedicated to popular government, the next great task was to demonstrate the permanency of our Union and to extend the principle of freedom to all inhabitants of our land. The master of this supreme accomplishment was Abraham Lincoln. Above all other national figures, he holds the love of his fellow countrymen. The work which Washington and Jefferson began, he extended to its logical conclusions.

That the principles for which these three men stood might be still more firmly established destiny raised up Theodore Roosevelt. To political freedom he strove to add economic freedom. By building the Panama Canal he brought into closer relationship the east and the west and realized the vision that inspired Columbus in his search for a new passage to the Orient.

The union of these four Presidents carved on the face of the everlasting hills of South Dakota will constitute a distinctly national monument. It will be decidedly American in conception, in its magnitude, in its meaning and altogether worthy of our Country. No one can look upon it understandingly without realizing that it is a picture of hope fulfilled. Its location will be significant. Here in the heart of the continent, on the side of a mountain which probably no white man had ever beheld in the days of Washington, in territory which was acquired by the action of Jefferson, which remained an unbroken wilderness beyond the days of Lincoln, which was especially beloved by Roosevelt, the people of the future will see history and art combined to portray the spirit of patriotism. They will know that the figure of these Presidents has been placed here because by following the truth they built for eternity. The fundamental principles which they represented have been wrought into the very being of our Country. They are steadfast as these ancient hills.

Other people have marveled at the growth and strength of America. . . . The progress of America has been due to the spirit of the people. It is in no small degree due to that spirit that we have been able to produce such great leaders. If coming generations are to maintain a like spirit, it will be because they continue to support the principles which these men represented. It is for that purpose that we erect memorials. We cannot hold our admiration for the historic figures which we shall see here without growing stronger in our determination to perpetuate the institutions which their lives revealed and established.

The fact that this enterprise is being begun in one of our new states not yet great in population, not largely developed in its resources, discloses that the old American spirit still goes where our people go . . . still inspires them to deeds of devotion and sacrifice. It is but another illustration of the determination of our people to use their material resources to minister to their spiritual life. This memorial will be another national shrine to which future generations will repair to declare their continuing allegiance to independence, to self-government, to freedom and to economic justice. It is an inspiring phase of American life.

Source: "Mount Rushmore." National Park Service. Available at https://www.nps.gov/moru/learn/historyculture/calvin-coolidge -dedication-speech.htm.

31. HERBERT HOOVER (1874–1964)

Presidential Term (1929–1933)

CHRONOLOGY

August 10, 1874—Herbert Hoover is born in West Branch, Iowa.

November 10, 1885—Now an orphan, Hoover moves to Newberg, Oregon, to live with his uncle.

October 1, 1891—Hoover enters Stanford University as a member of its first incoming class.

May 26, 1895—Hoover graduates from Stanford with a degree in geology.

March 1897—Hoover is hired by a British mining company to work in Australia.

February 10, 1899—Hoover marries his college sweetheart, Lou Henry; he leaves for China the next day.

June 10, 1900—While in Tientsin, the city is besieged during the Boxer Rebellion uprising against Western intervention in China.

1908—Hoover becomes an independent mining consultant and a millionaire.

November 5, 1914—Hoover organizes the Commission for Relief of Belgium and Northern France as World War I begins in Europe, beginning a career in public service.

November 12, 1914—Hoover organizes the American Relief Administration.

March 5, 1921—President Warren G. Harding names Hoover secretary of commerce.

November 6, 1928—Hoover defeats Democrat Al Smith to win the presidential election.

October 1929—The New York Stock Exchange crashes, beginning the Great Depression.

February 3, 1930—Hoover nominates Charles Evans Hughes for chief justice of the U.S. Supreme Court.

June 17, 1930—Hoover signs the Smoot-Hawley Tariff, raising tariffs on over 20,000 imported goods.

September 17, 1930—Construction of the Hoover Dam begins in Nevada.

March 3, 1931—President Hoover declares "The Star-Spangled Banner" the national anthem.

June 16, 1932—The Republican Party nominates Hoover for president.

July 28, 1932—Hoover orders the "Bonus Army," World War I veterans and their families seeking cash payments for service certificates, evicted from their protest camps in Washington, D.C.

November 8, 1932—Democrat Franklin Delano Roosevelt defeats Hoover in the presidential election.

October 19, 1936—Hoover is elected chairman of the Boys Clubs of America.

September 1, 1939—Germany invades Poland, beginning World War II.

August 14, 1945—V-J Day celebrates Japan's defeat and the end of World War II.

September 29, 1946—President Harry Truman appoints Hoover to chair a commission to study the executive branch of government, known as the First Hoover Commission.

September 29, 1953—President Dwight D. Eisenhower asks Hoover to chair a Second Hoover Commission.

August 10, 1962—The Hoover Presidential Library is dedicated in West Branch, Iowa.

October 20, 1964—President Hoover dies in the Waldorf Astoria hotel in New York.

BIOGRAPHICAL SKETCH

Herbert Clark Hoover was the 31st president of the United States. He is the only president Iowa ever

Herbert Hoover (Library of Congress)

One of them was Herbert Clark Hoover, who was born on August 10, 1874.

The Hoovers had been in West Branch since the town began. Eli Hoover had been among the original contingent of Ohio Quakers who had come to the area. Some took up farming; Eli was a carpenter. His son Jesse (1846–1880) was the town's blacksmith and sold farm tools on the side. Hulda Randall Minthorn (1849–1884) married Jesse on March 12, 1870. Herbert was the second of the couple's three children, preceded by his brother, Ted (1871–1955), and followed by his sister, Mary (1876–1953). By all accounts, it was a happy family and one that figured prominently in the town's doings. But that happiness was short-lived. Jesse Hoover died in 1880, and Hulda died four years later. Orphaned, Hoover and his siblings were passed back and forth between family and friends until 1885, when his late mother's brother agreed to take Herbert under his wing. It meant pulling up stakes and moving to Oregon. He went to high school for a while but dropped out to help his uncle run his real estate business. He kept up with his studies by going to night school, where he excelled at bookkeeping and mathematics.

In 1891, when Stanford University opened its doors, Herbert Hoover was a member of its incoming class. By most accounts, he was not a very good student. In fact, outside of mathematics, he failed every one of Stanford's entrance exams and had to be tutored to gain admission. Once in, he continued to struggle, not only to stay afloat academically but to find a major that appealed to him. The study of geology caught his eye, and a summer internship under the direction of John Branner of the U.S. Geological Service sold him on a career path. He graduated from Stanford in 1895 with a geology degree.

Unable to land a job right out of school, Hoover picked up part-time work in Nevada City and Grass Valley, two towns at the foot of California's Sierra Nevada Mountains, in the heart of the state's gold country. He was eventually hired by Louis Janin's firm, one of the leading gold mining concerns in the western United States, and was sent off to manage the company's interests in New Mexico before being assigned to the firm's head office in San Francisco. In 1897, Bewick-Moreing, mining consultants from

produced and was the first president born west of the Mississippi River. With a successful career as an engineer, a businessman, and a public official serving four U.S. presidents, he could have probably secured his place in American history. But it was his presidency, during which the United States suffered one of its deepest and longest economic collapses, that earned Herbert Hoover his legacy.

West Branch, Iowa, straddles the line separating Cedar and Johnson Counties. The name comes both from its location—it sits near the west branch of the Wapsinonoc Creek—and the people who would call it home; Quakers who migrated from Ohio brought the name of their gathering place, the West Branch Friends Meeting, with them. West Branch remained something of a legal nonentity after its establishment in the 1850s. But after the Civil War, the railroads were building their way across Iowa, so it made sense to officially put West Branch on the map. In 1875, a petition requesting incorporation was passed and approved. The town counted 375 people living within its limits.

London eager to capitalize on a gold boom in Australia, hired Hoover and sent him there. He initially did geology and mine engineering, part of Bewick-Moreing's drive to find gold deposits and increase its holdings. A year later, he was promoted to manage one of B-M's mining operations and soon earned junior partner status. That promotion made it possible for Hoover to marry Lou Henry, his Stanford sweetheart. He returned to California, and they became husband and wife on February 10, 1899.

Rather than returning to Australia, the Hoovers headed to China. Bewick-Moreing had an investment in gold mining there, and Hoover's geological, engineering, and management expertise were in demand. He managed the company's interests for a little over a year, improving its bottom line while also improving conditions for mine workers. Advocating on behalf of Chinese workers signaled a momentary change of heart; working in Australia, Hoover brought in immigrant workers to undercut the clout of miners' unions. He was also fundamentally opposed to minimum wage laws and workmen's compensation. He thought both were unfair to owners.

Hoover's industriousness, innovation, and insistence on protecting owners' rights did not go unnoticed. Bewick-Moreing had already made him a junior partner, but the company now gave him a healthy raise, a profit sharing plan, and control over a significant portion of its Australian holdings. He visited the continent four times between 1901 and 1907. The 1907 visit would be his last as a Bewick-Moreing partner. The following year, Herbert Hoover became his own boss and started a mining consulting firm. His business plan was simple: revive an underperforming mining operation by applying his technical and financial expertise in return for a share of the profits. By 1914, he had established a global reputation, not to mention a string of investments handled by his offices in San Francisco, New York, Paris, and London. As his list of achievements grew so did his personal wealth, not to mention his reputation as someone who could effectively operate on the international stage. That last quality would prove essential as the world slid into war.

World War I began in the summer of 1914, and Hoover, living in London, found himself, like other Americans abroad, caught in the cross fire between the Allied and Central Powers. Hoover took it upon himself to help American expatriates return home. He provided a full range of material support, including food, clothing, and even money. While he was putting out one humanitarian brush fire, Germany's Kaiser Wilhelm II started another by invading neutral Belgium in an attempt to outflank France. It was a bold but ultimately unsuccessful military gamble with fateful consequences. It forced Britain into the war to rescue Belgium. It also forced Belgians to the brink of starvation, as the German Army plundered its way from one end of the country to the other. Hoover's relief experience on behalf of his fellow Americans came in handy as he led the humanitarian efforts to feed hungry Belgians.

Hoover's efforts on the European side of the Atlantic had not gone unnoticed back home. When the United States entered the war in 1917, the marshaling of foodstuffs became just as important as any other resource, especially as the United States' allies were also counting on getting fed. President Woodrow Wilson put Herbert Hoover in charge of the U.S. Food Administration. His mandate was clear: feed Americans both in and out of uniform and U.S. allies. Hoover handled all three with precision and economy, selling Americans on voluntary abstinence, including days of the week when meat and bread were not on the table.

"Food will win the war" was a slogan Hoover created while head of the Food Administration. Both food and Hoover would be instrumental in keeping the peace once the war ended in 1918. President Wilson made the Food Administration a global operation, renaming it the American Relief Administration, and he sent Hoover back to Europe to make sure that millions of people did not go hungry. Hoover did the job; every friend, foe, and even communist was cared for.

Herbert Hoover was becoming well known on both sides of the Atlantic, especially at home—and just in time for the 1920 presidential election. Both the Democratic and Republican Parties thought he would be a good candidate. He had come out for the minimum wage, a shorter work week, and against child labor, making him the darling of progressives in both parties. And his journey from rags to riches was a compelling story that was guaranteed to attract voters. But Hoover never declared himself a Republican or a Democrat until March 1920, when he finally sided with the GOP. He hinted coyly that while he would not run for president, he would not say no if he were nominated. He may have seemed a catch, but Republicans passed. Hoover's stint as head of the Food Administration had made him an enemy of farmers, which constituted an important bloc to the party. Warren Harding was nominated and went on to a landslide victory in November. Hoover campaigned for Harding before stepping off the national stage and returning to private life.

Hoover's time out of the national spotlight would be brief. President-elect Harding needed to assemble his cabinet, and three slots, treasury, commerce, and interior, needed to be filled. He thought Hoover would be good for commerce. At first, Hoover refused, fearing a negative reaction from Senate Republicans. In time, though, Senate opposition softened, and Hoover took the job. It was a post he would hold until he became president himself.

Some people grow into a job, the presumption being that its expectations, challenging at first, come in time to be mastered. Herbert Hoover, on the other hand, grew the job of commerce secretary to meet his expectations. He saw the Commerce Department as the heart and soul of the United States' economic growth. Ultimately, everything in the U.S. government that had an impact on the economy would fall under Hoover's control. His reach into how the census was taken, how radio stations were regulated, and how air travel was conducted was viewed by some as overreach, and the joke in Washington was that Herbert Hoover was the secretary of commerce but the undersecretary of everything else. Undeterred, he set about to make the U.S. economy more productive by making it more efficient. He looked into job losses that occurred from foreign disputes and set about improving international trade by opening Commerce Department offices around the world. These outposts advised American businesses on how to capitalize on global opportunities. That opened a more cooperative era of government-business relations. But Hoover was just as interested in helping Middle America as Corporate America during the decade that would come to be

known as the roaring twenties. He kick-started home ownership by creating an alliance of bankers and the savings and loan industry to promote long-term mortgages. This stimulated the housing construction industry and put thousands of American families on the path to homeownership.

Hoover's accomplishments, along with tax breaks and a wave of government deregulation during the 1920s, helped to create prosperity and made him a likely presidential candidate in 1928—likely, but not necessarily, the favorite. He had stepped on a lot of toes as commerce secretary during the Harding and Coolidge years. In fact, something of an "anybody but Hoover" movement emerged within the GOP in the runup to the 1928 convention. But few could dispute Hoover's national reputation or would risk letting the White House go to the Democrats, and that was enough to give Hoover the nomination.

Eight years of prosperity had put voters in no mood to rock the boat, so Herbert Hoover cruised to victory in 1928. He promised to stay the economic course and to maintain the United States' isolationist foreign policy. His opponent, New York governor Al Smith, made the same promises, but he found himself fighting an uphill battle, being a Catholic, which worried Protestants, and an opponent of Prohibition. In the end, Hoover carried 41 of 48 states.

As president, Herbert Hoover intended to follow his predecessors in pursuit of, as he termed it, "the day when poverty will be banished from this nation." The key, as he saw it, was deregulation, the removal of government interference from the economy. To him, it ran counter to the nation's concepts of individualism and self-reliance. Most Americans seemed to agree; business was booming, the stock market was soaring, and credit was easy to get. But that all changed on October 29, 1929, when the stock market collapsed, plunging the United States into the Great Depression. Hoover tried just about everything to stop the slide short of direct federal intervention. He favored support for banks and railroads as a way to revive the national economy and called on local governments to aid the general public. After that, he backed public works projects. However, citing budget concerns, he balked at some efforts, including one to bring electric power to the Tennessee Valley.

When nothing seemed to work, Hoover turned to measures to protect American jobs and industries. He signed the Smoot-Hawley Tariff Act into law in 1930. The tariffs raised prices on imported industrial and agricultural products. It also set off a global trade war, as other nations retaliated. International trade ground to a standstill, and even more jobs were lost. Finally, in 1932, Hoover, who had opposed direct federal intervention because he feared putting Americans on the "dole," as he called it, would weaken the country, threw his support behind the Reconstruction Finance Corporation. The RFC, as it came to be known, parceled out federal support to banks, railroads, and local governments, hoping some kind of trickle-down effect would fund local relief efforts. It would turn out to be too little, too late.

Throughout the ordeal that came to be known as the Great Depression, Hoover's critics tried to portray him as incompetent and out of touch. In the summer of 1932, they would try to add heartless to the list. The World War Adjusted Compensation Act of 1924 had set 1945 as the year veterans would receive a bonus. But the Great Depression had wiped out the savings of many vets, and they descended on Washington to press Congress for immediate payment. Congress bought some of them off by funding their trips home, but many, who now called themselves members of the "Bonus Army" stayed and set up camp in the nation's capital. Things went from push, when Washington police tried and failed to disperse demonstrators, to shove, when Hoover sent in the U.S. Army to finish the job. The camp was burned to the ground, hundreds of protesters were injured, and the entire incident was another black eye for Hoover as he faced reelection in the fall.

Voters were angry as November approached. No one in the GOP wanted to take the brunt of that anger, so Hoover had no trouble winning the nomination. The fall campaign would be distinguished by two factors: the power of radio, which gave voters greater access to a candidate, and the treatment Hoover received on the campaign trail. The animosity, which included eggs pelting his motorcades, hecklers interrupting his speeches, death threats, and attempts to derail his train, was unheard of in terms of treatment given a sitting president at the time. And then there

were the Democrats, who successfully managed to blame Hoover for the Great Depression. Nothing he said could turn the tide, and in November, he and other Republicans bore the voters' wrath. Franklin Roosevelt carried 42 states and picked up over 57 percent of the popular vote. The years of Republican control of the presidency were over.

Herbert Hoover spent most of his postpresidential years trying to rebuild his image. He wrote more than two dozen books, some of which attacked FDR's New Deal programs. He campaigned for Republican presidential candidates in 1936 and 1940, secretly hoping the GOP might someday return to him. It was not to be. His contributions during World War II were limited, given his feelings toward Roosevelt and his opinion that FDR hurt chances for peace by provoking Japan and not supporting European efforts to work with Hitler. Roosevelt did not call on the former president once the United States entered the war in 1941.

In 1946, with the war over and a new president in the White House, Hoover's redemption began in earnest. Despite their ideological differences, and acknowledging his experience with food relief, Harry Truman asked Hoover to tour Germany and Austria and develop a plan to feed people. The war had obviously been hard on the farm economies in both countries. In Germany, the effects of crop failures and an absence of labor had reduced yields by 40 percent. Things were worse in Austria, where that country's harvest was half of what it had been before the war. Upon returning from his fact-finding mission, Hoover proposed a plan to address the nutritional needs of the men, women, and children living under Allied occupation. "Hoover Meals" delivered 40,000 tons of American food that had been portioned so that women and infants received their daily requirements of milk and fats and men received the calories they needed to put in a full day's work. He also developed a school meals program, which fed over 3 million students.

In 1947, Herbert Hoover was back in the White House, but in a different capacity than the last time he was there. Fresh off his successful food relief program, President Truman appointed him to lead a commission for the purpose of reorganizing the executive branch. The Hoover Commission recommended changes that would allow presidents greater control of departments under their supervision. It was something of a turnabout for Hoover; he had sharply criticized the way FDR had concentrated executive power during the Depression, but he now saw that different challenges required different approaches to governance. He chaired the Hoover Commission during both the Truman and Eisenhower administrations, leaving in 1961.

Publicly rehabilitated, honored by Republicans at their 1960 nominating convention, and recognized as the unofficial dean of living former presidents, Herbert Hoover returned to private life. He and his wife had lived in California after the 1932 election, but her death in 1944 sent him back east, where he lived at New York City's Waldorf Astoria hotel. He wrote, supported charitable causes, and oversaw the Hoover Institution, a conservative think tank at Stanford University. In 1962, he had a malignant tumor removed, but the procedure may have contributed to severe gastrointestinal bleeding, a condition that led to his death in New York on October 20, 1964.

HISTORICAL OVERVIEW

Just about anyone can lay claim to being a witness to history. But there is a difference between being a witness or a participant or being both. That last distinction belongs to few, but Herbert Hoover qualifies.

The country Hoover found waiting for him upon his birth in 1874 had 37 states and a total population of just over California's today. At least a third of his fellow citizens drew their livelihood from farming. Nearly three-quarters of them lived outside a city in houses lit by candles and kerosene. American democracy had not yet extended voting rights to women or even citizenship to Native Americans. When Americans went looking for diversion, it was likely to be found between the pages of a newspaper or a magazine and not via radio or television. And when they looked skyward, they most likely saw sun, clouds, and birds and nothing else. If they wondered about the world beyond the country's shores or what role the United States might play on the global stage, their imaginations as well as their expectations were limited.

Herbert Hoover was on hand for, and in some cases had a hand in, many of the changes Americans in the late 19th century could barely imagine. By the time of his death in 1964, he had seen the country grow from 37 to 50 states and the population swell to more than four times what it was at the time of his birth. It was more urban than rural, and more people worked a shift instead of the land. During the day, people could lose count of the planes flying overhead and wonder just how far into space the latest satellites were orbiting. And at night, they retreated indoors and gathered around a television to watch *Andy Griffith*, *Bonanza*, and *The Wonderful World of Disney*. Finally, the United States in 1964 that would bid Hoover farewell had more than established itself. Waves of economic growth and technological advancement as well leadership in two World Wars had put the country, to borrow a phrase, at the pinnacle of world power. It was a perch that Herbert Hoover had done much to help the United States reach.

Orphaned at 10, Herbert Hoover was sent to Oregon to live with an uncle. As he made his way across Iowa and into the Pacific Northwest, he must have seen the changes to the land and the people on it. The wheat fields of northern Iowa, home to many who had come from somewhere else, were changing. The wheat was still there, but some of the families were gone, driven out by falling prices, currency fluctuations, or just bad management. Farming practices were also changing. Combines—machines that both reap and bag the grain—cut harvest times and the number of men, women, and children needed to complete the job. Hoover's trip to Oregon gave him a front row seat to another vanishing act of sorts. Native American tribes, such as the Sioux, the Cheyenne, and the Shoshoni, that had ranged the land Hoover would cross were now being rounded up by the U.S. government and herded onto reservations, their nomadic days at an end.

Hoover arrived in Newburg, Oregon, in 1885. His uncle needed help with his real estate business. Oregon was filling up, as was the rest of the United States for that matter. Immigration, and people looking for something better were pulling up stakes in one part of the country and putting them down somewhere else. An endless stream of humanity forced the superintendent of the U.S. Census to declare in 1890 that for the first time in the country's existence, a frontier line no longer existed. The superintendent's pronouncement seemed to put an official stamp on what the Reverend Josiah Strong had warned of in a sermon in 1885: the available, productive lands of the world were disappearing. Historian Frederick Jackson Turner, speaking at the World's Columbian Exhibition in 1893, spoke of "the existence of an area of free land . . . and the advance of settlement westward" as a way to explain American development. In the years since Hoover's birth, the United States had admitted seven territories into statehood. All of this posed a provocative question: what forces might forge the American experience now that the frontier, or as some called it the Wild West, was no longer wild?

There may be no way of knowing whether the outlines of the United States' next chapter influenced Herbert Hoover as he began his own next chapter. He had entered Stanford University in the fall of 1891 and would leave with a degree in geology four years later. But just as Hoover was about to step into a new world, so was his country. The signs had been there for some time. The Alaskan territory was purchased in 1867, and in the same year, the U.S. flag was planted on Midway Island in the Pacific Ocean. In the following years, the United States added Hawaii, Guam, and the Philippines. The additions were deemed necessary by those convinced it was time to look outward, which was essential to national growth and welfare, and by those confident the United States had been marked to lead in the regeneration of the world.

By the end of the 19th century, American interests were focused on China. And, interestingly enough, so was Herbert Hoover. He had been hired by a London-based gold mining firm to help it increase its holdings, first in Australia and later in China. The country had all but disappeared under an avalanche of foreign incursions, beginning with the British in the 1840s. By the time Hoover and his wife, Lou, arrived in China, it had been sliced into spheres of influence controlled by France, Britain, Germany, Russia, and Japan. There was an American enclave as well, and when a nationalist anticolonial backlash broke out in 1900, the Boxer Rebellion, Hoover and other Americans were caught in the thick of it.

China would not be the last place Hoover would experience the potentially destructive forces of suppressed nationalism, but he probably never expected it to erupt in Europe and engulf most of the world. By 1914, Hoover, his wife, and his two children were living in London. He had gone into business for himself as a mining and engineering consultant. He must have seen, or at least felt, the tension building in the competition between Britain, France, and Germany for the largest army, navy, and empire. In the race to achieve the greatest landmass, the great powers ran roughshod over local populations, creating legions of subjects, but not citizens, and certainly not free ones. The continent and the globe became armed camps; treaties were made and alliances forged, in the event an accidental spark lit the fuse that would lead to war. The fuse was lit in Sarajevo that summer, and by autumn 1914, France, Britain, and Russia had squared off against Germany, Austria-Hungary, and Turkey in what would become the Great War, or, in more contemporary terms, World War I.

There were over 100,000 Americans in Europe in 1914 when World War I began. As citizens of a neutral country, their status was problematic for nations at war. The best course of action was to get them out of harm's way. Hoover helped lead efforts to get them home. He assembled over 500 volunteers and oversaw the distribution of food, clothing, and cash. In some cases, relief even included free steamship tickets. The repatriation campaign was humanitarian in nature, but also prophetic as far as Hoover was concerned. He was transitioning from the world of private enterprise to public service. He was also reaching the conclusion that the private sector in general, and individuals in particular, could solve problems without the intrusion of the federal government. The belief would become almost second nature to him.

While he was involved in bringing Americans home, Belgium was overrun by German troops. Kaiser Wilhelm II, seeking a quick victory over France, attacked his neutral neighbor to bypass French fortifications and capture Paris. The maneuver failed, but it widened the war by involving Britain, which had pledged to defend Belgian neutrality. It also affected Belgium's food supply, as advancing German forces plundered farms, villages, and towns. Britain's entry into the war made Belgium's food situation even worse. It imposed a naval blockade on Europe. The goal was to starve Germany into submission, but in the process, it deprived Belgium of crucial food imports. The American ambassador in London appealed to Hoover; would he head a semiofficial Belgian relief effort? Hoover agreed, and the Commission for Belgian Relief answered the call. Over the next four years, Hoover coordinated relief efforts with Belgian authorities and distributed 2 million tons of food. That meant acquiring the food, loading it on ships, getting those ships safely across the English Channel, and delivering it into the hands of hungry Belgians. To do that, Hoover's operation took on the trappings of an independent nation, sporting its own flag and using its own navy, factories, mills, and railroads. It made Hoover the face of international food relief, as he met regularly with world leaders to keep the operation running.

Just as Hoover's efforts on behalf of stranded Americans prepared him to handle the food crisis in Belgium, the Belgium achievement made him President Woodrow Wilson's choice to coordinate food efforts when the United States entered the war in April 1917. "Food will win the war," Hoover said on more than one occasion, and while that slogan became part of the government's advertising campaign, the enterprise faced a host of problems. The war was reaching a critical point in 1917. Russia, allied with Britain and France, had collapsed into revolution and withdrew from the war, allowing German troops to head west. Berlin gambled that France and Britain, depleted by three years of war and running short of food and supplies, would be unable to halt its spring 1918 offensive. The United States' entry would fill three gaping holes in the Allied effort: manpower, munitions, and food.

Hoover became the head of the U.S. Food Administration, which was charged with feeding U.S. troops, feeding U.S. allies, and feeding Americans at home. The stateside goal was voluntary abstinence, a departure from government-enforced rationing practiced elsewhere. To make that happen, Hoover appointed emissaries to help win the support of the political, agricultural, and business worlds. He forged a coalition with them and built an army of hundreds of thousands of women volunteers. He orchestrated an advertising campaign that prompted Americans to observe "Meatless Mondays" and "Wheatless Wednesdays." And despite the emphasis on volunteerism, he put some muscle behind the message; Hoover imposed a system of price controls and licensing regulations to prevent gouging.

The ink on the armistice ending the war in November 1918 had barely dried when Herbert Hoover returned to Europe. The war had changed the political and geographic outlines of Europe. It had ended the rule of the Romanovs in Russia, the Hapsburgs in Austria-Hungary, and the Hohenzollerns in Germany. It also brought the Baltic states of Estonia, Latvia, and Lithuania a step closer to independence, returned self-rule to Poland, and shattered the Austro-Hungarian empire into four independent nations: Austria, Hungary, Czechoslovakia, and Yugoslavia. The changes had raised questions about the continent's ability to function. Above all, it was unclear whether the new governments would be able to provide basic services to their constituents. Chief among those services was an adequate food supply.

Hoping to keep starvation from leading to anarchy, President Woodrow Wilson had decided to internationalize the Food Administration, renaming it the American Relief Administration (ARA), and he sent Hoover to run it. This time, the objective was not just aiding U.S. allies but also its former enemies. The ARA fed millions of German and Austro-Hungarian citizens and helped the United States avoid an embarrassment of riches. It had been so successful producing and preserving food that there was more than could be eaten. The ARA saw that it did not go to waste, even though the humanitarian effort raised eyebrows when its recipients included nations under communist control. It also prevailed despite Congress defunding the program in the summer of 1919, forcing Hoover to take the ARA private and rely on donations.

Hoover's understanding of conditions in Europe made him a valuable asset to Wilson at the Versailles Peace Conference that year. But he was wary of what was going on inside the palace's Hall of Mirrors. In fact, he had been wary of the war from the start, concerned that any alliance the United States might join would entangle the country for years to come. And while he sided with Wilson in opposing the harsh conditions the Allies imposed on Germany, he came out against any postwar alliance that did not take into consideration the United States' economic influence. He also parted with the president when he came out in favor of the reservations Congress attached to the treaty. Ever the realist, and despite the fact that the treaty contained an entanglement he dreaded—the League of Nations—Hoover campaigned for the treaty's ratification, congressional reservations and all, because further delay would have fostered global unrest. He returned to the United States in late 1919 convinced that the differences between the United States and Europe had grown too wide to bridge. He reportedly told the press waiting for him as he disembarked in New York that he was turning his back on Europe and hoped never to see it again.

He was not the only American to feel that way. Bloodied by war and disillusioned by peace, the United States turned inward in the 1920s. Rejecting diplomatic commitments, it also condemned "foreign" ideas and "un-American" lifestyles and turned away immigrants as well as foreign trade. Hoover had to navigate all this as a private citizen constantly in the public eye. His achievements as an international humanitarian and the driving force behind the Food Administration had made him one of the men of the hour. His chances of returning to the home he had built in California were lost in an endless series of speaking engagements and public appearances. He used the opportunity to champion infrastructure improvements, better health for children, more economic efficiency, less waste, and a way to do it all that showcased and celebrated individual effort and downplayed government interference. He was a man in demand.

Both the Democratic and Republican Parties thought Hoover would be a good presidential candidate. He had come out for the minimum wage and a shorter work week and against child labor, making him the darling of progressives in both parties. And his journey from rags to riches was a compelling story guaranteed to attract voters. But Hoover never publicly declared himself a Republican or a Democrat until March 1920, when he finally sided with the GOP. He hinted coyly that while he would not run for president, he would not say no if he were nominated. While

he may have seemed a catch, Republicans passed. Hoover's stint as head of the Food Administration had made him an enemy of farmers, which constituted an important bloc to the party. Warren Harding was nominated and went on to a landslide victory in November. Hoover campaigned for Harding before stepping off the national stage and returning to private life.

But his time out of the national spotlight would be brief. President-elect Harding needed to assemble his cabinet, and three slots, treasury, commerce, and interior, needed to be filled. He thought Hoover would be good for commerce. At first, Hoover refused, fearing a negative reaction from Senate Republicans. In time, opposition softened, and Hoover took the job. It was a post he would hold until he became president himself.

Some cabinet positions are stepping stones to the presidency. Being head of the Commerce Department is not one of them. For years, it was considered such a minor post that the specifics of its responsibilities and reach were hard to define. Hoover, on the other hand, saw the Commerce Department as the center of the universe as far as the nation's prosperity and stability were concerned. He overhauled the office, extended its reach and responsibilities, and, in the process, positioned himself for the 1928 presidential election.

Of course, he had some help. American prosperity seemed to flourish in the 1920s. The economy staggered briefly in 1920–1921, as it shifted from war to peace. But wartime government controls vanished quickly, and a succession of pro-business presidents—Warren Harding and Calvin Coolidge—worked to keep government out of the way. The Treasury Department cut taxes, mostly for the rich, between 1921 and 1926, and Congress raised tariffs on foreign goods to protect U.S. industries. In many respects, Hoover was not only a witness to all this but, as commerce secretary, an active participant. He had demanded from Harding, and had been given, the power to coordinate economic affairs throughout the U.S. government. He was on a mission to root out waste and ramp up efficiency, not only in government but also in business and industry. He made progress and enemies. Thanks to his intrusive manner, which sometimes resulted in his seizing control of responsibilities from other cabinet departments, Hoover became known as the "secretary of commerce and undersecretary of everything else."

If the elimination of waste was Hoover's goal, he had company. Henry Ford's famed Rouge River plant in Detroit, Michigan, pushed out a finished automobile every 10 seconds. Frederick Taylor, like Hoover an engineer, and the self-proclaimed "father of scientific management," sought to eliminate wasted motion in all things. Increasing efficiency across the board was another goal Hoover had set for himself. Commercial air travel was becoming a real possibility; the first transcontinental airmail flight took place in 1920, so moving passengers from coast to coast would only be a matter of time. Hoover wanted to give the industry more lift by providing indirect government subsidies and to bring farming into the air age by promoting the use of crop dusting to maximize harvests. He had to think his emphasis on promoting all things aeronautical enjoyed a bit of vindication when Charles Lindbergh, a former airmail pilot, flew the *Spirit of St. Louis* nonstop from New York to Paris in 1927.

The year 1927 was more than just the year Lindbergh and others broke barriers. It was also the year the lower Mississippi River, swollen by days of relentless rain, broke levees and flooded 10 states, killing at least 500 people and untold numbers of livestock and laying waste to 27,000 acres of land. It was a multistate tragedy with national implications, and the governors of 6 states along the Mississippi knew someone was needed to lead the relief effort who understood the complexities of dealing with state, regional, and national bureaucracies. Based on his track record for providing food and humanitarian relief during World War I, it was no surprise that President Coolidge put Hoover in charge. After creating 150 tent cities, gathering an armada of vessels to ferry survivors and supplies, and amassing a $17 million budget largely from private funding, Herbert Hoover had again become a household name, and just in time for the 1928 presidential election.

Economic prosperity along with his own performance had made Herbert Hoover the likely Republican presidential nominee in 1928. His chances were helped when Calvin Coolidge announced he would not seek another term. Those chances were not helped, however, by Coolidge's dislike of his secretary of commerce. In fact, something of an "anybody but Hoover" movement emerged within the GOP in the runup to the 1928 convention. But few could dispute Hoover's national reputation or would risk letting the White House go to the Democrats, and that was enough to win the nomination.

Voters were in no mood to rock the boat, and Herbert Hoover cruised to victory in 1928. He promised a steady economy and maintaining the United States' isolationist foreign policy. Tax cuts, higher tariffs on imported goods, a restrictive immigration policy, and several arms reductions treaties, all implemented by the Harding and Coolidge administrations, seemed to sit well with the electorate. His opponent, New York governor Al Smith, found himself fighting an uphill battle, being a Catholic, which worried Protestants, and an opponent of Prohibition. In the end, Hoover carried 41 of 48 states.

He may have been elected to pursue a stay-the-course administration with regard to national and international affairs, but Herbert Hoover's vision of how government should work was anything but status quo. He sought nothing less than an overhaul of regulatory agencies and a promotion of American individualism and self-reliance. In many ways, that sentiment was in keeping with the go-it-alone isolationist economic and foreign policies in place. But world events had been slowly intruding on American complacency during the 1920s. The country's refusal to participate in the postwar arrangements in Europe (the United States never signed the Versailles Peace Treaty or committed to the League of Nations) created something of a vacuum, which British and French ambitions quickly filled. Germany was forced to pay billions in reparations and surrender territory. The pain and humiliation of the settlement destabilized German politics, which later gave way to fascism and Hitler. Italy had already succumbed to fascism's appeal and elevated Mussolini to power. Despite American efforts to steer clear of Europe's economic and political problems, they landed on the United States' doorstep less than a year after Hoover took office. The U.S. economy stumbled, staggered, and ultimately crashed in October 1929, brought about in part by Britain's decision to raise its interest rates to lure back capital that had been invested in the United

States. That move, compounded by years of tax cuts, easy credit, and lax regulatory policies in the United States, contributed to a Wall Street meltdown. On October 29, 1929, "Black Tuesday," over 16 million shares changed hands. The stampede to get out of the market signaled the start of the downward spiral that would take the world into the Great Depression.

Hoover tried just about everything to stop the slide, short of direct federal intervention. He favored support for banks and railroads as a way to revive the national economy and called on local governments to aid the general public. After that, he backed public works projects. However, citing budget concerns, he balked at some efforts, including one to bring electric power to the Tennessee Valley. When nothing seemed to work, he turned to measures to protect American jobs and industries. He signed the Smoot-Hawley Tariff Act into law in 1930. The tariffs raised prices on imported industrial and agricultural products. It also set off a global trade war, as other nations retaliated. International trade ground to a standstill, and even more jobs were lost. Finally, in 1932, Hoover, who had opposed direct federal intervention out of fear that it would put Americans on the "dole," as he called it, threw his support behind the Reconstruction Finance Corporation (RFC). The RFC parceled out federal support to banks, railroads, and local governments, hoping some kind of trickle-down effect would fund local relief efforts. It would turn out to be too little, too late. The ripple effect of the Depression had spread from Wall Street to Main Street; businesses had defaulted on a record number of loans, and more than 5,000 banks had failed. Nearly a quarter of the American workforce was unemployed, many of them living in ramshackle shantytowns derisively referred to as "Hoovervilles."

Hoover's reluctance to turn the federal government's full attention to dealing with the Great Depression in some ways mirrored his approach to foreign policy. He had come into office determined to concentrate on domestic policy, and as a result, the fragile world order established after World War I began to disintegrate. While he kept the United States out of the League of Nations, allowing other nations to exploit the U.S. absence, he did devote time to encouraging global disarmament, putting U.S. support behind the London Naval Treaty. It was an extension of the 1922 Washington Naval Treaty, which sought to limit warship construction. He also spoke at the 1932 World Disarmament Conference in Geneva, urging cutbacks in tank and bomber production. His proposals fell on deaf ears, drowned out, perhaps, by the uproar generated by Japan's 1931 invasion of Manchuria, a Chinese province. Tokyo's forces had prevailed and claimed Manchuria as a puppet state. Outside of strong words and a declaration that the United States would not recognize territories taken by force, the Hoover administration did nothing more to challenge the aggression.

Incapable of leading the world into peace, and unable to lead the United States out of the Great Depression, Herbert Hoover faced bleak political prospects as the 1932 presidential election loomed. His critics tried to portray him as incompetent and out of touch. In the summer of 1932, they would try to add heartless to that list. The World War Adjusted Compensation Act of 1924 had set 1945 as the year veterans would receive a bonus. But the Great Depression had wiped out the savings of many vets, and they descended on Washington to press Congress for immediate payment. Congress bought some of them off by funding their trips home, but many, who now called themselves members of the "Bonus Army," stayed and set up camp in the nation's capital. Things went from push, when Washington police tried and failed to disperse demonstrators, to shove, when Hoover sent in the U.S. Army to finish the job. The camp was burned to the ground and hundreds of protesters were injured. The entire incident was another black eye for Hoover as he faced reelection in the fall.

Voters were angry as November approached. No one in the GOP wanted to take the brunt of that anger, so Hoover had no trouble winning renomination. The fall campaign would be distinguished by two factors: the power of radio, which gave voters greater access to a candidate, and the treatment Hoover received on the campaign trail. The animosity included eggs pelting his motorcades, hecklers interrupting his speeches, death threats, and attempts to derail his train. This treatment of a sitting president was unheard of at the time. And then the Democrats successfully managed to blame Hoover for the Great Depression. Nothing he said could turn the tide, and in November, he and other Republicans bore the voters' wrath. Franklin Roosevelt carried 42 states and picked up over 57 percent of the popular vote. The years of Republican control of the presidency were over.

Herbert Hoover spent most of his postpresidential years trying to rebuild his image. He wrote more than two dozen books, some of which attacked FDR's New Deal programs. He campaigned for Republican presidential candidates in 1936 and 1940, secretly hoping the GOP might someday return to him. It was not to be. His contributions during World War II were limited, given his feelings toward Roosevelt and his opinion that FDR hurt chances for peace by provoking Japan and not supporting European efforts to work with Hitler. Roosevelt did not call on the former president once the United States entered the war in 1941.

In 1946, with one war over, another one starting, and a new president in the White House, Hoover's redemption began in earnest. Despite their ideological differences, but acknowledging his experience with food relief, Harry Truman asked Hoover to tour Germany and Austria to develop a plan to feed people to keep them out of Soviet hands. Relations between the United States and the Soviet Union had never been good during the first half of the 20th century. Woodrow Wilson had hoped to kill communism by joining other nations in an ill-fated invasion, and when that did not work, he tried to isolate it, first by denying Moscow access to the League of Nations and then by refusing to diplomatically recognize the regime. Franklin Roosevelt ended the estrangement in 1933, but the seeds of bitterness and mistrust had been sown. Joseph Stalin's nonaggression pact with Hitler on the eve of World War II confirmed American mistrust. The two nations became allies by default when Hitler invaded the USSR and later declared war on the United States.

It was an awkward alliance; one nation was motivated to fight in the name of national self-determination and the other in the name of self-preservation. Those competing visions would be the backdrop in front of which the early years of the Cold War would be played out, as both nations staked their claims on territory, initially in Europe. The war had obviously been hard on Austria and Germany, with disastrous consequences

on the farm economies in both countries. In Germany, the effects of crop failures and an absence of labor had reduced yields by 40 percent. Things were worse in Austria, where that country's harvest was half of what it was before the war. A lack of food or faith in the future threatened to make both countries easy victims of communist expansion.

Upon returning from his fact-finding mission, Hoover proposed a plan to address the nutritional needs of the men, women, and children living under Allied occupation. "Hoover Meals" delivered 40,000 tons of American food that was portioned so that women and infants got their daily requirement of milk and fats and men got the calories they needed to put in a full day's work. He also developed a school meals program, which fed over 3 million students. Hoover's humanitarian achievement in Austria and Germany was a small first step in the American effort to confront a worldwide food crisis, although it may have gone unnoticed in the early days of the United States' postwar hopes and Cold War fears. There was, after all, the Truman Doctrine, the Marshall Plan, Containment, and the Iron Curtain to occupy world attention. Nonetheless, Hoover, by now well into his seventies, visited 38 nations and sought support from 7 kings, 36 prime ministers, and the Pope. He was also instrumental in advancing a proposal to the United Nations that eventually led to the creation of the United Nations International Children's Emergency Fund (UNICEF). He had little other use for the United Nations or any postwar alliance or organization that seemed to have a hand out for U.S. financial aid. His isolationist views were at odds with an interdependent world, and after 1950, outside of a few appearances and publications, he figured marginally in national matters.

Herbert Hoover died in New York on October 20, 1964. He was 90 and, at the time, the longest-living former president in American history. He had lived long enough to see Americans in 50 states and in outer space. He had seen radio give way to television. He had lived through two World Wars, and though not on hand for the horrors of human destruction, he had ensured there would be resources on hand to aid in human development once the shooting stopped. He was eulogized as someone who had fed more people and saved more lives than any other man in history, along with being, as he said himself, the only person to ever have had a depression named after him. His was a full and complicated life.

ANALYTICAL ESSAY

"Why are great men not chosen President," James Bryce asked in his 1888 study *The American Commonwealth*. Well, if Americans have not been able to answer the question posed by the British jurist and later ambassador to the United States, it is not for want of trying. Even before Bryce weighed in on the subject, time and effort were spent trying to come up with the qualifications that would attract the best and the brightest. The framers of the Constitution suggested that experience and fortitude were two qualities any successful president should possess. Alexander Hamilton said experience is "the parent of wisdom." His contemporaries defined fortitude as a combination of courage, steadfastness, firmness, trustworthiness, and integrity. Finding someone with those qualities was going to be a tall order. Bryce himself admitted as much when he tried to answer his own question, suggesting great men do not usually enter politics unless it is necessary, and when they do, he observed, there is no guarantee they will be elected.

The process of how presidents are elected has not changed all that much, but the sought-after traits have evolved over time. Americans still look for experience, but packaging is important. Sometimes voters take a chance on a risk-taker, someone willing to push the envelope but all the while recognizing the chances of failure. Other times, they opt for more predictable leadership. Other abilities are not quite so easily massaged. A record of accomplishment is always expected. Presidential wannabes cannot be one-hit wonders. They are expected to have been consistently successful in whatever they did up to that point. And do not forget judgment. This is not just the ability to correctly evaluate situations they are faced with, but the knack to see around the corner, for want of a better phrase, and tackle small problems before they become big ones. Successful presidents also have impeccable timing. They make difficult decisions at the right moments, thereby preventing the problems and the decisions to address them from becoming more difficult. Should

presidents be humble? Self-effacing? Have the ability to laugh at themselves or, at the very least, not take themselves too seriously? It is probably not a bad idea. Self-effacement humanizes. Should they also possess the personality to build relationships, win friends, influence people, charm and disarm opponents, consider all sides of an argument, and, above all, love the give and take of politics?

Herbert Clark Hoover had few of these qualities, yet he still managed to become president. Tens of thousands of Europeans owed their lives to Hoover's humanitarian relief efforts during and after World War I. Almost as many Americans owed their lives and livelihoods to his rescue efforts in the wake of the Mississippi River flood of 1927. His rags-to-riches story was the stuff of legends and outright admirable. He may have been admired by many Americans, but they did not feel a connection to him. To many, he appeared ill at ease. A 1928 magazine article asked, "Is Hoover Human?" A close associate commented that "there seems to be a broad feeling that he is too much a machine."

Many may have questioned Herbert Hoover's humanity, but few who truly knew him questioned his ambition to become president. As early as 1922, California senator Hiram Johnson was on record as saying, "Hoover has an ambition that overleaps itself. He is perfectly mad to be President." In 1926, almost a full year before Calvin Coolidge shocked the nation and the Republican Party by announcing he would not run in 1928, Hoover hired a publicity agent. He seemed a natural choice: humanitarian in chief to millions around the world during and after World War I, head of the U.S. Food Administration, and commerce secretary to two presidents during a period of sustained prosperity. Hoover exuded self-confidence and a feeling that he had never known failure. But he had his critics.

Those who knew Hoover, or at least worked with or around him, were less generous in their assessments. Andrew Mellon, who served as treasury secretary while Hoover held down the post at commerce, said Hoover was too rigid and inflexible to be president. "Hoover is an engineer," Mellon said. "He wants to run a straight line, just one line, and then say to everyone, 'this is the only line there is . . . come up to it, or else keep out.'" President Woodrow Wilson, despite having tapped Hoover to lead humanitarian efforts abroad and the Food Administration at home, questioned Hoover's trustworthiness: "I have a feeling that he would rather see a good cause fail than succeed if he were not head of it." Warren Harding, who picked Hoover to be commerce secretary warned that his subordinate should not be president because he was too "dictatorial and autocratic." Calvin Coolidge, who kept Hoover in the commerce post after Harding's death, said something to the effect that Hoover had given him years of unsolicited advice, all of it bad. As it became obvious that Hoover would be the GOP's nominee in 1928, the magazine *New Republic* thought it a "poor omen" that "Republicans . . . had so little liking of their own candidate." Their "suppressed uneasiness and irritation justify the prediction of . . . either a stormy or compromising career as President."

If Hoover was a difficult candidate for voters to warm up to, he was an even more difficult candidate to manage. He dreaded the campaign trail and the possibility that he might even meet some voters. When his advisers finally talked him into making a few token appearances, he gave in but warned, "I'll not kiss any babies." However, his reluctance to hit the hustings in search of votes did not prevent him from micromanaging his own campaign. Everything had to pass through him for approval. He even wrote his own speeches, a painstaking affair that Hoover equated to building bridges. "I write a speech as I build a bridge," he said, "step by step, and that takes time." And what he wrote and what he said often differed, depending on the audience. To progressives, he warned against government action against labor unions and supported public works jobs, an eight-hour workday, and financial support for farmers. Less progressive audiences were treated to Hoover's homage to "the American system of rugged individualism" and a condemnation of efforts by government to further regulate business. And while the messages differed, the one thing they had in common was their atrocious delivery. He was a horrendous public speaker. Little if anything was ever delivered off the cuff. He was tightly scripted, spoke in a monotone, made very few gestures to animate his presentation, and he mumbled.

Despite his sometimes grouchy nature and the impression he was cold toward people, Hoover won a convincing victory in 1928. He crushed New York governor Al Smith, his Democratic opponent, by over 6 million votes. Smith was battling the headwinds produced by eight years of economic prosperity under Republican presidents, plus the fact he was Catholic and anti-Prohibition. And there was Hoover's image, burnished by a sympathetic press, who hailed him as a "genius" and "as the most useful American citizen alive." The expectations that the good times would continue under Hoover were high. Unemployment at the time of his inauguration was just 3 percent, and during his inaugural address, he predicted that "we will soon . . . be in sight of the day when poverty will be banished from this nation." Perhaps those expectations were too high, a fact Hoover himself realized. "They (the people) have a conviction that I am a sort of superman," he told the editor of the *Christian Science Monitor*. "If some unprecedented calamity should come upon the nation . . . I would be sacrificed to the unreasoning disappointment of a people who expected too much." Eight months later, the stock market crashed, and the United States and then the world plunged into the Great Depression. In that same period, Hoover's administration went from one of great expectations to great disappointment.

But the disappointment had been building for some time. He had trouble working with Congress, although he was able to use Republican majorities in the House of Representatives and the Senate to secure passage of the Agricultural Marketing Act of 1929, making good on a campaign promise. Hoover had wanted to level the playing and enable "our farmers an income equal to those of other occupations." The act created a Federal Farm Board (FFB) with $500 billion to lend. It also set up a system where surplus crops were purchased to shrink supply and keep prices high. It was his sole legislative triumph in 1929, and while good, it might have been better. It was marred by his decision to select the president of International Harvester and not someone with farm experience to lead the FFB. Furthermore, he ordered the FFB to not buy up surplus farm commodities, one of its primary responsibilities. Apparently, anything that interrupted the natural rhythms of the marketplace, even to help those at risk, ran counter to Hoover's ideology. The Agricultural Marketing Act became law, but in the process, Hoover was exposed as being politically inept. He generally preferred to introduce or float ideas by assembling some kind of commission or conference instead of running them by Congress. That may have made sense to someone who relished the analytical process, but when a problem required specific and timely action, the commissions generally produced delay and muddle.

Hoover also did not seem to like politics; the give and take, the horse trading, and even the compromise implicit in the process repulsed him, and he made no attempt, not only as president but as leader of the Republican Party, to keep those behaviors to a minimum. More to the point, he just did not seem to like Congress very much. He told Secretary of State Henry Stimson that "he had bad impressions about every one of them." It was hard to get him to see another side of an issue besides his. Delegations of congressional representatives would come to the White House to pitch an idea only to find him unresponsive to any path but his own. His refusal to engage Congress, either in a consultative manner or by leveraging their support by taking his case to the public, paid negative dividends on a number of fronts, making him, in the words of an influential newspaper columnist at the time, "the most left-footed President politically the world ever saw."

If Herbert Hoover disappointed Congress with his reluctance to include it in his administration's activities, he compounded his problems by first delighting and then disappointing grassroots supporters. Progressives, liberals, and conservationists would find themselves wooed by Hoover only to be let down as he abandoned them in deference to what historian Kendrick Clements called Hoover's commitment to ideology over rationality. He thrilled progressives with his support of legislation that would limit legal action to break strikes. It was later revealed that he signed the bill into law only because he would have been subjected to a humiliating veto override by Congress. The luster of his progressive and liberal credentials were further dimmed when he made no effort to rein in the Labor Department's treatment of aliens, legal or otherwise. It was not just the round up and deportation that hurt him in the eyes of progressives, but what

happened after they were taken into custody. If their country of origin chose not to immediately repatriate them, they were jailed, in some cases for up to a year and a half, while their cases were resolved. He may have reassured liberals by his refusal to sign a restrictive covenant when he bought a second home in Washington, D.C., but he refused to denounce lynching and the segregation of mothers traveling to Europe to honor loved ones killed in World War I. He also nominated a man to the Supreme Court who opposed giving African Americans the right to vote. Every Republican in the U.S. Senate urged him to rescind the nomination, but Hoover resisted. When the Senate rejected his choice, the president suffered not only the embarrassment of a loss at the hands of his own party, but the loss of support among African Americans as well as liberals.

Conservationists were thrice-disappointed with Hoover's record on land, energy, and water. His Commission on the Conservation and Administration of the Public Domain was actually a funnel through which government-owned land flowed to the private sector, putting it at risk to special interests. His approach to the need to slow oil production was hobbled by bad leadership as well as a surprising misunderstanding about the finite nature of oil supplies. Lurking behind the vacillation on energy policy was Hoover's default position that government should not be involved in the marketplace, in which oil production and its sale played a significant role.

The outcome was the same when it came to water. Despite legislation that said towns and cities should get first crack at any power generated by government-funded hydroelectric projects, Hoover's Federal Power Commission ruled that the right of first refusal should go to private utility companies. There was a showdown in 1931. Congress passed legislation for federal control of the power station at Muscle Shoals, Alabama, and sent it to the president for his signature. The tone of Hoover's veto message was familiar: outrage at the thought that government would compete with privately owned utilities.

Herbert Hoover's demand for ideological adherence in relations between business and government; his refusal to directly engage Congress on matters of national importance; his inability to use the power of his office, the bully pulpit, as Teddy Roosevelt called it, to rouse public support for his agenda; and finally his actions, which tended to alienate the very people who supported him in 1928, left him politically isolated in the fall of 1929. And when the stock market crashed and the nation slid into depression, that isolation meant that Hoover, and Hoover alone, would bear the lion's share of the political consequences.

It took nearly two weeks for the Hoover administration to get its arms around the growing economic disaster soon to be known as the Great Depression. One of Hoover's first acts, and probably one of his more regrettable, was to banish the word "panic" to describe the economic crisis, preferring instead to refer to it as a "depression." The word choice would come back to haunt him. Outside of that wrinkle, the response was predictable. By the middle of November 1929, Hoover had consulted with leaders of industry, finance, construction, public utilities, farming, and labor. Even officials from the Federal Reserve System put in an appearance. The meetings were designed to encourage all sectors of the economy to stay the course; he asked factory owners not to cut wages and requested unions not to go on strike. In the early going, once the nation recovered from seeing the stock market perform like an out-of-control roller coaster, things seemed to be going Hoover's way. Management and labor cooperated, and the railroad industry pitched in by stepping up its timetable for scheduled maintenance projects. The president urged governors, mayors, and county commissioners not to wait any longer on those long overdue expansion projects in their jurisdictions. He tried to jump-start things by asking Congress for money for public works and for tax cuts.

But for all the cheerleading, and in some cases hectoring to get engaged, Hoover still felt government's role in the recovery should be restrained. He urged state and local governments to be "energetic yet prudent" in their relief efforts. Hoover's insistence that government relief efforts be muted, in keeping with his ideological bent, left a vacuum to be filled, presumably by the private sector. But business can only do so much, other than repeating the upbeat messages coming from the White House that the economic difficulties were temporary in nature. Even Hoover's political advisers calculated the economy might turn

around in time for him and the Republican Party to weather the 1930 midterm elections.

The odds of a turnaround dimmed as 1929 wound down. Unemployment kept climbing, and breadlines became a common sight in most American cities as the new year began. Everyone seemed to sense the country was not coming out of its economic funk—everyone, apparently, but President Hoover. Unemployment reached 4 million in April 1930, but Hoover remained oblivious, claiming that "a great economic experiment had succeeded to a remarkable degree." He seemed to suffer selective hearing loss when it came to joblessness. He just did not want to hear about unemployment figures, unless they were going down.

Hoover's refusal to face reality in the fall of 1929 was going to cost him whatever goodwill and support he might still have enjoyed. When he was commerce secretary, he was the darling of the press, accessible and quotable. Early in his presidency, the warm feelings continued when he told the White House press corps that he was relaxing the rules they had to follow when quoting the president. But as conditions worsened in the country and they were played out in the press, Hoover pulled back. He started by demanding that reporters submit their questions in advance of their meetings and followed that up with a requirement that all stories be submitted to the White House for review. Neither demand went over well, nor were they often observed. Hoover retaliated by refusing to say anything not printed in the press releases. The standoff resulted in a mass exodus of the press corps. What had once numbered in the hundreds was reduced to barely a dozen. And the goodwill that had defined the relationship in the early going had been replaced by frustration, which ultimately gave way to animosity on both sides. Hoover had alienated fellow Republicans in Congress and his grassroots supporters. Now, with the economy sliding into depression and everyone looking to him for solutions, he had antagonized the very group who could help explain those solutions and share his vision.

The string of miscues continued into 1930. Tariffs had been an oft-delayed topic, but with the economy on the verge of collapse, protectionist sentiment hung heavy in the air. Congress started things off, and high-tariff advocates began writing a bill featuring exorbitant duties on foreign products. Hoover, the consummate free trade advocate as well as the champion of economic nonintervention, did nothing to discourage the hikes. The Hawley-Smoot bill raised tariffs on nearly 900 items to the highest levels seen so far in the 20th century. Economists by the hundreds begged Hoover not to sign the bill into law. His secretary of state cautioned that the bill, if enacted into law, would destabilize an already shaky international financial community, and leading members of the financial community predicted it would lead to a global wave of economic nationalism. Once U.S. tariffs were imposed, other nations would surely retaliate, prolonging the depression and extending the public's misery by not exerting downward pressure on domestic prices.

On June 17, 1930, Herbert Hoover did what he rarely ever did; he disregarded the advice of experts outside of Congress and signed the Hawley-Smoot Tariff into law. He called tariffs "the largest encouragement to foreign trade." Outside the United States, Hawley-Smoot had the equivalency of a declaration of war, prompting the expected retaliation. The United States, on Hoover's watch, had seen banks, businesses, and farms fail. Now it was engaged in a trade war.

The year 1930 was significant for other events besides passage of the Hawley-Smoot Tariff. In October, President Hoover did something he had not done in the year since the stock market crashed; he addressed unemployment. Not surprisingly, the solution was another commission, the President's Emergency Committee for Employment. At the time of its creation, U.S. unemployment had climbed past 5 million. But it would not be the task of the committee to attack the problem by creating jobs. Instead, Hoover charged it with improving the mood of Americans to stop the growing chorus of voices calling for government relief. Not a penny was transferred from the committee's coffers to help local governments alleviate suffering. Instead, local leaders got press release after press release urging them to encourage constituents to hire a handyman to help spruce up their homes. When asked by state governors for copies of the committee's comprehensive plan to end unemployment, they were told bluntly that no plan existed.

November 1930 brought with it midterm congressional elections, the country's first opportunity to weigh in on Hoover's policies. Most presidents see the midterms for what they are: a referendum on how things are going. The party that controls Congress hopes that it can at least maintain power. That said, the 1930 congressional elections were a disaster for the GOP in general and Herbert Hoover in particular. Republican control in the House of Representatives was wiped out, giving Democrats their first taste of power in that chamber since 1919. In the Senate, the 17-seat Republican margin had been reduced to one.

Under normal circumstances, the reversal of fortune would be seen as a wake-up call, a time to reassess the problems caused by the Great Depression and, more to the point, to reassess policy approaches. But Herbert Hoover was having none of it. In his 1930 State of the Union address to Congress, a body all but in the hands of the opposition, he made it clear he was not going to engage in what he termed fiscal irresponsibility to address economic hardship. He had already turned down his own Committee for Employment's request for money to create jobs through public works projects. He delivered the same message to Congress. "Prosperity cannot be restored by raids upon the public Treasury," he said.

The State of the Union address was delivered against the backdrop of calamitous conditions in the banking industry. Six hundred banks failed in the last quarter of 1930, taking with them the life savings of hundreds of thousands of depositors. It would be a cruel December for many, and as a result, many looked to an improvement in 1931. To Senate Democrats, that improvement included the resuscitation of the president's very own Committee on Employment, a necessary tool to reduce joblessness. A bill proposing to do just that landed on Hoover's desk, awaiting his signature. But Hoover scoffed at the idea, convinced the suffering was minimal and, in any event, could be handled at the local level. Besides, he maintained in his veto message, "the primary duty of the government was to hold expenditures within our income, and rein in the big . . . spenders." The president's comments about the ability of local governments and charities to alleviate suffering were quickly challenged by the executive director of Philadelphia's Federation of Jewish Charities. Lessing Rosenwald said, "Private philanthropy is no longer capable of coping . . . with the bravest of intentions, the community chests are altogether unequal to the task ahead of us."

Herbert Hoover's reluctance to recognize or even deal with the pain of the Great Depression may have been borne out of ideological resistance to government overreach. But as that perceived reluctance filtered into the air supply fueling public opinion, it began to look more like indifference at the very least and insensitivity at the very worst, and that gave rise to growing public anger. By mid-1931, the jobless rate had climbed to 8 million, and by then, Hoover, the man hailed on inauguration day as the "Great Engineer" had become the "Great Scrooge." His relations with the press, the one outlet that could have helped him explain his actions and in the process make him appear human, were in tatters. The *New York Times* summed it up best: "Mr. Hoover thus far has failed as a party leader. He has failed as an economist. He has failed as a business leader. He has failed as a personality because of awkwardness of manner and speech and lack of mass magnetism." Outside of blaming World War I and the postwar complications without which, he stated flatly, "we should have no depression," he never acknowledged his own policies were failing.

Americans, on the other hand, were not so quick to let Hoover off the hook. He was booed mercilessly when he arrived in Philadelphia in October 1931 to watch the opening of the World Series. And earlier that month, bankers had forced him to create a National Credit Corporation (NCC) to provide banks with enough cash to allow them to remain open. The NCC and its $500 million budget proved to be either too little or too late. Whatever the reason, by the end of 1931, nearly 2,300 banks had failed. Earlier in the year, he had tried to staunch the bleeding on the jobs front by creating the President's Organization on Unemployment Relief. But like its predecessor, the President's Emergency Committee for Employment, whose chairperson, Arthur Woods, had resigned in frustration, it was just as useless, merely serving as a way to placate demands for direct government relief. Hoover would not commit to a government dole and said as much, again, in his 1931 State of the Union address. As far as he was concerned, it was unnecessary. Thanks to what he called "the sense of social responsibility in the Nation, our people have been protected from hunger and cold."

The country Herbert Hoover presided over in 1932 featured bank failures, mass unemployment, and the collapse of industry and agriculture on an unprecedented level. Hunger stalked the land, documented by actual reports of people starving to death. Homeless Americans became rootless, wandering from town to town in search of a job, a meal, or a place to stay. Some found refuge in abandoned freight cars, nicknamed "Hoover Pullmans," after the luxury sleeping cars found on cross-country trains, or in squalid tarpaper shacks in blighted areas of American cities, which its residents dubbed "Hoovervilles."

The year 1932 might also have been the moment Herbert Hoover realized that his leadership, based on his stubborn adherence to promoting self-reliance and extolling the virtues of "rugged individualism" by denying government help to people in need, had failed. But by then, he had alienated his own Republican Party, liberals, and progressives; nearly cost his party its control of Congress; and had certainly cost the GOP whatever advantage it might have had of retaining the presidency later that year.

Nonetheless, Hoover stuck to his guns. He was concerned about the shape of the federal government's finances, now in the red by nearly a billion dollars. The drain had been aggravated by the loss of gold reserves, and Hoover wanted a tax hike, coupled with cuts in spending, to address the issue. Congress was in no mood for either idea and countered with one of its own. It chartered the Reconstruction Finance Corporation and managed to gain Hoover's support for its plan to subsidize railroads, banks, and other institutions so they could stimulate economic activity at the local level. The idea of a "dole by any other name' may have appealed to Hoover, but progressives in and out of the Republican Party could not reconcile the action with his repeated refusal to provide relief directly to the American people. And it also placed the president in an awkward position; after being contemptuous of Congress and sure of his own intellect to the exclusion of others for so long, he was now following more than leading. He would become less of a leading figure in government efforts to rescue the economy and more of a target of ridicule for having let the suffering go on as long as it did.

Even having all but relinquished his role as recovery leader, he seemed to cling to the role of cheerleader. His administration issued a stream of highly optimistic yet generally unsubstantiated comments about economic and social improvement, such as national health being better than it ever had been and that children were getting more attention from their parents than when things were good. Hoover's leadership seemed not to be operating from within a vacuum so much as it was from a cocoon.

It would be hard to say whether Hoover's treatment of the "Bonus Army" in the spring of 1932 was the final straw or whether it was just more proof of his sense of estrangement from average Americans. World War I veterans had been promised bonuses for their service, and while that payday was still years away, the Depression made having the money sooner rather than later a pressing issue. In June, they descended on Washington to lobby Congress. When the Senate failed to act, most vets and their families went home. However, others stayed and built a small city of tents and tarpaper shacks. They showed no signs of dispersing, and after a couple of run-ins with the Washington, D.C., police, Hoover decided it was time for them to go. He gave the go-ahead to the U.S. Army and General Douglas MacArthur. MacArthur and his forces, infantry, cavalry, and armor, attacked the encampment in the middle of the night. Men, women, and children fled as the tanks rolled through, and soldiers set fire to the shelters. It was an unbelievable public relations nightmare and a story that did not fade away as summer gave way to fall and the 1932 presidential election. Rather than do everything he could to deprive the story of oxygen, Hoover seemed to fan the flames, first by refusing to condemn MacArthur's heavy-handed approach and then further enraging the public by claiming, without providing proof, that the veterans movement was riddled with criminals and communists.

The 1932 Republican National Convention was held in Chicago. Herbert Hoover was renominated, but it was a joyless occasion. The delegates and other Republican faithful knew what was coming because they knew what had happened during the last four years: millions unemployed, dispossessed, and homeless; thousands of insolvent banks; and deserted farms and factories. They felt that Republican policies, or at least the policies of one Republican, would be held accountable, and they wanted as little to do with that Republican as possible. That might explain why delegates at the convention found no pictures of the incumbent. They had an obligation to nominate Hoover, but that was it. He had charted his own course in the White House, turning up his nose at the offer of congressional help and preferring instead private sector experts or even his own counsel. And as the economy collapsed, he had turned a blind eye to the misery around him and a deaf ear to calls for him to enlist government as a tool to provide relief and recovery. He had stubbornly stuck to notions about self-reliance and rugged individualism, which, albeit romantic, proved inadequate in dealing with the Great Depression. Herbert Hoover had done things his way, and now voters would have their say.

The election results were not just a landslide repudiation of Herbert Hoover and his policies; they signaled a near obliteration of the Republican Party. Formerly safe GOP strongholds defected to Franklin Roosevelt and the Democratic Party, leaving Hoover and the GOP destroyed, dispirited, and disillusioned. Just four years ago, Hoover had carried 40 states; this time, he only carried 6, and when his home state of California went to FDR, Hoover conceded.

Successful presidencies consist of experienced, accomplished individuals exercising good judgment, in possession of an open mind, and blessed with impeccable timing. Factor in humility, personality, empathy, and warmth and few presidencies can falter. Herbert Hoover had experience, and he was accomplished. But it was not enough for him or the United States to weather the Great Depression.

John Morello

Further Reading

Burner, David. 1979. *Herbert Hoover: The Public Life.* New York: Knopf.

Byerly, Ross. 2006. "The Great Humanitarian: Herbert Hoover's Food Relief Efforts." https://www.cornellcollege.edu/history/courses/stewart/his260-3-2006/01%20one/graus.htm.

Clements, Kendrick A. 2010. *The Life of Herbert Hoover: Imperfect Visionary, 1918–1928*. New York: Palgrave MacMillan.

Gaddis, Vincent H. 2005. *Herbert Hoover, Unemployment, and the Public Sphere: A Conceptual History, 1919–1933*. Lanham, MD: University Press of America.

Hofstadter, Richard. 1948. *The American Political Tradition and the Men Who Made It*. New York: Knopf.

Leuchtenburg, William E. 2009. *Herbert Hoover*. The American President Series. Edited by Arthur M. Schlesinger Jr. and Sean Wilentz. New York: Times Books.

Lichtman, Allan J. 1979. *Prejudice and the Old Politics: The Presidential Election of 1928*. Chapel Hill: University of North Carolina Press

Lloyd, Craig. 1972. *Aggressive Introvert: A Study of Herbert Hoover and Public Relations Management, 1912–1933*. Columbus: Ohio State University Press.

Morris, Seymour, Jr. 2017. *Fit for The Presidency?: Winners, Losers, What-Ifs, and Also-Rans*. Lincoln: Potomac Books, an Imprint of the University of Nebraska Press.

Smith, Richard Norton. 1984. *An Uncommon Man: The Triumph of Herbert Hoover*. New York: Simon and Schuster.

Wilson, Joan Hoff 1975. *Herbert Hoover: Forgotten Progressive*. New York: Little, Brown.

Press Conference on the Depression (November 5, 1929)

At a press conference on November 5, President Hoover responded to the stock market crash and the evolving economic crisis. Voters had elected three Republican presidents, primarily on the belief that they would continue to provide economic growth and prosperity. The stock market collapse surprised both the public and President Hoover.

THE PRESIDENT. I haven't anything of any news here to announce. I thought perhaps you might like that I discuss the business situation with you just a little, but not from the point of view of publication at all—simply for your own information. I see no particular reasons for making any public statements about it, either directly or indirectly.

The question is one somewhat of analysis. We have had a period of over-speculation that has been extremely widespread, one of those waves of speculation that are more or less uncontrollable, as evidenced by the efforts of the Federal Reserve Board, and that ultimately results in a crash due to its own weight. That crash was perhaps a little expedited by the foreign situation, in that one result of this whole phenomenon has been the congestion of capital in the loan market in New York in the driving up of money rates all over the world.

The foreign central banks having determined that they would bring the crisis to an end, at least so far as their own countries were concerned, [p. 367] advanced money rates very rapidly in practically every European country in order to attract capital that had drifted from Europe into New York, back into their own industry and commerce. Incidentally, the effect of increasing discount rates in Europe is much greater on their business structure than it is with us. Our business structure is not so sensitive to interest rates as theirs is. So their sharp advancement of discount rates tended to affect this market, and probably expedited or even started this movement. But once the movement has taken place we have a number of phenomena that rapidly develop. The first is that the domestic banks in the interior of the United States, and corporations, withdraw their money from the call market.

There has been a very great movement out of New York into the interior of the United States, as well as some movement out of New York into foreign countries. The incidental result of that is to create a difficult situation in New York, but also to increase the available capital in the interior. In the interior there has been, in consequence, a tendency for interest rates to fall at once because of the unemployed capital brought back into interior points.

Perhaps the situation might be clearer on account of its parallel with the last very great crisis, 1907–1908. In that crash the same drain of money immediately took place into the interior. In that case there was no Federal Reserve System. There was no way to acquaint of capital movement over the country, and the interest rates ran up to 300 percent. The result was to bring about a monetary panic in the entire country.

Here with the Federal Reserve System and the activity of the Board, and the ability with which the situation has been handled, there has been a complete isolation of the stock market phenomenon from the rest of the business phenomena in the country. The Board, in cooperation with the banks in New York, has made ample capital available for the call market in substitution of the withdrawals. This has resulted in a general fall of interest rates, not only in the interior, but also in New York, as witness the reduction of the discount rate. So that instead of having a panic rise in interest rates with monetary rise following it, we have exactly the reverse phenomenon—we have a fallen interest [p. 368] rate. That is the normal thing to happen when capital is withdrawn from the call market through diminution in values.

The ultimate result of it is a complete isolation of the stock market phenomenon from the general business phenomenon. In other words, the financial world is functioning entirely normal and rather more easily today than it was 2 weeks ago, because interest rates are less and there is more capital available.

The effect on production is purely psychological. So far there might be said to be from such a shock some tendency on the part of people through alarm to decrease their activities, but there has been no cancellation of any orders whatsoever. There has been some lessening of buying in some of the luxury contracts, but that is not a phenomenon itself.

The ultimate result of the normal course of things would be that with a large release of capital from the speculative market there will be more capital available for the bond and mortgage market. That market has been practically starved for the last 4 or 5 months. There has been practically no—or very little at least—of mortgage or bond money available, practically no bond issues of any consequence. One result has been to create considerable reserves of business. A number of States have not been able to place their bonds for construction; a number of municipalities with bond issues have been held up because of the inability to put them out at what they considered fair rates. There are a great number of business concerns that would

proceed with their activities in expansion through mortgage and bond money which have had to delay. All of which comprises a very substantial reserve in the country at the present time. The normal result will be for the mortgage and bond market to spring up again and those reserves to come in with increased activities.

The sum of it is, therefore, that we have gone through a crisis in the stock market, but for the first time in history the crisis has been isolated to the stock market itself. It has not extended into either the production activities of the country or the financial fabric of the country, and for that I think we may give the major credit to the constitution of the Federal Reserve System.

And that is about a summary of the whole situation as it stands at this moment.

Source: *Public Papers of the Presidents of the United States.* Herbert Hoover, 1929. Washington, D.C.: Government Printing Office, 1974, 366–369.

Statement on Unemployment Relief (February 3, 1931)

In this statement, released by the White House on February 3, 1931, President Hoover discusses federal government funding of employment and relief efforts. He emphasizes the importance of mobilizing and organizing "self-help" agencies and state and local governments.

Certain Senators have issued a public statement to the effect that unless the President and the House of Representatives agree to appropriations from the Federal Treasury for charitable purposes they will force an extra session of Congress. I do not wish to add acrimony to a discussion, but would rather state this case as I see its fundamentals.

This is not an issue as to whether people shall go hungry or cold in the United States. It is solely a question of the best method by which hunger and cold shall be prevented. It is a question as to whether the American people on one hand will maintain the spirit of charity and mutual self-help through voluntary giving and the responsibility of local government as distinguished on the other hand from appropriations out of the Federal Treasury for such purposes. My own conviction is strongly that if we break down this sense of responsibility of individual generosity to individual and mutual self-help in the country in times of national difficulty and if we start appropriations of this character we have not only impaired something infinitely valuable in the life of the American people but have struck at the roots of self-government. Once this has happened it is not the cost of a few score millions, but we are faced with the abyss of reliance in future upon Government charity in some form or other. The money involved is indeed the least of the costs to American ideals and American institutions.

President Cleveland, in 1887, confronted with a similar issue stated in part:

A prevalent tendency to disregard the limited mission of this power and duty should, I think, be steadfastly resisted, to the end that the lesson should be constantly enforced that though the people support the Government, the Government should not support the people.

The friendliness and charity of our countrymen can always be relied upon to relieve their fellow citizens in misfortune. This has been repeatedly and quite lately demonstrated. Federal aid in such cases encourages the expectation of paternal care on the part of the Government and weakens the sturdiness of our national character, while it prevents the indulgence among our people of that kindly sentiment and conduct which strengthens the bonds of a common brotherhood.

And there is a practical problem in all this. The help being daily extended by neighbors, by local and national agencies, by municipalities, by industry and a great multitude of organizations throughout the country today is many times any appropriation yet proposed. The opening of the doors of the Federal Treasury is likely to stifle this giving and thus destroy far more resources than the proposed charity from the Federal Government.

The basis of successful relief in national distress is to mobilize and organize the infinite number of agencies of self-help in the community. That has been the American way of relieving distress among our own people and the country is successfully meeting its problem in the American way today.

We have two entirely separate and distinct situations in the country—the first is the drought area; the second is the unemployment in our large industrial centers—for both of which these appropriations attempt to make charitable contributions.

Immediately upon the appearance of the drought last August, I convoked a meeting of the Governors, the Red Cross and the railways, the bankers and other agencies in the country and laid the foundations of organization and the resources to stimulate every degree of self-help to meet the situation which it was then obvious would develop. The result of this action was to attack the drought problem in a number of directions. The Red Cross established committees in every drought county, comprising the leading citizens of those counties, with instructions to them that they were to prevent starvation among their neighbors and, if the problem went beyond local resources, the Red Cross would support them.

The organization has stretched throughout the area of suffering, the people are being cared for today through the hands and with sympathetic understanding and upon the responsibility of their neighbors who are being supported, in turn, by the fine spirit of mutual assistance of the American people. The Red Cross officials, whose long, devoted service and experience is unchallenged, inform me this morning that, except for the minor incidents of any emergency organization, no one is going hungry and no one need go hungry or cold.

To reinforce this work at the opening of Congress I recommended large appropriations for loans to rehabilitate agriculture from the drought and provision of further large sums for public works and construction in the drought territory which would give employment in further relief to the whole situation. These Federal activities provide for an expenditure of upward of $100 million in this area and it is in progress today.

The Red Cross has always met the situations which it has undertaken. After careful survey and after actual experience of several months with their part of the problem they have announced firmly that they can command the resources with which to meet any call for human relief in prevention of hunger and suffering in drought areas and that they accept this responsibility. They have refused to accept Federal appropriations as not being consonant either with the need or the character of their organization. The Government departments have given and are giving them every assistance. We possibly need to strengthen the Public Health Service in matters of sanitation and to strengthen the credit facilities of that area through the method approved by the Government departments to divert some existing appropriations to strengthen agricultural credit corporations.

In the matter of unemployment outside of the drought areas important economic measures of mutual self-help have been developed such as those to maintain wages, to distribute employment equitably, to increase construction work by industry, to increase Federal construction work from a rate of about $275 million a year prior to the depression to a rate now of over $750 million a year, to expand State and municipal construction-all upon a scale never before provided or even attempted in any depression. But beyond this to assure that there shall be no suffering, in every town and county voluntary agencies in relief of distress have been strengthened and created and generous funds have been placed at their disposal. They are carrying on their work efficiently and sympathetically.

But after and coincidently with voluntary relief, our American system requires that municipal, county, and State governments shall use their own resources and credit before seeking such assistance from the Federal Treasury.

I have indeed spent much of my life in fighting hardship and starvation both abroad and in the Southern States. I do not feel that I should be charged with lack of human sympathy for those who suffer, but I recall that in all the organizations with which I have been connected over these many years, the foundation has been to summon the maximum of self-help. I am proud to have sought the help of Congress in the past for nations who were so disorganized by war and anarchy that self-help was impossible. But even these appropriations were but a tithe of that which was coincidently mobilized from the public charity of the United States and foreign countries. There is no such

paralysis in the United States, and I am confident that our people have the resources, the initiative, the courage, the stamina and kindliness of spirit to meet this situation in the way they have met their problems over generations.

I will accredit to those who advocate Federal charity a natural anxiety for the people of their States. I am willing to pledge myself that, if the time should ever come that the voluntary agencies of the country together with the local and State governments are unable to find resources with which to prevent hunger and suffering in my country, I will ask the aid of every resource of the Federal Government because I would no more see starvation amongst our countrymen than would any Senator or Congressman. I have the faith in the American people that such a day will not come.

The American people are doing their job today. They should be given a chance to show whether they wish to preserve the principles of individual and local responsibility and mutual self-help before they embark on what I believe is a disastrous system. I feel sure they will succeed if given the opportunity.

The whole business situation would be greatly strengthened by the prompt completion of the necessary legislation of this session of Congress and thereby the unemployment problem would be lessened, the drought area indirectly benefited, and the resources of self-help in the country strengthened.

Source: *Public Papers of the Presidents of the United States. Herbert Hoover, 1931.* Washington, D.C.: Government Printing Office, 1976, 54–58.

Veto of the Bonus Bill (February 26, 1931)

Overseeing the federal government's economy and maintaining tight budgets to keep taxes low was a persistent aim of the Hoover administration. This objective clashed with the demands of World War I veterans and led to an incident politically damaging to the president's reelection chances.

A bonus bill seeking extra compensation for men who had served in the war was vetoed by President Harding in 1922. Another bill in 1924 passed over the veto of President Coolidge in a Congress controlled by his own party. That law provided compensation certificates payable in 1945, and on part of which veterans could borrow. In 1931, in response to demands from veterans, Congress passed a bill to increase the loan value available to veterans in the compensation certificates. Hoover considered the bill too expensive and returned it to Congress with his veto.

To the House of Representatives:

I return herewith, without my approval, H.R. 17054, "An Act to increase the loan basis of adjusted service certificates."

In order that it may be clearly understood, I may review that the adjusted compensation act (bonus bill) passed on May 19, 1924, awarded to 3,498,000 veterans approximately $1,365,000,000 further compensation for war service. To this sum was added 25 per cent, said to be consideration for deferring the payment until about 1945, the whole bearing 4 per cent compound interest. Immediate payment to dependents upon death was included, thus creating an endowment insurance policy represented by a certificate to each veteran showing the sum payable at the end of the period—the "face value." The total "face value" of the outstanding certificates to-day after paying the sums due of less than $50 and payments in full to dependents is $3,426,000,000 held by 3,397,000 veterans or an average of about $1,000 each.

The burden upon the country was to be an amount each year sufficient as a yearly premium to provide for the payment of the "face value" of these certificates in about 1945, and to date has involved an appropriation averaging $112,000,000 per annum. The accumulation of these appropriations is represented by Government obligations deposited in a reserve fund, which fund now amounts to about $750,000,000. A loan basis to certificate holders was established equal to 90 per cent of the reserve value of the certificates, such loans now in the sixth year being authorized to 22 1/2 per cent of the "face value."

When the bonus act was passed it was upon the explicit understanding of the Congress that the matter was closed and the Government would not be called upon to make subsequent enlargements. It is now proposed to enlarge the loan rate to 50 per cent of the

"face value," at a low rate of interest, thus imposing a potential cash outlay upon the Government of about $1,700,000,000, if all veterans apply for loans, less about $330,000,000 already loaned. According to the Administrator of Veterans' Affairs the probable number who will avail themselves of the privilege under this bill will require approximately $1,000,000,000. There not being a penny in the Treasury to meet such a demand, the Government must borrow this sum through the sale of the reserve fund securities together with further issues or we must need impose further taxation.

The sole appeal made for the reopening of the bonus act is the claim that funds from the National Treasury should be provided to veterans in distress as the result of the drought and business depression. There are veterans unemployed and in need to-day in common with many others of our people. These, like the others, are being provided the basic necessities of life by the devoted committees in those parts of the country affected by the depression or drought. The governments and many employers are giving preference to veterans in employment. Their welfare is and should be a matter of concern to our people. Inquiry indicates that such care is being given throughout the country, and it also indicates that the number of veterans in need of such relief is a minor percentage of the whole.

The utility of this legislation as relief to those in distress is far less than has been disclosed. The popular assumption has been that as the certificates average $1,000 then each veteran can obtain $500 by way of a loan. But this is only an average, and more than one-half will receive less than this amount. In fact over 800,000 men will be able to borrow less than $200, and of these over 200,000 will be able to borrow only an average of $75. Furthermore, there are 100,000 veterans whose certificates have been issued recently who under the proposed law will have no loan privilege until their certificates are two years old. It is therefore urgent in any event that local committees continue relief to veterans, but this legislation would lead such local committees and employers to assume that these veterans have been provided for by the Federal Treasury, and thereby threatens them with greater hardships than before.

The breach of fundamental principle in this proposal is the requirement of the Federal Government to provide an enormous sum of money to a vast majority who are able to care for themselves and who are caring for themselves.

Among those who would receive the proposed benefits are included 387,000 veterans and 400,000 dependents, who are already receiving some degree of allowance or support from the Federal Government. But in addition to these, it provides equal benefits for scores of thousands of others who are in the income-tax paying class, and for scores of thousands who are holding secure positions in the Federal, State, and local governments and in every profession and industry. I know that most of these men do not seek these privileges, they have no desire to be presented to the American people as benefitting by a burden put upon the whole people, and I have many manifestations from veterans on whom the times are bearing hardly that they do not want to be represented to our people as a group substituting special privilege for the idealism and patriotism they have rejoiced in offering to their country through their service.

It is suggested as a reason for making these provisions applicable to all veterans, that we should not make public distinction between veterans in need and the others who comprise the vast majority lest we characterize those deserving help as a pauper class. On the contrary, veterans in need are and should be a preferred class, that a grateful country would be proud to honor with its support. Adoption of the principle of aid to the rich or to those able to support themselves in itself sets up a group of special privilege among our citizens.

The principle that the Nation should give generous care to those veterans who are ill, disabled, in need or in distress, even though these disabilities do not arise from the war, has been fully accepted by the Nation. Pensions or allowances have been provided for the dependents of those who lost their lives in the war; allowances have been provided to those who suffered disabilities from the war; additional allowances were passed at the last session of Congress to all the veterans whose earning power at any time may be permanently impaired by injury or illness; free hospitalization is available not only to those suffering from the

results of war but to large numbers of temporarily ill. Together with war-risk insurance and the adjusted compensation, these services now total an annual expenditure of approximately $600,000,000 and under existing laws will increase to $800,000,000 per annum in a very few years for World War veterans alone. A total of five thousand millions of dollars has been expended upon such services since the war.

Our country has thus shown its sense of obligation and generosity, and its readiness at all times to aid those of its veterans in need. I have the utmost confidence that our service men would be amongst the first to oppose a policy of Government assistance to veterans who have property and means to support themselves, for service men are as devoted to the welfare of our country in peace as in war and as clearly foresee the future dangers of embarking on such a policy. It could but create resentments which would ultimately react against those who should be given care.

It is argued that the distribution of the hundreds of millions of dollars proposed by this bill would stimulate business generally. We can not further the restoration of prosperity by borrowing from some of our people, pledging the credit of all of the people, to loan to some of our people who are not in need of the money. If the exercise of these rights were limited to expenditure upon necessities only, there would be no stimulation to business. The theory of stimulation is based upon the anticipation of wasteful expenditure. It can be of no assistance in the return of real prosperity. If this argument of proponents is correct, we should make Government loans to the whole people.

It is represented that this measure merely provides loans against a future obligation and that, therefore, it will cost the American people nothing. That is an incomplete statement. A cost at once arises to the people when instead of proceeding by annual appropriation the Government is forced to secure a huge sum by borrowing or otherwise, especially in the circumstances of to-day when we are compelled in the midst of depression to make other large borrowings to cover deficits and refunding operations. An increased rate of interest which the Government must pay upon all long-term issues is inevitable. It imposes an additional burden of interest on the people which will extend through the whole term of such loans. Some cost arises to the people through the tendency to increase the interest rates which every State and municipality must pay in their borrowing for public works and improvements, as well as the rate which industry and business must pay. There is a cost to some one through the retardation of the speed of recovery of employment when Government borrowings divert the savings of the people from their use by constructive industry and commerce. It imposes a great charge upon the individual who loses such increased employment or continues unemployed. To the veteran this is a double loss when he has consumed the value of his certificate and has also lost the opportunity for greater earnings. There is a greater cost than all this: It is a step toward Government aid to those who can help themselves. These direct or indirect burdens fall upon the people as a whole.

The need of our people to-day is a decrease in the burden of taxes and unemployment, yet they (who include the veterans) are being steadily forced toward higher tax levels and lessened employment by such acts as this. We must not forget the millions of hardworking families in our country who are striving to pay the debts which they have incurred in acquiring homes and farms in endeavor to build protection for their future. They, in the last analysis, must bear the burden of increasing Government aid and taxes. It is not the rich who suffer. When we take employment and taxes from our people it is the poor who suffer.

There is a very serious phase of this matter for the wives and children of veterans and to the future security of veterans themselves. Each of these certificates is an endowment insurance policy. Any moneys advanced against them, together with its interest, will be automatically deducted from the value of the certificates in case of death or upon maturity. No one will deny that under the pressures or allurements of the moment, many will borrow against these certificates for other than absolutely necessary purposes. The loss to many families means the destruction of the one safeguard at their most critical time. It can not be contended that the interests of the families of our country are conserved by either cashing or borrowing upon their life-insurance policies.

I have no desire to present monetary aspects of the question except so far as they affect the human aspects.

Surely it is a human aspect to transfer to the backs of those who toil, including veterans, a burden of those who by position and property can care for themselves. It is a human aspect to incur the danger of continued or increased unemployment. It is a human aspect to deprive women and children of protection by reckless use of an endowment policy. Our country is rich enough to do any justice. No country is rich enough to do an injustice.

The patriotism of our people is not a material thing. It is a spiritual thing. We can not pay for it with Government aid. We can honor those in need by our aid. And it is a fundamental aspect of freedom among us that no step should be taken which burdens the Nation with a privileged class who can care for themselves.

I regard the bill under consideration as unwise from the standpoint of the veterans themselves, and unwise from the standpoint of the welfare of all the people. The future of our World War veterans is inseparably bound up with the future of the whole people. The greatest service that we can render both veterans and the public generally is to administer the affairs of our Government with a view to the well-being and happiness of all of the Nation.

The matter under consideration is of grave importance in itself; but of much graver importance is the whole tendency to open the Federal Treasury to a thousand purposes, many admirable in their intentions but in which the proponents fail or do not care to see that with such beginnings many of them insidiously consume more and more of the savings and the labor of our people. In aggregate they threaten burdens beyond the ability of our country normally to bear; and, of far higher importance, each of them breaks the barriers of self-reliance and self-support in our people.

Source: *Public Papers of the Presidents of the United States.* Herbert Hoover, 1932–33. Washington, D.C.: Government Printing Office, 1976, 103–109.

Campaign Speech in Madison Square Garden (October 21, 1932)

During the 1932 presidential campaign, Hoover defended his response to the depression and warned what the New Deal would do to American life. One of the more full-throated warnings came in this speech, delivered on October 21, 1932, in Madison Square Garden in New York.

This campaign in more than a contest between two men. It is more than a contest between two parties. It is a contest between two philosophies of government.

. . . The expressions of our opponents must refer to important changes in our economic and social system and our system of government; otherwise they would be nothing but vacuous words. And I realize that in this time of distress many of our people are asking whether our social and economic system is incapable of that great primary function of providing security and comfort of life to all of the firesides of 25 million homes in America, whether our social system provides for the fundamental development and progress of our people, and whether our form of government is capable of originating and sustaining that security and progress.

This question is the basis upon which our opponents are appealing to the people in their fear and their distress. They are proposing changes and so-called new deals which would destroy the very foundations of the American system of life.

Our people should consider the primary facts before they come to the judgment—not merely through political agitation, the glitter of promise, and the discouragement of temporary hardships—whether they will support changes which radically affect the whole system which has been builded during these six generations of the toil of our fathers. They should not approach the question in the despair with which our opponents would clothe it.

Our economic system has received abnormal shocks during the last 3 years which have temporarily dislocated its normal functioning. These shocks have in a large sense come from without our borders, and I say to you that our system of government has enabled us to take such strong action as to prevent the disaster which would otherwise have come to this Nation. It has enabled us further to develop measures and programs which are now demonstrating their ability to bring about restoration and progress.

We must go deeper than platitudes and emotional appeals of the public platform in the campaign if we will penetrate to the full significance of the changes which our opponents are attempting to float upon the wave of distress and discontent from the difficulties through which we have passed. We can find what our opponents would do after searching the record of their appeals to discontent, to group and sectional interest. To find that, we must search for them in the legislative acts which they sponsored and passed in the Democratic-controlled House of Representatives in the last session of Congress. We must look into both the measures for which they voted and in which they were defeated. We must inquire. whether or not the Presidential and Vice-Presidential candidates have disavowed those acts. If they have not, we must conclude that they form a portion and are a substantial indication of the profound changes in the new deal which is proposed.

And we must look still further than this as to what revolutionary changes have been proposed by the candidates themselves.

We must look into the type of leaders who are campaigning for the Democratic ticket, whose philosophies have been well known all their lives and whose demands for a change in the American system are frank and forceful. I can respect the sincerity of these men in their desire to change our form of government and our social and our economic system, though I shall do my best tonight to prove they are wrong. I refer particularly to Senator Norris, Senator La Follette, Senator Cutting, Senator Huey Long, Senator Wheeler, William Randolph Hearst, and other exponents of a social philosophy different from the traditional philosophies of the American people. Unless these men have felt assurance of support to their ideas they certainly would not be supporting these candidates and the Democratic Party. The zeal of these men indicates that they must have some sure confidence that they will have a voice in the administration of this Government.

I may say at once that the changes proposed from all these Democratic principals and their allies are of the most profound and penetrating character. If they are brought about, this will not be the America which we have known in the past. . . .

Now, our American system is rounded on a peculiar conception of self-government designed to maintain an equality of opportunity to the individual, and through decentralization it brings about and maintains these responsibilities. The centralization of government will undermine these responsibilities and will destroy the system itself.

Our Government differs from all 'previous conceptions, not only in the decentralization but also in the independence of the judicial arm of the Government.

Our Government is rounded on a conception that in times of great emergency, when forces are running beyond the control of individuals or cooperative action, beyond the control of local communities or the States, then the great reserve powers of the Federal Government should be brought into action to protect the people. But when these forces have ceased there must be a return to State, local, and individual responsibility.

The implacable march of scientific discovery with its train of new inventions presents every year new problems to government and new problems to the social order. Questions often arise whether, in the face of the growth of these new and gigantic tools, democracy can remain master in its own house and can preserve the fundamentals of our American system. I contend that it can, and I contend that this American system of our has demonstrated its validity and superiority over any system yet invented by human mind. It has demonstrated it in the face of the greatest test of peacetime history—that is the emergency which we have passed in the last 3 years.

When the political and economic weakness of many nations of Europe, the result of the World War and its aftermath, finally culminated in the collapse of their institutions, the delicate adjustments of our economic and social and governmental life received a shock unparalleled in our history. No one knows that better than you of New York. No one knows its causes better than you. That the crisis was so great that many of the leading banks sought directly or indirectly to convert their assets into gold or its equivalent with the result that they practically ceased to function as credit institutions is known to you; that many of our citizens sought flight for their capital to other countries; that many of them attempted to hoard gold in large amounts you know. These were but superficial indications of the flight of confidence and the belief that our Government could not overcome these forces.

Yet these forces were overcome—perhaps by narrow margins—and this demonstrates that our form of government has the capacity. It demonstrates what the courage of a nation can accomplish under the resolute leadership of the Republican Party. And I say the Republican Party because our opponents, before and during the crisis, proposed no constructive program, though some of their members patriotically supported ours for which they deserve on every occasion the applause of patriotism. Later on in the critical period, the Democratic House of Representatives did develop the real thought and ideas of the Democratic Party. They were so destructive that they had to be defeated. They did delay the healing of our wounds for months.

Now, in spite of all these obstructions we did succeed. Our form of government did prove itself equal to the task. We saved this Nation from a generation of chaos and degeneration; we preserved the savings, the insurance policies, gave a fighting chance to men to hold their homes. We saved the integrity of our Government and the honesty of the American dollar. And we installed measures which today are bringing back recovery. Employment, agriculture, and business—all of these show the steady, if slow, healing of an enormous wound. . . .

We have carried the first-line of trenches in a great national battle. It is of little difference who the commander in chief may be if the strategy and the policies and the subordinate captains and majors and colonels and generals are maintained and if the battle be continued. But that battle cannot be continued under our political system with a 4-month lapse between the election and the inauguration and a 12 month lapse thereafter while new strategies and new policies are being determined, no matter how admirable they may be.

Now, to go back to my major thesis—the thesis of the longer view. Before we enter into courses of deep-seated change and of the new deal, I would like you to consider what the results of this American system have been during the last 30 years—that is, a single generation. For if it can be demonstrated that by this means, our unequaled political, social, and economic system, we have secured a lift in the standards of living and the diffusion of comfort and hope to men and women, the growth of equality of opportunity, the widening of all opportunity such as had never been seen in the history of the world, then we should not tamper with it and destroy it, but on the contrary we should restore it and, by its gradual improvement and perfection, foster it into new performance for our country and for our children.

Now, if we look back over the last generation we find that the number of our families and, therefore, our homes, has increased from about 16 to about 25 million, or 62 percent. In that time we have builded for them 15 million new and better homes. We have equipped 20 million out of these 25 million homes with electricity; thereby we have lifted infinite drudgery from women and men. The barriers of time and space have been swept away in this single generation. Life has been made freer, the intellectual vision of every individual has been expanded by the installation of 20 million telephones, 12 million radios, and the service of 20 million automobiles. Our cities have been made magnificent with beautiful buildings, parks, and playgrounds. Our countryside has been knit together with splendid roads. We have increased by 12 times the use of electrical power and thereby taken sweat from the backs of men. In the broad sweep real wages and purchasing power of men and women have steadily increased. New comforts have steadily come to them. The hours of labor have decreased, the 12-hour day has disappeared, even the 9-hour day has almost gone. We are now advocating the 5-day week. During this generation the portals of opportunity to our children have ever widened. While our population grew by but 62 percent, yet we have increased the number of children in high schools by 700 percent, and those in institutions of higher learning by 300 percent. With all our spending, we multiplied by six times the savings in our banks and in our building and loan associations. We multiplied by 1,200 percent the amount of our life insurance. With the enlargement of our leisure we have come to a fuller life; we have gained new visions of hope; we are more nearly realizing our national aspirations and giving increased scope to the creative power of every individual and expansion of every man's mind.

Now, our people in these 30 years have grown in the sense of social responsibility. There is profound progress in the relation of the employer to the employed. We have more nearly met with a full hand the most sacred obligation of man, that is, the responsibility of a man to his neighbor. Support to our schools, hospitals, and institutions for the care of the afflicted surpassed in totals by billions the proportionate service in any period in any nation in the history of the world.

Now, 3 years ago there came a break in this progress. A break of the same type we have met 15 times in a century and yet have recovered from. But 18 months later came a further blow by the shocks transmitted to us from earthquakes of the collapse of nations throughout the world as the aftermath of the World War. The workings of this system of ours were dislocated. Businessmen and farmers suffered, and millions of men and women are out of jobs. Their distress is bitter. I do not seek to minimize it, but we may thank God that in view of the storm that we have met that 30 million still have jobs, and yet this does not distract our thoughts from the suffering of the 10 million.

But I ask you what has happened. This 30 years of incomparable improvement in the scale of living, of advance of comfort and intellectual life, of security, of inspiration, and ideals did not arise without right principles animating the American system which produced them. Shall that system be discarded because vote-seeking men appeal to distress and say that the machinery is all wrong and that it must be abandoned or tampered with? Is it not more sensible to realize the simple fact that some extraordinary force has been thrown into the mechanism which has temporarily deranged its operation? Is it not wiser to believe that the difficulty is not with the principles upon which our American system is founded and designed through all these generations of inheritance? Should not our purpose be to restore the normal working of that system which has brought to us such immeasurable gifts, and not to destroy it? . . .

The very essence of equality of opportunity in our American system is that there shall be no monopoly or domination by anybody—whether it be a group or section of the country, or whether it be business, or whether it be group interest. On the contrary, our American system demands economic justice as well as political and social justice; it is no system of laissez faire.

I am not setting up the contention that our American system is perfect. No human ideal has ever been perfectly attained, since humanity itself is not perfect. But the wisdom of our forefathers and the wisdom of the 30 men who have preceded me in this office hold to the conception that progress can be attained only as the sum of the accomplishments of free individuals, and they have held unalterably to these principles.

In the ebb and flow of economic life our people in times of prosperity and ease naturally tend to neglect the vigilance over their economic rights. Moreover, wrongdoing is obscured by an appearance of success in enterprise. Then insidious diseases and wrongdoings do grow apace. But we have in the past seen in times of distress and difficulty that wrongdoing and weakness come to the surface, and our people, in their endeavors to correct these wrongs, have been tempted to extremes which destroy rather than build.

It is men that do wrong, not our institutions. It is men who violate the laws and public rights. It is men, not institutions, that must be punished. . . .

Now, one of the most encouraging and inspiring phases of this whole campaign has been the unprecedented interest of our younger men and women. It is in this group that we find our new homes being founded and our new families in which the children are being taught these basic principles of love and faith and patriotism. It is in this group that we find the starting of business and professional careers with courage, with hopeful faces turned to the future and its promise. It is this group who must undertake the guardianship of our American system and carry it forward to its greater achievements.

Inevitably, in the progress of time, our country and its institutions will be entirely in their hands. The burdens of the depression have fallen on the younger generation, probably greater than even its severity on their elders. It has affected not only their economic well-being but has tended also to shatter many illusions. But their faith in our country and its institutions has not been shaken. I am confident that they will resist any destruction to our American system of political, economic, and social life.

It is a tribute to America and its past and present leaders, and even more a tribute to this younger generation, that, contrary to the experience of other countries, we can say tonight that the youth of America are more staunch than many of their elders. I can ask no higher tribute to the Republican Party, no greater aid in the maintenance of the American system and the program of this administration than the support being given by the younger men and women of our country. It has just been communicated to me that in every county and almost every precinct of our country, 3 million members of the Young Republican League are meeting tonight to listen to this address and to rally their support for the party on November 8. That in itself is a victory for the American system.

My countrymen, the proposals of our opponents represent a profound change in American life—less in concrete proposal, bad as that may be, than by implication and by evasion. Dominantly in their spirit they represent a radical departure from the foundations of 150 years which have made this the greatest Nation in the world. This election is not a mere shift from the ins to the outs. It means the determining of the course of our Nation over a century to come.

Source: *Public Papers of the Presidents of the United States. Herbert Hoover, 1932–33. Washington, D.C.: Government Printing Office, 1977, 656–680.*

32. FRANKLIN DELANO ROOSEVELT (1882–1945)

Presidential Term (1933–1945)

CHRONOLOGY

January 30, 1882—Franklin Delano Roosevelt is born at Hyde Park, New York.

September 6, 1901—Theodore Roosevelt, Franklin's uncle, becomes president after the assassination of President William McKinley.

June 24, 1903—Franklin Roosevelt receives an AB degree from Harvard University.

March 17, 1905—Roosevelt marries Anna Eleanor Roosevelt.

July 11–14, 1905—The Niagara Convention takes place, leading to the 1909 creation of the National Association for the Advancement of Colored People (NAACP).

November 8, 1910—Roosevelt is elected to the New York State Senate.

March 17, 1913—Roosevelt becomes assistant secretary of the navy under Woodrow Wilson and serves until 1920.

July–August 1914—World War I begins. President Woodrow Wilson declares U.S. neutrality.

April 2, 1917—The United States declares war on Germany and enters the war.

November 11, 1918—World War I ends; the Paris Peace Conference begins in December.

November 19, 1919—The U.S. Senate rejects American entry into the League of Nations.

November 2, 1920—Republicans Warren Harding and Calvin Coolidge defeat Democrats James Cox and Franklin Roosevelt in presidential election.

August 11–12, 1921—Thirty-nine-year-old Roosevelt is stricken with polio at his summer home in Campobello, New Brunswick, Canada.

November 6, 1928—Roosevelt is elected governor of New York.

October 29, 1929—The New York Stock Exchange crashes, beginning the Great Depression.

June 17, 1930—President Hoover signs the Smoot-Hawley Tariff Act, raising tariffs on over 20,000 imported goods; the act and retaliatory tariffs by trading partners exacerbate the economic depression.

1931—More than 2,000 banks fail, and unemployment increases to 16 percent.

November 8, 1932—Franklin Roosevelt, promising economic recovery with a "New Deal," defeats incumbent Herbert Hoover in his first of four presidential elections.

March 9, 1933—Roosevelt sends the Emergency Banking Act to Congress, which reopens banks with Treasury supervision, part of Roosevelt's "First 100 Days" of massive New Deal legislation to combat the Great Depression.

December 5, 1933—The Twenty-First Amendment ends Prohibition.

July 7, 1937—Japanese military forces invade China, beginning an eight-year war in Asia.

September 5, 1939—President Roosevelt declares U.S. neutrality as war looms in Europe; four days later, Germany invades Poland—the formal beginning of World War II.

September 16, 1940—Congress initiates peacetime military conscription.

March 11, 1941—Congress passes Lend-Lease legislation to supply nations fighting against Germany and Japan with war materiel; Roosevelt declares the United States to be the "arsenal of democracy."

August 14, 1941—Roosevelt and British prime minister Winston Churchill sign the Atlantic Charter, defining Allied goals for the war.

December 7, 1941—The Japanese attack Pearl Harbor, Hawaii, killing and wounding more than 3,400 Americans; a day later, Roosevelt delivers a speech to Congress calling for a declaration of war.

February 19, 1942—President Roosevelt signs Executive Order 9066, confining more than 75,000 Japanese Americans to internment camps.

June 3–6, 1942—The U.S. Navy defeats a Japanese aircraft carrier force near Midway Island and gains naval dominance in the Pacific Ocean.

November 8, 1942—U.S. troops invade North Africa; eight month later, on July 9, Allied forces land on the island of Sicily.

June 6, 1944—Known as D-Day, Allied forces invade Normandy, France.

February 4–11, 1945—Roosevelt's last meeting with Prime Minister Winston Churchill and Soviet premier Joseph Stalin—the "Big Three" allies in World War II—takes place at Yalta.

April 12, 1945—Franklin Roosevelt dies of a cerebral hemorrhage in Warm Springs, Georgia.

BIOGRAPHICAL SKETCH

Franklin Delano Roosevelt was the 32nd president of the United States and longest-serving chief executive. He was born on January 20, 1882, in the Hudson River valley town of Hyde Park, New York. The son of James Roosevelt and Sara Ann Delano, he grew up in a wealthy, prestigious family. His father's ancestors were Dutch immigrants who arrived in New York in the 17th century, and Sara Delano claimed her family had come on the *Mayflower*. Both the Roosevelts and Delanos made their fortunes as merchants, shipbuilders, and landowners. By the mid-1800s, they had joined an elite Hudson River "aristocracy."

Sara was James Roosevelt's second wife, and Franklin had a half-brother, James, from his father's previous marriage. The two siblings spent little time together growing up, and Sara Roosevelt doted on Franklin. She became a major influence in his life and once remarked, "My son Franklin is a Delano not a Roosevelt at all."

The family traveled regularly to Europe each summer during Franklin's youth, as most wealthy East Coast Americans did. He learned to speak conversational German and French as a result of the many visits. Franklin also developed a broad view of European society and culture that would later influence his thinking and attitude concerning foreign affairs and international relations. He was never a great athlete, but his father encouraged the boy's interests in sports and physical activity. Franklin learned to play polo, tennis, and golf, and he took a particular pleasure in sailing in the Hudson River near the family estate in Hyde Park. One can picture his youth as typical of the wealthy class of Americans who lived during the Gilded Age.

In his teens, Franklin attended Groton School, a prestigious private Episcopal prep school in Groton, Massachusetts. Its headmaster, Endicott Peabody, encouraged his wealthy students to adopt a noblesse oblige responsibility to help the less fortunate. He proved an important influence on Franklin's life. Peabody attended Franklin's marriage in 1905 and was a visitor at the White House after Roosevelt became president.

Roosevelt enrolled at Harvard University at the turn of the century. He was an average student, a member of Alpha Delta fraternity, and the editor of the *Harvard Crimson*, the school's newspaper. His father died in 1900 while Franklin was at Harvard, and Sara Roosevelt became more of an influence on the young man. He graduated in 1903 with an AB degree in history. The following year, he enrolled at Columbia University Law School in New York City. In 1907, he passed the New York State bar examination before graduating from law school and never earned a degree. In 1908, Roosevelt joined the prestigious New York City law firm Carter, Ledyard, and Milburn and practiced admiralty law.

In 1905, Roosevelt married his distant cousin, Eleanor Roosevelt, at a lavish ceremony in New York. President Theodore Roosevelt, Eleanor's uncle, gave the bride away. Just as Endicott Peabody had proved an important influence on Franklin, Theodore Roosevelt became one of his political mentors as well.

Franklin and Eleanor had begun a courtship in 1902, and against Sara's advice and approval, her son married Eleanor three years later. They moved to the family estate at Springwood in Hyde Park and lived in a home completely furnished, decorated, and dominated by Roosevelt's mother.

While Franklin was friendly, easygoing, and happy in the constant social life of his class, Eleanor was shy and tended to remain at Springwood. They had six children: Anna (1906), James (1907), Franklin (who died in infancy in 1909), Eliot (1910), Franklin (1914), and John (1916). Never comfortable with child-rearing, Eleanor hired nannies to raise them. Her husband, similarly, spent little time with the children. The couple may have admired and respected each other, but there was little passion in the marriage. Eleanor considered sex "an ordeal to be endured," perhaps reflective of the times and culture.

In any event, Franklin became involved in an extramarital affair with Eleanor's social secretary, Lucy Mercer, in 1914. The relationship lasted until 1918, when Eleanor discovered one of Mercer's love letters and confronted her husband. For political reasons, they did not divorce, and Franklin agreed not to see Mercer again. Their relationship, however, renewed once he was in the White House and after his mother died. Historians have also suggested that Roosevelt had affairs during his presidency with his private secretary, Margaret Leland, and Crown Princess Martha of Norway. After the initial issue with Lucy Mercer, Eleanor moved into a private residence at Hyde Park, Val-Kill, and would remain there for the rest of the marriage. The Roosevelts' relationship would continue as a pure political necessity.

Franklin Roosevelt never enjoyed the practice of law and told friends he wanted a career in politics. Although he admired President Theodore Roosevelt, a Republican, he became a member of the Democratic Party, his father's political faction. Democrats in his home district asked him to run for office in the New York State Assembly, but the incumbent Democrat chose to seek reelection. Franklin therefore opted to seek a seat in the state's senate. Running his own campaign, with his own money, he won the election and took his seat on January 11, 1911.

Franklin Delano Roosevelt (Library of Congress)

Although the senate met in Albany for only 10 weeks a year, Franklin made it a full-time job and joined a small group of "insurgent" Democrats who challenged the power of the New York City Tammany Hall ring of political bosses. As a supporter of the rising Progressive Movement in American politics, Roosevelt sat on the Agricultural Committee and advocated a series of reforms to benefit New York's small farmers. He gained a favorable reputation throughout New York and won reelection in 1912. At the same time, he aggressively supported the presidential campaign of New Jersey's Democratic governor, Woodrow Wilson, in 1912.

When Wilson won, he appointed Roosevelt assistant secretary of the navy, a position his relative Theodore had held at the beginning of the 1898 Spanish-American War. In March 1913, he joined Wilson's administration. Roosevelt performed well in the job, remained attentive to his responsibilities, and got on well with his boss, Navy Secretary Josephus Daniels. As president, Roosevelt would recall that during his time at the Navy Yard he gained a great deal of experience as to how the federal government operated. Once again, however, the desire to win political office beckoned.

In 1914, Roosevelt ran for the vacant U.S. Senate seat in New York. He failed badly in the Democratic primary against Tammany-backed James Gerard, who promptly lost the general election to a Republican, James Wadsworth. In a postmortem, FDR (an emerging new shorthand for Roosevelt) recognized that neither President Wilson nor the political bosses in Tammany Hall had backed him against Gerard. Accordingly, he met and made political peace with Charles Francis Murphy, the Tammany machine's major power broker.

Roosevelt returned to the Navy Department and served until 1920. The year 1920 was an election year, and Louis Howe, a New York journalist, political adviser, and friend since state senate days, convinced FDR to seek the Democratic nomination as vice president in the coming contest. When James Cox of Ohio earned the presidential nomination at the Democratic National Convention in San Francisco, California, Roosevelt joined the ticket to run against Warren Harding and Calvin Coolidge.

The Democrats did not have a good year in 1920. The Republicans held majorities in both houses of Congress. President Wilson's efforts to have the United States join the postwar League of Nations failed in the Senate after a lengthy and heated national public debate. Many Americans also seemed tired of the Progressive reform movement that had galvanized domestic policies and programs. Candidate Harding's promise to "Return to Normalcy" struck a positive chord. Cox and Roosevelt could only respond with "carbon copy" support of Wilson's postwar international and prewar domestic policies. They suffered a huge defeat. Harding won 404 electoral and 16 million popular votes. Cox managed to win 127 electoral and 9 million popular votes. The Republicans also maintained a majority in the House and the Senate. A decade of Republican Party power emerged in Washington until the Great Depression. FDR took some time to recover, lick his wounds, and plan for the next political battle. Tragically, a personal crisis took precedence.

After the 1920 defeat, FDR returned to New York to practice law and serve as a vice president with the Fidelity and Deposit Company. In August 1921, the family traveled to Campobello Island, their summer retreat in New Brunswick, Canada. After a swim in the cold waters, Roosevelt developed a fever and then his illness quickly worsened. Within a day or two, he was paralyzed from the waist down. Doctors believed he had suffered poliomyelitis and indicated the paralysis would be permanent. More recent diagnoses conclude that he suffered from Guillain-Barré syndrome, an autoimmune affliction, but either promised permanent paralysis.

Sara Roosevelt advised her son to retire from both law and politics and assume a private life in retirement. However, Eleanor and Louis Howe convinced FDR to stay involved in his political career. He agreed. Through hard physical exercise, Roosevelt learned to take short walks using heavy, painful braces and a cane. Although he used a wheelchair, he and his advisers made sure that the press and public never saw him in the chair. When he spoke publicly, it was usually standing with support from aides or his sons. In 1925, Roosevelt traveled south to test the political atmosphere, but he became interested in hydrotherapy as a means to ease his pain. In 1926, he bought and developed a treatment center in Warm Springs, Georgia. He would eventually purchase the Merriweather Inn in 1938, and Warm Springs would become a frequent resting place for the president.

In 1924, FDR reentered politics with a speech at the Democratic National Convention supporting candidate Al Smith, the governor of New York. Four years later, he repeated his support at the 1928 convention. In both elections, the Democrat lost by substantial margins. The strong economy and a peaceful international environment worked to the benefit of the Republicans, but the Democratic Party was also divided between Eastern urban leadership and Southern and Western agricultural interests. The party needed a leader who could bring the two sides together. Roosevelt saw himself as that possibility, but he also realized that Republican popularity precluded any realistic chance of his party's hopes to win the White House. If not Washington, then perhaps he could win in Albany.

In 1928, party leaders in New York convinced FDR to run for governor as Al Smith left office. His old political adviser Louis Howe ran Roosevelt's campaign, but newcomers such as James Farley and Frances Perkins joined the team and would play major roles during his presidency. During the governor's race. Roosevelt also began radio addresses, the forerunner of his presidential fireside chats, to inform New York voters of his goals. He faced a popular Republican opponent, New York attorney Albert Ottinger, but in a close election, he defeated Ottinger.

In Albany, FDR ran a progressive administration that often found him at odds with Tammany and chilled his relationship with Al Smith. He continued his "fireside chats" with New Yorkers and remained a popular governor. Then, in October 1929, the stock market crashed and began the Great Depression. Many political leaders in state government as well as Herbert Hoover in the White House predicted the depression would pass shortly. Roosevelt disagreed. He created a series of state programs, which included unemployment insurance, old age pensions, and other progressive legislation, that would follow him to Washington. To oversee those efforts, he found a new adviser, Harry Hopkins, another major figure in his presidential administration. The governor was putting together a strong team of loyal, hardworking advisers. In 1930, Roosevelt won reelection as governor easily, and he began preparations for the 1932 presidential contest. Many of the policies he tested in New York served as pilot programs for the New Deal.

The 1932 Republican National Convention convened in Chicago, Illinois, on June 27. FDR arrived as the front-runner, with broad support from Southern and Western delegates. His former political ally, but now an enemy, Al Smith, was his only competition. After three ballots, FDR held a majority, but he need two-thirds of the delegate votes to win. That occurred when John Nance Garner, the Texas Speaker of the House, convinced the Texas and California delegates to give their votes to Roosevelt. Accepting the party's nomination, Roosevelt's speech included the promise of a "new deal" for the American people, a phrase that would define his first term as president.

With more than 10 million unemployed Americans and a worsening depression, President Hoover and the Republicans in Congress faced a serious threat. The Democrats looked to end a decade of the opposition's control of the federal government. The nation's voters had supported a decade of Republican peace and prosperity. They were about to punish them for the economic depression. In November, FDR won 472 electoral votes and 22.8 million popular votes. Hoover carried only 6 states (59 electoral votes) and received 15.7 million popular votes. Congressional elections also swept the Republicans out of power. With a 59–36 split in the Senate and 313–117 in the House, FDR's party had a solid majority. Roosevelt had to wait until March 1933 to enter the White House, but plans for the new administration began immediately.

When Roosevelt came to the presidency in 1933, he was 51 years old, six feet one inches tall, and weighed roughly 180 pounds. Limited by his paralysis, he exercised his upper body and developed strong arms and shoulders. He smoked heavily, both cigarettes (in a cigarette holder) and cigars. FDR also liked to drink liquor, particularly scotch and brandy. On late afternoons in the White House, he regularly convened a happy hour group of friends and advisers, mixed gin martinis, and casually discussed the day's events. Gregarious and friendly, Roosevelt enjoyed the company of others but rarely exhibited a deep, personal affection for any of his advisers. He liked the company of women, and they were always at the gatherings. Eleanor rarely, if ever, attended. Through all of the crises, both domestic and international, that confronted FDR through four terms, he seemed to find his cocktail parties a relief from the pressures that confronted him as president.

FDR swore the oath of office in March and told Americans they "had nothing to fear, but fear itself" as the nation's economy confronted the greatest economic depression in its history. Between 1929 and 1932, industrial production had declined by 47 percent. Unemployment rose from 3.2 percent to 24.1 percent. More than 1,300 banks had closed. The U.S. gross domestic product (GDP) had fallen from $103 billion to $59 billion.

The Democrats had won the White House and Congress on pledges to confront the economic dilemma, and Roosevelt meant to do that. Rexford Tugwell, a Columbia University economics professor, joined FDR's growing brain trust of advisers. He convinced the president that the federal government needed to "control and coordinate" the economic recovery and not leave that responsibility to private business owners and bankers. Frances Perkins, the secretary of labor and first female cabinet member, agreed with Tugwell. The concept became the basis of the "First 100 days," or the "First New Deal." Between March and June 1933, with the broad support of Congress, the Roosevelt administration passed more economic legislation, programs, and policy actions than any previous government in U.S. history. The two basic control and coordination programs fell under the Agricultural Adjustment Act (AAA) and the National Industrial Recovery Act (NIRA). The press and public began to refer to the first New Deal as "alphabet soup," and many of the policies had some initial success.

By 1935, however, unemployment and economic recovery still lagged, and Roosevelt began to question the direction of the New Deal and its long-term success. The nation's GDP had climbed to only $13 billion, and unemployment was at 17 percent. At the same time, the Supreme Court delivered several devastating rulings, declaring the AAA and NIRA unconstitutional. In effect, the Court maintained the basic concept of "control and coordination" gave too much power to the president.

Always able to adjust, FDR focused on policies that provided new safeguards and security to protect the public against future economic crises. If the government could not prevent commercial depressions, as a natural aspect of free market economics, it could ease the burden on the public. The Social Security Act, the Federal Deposit Insurance Act (FDIC), the Security Exchange Commission (SEC), and other policies all aimed to address unregulated issues that had harmed Americans when the depression began. The Wagner Act opened the path to labor union rights to collective bargaining with owners, and the National Labor Relations Board (NLRB) protected union rights to do so. Critics on the right had accused FDR of moving down the path to socialism, but the president always believed in free market capitalism, so long as the federal government had some major oversight and regulatory authority.

The 1936 presidential election appeared a foregone conclusion. Roosevelt ran again against Alf Landon, the governor of Kansas. Almost conceding defeat, Landon offered a lackluster campaign, and FDR swept into his second term. He won the electoral votes of 46 of the 48 states and won 11 million more popular votes than his opponent. Democrats in the House and Senate won even larger majorities than they had in 1932. Although FDR's first four years had not ended the depression, most Americans believed he remained the proper choice to continue trying to do so.

The president appeared flexible in responding to the Court's decisions on the AAA and NIRA, and Roosevelt remained enough of a tough-minded politician to attack their rulings and move to change the Court. On February 5, 1937, he introduced a plan to add one new Supreme Court justice for every sitting judge over the age of 70 that failed to retire. Given the age of many of those justices, it would have raised the number on the Court to 15. FDR believed that his massive victory in 1936, along with huge Democratic majorities in Congress, would lead to the idea's success. It did not. Public opinion and newspaper editorials found the idea distasteful and a threat to the Constitution's separation of powers. Referring to the idea as "court packing," the plan ultimately died when Congress shelved the proposed bill.

Roosevelt made another political mistake when he delivered a foreign policy speech on October 5, 1937, in Chicago while dedicating a new bridge over Lake Shore Drive. He had long admired President Woodrow Wilson's attempt to end the United States' unilateral policy in international relations. He had supported the League of Nations and hoped for more direct American involvement in world affairs. The rise of totalitarian governments in Italy, Germany, and Japan and the outbreak of conflict in Asia and potential war in Europe led him to discuss the threats to the United States in his Chicago speech. FDR failed to name the "aggressor states," but he called for an international economic "quarantine" to address their behavior. Public opinion reacted negatively. Americans had elected Roosevelt to solve the depression, not to engage in foreign policy adventures. Recognizing that his "Quarantine Address" had made little impact, FDR bided his time and waited for world events to prove the significance of his concerns.

Roosevelt's misjudgments, in both instances, may have occurred as a result of the death of his most trusted adviser, Louis Howe, in April 1936. Howe seemed the only one able to control the president's political urges. Both the court-packing effort and quarantine address were issues Howe night have persuaded FDR to avoid. Roosevelt's oldest son, James, took Howe's place, but he never showed Howe's ability. In any event, the two actions convinced Republicans that Roosevelt was not invincible. Throughout his second term, they criticized and sought to block efforts to expand the New Deal. A brief economic recession in 1937 also indicated that the administration had failed to find a cure for the nation's ills. In the 1938 midterm elections, Republicans gained some seats in Congress, but the Democrats still held majorities.

The president had built a powerful constituency during his first two terms. Organized labor, urban voters, the Solid South, and minorities flocked to the party. His New Deal agricultural policies had also stolen traditional Republican voters in the Midwest and on the West Coast. FDR recognized that such a coalition would be virtually impossible to defeat. So even while further domestic legislation had stalled, he could count on the public's support.

By 1940, the world was at war. Across the Atlantic, Germany and Italy had conquered most of Western Europe and North Africa. Great Britain stood alone against the two Fascist governments. In Asia, the Japanese had invaded Manchuria and attacked China. Adolph Hitler already planned a massive invasion of the Soviet Union that would begin in June 1941. By tradition, the United States declared neutrality, and Congress legislated a series of neutrality acts to prevent the possibility of the nation being dragged into the worldwide conflict.

Unlike his mentor, President Wilson, who had hoped to keep the nation out of World War I, FDR never fully supported American neutrality. His Chicago "Quarantine Address" made that clear. Yet, he faced congressional legislation and a growing public "America first" attitude that demanded neutrality. Slowly, however, as international events grew worse,

he convinced both Congress and public opinion to finally accept a variety of policies to aid nations fighting against the Germans, Italians, and Japanese (the Axis powers). That broad action, ultimately defined as "all aid short of war," helped galvanize the American economy as U.S. industry accepted military contracts from the government. FDR's efforts would be tested in the 1940 presidential election. The president defied the two-term limit that had existed since George Washington and agreed to run for a third time.

In 1940, FDR defeated Wendell Willkie easily, but with electoral and popular votes less dominant than his victories in 1932 and 1936. American voters seemed more nervous and divided with the stalled economy and growing dangers abroad. However, the "Roosevelt coalition" held, and FDR resumed his residence in the White House. Two months before the election, the Axis powers had signed the Tripartite Pact. Concerned with Roosevelt's growing belligerence, it warned any neutral nation (obviously aimed at the United States) that an attack on any of them would result in war with all three.

Between 1940 and 1941, a domestic political debate grew in the United States. It pitted "America first" neutrality advocates and "all aid short of war" FDR supporters. It locked the nation in the most intense foreign policy debate since the post–World War I battle over the League of Nations. While most Americans generally supported Roosevelt's position regarding aid programs, they also clearly indicated that the nation should stay out of an actual war. In January 1941, a Gallup public opinion poll indicated that 88 percent wanted the administration to avoid war. Throughout the year, those numbers would remain high. That changed on December 7, 1941, when Japan attacked the United States at Pearl Harbor, Hawaii.

In 1940 and 1941, U.S. foreign policy had used a number of economic sanctions to force Japan to end its war with China. Those included freezing Japanese assets and embargoing the sale of aviation products and petroleum. Dependent on American fuel for its navy, the Japanese determined to assure a ready supply by invading the oil-rich Dutch East Indies. Part of that strategy ultimately led to the conclusion that Japan would have to destroy the American fleet at Pearl

Harbor, knowing it would provoke war. It did. Revisionist historians such as Charles Beard, *American Foreign Policy in the Making* (1946), and Charles Tansill, *Back Door to War* (1952), argued that FDR purposely provoked the attack to bring the United States into World War II. While there is no clear evidence of that charge—it surprised the president when the attack occurred—the Pearl Harbor attack worked.

On December 8, 1941, in a speech before Congress, FDR called the attack a "date which will live in infamy" and asked Congress for a declaration of war against the Japanese Empire. Jeanette Rankin, a Republican congresswoman from Montana and an avowed pacifist, cast the only negative vote. Three days later, Germany and Italy declared war on the United States. The national debate regarding U.S. neutrality ended.

In one of the most tragic domestic results of the Japanese attack. FDR issued Executive Order 9066 on February 19, 1942. It called for the deportation of Japanese and Japanese Americans from West Coast states, labeling them as "enemy aliens," to detention camps inland. More than 75,000 were moved; 67 percent were American citizens, and the rest had visas to be in the United States. Although the action, particularly in California, Washington, and Oregon, was prompted more by racism than fear of the Japanese as fifth column spies and saboteurs, the Supreme Court upheld EO 9066 in a 6–3 decision of *Korematsu v. United States* in 1944. Roosevelt seemed little concerned by his decision, and if he had concerns about civil liberties, he never mentioned them.

While the Pearl Harbor attack surprised President Roosevelt, he adopted his usual positive approach to what would become the largest and most complex military action in American history. Already in private conversations, and sometimes secret planning, with Great Britain, he and Prime Minister Winston Churchill had determined that war against Germany should be the primary goal. Japan would become a secondary theatre in the global conflict. Six months earlier, the Germans had invaded the Soviet Union. After early success, the Nazi military was stalled in Eastern Europe. As the massive power of the United States' industrial assets began to produce almost limitless weapons and ammunition, FDR and Churchill formed a coalition with the Soviets and China to confront the Axis powers. Over the next four years, American industrial power, Soviet and Chinese manpower, and British experience and geographical location would lead to the ultimate defeat of its enemies.

The U.S. industrial buildup ended the Great Depression. Government military contracts had filled the factories with workers, and farmers had been encouraged to expand their crop production. In all, the government spent $4 trillion (by today's value) using increased taxation, war bonds, and other revenue sources to fund the war. Unemployment in 1940 was 14.6 percent. By 1942, it had dropped to 4.7 percent, and in 1944, it bottomed at 1.2 percent. Around 350,000 women served in the military, and women in the civilian workforce climbed from 27 percent to 37 percent. At the same time, a massive federal bureaucracy grew to deal with the broad and complex needs necessary to confront the war. The growth of the government dwarfed the work of the New Deal.

On a personal level, President Roosevelt tended to conduct his own foreign policy with little assistance from Secretary of State Cordell Hull, who held the position from 1933 to 1944. In a series of prewar and wartime conferences, FDR met personally with Winston Churchill, Premier Joseph Stalin, and China's leader Chiang Kai-shek at various meetings to develop military and diplomatic plans. He began the policy of "summit diplomacy" that would bring the allied leaders, not just their staffs, to personally deal with issues. From the Arcadia Conference in December 1941 to the Yalta Conference in February 1945, Roosevelt led the U.S. delegations at numerous meetings.

Eleanor Roosevelt had consistently supported her husband's political career, campaigning for him throughout his presidency. She drew her own support and popularity as well as political enemies. As the more progressive element of the administration, she publicly supported civil rights for African Americans, while FDR courted white Southern Democrats to keep their electoral votes. In 1939, the world-renowned black opera singer Marian Anderson was scheduled to perform at Constitution Hall in Washington, D.C. The Daughters of the American Revolution (DAR) blocked her performance to sing before an integrated audience. In disgust, Eleanor Roosevelt resigned her membership in the DAR, and on April 9, she scheduled Anderson to perform at the Lincoln Memorial. She also met regularly with leaders in the African American community in an informal "kitchen cabinet" to discuss their concerns, If FDR did little to advance the rights of black Americans during his presidency, his wife prodded him to do more than he might have.

The 1944 election proved a fourth-term victory for the incumbent president. While margins were a bit closer, FDR easily defeated the Republican Thomas Dewey. The wartime economy still boomed, the war news looked promising, and voters were disinclined to change horses in midstream. Roosevelt had aged, however. He looked tired and needed more rest time from his duties. Some of his advisers concluded that he would not live through his fourth term. Still, he personally wanted the job, believed he could function as well as he ever had, and looked forward to the next four years.

The Roosevelts had not devoted a great deal of time to raising their children, and all of them had experienced problems growing to adulthood, Yet, during the war, each made contributions. Anna worked as an unpaid aide on her father's staff. James replaced Louis Howe and then became a marine officer, earning the Navy Cross and Silver Star in combat in the Pacific. Elliot flew 300 combat reconnaissance missions in Europe. Franklin Jr. and John, the youngest child, both served as naval officers in the Pacific.

By mid-1945, the Allies could predict victory. North Africa was under Allied control, and Italy, invaded earlier, had surrendered in September 1943. Russian forces were on the borders of Eastern Germany with a massive army. Their allies had invaded France in June 1945, and Germany had experienced regular strategic bombing raids from the United States and Britain. In the Pacific, between February and June, the key Japanese islands of Iwo Jima and Okinawa brought the Allies to Japan's doorstep. The U.S. massive aerial bombardment of Japan reached unparalleled dimensions.

Ominously, the United States had begun a top-secret program, the Manhattan Project, designed to create an atomic bomb. Between 1943 and 1946, working at Los Alamos, New Mexico, and elsewhere, hundreds of physicists, engineers, and military personnel created two nuclear weapons. Roosevelt had authorized, and the government had funded, the Manhattan Project; however, FDR died and Germany surrendered before the weapon was usable. Japan, still at war with the United States, remained a potential target.

In February 1945, after earlier summit meetings in Casablanca, Cairo, and Tehran during the war, FDR flew to Yalta, in the Soviet Crimea, to meet with Churchill and Stalin for the last time. The 7,000-mile trip tired the president. Observers thought he looked ill and 10 years older than his 62 years. For a week, the three world leaders hammered out postwar plans that included the military occupation of Germany, a Russia agreement to declare war on Japan, and the creation of a United Nations organization.

On March 1, Roosevelt delivered an address to Congress on the results of the conference. It was FDR's final formal speech. A few weeks later, he traveled to Warm Springs, Georgia, his Southern retreat, for a short vacation. Eleanor remained in Washington, and Lucy Mercer joined the president. At about 1:00 p.m., on April 12, while sitting with Mercer in the living room, Roosevelt said he had a severe headache. He collapsed unconscious, and when the doctors arrived, the president was pronounced dead of a cerebral hemorrhage at 3:30 p.m.

After being informed in Washington, Eleanor rushed to the White House and called for their daughter, Anna, to meet her. Franklin's sons, all serving in the military overseas, could not be with them. At 5:30 p.m., Vice President Harry Truman met with Mrs. Roosevelt. He had spent little time with the president, and FDR had rarely asked for his advice or opinions.

Many American adults had known no other president. Grief at the news was genuine and overwhelming. A special train carried Roosevelt's body to Washington on April 14, and a military procession brought the coffin from Union Station to the East Wing of the White House. An estimated 500,000 people gathered along the route to pay their respects. After a simple funeral service, FDR's caisson returned to the train station and traveled to Hyde Park, where he was buried.

HISTORICAL OVERVIEW

The way persons think and act are shaped by the times in which they live and often the places where they mature. Franklin Roosevelt spent his life, from 1882 to 1945, in a United States going through significant historic changes. Some he helped create during his presidency. Born during the Gilded Age into a New York, Hudson River valley family of wealth and privilege, FDR came to see the United States from that perspective. How his political actions responded to the broad evolution of U.S. society perhaps indicated FDR's ability to adapt to a quickly changing nation in the 20th century.

Demographics

In 1880, 50 million people populated the United States; 72 percent lived in rural areas, 86.5 percent were white and 13.1 percent black. Native Americans, Latinos, and Asians were so few that they were often uncounted in census reports. During the next 40 years, due to a massive wave of immigration and improving health conditions and rising birth rate, the population jumped to 106 million. By 1920, when Roosevelt ran as a Democratic vice presidential candidate, 53 percent of Americans lived in cities. When FDR ran for a third term as president, in 1940, 142 million people lived in the United States, 57 percent in urban locations, and the African American population had declined to 10 percent.

Most immigrant settlers from the colonial period to the Civil War in the 1860s had come from Northern Europe. Between 1880 and 1910, however, 15 million more arrived, and the majority had left homes in Southern and Eastern Europe. Many were Roman Catholic or Jewish, and they settled in urban locations, bringing different cultural backgrounds to the nation. A diverse society had begun to develop. On the West Coast, Japanese and Chinese immigrants joined the number of "different" people living in a country unaccustomed to the new demographics. The 1882 Chinese Exclusion Act virtually closed U.S. access to the Chinese. And the government began to create controlled "points of entry" to define who should or should not be in country. In 1892, Ellis Island, New York, opened to coordinate that effort on the East Coast. Even while the 1886 dedication of the Statue of Liberty had offered a symbolic beacon of hope to people seeking a new life, that symbolism overlooked the pragmatic factors that had encouraged immigration.

Industrial Revolution

The historian Richard Hofstadter wrote in *The Age of Reform* (1955) that "America was born in the country and moved to the city." The industrial revolution of mass machine production of goods and services exploded in the United States following the Civil War. Business entrepreneurs, with eager support from the government, invested capital in factories, railroads, and technical innovations to fuel the new economic system. With access to cheap natural resources, a growing population of consumers, and a generation of peace, the U.S. economy not only competed with Great Britain's and Western Europe's industrial growth. By 1913, the United States produced one-third of the world's production, more than Britain, Germany, and France combined. To produce those goods, business owners needed cheap labor. Mass immigration and the movement of African Americans from the South to northern cities provided that asset. Combined with natural resources, capital, and a compliant government, successful "robber baron" owners created personal wealth previously unknown in the nation.

The rapid change in the U.S. economy, however, had ill effects. Workers in the mills, mines, and factories faced dangerous, low-paid conditions; unhealthy tenements in the major cities grew; and efforts to create labor unions to protect industrial employees faced stiff resistance from owners and the government. As Franklin Roosevelt grew to political maturity, those issues would shape his thinking. Ultimately, the Democratic Party and the future president would seek to champion the large workforce and would earn their votes.

The Frontier

In 1860, most of territory between the Mississippi River and the West Coast remained unsettled except for the numerous Native American people who lived there. The United States had 36 states, and while it they "owned" the trans-Mississippi region, its citizens did not live there. In 1862, Congress passed the Homestead Act, which made free land available to anyone who moved into the territory and established permanent ownership there. To facilitate or encourage the move, the Central Pacific and Union Pacific began the construction of a transcontinental railroad. In 1869, the two joined the tracks at Ogden, Utah. During the next two decades, settlers moved into the former wilderness. Mining, timber, livestock, and farming businesses grew, and towns and cities rose along the rail lines. The U.S. government accepted the removal or engaged in wars against Native Americans to make space for the settlement, and in 1890, six new states joined the union.

In 1893, at the Chicago World's Fair, Frederick Jackson Turner read his essay "The Significance of the Frontier in American History." Turner, a history professor at the University of Wisconsin, had studied a map released by the Census Bureau in 1890. It no longer pictured the trans-Mississippi region as unsettled or frontier. Developing what scholars would call the "Frontier Thesis," Turner argued that the wilderness had shaped the nation's character since the colonial era. The constant battle to conquer and settle the wilderness helped create a unique form of American democracy, the "Americanization of immigrants," and other factors that made the nation and its people unique and exceptional. With the rise of urbanization, immigrant diversity, and the industrial revolution, Turner pondered how that might change the nation once a wilderness no longer existed to hone the United States' special character. Whether a myth or reality, which future historians debated, the "Frontier Thesis" has led to a serious discussion of U.S. uniqueness.

Whether the events that Turner discussed influenced an 11-year-old Roosevelt seems dubious, but it would matter later in his political life. Much of the isolationist sentiment that sought to hinder his and Woodrow Wilson's efforts to involve the United States in more active, direct, and shared international relations originated in the states that comprised the trans-Mississippi region.

Native Americans

In the year of FDR's birth, fewer than 250,000 Indians inhabited the United States, many in the frontier territories. Since the arrival of the first Europeans in colonial Jamestown and Plymouth, an ongoing, centuries-long struggle grew to control the American continent. Ultimately outnumbered and divided, Indian tribes in the western frontier confronted a nation with a larger population that was united and armed with modern technology and weapons. Forced to move onto reservations or fight, many Native American tribes opted to resist. A series of Indian Wars pitted U.S. cavalry and state militia forces against small bands of agile horsemen during the 30-year period following the Civil War. From Apache and Comanche in the Southwest, to Sioux, Cheyenne, and Arapaho in the Dakotas, the conflicts wore down Indian resistance. In June 1876, the epic defeat of George Custer's Seventh Cavalry at Little Big Horn, in the Dakotas, provided a brief moment of hope for Indian tribes in the region. However, it only enraged U.S. public opinion. General Philip Sheridan, the Civil War hero, had once referred to the Plains Indians as "the greatest light cavalry in history," but he was also reputed to remark that "the only good Indian is a dead Indian." That conclusion, for many Americans, may have led to the December 1890 massacre of Sioux women and children at the Wounded Knee reservation in South Dakota.

The U.S. government sought to resolve Indian relations as the wars slowly came to an end. While most Native Americans lived on reservations, the 1887 Dawes Act offered them an option to receive a free parcel of land to farm. Most Plains Indians, however, were not farmers. In *Century of Dishonor* (1881), Helen Hunt Jackson attacks years of government abuse and disregard of treaties. Yet, her solution, as with many white activists, seems to hinge on assimilating Indians into a basic Euro-Indian cultural lifestyle. Until well into the 20th century, a series of Indian residential schools opened to assimilate Indians students, with English-language classes, job training, and general European cultural values. The most famous, the Carlisle School in Pennsylvania, opened in 1879 and lasted until 1918. Its most noteworthy graduate, Jim Thorpe, became one of country's greatest athletes.

In 1924, Congress passed the Indian Citizenship Act, granting citizen options to Native Americans under the protection of the Fourteenth Amendment. Native Americans could select citizenship as an option or remain members of independent reservations. It, too, failed to provide a solution, as a number of states found ways to block Indians from voting. Then, in 1926–1928, the government commissioned an independent study from the Brookings Institute to examine the impact of U.S. Indian policy. It was a bleak analysis that questioned assimilation, Indian residential schools, and even the Citizenship Act as only minimally successful in improving the lives of the nation's Indian population.

As governor of New York, with a large Iroquois population, and as president, Franklin Roosevelt showed little interest in the issue. The 1934 Indian Reorganization Act offered subsidies to tribal reservation councils to adopt U.S.-style government systems. Beyond that, the New Deal failed to reach the reservations in any measurable way.

African Americans

African Americans arrived in the Jamestown settlement in 1619, a year before the *Mayflower*. Within a generation, the British North American colonists had established slave codes for blacks, and the long centuries of the nation's greatest tragedy took root. The African slave trade began in 1502, when Spain gave an *asiento* (contract) to Portugal to transport slaves from West and Central Africa to replace Indian populations dying in Spain's Caribbean colonies. While historians differ widely on how many African slaves made the notorious Middle Passage to the Americas, they certainly numbered in the millions. Demographics suggest that 38.5 percent went to Portugal's colony in Brazil; 18.5 percent to British colonies in the Caribbean islands; 17.5 percent to Spanish colonies, 13.6 percent to the French Caribbean, and 3.25 percent to the 13 English colonies in North America.

Slave codes subjugating African Americans grew strict and rigid by the end of the 1600s, particularly in the Southern colonies. By the American Revolution and the Constitutional Convention, more than 600,000 black slaves worked in Southern states, and the issue became a major factor in American politics. The three-fifths clause and fugitive slave clause in the Constitution technically made slavery legal, but battles between proslavery and antislavery advocates convulsed the nation throughout the 1800s. At the beginning of the American Civil War, 3.2 million slaves lived in the United States. The North and South went to war to resolve the issue. The North's victory under Republican leadership produced the Thirteenth, Fourteenth, and Fifteenth Amendments. They freed slaves, granted citizenship, and guaranteed civil liberties to millions of former slaves. Republican political leaders used Reconstruction policies to protect those guarantees, but the commitment slowly eroded. In the 1876 presidential election, Republican Rutherford Hayes won the contested vote, but white Southern Democrats had regained control of their states and demanded an end to protective Reconstruction. Hayes agreed.

While the nation's attention focused on the industrial revolution and settlement of the frontier. Southern Democrats passed a series of state laws that slowly blocked black voting rights, created sharecropping economic control of African Americans, and legislated numerous racist and restrictive laws to remove any substantial black civil rights in the region. The federal government made halfhearted efforts to limit what came to be called Jim Crow racism, but it rarely enforced its actions.

In 1896, the Supreme Court ruled (7–1) in the case of *Plessy v. Ferguson* that racial segregation was legal so long as "separate but equal" facilities in public transportation were available. The idea and practice soon spread to education and other public venues. In effect, the Court upheld the basic practice of Jim Crow. The shame and tragedy of slavery, which the Civil War and Constitutional amendments had ended, failed to address or correct the inherent racism that still existed and persisted in American society.

Numerous civil rights activists, such as Booker T. Washington, George Washington Carver, Mary Terrell, Ida Wells, and W. E. B. Dubois, mounted a new offensive to attack racism and civil rights injustice. The struggle was not about the abolition of slavery—the nation had accomplished that. It focused on fundamental rights and opportunities denied African Americans. However, black activists themselves often disagreed on the best ways to achieve the goal.

In 1905, DuBois and William Monroe Trotter convened a meeting of black and white civil rights activists at Niagara Falls and issued a manifesto calling for the end to racial segregation, full voting rights for African American men and women, and other clear social and economic rights. The Niagara Movement led to the ultimate creation of the National Association for Advancement of Colored People (NAACP) in 1909 at a conference in New York City. A year before, a race riot had occurred in Springfield, Illinois, the home of Abraham Lincoln and the first Northern city in decades to experience racial unrest. It prompted the NAACP's creation, and the organization became a focal point for black rights throughout the 20th century.

The efforts and sacrifice of African Americans, both in leadership and the general population, met with little support or changes of attitude among the broader society. Segregation and stark racism persisted throughout the new century. Prompted by Northern indifference and white Southern studied practice, blacks remained "other Americans." As late as Franklin Roosevelt's administrations in the 1930s, little had changed. A. Philip Randolph, an African American labor union leader during the Roosevelt era, found little support from FDR and only sympathy from Eleanor Roosevelt. The "modern" civil rights movement would not begin until after World War II.

Women's Rights

The initial goal of women's rights in the United States focused on the right to vote. The suffragette movement began in the 1840s and accelerated after the Civil War. Leaders such as Susan B. Anthony, Elizabeth Cady Stanton, and others organized various groups to agitate for the vote. In 1875, in the *Minor v. Happersett* ruling, the Supreme Court determined the "right to vote" was not protected by the Fourteenth Amendment. It led various and divided suffrage groups to unify, and they created the National American Woman Suffrage Association (NAWSA) in 1890. NAWSA served as the spear point of the suffragette movement throughout the early 1900s. Similar to African Americans, they faced initial disinterest, criticism, and hostility. As late as 1912, only nine states, all in the West, granted women the franchise, but over the years, public attitudes changed enough to lead to ratification of the Nineteenth Amendment in August 1920, securing women's right to vote throughout the United States. Ironically, African American women never fully gained voting rights until the 1960s.

While voting rights served as the first wave of the feminist movement, other economic and social equality issues for women remained an ongoing battle. Margaret Sanger's efforts to provide "productive rights" for women, equal pay, and other rights all faced resistance throughout the first half of the century. Eleanor Roosevelt had supported the voting rights amendment and sympathized with other aspects of the women's movement, but her husband rarely considered them during his political career. If women in the workforce gained as a result of New Deal legislation to protect unions, it was coincidental as a gender issue. Females still made less than men.

Progressive Era

The organizations that emerged to demand civil rights for African Americans and women were part of a broader reform movement. From the turn of the century to the end of World War I, the Progressive reform movement played a seminal role in changing American attitudes about the future of the nation as it entered the new century. In a grassroots, uncoordinated, middle-class conclusion, progressives believed that three basic problems confronted the nation. First, the industrial revolution had placed too much wealth and power in the hands of a few owners, who showed no fundamental concern for workers or consumers. Second, government, at all levels, proved unresponsive to the people. In many respects, it proved incompetent or corrupt and in the pocket of big business robber barons. And, third, progressives believed that the nation needed to develop a social conscience to defend and protect the rights and opportunities of those most harmed by the rapid changes occurring in the early 1900s.

Progressives failed to agree on the best methods to address and correct those concerns. Radicals, moderates, conservatives, liberals, Republicans, Democrats, socialists, and communists all argued progressive ideas, but they possessed different ways to create policy. The Republican and Democratic Parties ultimately filtered the basic concerns through their own broad constituencies and limited the influence of less mainstream solutions. While an Old Guard conservative group in the Republican Party sought to block any aspect of reform, it failed to stem the tide of progressive thinking and action.

At the municipal, county, and state levels, new and younger elected and hired officials, as well as private charities, worked to change the status quo. What Progressive reform determined, at almost all levels, centered on the conclusion that free market industrial capitalism had become too powerful and needed oversight and regulations to control its worst aspects. Individuals could not do so. Only government could provide a balance that allowed the marketplace to prosper and, at the same time, protect the workers and consumers who made that prosperity possible. Socialists, communists, and other progressive factions disagreed, but the two major parties pursued policies that supported free enterprise capitalism while acting to curb its increasing power.

From 1901 until 1920, three progressive presidents occupied the White House: Theodore Roosevelt (1901–1909), William Howard Taft (1909–1913), and Woodrow Wilson (1913–1921). The two Republicans and a Democrat had different approaches to reform, but they sought similar goals and objectives. The three leaders ran against each other in the 1912 presidential election, and Eugene Debs, the fourth candidate, was a Socialist Party leader.

Progressive reform, at the national level, produced four constitutional amendments: the Sixteenth (graduated personal income tax) and Seventeenth (popular election of U.S. senators) Amendments in 1913, the Eighteenth Amendment (Prohibition) in 1919, and the Nineteenth Amendment (female franchise) in 1920. At the same time, the Pure Food and Drug Act (1906) and other congressional legislation acted to protect consumers and workers. An early example of progressive action occurred at the local level when Jane Addams and Ellen Gates Starr opened Hull House in Chicago as a settlement home for immigrant women in 1889.

Their work had a major influence on Eleanor Roosevelt, who became involved and was an advocate for similar private charitable programs.

The reform movement created a major shift in thinking in the United States. It did not resolve every economic, political, and social problem in the country. Racism, sexism, and other forms of oppression continued to exist. It did, however, produce tangible results and drew attention to what Abraham Lincoln had termed "the better angels of our nature." It certainly influenced Franklin Roosevelt, whose political mentors, from Endicott Peabody at Groton prep school to Woodrow Wilson in the White House, had shaped his own progressive thinking.

The New Deal developed, in every respect, because Franklin Roosevelt believed that government could redress the balance that progressives hoped to achieve. The Great Depression gave him the perfect opportunity to pursue the goals they sought.

Foreign Policy

U.S. foreign policy had followed a long historical path of isolationism since George Washington's farewell address. The term did not suggest complete disinterest in international relations. Rather, it sought to prevent diplomatic and military alliances with foreign governments, particularly European states. Americans could and would trade with other nations and conduct other forms of contact, but it avoided direct alliances with them. Even during World War I, the United States fought as an associate power with the enemies of Germany.

Woodrow Wilson's efforts to join the United States to the League of Nations provoked a heated debate that hinged on the country's traditional isolationist history. The Senate's refusal to follow Wilson's lead proved how deeply the tradition had persuaded most Americans. Yet, by the second decade of the 20th century, the nation had become a world power, and some political leaders, including FDR, had begun to question the "isolationist impulse." He supported Wilson and maintained that position during the 1920 elections. Whether President Wilson, his relative Theodore Roosevelt, or other influences shaped his thinking, FDR pursued an internationalist perspective throughout his long career as chief executive. The outbreak of World War II provided the ultimate litmus test to follow a path of direct military alliances with other powers.

The American people, however, initially seemed unwilling to support the president. During the 1920s and 1930s, Republican Congresses had passed a series of Neutrality Acts to avoid the nation's being dragged into another war, as it had in 1917. Gerald P. Nye, a Republican senator from North Dakota, chaired a committee that blamed U.S. involvement in World War I on munitions manufacturers and other business leaders seeking profits. That Nye Committee helped prompt the neutrality legislation that blocked FDR from assuming a more direct U.S. response to ally with or even aid nations fighting against Germany, Japan, and Italy. While Roosevelt ultimately convinced Americans to support an "all aid short of war" policy, as late as November 1941, most of the country still hoped to keep the nation out of direct conflict.

The Japanese attack on Pearl Harbor in December 1941 changed American policy. The United States joined the war against the Axis powers as an active ally. During the conflict, as FDR met with other world leaders in the struggle, he made clear that the United States would lead the effort to create a United Nations organization and play a major role in postwar international affairs. The legacy of isolationism may have continued to influence the country; however, the hardcore commitment to that thinking had ended on December 7, 1941, and FDR had played the key role in ending it.

Conclusions

When Franklin Roosevelt died in Warm Springs, Georgia, in the spring of 1945, his life had dramatically changed from his patrician boyhood in Hyde Park, New York, the United States and its citizens had changed with him. Many of those shifts in politics, economics, and social concerns he had played a role in shaping. Others, in science, technology, and cultural innovations and offerings, he had not. Yet, FDR popularized some of those discoveries and their uses. His fireside chats, broadcast over commercial radio, utilized the new technology to significant advantage.

He even made the 5:00 p.m. cocktail gathering a trend that many Americans adopted. The use of new medicines and new weapons, even splitting the atom to produce a destructive force unknown until 1945, all evolved during the nation's massive commitment to wage war during his presidency. And from the White House, during that war, Roosevelt encouraged the public to continue going to movies and ballparks to enjoy the benefits of the nation's popular cultural options.

More than any of those influences, however, Franklin Roosevelt's presidency made major alterations in the nation's political and economic present and future, and those changes appeared to contradict his upbringing. FDR's actions as a political leader made little sense given his background of wealth and privilege as a boy and young man. In fact, many of the men and women in that circle of American elites despised him for what he was doing as a president.

Between 1932 and 1945, Roosevelt made the federal government and the presidency more powerful and involved in the day-to-day life of the people than any leader in the nation's history. The laws, regulations, and programs that the FDR years produced brought the center of power to Washington, D.C. Federal bureaus, departments, and agencies grew exponentially to implement, oversee, and enforce the New Deal. Regardless of the Supreme Court's efforts to curb the influence of the other two branches, a Democratic Congress and White House managed to control and direct domestic affairs to a degree never seen in the United States. That influence has remained to the present day.

As late as 1920s, the United States still opted to pursue its foreign policy based on unilateral or isolationist traditions. Here again, a historical overview suggests how Franklin Roosevelt's long commitment to internationalism changed that perspective and tradition as a result of American involvement in World War II. The president's personal involvement with world leaders in summit diplomacy; the postwar creation of the League of Nations, where the United States played a leading role; and the evolution of a number of multilateral regional alliances, such as the Organization of American States (OAS), signified a new direction in the nation's position as a world power.

Historians could claim that during the lifetime of any president, noteworthy changes occur in a historical overview of his or her life. In Franklin Roosevelt's case, they appear especially significant.

ANALYTICAL ESSAY

Franklin Delano Roosevelt came to the presidency in March 1933 with a set of political principles that he developed through years of experience and thought. An advocate of progressive reform in American society, he believed that government should play a direct role in assuring and promoting the "general welfare." An internationalist in the field of foreign affairs, he concluded that the nation's isolationist traditions no longer applied in a world where the United States existed as a major power. While those convictions remained clear, FDR had also learned a hard truth during his long political career. To accomplish goals, one had to win elections. That required compromises, deals, and alliances with those who did not necessarily share Roosevelt's views. To try and understand President Roosevelt, it remains essential to view him as both an adroit, careful politician and a committed progressive leader.

The Great Depression and World War II gave Roosevelt a grand laboratory to bring the range of his political strengths and genuine principles to the test. As tragic and complex as both events were to many Americans who suffered the years of depression and war, FDR saw them as challenges to his skills in gaining power and using it correctly according to his personal beliefs and convictions.

The Great Depression (1929–1941) was the worst economic collapse in U.S. history. Major depressions in the 1870s and 1890s had struck the national economy; however, they had lasted fewer years before recovery, and their damage remained more limited in scope. While statistics cannot define the full measure of the 1929 collapse in human terms, they can provide an idea of the crisis FDR's administration faced when it took office in March 1933. They also suggest how and why he attacked the Great Depression as he did.

The signal for the coming depression occurred when the New York Stock Exchange collapsed in October 1929. The signs of a coming depression, however, existed earlier. Overproduction had led to large inventories; sales orders had declined, and new construction of businesses, factories, and warehouses had also slowed or stopped. In basic economic terms of supply and demand, the supply far exceeded consumer demand. With fewer orders for new products, businesses cut production, and that meant a rise in unemployment. Gross domestic product (GDP) dropped from $103.8 billion to $55.7 billion in three years.

Yet, the financial investment in the American economy continued at a rapid and often dangerous pace. Commercial banks and private investors still poured billions of dollars into the money markets, assuming, incorrectly, that the prosperity and growth of the early 1920s would continue. The market crash provided an alarm bell. Perpetual prosperity and growth were a myth. Between 1929 and 1932, money markets lost 80 percent of their value as stocks were sold by banks and individuals at an alarming rate. Thousands of banks, unable to pay their investors, closed. The men and women who had placed their money in savings accounts or who had privately invested in the markets also went broke. Many of those individuals were also unemployed. The financial crisis only added to the supply and demand slow down. Unemployment grew with the loss of business and the financial collapse. In 1929, the unemployment number rested at 3.1 percent. By 1931, it had climbed to 15.6 percent, and in 1933, it reached 24.7 percent.

Farmers suffered as well. As prices for their products fell, many tried to harvest more crops to pay debts, taxes, and living expenses. Consumers, however, could not afford to buy the goods, and thousands of farmers went bankrupt and lost their land. At the same time, a series of dust storms ravaged the Southern and Plains states ruining more than a million acres of farmland. The impact of the growing depression had affected virtually every aspect of American life.

Before his presidential campaign in 1932, Governor Franklin Roosevelt had begun to address the problems of the depression in New York. Working with two of his top aides, Harry Hopkins and Frances Perkins, he instituted a series of work relief programs to combat unemployment concerns in the state. The 1920s had produced an attitude of limited government interference in the nation's, and his state's, economic affairs. Roosevelt, however, challenged that idea as governor, and it would continue to the 1932 campaign and the White House. In a speech before the state legislature, FDR summed up his broad view that would underpin the New Deal: "When widespread economic conditions render large numbers of men and women incapable of supporting themselves or their families," he told the legislators, "aid must be extended by the government as a matter of social duty."

At the 1932 Democratic National Convention in Chicago, FDR became one of three potential nominees, along with Alfred Smith and John Nance Garner. He worked with two political advisers, Louis Howe and James Farley, to portray himself as a moderate, and FDR promised Garner the vice presidency to remove the Texas politician from competition. That guaranteed Roosevelt the nomination. He spent the campaign attacking his opponent, President Herbert Hoover, for doing nothing to combat the depression effectively. Hoover had relied on protective tariffs, accusing European nations of creating the worldwide depression, and asking Americans to depend on their tradition of "rugged individualism" to combat the crisis. While Roosevelt refused to offer specific plans or policies to deal with the crisis, he promised the nation a "new deal" in Washington. Critics should have paid attention to his remarks before the New York State Assembly.

The campaign notwithstanding, the public had become frightened and dispirited. If it had supported the Republicans in the 1920s for "peace, prosperity, and security," it punished them in 1932 for failure to deliver. FDR won 472 electoral and 22.8 million popular votes. Hoover managed only 59 electoral and 15.7 million popular votes. Democrats won control of the Senate, 59–36. The House Democrats won almost 100 new seats, 313–117. Franklin Roosevelt and the Democratic Party possessed a popular mandate, and they planned to use it to confront the depression.

To implement the New Deal and pursue its basic policies and create its program, FDR had to win elections, and he did so, four times. Democrats in the House and Senate also maintained working majorities through his presidency. During his first term, President Roosevelt and his administration created a coalition of voters that changed the Democratic Party and kept it in power for decades. He gained the support of state party organizations; big city machine politicians; blue-collar and union laborers; minority voters (racial, ethnic, and religious); white Southern Democrats; intellectuals and most pundits; and even many farmers. While the popular vote matters, and he never lost that, FDR realized that electoral votes determined victory. The Southern Democrats controlled 150 electoral votes in 13 states. Urban, industrial, blue-collar states from New Jersey and west to Michigan controlled 231 electoral votes in 7 states. In those states' urban centers, diverse ethnic and religious populations made up significant portions of voter registration. African Americans seeking work and leaving the South also added to FDR's coalition in the North. Those electoral votes alone could guarantee 381 for Roosevelt. Only a few more from agricultural areas or California (22) secured four terms as chief executive. The president and his advisers knew it and planned accordingly.

One of the saddest and most tragic examples of FDR's broker coalition existed in his failure to seriously address black civil rights. Although he spoke out against lynching, poll taxes, and other forms of violence and oppression in the South, the president never promoted serious legislation or executive action to attack the racism. Major African American leaders, such as Mary McLeod Bethune and A. Philipp Randolph, met with Eleanor Roosevelt in a confidential "kitchen cabinet," but she remained one of the few of her husband's advisers who pressed him to take action. In those instances, FDR's realistic politics trumped her hopes.

The relationship between Franklin and Eleanor is a key aspect of any political analysis of his presidency. Their marriage may never have been a passionate or romantic relationship, but Eleanor's discovery of her husband's affair with Lucy Mercer cooled it permanently. Yet, she remained in the marriage, supported and encouraged his rising political career, and became, herself, an active member of his administration. The first lady championed the broad liberal agendas of the New Deal, which included civil rights, child welfare, and housing reform. Franklin used her to give speeches and visit with voters. In 1936, she began to publish a daily, syndicated newspaper column, "My Day," to also promote her various positions. She had many critics on the right, in the South, and even with moderate Democrats. However, the public as a whole admired and respected her commitment and common touch.

The Roosevelt administration's attack on the Great Depression began on the day after his inaugural in March 1933. His cabinet consisted of secretaries with experience and broad ability. Cordell Hull would remain his secretary of state until 1944. Harold Ickes stayed until 1945, and Frances Perkins, the first female cabinet secretary and his adviser from his New York days, remained until 1945. FDR also encouraged a group of university professors from Columbia University to join his "brain trust." The group included Raymond Moley, Rexford Tugwell, and Adolf Berle. Along with Harry Hopkins, Frances Perkins, Louis Howe, and Harold Ickes, his longtime advisers, they made up the team that planned the First New Deal.

In effect, Tugwell and Berle convinced the president that free enterprise business leaders had failed in their responsibility to address the problems that the depression created. Former President Hoover had depended on that possibility, but the selfishness and profit motivation of business owners prevented any serious effort to deal with the crisis. Cities and states lacked the funding or the organization to fully address the problem as well. What the country needed, therefore, was a massive federal legislative and executive initiative to combat the many factors that had led to the depression. It resulted in the "First 100 Days" of FDR's New Deal.

Between March 8 and June 16, President Roosevelt and Congress planned and legislated 15 separate bills to initiate the various programs. FDR's major goals included back-to-work programs, protection for the savings and homes of those who had lost them, and relief for the poor. On March 9, Congress passed the Emergency Banking Act (EBA), closed the banks, encouraged investors to put money back into them, criminalized forms of hoarding, and passed the 1933 Banking Act that created the Federal Deposit Insurance Corporation (FDIC). It provided government protection for individual investments.

The Federal Emergency Relief Administration (FERA) spent $500 million opening soup kitchens, nursery schools, and job planning programs. The Civilian Conservation Corps (CCC) created 2.5 million jobs for young men doing infrastructure work. The Agricultural Adjustment Act (AAA) set quotas and price controls on agriculture products to create price adjustments to protect farmers and consumers. The National Industrial Recovery Act (NIRA) legislated similar forms of quotas and price controls for the industrial sector. And the Tennessee Valley Authority (TVA) began a project to damn the Tennessee River and provide electricity and jobs in the region. Critics and supporters referred to the legislations as "alphabet soup."

President Roosevelt went on radio on March 12 to explain his policies to the public, the first of his noted "fireside chats." Enthusiastic and positive, in his usual style, he explained the philosophy behind the legislation, although critics on the left complained he had not gone far enough. One of his most vocal critics, Huey Long, Louisiana's governor, demanded more investment in the people and threatened to campaign against FDR in 1936. Another, Father Charles Coughlin, had a syndicated nationwide radio program that initially supported FDR but turned against him in 1935. He developed the same views as Long. The right attacked him for assuming too much power in directing the economy. Republicans seethed at the cost of the programs, almost $9 billion by 1936, and argued that rising taxes and deficit spending had threatened the financial structure of the federal government. Roosevelt, with his broad popularity intact and a generally supportive Congress, could brush off the critics. He failed, however, to control the U.S. Supreme Court.

In 1935 and 1936, the Supreme Court decided three cases that declared much of the First New Deal unconstitutional. *Schechter Poultry v. U.S.* (1935), *U.S. v. Butler* (1936), and *Carter v. Carter Coal Company* (1936) determined that the Agricultural Adjustment Act and the National Industrial Recovery Act, in many of their critical components, gave the federal government authority over the economy that the Constitution did not permit. At the time, the Court had four conservative justices, Pierce Butler, James Clark McReynolds, George Sutherland, and William Van Devanter (the "Four Horseman"); three liberals, Louis Brandeis, Benjamin Cardoza, and Harlan Stone (the "Three Musketeers"); and two swing votes, Chief

Justice Charles Evans Hughes and Owen J. Roberts. The conservative judges were able to win majority decisions in all three cases, and only the *Carter* case was a 5–4 decision.

The decisions effectively hobbled the early New Deal, and Democrats slammed the Supreme Court for intruding in the efforts of Congress and the president to combat the problems of the depression. FDR was enraged and concocted a plan to deal with the Court that proved his first major failure as chief executive—the "court-packing plan." On February 5, 1937, several months after his comfortable reelection to a second term, FDR asked Congress to consider a law that would encourage Supreme Court justices to retire at age 70 with full pensions. If they did not, the president could nominate "assistant" justices, with full voting rights, to add new members to the Court. As six of the sitting justices were 70 years old or older, it would conceivably allow FDR to nominate replacements and increase the number of justices to 15. With a Democratic majority in the Senate, it would allow Roosevelt to pack the Court with his judges.

The president's reelection convinced him that he would have the support of Congress and the public. He did not. Senator Carter Glass was so sure of support for Roosevelt's proposed legislation in Congress that he quipped, "Why, if the President asked Congress to commit suicide tomorrow they'd do it." Equally sure of himself, FDR expressed the same confidence. Public opinion, however, began to question the proposal as a political maneuver, not a needed reform measure. By April, it seemed clear both sides looked for a compromise. The Court's swing voters won a majority decision that upheld the government's authority to operate the National Labor Relations Board (NLRB) and the Social Security Act. The legislature used those decisions to shelve FDR's plan. The president's failure ultimately worked to his benefit. He had, whether he wanted to or not, preserved the dignity and traditions of the third branch of government. During the next eight years, he was able to appoint four new justices without changing the makeup of the Court. By 1945, "his" judges were on the bench of the Supreme Court.

While the court-packing plan brewed and boiled over between 1935 and 1937, Franklin Roosevelt worked to win a second term as president. At the Democratic National Convention in Philadelphia, the party faithful renominated FDR and John Nance Garner to run against Alf Landon, the governor of Kansas, and Frank Knox, a prominent newspaper editor. With little chance of defeating FDR, Landon ran a dispirited, lackluster campaign and suffered a humiliating defeat. Roosevelt won 98 percent of the nation's electoral votes and 60.8 percent of the popular vote. Congress maintained sizable majorities in both houses. That powerful mandate probably convinced Roosevelt to develop the court-packing plan, but its failure did little to stall his enthusiasm during the next four years. In fact, the president had already begun to see the attack on the depression from a new perspective.

If FDR and his advisers had hoped to coordinate and control the nation's economic recovery from Washington through the broad regulations of the NIRA and AAA, the Supreme Court had checked that plan. At the same time, after four years, the depression still lingered. Unemployment had dropped to 15 percent in 1937, but it rose to 19 percent a year later. Industrial and agricultural production remained weak, and the nation's GDP rose only slightly during Roosevelt's first term. Former President Hoover had warned that the federal government could not regulate an end to the depression. In a capitalist economy, he warned, cycles of rise and decline in the marketplace remained a natural part of the system. The Great Depression may have been the worst downward cycle in U.S. history, but it would pass. The current president was no enemy of capitalism. On the contrary, FDR's socialist and communist critics attacked him for his continued commitment to the economic system. In his second term, what he began to focus on were policies that would safeguard and secure the public in cycles of depression during his tenure and in the future.

Most of those policies already existed as a result of the First New Deal, and the Supreme Court had not declared them unconstitutional. The Federal Banking Act (1933) created the Federal Deposit Insurance Corporation (FDIC). It guaranteed federal protection (up to $5,000) for those who deposited their money in banks. The 1933 creation of the Securities Exchange Commission (SEC) established new government safeguards to protect investors in the stock markets. In

1935, Congress passed the Social Securities Act. Under the act, beginning in 1937, the government would collect a tax from working Americans to create a federal fund to provide old age benefits, unemployment insurance, accident benefits for work-related injuries, financial support for dependent mothers and children, and support for the physically and mentally disabled. The Wagner Act (1935) legalized the right of labor unions to collectively bargain with business owners over wages, benefits, and other concerns. The act created the National Labor Relations Board (NLRB), a three-member board, to serve as the final arbiter in future labor disputes with owners.

While many, if not most, of the massive control and coordination programs of the New Deal had short lives and disappeared, the safeguard and security policies and laws of the New Deal remain as a substantial social and economic safety net to the present day. Roosevelt's ability to shift his emphasis and direction suggest his flexibility in dealing with the frustration of his battle with the Supreme Court as well as his understanding of how best to deal with the depression.

Still, the government's efforts to pay for any of the programs cost money, and the United States lacked the funds to do so. During his first two terms, Roosevelt tended to support a federal balanced budget. In 1929, the government had a surplus of $734 million. By 1932, it had a deficit of $2.7 billion. With fewer taxes coming from families and businesses during the depression, that deficit continued. The highest tax rate in 1930 was 25 percent. By 1936, it was 79 percent. Those increases failed to erase the deficit. A fiscal debate developed between Henry Morgenthau, the treasury secretary, and Harry Hopkins, FDR's closest adviser, over how to deal with the issue. Morgenthau favored traditional conservative views on a balanced budget. Hopkins and others were influenced by the British economist John Maynard Keynes, who advocated necessary "deficit spending" and the redistribution of taxes, requiring more from the wealthy. The Keynesian advocates won the debate.

To offset large deficit spending during hard times and limited revenue, Keynes and his supporters believed that when economic trends became profitable again, governments might increase taxes and pay down the deficits created during hard times.

Unfortunately, World War II intervened, and deficits continued to rise. During his second term, Franklin Roosevelt had made two important domestic decisions. He turned his attention to safeguard and secure New Deal initiatives and abandoned his initial idea to control and coordinate the economy. At the same time, he altered his belief in a balanced budget and accepted the views of Keynes. Increasingly, however, FDR's concerns focused on international relations and the U.S. role in world affairs.

Although the United States failed to join the League of Nations in 1919, it still played a unilateral role in shaping international relations. In 1921–1922, the United States signed naval arms limitation agreements with other nations and signed the Nine Power Treaty, which was designed to protect China's sovereignty. In 1928, Secretary of State Frank Kellogg joined with Aristides Briand of France to develop an international agreement, with a number of other states, to "outlaw aggressive war." The League of Nations still functioned, but it would shortly prove incapable of preventing the rise of countries led by aggressive new leaders espousing new ideologies. In 1922, Benito Mussolini's Fascist Party gained control of the Italian government. In 1933, Adolph Hitler and the Nazi Party in Germany also won power at the ballot box and turned that nation into a dictatorship within two years. Japanese military leaders, such as Tojo Hideki, were slowly eroding Japan's democracy, and the Japanese military began to direct its nation's policies.

Shortly, those new governments would engage in growing belligerent military action. The Italians invaded Ethiopia, Libya, and Somalia to establish power in North Africa. In 1931, Japan seized Manchuria, in Northern China, and, in 1937, began a war with China. During the Spanish Civil War (1932–1939), Italy and Germany aided General Francisco Franco, and the Soviet Union's dictator, Joseph Stalin, sent support to Franco's enemies. The international climate appeared dangerous and unclear, which was clearly not the intention of diplomatic efforts shaped in the 1920s.

Franklin Roosevelt had supported President Wilson's efforts to join the League of Nations, and he believed that the United States should play a more direct part in world affairs. Never a believer in unilateral diplomacy or isolationism, FDR realized, however, that a majority of Americans did support those goals. While he recognized the emerging threats developing on the world scene, his primary focus on the depression and the clear American attitude opposed to direct involvement in those crises made him cautious. On October 5, 1937, dedicating the opening of a new bridge in Chicago, FDR delivered a speech that clearly expressed his foreign policy position. He condemned the actions of aggressive nations (without naming them) and called for some form of "international quarantine." Public reaction appeared either disinterested or critical. The American people had elected FDR to a second term to deal with the depression, not foreign affairs.

Congress agreed. In 1934, Republican senator Gerald P. Nye of North Dakota chaired a series of hearings on the causes that led America into World War I. The Nye Committee concluded that war profiteers and bankers, not legitimate foreign policy concerns, had motivated U.S. involvement. Congressional legislation between 1935 and 1937 created a series of Neutrality Acts to prevent the United States from pursuing policies it believed had drawn the nation into war in 1917. Those included prohibiting loans or supplies to nations at war, banning Americans from traveling on ships engaged in conflict, and other stipulations. Whether one termed the idea isolationism, unilateralism, or nonintervention, Congress sent a clear message that the United States should avoid involvement in the growing world conflict.

When Germany invaded Poland in September 1939, World War II began in Europe. France and England declared war on Germany. Italy and Japan were already allied with Hitler and engaged in their own conflicts in North Africa and China. The Soviet Union had signed a nonaggression agreement with Germany, but it remained a fragile, untrustworthy pact. In the Spring of 1940, an election year in the United States, the Nazis invaded France and the Low Countries and in a short time conquered most of Western Europe. Throughout the summer, German aircraft began a relentless bombing attack on England—the Battle of Britain.

Roosevelt hesitated to seek a third term in 1940. He recognized the long-standing tradition of a two-term limit. The fall of France and the attack on Great Britain, however, convinced him that he was the only one with the background and experience to deal with the world situation. Then, too, as an astute politician, he knew he would win. He took the Democratic nomination on the first ballot at its convention in Chicago and defeated his Republican opponent, Wendell Willkie, easily, but not with the large majorities he had won in 1932 and 1936. While the nation still lingered in the depression, its voters also seemed concerned about the world crisis. Yet, the powerful Roosevelt coalition held, and FDR could focus on foreign affairs.

Between 1939 and 1941, an intense political debate developed in the United States between isolationists and interventionists concerning the U.S. role in the war. Lobby groups such as the America First Committee supported the Neutrality Acts and demanded that the United States stay out of the conflict. The Committee to Defend America by Aiding the Allies supported FDR's efforts to play a more direct role against the Axis powers of Germany, Italy, and Japan.

One month after his election, on December 17, 1940, FDR held a press conference at the White House and announced a new Lend-Lease policy to aid the allies. In September, he had previously approved a "destroyer for bases" deal with Britain. The United States would supply the British with 50 older destroyers, and England would lease some of its bases in the Bahamas, Jamaica, Newfoundland, and elsewhere to the United States. Roosevelt suggested the idea of a Lend-Lease system to provide more aid and assistance. He used a simple analogy, remarking that a good neighbor would lend his garden hose to put out a neighbor's house fire. It would not only be the kind thing to do, but it would also prevent his own house from catching fire. The Lend-Lease Act became law in March 1941. Besides Britain, the United States offered the option to other nations at war with the Axis powers.

In Asia, the administration used economic sanctions and provided military aid to China to thwart Japanese actions in the Far East. The United States froze Japan's assets and embargoed the sale of aviation parts and fuel to the Japanese. Roosevelt may have hoped those pressures would lead Japan to end the war against the Chinese, but it failed. The oil embargo, however, put fatal burdens on the Japanese military. It either had to find another source for oil or give in to American economic pressure. It opted for the former, but that also influenced the decision to attack the U.S. fleet at Pearl Harbor.

By the fall of 1941, President Roosevelt had eliminated most of the restrictions of the Neutrality Acts and gained the support of the American people for an "all aid short of war" plan for the United States to aid the enemies of the Axis nations. The German invasion of the Soviet Union in June 1941 had increased the world threat and helped FDR's policies. On the other hand, most public opinion opposed direct U.S. involvement in the war. The Japanese attack on Pearl Harbor, Hawaii, on December 1941 changed American opinion.

In an address to a joint session of Congress on December 8, FDR charged that December 7, 1941, would remain "a date which will live in infamy" and asked for a declaration of war against Japan. By a vote of 82–0 in the Senate and 388-1 in the House (Republican Jeanette Rankin of Montana, an avowed pacifist, was the only dissenter), the United States entered World War II. Because of alliances with Japan, Germany and Italy declared war on the United States, and the United States reciprocated on December 11.

While no facts exist to verify the remarks, anecdotal history suggests that two U.S. enemies made prophetic remarks in early December. Admiral Ioroku Yamata, who had planned the attack at Pearl Harbor, is reputed to have said, "I fear all we have done is to awaken a sleeping giant and fill him with a terrible resolve." Albert Speer, Hitler's wartime production minister, confronted the Nazi leader and said, "We have lost the war."

Sixteen million men and women served in the U.S. armed forces during the war, and the U.S. industrial capacity dwarfed the other nations engaged in the conflict as its military production exploded between 1941 and 1945. The government spent more than $100 billion (in 1940s revenue value). Unemployment virtually disappeared as men and women flooded the factories to build the ships, planes, and equipment to supply American and Allied forces. While problems, mistakes, and actual corruption developed in the war industry, the Roosevelt administration's cooperation and support of private businesses worked well, and the bureaus of government tasked with that alliance did their job as President Roosevelt concentrated on wartime diplomacy.

One tragic decision would mar an otherwise positive presidential commitment to victory. On February 19, 1942, at the urging of California's governor and attorney general, FDR issued Executive Order 9066. It called for the internment of Japanese residents along the nation's West Coast as potential fifth column supporters of Japan. More than 100,000 Japanese, many American citizens, were sent to internment camps, even though no evidence existed that they posed a national security threat. The Supreme Court found the action legal, but many Americans, then and now, considered it more a reflection of blatant racism rather than a national security reality.

Even before war began, Roosevelt met Prime Minister Winston Churchill in August 1941 in Newfoundland. The conference produced the Atlantic Charter, basically a reaffirmation of Woodrow Wilson's Fourteen Points issued in 1917, declaring that Great Britain and the United States had no territorial or self-interested goals other than peace and the creation of a postwar United Nations organization. Months earlier, in his January 1941 State of the Union message, FDR's Four Freedoms remarks claimed U.S. goals sought a world that would guarantee freedom of speech, worship, and the elimination of want and fear. Both the Four Freedoms and Atlantic Charter aimed to establish lofty moral and ethical reasons for combating the Axis powers. There is little question that FDR saw the value of the declarations and clearly President Wilson was on his mind as he did so.

Roosevelt and Churchill met again in Washington with their staffs between December 22, 1941, and January 14, 1942. They determined to make Europe and the defeat of Germany the primary focus of the war. Japan would remain a second front. While many Americans wanted to focus on the Japanese, for obvious reasons, the strategic view prevailed. Thus began a long, deadly military effort that slowly led to Allied successes and were punctuated by Roosevelt's summit diplomacy to achieve final victory.

After a successful invasion of North Africa in 1943, driving German and Italian forces from the region, FDR and Churchill met at Casablanca, Morocco, in January 1943. Roosevelt announced he would accept no less than "unconditional surrender" from the Axis powers. He would not allow the kind of negotiated armistice that had ended World War I that had allowed Nazism to emerge in Germany. The two men discussed the time for an invasion of the European mainland in France, but the British convinced the Americans to secure the Mediterranean and Italy first. Invasions of Sicily and Italy began shortly.

Soviet premier Joseph Stalin criticized the decision and developed a serious distrust of British and U.S. motives. Suffering hundreds of thousands of casualties and fighting against almost 80 percent of the Nazi military, he could not accept the argument that a seaborne invasion of France required more time, supplies, and preparation. It remained a serious sore point throughout the war.

In November 1943, FDR met with Churchill and China's leader, Chiang Kai-shek, in Cairo, Egypt, to discuss the war in Asia. By late 1943, the United States had gained naval supremacy in the Pacific, and U.S. forces were "island hopping" across the central Pacific toward Japan, moving close enough to begin a major strategic bombing campaign against the Japanese homeland. FDR assured China's leader of continued support and continued recognition of his government in the postwar era. Roosevelt then flew to Tehran, Iran, where he had his first meeting with Stalin. FDR and Churchill briefed him on Operation Overlord, the Normandy invasion of France, and the president returned home convinced he could work with the Soviet leader.

The year 1944 was an election year. Throughout the spring and summer, as U.S. military successes continued, it appeared obvious that FDR would win nomination and a fourth term. Advisers worried about his health, and some predicted he would not live through to its end. He selected a relative unknown as a running mate, Senator Harry Truman of Missouri, and he again easily defeated his Republican opponent, Thomas Dewey, New York's governor. Moving into 1945, FDR continued a focused pace. In his first inaugural, he spoke of a "Good Neighbor" initiative toward Latin America, an idea that President Hoover had

begun. Through all his other issues and concerns, Roosevelt pursued "Good Neighborism" within the hemisphere, and a number of Latin American states allied with the United States during the war,

Ominously, President Roosevelt had agreed to fund a secret project to develop an atomic weapon. In December 1942, the top-secret Manhattan Project grew into a huge American-British project in Los Alamos, New Mexico, and elsewhere, and that finally resulted in a usable nuclear bomb in June–July 1945. After the 1944 victory, FDR still had no idea whether the project would prove successful. His successor, Harry Truman, would have to decide how to employ the weapon. After Italy and Germany surrendered, Japan remained the only enemy.

Between February 4 and 11, 1945, President Roosevelt flew to Yalta, in the Soviet Crimea, for a last meeting with Churchill and Stalin. They finalized postwar goals. Russia would declare war on Japan as soon as Germany surrendered. The Soviets also pledged to conduct free, democratic elections in areas of Eastern Europe they had freed from German control. The Allies would divide Germany into four military occupation zones. Russia would provide no direct support for the Communist revolution in China trying to overthrow Chiang Kai-shek. And Russia would support the creation of a postwar United Nations. Roosevelt returned to the United States persuaded that Stalin would uphold his pledges. With the exception of elections in Eastern Europe, he did so.

Cold War critics have suggested that FDR was too ill at Yalta to prove an effective summit diplomat, but there was little he or anyone could have done to block the Soviet Union, with more than 100 divisions in the East, from imposing its political will in the region. Whether he realized that or overlooked it still provokes debate.

President Roosevelt gave his last formal speech to Congress on the Yalta Conference on March 1, 1945. Fewer than six weeks later, he died at Warm Springs, Georgia, on April 12.

Jolyon P. Girard

Further Reading

Badger, Anthony. 2002. *The New Deal: The Depression Years, 1933–1940*. Chicago: Hill & Wang.

Brands, H. W. 2008. *Traitor to His Class: The Privileged and Radical Presidency of Franklin D. Roosevelt*. New York: Doubleday.

Burns, James MacGregor. 1956. *Roosevelt: The Lion and the Fox, 1882–1940*. New York: Harcourt, Brace and Company.

Burns, James MacGregor. 1970. *Roosevelt: The Soldier of Freedom, 1941–1945*. New York: Harcourt, Brace and Company.

Cole, Wayne S. 1983. *Roosevelt and the Isolationists*. Lincoln: University of Nebraska Press.

Dallek, Robert. 2017. *Franklin D. Roosevelt: A Political Life*. New York: Random House.

Franklin D. Roosevelt Papers. n.d. Franklin D. Roosevelt Presidential Library and Museum. http://www.fdrlibrary.marist.edu/archives/collections/list.html.

Goodwin, Doris Kearns. 1994. *No Ordinary Life: Franklin and Eleanor: The Homefront in World War II*. New York: Simon and Schuster.

Herman, Arthur. 2012. *Freedom's Forge: How American Business Produced Victory in World War II*. New York: Random House.

Shesol, Jeff. 2010. *Supreme Power: Franklin Roosevelt vs. the Supreme Court*. New York: W. W. Norton & Company.

First Inaugural Address (March 4, 1933)

President Roosevelt had easily defeated incumbent President Herbert Hoover in the 1932 election. The United States, in the midst of the most severe economic depression in its history, looked to the new president for some form of optimism regarding the future. From the steps of the U.S. Capitol, he delivered his address with the famous remark in his opening paragraph: "the only thing we have to fear is fear itself."

This is a day of national consecration. And I am certain that on this day my fellow Americans expect that on my induction into the Presidency I will address them with a candor and a decision which the present situation of our people impels. This is preeminently the time to speak the truth, the whole truth, frankly and boldly. Nor need we shrink from honestly facing conditions in our country today. This great Nation will endure as it has endured, will revive and will prosper. So, first of all, let me assert my firm belief that the only thing we have to fear is fear itself—nameless, unreasoning, unjustified terror which paralyzes needed efforts to convert retreat into advance. In every dark hour of our national life a leadership of frankness and vigor has met with that understanding and support of the people themselves which is essential to victory. I am convinced that you will again give that support to leadership in these critical days.

In such a spirit on my part and on yours we face our common difficulties. They concern, thank God, only material things. Values have shrunken to fantastic levels; taxes have risen; our ability to pay has fallen; government of all kinds is faced by serious curtailment of income; the means of exchange are frozen in the currents of trade; the withered leaves of industrial enterprise lie on every side; farmers find no markets for their produce; the savings of many years in thousands of families are gone.

More important, a host of unemployed citizens face the grim problem of existence, and an equally great number toil with little return. Only a foolish optimist can deny the dark realities of the moment.

Yet our distress comes from no failure of substance. We are stricken by no plague of locusts. Compared with the perils which our forefathers conquered because they believed and were not afraid, we have still much to be thankful for. Nature still offers her bounty and human efforts have multiplied it. Plenty is at our doorstep, but a generous use of it languishes in the very sight of the supply. Primarily this is because rulers of the exchange of mankind's goods have failed through their own stubbornness and their own incompetence, have admitted their failure, and have abdicated. Practices of the unscrupulous money changers stand indicted in the court of public opinion, rejected by the hearts and minds of men.

True they have tried, but their efforts have been cast in the pattern of an outworn tradition. Faced by failure of credit they have proposed only the lending of more money. Stripped of the lure of profit by which to induce our people to follow their false leadership, they have resorted to exhortations, pleading tearfully for restored confidence. They know only the rules of a generation of self-seekers. They have no vision, and when there is no vision the people perish.

The money changers have fled from their high seats in the temple of our civilization. We may now restore that temple to the ancient truths. The measure of the restoration lies in the extent to which we apply social values more noble than mere monetary profit.

Happiness lies not in the mere possession of money; it lies in the joy of achievement, in the thrill of creative effort. The joy and moral stimulation of work no longer must be forgotten in the mad chase of evanescent profits. These dark days will be worth all they cost us if they teach us that our true destiny is not to be ministered unto but to minister to ourselves and to our fellow men.

Recognition of the falsity of material wealth as the standard of success goes hand in hand with the abandonment of the false belief that public office and high political position are to be valued only by the standards of pride of place and personal profit; and there must be an end to a conduct in banking and in business which too often has given to a sacred trust the likeness of callous and selfish wrongdoing. Small wonder that confidence languishes, for it thrives only on honesty, on honor, on the sacredness of obligations, on faithful protection, on unselfish performance; without them it cannot live. Restoration calls, however, not for changes in ethics alone. This Nation asks for action, and action now.

Our greatest primary task is to put people to work. This is no unsolvable problem if we face it wisely and courageously. It can be accomplished in part by direct recruiting by the Government itself, treating the task as we would treat the emergency of a war, but at the same time, through this employment, accomplishing greatly needed projects to stimulate and reorganize the use of our natural resources.

Hand in hand with this we must frankly recognize the overbalance of population in our industrial centers and, by engaging on a national scale in a redistribution, endeavor to provide a better use of the land for those best fitted for the land. The task can be helped by definite efforts to raise the values of agricultural products and with this the power to purchase the output of our cities. It can be helped by preventing realistically the tragedy of the growing loss through foreclosure of our small homes and our farms. It can be helped by insistence that the Federal, State, and local governments act forthwith on the demand that their cost be drastically reduced. It can be helped by the unifying of relief activities which today are often scattered, uneconomical, and unequal. It can be helped by national planning for and supervision of all forms of transportation and of communications and other utilities which have a definitely public character. There are many ways in which it can be helped, but it can never be helped merely by talking about it. We must act and act quickly.

Finally, in our progress toward a resumption of work we require two safeguards against a return of the evils of the old order: there must be a strict supervision of all banking and credits and investments, so that there will be an end to speculation with other people's money; and there must be provision for an adequate but sound currency.

These are the lines of attack. I shall presently urge upon a new Congress, in special session, detailed measures for their fulfillment, and I shall seek the immediate assistance of the several States.

Through this program of action, we address ourselves to putting our own national house in order and making income balance outgo. Our international trade relations, though vastly important, are in point of time and necessity secondary to the establishment of a sound national economy. I favor as a practical policy the putting of first things first. I shall spare no effort to restore world trade by international economic readjustment, but the emergency at home cannot wait on that accomplishment.

The basic thought that guides these specific means of national recovery is not narrowly nationalistic. It is the insistence, as a first consideration, upon the interdependence of the various elements in and parts of the United States—a recognition of the old and permanently important manifestation of the American spirit of the pioneer. It is the way to recovery. It is the immediate way. It is the strongest assurance that the recovery will endure.

In the field of world policy, I would dedicate this Nation to the policy of the good neighbor—the neighbor who resolutely respects himself and, because he does so, respects the rights of others—the neighbor who respects his obligations and respects the sanctity of his agreements in and with a world of neighbors.

If I read the temper of our people correctly, we now realize as we have never realized before our interdependence on each other; that we cannot merely take but we must give as well; that if we are to go forward, we must move as a trained and loyal army willing to sacrifice for the good of a common discipline, because without such discipline no progress is made, no leadership becomes effective. We are, I know, ready and willing to submit our lives and property to such discipline, because it makes possible a leadership which aims at a larger good. This I propose to offer, pledging that the larger purposes will bind upon us all as a sacred obligation with a unity of duty hitherto evoked only in time of armed strife.

With this pledge taken, I assume unhesitatingly the leadership of this great army of our people dedicated to a disciplined attack upon our common problems.

Action in this image and to this end is feasible under the form of government which we have inherited from our ancestors. Our Constitution is so simple and practical that it is possible always to meet extraordinary needs by changes in emphasis and arrangement without loss of essential form. That is why our constitutional system has proved itself the most superbly enduring political mechanism the modern world has produced. It has met every stress of vast expansion of territory, of foreign wars, of bitter internal strife, of world relations.

It is to be hoped that the normal balance of Executive and legislative authority may be wholly adequate to meet the unprecedented task before us. But it may be that an unprecedented demand and need for undelayed action may call for temporary departure from that normal balance of public procedure.

I am prepared under my constitutional duty to recommend the measures that a stricken Nation in the midst of a stricken world may require. These measures, or such other measures as the Congress may build out of its experience and wisdom, I shall seek, within my constitutional authority, to bring to speedy adoption.

But in the event that the Congress shall fail to take one of these two courses, and in the event that the national emergency is still critical, I shall not evade the clear course of duty that will then confront me. I shall ask the Congress for the one remaining instrument to meet the crisis—broad Executive power to wage a war against the emergency, as great as the power that would be given to me if we were in fact invaded by a foreign foe.

For the trust reposed in me I will return the courage and the devotion that befit the time. I can do no less.

We face the arduous days that lie before us in the warm courage of national unity; with the clear consciousness of seeking old and precious moral values; with the clean satisfaction that comes from the stern performance of duty by old and young alike. We aim at the assurance of a rounded and permanent national life.

We do not distrust the future of essential democracy. The people of the United States have not failed. In their need they have registered a mandate that they want direct, vigorous action. They have asked for discipline and direction under leadership. They have made me the present instrument of their wishes. In the spirit of the gift I take it.

In this dedication of a Nation we humbly ask the blessing of God. May He protect each and every one of us. May He guide me in the days to come.

Source: Roosevelt, Franklin D. "Inaugural Address." March 4, 1933. Franklin D. Roosevelt Library, First Carbon Files, 1933–1945. National Archives.

"Quarantine" Speech (October 5, 1937)

Less than a year after winning a second term, President Roosevelt spoke in Chicago at the dedication of a new bridge over Lake Shore Drive. Calling attention to the aggressive national behavior of Germany, Japan, and Italy, he intimated that their actions were leading to the probability of global conflict. Although he did not specifically name those states, he called for an international "quarantine" to halt their behavior. The public response to his remarks was not positive. Most Americans wanted Roosevelt to continue to deal with domestic issues.

The political situation in the world, which of late has been growing progressively worse, is such as to cause grave concern and anxiety to all the peoples and nations who wish to live in peace and amity with their neighbors.

Some fifteen years ago the hopes of mankind for a continuing era of international peace were raised to great heights when more than sixty nations solemnly pledged themselves not to resort to arms in furtherance of their national aims and policies. The high aspirations expressed in the Briand-Kellogg Peace Pact and the hopes for peace thus raised have of late given way to a haunting fear of calamity. The present reign of terror and international lawlessness began a few years ago.

It began through unjustified interference in the internal affairs of other nations or the invasion of alien territory in violation of treaties; and has now reached a stage where the very foundations of civilization are seriously threatened. The landmarks and traditions which have marked the progress of civilization toward a condition of law, order and justice are being wiped away.

Without a declaration of war and without warning or justification of any kind, civilians, including vast numbers of women and children, are being ruthlessly murdered with bombs from the air. In times of so-called peace, ships are being attacked and sunk by submarines without cause or notice. Nations are fomenting and taking sides in civil warfare in nations that have never done them any harm. Nations claiming freedom for themselves deny it to others.

Innocent peoples, innocent nations, are being cruelly sacrificed to a greed for power and supremacy which is devoid of all sense of justice and humane considerations.

To paraphrase a recent author "perhaps we foresee a time when men, exultant in the technique of homicide, will rage so hotly over the world that every precious thing will be in danger, every book and picture and harmony, every treasure garnered through two millenniums, the small, the delicate, the defenseless— all will be lost or wrecked or utterly destroyed."

If those things come to pass in other parts of the world, let no one imagine that America will escape, that America may expect mercy, that this Western Hemisphere will not be attacked and that it will continue tranquilly and peacefully to carry on the ethics and the arts of civilization.

If those days come "there will be no safety by arms, no help from authority, no answer in science. The storm will rage till every flower of culture is trampled and all human beings are leveled in a vast chaos."

If those days are not to come to pass—if we are to have a world in which we can breathe freely and live in amity without fear—the peace-loving nations must make a concerted effort to uphold laws and principles on which alone peace can rest secure.

The peace-loving nations must make a concerted effort in opposition to those violations of treaties and those ignorings of humane instincts which today are creating a state of international anarchy and instability from which there is no escape through mere isolation or neutrality.

Those who cherish their freedom and recognize and respect the equal right of their neighbors to be free and live in peace, must work together for the triumph of law and moral principles in order that peace, justice and confidence may prevail in the world. There must be a return to a belief in the pledged word, in the value of a signed treaty. There must be recognition of the fact that national morality is as vital as private morality.

A bishop wrote me the other day: "It seems to me that something greatly needs to be said in behalf of ordinary humanity against the present practice of carrying the horrors of war to helpless civilians, especially women and children. It may be that such a protest might be regarded by many, who claim to be realists, as futile, but may it not be that the heart of mankind is so filled with horror at the present needless suffering that that force could be mobilized in sufficient volume to lessen such cruelty in the days ahead. Even though it may take twenty years, which God forbid, for civilization to make effective its corporate protest against this barbarism, surely strong voices may hasten the day."

There is a solidarity and interdependence about the modern world, both technically and morally, which makes it impossible for any nation completely to isolate itself from economic and political upheavals in the rest of the world, especially when such upheavals appear to be spreading and not declining. There can be no stability or peace either within nations or between nations except under laws and moral standards adhered to by all International anarchy destroys every foundation for peace. It jeopardizes either the immediate or the future security of every nation, large or small. It is, therefore, a matter of vital interest and concern to the people of the United States that the sanctity of international treaties and the maintenance of international morality be restored.

The overwhelming majority of the peoples and nations of the world today want to live in peace. They seek the removal of barriers against trade. They want to exert themselves in industry, in agriculture and in business, that they may increase their wealth through the production of wealth-producing goods rather than striving to produce military planes and bombs and machine guns and cannon for the destruction of human lives and useful property.

In those nations of the world which seem to be piling armament on armament for purposes of aggression, and those other nations which fear acts of aggression against them and their security, a very high proportion of their national income is being spent directly for armaments. It runs from thirty to as high as fifty percent. We are fortunate. The proportion that we in the United States spend is far less—eleven or twelve percent.

How happy we are that the circumstances of the moment permit us to put our money into bridges and boulevards, dams and reforestation, the conservation of our soil and many other kinds of useful works rather than into huge standing armies and vast supplies of implements of war.

I am compelled and you are compelled, nevertheless, to look ahead. The peace, the freedom and the security of ninety percent of the population of the world is being jeopardized by the remaining ten percent who are threatening a breakdown of all international order and law. Surely the ninety percent who want to live in peace under law and in accordance with moral standards that have received almost universal acceptance through the centuries, can and must find some way to make their will prevail.

The situation is definitely of universal concern. The questions involved relate not merely to violations of specific provisions of particular treaties; they are questions of war and of peace, of international law and especially of principles of humanity. It is true that they involve definite violations of agreements, and especially of the Covenant of the League of Nations, the Briand-Kellogg Pact and the Nine Power Treaty. But they also involve problems of world economy, world security and world humanity.

It is true that the moral consciousness of the world must recognize the importance of removing injustices and well-founded grievances; but at the same time it must be aroused to the cardinal necessity of honoring sanctity of treaties, of respecting the rights and liberties of others and of putting an end to acts of international aggression.

It seems to be unfortunately true that the epidemic of world lawlessness is spreading. When an epidemic of physical disease starts to spread, the community approves and joins in a quarantine of the patients in order to protect the health of the community against the spread of the disease.

It is my determination to pursue a policy of peace. It is my determination to adopt every practicable measure to avoid involvement in war. It ought to be inconceivable that in this modern era, and in the face of experience, any nation could be so foolish and ruthless as to run the risk of plunging the whole world into war by invading and violating, in contravention of solemn treaties, the territory of other nations that have done them no real harm and are too weak to protect themselves adequately. Yet the peace of the world and the welfare and security of every nation, including our own, is today being threatened by that very thing.

No nation which refuses to exercise forbearance and to respect the freedom and rights of others can long remain strong and retain the confidence and respect of other nations. No nation ever loses its dignity or its good standing by conciliating its differences, and by exercising great patience with, and consideration for, the rights of other nations.

War is a contagion, whether it be declared or undeclared. It can engulf states and peoples remote from the original scene of hostilities. We are determined to keep out of war, yet we cannot insure ourselves against the disastrous effects of war and the dangers of involvement. We are adopting such measures as will minimize our risk of involvement, but we cannot have complete protection in a world of disorder in which confidence and security have broken down.

If civilization is to survive the principles of the Prince of Peace must be restored. Trust between nations must be revived.

Most important of all, the will for peace on the part of peace-loving nations must express itself to the end that nations that may be tempted to violate their agreements and the rights of others will desist from such a course. There must be positive endeavors to preserve peace.

America hates war. America hopes for peace. Therefore, America actively engages in the search for peace.

Source: Roosevelt, Franklin D. "Address of the President at the Dedication of the Outerlink Bridge." Franklin D. Roosevelt— "The Great Communicator": The Master Speech Files, 1898, 1910–1945. File No. 1093. Franklin D. Roosevelt Presidential Library and Museum. Available at www.fdrlibrary.marist.edu /_resources/images/msf/msf01127.

Pearl Harbor Attack (December 8, 1941)

On December 7, 1941, without warning, the Japanese military attacked U.S. naval and air forces at Pearl Harbor and other U.S. sites in Hawaii, Guam, Wake, Midway, and the Philippines. The following day, addressing a joint session of Congress, Roosevelt asked for a declaration of war against the Japanese Empire, calling the day of the attack "a date which will live in infamy." Jeanette Rankin, a Republican member of the House of Representatives from Montana and an avowed pacifist, cast the only dissenting vote.

Yesterday, December 7, 1941—a date which will live in infamy—the United States of America was suddenly and deliberately attacked by naval and air forces of the Empire of Japan.

The United States was at peace with that Nation and, at the solicitation of Japan, was still in conversation with its Government and its Emperor looking toward the maintenance of peace in the Pacific. Indeed,

one hour after Japanese air squadrons had commenced bombing in the American Island of Oahu, the Japanese Ambassador to the United States and his colleague delivered to our Secretary of State a formal reply to a recent American message. And while this reply stated that it seemed useless to continue the existing diplomatic negotiations, it contained no threat or hint of war or of armed attack.

It will be recorded that the distance of Hawaii from Japan makes it obvious that the attack was deliberately planned many days or even weeks ago. During the intervening time the Japanese Government has deliberately sought to deceive the United States by false statements and expressions of hope for continued peace.

The attack yesterday on the Hawaiian Islands has caused severe damage to American naval and military forces. I regret to tell you that very many American lives have been lost. In addition, American ships have been reported torpedoed on the high seas between San Francisco and Honolulu.

Yesterday the Japanese Government also launched an attack against Malaya.

Last night Japanese forces attacked Hong Kong.

Last night Japanese forces attacked Guam.

Last night Japanese forces attacked the Philippine Islands.

Last night the Japanese attacked Wake Island. And this morning the Japanese attacked Midway Island.

Japan has, therefore, undertaken a surprise offensive extending throughout the Pacific area. The facts of yesterday and today speak for themselves. The people of the United States have already formed their opinions and well understand the implications to the very life and safety of our Nation.

As Commander in Chief of the Army and Navy I have directed that all measures be taken for our defense.

But always will our whole Nation remember the character of the onslaught against us.

No matter how long it may take us to overcome this premeditated invasion, the American people in their righteous might will win through to absolute victory. I believe that I interpret the will of the Congress and of the people when I assert that we will not only defend ourselves to the uttermost but will make it very certain that this form of treachery shall never again endanger us.

Hostilities exist. There is no blinking at the fact that our people, our territory, and our interests are in grave danger.

With confidence in our armed forces—with the unbounding determination of our people—we will gain the inevitable triumph, so help us God.

I ask that the Congress declare that since the unprovoked and dastardly attack by Japan on Sunday, December 7, 1941, a state of war has existed between the United States and the Japanese Empire.

Source: U.S. Department of State. *Peace and War: United States Foreign Policy, 1931–1941*. Washington, D.C.: U.S. Government Printing Office, 1943, 838–839.

Fireside Chat on the Home Front (October 12, 1942)

Between March 1933 and June 1944, President Roosevelt delivered 30 radio addresses to the American people. These "fireside chats" sought to inform the public of the major foreign policy and domestic issues that the nation confronted and how his administration was dealing with them. This October address informed the nation on how the United States was dealing with the nation's efforts to create a powerful military establishment to defeat the country's enemies through its efforts on the home front.

My fellow Americans:

As you know, I have recently come back from a trip of inspection of camps and training stations and war factories.

The main thing that I observed on this trip is not exactly news. It is the plain fact that the American people are united as never before in their determination to do a job and to do it well.

This whole nation of one hundred and thirty million free men, women and children is becoming one great fighting force. Some of us are soldiers or sailors, some of us are civilians. Some of us are fighting the war in airplanes five miles above the continent of Europe or the islands of the Pacific—and some of us are fighting it in mines deep doom in the earth of Pennsylvania or Montana. A few of us are decorated

with medals for heroic achievement, but all of us can have that deep and permanent inner satisfaction that comes from doing the best we know how—each of us playing an honorable part in the great struggle to save our democratic civilization.

Whatever our individual circumstances or opportunities—we are all in it, and our spirit is good, and we Americans and our allies are going to win— and do not let anyone tell you anything different.

That is the main thing that I saw on my trip around the country—unbeatable spirit. If the leaders of Germany and Japan could have come along with me, and had seen what I saw, they would agree with my conclusions. Unfortunately, they were unable to make the trip with me. And that is one reason why we are carrying our war effort overseas—to them.

With every passing week the war increases in scope and intensity. That is true in Europe, in Africa, in Asia, and on all the seas.

The strength of the United Nations is on the upgrade in this war. The Axis leaders, on the other hand, know by now that they have already reached their full strength, and that their steadily mounting losses in men and material cannot be fully replaced. Germany and Japan are already realizing what the inevitable result will be when the total strength of the United Nations hits them—at additional places on the earth's surface.

One of the principal weapons of our enemies in the past has been their use of what is called "The War of Nerves." They have spread falsehood and terror; they have started Fifth Columns everywhere; they have duped the innocent; they have fomented suspicion and hate between neighbors; they have aided and abetted those people in other nations—(even) including our own—whose words and deeds are advertised from Berlin and from Tokyo as proof of our disunity.

The greatest defense against all such propaganda, of course, is the common sense of the common people—and that defense is prevailing.

The "War of Nerves" against the United Nations is now turning into a boomerang. For the first time, the Nazi propaganda machine is on the defensive. They begin to apologize to their own people for the repulse of their vast forces at Stalingrad, and for the enormous casualties they are suffering. They are compelled to beg their overworked people to rally their weakened production. They even publicly admit, for the first time, that Germany can be fed only at the cost of stealing food from the rest of Europe.

They are proclaiming that a second front is impossible; but, at the same time, they are desperately rushing troops in all directions, and stringing barbed wire all the way from the coasts of Finland and Norway to the islands of the Eastern Mediterranean. Meanwhile, they are driven to increase the fury of their atrocities.

The United Nations have decided to establish the identity of those Nazi leaders who are responsible for the innumerable acts of savagery. As each of these criminal deeds is committed, it is being carefully investigated; and the evidence is being relentlessly piled up for the future purposes of justice.

We have made it entirely clear that the United Nations seek no mass reprisals against the populations of Germany or Italy or Japan. But the ring leaders and their brutal henchmen must be named, and apprehended, and tried in accordance with the judicial processes of criminal law.

There are now millions of Americans in army camps, in naval stations, in factories and in shipyards. . . .

In the last war, I had seen great factories; but until I saw some of the new present-day plants, I had not thoroughly visualized our American war effort. Of course, I saw only a small portion of all our plants, but that portion was a good cross-section, and it was deeply impressive.

The United States has been at war for only ten months and is engaged in the enormous task of multiplying its armed forces many times. We are by no means at full production level yet. But I could not help asking myself on the trip, where would we be today if the Government of the United States had not begun to build many of its factories for this huge increase more than two years ago, more than a year before war was forced upon us at Pearl Harbor?

We have also had to face the problem of shipping. Ships in every part of the world continue to be sunk by enemy action. But the total tonnage of ships coming out of American, Canadian and British shipyards, day by day, has increased so fast that we are getting ahead of our enemies in the bitter battle of transportation.

In expanding our shipping, we have had to enlist many thousands of men for our Merchant Marine. These men are serving magnificently. They are risking their lives every hour so that guns and tanks and planes and ammunition and food may be carried to the heroic defenders of Stalingrad and to all the United Nations' forces all over the world. . . .

As I told the three press association representatives who accompanied me, I was impressed by the large proportion of women employed—doing skilled manual (work) labor running machines. As time goes on, and many more of our men enter the armed forces, this proportion of women will increase. Within less than a year from now, I think, there will probably be as many women as men working in our war production plants. . . .

And of great importance to our future production was the effective and rapid manner in which the Congress met the serious problem of the rising cost of living. It was a splendid example of the operation of democratic processes in wartime.

The machinery to carry out this act of the Congress was put into effect within twelve hours after the bill was signed. The legislation will help the cost-of-living problems of every worker in every factory and on every farm in the land.

In order to keep stepping up our production, we have had to add millions of workers to the total labor force of the Nation. And as new factories came into operation, we must find additional millions of workers.

This presents a formidable problem in the mobilization of manpower.

It is not that we do not have enough people in this country to do the job. The problem is to have the right numbers of the right people in the right places at the right time.

We are learning to ration materials, and we must now learn to ration manpower.

The major objectives of a sound manpower policy are:

First, to select and train men of the highest fighting efficiency needed for our armed forces in the achievement of victory over our enemies in combat.

Second, to man our war industries and farms with the workers needed to produce the arms and munitions and food required by ourselves and by our fighting allies to win this war.

In order to do this, we shall be compelled to stop workers from moving from one war job to another as a matter of personal preference; to stop employers from stealing labor from each other; to use older men, and handicapped people, and more women, and even grown boys and girls, wherever possible and reasonable, to replace men of military age and fitness; to train new personnel for essential war work; and to stop the wastage of labor in all non-essential activities.

There are many other things that we can do, and do immediately, to help meet (the) this manpower problem.

The school authorities in all the states should work out plans to enable our high school students to take some time from their school year, (and) to use their summer vacations, to help farmers raise and harvest their crops, or to work somewhere in the war industries. This does not mean closing schools and stopping education. It does mean giving older students a better opportunity to contribute their bit to the war effort. Such work will do no harm to the students.

People should do their work as near their homes as possible. We cannot afford to transport a single worker into an area where there is already a worker available to do the job.

In some communities, employers dislike to employ women. In others they are reluctant to hire Negroes. In still others, older men are not wanted. We can no longer afford to indulge such prejudices or practices.

Every citizen wants to know what essential war work he can do the best. He can get the answer by applying to the nearest United States Employment Service office. There are four thousand five hundred of these offices throughout the Nation. They (are) form the corner grocery stores of our manpower system. This network of employment offices is prepared to advise every citizen where his skills and labors are needed most, and to refer him to an employer who can utilize them to best advantage in the war effort.

Perhaps the most difficult phase of the manpower problem is the scarcity of farm labor in many places. I have seen evidences of the fact, however, that the people are trying to meet it as well as possible.

In one community that I visited a perishable crop was harvested by turning out the whole of the high school for three or four days.

And in another community of fruit growers the usual Japanese labor was not available; but when the fruit ripened, the banker, the butcher, the lawyer, the garage man, the druggist, the local editor, and in fact every able-bodied man and woman in the town, left their occupations, (and) went out gathering(ed) the fruit, and sent it to market.

Every farmer in the land must realize fully that his production is part of war production, and that he is regarded by the Nation as essential to victory. The American people expect him to keep his production up, and even to increase it. We will use every effort to help him to get labor; but, at the same time, he and the people of his community must use ingenuity and cooperative effort to produce crops, and livestock and dairy products.

It may be that all of our volunteer effort—however well-intentioned and well administered—will not suffice wholly to solve (the) this problem. In that case, we shall have to adopt new legislation. And if this is necessary, I do not believe that the American people will shrink from it.

In a sense, every American, because of the privilege of his citizenship, is a part of the Selective Service.

The Nation owes a debt of gratitude to the Selective Service Boards. The successful operation of the Selective Service System and the way it has been accepted by the great mass of our citizens give us confidence that if necessary, the same principle could be used to solve any manpower problem. . . .

All of our combat units that go overseas must consist of young, strong men who have had thorough training. (A) An Army division that has an average age of twenty-three or twenty-four is a better fighting unit than one which has an average age of thirty-three or thirty-four. The more of such troops we have in the field, the sooner the war will be won, and the smaller will be the cost in casualties.

Therefore, I believe that it will be necessary to lower the present minimum age limit for Selective Service from twenty years down to eighteen. We have learned how inevitable that is—and how important to the speeding up of victory.

I can very thoroughly understand the feelings of all parents whose sons have entered our armed forces. I have an appreciation of that feeling and so has my wife.

I want every father and every mother who has a son in the service to know—again, from what I have seen with my own eyes—that the men in the Army, Navy and Marine Corps are receiving today the best possible training, equipment and medical care. And we will never fail to provide for the spiritual needs of our officers and men under the Chaplains of our armed services.

Good training will save many, many lives in battle. The highest rate of casualties is always suffered by units comprised of inadequately trained men.

We can be sure that the combat units of our Army and Navy are well manned, (and) well equipped, (and) well trained. Their effectiveness in action will depend upon the quality of their leadership, and upon the wisdom of the strategic plans on which all military operations are based. . . .

There are a few people in this country who, when the collapse of the Axis begins, will tell our people that we are safe once more; that we can tell the rest of the world to "stew in its own juice"; that never again will we help to pull "the other fellow's chestnuts from the fire"; that the future of civilization can jolly well take care of itself insofar as we are concerned.

But it is useless to win battles if the cause for which we fight these battles is lost. It is useless to win a war unless it stays won.

We, therefore, fight for the restoration and perpetuation of faith and hope and peace throughout the world.

The objective of today is clear and realistic. It is to destroy completely the military power of Germany, Italy and Japan to such good purpose that their threat against us and all the other United Nations cannot be revived a generation hence.

We are united in seeking the kind of victory that will guarantee that our grandchildren can grow and, under Gods may live their lives, free from the constant threat of invasion, destruction, slavery and violent death.

Source: Roosevelt, Franklin D. "Report on the Home Front." Franklin D. Roosevelt Presidential Library and Museum. Available at http://docs.fdrlibrary.marist.edu/101242.html.

Report on the Yalta Conference (March 1, 1945)

In his last major address, President Roosevelt gave a summation of his February meeting with Winston Churchill of Great Britain and Joseph Stalin of the Soviet Union at the Yalta Conference in the Crimea held February 4–11, 1945. The conference had agreed on final plans and goals for the defeat of Germany and Japan.

I come from the Crimea Conference with a firm belief that we have made a good start on the road to a world of peace.

There were two main purposes in this Crimea Conference. The first was to bring defeat to Germany with the greatest possible speed, and the smallest possible loss of Allied men. That purpose is now being carried out in great force. The German Army, and the German people, are feeling the ever-increasing might of our fighting men and of the Allied armies. Every hour gives us added pride in the heroic advance of our troops in Germany—on German soil—toward a meeting with the gallant Red Army.

The second purpose was to continue to build the foundation for an international accord that would bring order and security after the chaos of the war, that would give some assurance of lasting peace among the Nations of the world.

Toward that goal also, a tremendous stride was made.

At Teheran, a little over a year ago, there were long-range military plans laid by the Chiefs of Staff of the three most powerful Nations. Among the civilian leaders at Teheran, however, at that time, there were only exchanges of views and expressions of opinion. No political arrangements were made—and none was attempted.

At the Crimea Conference, however, the time had come for getting down to specific cases in the political field.

There was on all sides at this Conference an enthusiastic effort to reach an agreement. Since the time of Teheran, a year ago, there had developed among all of us a—what shall I call it?—a greater facility in negotiating with each other, that augurs well for the peace of the world. We know each other better.

I have never for an instant wavered in my belief that an agreement to insure world peace and security can be reached.

There were a number of things that we did that were concrete—that were definite. For instance, the lapse of time between Teheran and Yalta without conferences of civilian representatives of the three major powers has proved to be too long-fourteen months. During that long period, local problems were permitted to become acute in places like Poland and Greece and Italy and Yugoslavia.

Therefore, we decided at Yalta that, even if circumstances made it impossible for the heads of the three Governments to meet more often in the future, we would make sure that there would be more frequent personal contacts for the exchange of views, between the Secretaries of State and the Foreign Ministers of these three powers.

We arranged for periodic meetings at intervals of three or four months. I feel very confident that under this arrangement there will be no recurrences of the incidents which this winter disturbed the friends of world-wide cooperation and collaboration.

When we met at Yalta, in addition to laying our strategic and tactical plans for the complete and final military victory over Germany, there were other problems of vital political consequence.

For instance, first, there were the problems of the occupation and control of Germany—after victory—the complete destruction of her military power, and the assurance that neither the Nazis nor Prussian militarism could again be revived to threaten the peace and the civilization of the world.

Second—again for example—there was the settlement of the few differences that remained among us with respect to the International Security Organization after the Dumbarton Oaks Conference. As you remember, at that time, I said that we had agreed ninety percent. Well, that's a pretty good percentage. I think the other ten percent was ironed out at Yalta.

Third, there were the general political and economic problems common to all of the areas which had been or would be liberated from the Nazi yoke. This is a very special problem. We over here find it difficult to understand the ramifications of many of these problems in foreign lands, but we are trying to.

Fourth, there were the special problems created by a few instances such as Poland and Yugoslavia.

Days were spent in discussing these momentous matters and we argued freely and frankly across the table. But at the end, on every point, unanimous agreement was reached. And more important even than the agreement of words, I may say we achieved a unity of thought and a way of getting along together.

Of course, we know that it was Hitler's hope—and the German war lords'—that we would not agree—that some slight crack might appear in the solid wall of Allied unity, a crack that would give him and his fellow gangsters one last hope of escaping their just doom. That is the objective for which his propaganda ma- chine has been working for many months.

But Hitler has failed.

Never before have the major Allies been more closely united—not only in their war aims but also in their peace aims. And they are determined to continue to be united with each other-and with all peace-loving Nations—so that the ideal of lasting peace will become a reality.

The Soviet, British, and United States Chiefs of Staff held daily meetings with each other. They conferred frequently with Marshal Stalin, and with Prime Minister Churchill and with me, on the problem of coordinating the strategic and tactical efforts of the Allied powers. They completed their plans for the final knock-out blows to Germany. . . .

The German people, as well as the German soldiers must realize that the sooner they give up and surrender by groups or as individuals, the sooner their present agony will be over. They must realize that only with complete surrender can they begin to reestablish themselves as people whom the world might accept as decent neighbors.

We made it clear again at Yalta, and I now repeat that unconditional surrender does not mean the destruction or enslavement of the German people. The Nazi leaders have deliberately withheld that part of the Yalta declaration from the German press and radio. They seek to convince the people of Germany that the Yalta declaration does mean slavery and destruction for them—they are working at it day and night for that is how the Nazis hope to save their own skins, and deceive their people into continued and useless resistance.

We did, however, make it clear at the Conference just what unconditional surrender does mean for Germany.

It means the temporary control of Germany by Great Britain, Russia, France, and the United States. Each of these Nations will occupy and control a separate zone of Germany—and the administration of the four zones will be coordinated in Berlin by a Control Council composed of representatives of the four Nations.

Unconditional surrender means something else. It means the end of Nazism. It means the end of the Nazi Party—and of all its barbaric laws and institutions.

It means the termination of all militaristic influence in the public, private, and cultural life of Germany.

It means for the Nazi war criminals a punishment that is speedy and just—and severe.

It means the complete disarmament of Germany; the destruction of its militarism and its military equipment; the end of its production of armament; the dispersal of all its armed forces; the permanent dismemberment of the German General Staff which has so often shattered the peace of the world.

It means that Germany will have to make reparations in kind for the damage which has been done to the innocent victims of its aggression.

By compelling reparations in kind—in plants, in machinery, in rolling stock, and in raw materials—we shall avoid the mistake that we and other Nations made after the last war, the demanding of reparations in the form of money which Germany could never pay.

We do not want the German people to starve, or to become a burden on the rest of the world.

Our objective in handling Germany is simple—it is to secure the peace of the rest of the world now and in the future. Too much experience has shown that that objective is impossible if Germany is allowed to retain any ability to wage aggressive warfare.

These objectives will not hurt the German people. On the contrary, they will protect them from a repetition of the fate which the General Staff and Kaiserism imposed on them before, and which Hitlerism is now imposing upon them again a hundredfold. It will be removing a cancer from the German body politic which for generations has produced only misery and only pain to the whole world. . . .

Of equal importance with the military arrangements at the Crimea Conference were the agreements reached with respect to a general international organization for lasting world peace. . . .

A conference of all the United Nations of the world will meet in San Francisco on April 25, 1945.

There, we all hope, and confidently expect, to execute a definite charter of organization under which the peace of the world will be preserved and the forces of aggression permanently outlawed.

This time we are not making the mistake of waiting until the end of the war to set up the machinery of peace. This time, as we fight together to win the war finally, we work together to keep it from happening again. . . .

The structure of world peace cannot be the work of one man, or one party, or one Nation. It cannot be just an American peace, or a British peace, or a Russian, a French, or a Chinese peace. It cannot be a peace of large Nations—or of small Nations. It must be a peace which rests on the cooperative effort of the whole world.

It cannot be a structure of complete perfection at first. But it can be a peace—and it will be a peace—based on the sound and just principles of the Atlantic Charter—on the concept of the dignity of the human being—and on the guarantees of tolerance and freedom of religious worship. . . .

This is our chance to see to it that the sons and the grandsons of these gallant fighting men do not have to do it all over again in a few years.

The Conference in the Crimea was a turning point—I hope in our history and therefore in the history of the world. There will soon be presented to the Senate of the United States and to the American people a great decision that will determine the fate of the United States—and of the world—for generations to come.

There can be no middle ground here. We shall have to take the responsibility for world collaboration, or we shall have to bear the responsibility for another world conflict. . . .

I am confident that the Congress and the American people will accept the results of this Conference as the beginnings of a permanent structure of peace upon which we can begin to build, under God, that better world in which our children and grandchildren—yours and mine, the children and grandchildren of the whole world—must live, and can live.

Source: Roosevelt, Franklin D. "Message to Congress re the Yalta Conference." Franklin D. Roosevelt—"The Great Communicator": The Master Speech Files, 1898, 1910–1945. File No. 1572-A. Franklin D. Roosevelt Presidential Library and Museum. Available at www.fdrlibrary.marist.edu/_resources/images/msf/msfb0209.

33. HARRY S TRUMAN (1884–1972)

Presidential Term (1945–1953)

CHRONOLOGY

May 8, 1884—Harry S Truman is born in Lamar, Missouri.

April 1917—The United States enters World War I.

June 18, 1919—Truman marries Elizabeth "Bess" Virginia Wallace.

June 28, 1919—The signing of the Treaty of Versailles ends World War I.

November 6, 1934—Truman is elected to the U.S. Senate.

November 5, 1940—Truman is reelected to the U.S. Senate.

December 7, 1941—Japan attacks Pearl Harbor, leading to the United States entering World War II.

June 22, 1944—The Serviceman's Readjustment Act of 1944 (the GI Bill) is signed into law.

November 7, 1944—President Franklin D. Roosevelt is elected to his fourth term as president; Truman is elected vice president.

April 12, 1945—President Franklin Roosevelt dies; Truman becomes the 33rd president of the United States.

June 26, 1945—The United Nations charter is signed.

July 17–August 2, 1945—President Truman and Allied leaders meet at the Potsdam Conference.

August 6, 1945—U.S. forces drop the atomic bomb on Hiroshima, Japan; three days later, another bomb is dropped on Nagasaki.

August 15, 1945—Japan formally surrenders, ending World War II.March 12, 1947—President Truman announces the Truman Doctrine, which seeks to counter Soviet expansion.

June 5, 1947—Secretary of State George C. Marshall proposes what became known as the Marshall Plan to rebuild Europe in a speech at Harvard University.

November 2, 1948—Truman wins election as president; the *Chicago Daily Tribune* infamously declares Thomas Dewey's victory on its front page.

April 4, 1949—The North Atlantic Treaty Organization (NATO) is established.

February 9, 1950—Senator Joseph McCarthy of Wisconsin announces that he has a list of over 200 communists working in the government, beginning a four-year witch hunt.April 1950—The State Department issues National Security Paper 68 (NSC-68), an analysis of the Cold War.

June 25, 1950—North Korean forces cross the 39th parallel and invade South Korea, starting the Korean War.

July 5, 1950—The Battle of Osan is the first engagement between U.S. forces and North Korean troops.

February 27, 1951—The Twenty-Second Amendment limiting presidential tenure to two terms is ratified.

April 8, 1951—President Truman relieves General Douglas MacArthur of command of the UN forces in Korea.

November 4, 1952—Dwight D. Eisenhower is elected the 34th president of the United States.

July 27, 1953—An armistice ends fighting in the Korean War; however, there remains no peace treaty signed between the two sides to this day.

December 26, 1972—Harry S Truman dies in Kansas City, Missouri.

BIOGRAPHICAL SKETCH

Harry S Truman was the 34th president of the United States. Assuming the presidency in the aftermath of the death of Franklin Roosevelt, then in his 13th year

Harry S Truman (Harry S Truman Presidential Library)

Independence High School, he aspired to attend either West Point or Annapolis. However, those ambitions were thwarted by his poor eyesight. At the same time, he had developed into a skilled pianist, and his teacher even urged a career in music. But plans for the future gave way to the demands of the present when, in 1901, his father's financial fortunes took a disastrous turn. The recent high school graduate dropped plans for further schooling and instead got a job to help support the family.

In response to the family's needs, Truman undertook a range of jobs, including timekeeper for a railroad contractor, mailroom clerk for the *Kansas City Star*, clerk at the National Bank of Commerce in Kansas City, and bookkeeper at the Union National Bank in Kansas City. In 1906, he returned home at his father's request to help run the family farm near Grandview, Missouri. While he remained there until he entered the army in 1917, he also made some investments in a lead and zinc venture in 1915 and oil exploration in 1916, but neither panned out.

Truman served in the Missouri National Guard from 1905 to 1911. With the advent of World War I, he rejoined in May 1917, and his unit was incorporated into the regular army. He was a member of the 129th Field Artillery from August 1917 to May 1919. After basic training at Camp Doniphan, Fort Sill, Oklahoma, he shipped out to France in March 1918, anxious, the history-loving Truman said, to repay the nation's debt for the contributions Lafayette had rendered during the American Revolution. Truman was appointed commander of the 129th's Battery D, a group primarily consisting of Irish toughs from Kansas City, and despite his unimposing physical stature, he quickly earned the respect of his men. He and his men performed admirably, and while contributing effectively, they suffered only one fatality. Truman suffered no wounds and won no decorations, but he did earn a promotion from lieutenant to major.

Upon being mustered out, Truman married Elizabeth "Bess" Virginia Wallace on June 28, 1919, in Independence, Missouri. Bess was a spirited woman who had grown up a tomboy. The couple had met in Sunday school, when he was six and she was five. They were classmates through high school, but the relationship did not begin until after high school,

in the White House, Truman became responsible for leading the United States and its allies down the final road to victory in World War II while also beginning to chart a path for the United States in the radically different world that emerged from the global conflict.

Harry S Truman was born on May 8, 1884, in Lamar, Missouri. He was the oldest of three children born to John Anderson Truman and his wife, the former Martha Ellen Young. He was given a sole middle initial rather than a middle name in an effort to recognize both of his grandfathers, Anderson Shippe Truman and Solomon Young.

Truman grew up on farms in Harrisonville and Grandview, Missouri, before the family moved to Independence, which Truman would call home for the rest of his life. His thick glasses prevented him from engaging in the sports that were usually so much a part of a Midwestern boyhood, and he became a voracious reader with a deep interest in history. He received his early education in the Independence public schools, and as he approached his 1901 graduation from when Bess returned to Independence from the Barstow's finishing school she had attended in Kansas City. Bess's father had committed suicide about a year and half after her graduation from high school. While it was something she refused to ever speak about, as she was a notoriously private person, according to Margaret Truman, Bess was fearful that the issue would be brought up in one of Truman's campaigns, but it never was.

For part of Truman's Senate tenure, Bess, like many Senate wives, worked on his staff, and when the issue was raised, the ever-candid Truman made clear that she was fully earning her salary. As first lady, she was a marked contrast from Eleanor Roosevelt, taking no part in any formal governmental activities, although she was a sounding board and adviser to her husband, as she had been throughout his career. Bess willingly fulfilled the social commitments that went with being first lady, but given the major White House restoration that had the Trumans living in Blair House for much of their tenure, White House entertaining during the Truman years was limited. The couple had one child, a daughter, Mary Margaret (who went by Margaret), who was the object of her doting father's deep affections. A singer and later an author, who married Clifton Daniel Jr. of the *New York Times*, she was in the middle of one of Truman's more memorable and human moments when he fired off a less than diplomatic letter to a music critic from the *Washington Post* who had written an unflattering review of a concert performance by his daughter. Truman also had a sometimes rocky political relationship with his mother-in-law, whose family had Southern sympathies during the Civil War; she refused to stay in the Lincoln Bedroom when she visited the White House.

Following the war, Truman entered the business world, operating a postwar haberdashery that, while initially prosperous, went bankrupt in the recession of 1922. Rather than declare bankruptcy, Truman arranged to pay off his debts in installments, a task he completed over the next 12 years.

Truman began his political career in 1922. Securing the support of the Democratic machine headed by Thomas J. Pendergast, in November, Truman was elected judge for the Eastern District of Jackson County, Missouri. As an administrative post, it was essentially being the county executive. In that office, Truman reduced the county's debt and improved the roads, but despite those efforts, he was defeated for reelection in 1924. Out of a job, he worked selling memberships for the Kansas City Automobile Club. However, returning to the electoral arena, in 1926, he was elected presiding judge of Jackson County. In his role as chief executive, Truman secured passage of bond issues that provided for the construction of new roads, a new county hospital designed to serve the elderly, and a new courthouse. In addition, Truman demanded competitive bidding for the construction contracts as well as on-site inspections. He also reduced expense account abuses and cut much of the deadwood from the county's workforce.

In a reflection of his increasing political influence, in 1929, Truman became the head of the Democratic party for the Eastern District of Jackson County. The following year, he won reelection. That same year, in a testament to the job he was doing, Truman was named both president of the Greater Kansas City Plan Association as well as director of the National Council on City Planning. And in a further example of his increasing prominence, in 1933, the New Deal's Federal Emergency Relief Administration tapped him to serve as the reemployment director for the State of Missouri, for which he was paid $1 annually.

In 1934, Truman stepped onto the national stage, winning election to the U.S. Senate by almost 20 percentage points, 59.6 percent to 39.7 percent, over Republican Roscoe Conkling Patterson. From the beginning of his tenure, he was dogged by the perception that he was a puppet of Kansas City political boss Thomas J. Pendergast. Dubbed in some circles as the "Senator from Pendergast," Truman never denied the help Pendergast had given his career, but he was scrupulous in remaining apart from the corruption that was a part of the machine and which would ultimately result in Pendergast serving time in federal prison.

Initially serving on the Appropriations and Interstate Commerce Committees, the freshman senator was a reliable supporter of Franklin Roosevelt's New Deal, even loyally standing behind the president's controversial and ill-fated "court-packing plan." His first term also saw him help write and shepherd to passage the Civil Aeronautics Act of 1938, a bill aimed at regulating the developing airline industry as well as the Transportation Act of 1940, which enhanced the regulatory powers of the Interstate Commerce Committee. Generally seen as an ally of organized labor, Truman was also a comparative progressive on race relations. While Missouri's status as a border state in the Civil War reflected the somewhat tenuous nature of its race relations, Truman voted for federal anti-lynching legislation, an end to poll taxes, and the creation of the Fair Employment Practices Committee.

Despite a solid and productive first term, Truman's 1940 effort to win reelection was a fight for survival; it was a challenging contest but one from which Truman emerged victorious. Truman first had to defend himself within the state Democratic Party, where he ran head-on into the ambition of Governor Lloyd Stark. Although Stark had been supported by Thomas Pendergast, in the aftermath of his 1936 election victory, a campaign in which Pendergast's machine had been uncharacteristically sloppy and excessive in their efforts, Stark turned on Pendergast and helped in an investigation led by U.S. attorney Maurice M. Mulligan, which resulted in convictions on literally hundreds of charges. Not only was the machine left in tatters, but Pendergast himself was sent to federal prison. Truman had not only suddenly lost his powerful patron, but his association with Pendergast became a millstone around his neck as he sought reelection. Fortunately for the incumbent senator, the Democratic primary was not a head-to-head contest with Stark. Rather, Mulligan, whose brother Truman had defeated in the 1934 primary, also ran, seeking to benefit from his toppling of the machine. However, in the end, with Stark and Mulligan splitting the anti-Pendergast vote, Truman was able to slip in by less than 8,000 votes, winning renomination with 40.9 percent of the vote to Stark's 39.7 percent and Mulligan's 19.4.

But the primary victory was not the end of the story. While Truman had won in 1934 by almost 20 percent, he was now the candidate of a broken and deeply divided Democratic party headed by a presidential nominee Franklin Roosevelt, who, while still popular, was seeking an unprecedented and controversial third term. The result was an extraordinarily close election. But with possible war on the horizon, Truman touted his experience in World War I as well as the importance of both his experience and the value of maintaining continuity in the Senate. Ultimately, he was successful, winning reelection by less than 50,000 votes, 51.2 percent to 48.7 percent, over Republican nominee and former state senator Manvel H. Davis.

With his narrow victory behind him, Truman plunged back into his Senate responsibilities, and as the likelihood of U.S. involvement in the European war got ever stronger, he undertook an assignment that not only helped the war effort but gave him a national profile. Beginning in March of 1941, he served as chairman of the Special Committee to Investigate the National Defense Program, a body that identified and sought to correct problems relating to waste, inefficiency, and war profiteering in the defense effort. The Truman Committee, as it came to be called, was one of the most successful investigative efforts ever undertaken by the U.S. government. Its initial budget was only $15,000, and while that was expanded to $360,000 over three years, the committee was credited with saving upward of $10 billion—a huge sum at the time—as well as thousands of lives. It also gave Truman a political identity separate and apart from his controversial Pendergast ties, and it certainly did not hurt when the time came to select a running mate for Roosevelt in 1944.

The story behind Roosevelt's selection remains shrouded in mystery. Questions ranging from Roosevelt's real preference for a running mate to perceptions of his failing health—and thus the likelihood of the vice president becoming president—remain in search of definitive answers, although the broad outlines appear clear. On the matter of his health, anyone who saw the president with any degree of regularity knew that his health was failing, and while his doctor refused to acknowledge it directly, many knew—and would later admit they knew—that Roosevelt was unlikely to live out his fourth term if elected.

And yet, there still appears to have been little real concern over who would be the best next president. Rather, preconvention discussion was all about politics and electability. Indeed, once the president had been convinced that he could not keep Henry Wallace on the ticket, the talk turned to the least objectionable running mate. James F. Byrnes, for all his strengths and experience, was anathema to liberal on the issue of civil rights. Meanwhile, William O. Douglas, an FDR favorite whose brilliance was undeniable but whose political savvy was suspect, was the first choice of the liberals. Moderates thought that the senator from Missouri, who had shown his mettle as a campaigner in 1940 and had left nothing but a good impression by his work in the War Investigations Committee, was seen as safe.

According to one report, FDR told Democratic Party chairman Robert Hannegan, a Missouri native and Truman ally, that Douglas and Truman were both okay. But when Hannegan met with the other party chieftains, he switched the order, making it appear that Truman was the president's chosen heir apparent. While liberals were not pleased by the dumping of Wallace, Roosevelt still retained total control over the party, and so, despite some concerns, when the word went out that the Missouri senator was the choice, most party members fell in line. Truman was initially reluctant, but he acceded to the call and was nominated on the second ballot. He then proceeded to vigorously campaign on behalf of a ticket whose standard-bearer was not only in failing health but was focusing his energies on winning a still raging war while also trying to plan for the postwar world.

When the returns came in, the senator from Missouri found himself needing to prepare for an entirely different assignment. FDR and Truman defeated the Republican ticket of New York governor Thomas E. Dewey and Ohio governor John Bricker by a 53.4 percent to 45.9 percent margin in the popular vote and an even more resounding 432 to 99 vote victory in the Electoral College.

Truman's vice presidency was short and uneventful. He helped secure the confirmation of Wallace as secretary of commerce—Wallace's consolation prize for being dumped from ticket—and his tie-breaking vote prevented passage of a proposal by Senator Robert Taft that would have ended the Lend-Lease Act immediately upon the end of the war. But for the most part, Truman's time in office was the embodiment of the insignificance of which most of its previous occupants had spoken. He met only once with the president between the inauguration and FDR's death, and he was not included in any of the substantive conversations that were ongoing as efforts to end the war moved

into high gear. However, on the afternoon of April 12, 1945, amid a gathering in Speaker Sam Rayburn's office, Truman was called to the White House, where he was greeted by Eleanor Roosevelt, who told him simply, "Harry, the President is dead." And then, to his query, "Is there anything I can do for you?" the long-time first lady was reported to have responded, "Is there anything we can do for you? For you are the one in trouble now."

That night, at 7:09 p.m., standing in the White House Cabinet Room beneath a portrait of Woodrow Wilson, Truman was sworn into office by Chief Justice Harlan Fiske Stone, ushering in a new era. During the next four years, Truman would face a number of significant foreign and domestic concerns (covered in detail later). His presidency, from the beginnings of the Cold War to efforts at domestic reform in the post-New Deal, would prove important responsibilities, but by 1952, the nation had opted for a major change in the White House. Its voters would elect a Republican, Dwight Eisenhower, for the first time since 1928.

Following the inauguration of Dwight Eisenhower as president, Harry Truman retired to Independence, Missouri, where he spent almost another 20 years before his death on December 26, 1972. In retirement, Truman wrote a two-volume memoir of his White House years. Volume 1 was titled *Year of Decision* and volume 2 *Years of Trial and Hope 1946–1952*. Truman also oversaw the creation of the Harry S Truman Presidential Library & Museum in his hometown of Independence, Missouri.

To no one's surprise, Truman remained an active voice in Democratic Party politics, serving as both an elder statesman and an ever-candid partisan. While he originally opposed Kennedy's pursuit of the 1960 Democratic nomination, asserting that the Massachusetts senator was too young and inexperienced, he ultimately gave his full support and mourned his death. Ironically, Kennedy's assassination provided the opportunity for Truman and Eisenhower to patch up their differences. When they got together in the aftermath of Kennedy's funeral, the two old warriors had an informal dinner, hashing over the differences that had undercut their once cordial relations. Meanwhile, Truman's early effort to achieve at least a form of national health coverage was recognized and honored when Lyndon Johnson held the signing ceremony for Medicare at the Truman Library. With the beaming former president at his side, Johnson put his signature on the groundbreaking legislation. Johnson capped the tribute the following year when, as the program got up and running, he presented Truman and wife Bess with Medicare cards numbers one and two.

Harry Truman died on December 26, 1972, of old age. While an elaborate five-day state funeral had been planned years before and approved by Truman, he had made his approval subject to changes that his family might make. When the time came, everything was called back, in line with the former first lady's directive to "Keep it simple. Keep it simple." After a private service for the family at the local funeral home, the body lay in state in the lobby of the Truman Library. President Richard Nixon and his wife, Pat, came to pay their respects, as did former president Lyndon Johnson, who was accompanied by his wife, Lady Bird, and their family. In the end, 75,000 people passed by the casket before Truman was buried on the afternoon of December 28 in the courtyard of the library.

The burial was preceded by an Episcopal service in the small auditorium of the Truman Library. In a proceeding overseen by a Baptist minister and the Grand Masonic leader of Missouri, the feisty, dedicated public servant and unlikely leader of the free world, was remembered by a small contingent of invited guests, who included Averell Harriman, Clark Clifford, Harry Vaughan, and Sam Rosenman. There was no eulogy. His grave in the library's courtyard, topped by a tombstone that Truman had designed, lists his dates of his birth and death, the date of Margaret's birth, and his public offices, beginning with district judge and culminating with president of the United States. Bess died a decade later as the oldest former first lady in history; the marker over her grave reads, "First Lady of the United States."

HISTORICAL OVERVIEW

As Truman embarked upon the presidency, his cabinet represented a mix of some of the most respected and longest-serving members of the Roosevelt administration and recent newcomers, whose presence often represented the shifting focus of Roosevelt's years in the White House. Interior Secretary Harold Ickes and Secretary of Labor France Perkins had been with Roosevelt from the beginning in 1933. Perkins had actually served under him when he was governor of New York. Treasury Secretary Henry Morgenthau assumed his post less than a year into Roosevelt's term. In contrast, Secretary of State Edward R. Stettinius Jr. had been in office less than six months, having taken over from the ailing Cordell Hull on December 1, 1944. Meanwhile, Secretary of War Henry L. Stimson, a Washington veteran who had served in the cabinets of Presidents Taft and Hoover, joined the Roosevelt administration in 1940 as U.S. preparations for war were just getting under way. His role and influence in the young Truman administration were made clear by the fact that it was he who had informed the president of the existence of the Manhattan Project and the effort to develop atomic weapons, an initiative about which Truman as vice president had no knowledge.

With the war still raging, Truman had no time to ease into his new responsibilities. He did get some early good news when, on May 8, 1945, Germany surrendered. However, that did nothing to minimize the ongoing challenge of the Japanese, a topic that was at the top of the agenda when Truman attended his first summit meeting, which took place in Potsdam, Germany, from July 17 until August 2, 1945. This gathering provided Truman's introduction to Allied leaders Soviet premier Joseph Stalin and British prime minister Winston Churchill, as well as his successor, Clement Atlee, who had accompanied Churchill pending the results of a general election that had been held before their departures, the results of which were still unknown. After the July 26 announcement that Atlee's Labour Party had triumphed, Churchill departed, leaving Stalin the experienced member of the Allied triumvirate.

As the leaders discussed how best to deal with the now defeated Nazi Germany, they also sought to establish a global postwar order and the peace treaty issues while also seeking to address the inevitable effects of the war both in their own lands and globally. The central issue the leaders sought to address was how to handle Germany. They wanted to ensure that the country was both demilitarized and disarmed and decided that it would be divided into four zones of Allied occupation. They sought to remake Germany along democratic lines, repealing all of the discriminatory laws remaining from the Nazi era while also conducting a series of trials for those accused of being war criminals. In addition, the participants addressed issues related to the revised German-Soviet-Polish borders as well as the problem of the millions of Germans living in disputed territories. In the end, some of these issues, as well as others that remained unresolved, were left to further discussions and negotiations to be conducted by the Council of Foreign Ministers that they created and which was empowered to act on behalf of the United States, Great Britain, the Soviet Union, and China. Prior to Churchill's departure from Potsdam, Churchill, Truman, and Chiang Kai-shek, the chairman of the Nationalist Government of China (the Soviet Union was not at war with Japan) issued the Potsdam Declaration, which announced the basic terms of surrender for Japan as the Allies turned their full military attention to that front.

While Truman was at Potsdam, he received word that the United States had conducted a successful test of the atomic bomb, and while he did not reveal its existence to Stalin, he did advise the Soviet leader that the United States had developed a powerful new weapon. Stalin, whose spy network likely had left him better informed than Truman had been prior to Roosevelt's death, simply urged him to make good use of it.

The Allies received no response from the Japanese government, leaving them to believe that the Japanese planned to fight on. Consequently, on August 6, 1945, and then again on August 9, the United States dropped atomic bombs on Hiroshima and Nagasaki, respectively, in an effort to bring the war to a close. Although the decision remains controversial, Truman made it with the belief that both cities were legitimate military targets and that the bombing would bring about a quick end to the war, thus saving thousands of American lives. The effort seemed to work, as the Japanese announced their surrender on August 14, ending the war in Asia.

After a period of transition, Truman began to put his own stamp on his presidency. He had inherited a highly capable cabinet, but even those whose tenure under Roosevelt was not particularly long submitted

their resignations as the president got settled in. In response to Stettinius's resignation, Truman named his former Senate colleague—and a man who might well have looked at President Truman and thought, "That could be me"—James F. Byrnes to serve as secretary of state. Byrnes took over just in time to accompany Truman to Potsdam. He quickly backed away from his early inclination to try to cooperate with the Soviet Union, and his subsequent hard-line approach made him an early voice in urging the president to take steps to stop the Soviet Union's purported ambitions. As events moved along, Truman and Byrnes increasingly clashed, and on January 21, 1947, the secretary resigned. In choosing a replacement for Byrnes, the president quickly turned to General George C. Marshall. Although Marshall had retired, the president had already called upon the former army chief of staff to undertake a mission to bring peace between the warring factions in China. However, with no real leverage from which to mount the negotiations, Marshall was unsuccessful, and not long after he returned to the United States, Mao Zedong's Communists would defeat Chiang Kai-shek's Nationalist forces. That ultimate victory by the Chinese Communists would leave the Truman administration forever tarred with the politically charged, if erroneous, responsibility for having "lost China," a specter that would haunt U.S. foreign policy and the Democratic Party for decades.

As secretary of state, Marshall saw significantly greater success, including his overseeing the development and implementation of the Marshall Plan. Finally, in the aftermath of Truman's 1948 election victory, his health having become something of a concern, Marshall again retired. In his stead, Truman appointed Washington attorney Dean Acheson, who had served as undersecretary under Stettinius, Byrnes, and Marshall. Acheson would come to be recognized as one of the undisputed architects of the administration's Cold War containment policy, but past associations with Alger Hiss made him a target of Senator Joseph McCarthy and the Republicans, who charged that not only was he soft on communism but that he had harbored known communists in the State Department during his time as secretary.

As a result of the enactment of the National Security Act in July 1947, legislation that created the

National Security Council, the Central Intelligence Agency (CIA), the National Resources Board, and the Department of Defense, Truman appointed the first secretary of defense in the nation's history. He named James Forrestal, the then secretary of the navy, which was one of the departments being integrated into the new Defense Department, as the first secretary. Not surprisingly, Forrestal's tenure was marked by fierce interservice rivalries, a challenge he was never able to fix but one that likely contributed to the factors that led the troubled Forrestal to commit suicide in 1949. To succeed Forrestal, Truman chose Louis A. Johnson, who had served as Truman's lead fund-raiser for the 1948 campaign and whose tenure as defense secretary was focused on seeking greater unification of the armed forces. Presiding over a post–World War II scale back of the nation's security forces, he did not endear himself to the Defense personnel, who believed he should be fighting for a larger defense budget.

Johnson resigned shortly after the outbreak of the Korean War in June 1950. To replace him, Truman, as he had done before, turned to General George C. Marshall. Congress had to pass special legislation exempting Marshall from the statutory ban on military men leading the Defense Department, but it gladly did so in an effort to benefit from his unparalleled experience, especially as the nation sought to address the war in Korea. His stature and understanding of military life did much to improve morale in the Pentagon while also helping advance the war effort, and he provided Truman with support after the firing of General Douglas MacArthur. Marshall retired for a final time in September 1951 and was succeeded by Robert A. Lovett, who had served as deputy secretary under Marshall.

Truman inherited longtime FDR friend Henry Morgenthau Jr. as secretary of the treasury, but when Morgenthau demanded to accompany Truman to Potsdam, threatening to resign if he were not allowed to go, the president called his bluff by immediately accepting the resignation and sending Morgenthau back to private life. In his place, Truman named Frederick M. Vinson. At the time, Vinson was serving as the director of the Office of Economic Stabilization, but the former Kentucky congressman, who had also served on the U.S. court of appeals, was an old friend of the president. Vinson served as secretary until June 1946, when Truman selected him to serve as chief justice of the Supreme Court. Following that shift, Truman named John W. Snyder, who served for the remainder of Truman's term. He too was a longtime friend of the president, and in addition to leading the effort to tame the postwar economy, Snyder was a major advocate of U.S. savings bonds.

Truman's initial attorney general, inherited from Franklin Roosevelt, was Francis Biddle, who had been serving since 1941 and wanted to continue in the post. However, Truman opted for a change, naming Texan Tom Clark, who had been heading the Justice Department's Criminal Division, while convincing an unhappy Biddle to serve as an American judge at the Nuremberg trials. As attorney general, Clark oversaw a crackdown on communists, offering increased support for FBI efforts in this area. In addition, Clark inaugurated the United States Attorney General's List of Subversive Organizations, a catalog of groups and organizations that were deemed subversive by the attorney general. Ideologically, the groups that were included ranged from the Communist Party and Communist front organizations to the Ku Klux Klan and the Nazi Party.

When Truman appointed Clark to the Supreme Court in the summer of 1947, he named Rhode Island senator and former governor J. Howard McGrath to fill the vacancy. McGrath served until April 1952, when the president fired him for refusing to cooperate in an investigation into alleged corruption in the Justice Department. Truman replaced McGrath with James P. McGranery, a Philadelphia native who had previously served in the House and as a judge on the District Court for the Eastern District of Pennsylvania. McGranery pursued the thwarted investigation and ended up dismissing a number of employees as a result of their actions. In addition, McGranery approved prosecutions of communists under the Smith Act, and he also revoked the reentry permit of actor Charlie Chaplin after allegations that he was a communist.

Claude Wickard, whose tenure as secretary of agriculture had begun in September 1940 under Roosevelt, left the Truman administration in July. His successor, Clinton P. Anderson of New Mexico, served from 1945 until 1948. He directed the nation's postwar food relief programs, as the nation had to reorganize and redirect the farm economy from support for the war effort to addressing the worldwide need for food. Crossing partisan lines, Anderson convinced Truman to bring former president and World War I relief czar Herbert Hoover into the effort, and with Hoover's help and input, the United States was able to address and make a major impact on a global emergency. Intending to retire from government service, Anderson left the Department of Agriculture in May 1948, but he was soon convinced to run for the state's U.S. Senate seat. His subsequent victory that fall kicked off a 24-year Senate career. In his place, Truman appointed Charles F. Brannan of Colorado, who served through the end of the Truman presidency. Brannan had been the assistant secretary, and over the course of his time in office sought passage of the Brannan Plan, which, among other things, would have provided a guaranteed income for farmers; conservatives in Congress blocked the plan's passage. He was able to achieve a greater role for agricultural experts in the Foreign Service as the U.S. agricultural influence became more far-flung.

Secretary of Commerce Henry Wallace, whose original appointment by Roosevelt Truman had shepherded through the Senate to confirmation, was fired by the president in September 1946 after publicly criticizing the administration's policy toward the Soviet Union. The policy differences at the heart of that criticism formed the basis for his unsuccessful 1948 Progressive Party candidacy. To succeed him at Commerce, Truman chose W. Averell Harriman, heir to one of the country's largest railroad fortunes and a longtime Democratic benefactor and activist, who, after a long stint as ambassador to the Soviet Union, had been serving as ambassador to Great Britain at the time of Wallace's ouster. Harriman headed Commerce from October 1946 until April 1948, when he left to oversee implementation of the Marshall Plan. Harriman was succeeded at Commerce by Charles W. Sawyer, an attorney active in the Ohio Democratic Party. He had served as ambassador to Belgium under Roosevelt. As secretary of commerce, Sawyer, who held the office from May 1948 through the end of Truman's term, ordered the 1952 governmental seizure and operation of the nation's steel mills in an effort to end the labor stoppage that the president believed was hampering

the nation's ability to fight the war in Korea. Much to the president's distress, the Supreme Court invalidated the action.

Secretary of Labor Frances Perkins, FDR's barrier-breaking first female cabinet appointee, resigned at the end of June 1945. In her stead, Truman appointed Lewis Schwellenbach, a former federal judge and U.S. senator from Washington, who served from July 1, 1945, until June 10, 1948, when he suddenly died. It was a tumultuous time, as the nation was racked with strikes called by workers and unions seeking to make up ground lost during the war. After Schwellenbach's death, Truman appointed Maurice J. Tobin, a onetime mayor of Boston and governor of Massachusetts. Tobin was unable to achieve his major goal—the repeal of the Taft-Hartley Act. The Fair Labor Standards Amendments of 1949 raised the minimum wage and strengthened prohibitions on child labor. He also helped coordinate manpower needs during the Korean War. Although he and the president clashed when Tobin supported labor in the steel strike, he served ably through the end of Truman's term. Indeed, he defended the administration and the principle of freedom of speech by speaking out against the tactics of his fellow Irish Catholic senator, Joe McCarthy, and calling on all Catholics to repudiate McCarthy's irresponsible effort to shut down free thought in the United States.

In the Department of the Interior, FDR holdover Harold C. Ickes continued in office until 1946, when he resigned in protest over the appointment of Edwin Pauley as undersecretary of the navy. Truman named Julius Albert (J. A.) Krug to replace Ickes. As secretary, he was the administrator of coal mines in the United States, and in that capacity, he went head to head with John L. Lewis and the United Mine Workers in an unsuccessful effort to end a nationwide strike in 1946. When Krug resigned in 1949, the president appointed Oscar Chapman of Colorado to fill the position. The former assistant secretary would serve for the remainder of the Truman administration.

Frank C. Walker, who was appointed by Roosevelt in 1940, was serving as postmaster general when Truman took office, but he resigned in May 1945 owing to poor health. His successor, Robert Hannegan of Missouri, served for two years before his own health forced him to resign in December 1947, but not before he started having the service use helicopters to transport the mail from the airport to the downtown central post offices. Hannegan was replaced by Jesse M. Donaldson, also of Missouri. Donaldson had spent his whole career with the Postal Service, having begun as a letter carrier, but in a bow to a changing nation, he oversaw the shift from two residential deliveries a day to one.

With the military aspect of the war completed, Truman, still less than six months into his presidency, had to address the issue of economic reconversion, and on September 6, he gave Congress a 21-point Reconversion Plan. The proposal was both a response to the challenges presented by demobilization and the changeover from a wartime economy to a peacetime one and a declaration of independence by a president who had been following his predecessor's policies as he sought to bring World War II to a successful conclusion. Now charged with presiding over the peace, Truman offered a series of proposals that would ultimately serve as the basis for his legislative program. This would be called the Fair Deal.

At this point in his presidency, Truman simply outlined proposals intended to make the short-term transition from war to peace as smooth as possible, and he addressed some of the broader issues that the United States would begin to confront on the domestic side. Among the proposals the president made was a call for a major review and overhaul of the unemployment compensation system. Similarly, he called for both an increase in the minimum wage and an expansion of its coverage. Truman called for price controls to be extended so as to keep down the cost of living while the country moved toward a peacetime economy. At the same time, he urged a pragmatic approach to the elimination of wartime agencies and wartime controls, taking legal difficulties into account. Truman called for legislation to ensure full employment and also wanted the Fair Employment Practices Committee to be made permanent. Looking to build upon the New Deal's Wagner Act, Truman called for the maintenance of sound industrial relations, but recognizing the importance of a broad-based economy, he also wanted to increase aid to farmers and small businesses. The president called for the enactment of major new housing legislation as well as a major overhaul of the nation's tax system. He also called for an expansive public works program that could be coupled with renewed emphasis on conserving and building up natural resources. Truman also offered a number of proposals dealing with the disposal of wartime equipment and property, and he wanted multifaceted assistance for veterans. Finally, he called upon Congress to develop a decent pay scale for federal employees in all branches—executive, legislative, and judicial.

With a vision in place, Truman turned to the challenge of making it a reality. He secured passage the following February of the Employment Act of 1946, legislation that put a greater onus on the federal government to create a vibrant economy dedicated to full employment and production as well as purchasing power. In addition, recognizing the ever-greater complexity of the post–New Deal, postwar economy, a new Council of Economic Advisers was created to aid the president in developing economic policy. At the same time, Congress created the Joint Economic Committee, which was made up of both representatives and senators whose responsibility it was to review the government's economic policy at least annually. The law also required the president to submit a new and comprehensive annual economic report within 10 days of the submission of the national budget. This Economic Report of the President, as the act labeled it, was to forecast the future state of the economy, establish future national economic goals, and offer ideas on how to accomplish those goals.

Unfortunately, the law did little to address the concrete problems that Truman and the country were facing at the time. Foremost among these was the economy. Many economists and political leaders feared that a reconversion from the wartime economy would lead to another depression, and the Employment Act of 1946 was a recognition of the belief that the federal government had a new responsibility to lead the effort to achieve a healthy economy that served all its citizens.

Specific economic issues that arose following the war included the inevitable revival of the labor-management conflicts that had been sidelined in deference to the war effort as well as major shortages in housing and consumer goods. Too, with the economy again heating up, inflation became a new threat. While some wartime price controls remained, producers were often unwilling to sell at the artificially low prices. Farmers were foremost among these producers; despite a desperate need for grain both at home and overseas, they refused to sell it for months at a time in 1945 and 1946 until payments were significantly increased. When the price controls were finally lifted, the market was flooded. The meat market experienced a similar standoff.

Truman's efforts to address the inflation issue resulted in little public support and were often ridiculed. In addition, the end of rationing was followed by the end of price controls, both of which were magnified by a series of major strikes that plagued the country. A United Automobile Workers (UAW) strike against General Motors in November 1945 put 180,000 auto workers on the picket lines and was soon followed by strikes that had 800,000 steelworkers, over 200,000 electrical workers, and 150,000 packinghouse workers engaging in work stoppages in an effort to catch up in the postwar economy. These were all part of the labor turmoil that peaked in 1946, the worst year of labor strife in the nation's history, as the nation was hit by a wave of strikes that saw almost 5 million workers joining the picket lines. Perhaps the biggest crisis arose in May 1946, when, with the threat of a national railroad strike looming, the president seized the railroads. When two critical railway unions went on strike anyway, shutting down the nation's railways, Truman was livid. He appeared before Congress to ask for a new law that would draft railway workers into the army. When he got word midspeech that the strike had been settled, the still irate president completed the speech, and later that day, the House actually voted to draft the striking workers.

The record number of strikes, coupled with the modified wartime wage and price controls that allowed greater wage increases than price hikes, left an economy still struggling to find its footing and the administration and the Democrats easy targets for the nation's pent-up frustration. All of this frustration came to a head when voters went to the polls for the 1946 midterm elections. There, they administered a resounding rebuke to Truman and his Democratic Party. When all the votes were counted, the Democrats lost 55 seats in the House of Representatives, and the Senate saw 12 Democratic incumbents lose their seats. The electoral upheaval, one of the largest reversals in history, gave the Republicans majority control of both houses of Congress for the first time since 1930.

These overwhelming Republican victories left Truman on the political defensive. However, determined to protect the New Deal and its social programs, he consistently battled against Republican efforts to roll back FDR's advances. No piece of legislation was more symbolic of the battle than the Taft-Hartley Act. Officially known as the Labor Management Relations Act of 1947, the law was designed to roll back some of the rights accorded labor by the National Labor Relations Act (NLRA), also known as the Wagner Act, a central achievement of the New Deal that had been enacted in 1935. Passed over Truman's veto during the Republican-controlled 80th Congress, the law was in large part a reaction to the alleged immigrant-inspired upheaval and turmoil that marked the nation's economic resettlement in the aftermath of the end of World War II. While technically an amendment to the Wagner Act, the basic goal of its Republican sponsors was the revision of the original law so as to achieve a greater balance between the interests of management and labor.

The Republican majority, with support from Southern Democrats, was able to pass the bill early in the congressional session, but on June 20, 1947, Truman issued a veto declaring that the government would be too involved in labor-management relations under the act. However, with the president at the nadir of his political influence, both the House and Senate swiftly voted to override his veto, and the bill became law. In the end, while the law did represent a step back from the Wagner Act, the core concept of collective bargaining, one that the more practical management figures recognized had become an established part of the labor-management equation, remained. Those same management figures did believe that, overall, the revisions had done much to level the playing field between management and labor as they all worked to navigate through an often volatile postwar economy.

At the same time, the foreign policy challenges remained unrelenting. George Kennan's "Long Telegram" (1946) and "The Sources of Soviet Conduct" (the "X Article" [1947]) published in *Foreign Affairs* coupled with Winston Churchill's "Iron Curtain" speech at Westminster College had begun to sound the alarm about the extent of Soviet ambitions, leading to the beginnings of an American response. However, it was not until March 12, 1947, when Truman asked Congress for aid to help Greece and Turkey resist the spread of communism, and in doing so articulated the Truman Doctrine, that the United States fully asserted itself in the world community. In stating, "It must be the policy of the United States to support free peoples who are resisting subjugation by armed minorities or by outside pressures," Truman not only announced that United States was taking a stand against global communism, but also that he was cutting, once and for all, any remaining ties to the nation's isolationist past.

A central component in the development of long-term comprehensive Cold War containment was the National Security Council Paper No. 68, "United States Objectives and Programs for National Security," usually referred as NSC-68, a top-secret report prepared by the Department of State's Policy Planning Staff in April 1950. The report was written in response to Secretary Acheson's request for a comprehensive review of the U.S. containment strategy. The resulting paper put a new focus on the role of the military. While early containment efforts, based in part on Kennan's work, were primarily economics based, as seen in the support of Greece and Turkey following the articulation of the Truman Doctrine as well as the Marshall Plan, and even the shared defense alliance of NATO, NSC-68 argued that the United States needed to look at its military needs as it looked to fight the Cold War. Seeing the ever-greater military threat posed by the Soviet Union, one that was only getting stronger as the Soviets sought to put into effect their expansionist desires, the authors of NSC-68 argued the United States needed to respond in kind. They said that the massive Soviet arms buildup, one that would soon include nuclear weapons, needed to be met by a similar American increase and that President Truman needed to undertake an unprecedented increase of American weapon capacity—both conventional and nuclear.

While the report and its recommendations had many critics, including Secretary of Defense Louis

Johnson and respected Soviet experts and former ambassadors George Kennan and Charles Bohlen, all of whom maintained that the U.S. military was already superior to what the Soviets possessed, Kennan went further in arguing that economic and political means were the key to containing Soviet ambitions. However, the invasion of South Korea and the start of the Korean War in June put additional political pressure on an administration that had increasingly been defending itself against charges that it was soft on communism. All of this quickly tilted things in the direction of the report's recommendations, and the United States began a massive military buildup. NSC-68 made no specific recommendation as to how great an increase was needed, but in the final years of the Truman administration, in an effort that signaled the beginning of an arms race, the administration almost tripled defense spending as a percentage of the gross domestic product, taking it from 5 percent to 14.2 percent.

Then, in June 1947, the administration unveiled what would be one of its singular triumphs as the United States sought to address the increasingly clear threat both to freedom and American security, and in fact humanity, that was posed by the economic devastation that marked postwar Europe. In a speech at Harvard University, Secretary of State George C. Marshall proposed an economic aid package of unimaginable breadth that was aimed at addressing problems of similarly unprecedented magnitude. Indeed, the situation in Europe was dire. On some human level, millions were starving in countries across the continent, as the infrastructure and industrial capacity had been decimated. Similarly, their farmland and growing fields had been laid to ruin by the ravages of war. Politically, this economic and human carnage left people ripe for the promises of change and salvation, especially that offered by the Communists. Indeed, elections in Italy had already provided evidence of where things could lead. And yet, in assessing the situation, American policy makers knew that such an effort would not and could not succeed if it were seen as simply another gambit in the developing Cold War. Rather, while the political dividends could be real, the program had to focus on the humanitarian needs as well as provide a mechanism for each country to address its own needs. Thus, the Marshall Plan, formally the European Recovery Program, was open to any country—including the Soviet Union and its developing satellites—that sought to participate according to the prescribed guidelines. This put the onus on each participating country to develop recovery plans appropriate to their needs and economic capabilities. The United States was willing to invest in the European governments and their people, but the ideas and creativity would have to come from within.

In the end, in an example of impressive bipartisan support, the plan went through Congress about as fast as legislation can, and the first part of the ultimate total of $13 billion that the United States spent was on its way. Investing in a wide array of projects, the Marshall Plan ultimately saved lives and help lay the foundation for a continent-wide economic revival that would further develop and flourish in the coming decades. To no one's surprise, neither the Soviet Union nor any of its satellites chose to participate, but the spirt of openness and humanity that the plan represented transcended politics and conveyed a powerful message to the global community.

Another critical event in the evolution of the Truman administration's containment policy was the Berlin Airlift, which was a triumph of planning and execution. Faced with a direct challenge from Stalin, not to mention a potential humanitarian crisis, the administration put together one of the most impressive operations ever seen, with pilots and planes from the United States, the United Kingdom, France, Australia, Canada, New Zealand, and South Africa taking off around the clock. At its peak, the airlift planes were landing in West Belin every 30 seconds. The Allies were able to supply and feed the city for 15 months, beginning in June 1948, when the Soviets first blocked access, until the end of September 1949, when, although the blockade had officially been ended in May, the airlift was continued to build up supplies. Over the course of the blockade, the United States and its allies had flown in over 4 million tons of food and freight, experiencing 101 total fatalities, 31 of whom were Americans. It was a logistical triumph as well as a clear demonstration of the American determination to stop any ambitions the Soviet Union might have had to expand is reach. Coming in the aftermath of the launching of the Marshall Plan, the airlift reaffirmed the American commitment to the people threatened by communism and a loss of freedom.

As the reality of a Cold War set in, the United States asserted its leadership. With Europe beginning to get on its feet with the help of the Marshall Plan, attention was turned to the defensive needs of European nations. Seeking to develop a united front in the face of the Soviet Union's network of satellites countries, in 1949, Secretary of State Dean Acheson proposed an alliance of Western nations to serve as a counterforce to the Soviet-controlled bloc. The idea of a standing army in peacetime, especially one working with other nations, represented a radical departure from the nation's isolationist past, but as it had done with aid to Greece and Turkey, the administration convinced Congress of the need.

In some respects, the North Atlantic Treaty Organization (NATO) represented a logical next step in the Truman administration's containment policy. With the Marshall Plan helping the Western Europeans get back on their economic feet, a key element in helping them resist communism, and more specifically Soviet aggression, was a military alliance that would serve as an additional line of defense. At the same time, such a venture would represent a marked departure for a country whose historic isolationism kept it out of World War II until it was the victim of a direct attack on Pearl Harbor. But while the Marshall Plan had been aimed at addressing conditions that made countries receptive to communist doctrine, the threat in Turkey and Greece, which prompted the Truman Doctrine, and the Soviet's Berlin Blockade required a more forceful response, or at least the ability to mount one.

After much consideration and discussion with the United States' European allies, the idea of a European-American alliance that established a collective military defense force was agreed upon. In March 1948, the major Western European nations—Great Britain, France, Belgium, the Netherland, and Luxembourg—gathered in Brussels and signed the Treaty of Brussels, creating a mutual defense alliance. It provided for collective defense; if any of the signatories to the treaty were attacked, the others were committed to help defend it. Concurrently, the Truman administration, led by Secretary of State Dean Acheson, working with Republicans led by Senator Arthur H. Vandenburg, proposed a resolution that called on the president to pursue a security treaty with Western Europe. Negotiation with the European nations soon followed, and while some of the same concerns that had prevented U.S. involvement with the League of Nations were raised, an agreement was reached that changed the nature of the power balance in Europe, with the resulting agreement serving to put all of Western Europe under the American "nuclear umbrella," an arrangement that all hoped would serve as a deterrent to Soviet aggression in Europe. The Treaty was signed on April 4, 1949, and the organization, which outlasted the Cold War, became a central part of the West's containment efforts.

At the same time that the president was fighting communism abroad, he was also seeking to protect against that same threat on the home front, issuing an executive order, known as the "Loyalty Order," that established an employee loyalty program, whose goal was to ensure the anticommunist-based loyalty of all who worked in the federal government. Yet, the president was not unaware of the threats that such efforts had on civil liberties. Indeed, in 1950, Truman vetoed the McCarran Internal Security Act, only to have his veto overridden. The law, which required all communists to register with the government, also allowed the government to jail communists in a national emergency and to deny anyone who was a member of a totalitarian organization admission to the United States.

In 1949, Truman also introduced the Point Four Program, an initiative designed to further the U.S. effort to secure peace and expand freedom. A central component was a plan to make scientific advances and industrial progress more widely available in an effort to help with the growth and improvement of the world's less developed areas.

On Saturday, June 24, 1950, at about 9:20 p.m., Truman received a call from Secretary of State Dean Acheson informing him that the Communist forces of North Korea had invaded South Korea. Acheson advised the president that he already told UN Secretary-General Trygve Lie of Norway that he needed to call a meeting of the UN Security Council. While leaders awaited details, the invasion was widely seen in all quarters as the latest in the ongoing Communist effort to extend its reach as well as being a test of the Truman administration's containment policy.

Truman ultimately got authorization from the United Nations for a U.S.-led UN military force to repel the threat and force the North Koreans back to the other side of the 38th parallel—the demarcation line between the two nations. The UN-sponsored forces were under the leadership of General Douglas MacArthur, a military icon and the leader of the Pacific theater efforts in World War II. MacArthur undertook a daring maneuver that put the North Koreans back on their heels and over the 38th parallel, but disobeying Truman's order, he continued to push north toward the Chinese border. That led to a counterattack by the Chinese, who not only pushed American and UN forces back below the 38th parallel but injected a whole new element into the war by their involvement. Called to task by Truman, who reminded him that the United States and the United Nations were engaged in a peacekeeping effort, MacArthur publicly criticized the president. Reasserting the constitutionally mandated civilian control of the military, Truman then fired MacArthur for insubordination. Truman's decision ignited a political firestorm. A defiant MacArthur appeared before Congress, but it was short-lived effort to turn it into a presidential candidacy, which was a failure. In the end, analysts recognized that Truman's action was a wholly appropriate and necessary exercise of presidential power. Meanwhile, in Korea, both sides in the war settled in for what became a stalemate, which hurt the administration and Truman politically and that would not be resolved until Eisenhower became president.

For all the planning that had begun under Roosevelt, it was during the Truman administration that the United Nations came into being. Indeed, while Roosevelt had served in the Wilson administration and had both admired Wilson and learned from his errors related to the battle over the post–World War I League of Nations, lessons that were critical to the development of the United Nations, Truman's deep historical knowledge and understanding, as well as his early UN appointments and use of the organization, both in helping create Israel and in fighting the war in Korea, did much to give the body added credibility in the eyes of the world community.

Another hallmark of the Truman foreign policy was the critical role the United States played in the establishment of the State of Israel in 1948. With the end of the long-standing British mandate in Palestine scheduled to end in May 1948, in December 1947, the United Nations passed a resolution calling for the division of the area into two states, one Jewish and one Arab, once the mandate expired. Left to be determined was what to do with those areas with particular religious significance. From December to May, the State Department engaged in extensive discussions about how the United States should respond, but on May 14, 1948, the same day that the Jewish agency declared the creation of the Jewish State of Israel, President Truman, despite the opposition of Secretary Marshall and the State Department, whose objections included the fear that a war with Palestine might erupt, officially recognized Israel. It was an action that provided Israel immeasurable and immediate credibility as well as an ally whose backing was critical to Israel's early existence. Truman's decision, one many critics attributed to election year politics, also laid the foundation for an enduring political and international alliance.

Truman's greatest triumphs came in the area of foreign policy, as his record on the domestic side was more mixed. His Supreme Court appointments were, by most accounts, little more than serviceable. Indeed, although it is not really fair to refer to them, as critics often have, as a bunch of cronies, a particularly poignant small jibe when directed at a man who was forever trying to outrun his roots as the senator from the Pendergast machine, in fact, all four of the president's nominees—a former congressional colleague who later served as treasury secretary, Fred Vinson; Senate colleagues Harold Burton and Sherman Minton; and Attorney General Tom Clark—all shared a close bond with Truman but little else that would immediately lead one to think of them as justices on the Supreme Court. Truman had appointed Vinson as chief justice with the hope that the accomplished political operator would be able to use his well-honed political skills to bridge the divide among the FDR appointees on the Court, but it ultimately proved a task beyond his abilities, leaving the Vinson Court as one notable for the depths of its personal acrimony as well as its philosophical divisions. In the end, Truman's appointees

were recognized as dedicated public servants, justices who worked diligently, if unspectacularly, on a court whose stars were another part of the Roosevelt shadow in which Truman labored.

As the presidential election of 1948 loomed, Truman was a man under siege. Beleaguered at every turn and attacked by both the left (the Americans for Democratic Action, desperate to replace Truman with an appropriate liberal heir to FDR had made unsuccessful overtures to Dwight Eisenhower to run) and the right (the South was deeply distressed over the president's apparent sympathy to growing calls for civil rights and especially his executive order desegregating the military) within his own party, not to mention a Republican Party intent on getting back into the White House for the first time since 1933, Truman determined to take his case to the American people. Following the nomination of former Senate majority leader Alben Barkley of Kentucky as his running mate, in an address to a dispirited convention in the wee hours of the morning on August 15 in Philadelphia, Truman gave an old-fashioned stem-winder of a speech, one better suited to the stump—and the convention audience—than to the television audience that had long since gone to bed. In it, he challenged the Republican Party while energizing the Democrats, announcing his intention to call a late summer special session of Congress, where, as he cagily called them, the Republican-controlled "do nothing 80th Congress" with which he had long been fighting could make good on some of the high-minded promises—such as low-cost housing and the extension of Social Security—that Truman had been trying to achieve and that the Congress had contained. It was a rousing start, one which, at least briefly, lifted the pall that had descended over a party that at one point seemed to have adopted the waspish "To err is Truman" as its slogan.

As Truman expected, the special session yielded nothing of substance, but it did reinforce the image of the "do nothing 80th Congress" that he intended to hammer home to voters over the next two and a half months. Indeed, with the special session completed, the president took his message to the American people, undertaking a cross country train trip, where he proceeded to, in the words of one observer, "Give 'em hell"—although, as Truman explained, he was simply telling the truth, but the Republicans thought it was hell.

In addition to his down-home direct talk, Truman and his campaign strategists also decided to attack the issue of race head-on. Building upon his executive order to desegregate the military as well as the directives in the report "To Secure These Rights," Truman embraced the party's strong but controversial civil rights plank, consciously balancing the political risk of the potential defections by Southerners, who would in fact form their own party, known as the Dixiecrats, versus the potential gains in the North, where the urban African American vote could prove crucial in some of the big Electoral College states.

Beyond all this, Truman was also helped, however unwittingly, by an overconfident Republican nominee, New York governor Thomas E. Dewey, who cautiously and almost leisurely made his case for change, however vague and undefined, seemingly afraid to take any stance that might alienate what he and the Republicans believed was a receptive populace. Further complicating things, two third-party candidates were also running. Former FDR vice president Henry Wallace was on an independent Progressive Party ticket, and South Carolina governor Strom Thurmond was running as the States Rights Party candidate. Wallace and Thurmond were backed by the Southern delegation that had bolted the Democratic convention over the issue of civil rights. They operated around the edges while seeking to make their views on foreign policy and civil rights, respectively, a part of the national debate, and the major parties tried to determine just how much of an electoral impact these outsiders might have.

Yet, for all of these efforts and machinations, pundits were clear in their belief that the overmatched Truman would be heading back to Missouri and retirement come Inauguration Day. But when the final returns came in, Truman had pulled off an upset for the ages, with most of the voters who had flirted with the third and fourth parties ultimately staying in the Democratic fold and the Republicans being unable to surmount fears that they would turn back the clock (Truman had not hesitated to remind voters of how things had been the last time a Republican occupied the Oval Office). The incumbent Truman achieved a clear, if shocking, victory while also returning congressional control to the Democrats.

After a tumultuous term, as the 1952 presidential election approached, Truman was again a man under siege. The war in Korea had devolved into a veritable stalemate, Senator Joe McCarthy was hurling charges about the administration protecting the communists in their midst, and evidence of corruption among some of the president's aides had also emerged. To make matters worse, as the first primaries loomed, the president had given no indication of his intentions. With his failure to announce his intentions leaving a void, Tennessee senator Estes Kefauver, although only in his first term, stepped forward to fill it. Kefauver had earned major national attention the previous year when he presided over televised hearings investigating organized crime. As Kefauver undertook an active campaign, Truman, although still refusing to make a commitment, did allow his name to be placed on the New Hampshire ballot, although he was emphatic in stating his unwillingness to campaign. However, the situation blurred when on the morning after the March 11 primary, the nation awoke to the news that Kefauver had beaten Truman by over 10 percent of the vote and won all 12 of the state's convention delegates. The result added a whole new dimension to the race, and on March 29, when the embattled Truman announced his intention to step aside, the race took on a wholly different shape.

Truman's decision not to run did not mean that he did not intend to be involved. He was too much of a party man and too much of a political combatant to allow the White House to go to the Republicans without a fight. This became even more the case as Dwight Eisenhower, with whom Truman had had a falling out not long into his presidency, emerged as a viable Republican candidate. Initially, Truman tried to convince Illinois governor Adlai Stevenson to run, but he demurred. He also sounded out Averell Harriman in an effort to find someone to stop Kefauver, whom the president did not like but who had become the frontrunner upon Truman's withdrawal. Although the campaign was further complicated by the emergence of a number of state-based favorite son candidates, after Kefauver's early strength waned, a movement to draft Stevenson gained strength, and on the third ballot, the grandson of Grover Cleveland's vice president was nominated. To balance the ticket, while also trying to bring the once "Solid South" back into the fold after the Dixiecrat rebellion of 1948, the Democrats choose Alabama senator John J. Sparkman as his running mate.

On the Republican side, as Truman prepared to defend his and the party's record, his worst nightmare was realized when Dwight Eisenhower was nominated for president. The president's disdain for the general-turned-candidate was only heightened by one of the lowlights of the Eisenhower campaign. Disgusted by McCarthy's attacks on General Marshall, Ike's one-time mentor and backer, in an early campaign appearance in Wisconsin, Eisenhower planned to defend the man Truman had hailed as the "greatest living American." However, in the heat of the campaign, Eisenhower surrendered to the entreaties of the local politicians, who feared the impact of challenging the senator, especially on his home turf. Making matters worse, the speech had been released to the press in advance, so Eisenhower was not only criticized for failing to defend Marshall but also for having backed down in the face of the McCarthy threat.

No one was more outspoken in their attacks on Eisenhower than Truman, who saw the incident as a politically inspired betrayal and asserted that it was a true and sad indication of Eisenhower's character, if not his unfitness for the office of president. Truman was no less incensed by the scandal involving Nixon's secret fund. At the same time, he was frustrated by the lackluster Democratic campaign, and in the end, for all his efforts on behalf of Stevenson and Sparkman, he grudgingly realized that the end of an era had arrived. Eisenhower's overwhelming victory, while certainly a rebuke to Truman, was as much as anything a personal triumph for the revered World War II commander as well as a desire for change after an historic 20-year Democratic occupancy of the White House.

ANALYTICAL ESSAY

American presidents have come in all sizes and shapes, bringing a wide range of experiences to the office. However, by almost any measure, Harry Truman was an unlikely president, and his presidency was an unlikely successor to one of the undisputed iconic presidencies in the nation's history. Truman was the only 20th-century president who did not attend college, and as a senator, he was supported by the notorious Kansas City machine boss Tom Pendergast, which immediately made him suspect in the eyes of many. As if that were not enough, his politically motivated selection as the vice presidential nominee, a veritable afterthought of a president preoccupied by war, meant that there was no relationship with the incumbent, dying chief executive. In fact, at the time Harry Truman received the news that Franklin Roosevelt had died, he had only met with the president individually on one occasion since the inauguration, and knew nothing about the atomic bomb, whose development was then nearing completion. Yet, the failed haberdasher was tremendously well read and totally committed to serving the American people, and that knowledge and commitment, coupled with a previously unrecognized strength of character and leadership, served him and the nation extraordinarily well as he led the effort to develop the Cold War containment policy that would ultimately prove triumphant in the late 1980s.

Truman's start as president was certainly not one that inspired confidence. Only 82 days into his vice presidency, he was summoned to the White House to be told by First Lady Eleanor Roosevelt, "Harry, the president is dead." Most Americans would likely have agreed with Mrs. Roosevelt's follow-up comment, "Is there anything we can do for you, Harry? For you are the one in trouble now." It was a sentiment that not only spoke volumes about the situation but also reflected the fears of a nation facing a set of unprecedented challenges under new and unproven leadership. Indeed, the uncertainty and unfamiliarity that surrounded Truman's ascension to the presidency did nothing to convince a stunned and saddened nation that they were not all in trouble. And yet, over the course of the next almost eight years Harry Truman would respond to challenge after challenge in serving the nation in a most challenging time. He was not Franklin Roosevelt—and he knew it—but he was Harry Truman, and that proved to be something very good.

1032 | Presidents and Presidencies in American History

Truman's presidency was far from a perfect one, but it was one that helped the country pull together the many disparate strands that had emerged in the aftermath of both the Great Depression and World War II. Truman confronted an unprecedented set of challenges at home and abroad, and in responding to them, he began to recast American life at home and the United States' role in a changed international landscape. It was a role that saw the United States, under Truman's leadership, finally and unreservedly cast off the restraints of isolationism that harked back to the nation's beginnings in a very different time and in a very different world.

For Truman, there was no honeymoon period. He had no training period, and in quick succession, he attended an international summit conference and ordered the use of a previously unimagined atomic bomb—a weapon he did not even know existed when he assumed office—to bring the war to a close. He also helped launch the organization that leaders across the globe hoped would help prevent a third world war.

But with the war won, Truman then had to turn his and the country's attention to a no less arduous task—winning the peace. It was particularly challenging because the United States had emerged from the conflict in a singular position within the world community. He struggled to move the economy from its wartime footing to a peacetime one. At the same time, he was taking the country into a new era, where the experiments and advances of the New Deal would be tested in a society unsupported by the developing war economy. But not only was he ultimately successful in leading the county through that reconversion, but he even added some programs of his own through an agenda that became known as the Fair Deal. That effort reaffirmed the nation's commitment to a safety net for the less fortunate and, in doing so, helped to prevent the rollback that had occurred in the 1920s after World War I had interrupted the Progressive era. Truman's commitment to further strengthen and expand the New Deal, even in such areas as medical care that proved unsuccessful, helped make it all but impossible for Eisenhower and his immediate successors to roll back the welfare state and the protections it afforded so many Americans.

Indeed, on the domestic front, Truman faced an economy that presented a number of very different challenges. First, there was the matter of demobilization and the transformation of an army of soldiers into a workforce ready to make the peace. Too, there was the need to refit an industrial economy that had produced war materiel at an unprecedented level but now needed to redirect its energies, resources, and labor force to the consumer needs and desires that had been pent up over the last half decade of wartime sacrifice. And of course, there was a question lurking over all of this, one that a still scared and now scarred nation was afraid to ask: was the American economy reliant on the war for its health and vitality or was it in fact fully healthy and ready to move forward?

Over the course of his almost seven years in office, Truman faced and responded to numerous challenges. He oversaw the end of one war and the entry into another, albeit under the auspices of an international organization whose creation he had helped foster. But for all the many and difficult domestic challenges that Truman and the postwar nation faced, central to any assessment of the Truman presidency is the development and implementation of the containment policy as well as the auxiliary issues it spawned. From his initial articulation of the Truman Doctrine, the basic importance of the containment effort was certainly recognized, and with each passing year that a third world war was avoided, the impact and importance of the effort was only more appreciated and recognized. Yes, there were potential impacts that serve to perhaps blemish the overall effort. The degree to which Vietnam was an unfortunate manifestation of the policy remains a source of much debate, but, in general, that central aspect of Truman's presidency—and its ultimate success—has only enhanced his reputation with the passage of time.

At the same time, some elements of the administration's Cold War effort undermined, to at least some degree, its greater, more noble, and more effective efforts. The ultimate triumph of the Communists in China was in all likelihood inevitable, but there might have been a way to limit the collateral damage while avoiding the blame of losing China, a stigma that would resonate, to the detriment of Democrats and the country alike, for decades to come, especially in regard to Vietnam. Too, while the establishment of the loyalty and security program and the development of the Attorney General's List were aimed at making clear the administration's tough stance on communism, they not only trampled individual liberties, but, combined with his sometimes cavalier attitude or careless approach—embodied in such incidents as his own comment about it all being a "red herring" or Secretary of State Dean Acheson's personally admirable but politically suicidal loyalty to Alger Hiss—sowed confusion, opening the door to Joe McCarthy's further efforts. Indeed, the resulting political weakness that allowed the Republicans to get a Senate majority after the 1952 elections only added to the damage McCarthy was able to wreak, which would even spill over to his fellow Republican Dwight Eisenhower's administration.

Another domestic issue that Truman had to tackle was race relations. As had been true in the aftermath of World War I, African American soldiers who had fought overseas for democracy and freedom returned to the United States to find that they were guaranteed neither and that the nation's wartime rhetoric did not match its postwar reality. Holding up a mirror to the American dream, Truman and others had to face the reality of black soldiers—and their fellow African American citizens—wanting the same rights and opportunities they had not only fought to protect abroad but that most of their fellow American citizens, at least the white ones, took for granted. For Truman, it was not an easy choice. However, the senator from a Civil War border state, the leader of the party whose fragile electoral coalition began with a Solid South, nevertheless saw himself as president of the United States, and from using his power as commander in chief to desegregate the military to gambling his political career to support the civil rights platform at the 1948 Democratic convention, Truman established himself as president of the United States—all of it and all of its people. In many ways, Truman's work on the civil rights front was typical of his approach, reflecting both a political calculation and a recognition of a changing nation. In this case, fully understanding that the nation's best interests had been well served by many of the nation's African Americans, but that the postwar nation to which they returned was not serving

them, Truman stepped up, showing his best side as he fought for the little guy, the downtrodden, and the often forgotten.

In many ways, Harry Truman, as president, was a collection of contradictions. He could be the most partisan of politicians, seeing everything through a party-based lens, or he could be the national leader who rose above such partisan constraints, persuading Republicans such as Arthur Vandenberg to join with him to achieve some of the most notable and laudatory examples—things like the Marshall Plan and the Berlin Airlift—of governmental effectiveness that one can imagine. The contrast was telling and sometimes perplexing. Indeed, one aspect of the Truman presidency that illustrated these contrasting sides, as well as the changes in a man whose time in office was marked by extensive personal growth and the development of a national perspective, rather than the more regionally oriented perspective the senator from Missouri had first brought to Washington, was his personnel decisions. He was often and legitimately criticized for the role of the "Missouri gang," a group of long-time friends who the very loyal Truman appointed to a number of jobs for which they were often, at best, only marginally unqualified. This led to much criticism and, in some instances, corruption that did neither Truman nor the country any good.

At the same time, in appointing people like George C. Marshall and Dean Acheson to the post of secretary of state and George Kennan as head of policy planning, as well as other strong cabinet members, Truman showed an eye for talent as well as an ability to reach beyond his own limited background as he grew to meet the demands of the office. These people, among others, were central to the foreign policy initiatives and triumphs that represent both Truman's greatest accomplishments and remain his most enduring and noteworthy legacy. From the Truman Doctrine to the Berlin Airlift to the creation of NATO and the effort in Korea, not to mention the Marshall Plan, Truman set the stage for the United States to serve as a beacon for freedom for nations across the globe. Debates continue over whether Truman overreached and made the United States the world's policeman, or whether the foundation established by Truman in the effort to fight a perceived global communist threat made our tragic foray into Vietnam inevitable, but at the time, Truman and his team's strong and thoughtful response to a series of ongoing challenges from the Soviet Union represented an impressive exercise in presidential leadership.

In the end, Truman was a case of what you saw was what you got. He had an identification with the common man that the aristocratic FDR did not approach, and yet, while no one could doubt his commitment, his methods did not always resonate with those whose interests he sought to serve. He was at his best in the 1948 campaign, making the case on his own behalf. At the same time, he understood how he was perceived and its impact on the politics of the time, a realization that led him to put his ego aside and wisely rebuff those who sought to attach his name to the European Recovery Plan, recognizing that the difference between the Marshall Plan and the Truman Plan would likely be the difference between success or failure.

And yet, while he was fully conscious of his own weaknesses, both personal and political, Truman was an unapologetic defender of the office of the presidency, both as a vehicle for good on behalf of the American people and as a representative of its people. He respected the office and recognized the responsibility that came with the job. From a practical perspective, he was a consistent advocate of a strong presidency. Truman continued the centralization of power in the executive that FDR had taken to new levels, but he was not above overreaching, as in the steel seizure case and the proposed drafting of railroad strikers. And, of course, the firing of Douglas MacArthur not only reinforced the hallowed American tradition of civilian control of the military but also reaffirmed the strength and primacy of the presidency. Too, no small amount of the ire Truman felt toward MacArthur was rooted in what Truman saw as a lack of respect for the office itself.

In looking back over the more than six decades since he left the White House, Harry Truman stands as an embodiment of the ever-shifting and evolving nature of presidential reputations. He left the White House with record low approval ratings and was succeeded by the wildly popular Dwight Eisenhower. As the early historical assessments came in, he seemed to be lost in the middle between two hugely popular and charismatic figures in FDR and Ike. But with time and circumstances, things began to change.

Ironically, an old Truman foe, Richard Nixon, helped burnish the former president's reputation. First, for all the furor over Truman having "lost China," Nixon's diplomatic initiative and visit in early 1972 did much to reduce the stigma of that earlier effort. Then, with the nation mired in the Watergate scandal, the publication of the book *Plain Speaking: An Oral History of Harry S. Truman* reintroduced the American people to a man whose integrity and common man demeanor posed a stark contrast with the president under siege for countless crimes and misdeeds. As the House considered impeachment proceedings against Nixon, *Plain Speaking* climbed the best-seller lists, with Truman's popularity rising in a seemingly inverse relation to Nixon's. And the Truman revival did not end with Nixon's resignation, as 1975 saw the arrival of the play *Give 'em Hell, Harry!*, starring actor James Whitmore as the plain-spoken president. The work had its official opening in the spring of 1975 in a performance at Ford's Theater, which was attended by Gerald Ford, and after subsequent stage performances were videotaped, the resulting film was released in the fall of 1975. For his effort, Whitmore earned both Academy Award and Golden Globe nominations for Best Actor as well as a Grammy Award for Best Spoken Word Recording.

Truman would likely have found all of this highly amusing, while being unconcerned about the change. Like any politician, indeed anyone who subjects himself of herself to public scrutiny and approval, he preferred to be supported in his efforts, but he also understood full well the vagaries of public reactions. Indeed, having reportedly responded to a 1948 supporter who yelled, "Give 'em hell, Harry," by declaring, "I never did give them hell; I just told the truth, and they thought it was hell," the old partisan would likely have been more than comfortable simply knowing that he had told the truth and given his best effort to a country he had been proud to serve.

Bill H. Pruden

Further Reading

Cochran, Bert. 1973. *Harry Truman and the Crisis Presidency*. New York: Funk & Wagnalls Co.

Dallek, Robert. 2008. *Harry S. Truman*. The American Presidents Series. Edited by Arthur M. Schlesinger Jr. and Sean Wilentz. New York: Times Books/Henry Holt and Company.

Hamby, Alonzo L. 1995. *Man of the People: A Life of Harry S. Truman*. New York: Oxford University Press.

Harry S. Truman Papers. n.d. Harry S Truman Presidential Library & Museum. https://www.trumanlibrary.org/hst-pape.htm.

McCullough, David. 1992. *Truman*. New York: Simon & Schuster.

Miller, Merle. 1973. *Plain Speaking: An Oral History of Harry S. Truman*. New York: Berkley Publishing Corporation.

Truman, Margaret. 1993. *Harry S. Truman*. New York: Avon Books.

The Truman Doctrine (March 12, 1947)

The containment policy to block Soviet expansion following World War II was central to the Truman presidency. The president's address to Congress announcing the Truman Doctrine and requesting funds was an important step in the evolution of that policy. While the centerpiece of the address was the specific situation related to Greece and Turkey, Truman made clear the broader concerns and ideas underlying his request for aid. In doing so, he laid the groundwork for the containment policy. Consequently, this address offers a good explanation of the ideas behind the policy.

Mr. President, Mr. Speaker, Members of the Congress of the United States:

The gravity of the situation which confronts the world today necessitates my appearance before a joint session of the Congress. The foreign policy and the national security of this country are involved.

One aspect of the present situation, which I wish to present to you at this time for your consideration and decision, concerns Greece and Turkey.

The United States has received from the Greek Government an urgent appeal for financial and economic assistance. Preliminary reports from the American Economic Mission now in Greece and reports from the American Ambassador in Greece corroborate the statement of the Greek Government that assistance is imperative if Greece is to survive as a free nation.

I do not believe that the American people and the Congress wish to turn a deaf ear to the appeal of the Greek Government.

Greece is not a rich country. Lack of sufficient natural resources has always forced the Greek people to work hard to make both ends meet. Since 1940, this industrious and peace loving country has suffered invasion, four years of cruel enemy occupation, and bitter internal strife.

When forces of liberation entered Greece they found that the retreating Germans had destroyed virtually all the railways, roads, port facilities, communications, and merchant marine. More than a thousand villages had been burned. Eighty-five per cent of the children were tubercular. Livestock, poultry, and draft animals had almost disappeared. Inflation had wiped out practically all savings.

As a result of these tragic conditions, a militant minority, exploiting human want and misery, was able to create political chaos which, until now, has made economic recovery impossible.

Greece is today without funds to finance the importation of those goods which are essential to bare subsistence. Under these circumstances the people of Greece cannot make progress in solving their problems of reconstruction. Greece is in desperate need of financial and economic assistance to enable it to resume purchases of food, clothing, fuel and seeds. These are indispensable for the subsistence of its people and are obtainable only from abroad. Greece must have help to import the goods necessary to restore internal order and security, so essential for economic and political recovery.

The Greek Government has also asked for the assistance of experienced American administrators, economists and technicians to insure that the financial and other aid given to Greece shall be used effectively in creating a stable and self-sustaining economy and in improving its public administration.

The very existence of the Greek state is today threatened by the terrorist activities of several thousand armed men, led by Communists, who defy the government's authority at a number of points, particularly along the northern boundaries. A Commission appointed by the United Nations security Council is at present investigating disturbed conditions in northern Greece and alleged border violations along the frontier between Greece on the one hand and Albania, Bulgaria, and Yugoslavia on the other.

Meanwhile, the Greek Government is unable to cope with the situation. The Greek army is small and poorly equipped. It needs supplies and equipment if it is to restore the authority of the government throughout Greek territory. Greece must have assistance if it is to become a self-supporting and self-respecting democracy.

The United States must supply that assistance. We have already extended to Greece certain types of relief and economic aid but these are inadequate.

There is no other country to which democratic Greece can turn.

No other nation is willing and able to provide the necessary support for a democratic Greek government.

The British Government, which has been helping Greece, can give no further financial or economic aid after March 31. Great Britain finds itself under the necessity of reducing or liquidating its commitments in several parts of the world, including Greece.

We have considered how the United Nations might assist in this crisis. But the situation is an urgent one requiring immediate action and the United Nations and its related organizations are not in a position to extend help of the kind that is required.

It is important to note that the Greek Government has asked for our aid in utilizing effectively the financial and other assistance we may give to Greece, and in improving its public administration. It is of the utmost importance that we supervise the use of any funds made available to Greece; in such a manner that each dollar spent will count toward making Greece self-supporting, and will help to build an economy in which a healthy democracy can flourish.

No government is perfect. One of the chief virtues of a democracy, however, is that its defects are always visible and under democratic processes can be pointed out and corrected. The Government of Greece is not perfect. Nevertheless it represents eighty-five per cent of the members of the Greek Parliament who were chosen in an election last year. Foreign observers, including 692 Americans, considered this election to be a fair expression of the views of the Greek people.

The Greek Government has been operating in an atmosphere of chaos and extremism. It has made mistakes. The extension of aid by this country does not mean that the United States condones everything that the Greek Government has done or will do. We have condemned in the past, and we condemn now, extremist measures of the right or the left. We have in the past advised tolerance, and we advise tolerance now.

Greece's neighbor, Turkey, also deserves our attention.

The future of Turkey as an independent and economically sound state is clearly no less important to the freedom-loving peoples of the world than the future of Greece. The circumstances in which Turkey finds itself today are considerably different from those of Greece. Turkey has been spared the disasters that have beset Greece. And during the war, the United States and Great Britain furnished Turkey with material aid.

Nevertheless, Turkey now needs our support.

Since the war Turkey has sought financial assistance from Great Britain and the United States for the purpose of effecting that modernization necessary for the maintenance of its national integrity.

That integrity is essential to the preservation of order in the Middle East.

The British government has informed us that, owing to its own difficulties can no longer extend financial or economic aid to Turkey.

As in the case of Greece, if Turkey is to have the assistance it needs, the United States must supply it. We are the only country able to provide that help.

I am fully aware of the broad implications involved if the United States extends assistance to Greece and Turkey, and I shall discuss these implications with you at this time.

One of the primary objectives of the foreign policy of the United States is the creation of conditions in which we and other nations will be able to work out a way of life free from coercion. This was a fundamental issue in the war with Germany and Japan. Our victory was won over countries which sought to impose their will, and their way of life, upon other nations.

To ensure the peaceful development of nations, free from coercion, the United States has taken a leading part in establishing the United Nations, The United Nations is designed to make possible lasting freedom and independence for all its members. We shall not realize our objectives, however, unless we are willing to help free peoples to maintain their free institutions and their national integrity against aggressive movements that seek to impose upon them totalitarian regimes. This is no more than a frank recognition that totalitarian regimes imposed on free peoples, by direct or indirect aggression, undermine the foundations of international peace and hence the security of the United States.

The peoples of a number of countries of the world have recently had totalitarian regimes forced upon them against their will. The Government of the United States has made frequent protests against coercion and intimidation, in violation of the Yalta agreement, in Poland, Rumania, and Bulgaria. I must also state that in a number of other countries there have been similar developments.

At the present moment in world history nearly every nation must choose between alternative ways of life. The choice is too often not a free one.

One way of life is based upon the will of the majority, and is distinguished by free institutions, representative government, free elections, guarantees of individual liberty, freedom of speech and religion, and freedom from political oppression.

The second way of life is based upon the will of a minority forcibly imposed upon the majority. It relies upon terror and oppression, a controlled press and radio; fixed elections, and the suppression of personal freedoms.

I believe that it must be the policy of the United States to support free peoples who are resisting attempted subjugation by armed minorities or by outside pressures.

I believe that we must assist free peoples to work out their own destinies in their own way.

I believe that our help should be primarily through economic and financial aid which is essential to economic stability and orderly political processes.

The world is not static, and the status quo is not sacred. But we cannot allow changes in the status quo in violation of the Charter of the United Nations by such methods as coercion, or by such subterfuges as political infiltration. In helping free and independent nations to maintain their freedom, the United States

will be giving effect to the principles of the Charter of the United Nations.

It is necessary only to glance at a map to realize that the survival and integrity of the Greek nation are of grave importance in a much wider situation. If Greece should fall under the control of an armed minority, the effect upon its neighbor, Turkey, would be immediate and serious. Confusion and disorder might well spread throughout the entire Middle East.

Moreover, the disappearance of Greece as an independent state would have a profound effect upon those countries in Europe whose peoples are struggling against great difficulties to maintain their freedoms and their independence while they repair the damages of war.

It would be an unspeakable tragedy if these countries, which have struggled so long against overwhelming odds, should lose that victory for which they sacrificed so much. Collapse of free institutions and loss of independence would be disastrous not only for them but for the world. Discouragement and possibly failure would quickly be the lot of neighboring peoples striving to maintain their freedom and independence.

Should we fail to aid Greece and Turkey in this fateful hour, the effect will be far reaching to the West as well as to the East.

We must take immediate and resolute action.

I therefore ask the Congress to provide authority for assistance to Greece and Turkey in the amount of $400,000,000 for the period ending June 30, 1948. In requesting these funds, I have taken into consideration the maximum amount of relief assistance which would be furnished to Greece out of the $350,000,000 which I recently requested that the Congress authorize for the prevention of starvation and suffering in countries devastated by the war.

In addition to funds, I ask the Congress to authorize the detail of American civilian and military personnel to Greece and Turkey, at the request of those countries, to assist in the tasks of reconstruction, and for the purpose of supervising the use of such financial and material assistance as may be furnished. I recommend that authority also be provided for the instruction and training of selected Greek and Turkish personnel.

Finally, I ask that the Congress provide authority which will permit the speediest and most effective use, in terms of needed commodities, supplies, and equipment, of such funds as may be authorized.

If further funds, or further authority, should be needed for purposes indicated in this message, I shall not hesitate to bring the situation before the Congress. On this subject the Executive and Legislative branches of the Government must work together.

This is a serious course upon which we embark.

I would not recommend it except that the alternative is much more serious. The United States contributed $341,000,000,000 toward winning World War II. This is an investment in world freedom and world peace.

The assistance that I am recommending for Greece and Turkey amounts to little more than 1 tenth of 1 per cent of this investment. It is only common sense that we should safeguard this investment and make sure that it was not in vain.

The seeds of totalitarian regimes are nurtured by misery and want. They spread and grow in the evil soil of poverty and strife. They reach their full growth when the hope of a people for a better life has died. We must keep that hope alive.

The free peoples of the world look to us for support in maintaining their freedoms.

If we falter in our leadership, we may endanger the peace of the world—and we shall surely endanger the welfare of our own nation.

Great responsibilities have been placed upon us by the swift movement of events.

I am confident that the Congress will face these responsibilities squarely.

Source: *Public Papers of the Presidents of the United States. Harry S. Truman, 1947.* Washington, D.C.: Government Printing Office, 1963, 176–180.

Secretary of State George C. Marshall Outlines the Marshall Plan (June 5, 1947)

A major triumph of the Truman administration was the Marshall Plan. Although the program would prove to be an important cog in the nation's containment policy, Secretary of State George C. Marshall made clear that it was not simply a weapon to be used in the battle against communism. Rather, as it in fact proved to be, the plan was a response to human needs and a policy intended to help revive a war-torn continent still struggling in the aftermath of World War II.

I'm profoundly grateful and touched by the great distinction and honor and great compliment accorded me by the authorities of Harvard this morning. I'm overwhelmed, as a matter of fact, and I'm rather fearful of my inability to maintain such a high rating as you've been generous enough to accord to me. In these historic and lovely surroundings, this perfect day, and this very wonderful assembly, it is a tremendously impressive thing to an individual in my position. But to speak more seriously, I need not tell you, gentlemen, that the world situation is very serious. That must be apparent to all intelligent people. I think one difficulty is that the problem is one of such enormous complexity that the very mass of facts presented to the public by press and radio make it exceedingly difficult for the man in the street to reach a clear appraisement of the situation. Furthermore, the people of this country are distant from the troubled areas of the earth and it is hard for them to comprehend the plight and consequent reactions of the long-suffering peoples, and the effect of those reactions on their governments in connection with our efforts to promote peace in the world.

In considering the requirements for the rehabilitation of Europe, the physical loss of life, the visible destruction of cities, factories, mines and railroads was correctly estimated but it has become obvious during recent months that this visible destruction was probably less serious than the dislocation of the entire fabric of European economy. For the past 10 years conditions have been highly abnormal. The feverish preparation for war and the more feverish maintenance of the war effort engulfed all aspects of national economies. Machinery has fallen into disrepair or is entirely obsolete. Under the arbitrary and destructive Nazi rule, virtually every possible enterprise was geared into the German war machine. Long-standing commercial ties, private institutions, banks, insurance companies, and shipping companies disappeared, through loss of capital, absorption through nationalization, or by simple destruction. In many countries, confidence in the local currency has been severely shaken. The breakdown of the business structure of Europe during the war was complete. Recovery has been seriously retarded by the fact that two years after the close of hostilities a peace settlement with Germany and Austria has not been agreed upon. But even given a more prompt solution of these difficult problems the rehabilitation of the economic structure of Europe quite evidently will require a much longer time and greater effort than had been foreseen.

There is a phase of this matter which is both interesting and serious. The farmer has always produced the foodstuffs to exchange with the city dweller for the other necessities of life. This division of labor is the basis of modern civilization. At the present time it is threatened with breakdown. The town and city industries are not producing adequate goods to exchange with the food producing farmer. Raw materials and fuel are in short supply. Machinery is lacking or worn out. The farmer or the peasant cannot find the goods for sale which he desires to purchase. So the sale of his farm produce for money which he cannot use seems to him an unprofitable transaction. He, therefore, has withdrawn many fields from crop cultivation and is using them for grazing. He feeds more grain to stock and finds for himself and his family an ample supply of food, however short he may be on clothing and the other ordinary gadgets of civilization. Meanwhile people in the cities are short of food and fuel. So the governments are forced to use their foreign money and credits to procure these necessities abroad. This process exhausts funds which are urgently needed for reconstruction. Thus a very serious situation is rapidly developing which bodes no good for the world. The modern system of the division of labor upon which the exchange of products is based is in danger of breaking down.

The truth of the matter is that Europe's requirements for the next three or four years of foreign food and other essential products—principally from America—are so much greater than her present ability to pay that she must have substantial additional help or face economic, social, and political deterioration of a very grave character.

The remedy lies in breaking the vicious circle and restoring the confidence of the European people in the economic future of their own countries and of Europe as a whole. The manufacturer and the farmer throughout wide areas must be able and willing to exchange their products for currencies the continuing value of which is not open to question.

Aside from the demoralizing effect on the world at large and the possibilities of disturbances arising as a result of the desperation of the people concerned, the consequences to the economy of the United States should be apparent to all. It is logical that the United States should do whatever it is able to do to assist in the return of normal economic health in the world, without which there can be no political stability and no assured peace. Our policy is directed not against any country or doctrine but against hunger, poverty, desperation and chaos. Its purpose should be the revival of a working economy in the world so as to permit the emergence of political and social conditions in which free institutions can exist. Such assistance, I am convinced, must not be on a piecemeal basis as various crises develop. Any assistance that this Government may render in the future should provide a cure rather than a mere palliative. Any government that is willing to assist in the task of recovery will find full co-operation I am sure, on the part of the United States Government. Any government which maneuvers to block the recovery of other countries cannot expect help from us. Furthermore, governments, political parties, or groups which seek to perpetuate human misery in order to profit therefrom politically or otherwise will encounter the opposition of the United States.

It is already evident that, before the United States Government can proceed much further in its efforts to alleviate the situation and help start the European world on its way to recovery, there must be some agreement among the countries of Europe as to the requirements of the situation and the part those countries themselves will take in order to give proper effect to whatever action might be undertaken by this Government. It would be neither fitting nor efficacious for this Government to undertake to draw up unilaterally a program designed to place Europe on its feet economically. This is the business of the Europeans. The initiative, I think, must come from Europe. The role of this country should consist of friendly aid in the drafting of a European program and of later support of such a program so far as it may be practical for us to do so. The program should be a joint one, agreed to by a number, if not all European nations.

An essential part of any successful action on the part of the United States is an understanding on the part of the people of America of the character of the problem and the remedies to be applied. Political passion and prejudice should have no part. With foresight, and a willingness on the part of our people to face up to the vast responsibility which history has clearly placed upon our country, the difficulties I have outlined can and will be overcome.

I am sorry that on each occasion I have said something publicly in regard to our international situation, I've been forced by the necessities of the case to enter into rather technical discussions. But to my mind, it is of vast importance that our people reach some general understanding of what the complications really are, rather than react from a passion or a prejudice or an emotion of the moment. As I said more formally a moment ago, we are remote from the scene of these troubles. It is virtually impossible at this distance merely by reading, or listening, or even seeing photographs or motion pictures, to grasp at all the real significance of the situation. And yet the whole world of the future hangs on a proper judgment. It hangs, I think, to a large extent on the realization of the American people, of just what are the various dominant factors. What are the reactions of the people? What are the justifications of those reactions? What are the sufferings? What is needed? What can best be done? What must be done?

Thank you very much.

Source: Marshall, George C. "European Initiative Essential to Economic Recovery." *Department of State Bulletin* 16, no. 415 (1947): 1159–1160.

Relieving General MacArthur of His Command (April 11, 1951)

President Truman's "firing" of General Douglas MacArthur as the commander of UN forces in Korea was one of the most controversial acts of his presidency. Although it was politically damaging, it was an act that not only reaffirmed the supremacy of civilian control over the military in the American system, but it also revealed, not for the first time, Truman's deep respect (and indeed veneration) of his office. It was also yet another of his efforts to protect the power and authority of the presidency as the sole office that represented the American people.

Statement by the President:

With deep regret I have concluded that General of the Army Douglas MacArthur is unable to give his wholehearted support to the policies of the United States Government and of the United Nations in matters pertaining to his official duties. In view of the specific responsibilities imposed upon me by the Constitution of the United States and the added responsibility which has been entrusted to me by the United Nations, I have decided that I must make a change of command in the Far East. I have, therefore, relieved General MacArthur of his commands and have designated Lt. Gen. Matthew B. Ridgway as his successor.

Full and vigorous debate on matters of national policy is a vital element in the constitutional system of our free democracy. It is fundamental, however, that military commanders must be governed by the policies and directives issued to them in the manner provided by our laws and Constitution. In time of crisis, this consideration is particularly compelling.

General MacArthur's place in history as one of our greatest commanders is fully established. The Nation owes him a debt of gratitude for the distinguished and exceptional service which he has rendered his country in posts of great responsibility. For that reason I repeat my regret at the necessity for the action I feel compelled to take in his case.

Order by the President to General MacArthur:

I deeply regret that it becomes my duty as President and Commander in Chief of the United States military forces to replace you as Supreme Commander, Allied Powers; Commander in Chief, United Nations Command; Commander in Chief, Far East; and Commanding General, U.S. Army, Far East.

You will turn over your commands, effective at once, to Lt. Gen. Matthew B. Ridgway. You are authorized to have issued such orders as are necessary to complete desired travel to such place as you select.

My reasons for your replacement will be made public concurrently with the delivery to you of the foregoing order and are contained in the next following message.

Source: *Public Papers of the Presidents of the United States. Harry S. Truman, 1951.* Washington, D.C.: Government Printing Office, 1965, 222–227.

Farewell Address (January 15, 1953)

President Truman's farewell address was a recounting of the many things that he and his administration had achieved, a statement of patriotism, and a tribute to a country in which a boy from Missouri could become president and have the opportunity to serve its people and the world. Truman took pride in what he had done, but he also took pride in the principles and the ideas of the country and the people he had served, whose daily efforts made real the American dream. The farewell address was a fitting reflection of the man who gave it as well as his approach to the office he had faithfully occupied for almost eight years.

My fellow Americans:

I am happy to have this opportunity to talk to you once more before I leave the White House.

Next Tuesday, General Eisenhower will be inaugurated as President of the United States. A short time after the new President takes his oath of office, I will be on the train going back home to Independence, Missouri. I will once again be a plain, private citizen of this great Republic.

That is as it should be. Inauguration Day will be a great demonstration of our democratic process. I am glad to be a part of it—glad to wish General Eisenhower all possible success, as he begins his term—glad the whole world will have a chance to see how simply and how peacefully our American system transfers the vast power of the Presidency from my hands to his. It is a good object lesson in democracy. I am very proud of it. And I know you are, too.

During the last 2 months I have done my best to make this transfer an orderly one. I have talked with my successor on the affairs of the country, both foreign and domestic, and my Cabinet officers have talked with their successors. I want to say that General Eisenhower and his associates have cooperated fully in this effort. Such an orderly transfer from one party to another has never taken place before in our history. I think a real precedent has been set.

In speaking to you tonight, I have no new revelations to make—no political statements—no policy announcements. There are simply a few things in my heart that I want to say to you. I want to say "goodbye" and "thanks for your help." And I want to talk to you a little while about what has happened since I became your President.

I am speaking to you from the room where I have worked since April 12, 1945. This is the President's office in the West Wing of the White House. This is the desk where I have signed most of the papers that embodied the decisions I have made as President. It has been the desk of many Presidents, and will be the desk of many more.

Since I became President, I have been to Europe, Mexico, Canada, Brazil, Puerto Rico, and the Virgin Islands—Wake Island and Hawaii. I have visited almost every State in the Union. I have traveled 135,000 miles by air, 77,000 by rail, and 17,000 by ship. But the mail always followed me, and wherever I happened to be, that's where the office of the President was.

The greatest part of the President's job is to make decisions—big ones and small ones, dozens of them almost every day. The papers may circulate around the Government for a while but they finally reach this desk. And then, there's no place else for them to go. The President—whoever he is—has to decide. He can't pass the buck to anybody. No one else can do the deciding for him. That's his job.

That's what I've been doing here in this room, for almost 8 years. And over in the main part of the White House, there's a study on the second floor—a room much like this one—where I have worked at night and early in the morning on the papers I couldn't get to at the office.

Of course, for more than 3 years Mrs. Truman and I were not living in the White House. We were across the street in the Blair House. That was when the White House almost fell down on us and had to be rebuilt. I had a study over at the Blair House, too, but living in the Blair House was not as convenient as living in the White House. The Secret Service wouldn't let me walk across the street, so I had to get in a car every morning to cross the street to the White House office, again at noon to go to the Blair House for lunch, again to go back to the office after lunch, and finally take an automobile at night to return to the Blair House. Fantastic, isn't it? But necessary, so my guards thought—and they are the bosses on such matters as that.

Now, of course, we're back in the White House. It is in very good condition, and General Eisenhower will be able to take up his residence in the house and work right here. That will be much more convenient for him, and I'm very glad the renovation job was all completed before his term began.

Your new President is taking office in quite different circumstances than when I became President 8 years ago. On April 1945, I had been presiding over the Senate in my capacity as Vice President. When the Senate recessed about 5 o'clock in the afternoon, I walked over to the office of the Speaker of the House, Mr. Rayburn, to discuss pending legislation. As soon as I arrived, I was told that Mr. Early, one of President Roosevelt's secretaries, wanted me to call. I reached Mr. Early, and he told me to come to the White House as quickly as possible, to enter by way of the Pennsylvania Avenue entrance, and to come to Mrs. Roosevelt's study.

When I arrived, Mrs. Roosevelt told me the tragic news, and I felt the shock that all of you felt a little later—when the word came over the radio and appeared in the newspapers. President Roosevelt had died. I offered to do anything I could for Mrs. Roosevelt, and then I asked the Secretary of State to call the Cabinet together.

At 7:09 p.m. I was sworn in as President by Chief Justice Stone in the Cabinet Room.

Things were happening fast in those days. The San Francisco conference to organize the United Nations had been called for April 25th. I was asked if that meeting would go forward. I announced that it would. That was my first decision.

After attending President Roosevelt's funeral, I went to the Hall of the House of Representatives and told a joint session of the Congress that I would carry on President Roosevelt's policies.

On May 7th, Germany surrendered. The announcement was made on May 8th, my 61st birthday.

Mr. Churchill called me shortly after that and wanted a meeting with me and Prime Minister Stalin of Russia. Later on, a meeting was agreed upon, and Churchill, Stalin, and I met at Potsdam in Germany.

Meanwhile, the first atomic explosion took place out in the New Mexico desert.

The war against Japan was still going on. I made the decision that the atomic bomb had to be used to end it. I made that decision in the conviction it would save hundreds of thousands of lives—Japanese as well as American. Japan surrendered, and we were faced with the huge problems of bringing the troops home and reconverting the economy from war to peace.

All these things happened within just a little over 4 months—from April to August 1945. I tell you this to illustrate the tremendous scope of the work your President has to do.

And all these emergencies and all the developments to meet them have required the President to put in long hours—usually 17 hours a day, with no payment for overtime. I sign my name, on the average, 600 times a day, see and talk to hundreds of people every month, shake hands with thousands every year, and still carry on the business of the largest going concern in the whole world. There is no job like it on the face of the earth—in the power which is concentrated here at this desk, and in the responsibility and difficulty of the decisions.

I want all of you to realize how big a job, how hard a job, it is—not for my sake, because I am stepping out of it—but for the sake of my successor. He needs the understanding and the help of every citizen. It is not enough for you to come out once every 4 years and vote for a candidate, and then go back home and say, "Well, I've done my part, now let the new President do the worrying." He can't do the job alone.

Regardless of your politics, whether you are Republican or Democrat, your fate is tied up with what is done here in this room. The President is President of the whole country. We must give him our support as citizens of the United States. He will have mine, and I want you to give him yours.

I suppose that history will remember my term in office as the years when the "cold war" began to overshadow our lives. I have had hardly a day in office that has not been dominated by this all—embracing struggle—this conflict between those who love freedom and those who would lead the world back into slavery and darkness. And always in the background there has been the atomic bomb.

But when history says that my term of office saw the beginning of the cold war, it will also say that in those 8 years we have set the course that can win it. We have succeeded in carving out a new set of policies to attain peace—positive policies, policies of world leadership, policies that express faith in other free people. We have averted world war III up to now, and we may already have succeeded in establishing conditions which can keep that war from happening as far ahead as man can see.

These are great and historic achievements that we can all be proud of. Think of the difference between our course now and our course 30 years ago. After the First World War we withdrew from world affairs—we failed to act in concert with other peoples against aggression—we helped to kill the League of Nations—and we built up tariff barriers that strangled world trade. This time, we avoided those mistakes. We helped to found and sustain the United Nations. We have welded alliances that include the greater part of the free world. And we have gone ahead with other free countries to help build their economies and link us all together in a healthy world trade.

Think back for a moment to the 1930's and you will see the difference. The Japanese moved into Manchuria, and free men did not act. The Fascists moved into Ethiopia, and we did not act. The Nazis marched into the Rhineland, into Austria, into Czechoslovakia, and free men were paralyzed for lack of strength and unity and will.

Think about those years of weakness and indecision, and the World War II which was their evil result. Then think about the speed and courage and decisiveness with which we have moved against the Communist threat since World War II.

The first crisis came in 1945 and 1946, when the Soviet Union refused to honor its agreement to remove its troops from Iran. Members of my Cabinet came to me and asked if we were ready to take the risk that a firm stand involved. I replied that we were. So we took

our stand—we made it clear to the Soviet Union that we expected them to honor their agreement—and the Soviet troops were withdrawn from Iran.

Then, in early 1947, the Soviet Union threatened Greece and Turkey. The British sent me a message saying they could no longer keep their forces in that area. Something had to be done at once, or the eastern Mediterranean would be taken over by the Communists. On March 12th, I went before the Congress and stated our determination to help the people of Greece and Turkey maintain their independence. Today, Greece is still free and independent; and Turkey is a bulwark of strength at a strategic corner of the world.

Then came the Marshall plan which saved Europe, the heroic Berlin airlift, and our military aid programs.

We inaugurated the North Atlantic Pact, the Rio Pact binding the Western Hemisphere together, and the defense pacts with countries of the Far Pacific.

Most important of all, we acted in Korea. I was in Independence, Missouri, in June 1950, when Secretary Acheson telephoned me and gave me the news about the invasion of Korea. I told the Secretary to lay the matter at once before the United Nations, and I came on back to Washington.

Flying back over the flatlands of the Middle West and over the Appalachians that summer afternoon, I had a lot of time to think. I turned the problem over in my mind in many ways, but my thoughts kept coming back to the 1930's—to Manchuria, to Ethiopia, the Rhineland, Austria, and finally to Munich.

Here was history repeating itself. Here was another probing action, another testing action. If we let the Republic of Korea go under, some other country would be next, and then another. And all the time, the courage and confidence of the free world would be ebbing away, just as it did in the 1930's. And the United Nations would go the way of the League of Nations.

When I reached Washington, I met immediately with the Secretary of State, the Secretary of Defense, and General Bradley, and the other civilian and military officials who had information and advice to help me decide on what to do. We talked about the problems long and hard. We considered those problems very carefully.

It was not easy to make the decision to send American boys again into battle. I was a soldier in the First World War, and I know what a soldier goes through. I know well the anguish that mothers and fathers and families go through. So I knew what was ahead if we acted in Korea.

But after all this was said, we realized that the issue was whether there would be fighting in a limited area now or on a much larger scale later on—whether there would be some casualties now or many more casualties later.

So a decision was reached—the decision I believe was the most important in my time as President of the United States.

In the days that followed, the most heartening fact was that the American people clearly agreed with the decision.

And in Korea, our men are fighting as valiantly as Americans have ever fought—because they know they are fighting in the same cause of freedom in which Americans have stood ever since the beginning of the Republic.

Where free men had failed the test before, this time we met the test.

We met it firmly. We met it successfully. The aggression has been repelled. The Communists have seen their hopes of easy conquest go down the drain. The determination of free people to defend themselves has been made clear to the Kremlin.

As I have thought about our worldwide struggle with the Communists these past 8 years—day in and day out—I have never once doubted that you, the people of our country, have the will to do what is necessary to win this terrible fight against communism. I know the people of this country have that will and determination, and I have always depended on it. Because I have been sure of that, I have been able to make necessary decisions even though they called for sacrifices by all of us. And I have not been wrong in my judgment of the American people.

That same assurance of our people's determination will be General Eisenhower's greatest source of strength in carrying on this struggle.

Now, once in a while, I get a letter from some impatient person asking, why don't we get it over with? Why don't we issue an ultimatum, make all-out war, drop the atomic bomb?

For most Americans, the answer is quite simple: We are not made that way. We are a moral people. Peace is our goal, with justice and freedom. We cannot, of our own free will, violate the very principles that we are striving to defend. The whole purpose of what we are doing is to prevent world war III. Starting a war is no way to make peace.

But if anyone still thinks that just this once, bad means can bring good ends, then let me remind you of this: We are living in the 8th year of the atomic age. We are not the only nation that is learning to unleash the power of the atom. A third world war might dig the grave not only of our Communist opponents but also of our own society, our world as well as theirs.

Starting an atomic war is totally unthinkable for rational men.

Then, some of you may ask, when and how will the cold war end? I think I can answer that simply. The Communist world has great resources, and it looks strong. But there is a fatal flaw in their society. Theirs is a godless system, a system of slavery; there is no freedom in it, no consent. The Iron Curtain, the secret police, the constant purges, all these are symptoms of a great basic weakness—the rulers' fear of their own people.

In the long run the strength of our free society, and our ideals, will prevail over a system that has respect for neither God nor man.

Last week, in my State of the Union Message to the Congress—and I hope you will all take the time to read it—I explained how I think we will finally win through.

As the free world grows stronger, more united, more attractive to men on both sides of the Iron Curtain—and as the Soviet hopes for easy expansion are blocked—then there will have to come a time of change in the Soviet world. Nobody can say for sure when that is going to be, or exactly how it will come about, whether by revolution, or trouble in the satellite states, or by a change inside the Kremlin.

Whether the Communist rulers shift their policies of their own free will—or whether the change comes about in some other way—I have not a doubt in the world that a change will occur.

I have a deep and abiding faith in the destiny of free men. With patience and courage, we shall some day move on into a new era—a wonderful golden age—an age when we can use the peaceful tools that science has forged for us to do away with poverty and human misery everywhere on earth.

Think what can be done, once our capital, our skills, our science—most of all atomic energy—can be released from the tasks of defense and turned wholly to peaceful purposes all around the world.

There is no end to what can be done.

I can't help but dream out loud just a little here.

The Tigris and Euphrates Valley can be made to bloom as it did in the times of Babylon and Nineveh. Israel can be made the country of milk and honey as it was in the time of Joshua.

There is a plateau in Ethiopia some 6,000 to 8,000 feet high, that has 65,000 square miles of land just exactly like the corn belt in northern Illinois. Enough food can be raised there to feed a hundred million people.

There are places in South America—places in Colombia and Venezuela and Brazil—just like that plateau in Ethiopia—places where food could be raised for millions of people.

These things can be done, and they are self-liquidating projects. If we can get peace and safety in the world under the United Nations, the developments will come so fast we will not recognize the world in which we now live.

This is our dream of the future—our picture of the world we hope to have when the Communist threat is overcome.

I've talked a lot tonight about the menace of communism—and our fight against it—because that is the overriding issue of our time. But there are some other things we've done that history will record. One of them is that we in America have learned how to attain real prosperity for our people.

We have 62 1/2 million people at work. Businessmen, farmers, laborers, white-collar people, all have better incomes and more of the good things of life than ever before in the history of the world.

There hasn't been a failure of an insured bank in nearly 9 years. No depositor has lost a cent in that period.

And the income of our people has been fairly distributed, perhaps more so than at any other time in recent history.

We have made progress in spreading the blessings of American life to all of our people. There has been a tremendous awakening of the American conscience on the great issues of civil rights—equal economic opportunities, equal rights of citizenship, and equal educational opportunities for all our people, whatever their race or religion or status of birth.

So, as I empty the drawers of this desk, and as Mrs. Truman and I leave the White House, we have no regret. We feel we have done our best in the public service. I hope and believe we have contributed to the welfare of this Nation and to the peace of the world.

When Franklin Roosevelt died, I felt there must be a million men better qualified than I, to take up the Presidential task. But the work was mine to do, and I had to do it. And I have tried to give it everything that was in me.

Through all of it, through all the years that I have worked here in this room, I have been well aware I did not really work alone—that you were working with me.

No President could ever hope to lead our country, or to sustain the burdens of this office, save as the people helped with their support. I have had that help—you have given me that support—on all our great essential undertakings to build the free world's strength and keep the peace.

Those are the big things. Those are the things we have done together.

For that I shall be grateful, always.

And now, the time has come for me to say good night—and God bless you all.

Source: *Public Papers of the Presidents of the United States.* Harry S. Truman, 1952–1953. Washington, D.C.: Government Printing Office, 1966, 1197–1202.

34. DWIGHT D. EISENHOWER (1890–1969)

Presidential Term (1953–1961)

CHRONOLOGY

October 14, 1890—Dwight D. Eisenhower is born in Denison, Texas.

Spring 1915—Eisenhower graduates from West Point.

July 1, 1916—Eisenhower marries Mamie Doud.

April 1917—The United States enters World War I.

June 28, 1919—The Treaty of Versailles ending World War I is signed.

December 7, 1941—Japan attacks Pearl Harbor, leading to the U.S. entry into World War II.

June 6, 1944—Eisenhower oversees the D-Day operation on the beaches of Normandy.

June 26, 1945—The charter for United Nations is signed.

June 1948—Eisenhower assumes the presidency of Columbia University.

1949—The North Atlantic Treaty Organization (NATO) is established.

February 9, 1950—Senator Joseph McCarthy of Wisconsin announces that he has a list of over 200 communists working in the government; it is the start of a four-year witch hunt.

February 27, 1951—The Twenty-Second Amendment limiting presidential tenure to two terms is ratified.

November 4, 1952—Eisenhower is elected the 34th president of the United States.

March 5, 1953—Soviet leader Joseph Stalin dies.

June 19, 1953—Julius and Ethel Rosenberg are executed.

May 17, 1954—The U.S. Supreme Court issues a unanimous ruling in *Brown v. Board of Education of Topeka*, outlawing segregation in schools.

April 12, 1955—Dr. Jonas Salk announces the discovery of a polio vaccine.

May 1955—The Warsaw Pact is established.

September 24, 1955—President Eisenhower suffers a heart attack while vacationing in Colorado.

December 1955–December 1956—Dr. Martin Luther King Jr. heads the Montgomery, Alabama, bus boycott.

January 28, 1956—Elvis Presley makes his first appearance on national television.

November 6, 1956—President Eisenhower is elected to a second term as president.

September 9, 1957—President Eisenhower signs the Civil Rights Act of 1957.

September 24, 1957—President Eisenhower orders federal troops into Little Rock, Arkansas, to uphold the school desegregation order.

October 4, 1957—The Soviet Union launches Sputnik.

November 8, 1960—John F. Kennedy is elected the 35th president of the United States.

January 17, 1961—President Eisenhower delivers his now famous televised farewell address.

March 28, 1969—Eisenhower dies in Washington, D.C.

BIOGRAPHICAL SKETCH

Dwight David "Ike" Eisenhower was the 35th president of the United States. The nickname "Ike" seems to have been a one-syllable contraction of Eisenhower, and all the male children were referred to as "Ike." When he emerged from World War II as a national hero, leaders in both parties sought to turn the general's personal popularity into political power.

Ultimately elected in 1952 and reelected in 1956 as a Republican, Eisenhower presided over a period of economic prosperity and world peace. Although not without domestic strife and international tensions, the era nevertheless still represented a time of comparative calm following the tumultuous decades marked by the Great Depression and World War II and its immediate aftermath.

David Dwight Eisenhower was born on October 14, 1890, in Denison, Texas, to David Jacob Eisenhower and his wife, the former Ida Elizabeth Stover, the third of six boys. He was named David after his father, but to avoid confusion, he was called Dwight throughout his youth. By the time he enrolled at West Point, he was signing his name Dwight David Eisenhower.

The family moved to Abilene, Kansas, in 1891. In Abilene, the house of six growing boys was an active place, and roughhousing, not to mention fights, were the norm. So too was working. Dwight sold produce from the family garden while also working in a local creamery where he hauled ice and shoveled coal. He attended the local Abilene schools, going to Lincoln School for grades one through six followed by Garfield School for seventh and eighth grades.

At 15, Eisenhower developed blood poisoning after scraping his knee. To address the problem, the doctor initially recommended that his leg be amputated, but the active, athletic Eisenhower reacted so violently, asserting that he would rather die than be crippled, that his parent acceded to his wishes and pursued a less radical, but ultimately successful, treatment.

Eisenhower attended Abilene High School, where he graduated as a member of the class of 1909. While in high school, his favorite subjects were history and geometry, and in addition to organizing the school's athletic association, he played on both the football and baseball teams. Seeking a free college education, Eisenhower looked to the nation's service academies, first taking the exam for the United States Naval Academy. However, he was told that, having passed his 20th birthday, he was too old to be considered. He then focused his sights on the United States Military Academy at West Point, New York, and was admitted. He was a solid student, graduating 61st out of 164 cadets.

He turned in strong performances in engineering, ordnance, gunnery, and drill regulation, but his deportment record was not as strong as his academic record, as he ranked 95th in that area. Eisenhower would later say that his behavior suffered from his focus on sports; by his sophomore year, he was on track to be a star running back. However, an injury that year ended his career and caused him to consider leaving West Point. When he was given a chance to help coach the junior varsity team, he remained. Graduating in 1915, Eisenhower was commissioned a second lieutenant and assigned to the Nineteenth Infantry at Fort Sam Houston, Texas.

Shortly after he arrived in Texas, the young soldier was introduced to Marie Geneva "Mamie" Doud, to whom he would become engaged on Valentine's Day 1916 and would marry on July 1, 1916. The couple's first child, Doud Dwight, was born in September 1917; he tragically died of scarlet fever in January 1921. Their second son, John Sheldon Doud Eisenhower, was born on August 3, 1922, and he would follow his father into the military, graduating from West Point on June 6, 1944, D-Day, and then earning a reputation as a skilled military historian. Mamie's years as an army wife who followed her husband through numerous postings had made her an adaptable and gracious hostess, and she was just that as first lady. At the same time, also guarded her privacy, making her more like Bess Truman than Eleanor Roosevelt. She had long suffered from Ménière's disease, an inner ear condition that affects a person's equilibrium. Consequently, she would at times appear unsteady on her feet, a fact that resulted in unfounded rumors that the first lady had a drinking problem. Retiring with the president to Gettysburg in 1961, she looked after the president in his declining health until his death in 1969. She remained at Gettysburg until her own death in 1979. She is buried next to Eisenhower in Abilene.

Fort Sam Houston became the first stop on Dwight and Mamie's itinerant army journey, which Mamie later reported had included 28 moves before their retirement after his presidency. While at Fort Sam Houston, Eisenhower received promotions to first lieutenant in July 1916 and captain in May 1917. With the onset of World War I, Eisenhower sought an overseas assignment, but he was instead kept in the United

States, where he served as a training instructor at Fort Oglethorpe, Georgia; an organizer of the Sixty-Fifth Battalion Engineers at Camp Meade, Maryland; and commander of the Tank Corps Training Center at Camp Colt, Pennsylvania. These efforts earned him a temporary wartime promotion to major in June and lieutenant colonel in October of 1918, but once the war ended, he was back to the permanent rank of captain, although a promotion to major did come in June 1920.

During 1921 and the first part of 1922, Eisenhower served as a tank commander at Fort Dix, New Jersey; Fort Benning, Georgia; and then back again at Camp Meade. That was followed by an assignment to the Panama Canal Zone, where he was stationed from 1922 to 1924. He attended the Command and General Staff School at Ft. Leavenworth, Kansas, in 1925 and 1926, and he followed that with a stint at the Army War College in 1928 and 1929. From 1929 to 1932, Eisenhower served as special assistant to the assistant secretary of war, a post he left to join the staff of General Doulas MacArthur, an assignment that allowed him to be involved in MacArthur's effort to clear the Bonus Marchers from the capital. In 1935 he accompanied MacArthur to the Philippines, serving as his senior military assistant until 1939.

Having been promoted to lieutenant colonel in July 1936, Eisenhower returned to the United State upon assignment to Fort Lewis, Washington, where he served as executive officer of the Fifteenth Infantry Regiment for most of 1940 before being named chief of staff for infantry commander General Charles F. Thompson from November 1940 to the following March. Then, sporting a promotion to colonel, he served as chief of staff to General Kenyon A. Joyce of IX Corps from March to June 1941. He next assumed the post of chief of staff to General Walter Krueger, the III Corps commander, at Fort Sam Houston, where he served from June to December 1941. During the course of this assignment, he directed a number of large-scale training maneuvers, and with his efforts impressing his superiors, he earned a promotion to brigadier general.

In the aftermath of the attack on Pearl Harbor, Eisenhower was called to Washington and made assistant chief of staff in charge of war plans. He quickly

Dwight D. Eisenhower (Library of Congress)

distinguished himself, and in March 1942, he received a promotion to major general while being named chief of the general staff's operations division. A little over a year later, in June 1942, Eisenhower was named commander of U.S. forces in Europe, with a promotion to lieutenant general following a month later. Serving as Allied commander in chief, he oversaw the invasions of North Africa in November 1942, Sicily in July 1943, and Italy in September 1943. On August 30, Eisenhower received a permanent promotion to brigadier general and major general. In the aftermath of this series of successes, in December 1943, Roosevelt named Eisenhower the supreme Allied Commander and ordered him to mount an invasion of Europe with the goal of finally defeating Germany. The operation was named Overlord, and because of a combination of tides, moon phase, and the sunrise, June 5 was selected as D-Day. Weather forced a one-day postponement, but on June 6, 1944, the Allies were able to land at Normandy, France, and begin their movement inland toward Germany.

In December, Eisenhower was promoted to five-star general of the army. He continued to oversee the Allied efforts, including the final assault on Germany, and on May 7, 1945, he accepted their surrender in a ceremony in Reims, France. In November 1945, Eisenhower returned to the United States to assume the position of army chief of staff, succeeding the retired General George C. Marshall, who had been a mentor earlier in Eisenhower's career. General Eisenhower resigned from the army, where he had spent his whole adult life, in February 1948.

Eisenhower returned to the United States to assume the presidency of Columbia University in New York City. Accepting the position in June 1947, he assumed the role in June 1948, after having written his World War II memoir, *Crusade in Europe*. His tenure at Columbia, which officially went through January 1953, shortly before his inauguration as president of the United States, was interrupted by a number of things, including a call back to Washington in early 1949 to serve briefly as chairman of the Joint Chiefs of Staff as well as an adviser to the secretary of defense. An attack of ileitis sidelined him from mid-March 1949 to mid-May, at which point he returned to New York. Then, at the end of 1950, he acceded to a request by President Truman to assume the leadership of NATO in Europe. Although he offered to resign from the Columbia presidency, the university's trustees refused to accept the offer and instead granted him a leave of absence.

While Eisenhower's leadership proved to be largely ceremonial, he was deeply committed to ensuring that Columbia offered an education for citizenship, believing that a central aspect of education in a democracy was the preparation of people for the assumption of their responsibilities in the democratic process. It was a consistent refrain and one that he pursued whenever he had the opportunity. In addition, while honing and articulating that message, he further developed his views on democracy and politics, laying groundwork, however unintentionally, for the political career upon which he would soon embark.

While still technically the president of Columbia, Eisenhower spent much of the last two years of his prepresidential life serving as the first supreme commander of the North Atlantic Treaty Organization (NATO), and he was the obvious choice to make the unprecedented peacetime alliance a success. After his December 1950 appointment, he started the new year off by embarking on a tour of the European capitals in hopes of raising morale and convincing the residents of the importance of the alliance to their future security. It was not an easy task, but it was no more difficult than convincing the U.S. Congress, whom he addressed after the tour. Indeed, back in the United States, Ike convinced the reluctant congressmen of the importance of the U.S. role in the European defense effort, and he made it clear that it was not the United States' responsibility to do it alone. The effort was well received, and Eisenhower returned to Europe with Congress having approved the dispatch of four divisions overseas. Recognizing the critical importance of building support for NATO, Eisenhower maintained a consistent correspondence with a wide range of military, political, and civic leaders while also traveling around Europe to spread his message that support for Europe was critically important to American well-being.

By the January 1952 meeting of the North Atlantic Council in Lisbon, it was clear that Eisenhower had achieved his goal of establishing a stable NATO structure. The membership set some ambitious goals for the organization's military force, approving the contribution of West German divisions and welcoming Greece and Turkey into the fold as members of the developing alliance. With the foundation solid and complete, Eisenhower stepped down as Supreme Allied Commander on May 31 and returned to the United States to formally pursue the Republican nomination for president.

Eisenhower's decision to enter the political arena had not come easily. He had emerged from World War II as the most popular man in the United States, if not the world, and especially as President Truman struggled with the many economic and social challenges that emerged in the postwar world, leaders from both parties sought to induce Eisenhower to run for president. Although they would later clash, Truman is reported to have told Eisenhower shortly after the end of the war that he was willing to step aside if he wished to run, an offer the general quickly refused. At the same time, in advance of the 1948 election, liberal

Democrats, disenchanted with Truman, looked to Eisenhower as a possible alternative. Republicans were no less eager to turn the war hero's popularity into political capital, but Eisenhower made clear that he had no interest in being a candidate. Indeed, it was his hope that his resignation from the army and the assumption of the presidency of Columbia University would help reduce the pressure. And when Dewey was nominated by the Republicans in 1948 and appeared headed toward what everyone thought would be an easy victory, Eisenhower expected to go on with his life comfortably outside the political arena. However, when Truman unexpectedly defeated Dewey, Eisenhower's position as the head of one of the nation's leading universities, coupled with his return to service as the head of NATO forces, kept his political star shining.

Yet, for all his popularity, the nomination was not handed to him. Rather, the race had begun with Ohio senator Robert Taft, the son of the former president and chief justice and the head of the isolationist wing of the party, as the solid front-runner, but a coterie of East Coast Republican internationalists led by Massachusetts senator Henry Cabot Lodge Jr. and New York governor Dewey were determined to pursue Eisenhower, seeing him as an internationalist alternative as well as a potential winner. At the same time, Eisenhower, who had come away from a meeting with Taft in early 1951 disappointed with his isolationist views, was becoming increasingly open to the possibility, but he was still reluctant to enter the political arena. Meanwhile, although Lodge, Dewey, and company were making headway with Ike, they still had had to combat the party's inbred support for Taft as well as Eisenhower's ongoing, if wavering, reluctance, which was no small challenge given that ever since the war ended he had said he was not a candidate for president under either party's banner.

Determined to change Ike's mind and defeat Taft, Lodge and company set out to draft the reluctant Eisenhower. After entering him in a number of primaries, his fundamental appeal to voters quickly became evident, and after a visit from an old army colleague, where he was shown a tape of a rally supporting his effort, his lifelong service ethos took over, and he agreed to be a candidate. But that guaranteed nothing.

Taft had been preparing his candidacy for years and was a favorite of the grass roots, and while Eisenhower's performance in the primaries had demonstrated his appeal, it had little real impact in a nominating process that was controlled by state and local leaders.

In the end, after winning a couple of key procedural votes, the Eisenhower forces emerged victorious, with the general securing the nomination on the first ballot. Recognizing the need to balance the ticket, California senator Richard Nixon, only 39 years old but a recognized leader of the party's anticommunist forces, was chosen as the vice presidential nominee, providing an effective contrast to the older, New York–based Eisenhower.

The choice was warmly received by the convention, which also responded enthusiastically to Eisenhower's promise of a "Republican crusade . . . to sweep from office an administration which has fastened on every one of us the wastefulness, the arrogance and corruption in high places, the heavy burdens and anxieties which are the bitter fruit of a party too long in power."

In the general election, the political neophyte faced Democrat Adlai Stevenson, the governor of Illinois, who had secured the nomination after a race that had been a bit unusual. While it was assumed that Truman would seek another term, his failure to announce his intentions left a void, which first-term Tennessee senator Estes Kefauver, who had received major national attention the previous year while presiding over televised hearings investigating organized crime, readily filled. Truman had refused to make his intentions known, but he did allow his name to be placed on the New Hampshire ballot and made it clear that he would not campaign. In contrast, Kefauver conducted an active campaign, and on the morning after the March 11 primary, he awoke to the news that he had beaten the president by over 10 percent of the vote and won all 12 of the state's convention delegates. Then, on March 29, Truman, who was under siege on issues ranging from allegations of corruption in his administration to concerns about communists in the government, not to mention the ongoing stalemate in Korea, announced his intention to retire, and the race took on a wholly different shape.

Truman initially tried to convince Stevenson to run, but the Illinois statesman, who would develop a reputation for thoughtful indecisiveness, demurred. Meanwhile, other favorite son candidates emerged to challenge Kefauver, who had become the front-runner with Truman's withdrawal. Ultimately, a draft was organized, and after Kefauver's early strength waned, the Illinois governor, the grandson of Grover Cleveland's vice president, was nominated on the third ballot. To balance the ticket, while also trying to bring the once Solid South back into the fold after the Dixiecrat rebellion of 1948, the Democrats choose Alabama senator John J. Sparkman.

For all his popularity and leadership experience, Eisenhower was no politician nor did he want to be one. Indeed, over the course of a campaign in which he traveled over 30,000 miles by air and 20,000 by rail while visiting 45 states, he captivated audiences not through his policy proposals or high-flown oratory, but rather through his ability to connect with the American people, exuding a sincerity and a commitment to duty and service that not only reinforced his wartime image but transcended politics. At the same time, the realities of politics could not be completely avoided. One of the campaign's lowlights came when Eisenhower, at the last minute, excised a section of a speech in which he defended General Marshall against the reckless charges that Senator Joseph McCarthy had made against Ike's onetime mentor and backer. Planning to make the defense in McCarthy's home state of Wisconsin, he surrendered to the entreaties of the local politicians, who feared the repercussions of challenging the senator. Unhappily for Eisenhower, the speech had been released to the press in advance, so Eisenhower was criticized both for failing to defend Marshall and for having backed down in the face of the McCarthy threat.

The campaign faced another crisis when it was revealed that Nixon, while serving in the Senate, had an $18,000 fund intended to support his external political activities. This was legal, and in fact similar to a fund that Democratic nominee Stevenson maintained, but it raised concerns of improper influence and threatened to derail the whole campaign effort, especially when one of the campaign's major themes was to clean up Washington. Eisenhower was advised by many to drop Nixon from the ticket, but given that his selection of the vice presidential nominee had been

Ike's first major political decision, that option was not without its risks.

In the end, Nixon gave a controversial but memorable television speech in which he addressed the charges. Known to history as the "Checkers Speech," for its references to a dog that had been sent as a gift to his daughters, the speech saved his career, as the national response all but forced Eisenhower to keep him on the ticket, a place from which the young senator conducted a hard-hitting campaign that stirred the party faithful while also providing a valuable contrast with the more reserved and statesmanlike head of the ticket. At the same item, for all his gravitas and reserve, Eisenhower proved to be an effective personal campaigner, and his efforts were magnified and supplemented when the campaign's managers successfully introduced the use of television to promote Ike's candidacy, an innovation that would change forever the nature of national political discourse.

On Election Day, November 4, 1952, Eisenhower's victory over Stevenson was a resounding one. He garnered 55.2 percent of the popular vote, won 39 states, and secured 442 electoral votes. In looking at the full slate of results, it was clear that it was more a personal one for the popular war hero turned presidential candidate than an appeal to his political views or ideas.. However, he did seem to have limited coattails and with the vice president able to cast the tie-breaking vote, the Republicans achieved a majority in the Senate. That good news was tempered by the fact Senator Joe McCarthy would have a committee chairmanship from which to continue his efforts. How to deal with the rogue senator from Wisconsin would prove to be one of the president's earliest challenges.

Following the end of his presidency, in 1961, the Eisenhowers moved to a small farm they had purchased a number of years before in Gettysburg, Pennsylvania. It had been undergoing renovations during the presidency and was ready for occupancy upon the end of his term. It was the first permanent home the couple had had since their marriage.

As he prepared to leave office, Eisenhower made a request of President-elect John F. Kennedy and asked to be returned to his rank as a five-star general. JFK readily agreed. Congress restored the rank, and on

March 24, 1961, Eisenhower's five-star red pennant was added to the flagpole at the Gettysburg house.

In retirement, Eisenhower wrote his memoirs, *The White House Years*, which was published in two volumes. Volume one was titled *Mandate for Change, 1953–1956*, and volume two was titled *Waging Peace, 1956–1961*. They served as a follow-up to his postwar work that had been published in 1948, *Crusade in Europe*. Eisenhower also wrote a lighter work, *At Ease: Stories I Tell to Friends*. Retirement also allowed Eisenhower to further indulge his passion for painting, an activity that he had been introduced to by Winston Churchill during the war. Unlike golf, painting had become a source of under-the-radar pleasure and a means of relaxing during his presidency, and Gettysburg offered the time and venue he needed to paint the country scenes he so enjoyed.

While the politics of the presidency had undoubtedly been his least favorite part of the job, Ike nevertheless remained a major figure in the Republican Party after he left office. As the party's revered elder statesman and most effective campaigner, his blessing was sought by all presidential aspirants. At the same time, in typical fashion, the man who had essentially eschewed party labels and put service above all else was also consulted by both Kennedy and Johnson

Retirement did not spare Eisenhower from continuing health problems. He experienced a number of additional heart attacks (his first was in 1955), and each time, although he seemed to rally, his heart continued to weaken. In February 1969, following surgery to address a problem with his intestines, the then 78-year-old Eisenhower developed pneumonia, and in mid-March, his health significantly declined; he was suffering from congestive heart failure. Finally, on March 28, only months after his former vice president had become president and his favorite grandson, David, for whom Ike had renamed the presidential retreat Camp David, had married Julie Nixon, Eisenhower succumbed. He was buried in his military uniform in an army coffin in Abilene.

HISTORICAL OVERVIEW

As he turned his attention to assuming office, Eisenhower's first great task was to end the stalemate in Korea. In an election promise that had resonated with the American people, the former commander of the Allied forces had said he would go to Korea, and while the pledge was more the product of a speechwriter's inspiration than a well-considered plan, on December 2, 1952, Eisenhower followed through, arriving in Korea to assess the situation. He visited with troops and their commanders as well as South Korean leaders, and he received briefings on the military situation in the region. At the end of his visit, Eisenhower concluded, "We could not stand forever on a static front and continue to accept casualties without any visible results. Small attacks on small hills would not end this war." Given that assessment, when he took office, he used a combination of diplomacy and saber-rattling to try to end the conflict. Finally, an armistice, under which organized combat was stopped and the country's division—North and South along the 38th parallel—was retained, was signed on July 27, 1953.

As it had been in the army, a central component of Eisenhower's presidential leadership was a disciplined organizational structure, one that planned and then executed the plan. Consequently, the man who had made his initial military reputation in the planning realm installed a powerful White House chief of staff, former New Hampshire governor Sherman Adams, who he then empowered to oversee a structured weekly schedule that had the president meeting with congressional leaders on Mondays, holding press conferences on Wednesdays, chairing the National Security Council meeting on Thursdays, and meeting with his cabinet on Fridays. In addition, well aware of the importance of communication, he appointed James Hagerty, a former newspaperman who had been the press liaison during the campaign, press secretary. He also appointed Robert Cutler, a onetime World War II aide to General Marshall, as national security advisor. Meanwhile, in making his cabinet appointments Eisenhower relied heavily on the Republican establishment, which helped him assemble a team that one critic derisively dismissed as being made up of "eight millionaires and a plumber."

Eisenhower's first—and most obvious—appointment was attorney and longtime Republican foreign policy leader John Foster Dulles as secretary of state. Being the nephew of Wilson's secretary of state, Robert Lansing, and the grandson of John W. Foster, who had headed the State Department under President Benjamin Harrison, it seemed as though Dulles had been groomed since he was a boy to hold the position. Indeed, in addition to being one of Washington's top lawyers, he had served as a legal counsel at the 1919 Paris Peace Conference following World War I and was a member of the League of Free Nations Association that had pushed for U.S. membership in the league. He had also helped develop the Dawes Plan to address the problem of Germany's postwar reparations. A longtime foreign policy adviser to two-time Republican nominee Thomas E. Dewey, Dulles helped author the preamble to the United Nation's charter's and had served as a delegate to the UN General Assembly. In 1949, Dewey had appointed him to fill the Senate vacancy arising from the resignation of longtime senator Robert F. Wagner. His four-month stint on Capitol Hill came to an abrupt end when he was defeated by former governor Herbert F. Lehman in a special election. Dulles would serve under Eisenhower until April 1959, when, suffering from colon cancer, he resigned, only to die barely a month later.

As secretary of the treasury, Eisenhower selected George M. Humphrey of Ohio. An attorney and businessman, who at one time served as the president of steel manufacturer M.A. Hanna Company, Humphrey was the dominant voice on economic matters in the early days of the Eisenhower administration. He was an advocate of reducing spending and taxes and was committed to achieving a balanced budget. He served through the whole of Eisenhower's first term and resigned at the end of July 1957, at which point he was replaced by Robert B. Anderson, a Texas lawyer and businessman who was the secretary of the navy from 1953 to mid-1954. Eisenhower thought very highly of Anderson's talents, and when rumors were swirling in 1956 about possibly replacing Nixon on the ticket, Anderson's name surfaced as a very real option. He became the leading voice on economic policy after succeeding Humphrey as secretary, continuing to advocate for a balanced budget and urging the president to use any surplus to pay down the debt rather than providing a tax cut.

Eisenhower's choice for secretary of defense was Charles E. Wilson of Michigan, who was serving as president of General Motors at the time of his appointment. Wilson was probably best remembered for the assertion that "what was good for our country was good for General Motors, and vice versa." His term in office was marked by the implementation of budget cuts. With the end of the Korean War, he sought to reorder the nation's defense spending. When he left at the start of Eisenhower's second term, he was replaced by Neil H. McElroy, an Ohio businessman who had been president of Proctor & Gamble and who was himself succeeded by former secretary of the navy and deputy secretary of defense Thomas S. Gates Jr. in 1959. Under his watch, the department established a task force to set national nuclear priorities. Too, operating under the government's broad intelligence-gathering guidelines and in line with the program that had in fact been operating for years, Gates was the man who authorized the ill-fated U-2 flight of Francis Gary Powers.

For attorney general, Eisenhower selected Herbert Brownell Jr. A longtime confidant of Thomas E. Dewey, Brownell had been Eisenhower's campaign manager and was a well-regarded attorney. Given the pressures of the time, he established an Internal Security Division within the Justice Department, and following up on a Truman administration initiative, he undertook a program where many organizations with alleged communist ties were required to register with the attorney general's office. Under Brownell, the Justice Department became actively supportive of the developing civil rights movement, filing numerous suits in the aftermath of *Brown v. Board of Education*. When Brownell resigned in October 1957, he was succeeded by William P. Rogers, who had served as deputy attorney general and would remain as attorney general until Eisenhower left office. While in office, Rogers established the Civil Rights Division in the Justice Department and helped advise the president on how to respond to Arkansas governor Orval Faubus's recalcitrance during the desegregation of Little Rock's Central High School.

Serving as postmaster general for the whole of the Eisenhower years, Michigan's Arthur Summerfield, the Republican National Committee chairman during Eisenhower's successful campaign, gained notoriety for his unsuccessful effort to ban *Lady Chatterley's Lover* as part of a broader effort to rid the mails of obscene literature. In addition, Summerfield oversaw the decentralization of postal operations as the modernization of the department's accounting procedures.

Douglas McKay of Oregon served as Eisenhower's first secretary of the interior. The former governor was a fiscal conservative who reorganized the department, cutting numerous positions and hundreds of millions of dollars from the budget. At the same time, a penchant for economic development often put him at odds with conservation groups, who charged that he was not adequately protecting the nation's natural resources. McKay resigned in April 1956, with Eisenhower's blessing, to undertake an ultimately unsuccessful challenge against Democratic incumbent senator Wayne Morse. To replace McKay, the president selected Frederick Seaton, a Nebraska newspaperman and Republican activist who followed a short appointive stint in the U.S. Senate with a number of subcabinet posts under Eisenhower until he was appointed secretary. In that role, he oversaw the admission of Alaska and Hawaii to U.S. statehood and also worked on a project that sought to take drinking water from the ocean.

Secretary of Agriculture Ezra Taft Benson was one of the administration's stalwarts that served for the whole of Eisenhower's tenure. Benson was a free market advocate and worked hard to secure increased exports of American farm produce. But he also sought to reduce fixed price supports, a stance that put him at odds with much of the farm community.

Secretary of Commerce Sinclair Weeks held his office from the start of the administration until right after the midterm elections in 1958. A Massachusetts native who served a short appointive term in the U.S. Senate during World War II, Weeks's tenure as secretary was marked by an expansion of the nation's merchant marine as well as an increase in trade with the Communist Bloc countries in Europe. In addition, he was very involved in the beginnings of the Interstate Highway System and played a major role in developing its funding system. After Weeks resigned to attend

to his ailing wife, Eisenhower sought to appoint Lewis Strauss to succeed him, but acrimony and controversy dating back to Strauss's role in the 1954 revocation of Robert Oppenheimer's security clearance prevented his confirmation. Instead, the president promoted undersecretary Frederick Mueller. Upon confirmation, Mueller, who would serve until the end of Ike's term, implemented a trade embargo against Cuba and the newly installed Communist government.

The secretary of labor and "plumber" in the cabinet was Martin P. Durkin of Illinois. Durkin was the onetime president of the Plumbers and Pipe Fitters Union and a former director of labor for the state of Illinois. His tenure as secretary was short-lived, as he resigned in September 1953 in protest against the administration's refusal to seek revisions in the Taft-Hartley law. He was succeeded by James P. Mitchell of New Jersey, who remained in the post until the end of the Eisenhower administration.

As the first secretary of health, education, and welfare, Eisenhower appointed Texan Oveta Culp Hobby, only the second women to ever serve in the cabinet. As the first occupant to hold the office, it fell to Hobby to undertake the basic organization of the department that would soon be second to the Pentagon in terms of spending and personnel. Hobby resigned in the summer of 1955 and was succeeded by Marion Folsom, who had been serving as undersecretary of the treasury. Folsom served until the end of July 1958, when he was followed by Arthur Flemming, who also chaired the president's advisory committee on government organization. Flemming served until the end of the administration.

With this team in place, the president set about addressing the nation's problems. Given the ongoing nature of the Korean War that greeted him as well as the emergence of China as a threat on the Cold War landscape, upon taking office, Eisenhower directed the State Department to develop an alliance that would help contain communist aggression in the then free areas of Vietnam, Laos, and Cambodia, and Southeast Asia in general. Secretary of State Dulles undertook the assignment, and the result was the creation in September 1954 of a military alliance called the Southeast Asia Treaty Organization (SEATO). Other members of the alliance included France, Great Britain, Australia, New Zealand, the Philippines, Pakistan, and Thailand, all of which agreed to "act to meet the common danger" in the event of aggression against any signatory state. To clarify the reach of the commitment, a separate provision specified that Laos, Cambodia, and South Vietnam were the areas subject to the provisions of the treaty. SEATO did not include the kind of absolute mutual defense commitment that NATO did, but it provided for a collaborative defense structure that exceeded anything previously in existence in that region and was often used as a basis for U.S. involvement in Vietnam.

While the new efforts in Asia proved valuable, they quickly took a back seat to the changed Cold War landscape that Eisenhower, less than two months into his presidency, had to confront when Soviet premier Joseph Stalin died on March 5, 1953. Seeing an opportunity to take advantage of what he hoped might be a possible change in the Soviet Union's outlook, on April 16, Ike offered what became known as his "Chance for Peace" speech. He called on the superpowers to turn away from the ongoing arms race and urged them to instead devote those resources to building schools, hospitals, and infrastructure that would directly serve their citizens. While applauded by the press and widely circulated by the administration, the speech proved to be little more than an exercise in futility, an initiative soon forgotten as it quickly became clear that despite Stalin's death there would be no change in the Soviet Union's view of the Cold War. At the same time, for all his sincere desire to seek and maintain peace, Eisenhower never saw it as something that could be achieved from a position of weakness. In fact, throughout his presidency, the administration was always engaged in a two-track approach to national security—sincere words aimed at achieving and maintaining peace and consistent preparation for wars they hoped to never have to fight.

Nowhere was the paradox more clearly illustrated than in Eisenhower's approach to the newly emerging atomic age. Coming into office, Ike was greeted by the realty of the modern nuclear world. Just days before the election, the Atomic Energy Commission (AEC) had overseen the test of the first hydrogen bomb, with the Soviet Union testing its own version in August

1953. This reality, encapsulated in a report from a panel chaired by J. Robert Oppenheimer, meant that the world had reached a point where each of the superpowers could launch a potentially devastating attack against its counterpart, only to be met with a retaliatory response that would result in its own destruction. This shadow would both serve as the backdrop and incentive for Eisenhower's effort to secure peace for the whole of his presidency.

Although determined to reduce the threat of nuclear war, Eisenhower also desired to change the way people viewed atomic energy and the atomic threat. While he fully recognized the importance of secrecy and the tactical advantage that came with keeping aspects of U.S. atomic capabilities something that the Soviet Union could only wonder about, Ike also saw the whole nuclear issue as being about more than just weapons and defense. Consequently, he launched what became known as Operation Candor in an effort to help the American people better understand the positive advances that were resulting from the United States' scientific work with atomic energy as well as the risks and the rewards that were a part of the atomic age in which they all lived. One of these efforts to draw public attention and policy possibilities regarding the issue of nuclear development was his Atoms for Peace initiative. Speaking before the United Nations in December 1953, Eisenhower, the first man to be elected president after the advent of the atomic bomb, recognized how the world had changed, telling the assembled UN delegates, "I feel impelled to speak today in a language that in a sense is new—one which I, who have spent so much of my life in the military profession, would have preferred never to use. That new language is the language of atomic warfare." But then, reflective of a vision developed after but informed by the devastation of a world war, Eisenhower called for the distribution, in a peaceful and controlled manner, of nuclear technology to all countries in the world. In return for this shared knowledge, countries would agree to not pursue atomic weapons. The hope, Eisenhower explained, was that "this greatest of destructive forces can be developed into a great boon for the benefit of all mankind."

While the realities of the Cold War impacted the response to Eisenhower's proposal, preventing a full-scale embrace, many countries welcomed the overture. The United States not only benefited from the its attempt to serve as peacemaker, but it also launched a raft of efforts that included the training of foreign scientists, the declassification of large amounts of nuclear research, and the development of nuclear reactors worldwide. Although nations that already had nuclear weapons did not eliminate their stockpiles, the effort did seem to slow the development by others. Just as importantly, Eisenhower's proposal helped changed the focus from the development of weapons to the use of nuclear power and the accompanying technology for peaceful means.

Concurrently, one of Eisenhower's central concerns throughout his presidency was the threat of nuclear war. While horrified by the power and impact of the atomic bombs dropped on Hiroshima and Nagasaki, he hoped that their terrifying impact would serve as deterrent to any future use of the existing weapons. But their possible use as a deterrent was not enough for Eisenhower, so he worked throughout his presidency to reduce the chance that they could or would be used. One effort came on July 21, 1955, when, at a Four Power Summit in Geneva, Eisenhower called for the Soviet Union and the United States to exchange maps that would show the exact locations of every military installation in their respective countries. This proposal, known as the "Open Skies" initiative, would not only allow each superpower to perform surveillance of its counterparts, so as to ensure that they had abided by their agreed upon arms accord, but it was hoped that the ability to verify would be an additional incentive to do right by the agreements. While France and Great Britain were receptive, the Soviet Union rejected the idea, with Soviet leader Nikita Khrushchev calling it an "espionage plot." Although the idea was a noble—and sincere—one, it was later reported that Eisenhower had not expected the Soviet Union to be receptive, but he did feel that their dismissal of the idea not only diminished them in the eyes of the global community but made them appear to be the obstacle to the achievement of any meaningful arms control.

Not long afterward, in recognizing the importance of knowing where the Soviets stood, Eisenhower approved the use of the U-2, a high-altitude plane, to conduct surveillance over the Soviet Union.

Unhappily, on May 1, 1960, Francis Gary Powers's U-2 was shot down deep over Soviet territory. While the U.S. initially denied any knowledge, when Powers was produced, the United States was caught in a lie, and Eisenhower was embarrassed on the world stage. Khrushchev soon used the incident as an excuse to upend the Four Power Summit that met in Paris later that month. After making a series of accusations, he left the summit early, and he also rescinded an earlier invitation for Eisenhower to visit the Soviet Union. Eisenhower was deeply disappointed that a final push for peace had been lost, and while he defended the need for the flights, seeing them as a necessary defensive measure, he later said that he should have halted the U-2 flights as the summit neared.

As if the Cold War, not to mention the threat of nuclear war, did not present Eisenhower with sufficient external challenges, Senator Joseph McCarthy became even more of a problem after Eisenhower took office, as the president found himself confronting a Senator McCarthy who was occupying a more powerful official perch from which to pursue his anti-communist crusade. As chairman of the Senate's Permanent Subcommittee on Investigations, McCarthy continued the reckless attacks on the government, asserting that the State Department and others—including the army—were hiding and covering up for known communists. But this time, the charges were aimed at the Eisenhower administration. It was a difficult situation. Many Republicans, both in good faith and because of its believed political value, supported the senator's efforts, but others saw his efforts as a stain on the Senate and an obstacle for an administration seeking to chart a new path after two decades of Democratic rule.

Conscious of the power and authority of the presidency, Eisenhower believed that not only was there no value into getting down in the gutter with McCarthy but that it was beneath the office to do so and would only enhance McCarthy's stature. Rather, Eisenhower sought to bring pressure to bear behind the scenes. While McCarty aides Roy Cohn and David Schine were traipsing across Europe checking for objectionable books in army libraries, Eisenhower gave a powerful speech at Dartmouth College, where, without mentioning Cohn, Schine, or McCarthy, he defended freedom of thought and free inquiry while decrying the efforts of the "book burners." He also invoked executive privilege when McCarthy recklessly charged the army with knowingly covering for communists, a charge that led to the nationally televised Army-McCarthy hearings that would ultimately lead to the senator's downfall. While his role was not a highly public one, in using Nixon as a go-between while working with congressional leaders, Eisenhower clearly played a valuable and somewhat supportive role in bringing McCarthy's efforts to an end.

The next chapter of the Cold War unfolded in a surprising manner in the summer of 1956, for as Eisenhower and the United States looked ahead to the presidential election, events in the Middle East added a whole new dimension to the still developing conflict while also pitting the United States against two of its strongest allies. In late July 1956, following a period of escalating tensions between Egypt, Great Britain, and France, Egyptian president Gamal Abdel Nasser announced the nationalization of the Suez Canal Company, the joint British-French enterprise that had owned and operated the Suez Canal since its construction in 1869. Nasser offered full economic compensation for the company, but the action brought to a head the mutual fears and suspicions of the Europeans who were not only outraged by Nasser's action but were increasingly resentful of his apparent opposition to their influence in the region. Meanwhile, Nasser resented what he saw as their continuing efforts to maintain dominance over the region. The Eisenhower administration watched all this unfold, and concerned about the possible outbreak of hostilities, as well as possible intervention by the Soviet Union, it made an effort to mediate the British-French-Egyptian dispute. However, the Dulles-led effort was unsuccessful.

Meanwhile, from August to October, in conversations with the United States, the British refused to rule out the possible use of force to dealing with Nasser. In fact, unbeknownst to the United States, Britain, France, and Israel, which considered Nasser a threat to its own security, were holding discussions that resulted in a plan aimed at overthrowing the Egyptian leader. That effort moved beyond the planning stages on October 29, when Israeli forces launched an attack across Egypt's Sinai Peninsula, ultimately getting within 10 miles of the canal. Operating under the pretext of protecting the canal from the warring Middle East rivals, British and French troops were dispatched only days later.

The Eisenhower administration was not pleased by this turn of events. Balancing a desire to not be associated with European colonialism—a concern heighted by the country's harsh condemnation of the Soviet incursion into Hungary only days before—as well as the fear that the Soviets might come to Nasser's aid, they put pressure on Britain and France to accept a UN cease-fire on November 6. To more emphatically make the point, the United States voted for a UN resolution that publicly condemned the invasion while also approving the creation of a UN peacekeeping force. The American response led to short-term tension and ill will between the important allies, but by the following spring, relations had been restored. In the meantime, U.S. concerns about the ongoing status and influence of the European powers in the Middle East led to a reevaluation of American policies in that area.

In the end, there was no small irony to the fact that one of the more enduring aspects of the Eisenhower administration's foreign policy was in fact a product of the Suez Crisis, but in the aftermath of the U.S. rebuke of its allies, and amid concerns about the continuing influence of Britain in the region, in January 1957, as he headed into his second term, Eisenhower announced the Eisenhower Doctrine, a policy that was endorsed by Congress in March. In many ways, it built upon the Truman Doctrine by allowing a foreign nation to ask for U.S. economic or military aid if it was being threatened by armed outside aggression. In articulating the policy, the president did not hesitate to identify its main focus—the Soviet threat—as he made reference to the United States offering support to any country threatened by "overt armed aggression from any nation controlled by international communism."

The first substantive implementation of the Eisenhower Doctrine came in 1958 in Lebanon, although, ironically, the threat was neither armed nor Soviet inspired. Rather, Lebanon's president, Camille Chamoun, sought U.S. aid to prevent attacks from political rivals, some of whom had communist leanings, as well as from Syria and Egypt. Eisenhower sent U.S. troops into Lebanon to help maintain order, and while he never specifically cited the doctrine, the American action not only signaled support of Chamoun's pro-U.S. government, it also conveyed the clear message—to the Soviet Union and the rest of the world—that the United States was ready to act to protect its interests in the Middle East.

Amid all of this, the Eisenhower administration had to address the initial appearance of Vietnam, a longtime French colony, on the American international radar. Rebels said to be supported by the Communists had achieved a form of independence from France after the battle of Dien Bien Phu in May 1954. An international gathering in July, in Geneva, agreed to a split similar to the situation in Korea ,with the country divided at the 17th parallel. The North was to be controlled by the Communists, who were led by Ho Chi Minh, and the South, supported by the Western democracies, was governed by a group led by Ngo Dinh Diem. Under the terms of the Geneva Accords, free elections intended to result in one government for a unified Vietnam were to be held within two years. However, in large part because of U.S. resistance, based in the belief that such elections would result in a Communist victory, the elections were never held.

In the meantime, over the next six years, the Eisenhower administration poured money into South Vietnam in an effort to support the Diem regime against continuing aggression from the North. Well aware of the military challenges involved in fighting a war in the jungles of Southeast Asia, Eisenhower resisted calls for military assistance, but his articulation of what became known as the Domino Theory, the idea that the fall of one country to communism would lead to the fall of the adjoining one, and so on, until the whole region had fallen under Communist control, had a major impact on U.S. policy in the region. Indeed, the Domino Theory, coupled with the political shadow cast by the Truman administration's having "lost China," would play a prominent role in the development of U.S. policy in the region over the next two decades.

For all of the international events and incidents that crowded his calendar, Eisenhower still had more than few constitutional responsibilities that did not adhere to any formal timetable, and one of these was the appointment of judges to the federal bench.

Ironically, given that Eisenhower lacked the legal training that has been a part of so many of his presidential predecessor's backgrounds, one of the major legacies of his presidency lay in his appointments to the U.S. Supreme Court. When Eisenhower arrived in the White House there was not a single member of the Supreme Court who had been appointed by a Republican president. However, over the course of his eight years in office, he would not only remedy that partisan imbalance, but he would do so in way that has earned high praise from historians ever since. And it all began with the nomination for chief justice less than a year after he entered the White House.

Indeed, when Chief Justice Fred Vinson suddenly died of a heart attack in September 1953, Eisenhower was presented with a singular opportunity to impact the direction of the Court and the nation. Not surprisingly, given his organizational bent, the military-trained Eisenhower had established a very distinct set of criteria that he applied to his judicial nominees. These elements included having character and ability that would inspire "respect, pride and confidence" among the nation's citizens and a moderate common-sense philosophy, in the president's words, "the absence of extremes." He also sought geographic and religious balance, and, wanting both energy and impact from his appointees, he established an upper age limit of 62. Finally, all nominees had to pass a thorough FBI check and get American Bar Association (ABA) approval. These criteria did little to narrow the field, and the party's leaders offered many suggestions, including Dewey, Dulles, and New Jersey chief justice Arthur Vanderbilt. But when the dust had settled, the president and his political aides had narrowed their search to California governor Earl Warren, a man who fully met all of the president's requirements.

Political lore has it that Warren's appointment to the Supreme Court was the result of a convention promise made at a time when the California governor was in a position to influence the ultimate choice of the Republican presidential nominee. But whether true or not, the position of chief justice of the U.S. Supreme Court was one that proved ideally suited for Warren, a politician so skilled and so popular that in one of his gubernatorial reelection campaigns, he actually received the nomination of both parties. And those skills came into play faster than anyone might have expected as Warren guided a previously split Court to a unanimous decision in the landmark case of *Brown v. Board of Education*. Meanwhile, given that Warren took his seat as a result of a recess appointment on September 30, 1953, it was not until March 1, 1954, that Warren was actually confirmed in a voice vote.

Justice Robert Jackson's sudden death of a heart attack in October 1954 gave Eisenhower another seat to fill, and after being rebuffed by Thomas Dewey and his attorney general, Herbert Brownell, Ike turned to another highly respected New York lawyer and judge in their mold, John Marshall Harlan II, the grandson of the "Great Dissenter" of *Plessy v. Ferguson* fame. He easily satisfied all of Eisenhower's criteria, including the need for judicial experience, a factor that Ike reportedly added after his early disappointment with Warren. Harlan's recess appointment ran into some problems when some recalcitrant members of the Southern bloc sought to take out their frustrations over the *Brown* decision on the Court's newest potential member, but Harlan weathered the storm and was easily confirmed in March 1955.

Meanwhile, the appointment of William Brennan, a member of the New Jersey Supreme Court, was by all accounts a politically motivated choice, as the fall 1956 recess appointment of the Irish Catholic Democrat from a swing state in the middle of Eisenhower's reelection campaign had no political downside. Brennan's formal confirmation process the following January saw a last gasp inquisition from Senator Joe McCarthy, whom Brennan had criticized in a speech in the spring of 1954. But the senator, in ill health and in eclipse after his Senate censure, proved no threat. The New Jersey jurist was confirmed by a voice vote.

Eisenhower's final two appointments were noncontroversial appeals court judges who fully satisfied the president's criteria but whose careers went in markedly different directions. To replace retiring Stanley Reed, Eisenhower turned to Charles Whittaker of Missouri. Bedeviled by ill health, Whittaker retired after only five years. In contrast, Eisenhower's final choice was Potter Stewart, a member of a prominent Cincinnati family whose father had served as mayor and on the Ohio Supreme Court. Indeed, at age 39,

Stewart himself had served on the city council before being appointed by Eisenhower to the U.S. Court of Appeals for the Fifth Circuit. Four years later, when former Cleveland mayor and Ohio senator Harold Burton retired, Ike tapped the young judge for the high court. He was easily confirmed.

While Eisenhower was able through his appointments to influence the Court, the justices through their decisions were able to impact the domestic landscape to which the president then had to respond. Indeed, not long after taking office, Eisenhower and his administration found itself in the middle of the swiftly developing civil rights movement, a social and political force that was taken to a new level by the May 17, 1954, Supreme Court decision in *Brown v. Board of Education*. While the administration had, after some hesitation, submitted an amicus brief that basically supported the position of the NAACP, it could likely not have anticipated either the 9–0 ruling that the Eisenhower-appointed Chief Justice Earl Warren had managed to achieve, and it certainly could not have imagined the issues it would be forced to confront in the aftermath of the *Brown* decision. And yet, for all these unexpected developments, and as much as Eisenhower's civil rights legacy has been debated, once the Supreme Court had spoken, the president fulfilled his responsibility to enforce the law of the land.

In fact, following his impressive reelection victory and with a new Congress ready for action, the administration, under Attorney General Herbert Brownell's direction, prepared to introduce a new Civil Rights bill. While it, like most acts of Congress, would be impacted by the vagaries of the legislative process, including the longest individual filibuster in Senate history by South Carolina senator and former Dixiecrat presidential candidate Strom Thurmond, the Civil Rights Act of 1957, although an imperfect law, nevertheless represented an affirmative effort to address the issues that were coming to the fore in the aftermath of the *Brown* decision.

In the end, the act, the first civil rights measure passed since Reconstruction, was a substantive legislative advance in the effort to secure equal rights for the nation's African American population. While the act was watered down in the Senate, where the South had an influence belying their numbers—protection of voting rights in particular was a victim of Senate maneuverings—it nevertheless established a federal Civil Rights Commission with the power to investigate discrimination and then recommend ways to combat the inequalities, called for the creation of a new Civil Rights Section within the Justice Department, and provided some increased protection for the voting rights of African Americans. Achieving final congressional passage on August 27, Eisenhower signed the historic Civil Rights Act of 1957 on September 9, 1957, ironically only days after the integration effort at Central High School in Little Rock, Arkansas, had begun.

Indeed, the Little Rock crisis represented the next civil rights challenge the administration had to address. In the aftermath of the Supreme Court's decision in *Brown v. Board of Education*, the federal courts ordered Little Rock to begin desegregation in the fall of 1957. While school officials intended to comply, local citizens massed in opposition, taunting the young students and blocking their path to the school. Adding to the trouble was the fact that the police who were supposedly there to protect the black students often ignored their responsibilities. It quickly became clear that the state and local authorities were not going to provide the support and protection that was needed, and while eyes turned to Washington, Eisenhower hesitated to get involved, a stance that only encouraged the resistance. Indeed, Eisenhower initially refused to postpone a long-scheduled vacation at Newport, Rhode Island, and once there, he resisted suggestions to go back to the White House, responding in a way not unlike his efforts with Senator Joe McCarthy that he did not want to make the situation more than it was.

Finally, with Arkansas governor Orval Faubus still refusing to support the court-ordered desegregation, Eisenhower acceded to Faubus's suggestion of a meeting. Meeting at the Newport naval base, Eisenhower told Faubus that in a test of strength between a state and the federal government, the state would lose, adding that he had no desire to see a governor humiliated. Despite Eisenhower's belief that Faubus was returning to Arkansas ready to accept the desegregation effort, Faubus did not, and when a federal injunction removed all legal obstacles to the integration effort, Faubus responded by pulling out the National Guard while declaring that he had no responsibility for the preservation of order. The continuing effort to have the black students enter the school was again met by a threatening mob, and afraid for their safety, the students withdrew. With the world watching as Arkansas defied a direct order of the Supreme Court, the nation's chief executive finally acted, sending a detachment of 1,000 men of the 101st Airborne Division while also federalizing the state's National Guard. Within hours, army troops arrived in Little Rock and took up their posts, and the following day, September 25, Central High School was integrated.

Appearing on national television to explain his decision to send in the troops, Eisenhower offered a legalistic explanation of his responsibilities to enforce the law, but he failed to address any of the moral implications of that effort to achieve equality nor any of the human dimensions or the indignities and cruelties visited upon the black students. To many, it represented an opportunity lost. And in fact, it did not represent the end of the Little Rock saga, for while a small coterie of black students, protected by soldiers, did attend Central High for the rest of the 1957–1958 school year, the state's resistance to desegregation continued. Faubus closed Little Rock's high schools the following year, and the number of desegregated schools in the South dropped significantly in the aftermath of the Little Rock crisis. The issue of school desegregation would continue to rage into the 1970s.

Paradoxically perhaps, despite all this, in his final year in office, Eisenhower and his Justice Department made a final foray into the area of civil rights. While politicians and observers all acknowledged that the 1957 bill had represented a breakthrough, it was also acknowledged that the Southern bloc in the Senate had greatly weakened the first civil rights bill since Reconstruction. In 1960, with the clock running out, the administration, led by Attorney General William P. Rogers, determined to address some of the parts that had been watered down, even though they recognized that the same forces would try again to hold the line and limit progress. The result was the Civil Rights Act of 1960.

The 1960 act was focused on plugging the loopholes concerning voting rights that made the Fifteenth Amendment more symbol than reality, and in the end, it both established a system whereby the federal government could inspect local procedures and voters rolls and created penalties that could be imposed on anyone found guilty of interfering with a person's attempt to register to vote. In addition, the Civil Rights Commission that had been created by the Civil Rights Act of 1957 on a short-term basis was extended.

Although the act was largely symbolic, given that the 1957 and 1960 acts only led to a 3 percent increase in the black voter turnout in the 1960 election, the efforts did represent a step forward, however small, and served to highlight the South's deep opposition. Indeed, in seeking to stop the bill, the Southern senators organized what became the longest filibuster in Senate history. Beginning on February 29 and operating in teams of 6, the 18 senators were able to maintain control of the Senate floor for 125 straight hours with only a 15-minute break on the morning of March 2; 82 hours later, Senate Majority Leader Lyndon Johnson finally ended the 24-hours sessions he had been holding in hopes of breaking the effort. Ultimately, a limited bill was passed and signed by Eisenhower on May 6, to no great acclaim from anyone.

In the midst of his dealings with civil rights, as well as the unsettled international world, Eisenhower had to again face the American electorate. The 1956 general election ballot featured a rematch of the 1952 contest, with the same two names, Dwight D. Eisenhower for the Republicans and Adlai Stevenson for the Democrats, topping the tickets. While Tennessee senator Estes Kefauver again made a bid for the nomination, he had to console himself with the vice presidential nod, besting an emergent Massachusetts senator, John F. Kennedy, after Stevenson left the choice to the convention.

Meanwhile, although pressure had been exerted on Ike to drop Nixon from the Republican ticket, especially after concerns emerged about Ike's health, the Republicans stayed with their proven team and undertook a campaign aimed at promising the American people more of the same—peace and prosperity.

Indeed, with the ending of the Korean War only buttressing his reputation as a man of peace and the economy purring along, Eisenhower's only real challenge was to convince voters of his physical ability to perform the duties of the office. This he did through a controlled and consistent campaign that made clear

that he was ready to continue serving his country as he had for so many years. In the end, while the slogan may have been "I like Ike," the reality was something more. He was liked, respected, trusted, and admired, and on November 6, 1956, those feelings translated into an overwhelmingly victory. Winning 57.4 percent of the popular vote, 41 states, and 457 electoral votes, Eisenhower cruised to victory. But the personal dimension of the win was made clear by the fact that, despite Ike's dominance, the Democrats were able to retain control of both houses of Congress.

Like most presidents, Eisenhower's second term was less eventful or productive than his first, but accomplishments continued—some of which were about implementing earlier efforts, while others represented new ideas. One major accomplishment of the Eisenhower presidency that started in the first term but was furthered after his reelection was the creation of the Interstate Highway System, often called the Eisenhower Highway System. After numerous false starts that provided a minimal foundation, the administration, working closely with Congress, enacted the Federal-Aid Highway Act of 1954, which took the nation's commitment and investment to new levels as it authorized $175 million annually while changing the federal-state contribution ratio to 60–40.

However, this effort was overwhelmed in June 1956, when after years of political maneuvering, Congress passed a new version of the Federal-Aid Highway Act. This law dedicated $26 billion to finance the 41,000 miles of highway that were intended to go from coast to coast. The funding was to come from a tax on each gallon of gas, and the federal government would be footing the bill for 90 percent of the highway that would be created. To protect the fund, and recognizing that the project would not end with the building of the road but that maintenance would be necessary, the Federal-Aid Highway Act of 1956, which authorized the construction and the spending, was aided by the enactment of the Highway Revenue Act of 1956. That legislation created the funding mechanism by which the user taxes would be set aside for future highway purposes. The legislation established a Highway Trust Fund that was modeled on the Social Security Trust Fund. Reflective of the congressional and administrative cooperation that characterized the effort, the trust fund idea had been a suggestion of Eisenhower's treasury secretary, George Humphrey.

In addition to authorizing the construction of an interstate highway network, as well as a mechanism for the funding, the 1956 act established national standards for design, all of which were intended to make coast-to-coast travel easier, facilitate city evacuation in case of atomic attack, and replace slums with more attractive "ribbons of concrete." In fact, the increased highway mileage played a major role in the ways in which the nation's residential and housing patterns developed, hastening the growth of the suburbs.

Other legislative accomplishments of the Eisenhower years included the passage of the National Defense Education Act, which provided scholarships to students who specialized in mathematics and the sciences. In that same vein, following the Soviet's launching of Sputnik and Americans' recognition that the United States was lagging in the space race, Eisenhower established the President's Science Advisory Committee and also oversaw the creation of the National Aeronautics and Space Agency (NASA), to which was entrusted the responsibility for making up the deficit in the celestial battles that characterized the developing space race.

Another international accomplishment, albeit closer to home, was the enactment of the St. Lawrence Seaway Act, a 1954 law that provided for joint U.S.-Canadian construction of waterway upgrades that would open the Great Lakes to oceangoing vessels and thus expand trade opportunities for both nations. Eisenhower capped his presidency by overseeing the expansion of the United States, as Alaska and Hawaii were granted statehood in 1959.

For all the images and perceptions of the Eisenhower years as a period of calm and consistency, one undercurrent that disturbed that picture was the president's health. Eisenhower was a four-pack-a-day smoker, until he totally quit in 1949, and he had lived under great stress as head of Allied forces in World War II. He had also suffered a sudden heart attack in September 1955, an event that not only shocked the nation but raised questions about whether he would seek reelection. All of this put concerns about his health on the radar of the American public for the rest of his time in office. The heart attack in 1955 was

followed by surgery for a bowel obstruction in June 1956 and a November 1957 stroke. But in each case, he bounced back and continued to perform his duties as president.

However, there is now evidence that his health was continuing to deteriorate as his term came to an end. Indeed, while historians have long debated why the popular incumbent was not more active in his vice president's 1960 campaign to succeed him, it now appears that Nixon's reluctance to ask for Eisenhower's active involvement was not just a product of his own independence and desire to win on his own, but he was also influenced by a request from Mamie Eisenhower, backed up by Ike's physician, that the president's decreasing energies not be overtaxed. Ironically, in all likelihood, the frustration that Eisenhower felt at not being able to defend his record and support Nixon's effort did not help his condition. But there was no denying that his health was worsening, a reality that was made even clearer by the increasing heart trouble that marked his retirement years.

As he looked to a well-earned retirement after over 45 years of public service, Eisenhower sought to ensure a smooth transition of power. Meeting with the new president-elect, John F. Kennedy, the youngest man ever elected to the office, Eisenhower, the then oldest president in history, tried to impress upon the senator the often overwhelming nature of the job while also offering his help as needed, Then, only days before his presidency came to a close, and disappointed that he had not achieved even more in the effort to guarantee peace in an increasingly dangerous world, Eisenhower gave a heartfelt farewell address in which he warned about the power and influence of what he termed the *military industrial complex*, and he urged Americans of all stripes to be vigilant in their pursuit of peace and freedom. It was a fitting good-bye from a career military man whose tenure in office had been dedicated to both preserving the peace at hand while also doing all he could to achieve the conditions necessary for a peaceful future.

ANALYTICAL ESSAY

In the almost six decades since he left the presidency, Dwight D. Eisenhower's reputation as a chief executive has taken a dramatic turn. When he turned over the reins of power, he was seen as a little more than a placeholder, the man who everyone liked—and who even Kennedy acknowledged would likely have won a third term if it had been constitutionally permissible—but also a one who had not made any great impact. And yet, over the course of almost a half century marked by upheaval on the domestic and international fronts, it became clear that the comparative calm and its accompanying peace and prosperity that had marked the Eisenhower years was not an accident nor a run-of-the-mill occurrence. Those times were not just times to be appreciated; they were the result of effort and leadership that was equally deserving of recognition. While the glow of the Kennedy years that seemed both a contrast to Ike as well as a force that overshadowed him has been tarnished by subsequent historical study and reflection, Eisenhower has emerged to take his rightful place among the leading presidents in the nation's history, one who brought an end to an era of depression and war and who laid the groundwork for another admittedly fractious time of American advancement.

The Eisenhower presidency represented a distinctive era in American history. Coming after what was in many ways a series of wars—a defensive war against poverty (if not a war to defend and save capitalism) in terms of fighting its way out of the Great Depression, the obvious conflict of World War II, and then the fierce opening gambits of the Cold War—the Eisenhower years were, at least initially, seen as a period of passive conformity. They were a period of somnolence following the tumultuous decades that had preceded them. Some of this impression was shaped by the political needs of John F. Kennedy, who proclaimed that it was "time to get the country moving again" while also announcing "that the torch had been passed to a new generation." Kennedy played a vigorous game of touch football for the cameras while hiding his love for the old man's game, golf, from an admiring but restrained press. In undertaking to become the youngest man ever elected president, it was politically profitable to contrast all that his youth represented, especially as he was able to directly contrast it with an incumbent who was the oldest president in history. Framed in that way Kennedy's quest was less

audacious and more gallant, if not necessary, since the most powerful nation in the word could not be allowed to simply tread water, but rather needed to move forward. Youthful vigor, however illusory, not only provided a great contrast with a departing president, who had experienced multiple physical problems, but it was almost necessary, when it was compared to aging impotence and hesitation.

And yet, as time has passed and succeeding administrations have provided additional and valuable context, the true accomplishments of Eisenhower and his administration have come into focus, and the peace has replaced somnolence, wisdom has replaced lassitude and measured judgment, and war-tested restraint has replaced vigor in the hierarchy of values of the historical lexicon. Too, a more measured understanding of what "bearing any burden" and "paying any price" could mean when it moved from the page to policy, all in very different world, has left some analysts and historians shaking their heads at what they missed, both in terms of being blinded by the glamor and being caught napping by the more sophisticated use of power and the presidency than they had recognized.

Of course, for a long time, Eisenhower was overshadowed by the glitz and glamour of the Kennedy era. And yet, as time passed and more and more of JFK's foibles became known and his reality and rhetoric were analyzed, there came a greater recognition of just what the balding, aged war hero had accomplished—a presidency distinguished by eight years of peace and prosperity. One could perhaps quibble with the style, but the substance was undeniable. The man had first won World War II, and then he had turned around and proceeded to undertake the no less challenging task of winning the postwar peace.

Eisenhower's leadership and management skills often come up for consideration, with some seeing an efficient and well-honed machine and others seeing a disinterested chief executive, who delegated too much and was not really engaged in the process of governing. More recent studies make clear that while he did delegate, he was always the ultimate decision maker. In fact, Eisenhower's approach, not surprisingly, reflected his own experience, especially his work with Marshall, where he was one of those that the general entrusted to do a job. He surrounded himself with strong leaders who would address the problems at hand. Ike did not micromanage. He entrusted good people with responsibility, and in the context of the overarching philosophy he set out, he entrusted them with the responsibility to solve the given problem. But in the end, as evidenced in the ill-fated downed U-2 flight, the responsibility lay with the president, and he never failed to embrace it.

Indeed, in that same vein, the talk about Eisenhower's lack of political experience that often accompanied discussions of his leadership and management styles was shortsighted. Given the issues he would face as president, his experience as Supreme Allied Commander had offered a full-scale class in balancing competing interests, massaging delicate egos, and identifying and merging parties on behalf of their shared interests. It is of course true that Ike did not have the same type of electoral experience, but even there he proved something of a natural. Not known for his eloquence, he nevertheless offered a clear and articulate message that was based in common sense and that connected with voters.

Eisenhower had a presence that commanded every room he entered, but there was still a humanity and common man aspect to him that belied his heroic stature. As a statesman, he radiated a strength and sense of authority, indeed a kind of charisma, albeit different from the kind often associated with John Kennedy. It added to his effectiveness as a leader, someone who radiated calm, confident competence. Yet, for all his stature as the hero of the war, he was consistently reminding audiences that the soldiers, not the generals, had won the war, and in that same vein, he connected with the people as a leader who was working on their behalf. In assessing Eisenhower's political efforts and skills, it is important to recognize that he was likely as truly nonpartisan a president—excepting perhaps only Washington, who of course had warned from the beginning about the perils that he saw such a system bringing—as the nation has ever had.

Similarly, what historians have come to call Eisenhower's "hidden hand" approach to problem-solving was also in many ways a natural outgrowth of his military training, where results and not appearances were the determination of success or failure. A commanding general did not worry about spin, nor did he worry about the impact of perceptions and symbolic action on the upcoming election. Indeed, while the words may have been the same for Ike, the meaning of the political jargon and slogans during World War II, and their use from 1952 to 1960, could not have been more different. And yet, in both arenas, the concept of leadership was the same, and it was one in which Eisenhower excelled. The challenge of meshing the talents of ego-driven military leaders as diverse as Montgomery, Patton, and Bradley was an effective training ground for dealing with the likes of Robert Taft, Lyndon Johnson, and the like over the course of eight tumultuous years as chief executive.

For all of his supposed regrets about his choices, any assessment of the Eisenhower presidency must include a look at his Supreme Court appointments. While Eisenhower may not have gotten exactly the types of justices he wanted, his appointments, except for the beleaguered and overwhelmed Whittaker, were a credit to Eisenhower and the Court. Warren's leadership and Brennan's craftsmanship were critical to the nation's efforts to achieve equality and advance freedom. Meanwhile, Harlan and Stewart were talented legal minds who added much to the ongoing evolution of American law that was a central part of the Court's role during the 1950s through the 1970s. With all of their tenures extending well beyond Ike's own years in office, their shared efforts only magnify the important role they played in shaping his legacy.

At the same time, at least indirectly, Eisenhower's Court appointments helped hasten the development of another issue—civil rights—that remains a controversial part of his legacy. While the Court was in no way the sole force that led to the beginnings of a veritable political and social revolution, it played a substantive part. But while Ike can be given credit for appointments such as Warren and Brennan and their efforts in opening up new opportunities for the nation's African American population, they also helped put a spotlight on the president's own efforts, and not always to his credit. Indeed, Eisenhower's record on civil rights is a source of often heated debate among historians. He certainly took care that the laws were "faithfully executed," even going so far as to dispatch federal troops for the first time since Reconstruction, but at the same time, many observers and historians express legitimate disappointment, if not dismay, at his failure to use the presidency's bully pulpit to respond to the obvious angst and opposition that arose in response to *Brown* and subsequent efforts, such as the developing movement that was coming to the fore in the form of the Montgomery bus boycott and the lunch counter sit-ins that took place in the late winter and spring of 1960.

The singular and consistent complaint about Eisenhower and civil rights was the fact that at no time did he ever rise above the legal dictates of his office. Instead, choosing to adopt a neutral posture, he never used the extensive moral power of his office to move the cause of civil rights and equality forward. There can be little doubt that had Eisenhower, the president of the United States and the commander of the army that had triumphed in an all-out war to protect freedom, followed up on the *Brown* ruling with a national address that reminded the American people of their roots as a nation based in the ideal that all men are created equal and that the Supreme Court's ruling was the latest and most powerful chapter in the effort to achieve that goal, then the national response might have been very different.

No less problematic was Ike's refusal to give a national address on the issue of race, especially the reports that he rebuffed a request from Martin Luther King Jr. to give such a speech, explaining that he did not see what another speech could do. And yet, his actions in other areas, such as his Open Skies and Atoms for Peace addresses, not to mention his farewell address, clearly demonstrated that while never known for his high-flying rhetoric, he fully understood the value of such pronouncements coming from the unmatched bully pulpit of the presidency. Indeed, one can argue that Ike's civil rights record was in fact considerably more substantive than his successor's, but Kennedy's well-received television address, the one that framed the civil right struggle in moral terms, did much to enhance the former senator's record on civil rights, despite the fact that, from the Freedom Rides to Ole Miss to Birmingham, the Kennedy administration's efforts were even more reactive than Eisenhower's. It was unable to boast even a watered-down Civil Rights bill.

Indeed, the Eisenhower administration did oversee the passage of the first two civil rights acts since Reconstruction, but in its own way, that very fact highlights the contradictions central to the Eisenhower record. The Civil Rights Act of 1960, in many ways, embodies the challenges historians have faced in assessing Eisenhower's record and legacy in this area. On the one hand, the act broke no new ground, and Eisenhower was accused by some of simply ignoring the issue, leaving it to be handled by his successor. Meanwhile, defenders have argued that the effort to enact a new law reflected the recognition of a problem and a desire to address it that was ultimately hampered by the Democrats who controlled the Senate. At the very least, they say, the effort served to make the nation aware that a problem existed and needed to be addressed. Too, for all of their alleged lack of impact, they did serve to lay a foundation for the passage of the pieces of legislation, the 1964 Civil Rights Act and the 1965 Voting Rights Act, which soon followed. In addition, one of the law's important but overlooked provisions mandated that election officials in the county had to not only "retain and preserve" all voting-related records for 22 months but had to produce those records "upon demand in writing by the Attorney General." Utilizing this provision, Attorney General William P. Rogers and later Robert F. Kennedy of the Kennedy administration requested to inspect voting records in 26 Southern counties where African Americans had alleged discrimination. With those records as a starting point, investigations were undertaken that resulted in the Department of Justice filing almost 20 voter discrimination suits by the end of 1962. All of this fueled the debates that would ultimately lead to the passage of the Voting Rights Act as well as other efforts to make the promise of the Fifteenth Amendment a reality.

The challenges inherent in assessing Ike's presidency were evident back in 1956, when he was seeking reelection. Commentators of the time struggled to identify and explain exactly what Eisenhower represented. Viewed by all as optimistic and pragmatic, columnists wondered whether there was more to him than the attractive contrast that he represented to the previous two decades of war, depressions, and division. To many, it appeared that a promise to continue the calm of his first term was the centerpiece of his argument for reelection. Many were less benign, arguing that Ike himself was lazy and that the president had an obligation to affirmatively attack the problems still confronting the nation. It would take time for the understanding to come.

And while his second term was hurt by the U-2 incident as well as the usual inertia that historically marks second terms, the country continued to enjoy peace and prosperity, with a short term but not debilitating economic downturn being the only real blemish. Indeed, for all his campaign rhetoric about it being time for a change and how Americans needed to get the country moving again, John Kennedy acknowledged on numerous occasions that Eisenhower could have won a third term if he had been able to run again.

While it did not translate into any other policies, a consistent postwar concern and theme of Ike's, one he had articulated in his Columbia inauguration address as well as numerous other venues, was freedom and his fears for its future. He expressed his concerns about a world increasingly marked by states, including extensions of the New Deal, that were going beyond the reasonable safety net and undermining individual initiative and responsibility as people were increasingly content to let the government make decisions for them. He made no effort to roll back the New Deal, and, in fact, that reality during two terms of Republican rule did much to fully and finally cement the New Deal's place in American political culture, although his warnings about governmental overreach did offer future conservatives a philosophical point from which to base some of their "anti–big government" rhetoric.

Ike had worked vigilantly during his presidency to avoid war during his term in office and to lay a foundation for a more permanent peace. But as he left office, there remained loose ends and issues still to be resolved. To his credit, he had resisted the urgings of those who wanted him to pick up the banner from the French in Vietnam in the aftermath of their defeat in 1954 at Dien Bien Phu, and that decision has generally earned him plaudits from historians. At the same time, some saw him as not only abandoning the French but, to use his own terminology, allowing the first domino to fall, thus putting into play a policy that his successors would pursue.

Too, while Ike has been applauded for keeping the United States out of any major military engagements, it was during his administration, at the urging of then director Allen Dulles, that the CIA added covert operations to the Cold War playbook. Their efforts in such places as Iran and Guatemala, actions that would ultimately lead to the overthrow of democratically elected governments, opened up a new chapter in U.S. operations with results that would not become fully evident for decades. Similarly, it was under Ike that the United States upped its use of things like U-2 surveillance, efforts whose goals were certainly worthy but which, in the eyes of many, helped further develop the military industrial complex against which the exiting statesman would warn. Indeed, throughout his presidency Eisenhower walked a fine line, aggressively pursuing peace but never failing to prepare for war. He did it successfully, with his more adroit and restrained treatment of the use of nuclear weapons serving as an effective counterbalance to Dulles's more bellicose talk of massive retaliation. While the rhetoric sometimes got heated, in the end, Eisenhower ended the war in Korea and avoided U.S. involvement in any others.

It was only with the passage of time that Eisenhower's accomplishments came to be truly appreciated. Despite the turmoil that had preceded him, as he left office, there was a limited appreciation of just what he had accomplished. While his own popularity remained high, so too had Calvin Coolidge's upon leaving office and Warren Harding's upon his sudden death. And yet, unlike those two earlier conservative Republican standard-bearers, Ike's efforts have stood the test of time, and he has become appropriately recognized for the accomplishments of his tenure. The limits of the glitz and glamour of the Kennedy years, the almost frenetic activism of the Johnson years, and the disillusionment of Nixon, all served to help make clear that, although he had not been flashy, Eisenhower, the war-tested general, had nevertheless navigated the American ship of state through some rough political and international waters—even if most people had not really noticed at the time. Only when supposedly more eloquent, energetic, and politically experienced successors ran aground did the magnitude of his accomplishments come to be appreciated.

None of this would have truly surprised Eisenhower. Well versed in history, he understood the vagaries of public reputations. And as a proud and confident man, he did not need the external accolades. Instead, he took satisfaction in knowing, as he had from the moment he entered the army, that he had done his very best to serve the nation. If it took others longer to realize it, then so be it. The general knew that he had done his duty.

Bill H. Pruden

Further Reading

Dwight D. Eisenhower Presidential Library, Museum and Boyhood Home. n.d. https://www.eisenhower.archives.gov/research/online_documents.html.

Greenstein, Fred I. 1982. *The Hidden-Hand Presidency: Eisenhower as Leader*. New York: Basic Books.

Hitchcock, William I. 2018. *The Age of Eisenhower: America and the World in the 1950s*. New York: Simon & Schuster.

Newton, Jim. 2011. *Eisenhower: The White House Years*. New York: Doubleday.

Smith, Jean Edward. 2012. *Eisenhower in War and Peace*. New York: Random House.

Thomas, Evan. 2012. *Ike's Bluff: President Eisenhower's Secret Battle to Save the World*. New York: Little Brown.

Wicker, Tom. 2002. *Dwight D. Eisenhower*. The American Presidents Series. Edited by Arthur M. Schlesinger Jr. New York: Times Books/Henry Holt and Company.

"Atoms for Peace" Speech (December 8, 1953)

One of Eisenhower's central concerns throughout his presidency was the issue of atomic weapons. The "Atoms for Peace" speech represents his first effort to both address that threat and to reshape the conversation in an effort to help Americans, as well as the global community, see the full range of possibilities that atomic energy offered.

Madame President, Members of the General Assembly:

When Secretary General Hammarskjold's invitation to address this General Assembly reached me in Bermuda, I was just beginning a series of conferences with the Prime Ministers and Foreign Ministers of Great Britain and of France. Our subject was some of the problems that beset our world.

During the remainder of the Bermuda Conference, I had constantly in mind that ahead of me lay a great honor. That honor is mine today as I stand here, privileged to address the General Assembly of the United Nations.

At the same time that I appreciate the distinction of addressing you, I have a sense of exhilaration as I look upon this Assembly.

Never before in history has so much hope for so many people been gathered together in a single organization. Your deliberations and decisions during these somber years have already realized part of those hopes.

But the great tests and the great accomplishments still lie ahead. And in the confident expectation of those accomplishments, I would use the office which, for the time being, I hold, to assure you that the Government of the United States will remain steadfast in its support of this body. This we shall do in the conviction that you will provide a great share of the wisdom, the courage, and the faith which can bring to this world lasting peace for all nations, and happiness and well-being for all men.

Clearly, it would not be fitting for me to take this occasion to present to you a unilateral American report on Bermuda. Nevertheless, I assure you that in our deliberations on that lovely island we sought to invoke those same great concepts of universal peace and human dignity which are so clearly etched in your Charter.

Neither would it be a measure of this great opportunity merely to recite, however hopefully, pious platitudes.

I therefore decided that this occasion warranted my saying to you some of the things that have been on the minds and hearts of my legislative and executive associates and on mine for a great many months—thoughts I had originally planned to say primarily to the American people.

I know that the American people share my deep belief that if a danger exists in the world, it is a danger shared by all—and equally, that if hope exists in the mind of one nation, that hope should be shared by all.

Finally, if there is to be advanced any proposal designed to ease even by the smallest measure the tensions of today's world, what more appropriate audience could there be than the members of the General Assembly of the United Nations?

I feel impelled to speak today in a language that in a sense is new—one which I, who have spent so much of my life in the military profession, would have preferred never to use.

That new language is the language of atomic warfare.

The atomic age has moved forward at such a pace that every citizen of the world should have some comprehension, at least in comparative terms, of the extent of this development of the utmost significance to every one of us. Clearly, if the peoples of the world are to conduct an intelligent search for peace, they must be armed with the significant facts of today's existence.

My recital of atomic danger and power is necessarily stated in United States terms, for these are the only incontrovertible facts that I know. I need hardly point out to this Assembly, however, that this subject is global, not merely national in character.

On July 16, 1945, the United States set off the world's first atomic explosion. Since that date in 1945, the United States of America has conducted 42 test explosions.

Atomic bombs today are more than 25 times as powerful as the weapons with which the atomic age dawned, while hydrogen weapons are in the ranges of millions of tons of TNT equivalent.

Today, the United States' stockpile of atomic weapons, which, of course, increases daily, exceeds by many times the explosive equivalent of the total of all bombs and all shells that came from every plane and every gun in every theatre of war in all of the years of World War II.

A single air group, whether afloat or land-based, can now deliver to any reachable target a destructive cargo exceeding in power all the bombs that fell on Britain in all of World War II.

In size and variety, the development of atomic weapons has been no less remarkable. The development has been such that atomic weapons have virtually achieved conventional status within our armed services. In the United States, the Army, the Navy, the Air Force, and the Marine Corps are all capable of putting this weapon to military use.

But the dread secret, and the fearful engines of atomic might, are not ours alone.

In the first place, the secret is possessed by our friends and allies, Great Britain and Canada, whose scientific genius made a tremendous contribution to our original discoveries, and the designs of atomic bombs.

The secret is also known by the Soviet Union.

The Soviet Union has informed us that, over recent years, it has devoted extensive resources to atomic weapons. During this period, the Soviet Union has exploded a series of atomic devices, including at least one involving thermo-nuclear reactions.

If at one time the United States possessed what might have been called a monopoly of atomic power, that monopoly ceased to exist several years ago. Therefore, although our earlier start has permitted us to accumulate what is today a great quantitative advantage, the atomic realities of today comprehend two facts of even greater significance.

First, the knowledge now possessed by several nations will eventually be shared by others—possibly all others.

Second, even a vast superiority in numbers of weapons, and a consequent capability of devastating retaliation, is no preventive, of itself, against the fearful material damage and toll of human lives that would be inflicted by surprise aggression.

The free world, at least dimly aware of these facts, has naturally embarked on a large program of warning and defense systems. That program will be accelerated and expanded.

But let no one think that the expenditure of vast sums for weapons and systems of defense can guarantee absolute safety for the cities and citizens of any nation. The awful arithmetic of the atomic bomb does not permit of any such easy solution. Even against the most powerful defense, an aggressor in possession of the effective minimum number of atomic bombs for a surprise attack could probably place a sufficient number of his bombs on the chosen targets to cause hideous damage.

Should such an atomic attack be launched against the United States, our reactions would be swift and resolute. But for me to say that the defense capabilities of the United States are such that they could inflict terrible losses upon an aggressor—for me to say that the retaliation capabilities of the United States are so great that such an aggressor's land would be laid waste—all this, while fact, is not the true expression of the purpose and the hope of the United States.

To pause there would be to confirm the hopeless finality of a belief that two atomic colossi are doomed malevolently to eye each other indefinitely across a trembling world. To stop there would be to accept helplessly the probability of civilization destroyed-the annihilation of the irreplaceable heritage of mankind handed down to us generation from generation—and the condemnation of mankind to begin all over again the age-old struggle upward from savagery toward decency, and right, and justice.

Surely no sane member of the human race could discover victory in such desolation. Could anyone wish his name to be coupled by history with such human degradation and destruction.

Occasional pages of history do record the faces of the "Great Destroyers" but the whole book of history reveals mankind's never-ending quest for peace, and mankind's God-given capacity to build.

It is with the book of history, and not with isolated pages, that the United States will ever wish to be identified. My country wants to be constructive, not destructive. It wants agreements, not wars, among nations. It wants itself to live in freedom, and in the confidence that the people of every other nation enjoy equally the right of choosing their own way of life.

So my country's purpose is to help us move out of the dark chamber of horrors into the light, to find a way by which the minds of men, the hopes of men, the souls of men everywhere, can move forward toward peace and happiness and well being.

In this quest, I know that we must not lack patience.

I know that in a world divided, such as ours today, salvation cannot be attained by one dramatic act.

I know that many steps will have to be taken over many months before the world can look at itself one day and truly realize that a new climate of mutually peaceful confidence is abroad in the world.

But I know, above all else, that we must start to take these steps—now.

The United States and its allies, Great Britain and France, have over the past months tried to take some of these steps. Let no one say that we shun the conference table.

On the record has long stood the request of the United States, Great Britain, and France to negotiate with the Soviet Union the problems of a divided Germany.

On that record has long stood the request of the same three nations to negotiate an Austrian Peace Treaty.

On the same record still stands the request of the United Nations to negotiate the problems of Korea.

Most recently, we have received from the Soviet Union what is in effect an expression of willingness to hold a Four Power Meeting. Along with our allies, Great Britain and France, we were pleased to see that this note did not contain the unacceptable preconditions previously put forward.

As you already know from our joint Bermuda communique, the United States, Great Britain, and France have agreed promptly to meet with the Soviet Union.

The Government of the United States approaches this conference with hopeful sincerity. We will bend every effort of our minds to the single purpose of emerging from that conference with tangible results toward peace—the only true way of lessening international tension.

We never have, we never will, propose or suggest that the Soviet Union surrender what is rightfully theirs.

We will never say that the peoples of Russia are an enemy with whom we have no desire ever to deal or mingle in friendly and fruitful relationship.

On the contrary, we hope that this coming Conference may initiate a relationship with the Soviet Union which will eventually bring about a free intermingling of the peoples of the East and of the West—the one sure, human way of developing the understanding required for confident and peaceful relations.

Instead of the discontent which is now settling upon Eastern Germany, occupied Austria, and the countries of Eastern Europe, we seek a harmonious family of free European nations, with none a threat to the other, and least of all a threat to the peoples of Russia.

Beyond the turmoil and strife and misery of Asia, we seek peaceful opportunity for these peoples to develop their natural resources and to elevate their lives.

These are not idle words or shallow visions. Behind them lies a story of nations lately come to independence, not as a result of war, but through free grant or peaceful negotiation. There is a record, already written, of assistance gladly given by nations of the West to needy peoples, and to those suffering the temporary effects of famine, drought, and natural disaster.

These are deeds of peace. They speak more loudly than promises or protestations of peaceful intent.

But I do not wish to rest either upon the reiteration of past proposals or the restatement of past deeds. The gravity of the time is such that every new avenue of peace, no matter how dimly discernible, should be explored.

There is at least one new avenue of peace which has not yet been well explored—an avenue now laid out by the General Assembly of the United Nations.

In its resolution of November 18th, 1953, this General Assembly suggested—and I quote—"that the Disarmament Commission study the desirability of establishing a sub-committee consisting of representatives of the Powers principally involved, which should seek in private an acceptable solution . . . and report on such a solution to the General Assembly and to the Security Council not later than 1 September 1954."

The United States, heeding the suggestion of the General Assembly of the United Nations, is instantly prepared to meet privately with such other countries as may be "principally involved," to seek "an acceptable solution" to the atomic armaments race which overshadows not only the peace, but the very life, of the world.

We shall carry into these private or diplomatic talks a new conception.

The United States would seek more than the mere reduction or elimination of atomic materials for military purposes.

It is not enough to take this weapon out of the hands of the soldiers. It must be put into the hands of those who will know how to strip its military casing and adapt it to the arts of peace.

The United States knows that if the fearful trend of atomic military buildup can be reversed, this greatest of destructive forces can be developed into a great boon, for the benefit of all mankind.

The United States knows that peaceful power from atomic energy is no dream of the future. That capability, already proved, is here—now—today. Who can doubt, if the entire body of the world's scientists and engineers had adequate amounts of fissionable material with which to test and develop their ideas, that this capability would rapidly be transformed into universal, efficient, and economic usage.

To hasten the day when fear of the atom will begin to disappear from the minds of people, and the governments of the East and West, there are certain steps that can be taken now.

I therefore make the following proposals:

The Governments principally involved, to the extent permitted by elementary prudence, to begin now and continue to make joint contributions from their stockpiles of normal uranium and fissionable materials to an International Atomic Energy Agency. We would expect that such an agency would be set up under the aegis of the United Nations.

The ratios of contributions, the procedures and other details would properly be within the scope of the "private conversations" I have referred to earlier.

The United States is prepared to undertake these explorations in good faith. Any partner of the United States acting in the same good faith will find the United States a not unreasonable or ungenerous associate.

Undoubtedly initial and early contributions to this plan would be small in quantity. However, the proposal has the great virtue that it can be undertaken without the irritations and mutual suspicions incident to any attempt to set up a completely acceptable system of world-wide inspection and control.

The Atomic Energy Agency could be made responsible for the impounding, storage, and protection of the contributed fissionable and other materials. The ingenuity of our scientists will provide special safe conditions under which such a bank of fissionable material can be made essentially immune to surprise seizure.

The more important responsibility of this Atomic Energy Agency would be to devise methods whereby this fissionable material would be allocated to serve the peaceful pursuits of mankind. Experts would be mobilized to apply atomic energy to the needs of agriculture, medicine, and other peaceful activities. A special purpose would be to provide abundant electrical energy in the power-starved areas of the world. Thus the contributing powers would be dedicating some of their strength to serve the needs rather than the fears of mankind.

The United States would be more than willing—it would be proud to take up with others "principally involved" the development of plans whereby such peaceful use of atomic energy would be expedited.

Of those "principally involved" the Soviet Union must, of course, be one.

I would be prepared to submit to the Congress of the United States, and with every expectation of approval, any such plan that would:

First—encourage world-wide investigation into the most effective peacetime uses of fissionable material, and with the certainty that they had all the material needed for the conduct of all experiments that were appropriate;

Second—begin to diminish the potential destructive power of the world's atomic stockpiles;

Third—allow all peoples of all nations to see that, in this enlightened age, the great powers of the earth, both of the East and of the West, are interested in human aspirations first, rather than in building up the armaments of war;

Fourth—open up a new channel for peaceful discussion, and initiate at least a new approach to the many difficult problems that must be solved in both private and public conversations, if the world is to shake off the inertia imposed by fear, and is to make positive progress toward peace.

Against the dark background of the atomic bomb, the United States does not wish merely to present strength, but also the desire and the hope for peace.

The coming months will be fraught with fateful decisions. In this Assembly; in the capitals and military headquarters of the world; in the hearts of men everywhere, be they governors or governed, may they be the decisions which will lead this world out of fear and into peace.

To the making of these fateful decisions, the United States pledges before you—and therefore before the world—its determination to help solve the fearful atomic dilemma—to devote its entire heart and mind to find the way by which the miraculous inventiveness of man shall not be dedicated to his death but consecrated to his life.

I again thank the delegates for the great honor they have done me, in inviting me to appear before them, and in listening to me so courteously. Thank you.

Source: *Public Papers of the Presidents of the United States. Dwight D. Eisenhower, 1953.* Washington, D.C.: Government Printing Office, 1960, 813–822.

Address on Little Rock (September 24, 1957)

Civil rights were an issue that Eisenhower wrestled with throughout his presidency. In doing so, he faced ongoing criticism about his failure to make a speech that might have altered the nation's thinking about the emerging civil rights movement and about the Supreme Court decisions that were fueling it. Although such a broad-based speech never came, Eisenhower did make one televised address on the issue when he explained to the American people why he had sent federal troops to Little Rock, Arkansas, amid the effort to desegregate the city's Central High School. The speech offered a clear view of the way Eisenhower saw his role: as a chief executive empowered to enforce the law—and little else.

Good Evening, My Fellow Citizens: For a few minutes this evening I want to speak to you about the serious situation that has arisen in Little Rock. To make this talk I have come to the President's office in the White House. I could have spoken from Rhode Island, where I have been staying recently, but I felt that, in speaking from the house of Lincoln, of Jackson and of Wilson, my words would better convey both the sadness I feel in the action I was compelled today to take and the firmness with which I intend to pursue this course until the orders of the Federal Court at Little Rock can be executed without unlawful interference.

In that city, under the leadership of demagogic extremists, disorderly mobs have deliberately prevented the carrying out of proper orders from a Federal Court.

Local authorities have not eliminated that violent opposition and, under the law, I yesterday issued a Proclamation calling upon the mob to disperse.

This morning the mob again gathered in front of the Central High School of Little Rock, obviously for the purpose of again preventing the carrying out of the Court's order relating to the admission of Negro children to that school.

Whenever normal agencies prove inadequate to the task and it becomes necessary for the Executive Branch of the Federal Government to use its powers and authority to uphold Federal Courts, the President's responsibility is inescapable. In accordance with that responsibility, I have today issued an Executive Order directing the use of troops under Federal authority to aid in the execution of Federal law at Little Rock, Arkansas. This became necessary when my Proclamation of yesterday was not observed, and the obstruction of justice still continues.

It is important that the reasons for my action be understood by all our citizens. As you know, the Supreme Court of the United States has decided that separate public educational facilities for the races are inherently unequal and therefore compulsory school segregation laws are unconstitutional.

Our personal opinions about the decision have no bearing on the matter of enforcement; the responsibility and authority of the Supreme Court to interpret the Constitution are very clear. Local Federal Courts were instructed by the Supreme Court to issue such orders and decrees as might be necessary to achieve admission to public schools without regard to race—and with all deliberate speed.

During the past several years, many communities in our Southern States have instituted public school plans for gradual progress in the enrollment and attendance of school children of all races in order to bring themselves into compliance with the law of the land.

They thus demonstrated to the world that we are a nation in which laws, not men, are supreme.

I regret to say that this truth—the cornerstone of our liberties—was not observed in this instance.

It was my hope that this localized situation would be brought under control by city and State authorities. If the use of local police powers had been sufficient, our traditional method of leaving the problems in those hands would have been pursued. But when large gatherings of obstructionists made it impossible for the decrees of the Court to be carried out, both the law and the national interest demanded that the President take action.

Here is the sequence of events in the development of the Little Rock school case.

In May of 1955, the Little Rock School Board approved a moderate plan for the gradual desegregation of the public schools in that city. It provided that a start toward integration would be made at the present term in the high school, and that the plan would be in full operation by 1963. Here I might say that in a number of communities in Arkansas integration in the schools has already started and without violence of any kind. Now this Little Rock plan was challenged in the courts by some who believed that the period of time as proposed in the plan was too long.

The United States Court at Little Rock, which has supervisory responsibility under the law for the plan of desegregation in the public schools, dismissed the challenge, thus approving a gradual rather than an abrupt change from the existing system. The court found that the school board had acted in good faith in planning for a public school system free from racial discrimination.

Since that time, the court has on three separate occasions issued orders directing that the plan be carried out. All persons were instructed to refrain from interfering with the efforts of the school board to comply with the law.

Proper and sensible observance of the law then demanded the respectful obedience which the nation has a right to expect from all its people. This, unfortunately, has not been the case at Little Rock. Certain misguided persons, many of them imported into Little Rock by agitators, have insisted upon defying the law and have sought to bring it into disrepute. The orders of the court have thus been frustrated.

The very basis of our individual rights and freedoms rests upon the certainty that the President and the Executive Branch of Government will support and insure the carrying out of the decisions of the Federal Courts, even, when necessary with all the means at the President's command.

Unless the President did so, anarchy would result.

There would be no security for any except that which each one of us could provide for himself.

The interest of the nation in the proper fulfillment of the law's requirements cannot yield to opposition and demonstrations by some few persons.

Mob rule cannot be allowed to override the decisions of our courts.

Now, let me make it very clear that Federal troops are not being used to relieve local and state authorities of their primary duty to preserve the peace and order of the community. Nor are the troops there for the purpose of taking over the responsibility of the School Board and the other responsible local officials in running Central High School. The running of our school system and the maintenance of peace and order in each of our States are strictly local affairs and the Federal Government does not interfere except in a very few special cases and when requested by one of the several States. In the present case the troops are there, pursuant to law, solely for the purpose of preventing interference with the orders of the Court.

The proper use of the powers of the Executive Branch to enforce the orders of a Federal Court is limited to extraordinary and compelling circumstances. Manifestly, such an extreme situation has been created in Little Rock. This challenge must be met and with such measures as will preserve to the people as a whole their lawfully-protected rights in a climate permitting their free and fair exercise. The overwhelming majority of our people in every section of the country are united in their respect for observance of the law—even in those cases where they may disagree with that law.

They deplore the call of extremists to violence.

The decision of the Supreme Court concerning school integration, of course, affects the South more seriously than it does other sections of the country. In that region I have many warm friends, some of them in the city of Little Rock. I have deemed it a great personal privilege to spend in our Southland tours of duty while in the military service and enjoyable recreational periods since that time.

So from intimate personal knowledge, I know that the overwhelming majority of the people in the South—including those of Arkansas and of Little Rock—are of good will, united in their efforts to preserve and respect the law even when they disagree with it.

They do not sympathize with mob rule. They, like the rest of our nation, have proved in two great wars their readiness to sacrifice for America.

A foundation of our American way of life is our national respect for law.

In the South, as elsewhere, citizens are keenly aware of the tremendous disservice that has been done to the people of Arkansas in the eyes of the nation, and that has been done to the nation in the eyes of the world.

At a time when we face grave situations abroad because of the hatred that Communism bears toward a system of government based on human rights, it would be difficult to exaggerate the harm that is being done to the prestige and influence, and indeed to the safety, of our nation and the world.

Our enemies are gloating over this incident and using it everywhere to misrepresent our whole nation. We are portrayed as a violator of those standards of conduct which the peoples of the world united to proclaim in the Charter of the United Nations. There they affirmed "faith in fundamental human rights" and "in the dignity and worth of the human person" and they did so "without distinction as to race, sex, language or religion."

And so, with deep confidence, I call upon the citizens of the State of Arkansas to assist in bringing to an immediate end all interference with the law and its processes. If resistance to the Federal Court orders ceases at once, the further presence of Federal troops will be unnecessary and the City of Little Rock will return to its normal habits of peace and order and a blot upon the fair name and high honor of our nation in the world will be removed.

Thus, will be restored the image of America and of all its parts as one nation, indivisible, with liberty and justice for all.

Good night and thank you very much.

Source: *Public Papers of the Presidents of the United States. Dwight D. Eisenhower, 1957. Washington, D.C.: Government Printing Office, 1958, 689–694.*

Statement on the U-2 Incident (May 11, 1960)

The U-2 affair in the spring of 1960 represented both a major embarrassment for the Eisenhower administration as well as a major disappointment when it led to the ruin of the Four Power Summit. The administration initially sought to deny involvement, but when the Soviets produced downed pilot Gary Francis Powers, Eisenhower had to acknowledge his and the nation's role and responsibility. His remarks at the press conference do just that while also offering a thoughtful exposition on the important role of surveillance in the Cold War world.

I have made some notes from which I want to talk to you about this U-2 incident.

A full statement about this matter has been made by the State Department, and there have been several statesmanlike remarks by leaders of both parties.

For my part, I supplement what the Secretary of State has had to say with the following four main points. After that I shall have nothing further to say—for the simple reason that I can think of nothing to add that might be useful at this time.

First point is this: the need for intelligence-gathering activities.

No one wants another Pearl Harbor. This means that we must have knowledge of military forces and preparations around the world, especially those capable of massive surprise attack.

Secrecy in the Soviet Union makes this essential. In most of the world no large-scale attack could be prepared in secret. But in the Soviet Union there is a fetish of secrecy and concealment. This is a major cause of international tension and uneasiness today. Our deterrent must never be placed in jeopardy. The safety of the whole free world demands this.

As the Secretary of State pointed out in his recent statement, ever since the beginning of my administration I have issued directives to gather, in every feasible way, the information required to protect the United States and the free world against surprise attack and to enable them to make effective preparations for defense.

My second point: the nature of intelligence-gathering activities.

These have a special and secret character. They are, so to speak, "below the surface" activities.

They are secret because they must circumvent measures designed by other countries to protect secrecy of military preparations.

They are divorced from the regular, visible agencies of government, which stay clear of operational involvement in specific detailed activities.

These elements operate under broad directives to seek and gather intelligence short of the use of force, with operations supervised by responsible officials within this area of secret activities.

We do not use our Army, Navy, or Air Force for this purpose, first, to avoid any possibility of the use of force in connection with these activities and, second, because our military forces, for obvious reasons, cannot be given latitude under broad directives but must be kept under strict control in every detail.

These activities have their own rules and methods of concealment, which seek to mislead and obscure—just as in the Soviet allegations there are many discrepancies. For example, there is some reason to believe that the plane in question was not shot down at high altitude. The normal agencies of our Government are unaware of these specific activities or of the special efforts to conceal them.

Third point: How should we view all of this activity?

It is a distasteful but vital necessity.

We prefer and work for a different kind of world—and a different way of obtaining the information essential to confidence and effective deterrence. Open societies, in the day of present weapons, are the only answer.

This was the reason for my open-skies proposal in 1955, which I was ready instantly to put into effect, to permit aerial observation over the United States and the Soviet Union which would assure that no surprise attack was being prepared against anyone. I shall bring up the open-skies proposal again in Paris, since it is a means of ending concealment and suspicion.

My final point is that we must not be distracted from the real issues of the day by what is an incident or a symptom of the world situation today.

This incident has been given great propaganda exploitation. The emphasis given to a flight of an unarmed, nonmilitary plane can only reflect a fetish of secrecy.

The real issue are the ones we will be working on at the summit—disarmament, search for solutions affecting Germany and Berlin, and the whole range of East-West relations, including the reduction of secrecy and suspicion.

Frankly, I am hopeful that we may make progress on these great issues. This is what we mean when we speak of "working for peace."

And, as I remind you, I will have nothing further to say about this matter.

Source: *Public Papers of the Presidents of the United States. Dwight D. Eisenhower, 1960–61. Washington, D.C.: Government Printing Office, 1961, 403–404.*

Farewell Address (January 17, 1961)

President Eisenhower's farewell address was a valedictory address that looked back over almost five decades of service to the United States. It was at once a thank-you to the nation and its people for the opportunity to serve as well as a sharing of the lessons of history that he had so insightfully gleaned over his time in the military and the White House. Although the speech was initially overshadowed by much of the glitz and glamour of the Kennedys, its warning about the growth and influence of the "the military industrial complex" would, like so much of his record, later be recognized for its wisdom and sagacity.

My fellow Americans:

Three days from now, after half a century in the service of our country, I shall lay down the responsibilities of office as, in traditional and solemn ceremony, the authority of the Presidency is vested in my successor.

This evening I come to you with a message of leave-taking and farewell, and to share a few final thoughts with you, my countrymen.

Like every other citizen, I wish the new President, and all who will labor with him, Godspeed. I pray that the coming years will be blessed with peace and prosperity for all.

Our people expect their President and the Congress to find essential agreement on issues of great moment, the wise resolution of which will better shape the future of the Nation.

My own relations with the Congress, which began on a remote and tenuous basis when, long ago, a member of the Senate appointed me to West Point, have since ranged to the intimate during the war and immediate post-war period, and, finally, to the mutually interdependent during these past eight years.

In this final relationship, the Congress and the Administration have, on most vital issues, cooperated well, to serve the national good rather than mere partisanship, and so have assured that the business of the Nation should go forward. So, my official relationship with the Congress ends in a feeling, on my part, of gratitude that we have been able to do so much together.

II.

We now stand ten years past the midpoint of a century that has witnessed four major wars among great nations. Three of these involved our own country. Despite these holocausts America is today the strongest, the most influential and most productive nation in the world. Understandably proud of this pre-eminence, we yet realize that America's leadership and prestige depend, not merely upon our unmatched material progress, riches and military strength, but on how we use our power in the interests of world peace and human betterment.

III.

Throughout America's adventure in free government, our basic purposes have been to keep the peace; to foster progress in human achievement, and to enhance liberty, dignity and integrity among people and among nations. To strive for less would be unworthy of a free and religious people. Any failure traceable to arrogance, or our lack of comprehension or readiness to sacrifice would inflict upon us grievous hurt both at home and abroad.

Progress toward these noble goals is persistently threatened by the conflict now engulfing the world. It commands our whole attention, absorbs our very beings. We face a hostile ideology—global in scope, atheistic in character, ruthless in purpose, and insidious in method. Unhappily the danger it poses promises to be of indefinite duration. To meet it successfully, there is called for, not so much the emotional and transitory sacrifices of crisis, but rather those which enable us to carry forward steadily, surely, and without complaint the burdens of a prolonged and complex struggle—with liberty the stake. Only thus shall we remain, despite every provocation, on our charted course toward permanent peace and human betterment.

Crises there will continue to be. In meeting them, whether foreign or domestic, great or small, there is a recurring temptation to feel that some spectacular and costly action could become the miraculous solution to all current difficulties. A huge increase in newer elements of our defense; development of unrealistic programs to cure every ill in agriculture; a dramatic expansion in basic and applied research—these and many other possibilities, each possibly promising in itself, may be suggested as the only way to the road we wish to travel.

But each proposal must be weighed in the light of a broader consideration: the need to maintain balance in and among national programs-balance between the private and the public economy, balance between cost and hoped for advantage—balance between the clearly necessary and the comfortably desirable; balance between our essential requirements as a nation and the duties imposed by the nation upon the individual; balance between actions of the moment and the national welfare of the future. Good judgment seeks balance and progress; lack of it eventually finds imbalance and frustration.

The record of many decades stands as proof that our people and their government have, in the main, understood these truths and have responded to them well, in the face of stress and threat. But threats, new in kind or degree, constantly arise. I mention two only.

IV.

A vital element in keeping the peace is our military establishment. Our arms must be mighty, ready for instant action, so that no potential aggressor may be tempted to risk his own destruction.

Our military organization today bears little relation to that known by any of my predecessors in peacetime, or indeed by the fighting men of World War II or Korea.

Until the latest of our world conflicts, the United States had no armaments industry. American makers of plowshares could, with time and as required, make swords as well. But now we can no longer risk emergency improvisation of national defense; we have been compelled to create a permanent armaments industry of vast proportions. Added to this, three and a half million men and women are directly engaged in the defense establishment. We annually spend on military security more than the net income of all United States corporations.

This conjunction of an immense military establishment and a large arms industry is new in the American experience. The total influence—economic, political, even spiritual—is felt in every city, every State house, every office of the Federal government. We recognize the imperative need for this development. Yet we must not fail to comprehend its grave implications. Our toil, resources and livelihood are all involved; so is the very structure of our society.

In the councils of government, we must guard against the acquisition of unwarranted influence, whether sought or unsought, by the military-industrial complex. The potential for the disastrous rise of misplaced power exists and will persist.

We must never let the weight of this combination endanger our liberties or democratic processes. We should take nothing for granted. Only an alert and knowledgeable citizenry can compel the proper meshing of the huge industrial and military machinery of defense with our peaceful methods and goals, so that security and liberty may prosper together.

Akin to, and largely responsible for the sweeping changes in our industrial-military posture, has been the technological revolution during recent decades.

In this revolution, research has become central; it also becomes more formalized, complex, and costly. A steadily increasing share is conducted for, by, or at the direction of, the Federal government.

Today, the solitary inventor, tinkering in his shop, has been overshadowed by task forces of scientists in laboratories and testing fields. In the same fashion, the free university, historically the fountainhead of free ideas and scientific discovery, has experienced a revolution in the conduct of research. Partly because of the huge costs involved, a government contract becomes virtually a substitute for intellectual curiosity. For every old blackboard there are now hundreds of new electronic computers.

The prospect of domination of the nation's scholars by Federal employment, project allocations, and the power of money is ever present—and is gravely to be regarded.

Yet, in holding scientific research and discovery in respect, as we should, we must also be alert to the equal and opposite danger that public policy could itself become the captive of a scientific-technological elite.

It is the task of statesmanship to mold, to balance, and to integrate these and other forces, new and old, within the principles of our democratic system—ever aiming toward the supreme goals of our free society.

V.

Another factor in maintaining balance involves the element of time. As we peer into society's future, we—you and I, and our government-must avoid the impulse to live only for today, plundering, for our own ease and convenience, the precious resources of tomorrow. We cannot mortgage the material assets of our grandchildren without risking the loss also of their political and spiritual heritage. We want democracy to survive for all generations to come, not to become the insolvent phantom of tomorrow.

VI.

Down the long lane of the history yet to be written America knows that this world of ours, ever growing smaller, must avoid becoming a community of dreadful fear and hate, and be, instead, a proud confederation of mutual trust and respect.

Such a confederation must be one of equals. The weakest must come to the conference table with the same confidence as do we, protected as we are by our moral, economic, and military strength. That table, though scarred by many past frustrations, cannot be abandoned for the certain agony of the battlefield.

Disarmament, with mutual honor and confidence, is a continuing imperative. Together we must learn how to compose differences, not with arms, but with intellect and decent purpose. Because this need is so sharp and apparent I confess that I lay down my official responsibilities in this field with a definite sense of disappointment. As one who has witnessed the horror and the lingering sadness of war—as one who knows that another war could utterly destroy this civilization which has been so slowly and painfully built over thousands of years—I wish I could say tonight that a lasting peace is in sight.

Happily, I can say that war has been avoided. Steady progress toward our ultimate goal has been made. But, so much remains to be done. As a private citizen, I shall never cease to do what little I can to help the world advance along that road.

VII.

So—in this my last good night to you as your President—I thank you for the many opportunities you have given me for public service in war and peace. I trust that in that service you find some things worthy; as for the rest of it, I know you will find ways to improve performance in the future.

You and I—my fellow citizens—need to be strong in our faith that all nations, under God, will reach the goal of peace with justice. May we be ever unswerving in devotion to principle, confident but humble with power, diligent in pursuit of the Nation's great goals.

To all the peoples of the world, I once more give expression to America's prayerful and continuing aspiration:

We pray that peoples of all faiths, all races, all nations, may have their great human needs satisfied; that those now denied opportunity shall come to enjoy it to the full; that all who yearn for freedom may experience its spiritual blessings; that those who have freedom will understand, also, its heavy responsibilities; that all who are insensitive to the needs of others will learn charity; that the scourges of poverty, disease and ignorance will be made to disappear from the earth, and that, in the goodness of time, all peoples will come to live together in a peace guaranteed by the binding force of mutual respect and love.

Source: *Public Papers of the Presidents of the United States.* Dwight D. Eisenhower, 1960–61. Washington, D.C.: Government Printing Office, 1961, 1035–1040.